Lecture Notes in Computer Science 13485

More information about this series at https://link.springer.com/bookseries/558

Björn Andres · Florian Bernard ·
Daniel Cremers · Simone Frintrop ·
Bastian Goldlücke · Ivo Ihrke (Eds.)

Pattern Recognition

44th DAGM German Conference, DAGM GCPR 2022
Konstanz, Germany, September 27–30, 2022
Proceedings

Springer

Editors
Björn Andres (iD)
TU Dresden
Dresden, Germany

Florian Bernard
University of Bonn
Bonn, Germany

Daniel Cremers (iD)
Technical University of Munich
Munich, Germany

Simone Frintrop (iD)
University of Hamburg
Hamburg, Germany

Bastian Goldlücke
University of Konstanz
Konstanz, Germany

Ivo Ihrke
University of Siegen
Siegen, Germany

ISSN 0302-9743   ISSN 1611-3349 (electronic)
Lecture Notes in Computer Science
ISBN 978-3-031-16787-4   ISBN 978-3-031-16788-1 (eBook)
https://doi.org/10.1007/978-3-031-16788-1

This Springer imprint is published by the registered company Springer Nature Switzerland AG
The registered company address is: Gewerbestrasse 11, 6330 Cham, Switzerland

Preface

It was a pleasure to organize the 44th DAGM German Conference on Pattern Recognition (DAGM GCPR 2022), which was held from September 27 to September 30, 2022, at the Konstanz University of Applied Sciences (HTWG). This year, it again took place jointly with the International Symposium on Vision, Modeling and Visualization (VMV). The conference also hosted four Special Tracks on Computer Vision Systems and Applications, Pattern Recognition in the Life and Natural Sciences, Photogrammetry and Remote Sensing, and Robot Vision. The four-day program included one day for tutorials and workshops and three main conference days, with a welcome reception at the historic council building at the harbour of Konstanz and a conference dinner on Mainau Island.

We received 78 submissions. Out of the 78 submissions, three were desk rejected due to violation of the submission policy. The remaining papers underwent a rigorous double-blind reviewing procedure with three Program Committee (PC) members assigned to each paper. Afterwards, one of the involved PC members served as moderator for a discussion among the reviewers and prepared a consolidation report that was also forwarded to the authors in addition to the reviews. As a result of this rigorous reviewing procedure, 36 out of 78 submissions were accepted, which corresponds to an acceptance rate of 46.1%. All accepted papers are published in these proceedings and they cover the entire spectrum of pattern recognition, machine learning, optimization, action recognition, video segmentation, generative models, self-supervised learning, 3D modeling, and applications.

The conference was attended by over 120 registered participants. We were very happy to have three internationally renowned researchers as our invited speakers to present their work in fascinating areas: Michael Bronstein (University of Oxford and Google Deepmind), Iain Couzin (Max Planck Institute of Animal Behavior and University of Konstanz), and Paolo Favaro (University of Bern). Furthermore, we invited submissions to a Nectar Track on Machine Learning, Pattern Recognition and Computer Vision. In the Nectar Track, six selected excellent publications which have been recently published in high-ranking conferences or journals were presented by their authors in two special oral sessions at the conference. Finally, a Tutorial on Graph and Multi-Graph Matching was organized by Florian Bernard (University of Bonn), Dagmar Kainmüller (MDC Berlin), Carsten Rother (TU Dresden), Bogdan Savchynskyy (HCI Heidelberg), and Paul Swoboda (Max Planck Institute for Informatics).

The success of DAGM GCPR 2022 would not have been possible without the support of many people. First of all, we would like to thank all authors of the submitted papers and the speakers for their contributions. All PC members and Special Track Chairs deserve great thanks for their timely and competent reviews. We are grateful to our sponsors for their support as well. Finally, special thanks go to the support staff, in particular the conference secretaries for their outstanding administrative help and the organization of the social events, as well as the staff at HTWG and their Institute for Optical Systems for hosting the conference on their campus. We would like to thank Springer for giving us the opportunity of continuing to publish the DAGM GCPR proceedings in the LNCS series.

September 2022

Björn Andres
Florian Bernard
Daniel Cremers
Simone Frintrop
Bastian Goldlücke
Ivo Ihrke

Organization

General Chairs

GCPR
Bastian Goldlücke   University of Konstanz, Germany

VMV
Oliver Deussen   University of Konstanz, Germany

Venue
Georg Umlauf   HTWG Konstanz, Germany

Program Chairs

Björn Andres   TU Dresden, Germany
Florian Bernard   University of Bonn, Germany
Daniel Cremers   TU Munich, Germany
Simone Frintrop   University of Hamburg, Germany
Ivo Ihrke   University of Siegen, Germany

Special Track Chairs

Joachim Denzler   University of Jena, Germany
Friedrich Fraundorfer   Graz University of Technology, Austria
Xiaoyi Jiang   University of Münster, Germany
Helmut Mayer   Bundeswehr University Munich, Germany
Bodo Rosenhahn   Leibniz University Hannover, Germany
Uwe Sörgel   University of Stuttgart, Germany
Carsten Steger   MVTec Software GmbH and TU Munich, Germany
Jörg Stückler   Max Planck Institute for Intelligent Systems, Germany

Program Committee

Aamir Ahmad   Max Planck Institute for Intelligent Systems, Germany
Christian Bauckhage   Fraunhofer IAIS, Germany

Jens Behley	University of Bonn, Germany
Csaba Beleznai	Austrian Institute of Technology, Austria
Horst Bischof	Graz University of Technology, Austria
Thomas Brox	University of Freiburg, Germany
Joachim Buhmann	ETH Zurich, Switzerland
Dongliang Cao	University of Bonn, Germany
Xun Cao	Nanjing University, China
Joachim Denzler	University of Jena, Germany
Peter Eisert	Fraunhofer Heinrich Hertz Institute, Germany
Michael Felsberg	Linköping University, Sweden
Gernot A. Fink	TU Dortmund, Germany
Boris Flach	Czech Technical University in Prague, Czech Republic
Mario Fritz	Helmholtz Center for Information Security, Germany
Jürgen Gall	University of Bonn, Germany
Guillermo Gallego	TU Berlin, Germany
Margrit Gelautz	TU Wien, Austria
Bastian Goldluecke	University of Konstanz, Germany
Ronny Haensch	IEEE Geoscience and Remote Sensing Society, USA
Ramon Hegedus	TH-EXOVISION Ltd., Hungary
Matthias Hein	University of Tübingen, Germany
Christian Heipke	Leibniz Universität Hannover, Germany
Vaclav Hlavac	Czech Technical University in Prague, Czech Republic
Ivo Ihrke	University of Siegen, Germany
Jannik Irmai	TU Dresden, Germany
Dorota Iwaszczuk	TU Darmstadt, Germany
Xiaoyi Jiang	University of Münster, Germany
Ole Johannsen	University of Konstanz, Germany
Ullrich Köthe	University of Heidelberg, Germany
André P. Kelm	University of Hamburg, Germany
Margret Keuper	University of Mannheim, Germany
Reinhard Koch	Kiel University, Germany
Arjan Kuijper	Fraunhofer IGD and TU Darmstadt, Germany
Christoph H. Lampert	IST Austria, Austria
Bastian Leibe	RWTH Aachen University, Germany
Hendrik P. A. Lensch	University of Tübingen, Germany
Andreas Maier	University of Erlangen-Nuremberg, Germany
Julio Marco	Universidad de Zaragoza, Spain
Helmut Mayer	Bundeswehr University Munich, Germany

Support Staff

Conference Secretariat and Social Events

Ingrid Baiker   University of Konstanz, Germany
Claudia Widmann   University of Konstanz, Germany

Web Page and Tutorial Organizer

Ole Johannsen   University of Konstanz, Germany

Organization and Management of Student Helpers

Urs Waldmann   University of Konstanz, Germany

Sponsors

Gold

Carl Zeiss AG, Oberkochen, Germany

Silver

Amazon, Research Center Tübingen, Germany

Bronze

Knime AG, Konstanz, Germany
Sony Europe B.V., Stuttgart Technology Center, Germany

Contents

Detection and Recognition

Language and Vision

Scene Understanding

Photogrammetry and Remote Sensing

Pattern Recognition in the Life and Natural Sciences

Systems and Applications

Machine Learning Methods

InvGAN: Invertible GANs

Partha Ghosh[1]([envelope]), Dominik Zietlow[1,2], Michael J. Black[1,2], Larry S. Davis[2], and Xiaochen Hu[2]

[1] MPI for Intelligent Systems, Tübingen, Germany
pghosh@tuebingen.mpg.de
[2] Amazon.com, Inc., Seattle, USA
{zietld,mjblack,lrrydav,sonnyh}@amazon.com

Abstract. Generation of photo-realistic images, semantic editing and representation learning are only a few of many applications of high-resolution generative models. Recent progress in GANs have established them as an excellent choice for such tasks. However, since they do not provide an inference model, downstream tasks such as classification cannot be easily applied on real images using the GAN latent space. Despite numerous efforts to train an inference model or design an iterative method to invert a pre-trained generator, previous methods are dataset (e.g. human face images) and architecture (e.g. StyleGAN) specific. These methods are nontrivial to extend to novel datasets or architectures. We propose a general framework that is agnostic to architecture and datasets. Our key insight is that, by training the inference and the generative model together, we allow them to adapt to each other and to converge to a better quality model. Our **InvGAN**, short for Invertible GAN, successfully embeds real images in the latent space of a high quality generative model. This allows us to perform image inpainting, merging, interpolation and online data augmentation. We demonstrate this with extensive qualitative and quantitative experiments.

1 Introduction

The ability to generate photo-realistic images of objects such as human faces or fully clothed bodies has wide applications in computer graphics and computer vision. Traditional computer graphics, based on physical simulation, often fails to produce photo-realistic images of objects with complicated geometry and material properties. In contrast, modern data-driven methods, such as deep learning-based generative models, show great promise for realistic image synthesis [23,24]. Among the four major categories of generative models –generative adversarial networks (GANs), variational auto-encoders (VAEs), normalizing flows and autoregressive models– GANs deliver images with the best visual quality. Although recent efforts in VAEs [13,34] have tremendously improved their generation quality, they still use larger latent space dimensions and deliver lower

---

Supplementary Information The online version contains supplementary material available at https://doi.org/10.1007/978-3-031-16788-1_1.

B. Andres et al. (Eds.): DAGM GCPR 2022, LNCS 13485, pp. 3–19, 2022.
https://doi.org/10.1007/978-3-031-16788-1_1

quality images. Autoregressive models are very slow to sample from and do not provide a latent representation for the trained data. Flow-based methods do not perform dimensionality reduction and hence produce large models and latent representations. On the other hand, GANs offer great generation quality, but do not provide a mechanism to embed real images into the latent space. This limits them as a tool for image editing and manipulation. Specifically, while several methods exist [2,4,6,46], there is no method that trains the generative and the inference model together[1]. To that end, we propose *InvGAN*, an invertible GAN in which the discriminator acts as an inference module. InvGAN enables a wide range of applications, as described in the following paragraphs.

GANs learn a latent representation of the training data. This representation has been shown to be well-structured [10,23,24], allowing GANs to be employed for a variety of downstream tasks (e.g. classification, regression and other supervised tasks) [28,33]. We extend the GAN framework to include an inference model that embeds real images into the latent space. InvGAN can be used to support representation learning [11,27], data augmentation [10,37] and algorithmic fairness [7,38,39]. Previous methods of inversion rely on computationally expensive optimization of inversion processes [3,4], limiting their scope to offline applications, e.g. data augmentation has to happen before training starts. Efficient, photo-realistic, semantically consistent, and model-based inversion is the key to online and adaptive use-cases.

Recent work shows that even unsupervised GAN training isolates several desirable generative characteristics [29,43]. Prominent examples are correspondences between latent space directions and e.g. hairstyle, skin tone and other visual characteristics. Recent works provide empirical evidence suggesting that one can find paths in the latent space (albeit non-linear) that allow for editing individual semantic aspects. GANs therefore have the potential to become a high-quality graphics editing tool [18,41]. However, without a reliable mechanism for projecting real images into the latent space of the generative model, editing of real data is impossible. InvGAN take a step towards addressing this problem.

2   Related Work

The task, GAN inversion, refers to the task of (approximately) inverting the generator network. It has been addressed in two primary ways (1) using an inversion model (often a deep neural network) (2) using an iterative optimization-based method, typically initialized with (1). Although, invertibility of generative models span beyond specific data domains (images, speech, language etc..), we study InvGAN applied to image data only. Its applications of generation of sound, language etc.. is left as future work.

---

[1] Except for BiGAN [14] and ALI [16]. We discuss the differences in Sect. 2.

Optimization Based: iGAN [53] optimizes for a latent code while minimizing the distance between a generated image and a source image. To ensure uniqueness of the preimage of a GAN-generated data point, Zachary et al. [26] employ stochastic clipping. As the complexity of the GAN generators increases, an inversion process based on gradient descent and pixel space MSE is insufficient. Addressing this, Rameen et al. specifically target StyleGAN generators and optimize for perceptual loss [3,4]. However, they invert into the $W+$ space, the so-called extended W space of StyleGAN. This results in high dimensional latent codes and consequently prolongs inversion time. This can also produce out-of-distribution latent representations, which makes them unsuitable for downstream tasks. Contrary to these, InvGAN offers fast inference embedding in the non-extended latent space.

Model Based: BiGAN [14] and ALI [16] invert the generator of a GAN during the training process by learning the joint distribution of the latent vector and the data in a completely adversarial setting. However, the quality is limited, partially because of the choice of DCGAN [32] and partially because of the significant dimensionality and distribution diversity between the latent variable and the data domain [15]. More recent models target the StyleGAN architecture [35,44,52] and achieve impressive results. Most leverage StyleGAN peculiarities, i.e., they invert in the $W+$ space, so adaptation to other GAN backbones is nontrivial. Adversarial latent auto-encoders [31] are closest to our current work. Our model and adversarial autoencoders can be made equivalent with a few alterations to the architecture and to the optimization objective. We discuss this more in detail in Sect. 3.2. Our method, on the other hand, neither uses any data set specific loss nor does it depend upon any specific network architecture.

Hybrid Optimization and Regression Based: Guan et al. [20] train a regressor that is used to initialize an optimization-based method to refine the regressor's guess. However, is specific to human face datasets. Zhu et al. [51] modify the general hybrid approach with an additional criterion that encourages the recovered latent must belong to the semantically meaningful region learned by the generator by assuming that the real image can be reconstructed more faithfully in the immediate neighbourhood of an initial guess given by a model-based inversion mechanism. Yuval et al. [5] replace gradient-based optimization with an iterative encoder that encodes the current generation and target image to the estimated latent code difference. They empirically show that this iterative process converges and that the recovered image improves over iterations. However, this method requires multiple forward passes in order to achieve a suitable latent code. In contrast to the work above, the inference module obtained by our method infers the latent code in one shot. Hence, it is much faster and does not run the risk of finding a non-meaningful latent code.

The inversion mechanisms presented so far do not directly influence the generative process. In most of the cases, they are conducted on a pre-trained frozen generator. Although in the case of ALI [16] and BiGAN [14] the inference model loosely interacts with the generative model at training time, the interaction is only indirect; i.e. through the discriminator. In our work, we tightly couple the inference module with the generative module.

Joint Training of Generator and Inference Model: We postulate that jointly training an inference module will help regularize GAN generators towards invertibility. This is inspired by the difficulty of inverting a pre-trained high-performance GAN. For instance, Bau et al. [8] invert PGAN [22], but for best results a two-stage mechanism is needed. Similarly, Image2StyleGAN [2] projects real images into the extended W^+ space of StyleGAN, whereas, arguably, all the generated images can be generated from the more compact z or w space. This is further evident from Wulff et al. [45] who find an intermediate latent space in StyleGAN that is more Gaussian than the assumed prior. However, they too use an optimization-based method and, hence, it is computationally expensive and at the same time specific to both the StyleGAN backend and the specific data set. Finally, we refer the readers to 'GAN Inversion: A Survey' [46] for a comprehensive review of relate work.

3   Method

Goal: Our goal is to learn an inversion module alongside the generator during GAN training. An inversion module is a mechanism that returns a latent embedding of a given data point. Specifically, we find a generator $G : \mathbb{W} \to \mathbb{X}$ and an inference model $D : \mathbb{X} \to \mathbb{W}$ such that $x \approx G(D(x \sim \mathbb{X}))$, where $\mathbb{X}$ denotes the data domain and $\mathbb{W}$ denotes the latent space. We reuse the GAN discriminator to play the role of this inference model D in practice.

3.1   Architecture

We demonstrate InvGAN using DC-GAN, BigGAN and StyleGAN as the underlying architectures. Figure 1 represents the schematic of our model. We follow the traditional alternate generator-discriminator training mechanism. The generative part consists of three steps 1. sampling latent code: $z \sim \mathcal{N}(0, I)$, 2. mapping the latent code to w space: $w = M(z)$, 3. using mapped code to generate fake data: $x = G(w)$, where M is a mapping network, G is the generator, D is the discriminator, and $\mathcal{N}(0, I)$ is the standard normal distribution. In practice, the discriminator, besides outputting real/fake score, also outputs inferred w parameter, which was found to work better empirically over designs with two different networks for discrimination and inference. From here on, we use $\tilde{w}, c = D(x)$ to denote the inferred latent code ($\tilde{w}$) using the discriminator D and c to denote the real-fake classification decision for the sample $x \in \mathbb{X}$. Wherever obvious, we simply use $D(x)$ to refer to c, the discrimination decision only.

3.2   Objective

GAN Objective: The min-max game between the discriminator network and the generator network of vanilla GAN training is described as

$$\min_{G,M} \max_{D} \mathcal{L}_{\text{GAN}} = \min_{G,M} \max_{D} \left[\mathbb{E}_{x \in \mathbb{X}}[\log D(x)] + \mathbb{E}_{z \in \mathbb{Z}}[\log(1 - D(G(M(z))))] \right]. \tag{1}$$

A naive attempt at an approximately invertible GAN would perform $\min_G \max_D \mathcal{L}_{\text{GAN}} + \min_{G,D} \|w - \tilde{w}\|_p$, where $\|\bullet\|_p$ denotes an L_p norm. This loss function can be interpreted as optimal transport cost. We discuss this in more detail at the end of this section. However, this arrangement, coined the "naive model", does not yield satisfactory results, cf. Sect. 4.4. This can be attributed to three factors: (1) w corresponding to real images are never seen by the generator; (2) no training signal is provided to the discriminator for inferring the latent code corresponding to real images (w_R); (3) the distribution of w_R might differ from prior distribution of w. We address each of these concerns with a specific loss term designed to address the said issues. Our naive model corresponds to the adversarial autoencoders [31] if the real-fake decision is derived from a common latent representation. However, this forces the encoding of real and generated images to be linearly separable and contributes to degraded inference performance.

Minimizing Latent Space Extrapolation: Since, in the naive version, neither the generator nor the discriminator gets trained with w_R, it relies completely upon its extrapolation characteristics. In order to reduce the distribution mismatch for the generator, we draw half the mini batch of latent codes from the prior and the other half consists of w_R; i.e., $w_{\text{total}} = w \mathbin{+\!\!+} w_R$, $w \sim P(W)$ where $+\!\!+$ denotes a batch concatenation operation. By $w \sim P(W)$, we denote the two stage process given by the following $w = M(z \sim P(Z))$. Together with the naive loss this forms the first three terms of our full objective function given in Eq. 3

Pixel Space Reconstruction Loss: Since latent codes for real images are not given, the discriminator cannot be trained directly. However, we recover a self-supervised training signal by allowing the gradients from the generator to flow into the discriminator. Intuitively, the discriminator tries to infer latent codes from real images that help the generator reproduce that image. As shown in Sect. 4.4, this improves real image inversion tremendously. We enforce further consistency by imposing an image domain reconstruction loss between input and reconstructed real images. However, designing a meaningful distance function for images is a non-trivial task. Ideally, we would like a feature extractor function f that extracts low- and high-level features from the image such that two images can be compared meaningfully. Given such a function, a reconstruction loss can be constructed as

$$\mathcal{L}_{\text{fm}} = \|\mathbb{E}_{x \in \mathbb{X}}(f(x) - f(G(w \sim P(W|x))))\|_p \tag{2}$$

A common practice in the literature is to use a pre-trained VGG [21,50] network as a feature extractor f. However, it is well known that deep neural networks are susceptible to adversarial perturbations [47]. Given this weakness, optimizing for perceptual loss is error-prone. Hence, a combination of a pixel-domain L_2 and feature-space loss is typically used, but this often results in degraded quality. Consequently, we take the discriminator itself as the feature extractor function f. Due to the min-max setting of GAN training, we are guaranteed to avoid the perils of adversarial and fooling samples, if we use the discriminator features, instead of VGG features. The feature loss is shown in the second half of Fig. 1. Although this resembles the feature matching described by Salimans et al. [36], it has a crucial difference. As seen in Eq. 2 the latent code fed into the generator is drawn from the conditional distribution $P(W|x) := \delta_{D(x)}(w)$ rather than the prior $P(W)$, where $\delta(x)$ represents the Dirac delta function located at x. This forces the distribution of the features to match more precisely as compared to the simple first-moment matching proposed by Salimans et al. in [36].

Addressing Mismatch Between Prior and Posterior: Finally, we address the possibility of mismatch between inferred and prior latent distributions (point (3) described above) by imposing a maximum mean discrepancy (MMD) loss between the sets of samples of the said two distributions. We use an RBF kernel to compute this. The loss improves the random sampling quality by providing a direct learning signal to the mapping network. This forms the last term of our objective function as shown in Eq. 3.

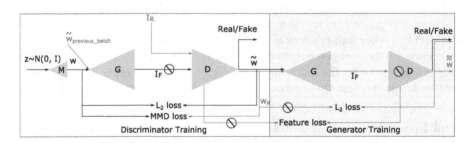

Fig. 1. We train InvGAN following a regular GAN. We use a second output head in the discriminator besides the real fake decision head, to infer the latent-code z of a given image. Here ⊘ denotes no gradient propagation during back propagation step. It also denotes 'no training' when it is placed on a model. We use red color to show data flow corresponding to real images.

Putting everything together gives the objective of our complete model. It is as shown in Eq. 3. Note that here the expectation operator $\mathbb{E}_{w+w_R}$ acts on several loss terms that are independent of w_R or w. In such cases keeping in mind the identity $c = \mathbb{E}[c]$, where c is a constant, can add clarity. Furthermore, here and in the rest of the paper we use a plus operator $+$, between two optimization process, to indicate that both of them are performed simultaneously.

$$\min_{G,M}\left[\max_{D}\mathcal{L}_{\mathrm{GAN}} + \min_{D}\left[\mathbb{E}_{w+w_R}\left[\left\|M(z)-\tilde{w}\right\|_2^2 + \left\|(\tilde{w}+w_R)-\tilde{\tilde{w}}\right\|_2^2 + \mathcal{L}_{\mathrm{fm}}\right.\right.\right. \\ \left.\left.\left. + \mathrm{MMD}\{w,w_R\}\right]\right]\right] \tag{3}$$

An Optimal Transport Based Interpretation: Neglecting the last three terms described in Eq. 3, our method can be interpreted as a Wasserstein autoencoder (the GAN version) (WAE-GAN) [42]. Considering a WAE with its data domain set to our latent space and its latent space assigned to our image domain, if the encoder and the discriminator share weights the analogy is complete. Our model can, hence, be thought of as learning the latent variable model $P(W)$ by randomly sampling a data point $x \sim \mathbb{X}$ from the training set and mapping it to a latent code w via a deterministic transformation. In terms of density, it can be written as in Eq. 4.

$$P(W) := \int_{x \in \mathbb{X}} P(w|x)P(x)\mathrm{d}x. \tag{4}$$

As proven by Olivier et al. [9], under this model the optimal transport problem $W_c(P(W), P_D(W)) := \inf_{\Gamma \in P(w_1 \sim P(W), w_2 \sim P_D(W))} [\mathbb{E}_{w_1,w_2 \sim \Gamma} [c(w_1, w_2)]]$ can be solved by finding a generative model $G(X|W)$ such that its X marginal, $P_G(X) = \mathbb{E}_{w \sim P(W)} G(X|w)$ matches the image distribution $P(X)$. We ensure this by considering the Jensen-Shannon divergence $D_{\mathrm{JS}}(P_G(X), P(X))$ using a GAN framework. This leads to the cost function given in Eq. 5, when we choose the ground cost function $c(w_1, w_2)$ to be squared L_2 norm.

$$\min_{G,M}\max_{D}\mathcal{L}_{\mathrm{GAN}} + \min_{G,M}\min_{D}\left\|w-\tilde{w}\right\|_2^2 \tag{5}$$

Finally, we find that by running the encoding/decoding cycle one more time, we can impose several constraints that improve the quality of the encoder and the decoder network in practice. This leads to our full optimization criterion, as described in Eq. 3. Note that our method because of this extra cycle is less efficient computationally as compared to vanilla VAEs or WAEs, but by incurring this computational penalty we successfully avoid having to define a loss function in the image domain. This results in sharper image generation.

3.3 Dealing with Resolutions Higher Than the Training Resolution

Although StyleGAN [24] and BigGAN [10] have shown that it is possible to generate relatively high-resolution images, in the range of 1024×1024 and 512×512, their training is resource intense and the models are difficult to tune for new data sets. Equipped with invertibility, we explore a tiling strategy to improve the output resolution. First, we train an invertible GAN at a lower resolution $(m \times m)$ and simply tile them $n \times n$ times with n^2 latent codes to obtain a higher resolution $(mn \times mn)$ final output image. The new latent space containing n^2 latent codes obtained using the inference mechanism of the invertible GAN can now be used for various purposes, as described in Sect. 4.3 and reconstructions are visualized in Fig. 3. This process correlates in spirit somewhat to COCO-GAN [25]. The main difference, however, is that our model at no point learns to assemble neighbouring patches. Indeed, the seams are visible if one squints at the generated images, e.g., in Fig. 3. However, a detailed study of tiling for generation of higher resolution images than the input domain is beyond the scope of our paper. We simply explore some naive settings and their applications in Sect. 4.3.

4 Experiments

We test InvGAN on several diverse datasets (MNIST, ImageNet, CelebA, FFHQ) and multiple backbone architectures (DC-GAN, BigGAN, StyleGAN). For the mapping network in the generator, we use the standard 8-layer mapping network with StyleGAN and add a 2-layer mapping network to BigGAN and DC-GAN. Our method is evaluated both qualitatively (via style mixing, image inpainting etc.) and quantitatively (via the FID score and the suitability for data augmentation for discriminative tasks such as classification). We found that relative weights of different terms in our objective function do not impact the model's performance significantly. Therefore, keeping simplicity in mind, we avoid tuning and simply set them to be one.

Table 1 shows random sample FIDs, middle point linear interpolation FIDs and test set reconstruction mean absolute errors (MAEs) of our generative model. We note here that interpolation FID and random generation FID are comparable to non-inverting GANs. This leads us to conclude that the inversion mechanism does not adversarially impact the generative properties. We provide a definition, baseline and understanding of inversion of a high-quality generator for uniform comparison of future works on GAN inversion. We highlight model-based inversion, joint training of generative and inference model and its usability in downstream tasks. We demonstrate that InvGAN generalizes across architectures, datasets, and types of downstream task.

Table 1. Here we report random sample FID (RandFID), FID of reconstructed random samples (RandRecFID), FID of reconstructed test set samples (TsRecFID), FID of the linear middle interpolation of test set images (IntTsFID) and reconstruction per pixel per color channel mean absolute error when images are normalized between ± 1, also from test set. All FID scores are here evaluated against train set using 500 and 50000 samples. They are separated by '/'. For the traditional MSE optimization based and In-Domain GAN inversion, the MSE errors are converted to MAE by taking square root and averaging over the color channels and accounting for the re-normalization of pixel values between ± 1 (MAE± 1). Runtime is given in seconds per image. We ran them on a V100 32GB GPU and measured wall clock time.

Models	RandFID	RandRecFID	TsRecFID	IntTsFID	MAE ± 1	Run Time
FFHQ [48]	49.65/14.59	56.71/23.93	-/13.73	68.45/38.01	0.129	0.045
FFHQ Enc. [51]	46.82/14.38	-/-	88.48/ -	-/-	0.460	
FFHQ MSE opt. [51]	46.82/14.38	-/-	58.04/ -	-/-	0.106	
FFHQ In-D. Inv. [51]	46.82/14.38	52.02/-	42.64/ -	71.83/-	0.115	99.76
DCGAN, MNIST	17.44/6.10	16.76/4.25	17.77/4.70	26.04/11.44	0.070	$3.3 \cdot 10^{-5}$
StyleGAN, CelebA	26.63/4.81	24.35/3.51	24.37/4.14	32.37/15.60	0.150	$1.0 \cdot 10^{-3}$
StyleGAN, FFHQ	49.14/12.12	44.42/8.85	41.14/7.15	49.52/14.36	0.255	$2.0 \cdot 10^{-3}$

We start with a StyleGAN-based architecture on FFHQ and CelebA for image editing. Then we train a BigGAN-based architecture on ImageNet, and show super resolution and video key-framing by tiling in the latent domain to work with images and videos that have higher resolution than training data. We also show ablation studies with a DC-GAN-based architecture on MNIST. In the following sections we evaluate qualitatively by visualizing semantic editing of real images and quantitatively on various downstream tasks including classification fairness, image super resolution, image mixing, etc.

4.1 Semantically Consistent Inversion Using InvGAN

GANs can be used to augment training data and substantially improve learning of downstream tasks, such as improving fairness of classifiers of human-facial attributes [7,33,38,39]. There is an important shortcoming in using existing GAN approaches for such tasks: the labeling of augmented data relies on methods that are trained independently on the original data set, using human annotators or compute-expensive optimization-based inversion. A typical example is data-set debasing by Ramaswamy et al. [33]. For each training image, an altered example that differs in some attribute (e.g. age, hair color, etc..) has to be generated. This can be done in one of two ways, 1. by finding the latent representation of the ground truth image via optimization and 2. by labeling random samples using pre-trained classifiers on the biased data set. Optimization-based methods are slow and not a viable option for on-demand/adaptive data augmentation. Methods using pre-trained classifiers inherit their flaws, e.g. spurious correlation induced dependencies. However, having access to a high-quality inversion mechanism help us overcome such problems [54].

To verify that InvGAN is indeed suitable for such tasks, we train ResNet50 attribute classifiers on the CelebA dataset. We validate that the encoding and decoding of InvGAN results in a semantically consistent reconstruction by training the classifier only on reconstructions of the full training set. As a baseline, we use the same classifier trained on the original CelebA. We produce two reconstructed training sets by using the tiling-based inversion (trained on ImageNet) and by training InvGAN on CelebA (without tiling). For each attribute, a separate classifier has been trained for 20 epochs. The resulting mean average precisions are reported in Table 2. We see that training on the reconstructions allows for very good domain transfer to real images, indicating that the reconstruction process maintained the semantics of the images.

Table 2. Mean average precision for a ResNet50 attribute classifier on CelebA, averaged over 20 attributes. We report the performance for training on the original dataset, the reconstructed dataset using the tiling-based method pre-trained on ImageNet and the reconstruction on InvGAN trained on the CelebA training set directly.

Train on → Eval. on ↓	Original	Tile Recon.	Full Recon.
Original	0.81 ± 0.15	0.77 ± 0.16	0.79 ± 0.15
Tile recon.	0.79 ± 0.16	0.80 ± 0.15	0.78 ± 0.16
Full recon.	0.81 ± 0.15	0.78 ± 0.16	0.81 ± 0.14
Recon. Vis.			

4.2 Suitability for Image Editing

GAN inversion methods have been proposed for machine supported photo editing tasks [12,30,51]. Although there is hardly any quantitative evaluation for the suitability of a specific inversion algorithm or model, a variety of representative operations have been reported [3,4,51]. Among those are in-painting cut out regions of an image, image-merging and improving on amateur manual photo editing. Figures 2 and 8 in the appendix visualize those operations performed on FFHQ and CelebA images, respectively. We demonstrate in-painting by zeroing out a randomly positioned square patch and then simply reconstructing the image. Image-merging is performed by reconstructing an image which is composed out of two images by simply placing them together. By reconstructing an image that has undergone manual photo editing, higher degrees of photo-realism are achieved. Quantitative metric for such tasks are hard to define and hence is scarcely found in prior art, since they depend upon visual quality of the results. We report reconstruction and interpolation FIDs in Table 1, in an effort to establish a baseline for future research. However, we do acknowledge that a boost in pixel fidelity in our reconstruction will greatly boost the performance of InvGAN on photo editing tasks. The experiments clearly show the general suitability of the learned representations to project out of distribution images to the learned posterior manifold via reconstruction.

Fig. 2. Benchmark image editing tasks on FFHQ (128 px). Style mixing: we transfer the first $0, 1, 2, \ldots, 11$ style vectors from one image to another. For the other image editing tasks, pairs of images are input image (left) and reconstruction (right).

4.3   Tiling to Boost Resolution

Limitations in video RAM and instability of high resolution GANs are prominent obstacles in generative model training. One way to bypass such difficulties is to generate the image in parts. Here we train our invertible generative model, a BigGAN architecture, on 32×32 random patches from ImageNet. Once the inversion mechanism and the generator are trained to satisfactory quality, we reconstruct both FFHQ and ImageNet images. We use 256×256 resolution and tile 32 patches in an 8×8 grid for FFHQ images, and 128×128 resolution and tiling 32 patches in a 4×4 grid for ImageNet images. The reconstruction results are shown in Fig. 3. Given the successful reconstruction process, we explore the tiled latent space for tasks such as image deblurring and time interpolation of video frames.

Image De-blurring: Here we take a low-resolution image, scale it to the intended resolution using bicubic interpolation, invert it patch by patch, Gaussian blur it, invert it again and linearly extrapolate it in the deblurring direction. The deblurring direction is simply obtained by subtracting the latent code of the given low resolution but bicubic up sampled image from the latent code of the blurred version of it at the same resolution. The exact amount of extrapolation desired is left up to the user. In Fig. 4 we show the effect of three different levels of extrapolation. Although our method is not trained for the task of super resolution, by virtue of a meaningful latent space we can enhance image quality.

(a)   (b)

Fig. 3. Tiled reconstruction of random (a) FFHQ images and (b) ImageNet images. The left column shows the real images, the second shows the patch by patch reconstructions, and the third shows the absolute pixel-wise differences. Note that interestingly though the patches are reconstructed independent of each other, the errors lie mostly on the edges of the objects in the images, arguably the most information dense region of the images.

Fig. 4. Super resolution using extrapolation in the tiled latent space. From left, we visualize the original image, the low-resolution version of it, the reconstruction of the low-resolution version, and progressive extrapolation to achieve deblurring.

Temporal Interpolation of Video Frames: Here we boost the frame rate of a video post capture. We infer the tiled latent space of consecutive frames in a video, and linearly interpolate each tile to generate one or more intermediate frames. Results are shown in Figure 6 in the appendix and in the accompanying videos in supplementary material. We find the latent code of each frame in a video sequence, and then derive intermediate latent codes by weighted averaging neighboring latent codes using a Gaussian window. We use the UCF101 data set [40] for this task. Note however that since there is no temporal constraint and each patch is independently interpolated, one can notice flicker effect. Further-studies into this matter are left to future work.

As can also be seen, this process produces discontinuities at the boundaries of the patches. This is because neighboring patches are modeled independently of one another in this work. This can be dealt with in a variety of ways, namely, by carefully choosing overlapping patch patterns and explicitly choosing a pre-determined or learning-based stitching mechanism, seam detection and correction [1, 49]. However, a thorough study in this direction is considered out of scope for the current work.

4.4   Ablation Studies

Recall that the naive model defined in Sect. 3.2 uses the optimization $\min_{G,M} \left[\max_D L_{\text{GAN}} + \min_D \mathbb{E}_{z \sim P(Z)} \| M(z) - \tilde{w} \|_p \right]$ to train (also given in Equation 5), In Fig. 5a we show how our three main components progressively improve the naive model. As is apparent from the method section, the first major improvement comes from exposing the generator to the latent code inferred from real images. This is primarily due to the difference in the prior and the induced posterior distribution. This is especially true during early training, which imparts a lasting impact. The corresponding optimization is $\min_{G,M} \left[\max_D L_{\text{GAN}} + \min_D \mathbb{E}_{w = M(z \sim P(Z)) + w_R} \| w - \tilde{w} \|_p \right]$. This simply reduces the distribution mismatch between prior and posterior by injecting inferred latent codes, improves inversion quality. This is visualized in Fig. 5b. We call this model the augmented naive model. However, this modification unlocks the possibility to enforce back propagation of generator loss gradients to the discriminator and real-image, generated-image pairing, as detailed in Sect. 3.2. This leads to our model and the results are visualized in Fig. 5c.

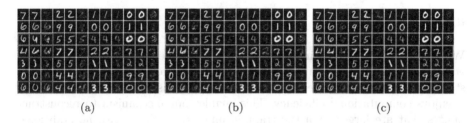

(a)   (b)   (c)

Fig. 5. Inversion of held out test samples. Columns are in groups of three: the first column holds real images, second their reconstruction and third the absolute pixel-wise difference. (a) Inversion using naive model, i.e. only z reconstruction loss is used (b) inversion using model that uses latent codes from real samples, i.e., the augmented naive model. (c) our full model. Notice how the imperfections in the reconstructions highlighted with red boxes gradually vanishes as the model improves. (Color figure online)

5   Discussion and Future Work

While InvGAN can reliably invert the generator of a GAN, it still can benefit from an improved reconstruction fidelity for tasks such as image compression, image segmentation, etc. We observe that the reconstruction of rare features, such as microphones, hats or background, tend to have lower quality, as seen in the appendix in Figure 7 bottom row 3rd and 4th columns. This combined with the fact that the reconstruction loss during training tends to saturate even when the weights are sufficiently high indicates that even well-engineered architectures such as StyleGAN and BigGAN lack representative power to provide sufficient data coverage.

Strong inductive biases in the generative model have the potential to improve the quality of the inference module. For instance, GIF [18] and hologan [29] among others introduce strong inductive bias from the underlying 3D geometry and lighting properties of a 2D image. Hence, an inverse module of these generative mechanism has the potential to outperform their counterparts, which are trained fully supervised on the labelled training data alone at estimating 3D face parameters from 2D images.

As was shown by the success of RAEs [17], there is often a mismatch between the induced posterior and the prior of generative models, which can be removed by an ex-post density estimator. InvGAN is also aminable to ex-post density estimation. When applied to the tiled latent codes, it estimates a joint density of the tiles for unseen data. This would recover a generative model without going through the unstable GAN training.

We have shown that our method scales to large datasets such as ImageNet, CelebA, and FFHQ. A future work that is able to improve upon reconstruction fidelity, would be able to explore adversarial robustness by extending [19] to larger datasets.

6   Conclusion

We presented InvGAN, an inference framework for the latent generative parameters used by a GAN generator. InvGAN enjoys several advantages compared to state-of-the-art inversion mechanisms. Since InvGAN is a model-based approach, it enjoys computational efficiency. This enables our mechanism to reconstruct images that are larger than the training images by tiling, with no additional merging step. Furthermore, the inversion mechanism is integrated into the training phase of the generator, this encourages the generator to cover all modes. We further demonstrated that the inferred latent code for a given image is semantically meaningful, i.e., it falls inside the structured part of the latent space learned by the generator.

Acknowledgement. We thank Alex Vorobiov, Javier Romero, Betty Mohler Tesch and Soubhik Sanyal for their insightful comments and intriguing discussions. While PG and DZ are affiliated with Max Planck Institute for Intelligent Systems, this project was completed during PG's and DZ's internship at Amazon. MJB performed this work while at Amazon.

References

1. Seamless color mapping for 3D reconstruction with consumer-grade scanning devices

2. Abdal, R., Qin, Y., Wonka, P.: Image2StyleGAN: how to embed images into the styleGAN latent space? In: Proceedings of the IEEE International Conference on Computer Vision, pp. 4432–4441 (2019)
3. Abdal, R., Qin, Y., Wonka, P.: Image2StyleGAN: how to embed images into the styleGAN latent space? arXiv:1904.03189 (2019)
4. Abdal, R., Qin, Y., Wonka, P.: Image2StyleGAN++: how to edit the embedded images? In: Proceedings of the IEEE Conference on Computer Vision and Pattern Recognition (CVPR) (2020)
5. Alaluf, Y., Patashnik, O., Cohen-Or, D.: Restyle: a residual-based styleGAN encoder via iterative refinement (2021)
6. Alaluf, Y., Tov, O., Mokady, R., Gal, R., Bermano, A.H.: Hyperstyle: StyleGAN inversion with hypernetworks for real image editing (2021). arXiv:2111.15666, https://doi.org/10.48550/ARXIV.2111.15666
7. Balakrishnan, G., Xiong, Y., Xia, W., Perona, P.: Towards causal benchmarking of bias in face analysis algorithms. In: Vedaldi, A., Bischof, H., Brox, T., Frahm, J.-M. (eds.) ECCV 2020. LNCS, vol. 12363, pp. 547–563. Springer, Cham (2020). https://doi.org/10.1007/978-3-030-58523-5_32
8. Bau, D., Strobelt, H., Peebles, W., Zhou, B., Zhu, J.Y., Torralba, A., et al.: Semantic photo manipulation with a generative image prior. arXiv preprint arXiv:2005.07727 (2020)
9. Bousquet, O., Gelly, S., Tolstikhin, I., Simon-Gabriel, C.J., Schoelkopf, B.: From optimal transport to generative modeling: the vegan cookbook. arXiv preprint arXiv:1705.07642 (2017)
10. Brock, A., Donahue, J., Simonyan, K.: Large scale GAN training for high fidelity natural image synthesis. arXiv:1809.11096 (2018)
11. Chen, M., Radford, A., Child, R., Wu, J., Jun, H., Luan, D., Sutskever, I.: Generative pretraining from pixels. In: III, H.D., Singh, A. (eds.) Proceedings of the 37th International Conference on Machine Learning, Proceedings of Machine Learning Research, 13–18 Jul 2020, vol. 119, pp. 1691–1703. PMLR (2020). https://proceedings.mlr.press/v119/chen20s.html
12. Cheng, Y., Gan, Z., Li, Y., Liu, J., Gao, J.: Sequential attention GAN for interactive image editing. arXiv preprint arXiv:1812.08352 (2020)
13. Child, R.: Very deep VAEs generalize autoregressive models and can outperform them on images. In: International Conference on Learning Representations (2021). https://openreview.net/forum?id=RLRXCV6DbEJ
14. Donahue, J., Krähenbühl, P., Darrell, T.: Adversarial feature learning. arXiv preprint arXiv:1605.09782 (2016)
15. Donahue, J., Simonyan, K.: Large scale adversarial representation learning. arXiv:1907.02544 (2019)
16. Dumoulin, V., et al.: Adversarially learned inference. arXiv preprint arXiv:1606.00704 (2016)
17. Ghosh, P., Sajjadi, M.S.M., Vergari, A., Black, M.J., Schölkopf, B.: From variational to deterministic autoencoders. In: 8th International Conference on Learning Representations (ICLR) (2020). https://openreview.net/forum?id=S1g7tpEYDS
18. Ghosh, P., Gupta, P.S., Uziel, R., Ranjan, A., Black, M.J., Bolkart, T.: GIF: generative interpretable faces. In: International Conference on 3D Vision (3DV) (2020). http://gif.is.tue.mpg.de/
19. Ghosh, P., Losalka, A., Black, M.J.: Resisting adversarial attacks using gaussian mixture variational autoencoders. In: Proceedings AAAI Conference Artificial Intelligence, vol. 33, pp. 541–548 (2019). https://doi.org/10.1609/aaai.v33i01.3301541. https://ojs.aaai.org/index.php/AAAI/article/view/3828

20. Guan, S., Tai, Y., Ni, B., Zhu, F., Huang, F., Yang, X.: Collaborative learning for faster styleGAN embedding. arXiv:2007.01758 (2020)
21. Johnson, J., Alahi, A., Li, F.: Perceptual losses for real-time style transfer and super-resolution. arXiv:1603.08155 (2016)
22. Karras, T., Aila, T., Laine, S., Lehtinen, J.: Progressive growing of GANs for improved quality, stability, and variation. arXiv preprint arXiv:1710.10196 (2017)
23. Karras, T., Laine, S., Aila, T.: A style-based generator architecture for generative adversarial networks. In: Proceedings of the IEEE Conference on Computer Vision and Pattern Recognition (CVPR), pp. 4401–4410 (2019)
24. Karras, T., Laine, S., Aittala, M., Hellsten, J., Lehtinen, J., Aila, T.: Analyzing and improving the image quality of StyleGAN. In: Proceedings of the IEEE Conference on Computer Vision and Pattern Recognition (CVPR), pp. 8110–8119 (2020)
25. Lin, C.H., Chang, C., Chen, Y., Juan, D., Wei, W., Chen, H.: COCO-GAN: generation by parts via conditional coordinating. arXiv:1904.00284 (2019)
26. Lipton, Z.C., Tripathi, S.: Precise recovery of latent vectors from generative adversarial networks. arXiv preprint arXiv:1702.04782 (2017)
27. Locatello, F., et al.: Challenging common assumptions in the unsupervised learning of disentangled representations. In: International Conference on Machine Learning, pp. 4114–4124. PMLR (2019)
28. Marriott, R.T., Madiouni, S., Romdhani, S., Gentric, S., Chen, L.: An assessment of GANs for identity-related applications. In: 2020 IEEE International Joint Conference on Biometrics (IJCB), pp. 1–10 (2020). https://doi.org/10.1109/IJCB48548.2020.9304879
29. Nguyen-Phuoc, T., Li, C., Theis, L., Richardt, C., Yang, Y.L.: HoloGAN: unsupervised learning of 3D representations from natural images. In: Proceedings of the IEEE International Conference on Computer Vision (ICCV), pp. 7588–7597 (2019)
30. Perarnau, G., Van De Weijer, J., Raducanu, B., Álvarez, J.M.: Invertible conditional GANs for image editing. arXiv preprint arXiv:1611.06355 (2016)
31. Pidhorskyi, S., Adjeroh, D.A., Doretto, G.: Adversarial latent autoencoders. arXiv:2004.04467 (2020)
32. Radford, A., Metz, L., Chintala, S.: Unsupervised representation learning with deep convolutional generative adversarial networks. arXiv preprint arXiv:1511.06434 (2015)
33. Ramaswamy, V.V., Kim, S.S., Russakovsky, O.: Fair attribute classification through latent space de-biasing. arXiv preprint arXiv:2012.01469 (2020)
34. Razavi, A., van den Oord, A., Vinyals, O.: Generating diverse high-fidelity images with VQ-VAE-2. In: Advances in Neural Information Processing Systems, pp. 14866–14876 (2019)
35. Richardson, E., et al.: Encoding in style: a styleGAN encoder for image-to-image translation. arXiv:2008.00951 (2020)
36. Salimans, T., Goodfellow, I.J., Zaremba, W., Cheung, V., Radford, A., Chen, X.: Improved techniques for training GANs. arXiv:1606.03498 (2016)
37. dos Santos Tanaka, F.H.K., Aranha, C.: Data augmentation using GANs. arXiv:1904.09135 (2019)
38. Sattigeri, P., Hoffman, S.C., Chenthamarakshan, V., Varshney, K.R.: Fairness GAN. arXiv preprint arXiv:1805.09910 (2018)
39. Sharmanska, V., Hendricks, L.A., Darrell, T., Quadrianto, N.: Contrastive examples for addressing the tyranny of the majority. arXiv preprint arXiv:2004.06524 (2020)

40. Soomro, K., Zamir, A.R., Shah, M.: UCF101: a dataset of 101 human actions classes from videos in the wild. arXiv:1212.0402 (2012)
41. Tewari, A., et al.: Stylerig: rigging StyleGAN for 3D control over portrait images. In: IEEE Conference on Computer Vision and Pattern Recognition (CVPR). IEEE (2020)
42. Tolstikhin, I., Bousquet, O., Gelly, S., Schoelkopf, B.: Wasserstein auto-encoders. In: International Conference on Learning Representations (2018). https://openreview.net/forum?id=HkL7n1-0b
43. Voynov, A., Babenko, A.: Unsupervised discovery of interpretable directions in the GAN latent space. arXiv preprint arXiv:2002.03754 (2020)
44. Wei, T., et al.: A simple baseline for StyleGAN inversion. arXiv:2104.07661 (2021)
45. Wulff, J., Torralba, A.: Improving inversion and generation diversity in StyleGAN using a gaussianized latent space. arXiv preprint arXiv:2009.06529 (2020)
46. Xia, W., Zhang, Y., Yang, Y., Xue, J.H., Zhou, B., Yang, M.H.: Gan inversion: a survey. arXiv preprint arXiv:2101.05278 (2021)
47. Xu, H., et al.: Adversarial attacks and defenses in images, graphs and text: a review. arXiv:1909.08072 (2019). https://doi.org/10.48550/ARXIV.1909.08072
48. Xu, Y., Shen, Y., Zhu, J., Yang, C., Zhou, B.: Generative hierarchical features from synthesizing images. In: CVPR (2021)
49. Yu, J., et al.: Vector-quantized image modeling with improved VQGAN. In: International Conference on Learning Representations (ICLR) (2022)
50. Zhang, R., Isola, P., Efros, A.A., Shechtman, E., Wang, O.: The unreasonable effectiveness of deep features as a perceptual metric. In: CVPR (2018)
51. Zhu, Jiapeng, Shen, Yujun, Zhao, Deli, Zhou, Bolei: In-domain GAN inversion for real image editing. In: Vedaldi, Andrea, Bischof, Horst, Brox, Thomas, Frahm, Jan-Michael. (eds.) ECCV 2020. LNCS, vol. 12362, pp. 592–608. Springer, Cham (2020). https://doi.org/10.1007/978-3-030-58520-4_35
52. Zhu, J., Zhao, D., Zhang, B.: LIA: latently invertible autoencoder with adversarial learning. arXiv:1906.08090 (2019)
53. Zhu, J.-Y., Krähenbühl, P., Shechtman, E., Efros, A.A.: Generative visual manipulation on the natural image manifold. In: Leibe, B., Matas, J., Sebe, N., Welling, M. (eds.) ECCV 2016. LNCS, vol. 9909, pp. 597–613. Springer, Cham (2016). https://doi.org/10.1007/978-3-319-46454-1_36
54. Zietlow, D., et al.: Leveling down in computer vision: pareto inefficiencies in fair deep classifiers. arXiv:2203.04913 (2022). https://doi.org/10.48550/ARXIV.2203.04913

Auto-Compressing Subset Pruning for Semantic Image Segmentation

Konstantin Ditschuneit$^{(\boxtimes)}$ (iD) and Johannes S. Otterbach (iD)

Merantix Labs GmbH, Berlin, Germany
{konstantin.ditschuneit,johannes.otterbach}@merantix.com

Abstract. State-of-the-art semantic segmentation models are characterized by high parameter counts and slow inference times, making them unsuitable for deployment in resource-constrained environments. To address this challenge, we propose AUTO-COMPRESSING SUBSET PRUNING, ACoSP, as a new online compression method. The core of ACoSP consists of learning a channel selection mechanism for individual channels of each convolution in the segmentation model based on an effective temperature annealing schedule. We show a crucial interplay between providing a high-capacity model at the beginning of training and the compression pressure forcing the model to compress concepts into retained channels. We apply ACoSP to SegNet and PSPNet architectures and show its success when trained on the CAMVID, CITYSCAPES, PASCAL VOC2012, and ADE20K datasets. The results are competitive with existing baselines for compression of segmentation models at low compression ratios and outperform them significantly at high compression ratios, yielding acceptable results even when removing more than 93% of the parameters. In addition, ACoSP is conceptually simple, easy to implement, and can readily be generalized to other data modalities, tasks, and architectures. Our code is available at https://github.com/merantix/acosp.

1 Introduction

Recent years have seen significant advances in training convolutional neural networks (CNNs), enabling new applications in semantic segmentation. However, these advances come at the cost of high computational resource requirements.

To reduce the computational burden of existing state-of-the-art models and maintain a high performance across tasks, the community is actively researching methods to efficiently compress and speed up neural networks. Pruning as a compression technique has been studied in great depth for image classification tasks [2], but it has received less attention in the context of semantic segmentation. Latter, to the best of our knowledge, has only been discussed in a few prior works [9,16,26,32,39].

Supplementary Information The online version contains supplementary material available at https://doi.org/10.1007/978-3-031-16788-1_2.

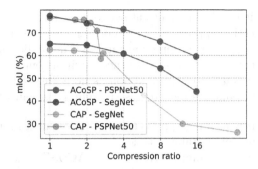

Fig. 1. Mean Intersection-over-Union (mIoU) as a function of the compression ratio for ACoSP and the baseline CAP [16]. The data is obtained by training SegNet and PSP-Net models on the CITYSCAPES dataset. For training details, see Sect. 4. We can clearly see that we are competitive with CAP at small compression ratios and significantly outperform it at high compression ratios.

In this work, we focus on model compression for semantic image segmentation using CNNs. We introduce a new pruning approach called AUTO-COMPRESSING SUBSET PRUNING, ACoSP for short, based on a modification of *Differential Subset Pruning* which was first introduced in Li et al. [24]. ACoSP efficiently reduces the number of convolution filters in the pruned model, resulting in a *thin* network compared to the unpruned counterpart. While most pruning approaches focus on finding the parameters or filters that can safely be removed, ACoSP focuses on the removal process itself. Moreover, the chip design of current accelerator hardware, such as GPUs or TPUs, limits their ability to efficiently deal with arbitrarily and sparsely connected networks resulting from unstructured pruning approaches, resulting in significant engineering efforts for efficient deployment [12,40]. Hence, the goal of ACoSP is to combine the parameter efficiency of unstructured pruning while preserving a structured architecture to ease the model deployment on current hardware. In short, ACoSP produces a thin, densely connected, and structured model.

To this end, we leverage the observation that higher parameter counts correlate with a decrease in the number of training steps required to train a model to a certain performance, as studied in transformer-based models [19,35] and image classification [31]. At the same time, the *Lucky Lottery Hypothesis* [10] tells us that only a few model parameters are relevant for training a model successfully, leading to sparsely connected network graphs. The key insight is to let the model use all of the parameters at the beginning of the training and then gradually decrease the importance of most convolution filters during training. In this way, we incentivize the model to compress most of the relevant parameters into the non-pruned layers while leveraging the lucky initialization and sample efficiency of large models at the beginning of the training.

With this approach, we turn pruning into a form of continuous auto-compression during the training, thus combining the benefits of high parameter counts during training with thin, efficient networks at inference time. In contrast to other learned selection approaches, our approach offers a simple selection process with a strictly enforced compression rate, and no additional loss function. This aids deployment in resource-constrained environments and preserves the guarantees of the original objective function as no additional losses need to be optimized during the compression process. To summarize our contributions:

- We introduce a new pruning approach for image segmentation that gradually compresses the model at training time,
- We demonstrate the competitiveness of ACoSP with other pruning approaches by applying it to two widely used image segmentation model architectures trained on the CamVid, Cityscapes, Pascal VOC2012, and ADE20k benchmark datasets,
- We demonstrate the importance of ACoSP's auto-compression and conclude with a study of the interaction of pruning and training.

The remainder of the paper is structured as follows: In Sect. 2, we give an overview of related pruning approaches. Section 3 lays out the fundamentals of pruning and subset selection. Section 3.2 introduces our approach and we demonstrate its application to semantic segmentation models. In Sect. 4, we show experiments and discuss results and analyses before we conclude our work in Sect. 5.

2   Related Work

Parameter reduction techniques, such as pruning fully connected neural networks (FCN) in an unstructured way, date back to the early days of neural networks with seminal works of LeCun et al. [22] and Hassibi and Stork [15]. Since then, many advances have been achieved. Neill [29] reviews various techniques. To give a few examples, Denil et al. [6] exploit that parameters in FCN and CNN exhibit structures that enable prediction of 95% of the model's weights using only 5% of the trained weights. In a different approach to pruning FCNs and CNNs, Srinivas and Babu [34] exploit redundancies in the models by removing individual neurons rather than individual weights from the network. Lebedev and Lempitsky [21] build upon these works and aim at preserving the structural advantages of having few but dense layers. They propose to remove individual filters in a convolution based on their matrix multiplication form in conjunction with approaches developed in LeCun et al. [22]. Li et al. [23] simplify the objective function to prune convolutional filters based on their ℓ_1-norm to induce thin networks. To regain lost accuracy, they introduce a second retraining step. Finally, a different route to compression of CNNs is taken by Liu et al. [25], who reduce the parameter counts in a network by exploiting the redundancy in parameters by using a sparse decomposition of the convolutional kernels. This allows them to express the full network with a significantly reduced memory footprint.

The above methods rely on removing parameters post-training and regaining lost accuracy through few-step retraining. To the best of our knowledge, Weigend et al. [37] are the first to introduce a method that incorporates pruning into the training procedure. Bejnordi et al. [1] pick up the idea of dynamic pruning and learn a gating function that switches on and off the convolution operator on certain filters of the convolution dynamically based on the feature input to the convolution block. A similar approach is followed by Kim et al. [20] who are learning a discrete rather than continuous gating function by introducing a relaxation of a non-differentiable discrete loss. Luo and Wu [28] predict the next layer's gating function from the previous layer's activations instead of the feature maps. Su et al. [36] use the weights of a pre-trained model to learn a gating function of the next layer. This lets them also optimize for the computational budget of the model through an added loss term on the objective function. A commonality of all these approaches is their reliance on additional loss terms in the objective function or on discrete, non-smooth removals of whole filters. This can lead to sub-optimal solutions or shocks in the model's training dynamics.

Most work studying pruning for computer vision focuses on image classification [2] leaving the question of transferability of these results to pixel-wise classification, as done in semantic segmentation, largely open. In contrast to the high information redundancy of classification-labels, semantic segmentation needs to preserve detailed pixel-level structures in the prediction map. When pruning indiscriminately, these structures can be lost, resulting in a lower performance of the model, which might not be recoverable with re-training [11]. We are aware of a few works that extend the investigations of pruning to semantic segmentation networks [9,16,26,32,39]; with only three of them [16,32,39] reporting results on commonly used benchmark datasets: He et al. [16] introduce a context-aware guidance module that leverages local context-aware features to control the channel scaling factors in the batch-normalization layers. They demonstrate the approach's efficacy on a set of different model architectures trained on CITYSCAPES and CAMVID. Schoonhoven et al. [32] view CNNs as computational graphs and use a longest-path algorithm to find relevant chains of computation greedily. They train models on a synthetic dataset and CAMVID. However, their reported results are not directly comparable to channel pruning, as they prune individual filter maps of a convolution rather than output channels. Finally, You et al. [39], introduce a channel-wise scaling factor whose importance is estimated through sensitivity analysis of the loss-function w.r.t., these parameters. They train these models on the PASCAL VOC2011 dataset [7] by iterating between training the model for a fixed set of iterations and a sensitivity estimation followed by a sparsification phase.

3 Auto-Compressing Subset Pruning

In contrast to the previous approaches, ACoSP learns channel-importance weights during training through annealing, thus avoiding shocks in the system. The dependency on the annealing schedule is weak and we show that it can even

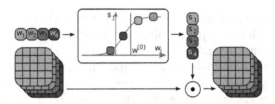

Fig. 2. ACoSP is applied to every convolution layer. It multiplies each output channel by a scaling factor s_j parameterized by a logit ω_j. An additional offset $\omega^{(0)}$ ensures that a predefined number is selected. A temperature variable is gradually decreased, annealing the SIGMOID to a step function until a binary channel selection mask remains.

be replaced with an arbitrary subset of filters to keep while slowly annealing all others weights to zero. Moreover, ACoSP does not rely on additional loss functions that compete with the original objective and removes the complicated trade-off of weighting these losses against each other. As an additional benefit, ACoSP also allows for fine-grained control of the final compression ratio. While we study ACoSP in the context of segmentation, it should be noted that the method is task-agnostic and can readily be applied to other problems.

These results are achieved by using a modification of Differential Subset Pruning introduced in the context of pruning transformer heads in large NLP models [24]. We exchange the SOFTMAX weighting with a simple SIGMOID and shifting operation to simulate an effective TOP-K operation and show how to apply this approach to CNN-based segmentation networks. This is in contrast to Xie et al. [38] who are using an optimal-transport-based differentiable TOP-K relaxation at a much higher computational cost.

3.1 Introduction

We are focusing on four key elements that need to be considered when pruning: (i) the inductive bias of the final compressed model (ii) the criteria to decide what should be pruned (iii) the schedule when to prune the elements, and (iv) how much should be pruned. To briefly recap:

Pruning Structure. To facilitate easy deployment on modern, specialized hardware, such as GPUs or TPUs, ACoSP aims at preserving the model structure to create thin, but densely connected networks. The trade-off compared to unstructured pruning, is a higher drop in performance, which is typically acceptable given the hardware constraints and increased ease of deployment.

Pruning Criteria. We avoid the introduction of additional loss functions based on heuristics, such as the ℓ_1-weight norm, by choosing a learned pruning approach. ACoSP learns a gate vector **s** whose number of elements corresponds to the number of convolution output channels for each convolution in our segmentation network (see Fig. 2). If certain components of the gate are almost closed, subsequent layers depend on these features only weakly, if at all. By forcing the gate signal to be close to zero or one, we remove or retain the respective filters, effectively compressing the model into the filters with open gates.

Pruning Schedule. To determine when to prune the chosen elements, we have several options: pruning before, after, or during the training and interleaving them in so-called tick-tock schedules [39].

Algorithm 1. ACoSP

Input: data x_i, model $\mathcal{M}$, epoch E, temp. schedule T
Output: train & pruned model $\mathcal{M}$
for e in $[1, \ldots, E]$ **do**
$\quad \tau \leftarrow T(e)$
$\quad$ **for** CONV c in $\mathcal{M}$ **do**
$\quad\quad \omega_{c,j} \leftarrow$ GETFILTERWEIGHT(c)
$\quad\quad \omega_c^{(0)} \leftarrow$ QUANTILE$_K(\omega_{c,j})$
$\quad\quad s_{c,j} \leftarrow$ SIGMOID $\left((\omega_{c,j} - \omega_c^{(0)}) \, / \, \tau\right)$
$\quad$ **end for**
$\quad \mathcal{M}.\text{update}()$
end for

Removing weights in a structured fashion after training, introduces shocks into the system, due to the removal of important weights of the underlying, unstructured *lottery winner* [10]. This is associated with strong performance degradation, which can only partially be recovered through retraining. To avoid such shocks, ACoSP compresses the model during training to transfer the information of the unstructured lottery winner into the remaining dense and structured filters. This is achieved by forcing the gating vectors to approach a binary value in $\{0, 1\}$ by using a SIGMOID-parameterization (see Fig. 2) and an effective temperature schedule.

Compression Ratio – Subset Selection. Typical online pruning techniques enforce compression ratios via additional loss functions. As a consequence, the final compression ratio is non-deterministic and hard to set at the outset of training. Posthoc methods, on the other hand, can easily be tailored to a target compression ratio, but suffer from the pruning shock as outlined above. ACoSP addresses this by approaching structured pruning via a subset selection process. Given a finite set $\mathcal{E} = \{1, \ldots, N\} \subset \mathbb{N}$ of elements and a pruning target fraction of $0 < r < 1$, the operation of removing $r \cdot N$ elements is equivalent to the selection of $K = \lfloor (1 - r) \cdot N \rfloor$ remaining elements. Hence, pruning to the given fraction r is equivalent to selecting a subset $\mathcal{S} \subseteq \mathcal{E}$ of cardinality K that maximizes the objective function. In the following, we will refer to this as a TOP-K operation.

Mathematically, we express the selection of element $j \in \mathcal{S}$ through the scaling factors $s_j \in \{0, 1\}$ and an additional constraint equation:

$$j \in \mathcal{S} \Leftrightarrow s_j = 1, \text{ subject to } \sum_j s_j = K. \tag{1}$$

Solving this constraint optimization problem while maximizing the objective function allows us to compress the model by selecting K individual elements under the observation of the total number of allowed selections. In our approach, this can be achieved by shifting the SIGMOID operation accordingly as indicated in Fig. 2.

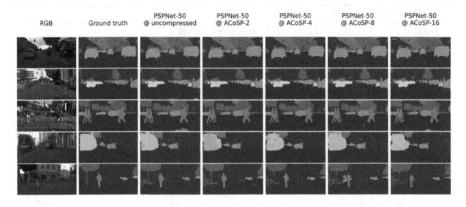

Fig. 3. Impact of the ACoSP strategy on the performance of a PSPNet-50, trained on CITYSCAPES, compared to the ground-truth at varying compression ratios. As can be expected, compression mostly impacts the resolution of fine details (clearly seen in the first row in the blue overhead bar and the vanishing of traffic poles in the second row). However, it is encouraging to see that the ACoSP does not forget concepts. For instance, the person crossing the street is discovered at all compression ratios. (Color figure online)

3.2   Details of the Algorithm

Leveraging subset selection to compress models efficiently is a general technique not limited to segmentation. We first describe it in an abstract setting and apply it to CNNs in a subsequent step.

General Framework of SIGMOID-Based Subset Selection. A first challenge is to find a differentiable relaxation of the TOP-K operator. While there are existing derivations of such operators [13,24,38], we have found them to be numerically unstable and/or inefficient when applied to vectors with thousands of entries; which we require to select channels from CNNs. The recursive Gumbel-softmax approach used in [24], in particular, requires one recursion for each selected element out of the Top-K. We, therefore, introduce a parallel, simple, stable, and differentiable approximation of the TOP-K operator that is applicable to a large set of elements.

We introduce the scaling factors $s_{c,j} \in [0,1]$, $j \in \{1,\ldots,N_c\}$, $c \in \{1,\ldots,C\}$, where N_c is the number of elements in a layer c, e.g., channels in the case of convolution, and C is the total number of layers in the model. The $s_{c,j}$ are parameterized via learnable weights $\omega_{c,j}$ and constrain them to the unit interval by using the SIGMOID function (see Fig. 2). We introduce a temperature variable $\tau \in \mathbb{R}^+$ to achieve gradual annealing of the SIGMOID selection into a binary mask. In the limit of $\tau \longrightarrow 0$, the SIGMOID turns into the Heaviside-step function $\Theta(\omega_{c,j}) = \mathbf{1}_{\omega_{c,j}>0}$. Here, $\mathbf{1}_x$ is the indicator function of condition x. Since SIGMOID is differentiable, gradients can be back-propagated through the gating operation, and the $\omega_{c,j}$ can be learned via gradient descent. The relaxed TOP-K operation is achieved by determining the offset value $\omega_c^{(0)}$, such that $\sum_j^N \mathbf{1}_{\omega_{c,j}>\omega_c^{(0)}} = K$. This is an extreme value problem, but it can easily be solved using a quantile function, or by selecting the K-th value of a reversely sorted array. The offset value allows us to shift the weights, and hence the scaling factors, in such a way that only the TOP-K elements fulfill.

$$\tilde{\omega}_{c,j} = \omega_{c,j} - \omega_c^{(0)} \begin{cases} > 0, & \text{if } j \in \mathcal{S} \\ < 0, & \text{otherwise.} \end{cases} \qquad (2)$$

Putting it together with the annealing schedule induced by the effective temperature, we can hence learn the channel selection mask via

$$s_{c,j} = \text{SIGMOID}\left(\frac{\tilde{\omega}_{c,j}}{\tau}\right) \xrightarrow{\tau \to 0} \begin{cases} 1, & \text{if } j \in \mathcal{S} \\ 0, & \text{otherwise.} \end{cases} \qquad (3)$$

The full algorithm is summarized as pseudocode in Algorithm 1. The key is to adjust the offset in each step to fix TOP-K elements that fulfill the Heaviside condition and slowly anneal the temperature to zero. The free choice of K allows us to control the final compression ratio during training and, more importantly, does not require any hyper-parameters.

While the gating factors $s_{c,j}$ are differentiable with respect to the weights $\omega_{c,j}$, the operation is not fully differentiable, because $\omega_c^{(0)}$ depends on all $\omega_{c,j}$ in a non-differentiable way.

Subset Selection for CNNs. The subset selection approach is general and can be applied to all problems involving a TOP-K operation. As a demonstration, we apply it to CNNs. As depicted in Fig. 2, we introduce a channel-wise scaling factor, i.e., a learnable gating vector whose elements are the weights for scaling values for each channel. For simplicity of the implementation, we note that due to the linearity of the convolution operator, it is sufficient to multiply the activations of the convolution with the corresponding scaling factors rather than the weights of the convolution.

Table 1. Detailed results of our ACoSP compressing strategy on the CITYSCAPES [4], PASCAL VOC2012 [8] and ADE20K [42] datasets. Unless otherwise noted, all experiments use a PSPNet with a ResNet-50 backbone pretrained on Imagenet [5] (for more detailed results on SegNet we refer to the appendix). For CITYSCAPES, we report the mIoU on the test set if available and the validation set in parenthesis. The table clearly shows the strength of ACoSP to keep a high performance despite a high compression ratio. †: Numbers are taken from [16]. *: Numbers taken from Bejnordi et al. [1]; Numbers were calculated on the CITYSCAPES validation set.; While not technically compression the network, they do reduce the required MACs due to their gating process. Numbers are reflecting the performance with the gating mechanism and without the mechanism in parenthesis.#: Numbers taken from You et al. [39]; the numbers are not directly comparable due to architectural differences (FCN-32 with VGG-16 backbone compared to a PSPNet50) as well as training being done on the *extended* PASCAL VOC 2011 dataset [7,14]. Mean inference time per sample t and standard deviation have been measured on a NVIDIA T4 on models trained on CITYSCAPES.

Method	CITYSCAPES			PASCAL VOC 2012 #	ADE20K
	mIoU (%)	Params [M] (↓ %)	Inference time t [ms]	mIoU (%)	mIoU (%)
Unpruned (OURS)	77.37 (78.0)	49.08	183.5 ± 24.6	72.71	41.42
CCGN [1] (from scratch) *	71.9 (70.6)	(23.7 % ↓)			
CCGN (pretrained)*	74.4 (73.9)	(23.5 % ↓)			
GBN [39]#				62.84 (62.86)	
FPGM [17] †	74.59	27.06 (47.40 % ↓)			
NS-20% [27]†	73.57	23.61 (54.11 % ↓)			
BN-Scale-20%†	73.85	23.59 (54.15 % ↓)			
CAP-60% [16]†	n/a (75.59)	27.31 (46.92 % ↓)			
CAP-70% †	n/a (73.94)	23.78 (53.78 % ↓)			
ACoSP-2 (Ours)	74.57 (74.1)	24.57 (50.00 % ↓)	90.54 ± 2.42 (2.03x)	72.70	38.97
ACoSP-4 (Ours)	71.05 (71.5)	12.32 (74.90 % ↓)	46.58 ± 1.22 (3.94x)	65.84	33.67
ACoSP-8 (Ours)	66.63 (66.1)	6.19 (87.39 % ↓)	23.30 ± 0.50 (7.88x)	58.26	28.04
ACoSP-16 (Ours)	59.50 (59.5)	3.14 (93.60 % ↓)	12.59 ± 0.18 (14.6x)	48.05	19.39

We determine the desired compression by assigning each convolution in the network a number of remaining channels $K_c \in \mathbb{Z}^+$ and lower-bound it by a minimal number of channels K_{min}. We choose $K_{min} = 8$ in our experiments. We then define a weight vector w_c to represent the gate, containing the weights $\omega_{c,j}$. The convolution blocks of the models in our experiment follow the post-activation pattern CONV → BATCHNORM → ACTIVATION.

Initialization and Temperature Annealing Schedule. During the calculation of the scaling factors, we normalize the weights $\omega_{c,j}$ of our gate vector w_c to avoid saturation of the SIGMOID function and to keep gradients finite and non-zero. This also allows us to use a single temperature value for every scaling operator in the network, even if the gradients are significantly different in magnitude. We initialize all $\omega_{c,j}$ by drawing values from a uniform distribution instead of using a constant value.

Finally, in order to encourage the transfer of concepts and the compression of models, we anneal the temperature over time. In the spirit of Li et al. [24], we choose an exponential decaying temperature schedule to keep a constant selection pressure during training. The exponential decay is fully determined by the decay constant, or the *pruning duration* for simplicity, which constitutes a hyper-parameter in our setup. After the final temperature has been reached, the SIGMOID is close to a step function and the masking layer has turned into a binary selection. The gate weights receive no gradient updates anymore, and the pruning selection is final.

4   Experiments

We evaluate the performance of ACoSP on the semantic segmentation benchmarks CAMVID [3], CITYSCAPES [4], PASCAL VOC2012 [8], and ADE20K [42]. For our experiments, we use the SegNet architecture with a VGG-16 backbone and a PSPNet with a ResNet-50 backbone. Both backbones are pretrained on IMAGENET [5].

To be able to evaluate ACoSP, we choose He et al. [16], You et al. [39], and Bejnordi et al. [1] as baselines, which motivates our choice of datasets and architectures. Most notably, this excludes state-of-the-art semantic segmentation architectures, and we leave the study of these architectures to future work. We note that we do not have access to either implementation or pretrained checkpoints of the references we compare ourselves to. Hence, we tried to reproduce these uncompressed baselines to the best of our knowledge.

We train each model on the respective datasets using the procedure described in the supplementary material and use ACoSP to prune the filters of all convolution and deconvolution layers of the architectures, except for the final output layer to retain expressivity. A global compression ratio is used to compute the retained number of channels for each convolution. However, independent of the compression ratio, at least 8 channels are being kept. We found this minimal number of channels to be beneficial during training and of negligible impact on parameters and floating point operations (FLOPs).

We run multiple ablation studies varying compression ratios and pruning durations, and additionally analyze the learned filter selection. To evaluate our trained models, we calculate the mean Intersection-over-Union (mIoU). Here we follow the evaluation pattern of Zhao et al. [41] and use a sliding window over the full input image.

Qualitative Assessment. Fig. 3 shows a subset of segmentation mask from a PSPNet trained on CITYSCAPES at varying degrees of compression (see supplementary materials for masks of other models and datasets). The samples have been chosen explicitly to highlight the impact of ACoSP on a variety of classes as well as small and large image features. ACoSP is able to preserve the major class information even with a compression ratio of 16 – a reduction of more than one order of magnitude in numbers of parameters – with degradations mostly limited to fine features such as sign posts and lamps. Moreover, it is important to note that ACoSP does not result in forgetting concepts but rather only a loss in boundary precision. Since we train the models using cross-entropy losses there is reason to believe that some of this loss can be recovered by using a more tailored loss function [18,30] such as the DICE-loss of Sørenson [33].

Compression Ratio. A major benefit of ACoSP is its ability to specify the compression ratio *a-priori*, in contrast to methods that require implicit methods, such as additional loss functions. We choose the compression ratios of our experiments $R = \{2^k \,|\, k = 0, \ldots, 4\} = \{1, 2, 4, 8, 16\}$ in a way that halves the remaining filters for every experiment in the series.

As can be seen in Fig. 1, we compare favorably to the baselines on the CITYSCAPES dataset for small compression ratios and outperform them significantly at high compression ratios for both architectures, SegNet and PSPNet. We report more exhaustive numbers in Table 1, to show that this behavior is consistent across datasets. To underline the focus on real-world model deployments, we also report parameter reductions and inference speed ups for the models trained on CITYSCAPES. We report similar results on SegNet and CITYSCAPES in the appendix.

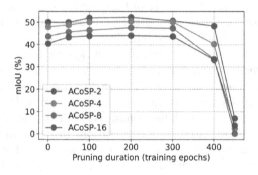

Fig. 4. mIoU as a function of pruning durations. The results are obtained using a SegNet architecture trained on CAMVID. The different curves show similar behavior for all tested compression ratios. Moreover, the performance of the final model is fairly robust w.r.t. the exact choice of the pruning duration. The performance drop due to the pruning shock of *post-hoc* pruning is clearly visible, and a minor drop due to a-priori training as well. Latter is likely due to the limited available capacity of the model.

Pruning Duration. Since ACoSP introduces the pruning duration as a new hyper-parameter via the temperature annealing schedule, we investigate the dependence of the results on the choice of this parameter. We fix the initial and final temperature at 1 and 0.001, respectively, and vary the annealing duration of the exponential schedule according to $D = \{0, 50, 100, 200, 300, 400, 450\}$. Note that $D = 0$ corresponds to a-priori pruning, i.e., pruning at the start of the training, while $D = 450$ corresponds to pruning after training, i.e., post-hoc compression. Intuitively the pruning duration controls the time the model has to compress relevant concepts into layers that are not pruned in the end.

Due to computational budget reasons, we perform this ablation by training a SegNet on the CAMVID dataset. The results are shown in Fig. 4 and indicate that the approach is fairly robust with respect to the exact choice of the pruning duration. As expected, pruning at initialization has slightly inferior performance due to the restricted capacity of the model. It can be expected that a more complicated and/or larger dataset will show a significantly more pronounced effect in the a-priori pruning case due to under-parametrization. Similarly, pruning at the end of training introduces a big shock to the system, resulting in a significant drop in performance. Otherwise, ACoSP is not sensitive with respect to the choice of the pruning duration. This behavior generally aligns with the intuition that the model needs the additional capacity to train efficiently in the beginning. Later in the training, the concepts can be gradually compressed into the remaining layers.

Generalization of the Approach. The mechanism behind ACoSP is generally applicable to all CNN-based architectures and with more modifications also to other model architectures. Hence it can also be used for other tasks and is not specific to semantic image segmentation. To demonstrate the transferability, we also evaluate ACoSP on the CIFAR10 image classification task using ResNet-18 resulting in a drop from 89.71% to 76.85% top-1 accuracy when reaching the maximum compression level. As the results are qualitatively similar to results obtained for the semantic segmentation task, we choose to omit the discussion from the main body and refer the reader to the supplementary material for more details.

5   Summary and Outlook

In this work, we focus on compressing semantic segmentation models to produce densely connected but thin architectures out of large state-of-the-art model architectures. The resulting models can easily be deployed in environments constrained by available compute and memory resources.

We introduce ACoSP, a new online compression method that selects convolutional channels during training using a learnable gate vector parameterized by a shifted-SIGMOID layer in conjunction with a temperature annealing schedule. Major advantages of this method are (i) its ability to specify the compression ratio a-priori and (ii) its independence of additional loss objectives that need tuning while at the same time (iii) being easy to implement. This comes at the expense of an additional hyper-parameter. However, we demonstrate that the method is robust with respect to the exact choice of this parameter. We show that our approach is robust with respect to model architectures and dataset choices and is competitive with existing segmentation baselines in the low-compression regime. Moreover, ACoSP outperforms previous approaches significantly in the high-compression regime on most datasets, with decent results even when discarding more than 93% of the model. We show that the success of ACoSP is not based on its exact selection mechanism but rather on the availability of large model capacity at the beginning of training working together with a compression pressure induced by the temperature annealing schedule driving the selection process.

While we studied this method in connection with semantic segmentation using CNNs, the underlying approach is generic. It can readily be applied to other data modalities and tasks and model architectures as demonstrated by a proof of concept using an image classification task. We leave further explorations as well as the application of ACoSP to state-of-the-art architectures, different tasks and data modalities and the study of more tailored loss functions to future work.

Our work contributes to the field of online model compression methods and rephrases the process in terms of self-compression via concept transfer. It enables us to leverage the advantage of large, over-parameterized state-of-the-art models while at the same time being able to tailor the resulting model to a given resource-constrained environment. We hope this work inspires more research investigating the transfer of relevant unstructured model weights into unpruned subsets of a more structured model.

6 Author Contributions, Acknowledgements and Disclosure of Funding

The authors would like to thank Thomas Wollmann, Stefan Dietzel, and Alexandra Lindt for valuable discussions and proofreading the manuscript. We also thank NVIDIA for generously providing us with compute resources as part of the partnership with the AI Campus, Berlin, as well as Altair for their IT support.

K.D. contributed to the design and implementation of the research, performed the experiments and analysis, and wrote the paper. J.S.O. contributed to the design of the research, wrote the paper, and supervised the work. All authors discussed the results and contributed to the final manuscript.

This work has been funded by EU ECSEL Project SECREDAS Cyber Security for Cross Domain Reliable Dependable Automated Systems (Grant Number: 783119). The authors would like to thank the consortium for the successful cooperation.

References

1. Bejnordi, B.E., Blankevoort, T., Welling, M.: Batch-shaping for learning conditional channel gated networks. arXiv:1907.06627 [cs, stat] (2020)
2. Blalock, D.W., Ortiz, J.J.G., Frankle, J., Guttag, J.V.: What is the state of neural network pruning? arXiv:2003.03033 (2020)

3. Brostow, G.J., Fauqueur, J., Cipolla, R.: Semantic object classes in video: a high-definition ground truth database. Patt. Recognit. Lett. **30**, 88–97 (2009)
4. Cordts, M., et al.: The cityscapes dataset for semantic urban scene understanding. arxiv:1604.01685 [cs] (2016)
5. Deng, J., Dong, W., Socher, R., Li, L.J., Li, K., Li, F.F.: ImageNet: a large-scale hierarchical image database. In: CVPR, pp. 248–255 (2009). https://doi.org/10.1109/CVPR.2009.5206848
6. Denil, M., Shakibi, B., Dinh, L., Ranzato, M., de Freitas, N.: Predicting parameters in deep learning. In: NIPS (2013)
7. Everingham, M., Van Gool, L., Williams, C.K.I., Winn, J., Zisserman, A.: The PASCAL visual object classes challenge 2011 (VOC2011) results. http://www.pascal-network.org/challenges/VOC/voc2011/workshop/index.html (2011)
8. Everingham, M., Van Gool, L., Williams, C.K.I., Winn, J., Zisserman, A.: The PASCAL visual object classes challenge 2012 (VOC2012) results. http://www.pascal-network.org/challenges/VOC/voc2012/workshop/index.html (2012)
9. Fernandes Junior, F.E., Nonato, L.G., Ranieri, C.M., Ueyama, J.: Memory-based pruning of deep neural networks for IoT devices applied to flood detection. Sensors **21**(22), 7506 (2021). https://doi.org/10.3390/s21227506. https://www.mdpi.com/1424-8220/21/22/7506
10. Frankle, J., Carbin, M.: The lottery ticket hypothesis: finding sparse, trainable neural networks. In: 7th International Conference on Learning Representations, ICLR 2019, 6–9 May 2019, New Orleans, LA, USA (2019). https://openreview.net/forum?id=rJl-b3RcF7
11. Frankle, J., Schwab, D.J., Morcos, A.S.: The early phase of neural network training. In: International Conference on Learning Representations (2020). https://openreview.net/forum?id=Hkl1iRNFwS
12. Gajurel, A., Louis, S.J., Harris, F.C.: GPU acceleration of sparse neural networks. arXiv:2005.04347 (2021)
13. Grover, A., Wang, E., Zweig, A., Ermon, S.: Stochastic optimization of sorting networks via continuous relaxations. In: 7th International Conference on Learning Representations, ICLR 2019, New Orleans, LA, USA, 6–9 May 2019 (2019). https://openreview.net/forum?id=H1eSS3CcKX
14. Hariharan, B., Arbeláez, P., Bourdev, L., Maji, S., Malik, J.: Semantic contours from inverse detectors. In: 2011 International Conference on Computer Vision, pp. 991–998 (2011). https://doi.org/10.1109/ICCV.2011.6126343
15. Hassibi, B., Stork, D.G.: Second order derivatives for network pruning: optimal brain surgeon. In: NIPS (1992). https://openreview.net/forum?id=HyZ7eYbOWH
16. He, W., Wu, M., Liang, M., Lam, S.K.: CAP: context-aware pruning for semantic segmentation. In: Proceedings of the IEEE/CVF Winter Conference on Applications of Computer Vision (WACV), pp. 960–969 (2021). https://openaccess.thecvf.com/content/WACV2021/papers/He_CAP_Context-Aware_Pruning_for_Semantic_Segmentation_WACV_2021_paper.pdf
17. He, Y., Liu, P., Wang, Z., Hu, Z., Yang, Y.: Filter pruning via geometric median for deep convolutional neural networks acceleration. In: 2019 IEEE/CVF Conference on Computer Vision and Pattern Recognition (CVPR), pp. 4335–4344 (2019). https://doi.org/10.1109/CVPR.2019.00447
18. Jadon, S.: A survey of loss functions for semantic segmentation. In: 2020 IEEE Conference on Computational Intelligence in Bioinformatics and Computational Biology (CIBCB), pp. 1–7 (2020)
19. Kaplan, J., et al.: Scaling laws for neural language models. arXiv:2001.08361 [cs, stat] (2020)

20. Kim, J., youn Park, C., Jung, H., Choe, Y.: Plug-in, trainable gate for streamlining arbitrary neural networks. In: AAAI (2020)
21. Lebedev, V., Lempitsky, V.S.: Fast convnets using group-wise brain damage. In: 2016 IEEE Conference on Computer Vision and Pattern Recognition (CVPR), pp. 2554–2564 (2016)
22. LeCun, Y., Denker, J., Solla, S.: Optimal brain damage. In: Touretzky, D. (ed.) Advances in Neural Information Processing Systems, vol. 2. Morgan-Kaufmann (1990). https://proceedings.neurips.cc/paper/1989/file/6c9882bbac1c7093bd25041881277658-Paper.pdf
23. Li, H., Kadav, A., Durdanovic, I., Samet, H., Graf, H.P.: Pruning filters for efficient convNets. arXiv:1608.08710 [cs] (2017)
24. Li, J., Cotterell, R., Sachan, M.: Differentiable subset pruning of transformer heads. Trans. Assoc. Comput. Linguist. **9**, 1442–1459 (2021)
25. Liu, B., Wang, M., Foroosh, H., Tappen, M., Pensky, M.: Sparse convolutional neural networks. In: Proceedings of the IEEE Conference on Computer Vision and Pattern Recognition (CVPR) (2015)
26. Liu, Y., Wang, Y., Qi, H., Ju, X., Wang, P.: SuperPruner: automatic neural network pruning via super network. Sci. Program. **2021**, 1–11 (2021). https://doi.org/10.1155/2021/9971669
27. Liu, Z., Li, J., Shen, Z., Huang, G., Yan, S., Zhang, C.: Learning efficient convolutional networks through network slimming. In: 2017 IEEE International Conference on Computer Vision (ICCV), pp. 2755–2763 (2017)
28. Luo, J.H., Wu, J.: AutoPruner: an end-to-end trainable filter pruning method for efficient deep model inference. arXiv:1805.08941 [cs] (2019)
29. Neill, J.O.: An overview of neural network compression. arxiv:2006.03669 [cs] (2020)
30. Reinke, A., et al.: Common limitations of image processing metrics: a picture story. arXiv:2104.05642 (2021)
31. Rosenfeld, J.S., Rosenfeld, A., Belinkov, Y., Shavit, N.: A constructive prediction of the generalization error across scales. arXiv:1909.12673 (2020)
32. Schoonhoven, R., Hendriksen, A.A., Pelt, D.M., Batenburg, K.J.: LEAN: graph-based pruning for convolutional neural networks by extracting longest chains. arXiv:2011.06923 (2020)
33. Sørenson, T.: A Method of Establishing Groups of Equal Amplitude in Plant Sociology Based on Similarity of Species Content and Its Application to Analyses of the Vegetation on Danish Commons. Biologiske skrifter, I kommission hos E. Munksgaard (1948). https://books.google.de/books?id=rpS8GAAACAAJ
34. Srinivas, S., Babu, R.V.: Data-free parameter pruning for deep neural networks. arxiv:1507.06149 [cs] (2015)
35. Strudel, R., Pinel, R.G., Laptev, I., Schmid, C.: Segmenter: transformer for semantic segmentation. In: 2021 IEEE/CVF International Conference on Computer Vision (ICCV), pp. 7242–7252 (2021)
36. Su, X et al.: Data agnostic filter gating for efficient deep networks. arXiv:2010.15041 [cs] (2020)
37. Weigend, A., Rumelhart, D., Huberman, B.: Generalization by weight-elimination with application to forecasting. In: Lippmann, R., Moody, J., Touretzky, D. (eds.) Advances in Neural Information Processing Systems, vol. 3. Morgan-Kaufmann (1990). https://proceedings.neurips.cc/paper/1990/file/bc6dc48b743dc5d013b1abaebd2faed2-Paper.pdf
38. Xie, Y., et al.: Differentiable top-k operator with optimal transport. arXiv:2002.06504 (2020)

39. You, Z., Yan, K., Ye, J., Ma, M., Wang, P.: Gate decorator: global filter pruning method for accelerating deep convolutional neural networks. In: Advances in Neural Information Processing Systems (NeurIPS) (2019)
40. Zhang, S., et al.: Cambricon-x: an accelerator for sparse neural networks. In: 2016 49th Annual IEEE/ACM International Symposium on Microarchitecture (MICRO), pp. 1–12 (2016)
41. Zhao, H., Shi, J., Qi, X., Wang, X., Jia, J.: Pyramid scene parsing network. In: 2017 IEEE Conference on Computer Vision and Pattern Recognition (CVPR), pp. 6230–6239 (2017)
42. Zhou, B., Zhao, H., Puig, X., Fidler, S., Barriuso, A., Torralba, A.: Scene parsing through ade20k dataset. In: 2017 IEEE Conference on Computer Vision and Pattern Recognition (CVPR), pp. 5122–5130 (2017)

Improving Robustness and Calibration in Ensembles with Diversity Regularization

Hendrik Alexander Mehrtens[1,2]([✉]) [ID], Camila Gonzalez[1] [ID],
and Anirban Mukhopadhyay[1] [ID]

[1] Technische Universität Darmstadt, 64289 Darmstadt, Germany
hendrikalexander.mehrtens@dkfz.de,
{camila.gonzalez,anirban.mukhopadhyay}@gris.tu-darmstadt.de
[2] Deutsches Krebsforschungszentrum, 69120 Heidelberg, Germany

Abstract. Calibration and uncertainty estimation are crucial topics in high-risk environments. Following the recent interest in the diversity of ensembles, we systematically evaluate the viability of explicitly regularizing ensemble diversity to improve robustness and calibration on in-distribution data as well as under dataset shift. We introduce a new diversity regularizer for classification tasks that uses out-of-distribution samples and increases the overall accuracy, calibration and out-of-distribution detection capabilities of ensembles. We demonstrate that diversity regularization is highly beneficial in architectures where weights are partially shared between the individual members and even allows to use fewer ensemble members to reach the same level of robustness. Experiments on CIFAR-10, CIFAR-100, and SVHN show that regularizing diversity can have a significant impact on calibration and robustness, as well as out-of-distribution detection.

Keywords: Diversity · Ensembles · Robustness · Calibration

1 Introduction

When a machine learning system is used in high-risk environments, such as medicine and autonomous driving, a well-calibrated estimate of the uncertainty is necessary. A model is said to be *calibrated* [9] if the confidence of its predictions reflects its true probability of being correct. However, deep neural networks tend to be overconfident in their predictions [9] leading to multiple recent approaches attempting to improve their calibration [2,32]. Furthermore, models need to be robust to shifts in the data domain, which can for example arise in the data shift between the training and deployment domains.

Supplementary Information The online version contains supplementary material available at https://doi.org/10.1007/978-3-031-16788-1_3.

B. Andres et al. (Eds.): DAGM GCPR 2022, LNCS 13485, pp. 36–50, 2022.
https://doi.org/10.1007/978-3-031-16788-1_3

To this day, Deep Ensembles [21] outperform most other approaches. A common explanation for the improved performance is the high diversity of solutions in the ensemble [4,6,27], which is mostly generated by training from different parameter initializations. While this approach works well empirically, distance in parameter space generated through training from different starting positions does not guarantee diversity in the solution space, which we refer to as *functional diversity* [43]. However, ensuring a diverse set of solutions in an ensemble is critical to its performance [6,43].

Following recent interest in the topic of diversity in neural networkbreak ensembles [6], many publications try to implicitly generate diversity by training with different architectures [1,45], different data augmentations [38] and different hyperparameters [42]. However, this approach to generate diversity is suboptimal, as it does not guarantee diversity. Additionally, choosing the right architectures and hyperparameters requires a lot of design decisions and is thereby time-consuming.

On the other side, functional diversity can be regularized explicitly [27], an idea recently used to improve adversarial robustness in ensembles [16,33]. Although these explicit approaches guarantee diversity of predictions, they rely on diversity measures on the original training data, which can lead to a degradation in accuracy. Additionally, these approaches do not perform well in tasks of out-of-distribution detection and the naive implementation requires the simultaneous training of multiple ensemble members, which is expensive and can be prohibitive in some tasks.

In our experiments, we put a special focus on ensembles that share parameters between the members. While these architectures require much less computational time, the lower ratio of independent parameters per member leads to a reduction of diverse predictions [25], which naturally lends itself to using explicit diversity maximization. For this, we use ensemble architectures with an increasing ratio of shared parameters between members and show that the effect of diversity regularization on robustness and calibration increases with a higher ratio of shared parameters.

We introduce the **Sample Diversity regularizer (SD)** that instead of using in-distribution images to diversify the predictions, uses out-of-distribution images. This, as we show, can be sampled from noise, not requiring an external dataset and increases accuracy and calibration under dataset shift, while also increasing the out-of-distribution detection capabilities of the model, contrary to our other baseline regularizers. The proposed regularizer can also be combined for greater effect with the other explicit diversity regularizers. Taking inspiration from the methods of Shui et al. [35], we systematically evaluate the effectiveness of explicit diversity regularization, coming to the conclusion that diversity regularization is especially useful when encountering dataset shift [32], even reducing the number of ensemble members needed for the same performance and allowing for the training of light-weight approximate ensemble architectures instead of full ensembles.

To summarize, our contributions are as follows:

- We demonstrate that diversity regularization **is highly effective for architectures with a high ratio of shared parameters**, reducing the number of needed ensemble members under dataset shift and allowing for smaller architectures.
- We introduce the **Sample Diversity regularizer**, which **increases the accuracy and calibration under dataset shift, as well as the out-of-distribution detection capabilities** and can be combined with existing diversity regularizers for greater effect.

2   Related Work

In recent years, calibration of deep neural networks has become a focus in machine learning research. Although multiple approaches, from temperature scaling [9], MC Dropout [7,18] to Variational Inference methods [3,28] have been explored, neural network ensembles have demonstrated that they produce the best-calibrated uncertainty estimates [2,21,32].

An important property of well-calibrated models is whether they still give reasonable uncertainties when encountering dataset shift, as this setting better reflects real-world conditions. Ovadia et al. [32] compared multiple approaches using the CIFAR-10-C, CIFAR-100-C and ImageNet-C datasets by Hendrycks et al. [12], coming to the conclusion that Deep Ensembles [22] outperformed every other approach, making them the de-facto standard for uncertainty estimation and robustness.

The superiority of ensembles in these task has been partly attributed to the diversity between the individual members [6]. Ensemble diversity, in general, has long been a research topic in machine learning with many early works recognizing it as a key principle in the performance of ensembles [4,27]. Recently, a greater focus has been placed on improving diversity in neural network ensembles by different *implicit* means, for example by providing each ensemble member with differently augmented inputs [38], building ensembles out of different neural network architectures [1,36,45] or training ensemble members with different hyperparameters [42].

Explicit approaches on the other hand try to maximize the diversity between ensemble members by orthogonalizing their gradients [16], decorrelating their predictions on all classes [27,35] or on randomly sampled noise inputs [15] or orthogonalizing only on non-correct classes [33]. Another strategy is to increase diversity in the internal activations or parameters of the ensemble members [23,34,37], which forms a promising direction but requires computationally expensive adversarial setups. Finally, there are sampling-based methods that try to maximize the diversity of the sampling procedure, for example through Determinantal Point Processes [20,40]. The advantage of these explicit approaches is that they can directly control the diversity in the ensemble and do not rely on decisions with indirect and often unclear consequences.

As training ensembles is expensive, multiple methods have tried to reduce training costs. Snapshot-based methods [8, 14] save multiple epochs along a training trajectory, Batch Ensembles [41] generate individual ensemble members by addition of a per-member Rank-1 Hadamard-product and TreeNets [25] approximate a Deep Ensemble by sharing the lower levels of a network between members. Furthermore, distillation approaches were proposed [39, 44] that try to compress multiple networks into a single one. However, these approaches tend to reduce the diversity between the individual members, by either sharing parameters between them or not training them independently, leading to a reduction in accuracy and calibration.

In this work we show that diversity regularization is highly useful in parameter shared ensembles and that diversity regularization can not only help with accuracy and under dataset shift but also with out-of-distribution detection. Taking inspiration from Jain et al. [15] we introduce an explicit diversity regularizer for classification that uses out-of-distribution samples, leaving the predictions on the original data intact.

3   Methods and Metrics

For our evaluation, we consider a classification task with C classes. Given a data point $x \in \mathbb{R}^L$ out of a dataset with N entries and its corresponding one-hot label $\hat{y} \in \mathbb{R}^C$, the prediction of the j-*th* member of an ensemble with M members is called $f(x, \theta_j) = y_j$, where $\theta_j \in \mathbb{R}^P$ are the parameters of the jth ensemble member. We refer to the mean of all predictions as $\bar{y}$.

In this section, we describe the evaluated regularization functions, architectures, and metrics as well as introduce our novel approach to diversity regularization.

3.1   Regularizers

Given an image x, a label $\hat{y}$ and the ensemble predictions $y_i, i \in [1, ..., M]$, all regularizers $\mathcal{L}_{reg}$, which will be introduced in the following paragraphs, work as a regularizer to the cross-entropy (CE) loss, where λ_{reg} is a hyper-parameter that is chosen for each individual method.

$$\mathcal{L}_{total}(\hat{y}, y_1, ..., y_M) = \mathcal{L}_{CE}(\hat{y}, \bar{y}) - \lambda_{reg}\mathcal{L}_{reg}(...) \tag{1}$$

For our experiments, we select a set of regularization functions that compute a measure of similarity of the individual ensemble members' predictions. An illustration of the general structure can be seen in Fig. 1.

Regularizers under consideration are our *Sample Diversity* regularizer, the *ADP* [33] regularizer, which was recently introduced for increasing robustness in ensembles to adversarial attacks, and the *Negative Correlation* regularizer.

Additionally we consider the average pair-wise χ^2 distance (see Eq. 4). All these regularizers encourage the individual members to have diverse predictions given the same input and can therefore be seen as increasing the functional diversity.

Negative Correlation: The *Negative Correlation* regularizer was first used by Liu et al. [27] to increase the diversity in neural network ensembles. The key insight was that the error of an ensemble depends upon the correlation of the errors between individual members [4]. Originally designed for regression tasks, it was already used by Shui et al. [35] to improve the diversity and calibration in neural network ensembles in classification tasks. This approach however reduces the accuracy of the ensemble and can lead to training instabilities.

$$NegCorr(y_1, ..., y_M) = -\sum_i^C ((y_i - \bar{y}) \cdot (\sum_{i \neq j} y_j - \bar{y})) \tag{2}$$

ADP: The *ADP* regularizer [33] orthogonalizes the predictions of the ensemble members on the non-correct classes during training.

Given a correct class k, the vector of the predictions for the non-correct classes are formed $y_i^{\setminus k} = (y_i^1, \ldots, y_i^{k-1}, y_i^{k+1}, \ldots, y_i^C)$, re-normalized and stacked into a matrix $Y_{\setminus k} \in \mathbb{R}^{(C-1) \times M}$. Furthermore an entropy regularizer (H) is used to prevent extreme solutions. Together the regularizer is optimized using the hyperparameters α and β.

$$ADP(\bar{y}^{\setminus k}, y_1^{\setminus k}, \ldots, y_C^{\setminus k}) = \alpha \cdot H(\bar{y}^{\setminus k}) + \beta \log(det(Y_{\setminus k}^T \cdot Y_{\setminus k})) \tag{3}$$

χ^2 **distance:** As a distance measure between distributions, we implement the average pair-wise χ^2 distance between the members' predictive distributions as a regularizer. Like the likelihood, the measure lives on the range $[0, 1]$ and the regularizer can be computed as

$$\chi^2(y_1, ..., y_M) = \log\left(\frac{1}{M \cdot (M-1)} \sum_{i \neq j} \sum_{k=1}^C \frac{y_i^{(k)} - y_j^{(k)}}{y_i^{(k)} + y_j^{(k)}}\right) \tag{4}$$

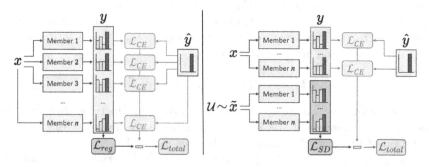

Fig. 1. Conceptual figure showcasing the differences between approaches. (left) Given an input x, the individual members are not only optimized individually with regard to the cross-entropy loss but the predictions are additionally regularized by a diversity regularizer (L_{reg}). The predictions of the individual members on the original input are compared by a diversity regularizer. (right) Our *Sample Diversity* (L_{SD}) approach utilizes additional inputs, sampled from the uniform distribution, to compute a measure of diversity as a regularizer. This preserves the original predictions on the training data.

Sample Diversity

Building on the work of Jain et al. [15] and the loss-formulation of *ADP* [33], we introduce a similar regularizer for classification tasks, which we illustrate in Fig. 1. Instead of regularizing diversity on the predictions of in-distribution data points, which could degrade performance, we generate out-of-distribution data points and enforce predictive orthogonality there. The loss reaches a minimum if all predictions are orthogonal on the sampled data points and thereby diverse but correct on the in-distribution data. Image batches are sampled from the uniform probability distribution (white noise). Given all logits outputs for a sampled data point $\tilde{x} \sim U^{H \times W}$, of all M ensemble members $(\tilde{y}_1, ..., \tilde{y}_M)$, normalized to length one and stacked in a matrix $\tilde{Y} \in \mathbb{R}^{C \times M}$, we maximize Eq. 5 as our regularizer.

$$SampleDiversity(\tilde{y}_1, ..., \tilde{y}_M) = log(det(\tilde{Y}^T \cdot \tilde{Y})) \qquad (5)$$

Other possible formulations are evaluated in the supplemental material, for comparability we stick to the *ADP* loss formulation. In the out-of-distribution detection literature, multiple other approaches that utilize OOD data during training exist, however these approaches act on single neural networks, utilize adversarial generators and experiment in the out-of-distribution detection domain [13,24,29]. Our goal is to formulate a practical functional diversity regularizer that utilizes the strength of ensembles, while not requiring expensive adversarial training.

3.2 Architectures

As more shared parameters reduce the computational resources required when training an ensemble but also the diversity of the ensemble, we study if higher dependency between members, increases the viability of diversity regularization. To this end, we compare the independently trained Deep Ensembles of randomly initialized neural networks [21] without adversarial training with TreeNets [25] that approximate a Deep Ensemble by sharing a base part of the network with each member, as well as Batch Ensembles [41] that generate their members by adding a Rank-1 Hadamard product to the parameter matrices of a base network and have the least number of independent parameters. We limit the scope of our study to the aforementioned architectures, although other architectures like the MiMo architecture [10] exist, as they are closest in structure to the Deep Ensemble.

3.3 Metrics

When working with calibration it is not only important to be well-calibrated on the original data but also under reasonable dataset shifts, which is crucial for real-world application. To evaluate this, corrupted datasets are used that simulate realistic noise and corruptions settings. All our metrics will be reported on the original datasets, as well as under dataset shift. In addition to accuracy and negative log-likelihood (NLL), we measure additional metrics, which are explained in the following:

Calibration: A commonly used measure of calibration is the *Expected Calibration Error* (ECE) [30]. As noticed by Ashuka et al. [2] this metric may not produce consistent rankings between models. For this reason, temperature scaling [9] with five-fold cross-validation on the test-set is deployed to generate consistent results. The temperature is computed for each dataset on the uncorrupted version. Our scores are computed after applying temperature scaling to the predictions. The temperature is chosen to minimize the negative log-likelihood, as proposed by Guo et al. [9].

AUC-ROC: The ability of detecting out-of-distribution data is tested, as intuitively more diverse ensemble members should produce more diverse predictions when evaluated on out-of-distribution data. We use the confidence of the average prediction of the ensemble as threshold classifier for distinguishing between in-distribution (ID) and out-of-distribution (OOD) data. Following [2] the AUC-ROC metric is reported for OOD detection.

Table 1. Experiments on CIFAR-10. Comparison of diversity regularization on different architectures with ensemble size 5 under dataset shift on the original (org.) data and highest corruption level (corr.).

Model	Method	Accuracy ↑		ECE ↓	
		org.	corr.	org.	corr.
DeepEns.	ind.	$\mathbf{0.936}_{\pm 0.001}$	$0.543_{\pm 0.010}$	$0.023_{\pm 0.001}$	$0.170_{\pm 0.014}$
	ADP	$0.933_{\pm 0.000}$	$0.549_{\pm 0.005}$	$0.032_{\pm 0.002}$	$\mathbf{0.126}_{\pm 0.010}$
	NegCorr.	$0.934_{\pm 0.001}$	$0.538_{\pm 0.002}$	$0.023_{\pm 0.001}$	$0.164_{\pm 0.007}$
	χ^2	$0.934_{\pm 0.001}$	$0.542_{\pm 0.006}$	$0.023_{\pm 0.000}$	$0.171_{\pm 0.008}$
	SampleDiv.	$0.933_{\pm 0.001}$	$\mathbf{0.579}_{\pm 0.004}$	$\mathbf{0.022}_{\pm 0.001}$	$0.134_{\pm 0.007}$
TreeNet	ind.	$0.919_{\pm 0.002}$	$0.523_{\pm 0.01}$	$0.035_{\pm 0.001}$	$0.234_{\pm 0.010}$
	ADP	$0.917_{\pm 0.002}$	$0.535_{\pm 0.019}$	$\mathbf{0.024}_{\pm 0.000}$	$\mathbf{0.180}_{\pm 0.031}$
	NegCorr.	$0.918_{\pm 0.003}$	$0.528_{\pm 0.013}$	$0.027_{\pm 0.002}$	$0.200_{\pm 0.014}$
	χ^2	$\mathbf{0.920}_{\pm 0.004}$	$0.517_{\pm 0.013}$	$0.027_{\pm 0.001}$	$0.238_{\pm 0.013}$
	SampleDiv.	$0.916_{\pm 0.002}$	$\mathbf{0.545}_{\pm 0.007}$	$0.030_{\pm 0.002}$	$0.213_{\pm 0.014}$
BatchEns.	ind.	$0.905_{\pm 0.001}$	$0.512_{\pm 0.019}$	$0.097_{\pm 0.002}$	$0.285_{\pm 0.014}$
	ADP	$\mathbf{0.906}_{\pm 0.002}$	$0.517_{\pm 0.011}$	$\mathbf{0.032}_{\pm 0.008}$	$\mathbf{0.171}_{\pm 0.049}$
	NegCorr.	$0.904_{\pm 0.001}$	$0.503_{\pm 0.002}$	$0.072_{\pm 0.021}$	$0.258_{\pm 0.030}$
	χ^2	$0.905_{\pm 0.002}$	$0.503_{\pm 0.014}$	$0.058_{\pm 0.007}$	$0.265_{\pm 0.030}$
	SampleDiv.	$0.904_{\pm 0.000}$	$\mathbf{0.545}_{\pm 0.007}$	$0.037_{\pm 0.015}$	$0.175_{\pm 0.032}$

4   Experiments and Results

We first describe the general setup that is used in all of our experiments. After that, we test the effect of our different diversity regularizers on the accuracy, *NLL* and calibration and later focus on out-of-distribution detection.

4.1   Datasets, Models, and Training

The base architecture for all our experiments is a ResNet-20 [11]. We train our models on the CIFAR-10, CIFAR-100 [19] and SVHN [31] datasets. For experiments under dataset shift, we use the corrupted versions of the CIFAR-10 and CIFAR-100 datasets created by Hendrycks et al. [12] and additionally create a corrupted version of the SVHN dataset using all 19 corruptions with 5 levels of corruption intensity.

All experiments are conducted, unless otherwise stated, with a learning rate of $1e - 4$, a L_2 weight decay of $2e - 4$, a batch size of 128 and Adam [17] as the optimizer, with the default β_1 and β_2 parameters. Each model is trained for 320 epochs. For augmentation, we use random crops and random horizontal flips, as described by Kaiming et al. [11]. The optimal temperatures are computed by five-fold cross-validation on the test dataset, as suggested by Ashukha et al. [2].

When using the TreeNet architecture the ResNet is split after the second pooling operation. The cross-entropy loss is computed for each member individually and then combined. When training the Batch Ensemble, each member is trained with the same inputs at each step, so it is possible to compare the predictions of the individual members. Batch Ensemble was originally trained by splitting a batch over the ensemble members in each step. When evaluating the impact of this change, we found no significant differences between the two training methods. The comparison can be found in the supplemental material.

Each experiment is performed 3 times and we report the mean performance together with the standard deviation. Whenever possible, hyperparameters are chosen as presented in the original papers. All other parameters were fine-tuned by hand on a 10% split of the training data.

When training with the *ADP* regularizer, we use the parameters $\alpha = 0.125$, $\beta = 0.5$ which performed best for us in preliminary experiments. Those are the original parameters reported in the paper scaled by a factor of 0.25. For the *Sample Diversity* regularizer, we choose the number of sampled images equal to the original batch size. The images are sampled uniformly on all 3 channels in the range $[0, 1]$. We then choose $\lambda_{SD} = 0.5$ for training. The χ^2 baseline used $\lambda_{\chi^2} = 0.25$. The *Negative Correlation* regularizer proved hard to train in a stable manner. We use $\lambda_{NC} = 1e - 5$, as values above this threshold destabilized the training process.

4.2   Diversity Regularization Under Dataset Shift

We train the Deep Ensemble, TreeNet, and Batch Ensemble architectures on CIFAR-10, CIFAR-100, and SVHN. The experiments are performed with 5 ensemble members. On all three datasets, we compare the independently trained ensembles, which we refer to as 'ind.' in our figures, with the regularized variants. We then evaluate all models on the corrupted versions of the datasets, comparing the accuracy, NLL and ECE.

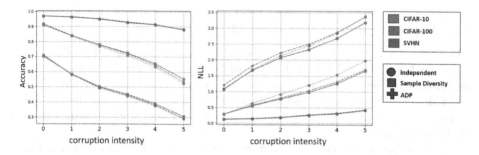

Fig. 2. Accuracy (left) and NLL (right) with different regularizers over different datasets.

Table 1 shows the results of our experiments on CIFAR-10 and the corrupted variant with all architectures. We compare the accuracy and ECE on the original data and on the highest corruption level. The results for the CIFAR-100 and SVHN datasets can be found in the supplemental material.

The *Sample Diversity* regularizer outperforms all other regularization functions in terms of accuracy on the corrupted data, improving the accuracy under dataset shift by 3.6% (Deep Ensemble), 2.3% (TreeNet) and 3.3% (Batch Ensemble), as can be seen on all architectures under dataset shift. Both the *Sample Diversity* and *ADP* regularizer outperform the other approaches in terms of ECE. The only exception occurs on the non-corrupted data with the Deep Ensembles architecture, where the *ADP* regularizer slightly decreases the calibration. Overall the χ^2 and *Negative Correlation* regularizer perform worse. This is most likely due to the fact that the diversity in these regularizers is also enforced on the correct class. When training these regularizers we also observed training instabilities.

As hypothesized the diversity regularization is effective when using constrained ensemble architectures. This is particularly noticeable for the Batch Ensemble architecture, which has the highest amount of shared weights per member, but also on the TreeNet architecture, a significant decrease of the ECE is observable, even on the original data, compared to the Deep Ensemble architecture, where diversity regularization performs worse. An interesting observation is that the TreeNet and Batch Ensemble regularized with the *Sample Diversity* loss outperform the Deep Ensemble of the same size (54.5% on both architectures, compared to 54.3% for the unregularized Deep Ensemble) on the corrupted data in terms of classification accuracy. Looking at the results it is clear that regularizing diversity helps in improving robustness to dataset shifts. It improves ensemble calibration, lowering the ECE under dataset shift significantly.

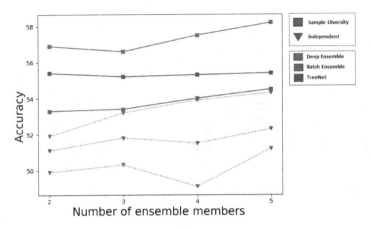

Fig. 3. Comparison of the three different architectures over the ensemble sizes 2 to 5 on the highest corruption level on CIFAR-10.

The displayed metrics show a clear split between *ADP* and *Sample Diversity* on one side and the normal training routine on the other side.

Figure 2 compares the mean accuracy and negative log-likelihood of the *Sample Diversity* and *ADP* regularizer over all three datasets. We use a TreeNet with 5 members. The x-axis denotes the corruption level, the colors encode the dataset, while the line style and marker encode the regularizer. The *Sample Diversity* regularizer (solid, square) consistently improves the accuracy and decreases the negative log-likelihood under dataset shift. This difference is especially noticeable for the CIFAR-10 and CIFAR-100 datasets, on SVHN all methods stay relatively close to each other. The *ADP* (dashed, plus) regularizer on the other hand can even strongly decrease the negative log-likelihood on the original data, as can be seen with the CIFAR-100 results.

Figure 3 compares the effectiveness of *Sample Diversity* regularization on the highest corruption level of CIFAR-10 over the different ensemble sizes 2 to 5, comparing the mean accuracy, *NLL* and *ECE*. The colors encode the architecture, while the line style and marker encode the regularizer (*Sample Diversity* or independent training). As can be seen in the figure, diversity regularization is even highly effective when using as few as 2 ensemble members and does not require a large pool of members. Even a TreeNet or BatchEnsemble with 2 members, outperforms the unregularized equivalent with 5 members. This strongly reduces the number of ensemble members required for the same performance and shows that even lightweight ensemble architectures can outperform a Deep Ensemble. A table with detailed results can be found in the supplemental material.

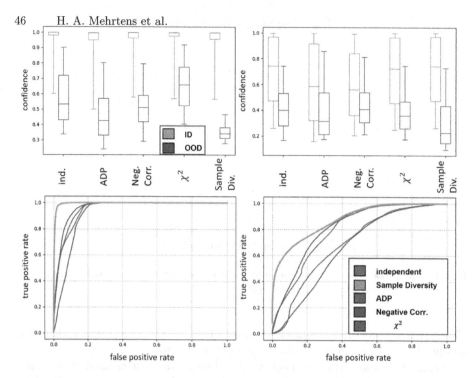

Fig. 4. Distribution of confidence (top) and ROC curve for distinguishing between ImageNet and ID data (bottom) for a TreeNet architecture with 5 members with different regularization's on CIFAR-10 (left) and CIFAR-100 (right).

4.3   Out-of-Distribution Detection

Figure 4 shows the distribution of confidence and the receiver operating characteristic (ROC) for differentiating between in-distribution and out-of-distribution data, which was in this experiment chosen as tinyImageNet [26], a 200-class subset of the ImageNet [5] dataset. The evaluated models are TreeNet architectures with 5 members, trained on CIFAR-10 and CIFAR-100. We do not report on SVHN, as every model there reached a near-perfect separation between in- and out-of-distribution data.

Looking at the ROC on CIFAR-10, *Negative Correlation* and *ADP* improve the separation slightly, while *Sample Diversity* strongly increases the dataset separation. Things look different on CIFAR-100 where all regularizers but *Sample Diversity* decrease the separation of the two datasets compared to independent training. To explain this, we take a look at the differences in the confidence distributions across the datasets. While all models are fairly confident in their predictions on CIFAR-10, most likely due to the few well-separated classes, on CIFAR-100 every model is highly uncertain, with confidence distributions between in-distribution data and OOD highly overlapping. There, the increased uncertainty that *Negative Correlation* and *ADP* introduce on in-distribution predictions is a disadvantage as the confidence distributions now tend to overlap more. On the other hand, *Sample Diversity* that only encourages orthogonality on OOD data improves the OOD detection capability.

Table 2. AUC-ROC over three runs, on separating in-distribution data and out-of-distribution data. Entries marked with '-' diverged.

Model	Method	AUC-ROC ↑	
(trained on)		CIFAR-10	CIFAR-100
DeepEns.	indi.	$0.980_{\pm 0.014}$	$0.798_{\pm 0.025}$
	ADP	$0.965_{\pm 0.017}$	$0.804_{\pm 0.034}$
	NCL	$\mathbf{0.993}_{\pm 0.001}$	$0.729_{\pm 0.038}$
	χ^2	$0.983_{\pm 0.011}$	$0.834_{\pm 0.037}$
	SD	$0.982_{\pm 0.012}$	$\mathbf{0.919}_{\pm 0.026}$
TreeNet	indi0.	$0.947_{\pm 0.044}$	$0.799_{\pm 0.049}$
	ADP	$0.952_{\pm 0.008}$	$0.695_{\pm 0.050}$
	NCL	$0.960_{\pm 0.011}$	$0.663_{\pm 0.097}$
	χ^2	$0.916_{\pm 0.020}$	$0.815_{\pm 0.019}$
	SD	$\mathbf{0.995}_{\pm 0.003}$	$\mathbf{0.877}_{\pm 0.122}$
BatchEns.	indi.	$0.928_{\pm 0.008}$	$0.497_{\pm 0.187}$
	ADP	$0.909_{\pm 0.026}$	$0.595_{\pm 0.110}$
	NCL	$0.934_{\pm 0.076}$	-
	χ^2	$0.974_{\pm 0.008}$	$\mathbf{0.809}_{\pm 0.122}$
	SD	$\mathbf{0.991}_{\pm 0.004}$	$0.614_{\pm 0.080}$

Table 2 reports the AUC-ROC, as suggested by Ashuka et al. [2], for all our evaluated models. None of the baseline regularizers is able to consistently increase the AUC-ROC over the level reached by independent training. *Sample Diversity*, even though it is not the best in every single experiment, outperforms independent training and nearly all other regularizers consistently in every setting. We conclude that *Sample Diversity* can not only increase the robustness and calibration but at the same time also the out-of-distribution detection capabilities of the model, while only requiring uninformative out-of-distribution noise and no additional datasets.

Ablation studies, as well as more detailed results can be found in the supplemental material. There the experiments indicate that the *ADP* loss formulation is sub-optimal and future research could increase the viability of diversity regularization further. Furthermore, adversarial training for the image generation of *Sample Diversity* or using real out-of-distribution data like ImageNet instead of the uniformly sampled noise images, does not lead to any further improvements. We also conduct experiments, measuring the impact of distance in parameter space and the different behaviors of our tested regularizers. Finally, we test other architectures are tested to confirm our results.

5   Conclusion

We conduct a comprehensive study comparing different popular diversity regularization methods on robustness, calibration and out-of-distribution detection benchmarks, over multiple datasets and architectures. Furthermore, we introduce the *Sample Diversity* regularizer, which is well suited for **improving accuracy and ECE and can be combined with the *ADP* regularizer for greater effect**. Contrary to other regularizers, our regularizer **also increases the out-of-distribution detection capabilities**. Our experiments show that **diversity regularized ensembles are better in terms of accuracy and calibration under dataset shift**. Regularizing ensembles beyond the diversity reached by independent training especially on architectures with shared parameters is beneficial. Even **the TreeNet and Batch Ensemble can outperform a Deep Ensemble in terms of robustness to dataset shift when diversity regularization is used**, even when we use fewer members.

Acknowledgements. I would like to thank the Deutsches Krebsforschungszentrum (DKFZ) for supporting the publication of this paper. I am grateful for everyone who proof-read the present and earlier versions of the manuscript, providing helpful insights.

References

1. Antorán, J., Allingham, J.U., Hernández-Lobato, J.M.: Depth uncertainty in neural networks. In: Advances in Neural Information Processing Systems (2020)
2. Ashukha, A., Lyzhov, A., Molchanov, D., Vetrov, D.: Pitfalls of in-domain uncertainty estimation and ensembling in deep learning. In: International Conference on Learning Representations (2020)
3. Blundell, C., Cornebise, J., Kavukcuoglu, K., Wierstra, D.: Weight uncertainty in neural networks. In: Proceedings of the 32nd International Conference on Machine Learning (ICML 2015) (2015)
4. Brown, G.: Diversity in Neural Network Ensembles. Ph.D. thesis, University of Manchester, March 2004
5. Deng, J., Dong, W., Socher, R., Li, L.J., Li, K., Fei-Fei, L.: Imagenet: a large-scale hierarchical image database. In: 2009 IEEE Conference on Computer Vision and Pattern Recognition, pp. 248–255. IEEE (2009)
6. Fort, S., Hu, H., Lakshminarayanan, B.: Deep ensembles: a loss landscape perspective (2019)
7. Gal, Y., Ghahramani, Z.: Dropout as a Bayesian approximation: representing model uncertainty in deep learning. In: International Conference on Machine Learning, pp. 1050–1059 (2016)
8. Garipov, T., Izmailov, P., Podoprikhin, D., Vetrov, D., Wilson, A.G.: Loss surfaces, mode connectivity, and fast ensembling of DNNs. In: Advances in Neural Information Processing Systems (2018)
9. Guo, C., Pleiss, G., Sun, Y., Weinberger, K.Q.: On calibration of modern neural networks. In: Precup, D., Teh, Y.W. (eds.) Proceedings of the 34th International Conference on Machine Learning. Proceedings of Machine Learning Research, vol. 70, pp. 1321–1330. PMLR, 06–11 August 2017

10. Havasi, M., et al.: Training independent subnetworks for robust prediction. In: Ninth International Conference on Learning Representations (ICLR 2021) (2021)
11. He, K., Zhang, X., Ren, S., Sun, J.: Deep residual learning for image recognition. In: 2016 IEEE Conference on Computer Vision and Pattern Recognition (CVPR) (2016)
12. Hendrycks, D., Dietterich, T.: Benchmarking neural network robustness to common corruptions and perturbations. In: International Conference on Learning Representations (2019)
13. Hendrycks, D., Mazeika, M., Dietterich, T.: Deep anomaly detection with outlier exposure. In: International Conference on Learning Representations (2019)
14. Huang, G., Li, Y., Pleiss, G., Liu, Z., Hopcroft, J.E., Weinberger, K.Q.: Snapshot ensembles: Train 1, get m for free (2017)
15. Jain, S., Liu, G., Mueller, J., Gifford, D.: Maximizing overall diversity for improved uncertainty estimates in deep ensembles. In: Proceedings of the AAAI Conference on Artificial Intelligence, vol. 34, pp. 4264–4271 (2020)
16. Kariyappa, S., Qureshi, M.K.: Improving adversarial robustness of ensembles with diversity training (2019)
17. Kingma, D.P., Ba, J.: Adam: a method for stochastic optimization. In: Bengio, Y., LeCun, Y. (eds.) 3rd International Conference on Learning Representations, ICLR 2015, San Diego, CA, USA, May 7–9, 2015, Conference Track Proceedings (2015)
18. Kingma, D.P., Salimans, T., Welling, M.: Variational dropout and the local reparameterization trick. In: Advances in Neural Information Processing Systems, pp. 2575–2583 (2015)
19. Krizhevsky, A.: Learning multiple layers of features from tiny images (2009)
20. Kulesza, A.: Determinantal point processes for machine learning. In: Foundations and Trends®in Machine Learning, vol. 5, p. 123–286. Now Publishers (2012)
21. Lakshminarayanan, B., Pritzel, A., Blundell, C.: Simple and scalable predictive uncertainty estimation using deep ensembles. In: Advances in Neural Information Processing Systems (2017)
22. Lakshminarayanan, B., Pritzel, A., Blundell, C.: Simple and scalable predictive uncertainty estimation using deep ensembles. In: Advances in Neural Information Processing Systems, vol. 30 (2017)
23. Larrazabal, A.J., Martínez, C., Dolz, J., Ferrante, E.: Orthogonal ensemble networks for biomedical image segmentation. In: de Bruijne, M., et al. (eds.) MICCAI 2021. LNCS, vol. 12903, pp. 594–603. Springer, Cham (2021). https://doi.org/10.1007/978-3-030-87199-4_56
24. Lee, K., Lee, H., Lee, K., Shin, J.: Training confidence-calibrated classifiers for detecting out-of-distribution samples. In: International Conference on Learning Representations (2018)
25. Lee, S., Purushwalkam, S., Cogswell, M., Crandall, D., Batra, D.: Why m heads are better than one: training a diverse ensemble of deep networks (2015)
26. Li, F.F., Karpathy, A., Johnson, J.: The tinyimagenet dataset - kaggle. http://www.kaggle.com/c/tiny-imagenet
27. Liu, Y., Yao, X.: Ensemble learning via negative correlation. In: Neural Networks, vol. 12 (1999)
28. Maddox, W.J., Izmailov, P., Garipov, T., Vetrov, D.P., Wilson, A.G.: A simple baseline for bayesian uncertainty in deep learning. In: Advances in Neural Information Processing Systems, pp. 13153–13164 (2019)
29. Malinin, A., Gales, M.: Reverse kl-divergence training of prior networks: improved uncertainty and adversarial robustness. In: Advances in Neural Information Processing Systems (2019)

30. Naeini, M.P., Cooper, G.F., Hauskrecht, M.: Obtaining well calibrated probabilities using Bayesian binning. In: AAAI. AAAI 2015, pp. 2901–2907. AAAI Press (2015)
31. Netzer, Y., Wang, T., Coates, A., Bissacco, A., Wu, B., Ng, A.Y.: Reading digits in natural images with unsupervised feature learning. In: NIPS Workshop on Deep Learning and Unsupervised Feature Learning 2011 (2009)
32. Ovadia, Y., et al.: Can you trust your model's uncertainty? Evaluating predictive uncertainty under dataset shift. In: Advances in Neural Information Processing Systems, pp. 13991–14002 (2019)
33. Pang, T., Xu, K., Du, C., Chen, N., Zhu, J.: Improving adversarial robustness via promoting ensemble diversity. In: Chaudhuri, K., Salakhutdinov, R. (eds.) Proceedings of the 36th International Conference on Machine Learning. Proceedings of Machine Learning Research, vol. 97, pp. 4970–4979. PMLR, 09–15 June 2019
34. Rame, A., Cord, M.: Dice: diversity in deep ensembles via conditional redundancy adversarial estimation. In: International Conference on Learning Representations (2021)
35. Shui, C., Mozafari, A.S., Marek, J., Hedhli, I., Gagné, C.: Diversity regularization in deep ensembles. In: International conference on Learning Representations (2018)
36. Singh, S., Hoiem, D., Forsyth, D.: Swapout: learning an ensemble of deep architectures (2016)
37. Sinha, S., Bharadhwaj, H., Goyal, A., Larochelle, H., Garg, A., Shkurti, F.: Dibs: diversity inducing information bottleneck in model ensembles. In: Proceedings of the AAAI Conference on Artificial Intelligence, vol. 35, pp. 9666–9674 (2021)
38. Stickland, A.C., Murray, I.: Diverse ensembles improve calibration. In: ICML 2020 Workshop on Uncertainty and Robustness in Deep Learning (2020)
39. Tran, L., et al.: Hydra: preserving ensemble diversity for model distillation. In: ICML 2020 Workshop on Uncertainty and Robustness in Deep Learning (2020)
40. Tsymbalov, E., Fedyanin, K., Panov, M.: Dropout strikes back: improved uncertainty estimation via diversity sampling (2020)
41. Wen, Y., Tran, D., Ba, J.: Batchensemble: an alternative approach to efficient ensemble and lifelong learning. In: Eighth International Conference on Learning Representations (ICLR 2020) (2020)
42. Wenzel, F., Snoek, J., Tran, D., Jenatton, R.: Hyperparameter ensembles for robustness and uncertainty quantification. In: Advances in Neural Information Processing Systems (2020)
43. Wilson, A.G., Izmailov, P.: Bayesian deep learning and a probabilistic perspective of generalization. In: Advances in Neural Information Processing Systems (2020)
44. Wortsman, M., et al.: Model soups: averaging weights of multiple fine-tuned models improves accuracy without increasing inference time (2022). https://doi.org/10.48550/ARXIV.2203.05482
45. Zaidi, S., Zela, A., Elsken, T., Holmes, C., Hutter, F., Teh, Y.W.: Neural ensemble search for performant and calibrated predictions (2020)

Unsupervised, Semi-supervised and Transfer Learning

FastSiam: Resource-Efficient Self-supervised Learning on a Single GPU

Daniel Pototzky[1,2](✉), Azhar Sultan[1], and Lars Schmidt-Thieme[2]

[1] Robert Bosch GmbH, Hildesheim, Germany
daniel.pototzky@de.bosch.com
[2] Information Systems and Machine Learning Lab, University of Hildesheim, Hildesheim, Germany

Abstract. Self-supervised pretraining has shown impressive performance in recent years, matching or even outperforming ImageNet weights on a broad range of downstream tasks. Unfortunately, existing methods require massive amounts of computing power with large batch sizes and batch norm statistics synchronized across multiple GPUs. This effectively excludes substantial parts of the computer vision community from the benefits of self-supervised learning who do not have access to extensive computing resources.

To address that, we develop FastSiam with the aim of matching ImageNet weights given as little computing power as possible. We find that a core weakness of previous methods like SimSiam is that they compute the training target based on a single augmented crop (or "view"), leading to target instability. We show that by using multiple views per image instead of one, the training target can be stabilized, allowing for faster convergence and substantially reduced runtime. We evaluate FastSiam on multiple challenging downstream tasks including object detection, instance segmentation and keypoint detection and find that it matches ImageNet weights after 25 epochs of pretraining on a single GPU with a batch size of only 32.

Keywords: Resource-efficient · Self-supervised learning

1 Introduction

Self-supervised pretraining aims at learning transferable representations given large amounts of unlabeled images. The resulting weights can be used as initialization for finetuning on a small, labeled dataset.

In recent years, methods that compare views of images have increasingly attracted attention [3,6,8,17,18]. The underlying idea is that even if it is unknown what kind of object is depicted on an image, two augmented crops of

---

Supplementary Information The online version contains supplementary material available at https://doi.org/10.1007/978-3-031-16788-1_4.

B. Andres et al. (Eds.): DAGM GCPR 2022, LNCS 13485, pp. 53–67, 2022.
https://doi.org/10.1007/978-3-031-16788-1_4

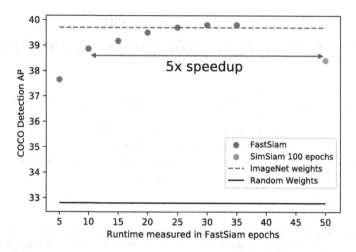

Fig. 1. Finetuning pretrained weights for object detection on MS COCO [22] following the 1x evaluation protocol with a Mask R-CNN and FPN-backbone as first described in MoCo [18]. FastSiam matches ImageNet weights if trained with a batch size of 32 on a single GPU for 25 epochs. FastSiam uses 4 views per image whereas SimSiam uses 2. Because of that FastSiam requires twice as long per epoch than SimSiam does but overall runtime to match SimSiam is still cut by a factor of more than 5.

it should still result in similar features. State-of-the-art methods based on this idea such as BYOL [17] and SwAV [3] have been shown to match or even outperform ImageNet weights. These approaches are typically trained with large batch sizes (i.e. up to 4096) and batch-norm statistics synchronized across multiple GPUs for up to 1000 epochs. Just reproducing them requires massive amounts of computing power. We argue that the dependence on large batch sizes and long training schedules effectively excludes large parts of the computer vision community from the benefits of self-supervised learning.

To understand why conventional self-supervised methods are very compute-intensive, compare them to supervised learning. The training targets in supervised learning are determined by the respective labels for each image that do not change throughout training. Conversely, the training targets of self-supervised pretraining methods are usually computed on the fly and change throughout training, depending on many factors including which crops are sampled for target computation. This property of ever-changing training targets slows down convergence.

In addition, self-supervised methods typically require large batch sizes to work well. One reason for this is that some methods contrast a positive view with another positive view from the same image and thousands of negative views from other images [6]. Only if many negative examples are included in a batch, the task of distinguishing views from the same image from those of other images gets sufficiently difficult. Even methods that do not use negative examples explicitly like BYOL [17] observe a decrease in performance if the batch size is small.

In contrast, SimSiam [8], which also does not use negative examples, is somewhat less dependent on large batches and works best with a batch size of 256. Our method FastSiam improves upon the shortcomings of SimSiam, in particular, by stabilizing the training target using multiple views per image instead of one. The suggested changes allow for training with smaller batch sizes, i.e. less unique images (32 vs. 256) and fewer views (128 vs. 512), and lead to much faster convergence and reduced computing requirements (see Fig. 1).

We show in experiments that FastSiam matches ImageNet weights on a variety of downstream tasks including object detection, instance segmentation and keypoint detection after 25 epochs of self-supervised pretraining on a single GPU with a batch size of only 32. We believe these findings to be very relevant for a large number of computer vision researchers who have only limited access to computing resources. FastSiam may allow them to benefit from recent progress in self-supervised pretraining. Overall, our contributions can be summarized as follows:

- We propose FastSiam, a self-supervised pretraining method that works best with small batch sizes and that converges much faster than competing methods.
- We identify target instability as a core reason why existing methods require very long training schedules and large batch sizes. We show that by stabilizing the training target, convergence can be reached much faster and a batch size of only 32 is found to be best.
- Weights trained by FastSiam for only 25 epochs on a single GPU match or improve upon ImageNet weights on a variety of downstream tasks including object detection, instance segmentation and keypoint detection.

2   Related Work

Self-supervised pretraining attempts to learn transferable image representations by only having access to a large number of unlabeled images. Early methods in the field focus on handcrafted pretext tasks including colorization [20], rotation prediction [16], clustering [2], solving jigsaw puzzles [24] and others [14].

In recent years, approaches that compare views of images have gained attention [3,6–8,10,15,17,18,33]. Some of these methods are called contrastive methods because they compare views of the same image with those of other images, either maximizing or minimizing feature similarity [6,7,10,15,18,33]. Among them, SimCLR [6] shows that contrastive methods benefit from strong data augmentation, large batch sizes and many epochs of training. Different from contrastive methods, BYOL [17] and SimSiam [8] find that using negative examples is not even necessary if an asymmetric architecture, as well as a momentum encoder or a stop-gradient operation, are applied. Moreover, SwAV [3] uses an online clustering of output features and enforces consistency between cluster assignments. Instead of contrasting per-image features, some methods compare class predictions [4].

One property of all these approaches is that they compute a global feature vector or a per-image class prediction. Conversely, other self-supervised methods are specifically designed for object detection or segmentation downstream tasks by comparing local patches [5, 13, 23, 28, 31] or even pixels [25] across views instead of entire images.

Recently, self-supervised methods that were originally developed for convolutional neural networks have also been applied to transformers [10, 32] and vice versa [4]. Furthermore, some approaches have been developed which make use of transformer-specific properties [1, 12, 34].

While the vast majority of methods that compare views of images use two of them, some approaches include more than that [3, 4]. The clustering-based approach SwAV [3], in particular, combines two views of the normal resolution with multiple smaller ones, resulting in an increase in performance. However, SwAV does not observe a speedup of convergence.

Typically, self-supervised methods are trained between 200 and 1000 epochs with batch sizes of up to 4096. While several methods report a strong decrease in performance given smaller batch sizes [17], others show only a moderate decline. For example, the performance of SwAV [3] only decreases somewhat if the batch size is reduced from 4096 to 256 unique images (with 6 to 8 views per image, some of which are of lower resolution). Different from competing methods, MoCov2 [7] is trained with a batch size of 256 by default, which is made possible by keeping a large queue of negative samples. By doing so, MoCov2 decouples the batch size from the number of negative instances used in the loss. Moreover, DINO [4] shows only a moderate decline in performance with a batch size of 128 when evaluating on a k-NN classification task. In addition, SimSiam [8], DenseCL [28] and DetCo [31] use a batch size of 256 by default.

Overall, some methods are moderately robust to small batch sizes, but they still observe a substantial decrease in performance for batch sizes lower than 128. No method matches ImageNet weights with a very short training schedule on a single GPU while only requiring a small batch size. This essentially means that there is no self-supervised method that is suited for computer vision researchers who have limited access to computing power. FastSiam addresses this issue and matches ImageNet weights after only 25 epochs of training on a single GPU with batch size as low as 32.

3   Method

In this section, we describe the core properties of FastSiam, which allow for fast convergence and training with small batch sizes on a single GPU. FastSiam extends upon SimSiam and addresses a core weakness of it, namely target instability.

3.1   Background

SimSiam inputs two augmented crops of an image, $x_1 \in \mathbb{R}^{H \times W \times C}$ and $x_2 \in \mathbb{R}^{H \times W \times C}$. The view x_1 is fed into the prediction branch which consists of an encoder network f (e.g. a ResNet50 with an MLP on top) and a predictor head h (e.g. another MLP), resulting in prediction $p_1 \triangleq h(f(x_1))$. The target branch computes a vector that serves as a target by processing x_2 through the same encoder f that the prediction branch also uses, i.e. $z_2 \triangleq f(x_2)$. Gradients are not backpropagated on the target branch as a stop-gradient operation is applied. Overall, the network is trained to make the output features from the prediction branch similar to those of the target branch by minimizing their negative cosine similarity (see Eq. 1).

$$L(p_1, z_2) = -\frac{p_1}{\|p_1\|_2} \cdot \frac{z_2}{\|z_2\|_2} \tag{1}$$

3.2 Stabilizing the Training Target

SimSiam and other methods that compare views of images implicitly assume that the sampled views show at least parts of the same object. However, this is often not the case when applying the usual cropping strategy to object-centric images. Maximizing the feature similarity of views that show different objects is arguably not an ideal training strategy and may lead to training instability. Furthermore, even if both views show parts of the same object, target vectors may differ strongly depending on which views are sampled and how they get augmented.

Computing the target vector for all possible views of an image results in a multivariate distribution. Assume, for simplicity, that this distribution has the mean μ and the variance Σ. We argue that SimSiam and other self-supervised methods suffer from target instability because they sample only one instance T_1 from this distribution (see Eq. 2). After all, a target vector generated from a single view may differ substantially from the overall properties of the distribution like the mean value, leading to target instability.

$$\mathbb{E}(T_1) = \mu, \quad Var(T_1) = \Sigma \tag{2}$$

To address this issue, we propose to use multiple views for target computation to get a more stable estimate of the mean value. This can be seen as a way of avoiding outliers to determine the training target. Sampling and averaging K independent and identically distributed target vectors is equivalent to sampling from a distribution with the same mean but reduced variance (see Eq. 3). Increasing the number of samples by a factor of four reduces the variance by a factor of four and the resulting standard error of the mean by a factor of two if samples are uncorrelated. More details on this connection are included in the supplementary material.

$$\mathbb{E}(\bar{T}_K) = \mu, \quad Var(\bar{T}_K) = \frac{\Sigma}{K} \tag{3}$$

Figure 2a depicts the distribution of the first dimension of a 2048-dimensional vector in the case of varying amounts of samples K that were drawn from $\mathcal{N}(0, I)$.

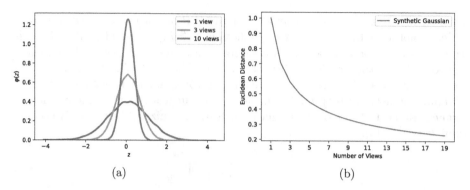

Fig. 2. Target statistics for varying numbers of sampled views if the underlying distribution is Gaussian. The more views are used for target computation, the sharper the distribution of target vectors centers around its mean (a), and the smaller the average Euclidean distance to the target vector computed based on all possible views becomes (b). For visualization purposes, we only plot results for the first of 2048 dimensions of the target vector in (a).

The more views are used for target computation, the sharper the resulting distribution centers around its mean. Based on that, Fig. 2b shows the decreasing average Euclidean distance between the sampled target and the mean of using all possible views. If few views are provided, adding one more results in a strong decrease. Conversely, if already many views are available, including another one has only a small effect.

FastSiam makes use of the connection that averaging multiple samples reduces the standard error of the mean (see Fig. 3). By doing so, the training target becomes much more stable, allowing for faster convergence and training with smaller batch sizes both in terms of unique images and the total number of views. The resulting loss function in which multiple views are combined for target generation is shown in Eq. 4.

$$L(z_1, z_2, z_3, ..., z_K, p_{K+1}) = -\frac{p_{K+1}}{\|p_{K+1}\|_2} \cdot \frac{\frac{1}{K}\sum_{i=1}^{K} z_i}{\|\frac{1}{K}\sum_{i=1}^{K} z_i\|_2} = -\frac{p_{K+1}}{\|p_{K+1}\|_2} \cdot \frac{\bar{T}_K}{\|\bar{T}_K\|_2}$$

(4)

The total loss that is optimized is formulated in Eq. 5. Each view is passed through the prediction branch once and the remaining views are used for target computation. We find $K = 3$ to be best, meaning that the combination of three views is used for target computation.

$$L_{total} = \sum_{i=1}^{K+1} \frac{1}{K+1} L(\{z_j | j \neq i \wedge 1 \leq j \leq K+1\}, p_i)$$

(5)

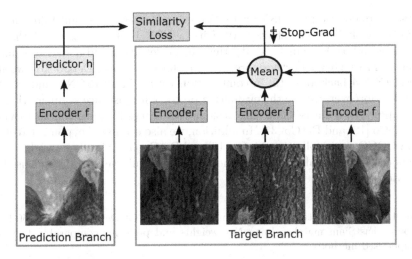

Fig. 3. Overall setup of FastSiam. On the target branch, FastSiam combines the information from multiple views to increase target stability. Gradients are not backpropagated, meaning that the target vector can be seen as a constant. On the prediction branch, only one view is used. The resulting prediction is trained to be similar to the output of the target branch. By increasing target stability, convergence can be reached much faster and with smaller batch sizes both in terms of unique images and the total number of views.

4 Experiments

The overall experimental setup is divided into two parts. First, FastSiam is pretrained without labels. Second, the resulting weights are evaluated by finetuning them on a diverse set of downstream tasks. These include object detection, instance segmentation and keypoint detection on MS COCO [22] and CityScapes [11]. We show that FastSiam matches or exceeds the performance of ImageNet weights and is competitive with other self-supervised methods while requiring much less computing power.

4.1 Experimental Setup

Pretraining Setup. For self-supervised pretraining we use ImageNet [26], which contains 1.2 million images from 1000 classes. We follow the training setup in SimSiam [8] including, for example, the augmentation pipeline. By default, we train for 25 epochs with a cosine learning rate decay schedule. The learning rate is set to 0.125 for a batch size of 32. In the case of larger batch sizes, the learning rate is scaled linearly. We use three views per image for target computation.

Evaluation Protocols. We evaluate the pretrained weights on a variety of downstream tasks using common protocols that are implemented in Detectron2 [29]. We adopt two different protocols for evaluating object detection and instance segmentation on MS COCO. Following DenseCL [28] and InfoMin [27] we use a Mask R-CNN detector [19] with a FPN backbone [21] and the 1× schedule with 90,000 steps for evaluating object detection and instance segmentation on MS COCO. Furthermore, like in MoCo [18] and DetCo [31] we use a ResNet50-C4 backbone [19] in combination with a Mask R-CNN and the 1× schedule. Moreover, we use the evaluation protocol for instance segmentation on CityScapes [11], a dataset covering urban street scenes for autonomous driving, from MoCo [18] and DetCo [31]. In addition, we also evaluate keypoint detection on MS COCO again following MoCo [18] and DetCo [31]. SimSiam weights after 100 epochs were downloaded from the author's github website [9] and used in evaluations.

Table 1. Object Detection and Segmentation on MS COCO with a ResNet50-FPN Backbone. FastSiam matches ImageNet weights and performs comparably to other self-supervised methods.

Method	Epoch	Batch	Views	AP^{bb}	AP^{bb}_{50}	AP^{bb}_{75}	AP^{mk}	AP^{mk}_{50}	AP^{mk}_{75}
Random	-	-	-	32.8	50.9	35.3	29.9	47.9	32.0
ImageNet	90	256	1	39.7	59.5	43.3	35.9	56.6	38.6
InsDis [30]	200	256	1	37.4	57.6	40.6	34.1	54.6	36.4
MoCo [18]	200	256	2	38.5	58.9	42.0	35.1	55.9	37.7
MoCov2 [7]	200	256	2	38.9	59.4	42.4	35.5	56.5	38.1
SwAV [3]	200	4096	8	38.5	60.4	41.4	35.4	57.0	37.7
DetCo [31]	200	256	20	40.1	61.0	43.9	36.4	58.0	38.9
SimCLR [6]	200	4096	2	38.5	58.0	42.0	34.8	55.2	37.2
DenseCL [28]	200	256	2	40.3	59.9	44.3	36.4	57.0	39.2
BYOL [17]	200	4096	2	38.4	57.9	41.9	34.9	55.3	37.5
SimSiam [8]	100	256	2	38.4	57.5	42.2	34.7	54.9	37.1
FastSiam	10	32	4	38.9	58.3	42.6	35.2	55.5	37.9
FastSiam	25	32	4	39.7	59.4	43.5	35.7	56.5	38.2

4.2   Main Results

Object Detection and Instance Segmentation on MS COCO. Table 1 shows the results on MS COCO for object detection and instance segmentation using a ResNet50-FPN backbone. FastSiam trained for 25 epochs with a batch size of 32 results in comparable performance to state-of-the-art self-supervised methods and also matches ImageNet weights. Even if FastSiam is only trained for 10 epochs, performance is comparable to many other self-supervised methods including SimSiam trained for 100 epochs while greatly outperforming a random initialization. Furthermore, in Table 2 we report results on MS COCO with a

ResNet-C4 backbone. If FastSiam is trained for 25 epochs, performance matches ImageNet weights and most other self-supervised methods. Notably, FastSiam clearly outperforms SimSiam trained for 100 epochs and almost matches the performance of it trained for 200 epochs. In the case of training FastSiam for only 10 epochs, performance remains competitive with other self-supervised methods while greatly improving upon a random initialization.

Table 2. Object Detection and Instance Segmentation on MS COCO with a ResNet50-C4 Backbone. FastSiam matches ImageNet weights and performs comparably to other self-supervised methods

Method	Epoch	Batch	Views	AP^{bb}	AP^{bb}_{50}	AP^{bb}_{75}	AP^{mk}	AP^{mk}_{50}	AP^{mk}_{75}
Random	-	-	-	26.4	44.0	27.8	29.3	46.9	30.8
ImageNet	90	256	1	38.2	58.2	41.2	33.3	54.7	35.2
InsDis [30]	200	256	1	37.7	57.0	40.9	33.0	54.1	35.2
MoCo [18]	200	256	2	38.5	58.3	41.6	33.6	54.8	35.6
MoCov2 [7]	200	256	2	38.9	58.4	42.0	34.2	55.2	36.5
SwAV [3]	200	4096	8	32.9	54.3	34.5	29.5	50.4	30.4
DetCo [31]	200	256	20	39.8	59.7	43.0	34.7	56.3	36.7
SimSiam [8]	200	256	2	39.2	59.3	42.1	34.4	56.0	36.7
SimSiam [8]	100	256	2	35.8	54.5	38.7	31.7	51.5	33.7
FastSiam	10	32	4	37.3	56.9	40.2	32.8	53.8	34.7
FastSiam	25	32	4	38.5	58.0	41.6	33.7	54.8	35.8

Instance Segmentation on CityScapes. Table 3 shows results for instance segmentation on CityScapes. FastSiam trained for 25 epochs outperforms ImageNet weights and is competitive with other self-supervised methods while being trained for fewer epochs and with much smaller batch size. Even when training FastSiam for only 10 epochs, downstream performance almost matches ImageNet weights while being clearly superior to a random initialization.

Keypoint Detection on MS COCO. In Table 4 we report results for keypoint detection on MS COCO. FastSiam trained for only 10 epochs improves upon ImageNet weights and performs comparably to other self-supervised methods including SimSiam while requiring much less computing power. If FastSiam is trained for 25 epochs, detection performance is only slightly better than after 10 epochs.

Runtime Analysis. In this section, we compare the runtime of FastSiam with that of SimSiam. In particular, we investigate how much runtime by FastSiam is

Table 3. Instance Segmentation on CityScapes. FastSiam matches competing methods and improves upon ImageNet weights.

Method	Epoch	Batch	Views	AP^{mk}	AP^{mk}_{50}
Random	-	-	-	25.4	51.1
ImageNet	90	256	1	32.9	59.6
InsDis [30]	200	256	1	33.0	60.1
MoCo [18]	200	256	2	32.3	59.3
MoCov2 [7]	200	256	2	33.9	60.8
SwAV [3]	200	4096	8	33.9	62.4
DetCo [31]	200	256	20	34.7	63.2
SimSiam [8]	100	256	2	32.9	60.9
FastSiam	10	32	4	32.6	59.9
FastSiam	25	32	4	34.0	60.7

Table 4. Keypoint Detection on MS COCO. FastSiam matches competing methods and outperforms ImageNet weights.

Method	Epoch	Batch	Views	AP^{kp}	AP^{kp}_{50}	AP^{kp}_{75}
Random	-	-	-	65.9	86.5	71.7
ImageNet	90	256	1	65.8	86.9	71.9
InsDis [30]	200	256	1	66.5	87.1	72.6
MoCo [18]	200	256	2	66.8	87.4	72.5
MoCov2 [7]	200	256	2	66.8	87.3	73.1
SwAV [3]	200	4096	8	66.0	86.9	71.5
DetCo [31]	200	256	20	67.2	87.5	73.4
SimSiam [8]	100	256	2	66.4	87.1	72.2
FastSiam	10	32	4	66.5	87.2	72.4
FastSiam	25	32	4	66.6	87.2	72.6

needed to match the performance of SimSiam and supervised ImageNet weights. Figure 4 shows results for AP^{bb} for object detection on MS COCO and AP^{mk} for instance segmentation on CityScapes. FastSiam requires almost exactly twice as much time per epoch as SimSiam because it uses four views per image instead of two. Therefore, four forward and backward paths are computed instead of two. Test are conducted on NVIDIA GeForce RTX 2080 Ti. Because time measurements in GPU hours depend on the specific hardware, we report the relative runtime measured in equivalents of FastSiam epochs. In terms of computing requirements, 100 epochs of SimSiam are equivalent to 50 FastSiam epochs. However, the total runtime of FastSiam is between 5 and 10 times lower because training converges significantly faster due to increased target stability.

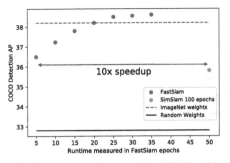 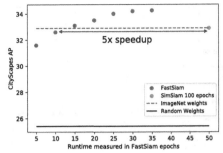

(a) Object Detection on MS COCO with a ResNet50-C4 Backbone.

(b) Instance Segmentation on CityScapes with a Mask RCNN.

Fig. 4. Runtime comparison between FastSiam and SimSiam. Performance of pre-trained weights is evaluated on object detection and instance segmentation. FastSiam reaches the same downstream performance as SimSiam with a speedup between factor 5 and 10.

4.3 Ablations

The Optimal Number of Views. We investigate what number of views is optimal for target computation. Figure 5 shows downstream performance for object detection on MS COCO and instance segmentation on CityScapes given a varying number of views for target computation, ranging from one to four. To ensure a fair comparison, we use a fixed amount of computing power (equivalent to 50 epochs in case of three views) and the same number of views per batch (512). If only one view is used like in SimSiam, the training target is unstable. Conversely, one could use as many views as fit in the batch taken from a single image. While this would maximize target stability, the diversity within each batch would be very low. We find that using three views for target computation offers the best trade-off and results in the highest transfer performance, hence we choose it as our default.

Effect of Batch Size on Performance. We investigate the effect that the chosen batch size in FastSiam has on the downstream performance. In Table 5 we compare AP^{bb} for object detection on MS COCO, AP^{mk} for instance segmentation on CityScapes and AP^{kp} for keypoint detection on MS COCO given different batch sizes in pretraining. We find that increasing batch size from the default of 32 to 64 or 128 does not lead to better downstream performance. Whereas other self-supervised methods [17] report that reducing the batch size to 256 or below decreases performance, FastSiam even works best with a batch size of 32. Reducing the batch size below 32 has no practical value because it already fits on a single GPU.

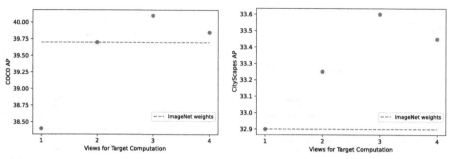

(a) Detection on MS COCO with FPN.   (b) Instance Segmentation on CityScapes.

Fig. 5. The downstream performance for varying numbers of views used for target computation, three being the default in FastSiam. Total compute as well as the number of views per batch is the same for all settings.

Table 5. Effect of Batch Size on Downstream Performance. We compare AP^{bb} for object detection on MS COCO, AP^{mk} for instance segmentation on CityScapes and AP^{kp} for keypoint detection on MS COCO given different batch sizes in pretraining.

Method	Epoch	Batch	COCO FPN	COCO C4	CityScapes	Keypoint
Random	-	-	32.8	26.4	25.4	65.9
ImageNet	90	256	39.7	38.2	32.9	65.8
FastSiam	25	32	39.7	38.5	34.0	66.6
FastSiam	25	64	39.7	38.4	33.6	66.6
FastSiam	25	128	39.8	38.5	33.3	66.6

Activation Maps. We visualize activation maps for FastSiam trained for 25 epochs and SimSiam trained for 100 epochs (see Fig. 6). FastSiam activates more precise object regions than SimSiam does. This property is particularly important for downstream tasks that involve localization.

Qualitative Analysis. In this section, we qualitatively analyze which views of images result in target vectors that are either close to the mean vector or very far away from it. For this, we input 200 views for each randomly selected image in an untrained encoder network. We then determine the views corresponding to the three most similar and three most distant target vectors relative to the mean vector. The result is shown in Fig. 7. The first column depicts the original image. Columns 2–4 show the views corresponding to the three target vectors with the smallest difference to the mean. The remaining columns 5–7 show the three views which lead to the most distant target vectors. These outlier vectors result from views that either do not contain the object of interest (e.g. a dog) or are very heavily augmented (e.g. strong color jitter or conversion to greyscale).

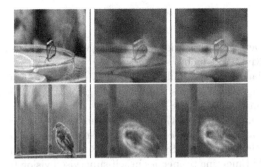

Fig. 6. Activation maps for FastSiam (middle column) and SimSiam (right column). FastSiam generates more precise object regions than SimSiam does.

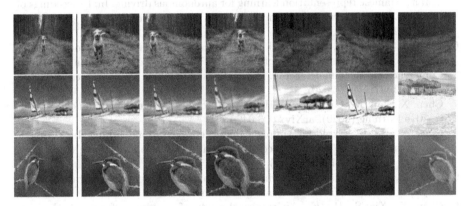

Fig. 7. Views of images that result in target vectors that are closest or most distant to the mean target. Column 1 shows the original image, columns 2–4 the three views which result in target vectors with the smallest distance to the mean, whereas columns 5–7 shows the three views that result in the most distant target vectors. Views corresponding to outlier vectors often do not contain the object of interest (e.g. a dog) or are heavily augmented.

5   Conclusion

In this work, we propose FastSiam, a self-supervised pretraining method that is optimized for fast convergence, small batch sizes and low computing requirements. On a diverse set of downstream tasks including object detection, instance segmentation and keypoint detection, FastSiam matches ImageNet weights and performs comparably to other self-supervised methods while requiring much less computing power. We believe that FastSiam is of particular interest for computer vision researchers who have only limited access to computing resources, finally allowing them to benefit from self-supervised pretraining.

References

1. Bar, A., et al.: Detreg: unsupervised pretraining with region priors for object detection (2021). arXiv:2106.04550
2. Caron, M., Bojanowski, P., Joulin, A., Douze, M.: Deep clustering for unsupervised learning of visual features. In: Proceedings of the European Conference on Computer Vision (ECCV) (2018)
3. Caron, M., Misra, I., Mairal, J., Goyal, P., Bojanowski, P., Joulin, A.: Unsupervised learning of visual features by contrasting cluster assignments. In: Advances in Neural Information Processing Systems, vol. 33, pp. 9912–9924 (2020)
4. Caron, M., et al.: Emerging properties in self-supervised vision transformers (2021). arXiv:2104.14294
5. Chen, K., Hong, L., Xu, H., Li, Z., Yeung, D.Y.: Multisiam: self-supervised multi-instance siamese representation learning for autonomous driving. In: Proceedings of the IEEE/CVF International Conference on Computer Vision (ICCV), pp. 7546–7554 (2021)
6. Chen, T., Kornblith, S., Norouzi, M., Hinton, G.: A simple framework for contrastive learning of visual representations. In: Proceedings of the 37th International Conference on Machine Learning. Proceedings of Machine Learning Research, vol. 119, pp. 1597–1607 (2020)
7. Chen, X., Fan, H., Girshick, R., He, K.: Improved baselines with momentum contrastive learning (2020). arXiv:2003.04297
8. Chen, X., He, K.: Exploring simple siamese representation learning. In: Proceedings of the IEEE/CVF Conference on Computer Vision and Pattern Recognition (CVPR), pp. 15750–15758 (2021)
9. Chen, X., He, K.: Simsiam: exploring simple siamese representation learning (2021). https://github.com/facebookresearch/simsiam
10. Chen, X., Xie, S., He, K.: An empirical study of training self-supervised vision transformers. In: Proceedings of the IEEE/CVF International Conference on Computer Vision (ICCV), pp. 9640–9649 (2021)
11. Cordts, M., et al.: The cityscapes dataset for semantic urban scene understanding (2016). arXiv:1604.01685
12. Dai, Z., Cai, B., Lin, Y., Chen, J.: UP-DETR: unsupervised pre-training for object detection with transformers. In: Proceedings of the IEEE/CVF Conference on Computer Vision and Pattern Recognition (CVPR), pp. 1601–1610 (2021)
13. Ding, J., et al.: Unsupervised pretraining for object detection by patch reidentification (2021). arXiv:2103.04814
14. Doersch, C., Gupta, A., Efros, A.A.: Unsupervised visual representation learning by context prediction. In: Proceedings of the IEEE International Conference on Computer Vision (ICCV) (2015)
15. Gidaris, S., Bursuc, A., Puy, G., Komodakis, N., Cord, M., Perez, P.: Obow: online bag-of-visual-words generation for self-supervised learning. In: Proceedings of the IEEE/CVF Conference on Computer Vision and Pattern Recognition (CVPR), pp. 6830–6840 (2021)
16. Gidaris, S., Singh, P., Komodakis, N.: Unsupervised representation learning by predicting image rotations. In: International Conference on Learning Representations ICLR (2018)
17. Grill, J.B., et al.: Bootstrap your own latent: a new approach to self-supervised learning (2020). arXiv:2006.07733

18. He, K., Fan, H., Wu, Y., Xie, S., Girshick, R.: Momentum contrast for unsupervised visual representation learning. In: Proceedings of the IEEE/CVF Conference on Computer Vision and Pattern Recognition (CVPR) (2020)
19. He, K., Gkioxari, G., Dollar, P., Girshick, R.: Mask R-CNN. In: Proceedings of the IEEE International Conference on Computer Vision (ICCV), October 2017
20. Larsson, G., Maire, M., Shakhnarovich, G.: Colorization as a proxy task for visual understanding. In: Proceedings of the IEEE Conference on Computer Vision and Pattern Recognition (CVPR) (2017)
21. Lin, T.Y., Dollár, P., Girshick, R., He, K., Hariharan, B., Belongie, S.: Feature pyramid networks for object detection (2017). arXiv:1612.03144
22. Lin, T.Y., et al.: Microsoft coco: common objects in context (2015). arXiv:1405.0312
23. Liu, S., Li, Z., Sun, J.: Self-EMD: self-supervised object detection without imagenet. CoRR (2020). arXiv:2011.13677
24. Noroozi, M., Favaro, P.: Unsupervised learning of visual representations by solving jigsaw puzzles. In: Leibe, B., Matas, J., Sebe, N., Welling, M. (eds.) ECCV 2016. LNCS, vol. 9910, pp. 69–84. Springer, Cham (2016). https://doi.org/10.1007/978-3-319-46466-4_5
25. Pinheiro, P., Almahairi, A., Benmalek, R., Golemo, F., Courville, A.: Unsupervised learning of dense visual representations. In: Advances in Neural Information Processing Systems, vol. 33, pp. 4489–4500 (2020)
26. Russakovsky, O., et al.: Imagenet large scale visual recognition challenge (2015). arXiv:1409.0575
27. Tian, Y., Sun, C., Poole, B., Krishnan, D., Schmid, C., Isola, P.: What makes for good views for contrastive learning? In: Larochelle, H., Ranzato, M., Hadsell, R., Balcan, M.F., Lin, H. (eds.) Advances in Neural Information Processing Systems, vol. 33, pp. 6827–6839. Curran Associates, Inc. (2020)
28. Wang, X., Zhang, R., Shen, C., Kong, T., Li, L.: Dense contrastive learning for self-supervised visual pre-training. In: Proceedings of the IEEE/CVF Conference on Computer Vision and Pattern Recognition (CVPR), pp. 3024–3033 (2021)
29. Wu, Y., Kirillov, A., Massa, F., Lo, W.Y., Girshick, R.: Detectron2 (2019). https://github.com/facebookresearch/detectron2
30. Wu, Z., Xiong, Y., Yu, S.X., Lin, D.: Unsupervised feature learning via non-parametric instance discrimination. In: Proceedings of the IEEE Conference on Computer Vision and Pattern Recognition (CVPR), June 2018
31. Xie, E., et al.: DetCo: unsupervised contrastive learning for object detection. In: Proceedings of the IEEE/CVF International Conference on Computer Vision (ICCV), pp. 8392–8401 (2021)
32. Xie, Z., et al.: Self-supervised learning with swin transformers (2021). arXiv:2105.04553
33. Zbontar, J., Jing, L., Misra, I., LeCun, Y., Deny, S.: Barlow twins: self-supervised learning via redundancy reduction. In: International Conference on Machine Learning (ICML) (2021)
34. Zhou, J., et al.: iBOT: image BERT pre-training with online tokenizer (2021). arXiv:2111.07832

Reiterative Domain Aware Multi-target Adaptation

Sudipan Saha[1]($\boxtimes$) (iD), Shan Zhao[1] (iD), Nasrullah Sheikh[2] (iD),
and Xiao Xiang Zhu[1,3] (iD)

[1] Department of Aerospace and Geodesy, Chair of Data Science in Earth
Observation, Technical University of Munich, Ottobrunn 85521, Germany
{sudipan.saha,shan.zhao}@tum.de
[2] IBM Research Almaden, San Jose, CA, USA
nasrullah.sheikh@ibm.com
[3] Remote Sensing Technology Institute, German Aerospace Center (DLR),
Weßling 82234, Germany
xiaoxiang.zhu@dlr.de

Abstract. Multi-Target Domain Adaptation (MTDA) is a recently popular powerful setting in which a single classifier is learned for multiple unlabeled target domains. A popular MTDA approach is to sequentially adapt one target domain at a time. While only one pass is made through each target domain, the adaptation process for each target domain may consist of many iterations. Inspired by the spaced learning in neuroscience, we instead propose a reiterative approach where we make several passes/reiterations through each target domain. This leads to a better episodic learning that effectively retains features for multiple targets. The reiterative approach does not increase total number of training iterations, as we simply decrease the number of iterations per domain per reiteration. To build a multi-target classifier, it is also important to have a backbone feature extractor that generalizes well across domains. Towards this, we adopt Transformer as a feature extraction backbone. We perform extensive experiments on three popular MTDA datasets: Office-Home, Office-31, and DomainNet, a large-scale dataset. Our experiments separately show the benefits of both reiterative approach and superior Transformer-based feature extractor backbone.

Keywords: Domain adaptation · Multi-domain analysis · Spaced learning · Transformers

1 Introduction

Despite the impressive performance of deep learning models in vision tasks [15,16,28,45,49], they often fail to generalize when exposed to a new environment. This is caused by a misalignment between the source and the target

Supplementary Information The online version contains supplementary material available at https://doi.org/10.1007/978-3-031-16788-1_5.

data distributions [66]. To solve this problem, unsupervised domain adaptation (UDA) [11,33,35,39] exploits the labeled source and unlabeled target data to learn a robust classifier for the target domain(s). Most existing UDA methods are designed to adapt to a single unlabeled target from a single labeled source domain [2,23,43,56]. Such models are not suitable for practical settings where we may come across many target domains, due to which a separate model needs to be trained for each target domain. Recently, some works in the literature have addressed this issue by designing methods to adapt to multiple domains simultaneously from a single source domain [40]. This domain adaptation setting, called Multi-Target Domain Adaptation (MTDA), is challenging as the increase of the domains brings more difficulty in aligning feature distributions among them.

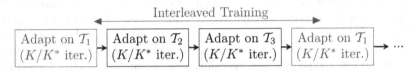

Fig. 1. Reiterative training approach assuming three target domains T_1, T_2, and T_3 (in that order of closeness to the source domain). Inspired by the spaced learning in neuroscience [51], instead of training for K iterations at one pass, the training process is decomposed into K^* interleaved training passes of K/K^* iterations each.

A popular strategy for MTDA is to first train the model on the source dataset and then sequentially adapt the model on the target datasets. Following this strategy, Roy *et al.* [47] proposed Domain-aware Curriculum Graph Co-Teaching (D-CGCT) that makes one pass through all target domains, starting from the easiest domain or the domain showing most resemblance to the source domain. Each domain is adapted for K iterations, after which the pseudo-labeled samples (henceforth called pseudo-samples) are selected and are used along with the source domain samples for processing the following target domains. The crux of the idea is that pseudo-samples from the easier domains assist in adapting the classifier on the more difficult target domains. One caveat of merely making only one pass through each target domain is that by the time the final model is obtained after adapting for all target domains, model may have lost knowledge of some of the target domains.

In neuroscience, interleaved repetition (spaced learning) has been shown to benefit memory compared with restudying the material in immediate succession (massed learning) [8,54]. Repeated stimuli separated by timed spaces can initiate long-term memory encoding [26]. Motivated by this, we postulate that instead of adapting a specific target domain for K iterations at one pass (equivalent of massed learning), we can make K^* passes (or reiterations) through each target domain of reduced (K/K^*) iterations each. The learning on a specific target domain is interleaved by the learning on the other target domains. Thus, similar to spaced learning we make interleaved repetitions on the target domains that enhance the capability of the learned model to jointly handle all target domains.

After each pass/reiteration over a target domain, some of the target domain samples are added to the pseudo-samples. The reiterative training concept is visualized in Fig. 1.

Composition of a training minibatch is an important factor in learning a better MTDA model. Even though our goal is to adapt the classifier on the target domains, the primary reference of guidance for the classifier is the labeled source samples. Based on this, we postulate that more source samples than target samples in each minibatch during training can improve the adaptation performance.

The generalization ability of the backbone feature extractor may play a crucial role in multi-target adaptation. Transformers have recently shown excellent capability in many computer vision tasks [19]. Unlike CNN which generally concentrates on the local features, the Vision Transformer (ViT) [6] exploits the attention across the patches to capture the long-distance features and acquires global information. Moreover, Transformer-based models have shown good performance in transfer learning and domain adaptation [7,37,62]. Motivated by this, we propose to use pre-trained Transformer as a feature extractor for MTDA. We hypothesize that the strong generalization capability of Transformer-based features will enhance the adaptation ability across multiple target domains.

The main contributions of this work are as follows:

1. Inspired by neuroscience, we introduce a reiterative approach for multi-target adaptation. The proposed reiterative approach conserves computation cost, however makes better multi-target adaptation by making multiple adaptation passes through each target domain.
2. We furthermore show that choosing more source samples than target samples in the training minibatch improves MTDA performance.
3. We introduce Transformer in the context of multi-target adaptation. We combine Transformer and GNN in the same framework to obtain a superior MTDA framework that benefits simultaneously from the excellent generalization ability of the Transformer backbone and feature aggregation capability of GNN.
4. We experimentally validate on three popular benchmark datasets showing a significant improvement over the existing domain-aware MTDA frameworks. Our experiments clearly show that the reiterative approach itself is sufficient to improve performance over the existing state-of-the-art methods, without using Transformer as backbone. However, using Transformer as backbone feature extractor further enhances the performance.

The rest of the paper is organized as follows: In Sect. 2 we described the state-of-the-art, and in Sect. 3 we present our proposed solution. Section 4 provides the experimental setup and evaluation of our proposed approach, and finally we conclude in Sect. 5.

2   Related Works

Mitigating the discrepancy between the training and test data distributions is a long lasting problem. The machine learning and computer vision literature is rich in domain adaptation techniques for several problems including image classification, semantic segmentation, and object recognition [66]. In this regard, domain adaptation aligns the data distribution using generative modeling [2, 23], adversarial training [34,56], and standard divergence measures [30,43]. The domain adaptation problem can be presented in various flavors depending on the overlap of classes between domains (closed-set, open-set) [25,42,50] or number of sources and targets, e.g., single-source-single-target, multi-source [14,52,65], multi-target [13,24,64].

Multi-target domain adaptation [4,24,40,47,63,64] transfers a network learned on a single labeled source dataset to multiple unlabeled target datasets. This line of research is quite new and there are only few methods towards this direction. While there has been extensive research on single-target domain adaptation, those methods cannot be trivially applied in the multi-target setting. The method in [4] clusters the blended target domain samples to obtain sub-targets and subsequently applies a single-target domain adaptation method on the source and the obtained sub-targets. Multi-teacher MTDA (MT-MTDA) [40] uses knowledge distillation to distill target domain knowledge from multiple teachers to a common student.

Sequentially adapting the source classifier to each target domain for multi-target adaptation is related to incremental learning. Incremental learning [46] continually trains a classifier for sequentially available data for novel tasks. There are only few existing works in the domain adaptation literature [38,61] in this line.

Learning from noisy labels is an important topic in weakly supervised learning. A recently popular approach to handle noisy labels is co-teaching [18] that cross-trains two deep networks that teach each other given every minibatch. While the predictions from the two classifiers may strongly disagree at the beginning, the two networks converge towards consensus with the increase of training epochs.

Graph Neural Networks (GNNs) are neural networks applied on the graph-structured data. GNNs can capture the relationships between the nodes (objects) in a graph using the edges [17,27,44]. GNNs [27] have been recently adopted for progressive/incremental domain adaptation [36,47]. Progressive Graph Learning (PGL) [36] operates in single-target setting where a graph neural network with episodic training is integrated to suppress the underlying conditional shift and to close the gap between the source and target distributions. Further extending this concept, [47] proposes a method for multi-target domain adaptation. As discussed in Sect. 1, our method is closely related to [47]. While their method is applicable to both domain-agnostic and domain-aware setting, in our work we focus on the domain-aware setting in [47], i.e., D-CGCT. A heterogeneous Graph Attention Network (HGAN) is used for MTDA in [63].

Transformer is a recently popular deep learning architecture. The fundamental building block of a Transformer is self-attention. Attention mechanism computes the responses at each token in a sequence by attending it to all tokens and gathering the corresponding embeddings based on the attention scores accordingly [19]. To extend the application of Transformer to the grid-like data, ViT is proposed, which uses a pure Transformer and formulates the classification problem as a sequential problem by splitting the image into a sequence of patches. It is composed of three main components: a linear layer to project flattened image patches to lower dimensional embeddings, the standard Transformer encoder with multi-head self-attention to compute independent scoring functions from different subspaces, and a MLP head for classification score prediction. Different variants of image-based Transformers have been proposed, e.g., Data-efficient image Transformers (DeiT) [55], Convolutional vision Transformer (CvT) [59], Compact Convolutional Transformer (CCT) [20], and LocalViT [31]. Recently the application of Transformers in computer vision tasks including image generation [29], object detection [1], classification and segmentation [60] has sprung up due to its advantageous capability. The Transformer encoder in ViTs can be regarded as a feature extractor naturally, due to their capability to capture the long distance features. Transformers have shown good performance in transfer learning [37], e.g. in medical image analysis [7]. Furthermore, Transformers have been shown to be useful for source-free domain adaptation in [62]. They make the observation that focusing attention on the objects in the image plays an important role in domain adaptation.

Understanding human learning and memory is a long-standing problem. Spaced learning [54] is such a technique that achieves efficient memorization by using repeated review of the content following a schedule to improve long-term retention [53]. This is inspired by the idea that just learning once is not enough to generate long term retention of a content (that has to be learned) and it is important to revisit the content from time to time. Opposite to restudying the material in immediate succession (massed learning), multiple learning sessions with interleaved repetition (spaced learning) lead to better retention of knowledge. There are various theoretical models that attempt to explain the superiority of spaced learning over massed learning, e.g., Wagner *et al.* [58] proposed that spaced learning reduces neural repetition suppression, which results in enhanced neural activity. Spaced learning has found application in several disciplines, including language learning [41], primary school education [12], learning for individuals with Parkinson's disease [9].

Similar to [62], our work exploits Transformer as the backbone feature extractor to capitalize on its ability to generalize across domains. MTDA is a relatively new area, where our work is related to [47]. However, in contrast to [47], we use a reiterative approach, inspired by spaced learning, to effectively ingest target domain pseudo-samples. The learning of the dual-classifier head is based on co-teaching [18] and follows similar episodic training as in [36].

3   Proposed Method

For the proposed multi-target domain adaptation, we are provided with a source dataset S containing n_s labeled samples $(\mathbf{x}_{s,i}, y_{s,i})_{i=1}^{n_s}$ and N target datasets $\mathcal{T} = \{\mathcal{T}_j\}_{j=1}^N$. The underlying data distributions of the source and the N target domains are different from each other. However, they share the same label space and for each target sample their domain is known. Our goal is to learn predictor for the N target domains by using the labeled data S and the unlabeled data $\mathcal{T}$.

Towards this end, our proposed model consists of a feature extractor F, a MLP classifier G_{mlp}, and a Graph Neural Network module G_{gnn}, and a domain discriminator network D. The G_{gnn} module consists of an edge-based network f_{edge}, and a node classifier f_{node}. For a given sample, $\mathbf{x}$, feature extractor network F extracts the features f given as $f = F(\mathbf{x})$. These features are then fed to G_{mlp} and f_{edge}, and their output is fed to node classifier f_{node}. The parameters of networks $F, D, G_{mlp}, f_{edge}, f_{node}$ are represented as $\theta, \psi, \phi, \varphi, \varphi'$, respectively. The network structure and the basic on GNN is provided in Appendix A. In the following subsections below, we explain in detail the architecture and training of our proposed model.

3.1   Transformer-Based Feature Extractor

We adopt the Transformer-based feature extractor from TransUNet [3] as a pre-trained feature extractor F. Instead of using a pure Transformer, a CNN-Transformer hybrid model is used. CNN is first applied to the input image to generate feature map and subsequently patch embedding is applied to 1×1 patches extracted from the CNN feature map to compute the input of the Transformer. Such hybrid CNN-Transformer encoder has shown good performance both in image segmentation [3] and domain adaptation [62]. For the CNN, we specifically employ ResNet-50 model [21]. The feature extractor backbone is pre-trained on ImageNet dataset [5]. Transformer is further elaborated in Appendix B.

3.2   Training on the Source Dataset

Before adapting on the targets $\mathcal{T}$, the source labeled samples $(\mathbf{x}_{s,i}, y_{s,i})_{i=1}^{n_s}$ are used to train the model F and G_{mlp}, thus updating the parameters θ and ϕ, respectively. While F consists of ResNet-Transformer model as described in Sect. 3.1, the G_{mlp} is a fully connected output layer consisting of n_c logits. Cross-entropy loss ℓ_{ce}^{mlp} computed from the source samples is used for training and the target samples are not used at this stage.

3.3   Target Adaptation

At each step of the target adaptation, we treat a selected set of samples $\hat{S}^{total}$ as the samples for which we are confident about their labels. These samples are called pseudo-source ($\hat{S}^{total}$) and is initialized with source samples S after the step in Sect. 3.2. However target samples are slowly added to it, as explained in the following subsections.

In this step the model performs feature adaptation on the target domains, one domain at a time, starting from the easiest domain and gradually moving to the more difficult ones. The easiest domain is defined as the domain closest to the source domain, which is measured by the uncertainty ($H(T_j)$ for domain T_j) in the target predictions with the source-trained model [10, 47]. Confident samples tend to have greater maximum softmax probabilities, while uncertain samples produce lower maximum softmax probability [22]. The negative of maximum of softmax for domain (T_j) of the predictions returned by the source-trained model is used to characterize the uncertainty of the target domain [47]. $H(T_j)$ is computed by considering all samples belonging to the domain T_j.

Once one target domain to be processed is fixed, adaptation is performed for K iterations. In each iteration, some source samples ($\hat{\mathcal{B}}_s^q$) and some target samples ($\hat{\mathcal{B}}_t^q$) are drawn to form a minibatch. Each minibatch of images is fed to the feature extractor to obtain features corresponding to them and then fed to the G_{mlp} and G_{gnn}. The G_{gnn} consists of the edge network f_{edge} and the node classifier f_{node}. The G_{mlp} does not aggregate features from different samples, rather predicts based on only the sample of interest. On the other hand GNN-based classifier aggregates the features of the samples in the batch. In other words, prediction from G_{gnn} not only accounts for a sample $\mathbf{x}$, rather also for the other samples in the minibatch. While this leads to potentially better context-aware learning paradigm, naively using it may lead to noisy feature degrading the classification performance. The MLP classifier and the GNN classifier capture different aspects, thus they are further exploited to provide feedback to each other, similar to co-teaching [18]. The output from the MLP head is obtained as:

$$\hat{y} \leftarrow \texttt{softmax}(G_{mlp}(F(\mathbf{x}))) \tag{1}$$

Similarly, the output from the GNN head is obtained as:

$$\bar{y} \leftarrow \texttt{softmax}(G_{gnn}(F(\mathbf{x}))) \tag{2}$$

The G_{mlp} and f_{node} of G_{gnn} is trained with cross-entropy loss ℓ_{ce}^{mlp} and ℓ_{ce}^{edge}, respectively, computed over the source/pseudo-source samples.

Feedback from MLP to GNN: For edge network f_{edge} to learn the pairwise similarity between samples, a target matrix $\hat{A}^{tar}$ is formed such that an element $\hat{a}^{tar}$ in $\hat{A}^{tar}$ is 1 if the labels of i-th and j-th sample are the same. While label information is known from the source samples ($\hat{\mathcal{B}}_s^q$), they are not known for the target samples ($\hat{\mathcal{B}}_t^q$). Thus, pseudo-labels of target samples are formed using prediction of G_{mlp}. In this way G_{mlp} teaches G_{gnn}. A (binary-cross-entropy) edge loss between elements of affinity matrix $\hat{A}$ (produced by f_{edge}) and the target matrix $\hat{A}^{tar}$ is computed as ℓ_{bce}^{edge}.

Feedback from GNN to MLP: At the end of processing each target domain, a score w_j is assigned to each sample $\mathbf{x}_{t,j}$ in the target domain as:

$$w_j \leftarrow \max_{c \in n_c} p(\bar{y}_{t,j} = c | \mathbf{x}_{t,j}) \tag{3}$$

w_j indicates the confidence of prediction of G_{gnn} for the sample j. If w_j is greater than a score τ, then this sample is appended to the list of pseudo-labeled samples $\hat{S}^{total}$ that are used while processing the subsequent target domains. In this way, the G_{gnn} creates a set of context-aware pseudo-samples after processing each target domain, thus enabling more effective learning of G_{mlp}.

Domain Discriminator: In addition to the MLP and GNN based networks, a domain discriminator D is used to predict the domain of the samples [11,34]. The output from this is obtained as:

$$\hat{d} \leftarrow \mathtt{sigmoid}(D(F(\mathbf{x}))) \tag{4}$$

The domain discriminator in conjunction with a gradient reversal layer (GRL) is trained with an adversarial loss ℓ_{adv}. This further pushes the feature extractor to learn features such that the source and different target features appear as if they are coming from the same distribution.

3.4   Reiterative Target Adaptation

As discussed in Sect. 2, spaced learning [54] promotes efficient memory retention by using repeated and interleaved review of the content [53]. Multiple learning sessions with interleaved repetition leads to a better retention of knowledge in comparison to restudying the same topic in immediate succession (massed learning). In neuroscience, massed learning may lead to repetition suppression, a diminished neural activation that results from the continuous repeated presentation of a stimulus. Merely training continuously over a specific target domain for K iterations is similar to massed learning. Like diminished neural activation, in our case such continuous adaptation on one target may produce large softmax values even for samples for which model is not confident, thus yielding unreliable pseudo-samples. Motivated by the interleaved repetition of spaced learning [8,54], we propose to make multiple (K^*) passes of adaptation (we call it reiteration) over each target domain.

In more details, if there are only three target domains T_1, T_2, and T_3 (in that order of difficulty), the target adaption in Sect. 3.3 processes it only once in the order T_1, T_2, and T_3. Instead, using the reiterative strategy, if $K^* = 2$, proposed method processes the target domains in the order T_1, T_2, T_3, T_1, T_2, and T_3.

We also propose to scale down the number of training iterations (per reiteration) by a factor of K^*. In this way, proposed method with K^* reiteration passes uses the same number of iterations as original D-CGCT with K adaptation iterations per target domain. Using less number of adaptation iteration per pass/reiteration also reduces the massed learning effect. By only iterating K/K^* times per target domain in a reiteration, the target adaptation process does not push itself too hard, thus avoiding to produce high softmax values for low-confident samples. On the other hand, with increasing reiterative passes, the adaptation process unfolds slowly, however in a more effective manner.

3.5   Emphasizing Source Samples

We furthermore postulate that more source samples in a minibatch can lead to more effective target adaptation. In other words, instead of setting $B_s = B_t = B$, we propose to set $B_s > B_t$. Such a modification does not affect the number of training iterations. Moreover, $B_s + B_t$ can be kept fixed by simply decreasing B_t while increasing B_s.

The proposed algorithm is detailed in the Appendix. Once the proposed MLP-GNN dual head model is trained, either head can be used during inference to determine the class of a target test sample. However, as noted in [47], the GNN head requires mini-batch of samples, that may not be available during real-world inference. Hence, once trained, it is more practical to use the MLP head for inference.

4   Experimental Validation

In this section, we describe the datasets for evaluation, and describe the evaluation protocol of our proposed approach.

4.1   Datasets

We conducted experiments on standard three domain adaptation datasets.

Office-Home has 4 domains (Art, Clipart, Product, Real), 65 classes [57].

Office-31 has 3 domains (Amazon, DSLR, Webcam) and 31 classes [48].

DomainNet has 6 domains and 345 classes [43] and is very large scale containing 0.6 million images. The 6 domains are Real (R), Painting (P), Sketch (S), Clipart (C), Infograph (I), Quickdraw (Q).

4.2   Evaluation Protocol and Settings

Like previous works on MTDA [47], we use the classification accuracy to evaluate the performance of proposed method. The performance for a given source is given by setting the remaining domains as target domains and averaging the accuracy on all the target domains.

For sake of fairness of comparison, we use the same set of hyperparameters as reported in [47]. In addition to D-CGCT [47], comparison is shown to MT-MTDA [40] and Conditional Adversarial Domain Adaptation (CDAN) [34] along with domain-aware curriculum learning (DCL), i.e., CDAN+DCL, as shown in [47]. For DomainNet, comparison is also provided to HGAN [63].

Please note that our experimental results can be broadly categorized into two groups. The results in Table 1, 2 and 3 mainly show the benefits of using the proposed reiterative approach and more source samples in training minibatch. This benefit is irrespective of the backbone feature extractor. Results presented in the remaining Tables also bring in the benefits brought by using superior backbone feature extractor (Transformer).

More details about implementation and experimental settings can be found in https://github.com/sudipansaha/reiterDA22.

4.3 Analyses on Office-Home Dataset

We perform several analyses and ablation studies on the Office-Home dataset. These experiments simply use ResNet-50 (not Transformer) backbone as in [47], unless otherwise stated.

Table 1. Accuracy w.r.t. K^* on Office-Home dataset, source - Art, target - rest.

K^*	1	3	5	10	20
Accuracy	70.5	72.4	73.4	**73.6**	72.8

Table 2. The performance variation w.r.t. source and target samples in a minibatch (B_s, B_t) on Office-Home dataset, source - Art, target - rest.

B_s, B_t	32,32	48,16	48,32
Target accuracy	73.6	73.7	75.1

Table 3. Correct pseudo-sample. (Office-Home, source: Art, target: rest.)

K^*, B_s, B_t	#Real	#Product	#Clipart
1,32,32	2969	3047	1971
10,48,16	3537	3480	2580

Taking Art as source and rest as target, we vary the number of reiteration (K^*) in Table 1. In this experiment, we use $B_s = 32, B_t = 32$. Here, $K^* = 1$ is equivalent to using D-CGCT. We observe that the target accuracy improves as K^* increases. The best target accuracy is obtained at $K^* = 10$. Following [47], we used $K = 10000$. Thus, $K^* = 10$ implies decomposing the adaptation process into 10 reiterations of $\frac{K}{K^*} = 1000$ iterations each. In the rest of the experiments related to Office-Home dataset, $K^* = 10$ is used. After each reiteration, some new target samples are added to the pseudo-source $\hat{S}^{total}$. We show this process in Appendix C.

We hypothesized in Sect. 3.5 that using more source samples in the training minibatch may improve the target adaptation. To examine this, we vary value of B_s and B_t, as shown in Table 2 taking Art as source and rest as target. Among the three compared settings, $B_s = 48$, $B_t = 32$ obtains the best result. Even with $B_s = 48$ and $B_t = 16$, improvement is observed over $B_s = B_t = 32$. Though $B_s = 48$, $B_t = 32$ is better, we use $B_s = 48$, $B_t = 16$ combination for subsequent experiments, to keep $B_s + B_t$ value same as in [47]. We further show in Table 3 that the correctly chosen pseudo-samples increase after employing reiterative strategy and using more source samples in minibatch. Using Transformer as the backbone feature extractor further improves the performance of the proposed method, as shown in Table 4.

Finally we show that the proposed reiterative strategy outperforms D-CGCT [47] in most cases irrespective of the feature extractor backbone. This is shown on all 4 domains (Art, Clipart, Product, Real) as source, while treating other three as target. Performance improvement is consistent for ResNet-18, ResNet-50, and Transformer (except one case), as shown in Table 5.

Henceforth, the proposed method is shown with Transformer-based feature extractor, as detailed in Sect. 3.1. Accuracy reported for D-CGCT is however from [47], with architecture of their choice.

Table 4. Variation of 4 components of the proposed method (k^*, B_s, B_t, and backbone) on Office-Home dataset, source: Art, target: rest.

k^*	B_s	B_t	Backbone	Accuracy
1	32	32	ResNet-50	70.5
10	32	32	ResNet-50	73.6
10	48	16	ResNet-50	73.7
10	48	16	Transformer	80.8

Table 5. The performance comparison on the Office-Home dataset when using different architectures as the backbone.

Method	Art	Clipart	Product	Real
D-CGCT (ResNet-18)	61.4	60.7	57.3	63.8
Proposed (ResNet-18)	**64.9**	**65.4**	**61.8**	**66.7**
D-CGCT (ResNet-50)	70.5	71.6	66.0	71.2
Proposed (ResNet-50)	**73.7**	**76.0**	**68.7**	**72.7**
D-CGCT (Transformer)	77.0	78.5	77.9	**80.9**
Proposed (Transformer)	**80.8**	**81.8**	**80.7**	78.8

4.4 Quantitative Comparisons

Office-Home: The proposed method outperforms D-CGCT (and other compared methods) for all four domains. The performance improvement is quite prominent, Art (10.3%), Clipart (10.2%), Product (14.7%), and Real (7.6%).

This may be attributed to both use of Transformer as backbone feature extractor and the reiterative training strategy. The performance improvement is almost uniform for all domains, except for the Real domain. On average it outperforms D-CGCT by 10.7%. The quantitative result of Office-Home dataset is shown in Table 6.

Table 6. Office-Home: the classification accuracy is reported for each source and the rest set as target, with each source domain being indicated in the columns.

Method	Art	Clipart	Product	Real
MT-MTDA	64.6	66.4	59.2	67.1
CDAN+DCL	63.0	66.3	60.0	67.0
D-CGCT	70.5	71.6	66.0	71.2
Proposed	**80.8**	**81.8**	**80.7**	**78.8**

Office-31: Originally in [47], target adaptation iterations K is set as 3000 for Office-31 dataset. We set the number of reiterations $K^* = 3$ to keep $\frac{K}{K^*} = 1000$, as in Office-Home.

The proposed method outperforms D-CGCT for DSLR (3.4%) and Webcam (2.8%) and obtains similar performance for Amazon. Remarkably, proposed method shows the least improvement for Amazon as source, which has the most number of images in Office-31 dataset. This indicates a possibility that the improvement brought by the proposed method diminishes if there are abundant images in the labeled source domain, which is often not the case in practice. The quantitative result of the Office-31 dataset is shown in Table 7.

Table 7. Office-31: the classification accuracy is reported for each source and the rest set as target, with each source domain being indicated in the columns.

Method	Amazon	DSLR	Webcam
MT-MTDA	87.9	83.7	84.0
CDAN+DCL	92.6	82.5	84.7
D-CGCT	93.4	86.0	87.1
Proposed	**93.4**	**89.4**	**89.9**

DomainNet: Like other two datasets, we chose K^* such that $\frac{K}{K^*} = 1000$. The quantitative result for the different source $\rightarrow$ target combinations are shown in Table 8, following the format in [63]. Performance improves over D-CGCT in most cases, e.g., R→S (10.2%), R→C (8.1%), R→I (5.6%), R→P (5.4%), P→S (2.2%) and P→I (2.5%). However, there is strong variation in improvement depending on the source and target. This may be attributed to relative dissimilarity in certain domains, e.g., Infograph contains images of objects that are surrounded by text, which introduces additional difficulty in adaptation. Additional quantitative comparison on this dataset is provided in the Appendix D.

Table 8. DomainNet: Domains are Real (R), Painting (P), Sketch (S), Clipart (C), and Infograph (I). R->S indices Real as source and Sketch as target.

Method	R→S	R→C	R→I	R→P	P→S	P→R	P→C	P→I
HGAN	34.3	43.2	17.8	43.4	35.7	52.3	35.9	15.6
CDAN+DCL	45.2	58.0	23.7	54.0	45.0	**61.5**	50.7	20.3
D-CGCT	48.4	59.6	25.3	55.6	45.3	58.2	**51.0**	21.7
Proposed	**58.6**	**67.7**	**30.9**	**61.0**	**47.5**	55.9	48.6	**24.2**

5 Conclusion

While single-source single-target domain adaptation has been long studied in the literature, its practical applications are limited. Thus domain adaptation is moving beyond this simple setting towards more practical and complex settings, e.g., multi-target adaptation. Our work takes forward multi-target adaptation by proposing a reiterative adaptation strategy that enhances the target adaptation performance by ensuring the long term retention of the learning across different target domains. We further exploit Transformer along with graph neural network for effectively capturing the relationship among source and target samples. While the reiterative adaptation strategy and usage of Transformer are two different contributions, our experiments separately show benefits of both. The proposed method consistently improves the performance for Office-Home and Office-31 datasets and almost always for the DomainNet dataset. In future, we plan to further improve the theoretical understanding of our method by taking inspiration from optimization, e.g., by formulating it in terms of an alternating minimization approach [32]. The proposed method requires data from the source domain while adapting the model to target. This may potentially limit its practical application and needs to be addressed in the future by modifying the proposed method for source-free adaptation.

Acknowledgments. This work is supported by the German Federal Ministry of Education and Research in framework of the international future AI lab "AI4EO – Artificial Intelligence for Earth Observation: Reasoning, Uncertainties, Ethics and Beyond" (grant number: 01DD20001) and by German Federal Ministry of Economics and Technology in the framework of the "national center of excellence ML4Earth" (grant number: 50EE2201C).

References

1. Beal, J., Kim, E., Tzeng, E., Park, D.H., Zhai, A., Kislyuk, D.: Toward transformer-based object detection. arXiv preprint arXiv:2012.09958 (2020)

2. Bousmalis, K., Silberman, N., Dohan, D., Erhan, D., Krishnan, D.: Unsupervised pixel-level domain adaptation with generative adversarial networks. In: Proceedings of the IEEE Conference on Computer Vision and Pattern Recognition, pp. 3722–3731 (2017)
3. Chen, J., et al.: TransUNet: transformers make strong encoders for medical image segmentation. arXiv preprint arXiv:2102.04306 (2021)
4. Chen, Z., Zhuang, J., Liang, X., Lin, L.: Blending-target domain adaptation by adversarial meta-adaptation networks. In: Proceedings of the IEEE/CVF Conference on Computer Vision and Pattern Recognition, pp. 2248–2257 (2019)
5. Deng, J., Dong, W., Socher, R., Li, L.J., Li, K., Fei-Fei, L.: ImageNet: a large-scale hierarchical image database. In: 2009 IEEE Conference on Computer Vision and Pattern Recognition, pp. 248–255. IEEE (2009)
6. Dosovitskiy, A., et al.: An image is worth 16x16 words: transformers for image recognition at scale. arXiv preprint arXiv:2010.11929 (2020)
7. Duong, L.T., Le, N.H., Tran, T.B., Ngo, V.M., Nguyen, P.T.: Detection of tuberculosis from chest X-Ray images: boosting the performance with vision transformer and transfer learning. Expert Syst. Appl. **184**, 115519 (2021)
8. Feng, K., et al.: Spaced learning enhances episodic memory by increasing neural pattern similarity across repetitions. J. Neurosci. **39**(27), 5351–5360 (2019)
9. Fernandes, H.A., Park, N.W., Almeida, Q.J.: Effects of practice and delays on learning and retention of skilled tool use in Parkinson's disease. Neuropsychologia **96**, 230–239 (2017)
10. Gal, Y.: Uncertainty in deep learning (2016)
11. Ganin, Y., Lempitsky, V.: Unsupervised domain adaptation by backpropagation. In: International Conference on Machine Learning, pp. 1180–1189. PMLR (2015)
12. Garzia, M., Mangione, G.R., Longo, L., Pettenati, M.C.: Spaced learning and innovative teaching: school time, pedagogy of attention and learning awareness. Res. Educ. Media **8**(1), 22–37 (2016)
13. Gholami, B., Sahu, P., Rudovic, O., Bousmalis, K., Pavlovic, V.: Unsupervised multi-target domain adaptation: an information theoretic approach. IEEE Trans. Image Process. **29**, 3993–4002 (2020)
14. Gong, R., Dai, D., Chen, Y., Li, W., Van Gool, L.: mDALU: multi-source domain adaptation and label unification with partial datasets. In: Proceedings of the IEEE/CVF International Conference on Computer Vision, pp. 8876–8885 (2021)
15. Goodfellow, I., Bengio, Y., Courville, A.: Deep Learning. MIT Press, Cambridge (2016)
16. Guo, X., Liu, X., Zhu, E., Yin, J.: Deep clustering with convolutional autoencoders. In: Liu, D., Xie, S., Li, Y., Zhao, D., El-Alfy, E.S. (eds.) ICONIP 2017. LNCS, vol. 10635, pp. 373–382. Springer, Cham (2017). https://doi.org/10.1007/978-3-319-70096-0_39
17. Hamilton, W.L., Ying, R., Leskovec, J.: Inductive representation learning on large graphs. In: Proceedings of the 31st International Conference on Neural Information Processing Systems, pp. 1025–1035 (2017)
18. Han, B., et al.: Co-teaching: robust training of deep neural networks with extremely noisy labels. arXiv preprint arXiv:1804.06872 (2018)
19. Han, K., et al.: A survey on visual transformer. arXiv preprint arXiv:2012.12556 (2020)
20. Hassani, A., Walton, S., Shah, N., Abuduweili, A., Li, J., Shi, H.: Escaping the big data paradigm with compact transformers. arXiv preprint arXiv:2104.05704 (2021)

21. He, K., Zhang, X., Ren, S., Sun, J.: Deep residual learning for image recognition. In: Proceedings of the IEEE Conference on Computer Vision and Pattern Recognition, pp. 770–778 (2016)

22. Hendrycks, D., Gimpel, K.: A baseline for detecting misclassified and out-of-distribution examples in neural networks. arXiv preprint arXiv:1610.02136 (2016)

23. Hong, W., Wang, Z., Yang, M., Yuan, J.: Conditional generative adversarial network for structured domain adaptation. In: Proceedings of the IEEE Conference on Computer Vision and Pattern Recognition, pp. 1335–1344 (2018)

24. Isobe, T., et al.: Multi-target domain adaptation with collaborative consistency learning. In: Proceedings of the IEEE/CVF Conference on Computer Vision and Pattern Recognition, pp. 8187–8196 (2021)

25. Jing, T., Liu, H., Ding, Z.: Towards novel target discovery through open-set domain adaptation. arXiv preprint arXiv:2105.02432 (2021)

26. Kelley, P., Whatson, T.: Making long-term memories in minutes: a spaced learning pattern from memory research in education. In: Frontiers in Human Neuroscience, p. 589 (2013)

27. Kipf, T.N., Welling, M.: Semi-supervised classification with graph convolutional networks. arXiv preprint arXiv:1609.02907 (2016)

28. LeCun, Y., Bengio, Y., Hinton, G.: Deep learning. Nature **521**(7553), 436–444 (2015)

29. Lee, K., Chang, H., Jiang, L., Zhang, H., Tu, Z., Liu, C.: ViTGAN: training GANs with vision transformers. arXiv preprint arXiv:2107.04589 (2021)

30. Li, Y., Wang, N., Shi, J., Hou, X., Liu, J.: Adaptive batch normalization for practical domain adaptation. Pattern Recogn. **80**, 109–117 (2018)

31. Li, Y., Zhang, K., Cao, J., Timofte, R., Van Gool, L.: LocalViT: bringing locality to vision transformers. arXiv preprint arXiv:2104.05707 (2021)

32. Liang, J., He, R., Sun, Z., Tan, T.: Distant supervised centroid shift: a simple and efficient approach to visual domain adaptation. In: Proceedings of the IEEE/CVF Conference on Computer Vision and Pattern Recognition, pp. 2975–2984 (2019)

33. Liang, J., Hu, D., Feng, J.: Do we really need to access the source data? Source hypothesis transfer for unsupervised domain adaptation. In: International Conference on Machine Learning, pp. 6028–6039. PMLR (2020)

34. Long, M., Cao, Z., Wang, J., Jordan, M.I.: Conditional adversarial domain adaptation. arXiv preprint arXiv:1705.10667 (2017)

35. Long, M., Zhu, H., Wang, J., Jordan, M.I.: Unsupervised domain adaptation with residual transfer networks. arXiv preprint arXiv:1602.04433 (2016)

36. Luo, Y., Wang, Z., Huang, Z., Baktashmotlagh, M.: Progressive graph learning for open-set domain adaptation. In: International Conference on Machine Learning, pp. 6468–6478. PMLR (2020)

37. Malpure, D., Litake, O., Ingle, R.: Investigating transfer learning capabilities of vision transformers and CNNs by fine-tuning a single trainable block. arXiv preprint arXiv:2110.05270 (2021)

38. Mancini, M., Bulo, S.R., Caputo, B., Ricci, E.: AdaGraph: unifying predictive and continuous domain adaptation through graphs. In: Proceedings of the IEEE/CVF Conference on Computer Vision and Pattern Recognition, pp. 6568–6577 (2019)

39. Na, J., Jung, H., Chang, H.J., Hwang, W.: FixBi: bridging domain spaces for unsupervised domain adaptation. In: Proceedings of the IEEE/CVF Conference on Computer Vision and Pattern Recognition, pp. 1094–1103 (2021)

40. Nguyen-Meidine, L.T., Belal, A., Kiran, M., Dolz, J., Blais-Morin, L.A., Granger, E.: Unsupervised multi-target domain adaptation through knowledge distillation. In: Proceedings of the IEEE/CVF Winter Conference on Applications of Computer Vision, pp. 1339–1347 (2021)
41. Noor, N.M., Yunus, K., Yusoff, A.M.H., Nasir, N.A.M., Yaacob, N.H.: Spaced learning: a review on the use of spaced learning in language teaching and learning. J. Lang. Linguist. Stud. **17**(2), 1023–1031 (2021)
42. Panareda Busto, P., Gall, J.: Open set domain adaptation. In: Proceedings of the IEEE International Conference on Computer Vision, pp. 754–763 (2017)
43. Peng, X., Bai, Q., Xia, X., Huang, Z., Saenko, K., Wang, B.: Moment matching for multi-source domain adaptation. In: Proceedings of the IEEE/CVF International Conference on Computer Vision, pp. 1406–1415 (2019)
44. Qin, X., Sheikh, N., Reinwald, B., Wu, L.: Relation-aware graph attention model with adaptive self-adversarial training. Proc. AAAI Conf. Artif. Intell. **35**(11), 9368–9376 (2021)
45. Ronneberger, O., Fischer, P., Brox, T.: U-Net: convolutional networks for biomedical image segmentation. In: Navab, N., Hornegger, J., Wells, W.M., Frangi, A.F. (eds.) MICCAI 2015. LNCS, vol. 9351, pp. 234–241. Springer, Cham (2015). https://doi.org/10.1007/978-3-319-24574-4_28
46. Rosenfeld, A., Tsotsos, J.K.: Incremental learning through deep adaptation. IEEE Trans. Pattern Anal. Mach. Intell. **42**(3), 651–663 (2018)
47. Roy, S., Krivosheev, E., Zhong, Z., Sebe, N., Ricci, E.: Curriculum graph co-teaching for multi-target domain adaptation. In: Proceedings of the IEEE/CVF Conference on Computer Vision and Pattern Recognition, pp. 5351–5360 (2021)
48. Saenko, K., Kulis, B., Fritz, M., Darrell, T.: Adapting visual category models to new domains. In: Daniilidis, K., Maragos, P., Paragios, N. (eds.) ECCV 2010. LNCS, vol. 6314, pp. 213–226. Springer, Heidelberg (2010). https://doi.org/10.1007/978-3-642-15561-1_16
49. Saha, S., Sudhakaran, S., Banerjee, B., Pendurkar, S.: Semantic guided deep unsupervised image segmentation. In: Ricci, E., Rota Bulò, S., Snoek, C., Lanz, O., Messelodi, S., Sebe, N. (eds.) ICIAP 2019. LNCS, vol. 11752, pp. 499–510. Springer, Cham (2019). https://doi.org/10.1007/978-3-030-30645-8_46
50. Saito, K., Yamamoto, S., Ushiku, Y., Harada, T.: Open set domain adaptation by backpropagation. In: Ferrari, V., Hebert, M., Sminchisescu, C., Weiss, Y. (eds.) ECCV 2018. LNCS, vol. 11209, pp. 156–171. Springer, Cham (2018). https://doi.org/10.1007/978-3-030-01228-1_10
51. Smolen, P., Zhang, Y., Byrne, J.H.: The right time to learn: mechanisms and optimization of spaced learning. Nat. Rev. Neurosci. **17**(2), 77–88 (2016)
52. Sun, S., Shi, H., Wu, Y.: A survey of multi-source domain adaptation. Inf. Fus. **24**, 84–92 (2015)
53. Tabibian, B., Upadhyay, U., De, A., Zarezade, A., Schölkopf, B., Gomez-Rodriguez, M.: Enhancing human learning via spaced repetition optimization. Proc. Natl. Acad. Sci. **116**(10), 3988–3993 (2019)
54. Toppino, T.C., Gerbier, E.: About practice: repetition, spacing, and abstraction. In: Psychology of Learning and Motivation, vol. 60, pp. 113–189. Elsevier (2014)
55. Touvron, H., Cord, M., Douze, M., Massa, F., Sablayrolles, A., Jégou, H.: Training data-efficient image transformers & distillation through attention. In: International Conference on Machine Learning, pp. 10347–10357. PMLR (2021)
56. Tzeng, E., Hoffman, J., Saenko, K., Darrell, T.: Adversarial discriminative domain adaptation. In: Proceedings of the IEEE Conference on Computer Vision and Pattern Recognition, pp. 7167–7176 (2017)

57. Venkateswara, H., Eusebio, J., Chakraborty, S., Panchanathan, S.: Deep hashing network for unsupervised domain adaptation. In: Proceedings of the IEEE Conference on Computer Vision And Pattern Recognition, pp. 5018–5027 (2017)
58. Wagner, A.D., Maril, A., Schacter, D.L.: Interactions between forms of memory: when priming hinders new episodic learning. J. Cogn. Neurosci. **12**(Supplement 2), 52–60 (2000)
59. Wu, H., et al.: CVT: introducing convolutions to vision transformers. arXiv preprint arXiv:2103.15808 (2021)
60. Wu, S., Wu, T., Lin, F., Tian, S., Guo, G.: Fully transformer networks for semantic image segmentation. arXiv preprint arXiv:2106.04108 (2021)
61. Wulfmeier, M., Bewley, A., Posner, I.: Incremental adversarial domain adaptation for continually changing environments. In: 2018 IEEE International Conference on Robotics and Automation (ICRA), pp. 4489–4495. IEEE (2018)
62. Yang, G., et al.: Transformer-based source-free domain adaptation. arXiv preprint arXiv:2105.14138 (2021)
63. Yang, X., Deng, C., Liu, T., Tao, D.: Heterogeneous graph attention network for unsupervised multiple-target domain adaptation. IEEE Trans. Pattern Anal. Mach. Intell. (2020)
64. Yu, H., Hu, M., Chen, S.: Multi-target unsupervised domain adaptation without exactly shared categories. arXiv preprint arXiv:1809.00852 (2018)
65. Zhang, K., Gong, M., Schölkopf, B.: Multi-source domain adaptation: a causal view. In: Twenty-Ninth AAAI Conference on Artificial Intelligence (2015)
66. Zhang, Y., Liu, T., Long, M., Jordan, M.: Bridging theory and algorithm for domain adaptation. In: International Conference on Machine Learning, pp. 7404–7413. PMLR (2019)

Augmentation Learning
for Semi-Supervised Classification

Tim Frommknecht[1]([✉]), Pedro Alves Zipf[1], Quanfu Fan[2], Nina Shvetsova[1],
and Hilde Kuehne[1,2]

[1] Goethe University Frankfurt, Frankfurt, Hesse, Germany
tim.frommknecht@gmx.de
[2] MIT-IBM Watson AI Lab, Cambridge, MA, USA

Abstract. Recently, a number of new Semi-Supervised Learning methods have emerged. As the accuracy for ImageNet and similar datasets increased over time, the performance on tasks beyond the classification of natural images is yet to be explored. Most Semi-Supervised Learning methods rely on a carefully manually designed data augmentation pipeline that is not transferable for learning on images of other domains. In this work, we propose a Semi-Supervised Learning method that automatically selects the most effective data augmentation policy for a particular dataset. We build upon the Fixmatch method and extend it with meta-learning of augmentations. The augmentation is learned in additional training before the classification training and makes use of bi-level optimization, to optimize the augmentation policy and maximize accuracy. We evaluate our approach on two domain-specific datasets, containing satellite images and hand-drawn sketches, and obtain state-of-the-art results. We further investigate in an ablation the different parameters relevant for learning augmentation policies and show how policy learning can be used to adapt augmentations to datasets beyond ImageNet.

Keywords: Semi-Supervised Learning · Augmentation learning · Meta learning

1 Introduction

Convolutional Neural Networks (CNNs) are widely used in many computer vision applications and achieve state-of-the-art performance in many different tasks across various domains. However, training CNNs requires a large amount of data with proper annotation. Data annotation is often done by humans and thus expensive on a large scale, especially if the labeling requires an educated domain expert (e.g., in the case of medical images). Many methods have been proposed to address that problem. One possible solution to avoid an expensive annotation process is utilizing Semi-Supervised Learning [1–3,11,15,19,21,22] that requires labeling for only a small fraction of the data and combines training from labeled data with learning from large-scale unlabeled data. Such training

B. Andres et al. (Eds.): DAGM GCPR 2022, LNCS 13485, pp. 85–98, 2022.
https://doi.org/10.1007/978-3-031-16788-1_6

can lead to huge improvements [1–3, 15, 19, 21, 22], and unlabeled data can often be gathered at low cost, making Semi-Supervised Learning a cheap option to increase performance on datasets with a limited amount of labeled data.

In most modern Semi-Supervised Learning methods unlabeled data is utilized by applying an augmentation technique in some form. [1–3, 11, 15, 19, 21, 22]. Image augmentation [4, 5, 14, 18] is an effective way to alter images while keeping their class information. However, augmentation can not only alter inessential features of the image but also lead to a loss of relevant information. Augmentation that changes the colors of an image can be useful for the task of distinguishing between a tractor and a chair but can be harmful to the task of predicting the condition of a diseased tomato leaf. Most modern Semi-Supervised Learning methods [1–3, 11, 15, 19, 21, 22] are mostly evaluated on the ImageNet dataset [6] or similar natural image datasets like CIFAR-10 [10] and CIFAR-100 [10], where the classification task is to recognize full objects in real life images. And so far the selection of augmentation has mostly been based on the incentive to improve performance on these datasets. Hence, the used augmentations might not be optimal for all datasets, so the methods might not be able to unfold their full potential on domain-specific datasets with unique properties such as medical images or pencil sketches.

To address this problem, we propose a Semi-Supervised Learning method that performs data augmentation policy learning, to optimize the Semi-Supervised Learning training for each individual, domain-specific dataset. Inspired by recent advances in augmentation training in self-supervised learning setups, such as AutoAugment [4], Fast AutoAugment [14], or DADA [13], we propose a way to integrate the augmentation learning pipeline into a Semi-Supervised setup. We combine FixMatch [19], a recently published method for Semi-Supervised Learning , with the augmentation learning approach of DADA [13]. This is done by building a bi-level-optimization loop around FixMatch which iteratively updates augmentation parameters to maximize classification accuracy in future epochs. The augmentation parameters include a weight determining how frequently the augmentation is applied. The learned augmentation is then applied during follow-up training. To make the best use of the learned augmentation we propose to add a sharpening step, to further improve our results. In an experimental evaluation, we compare our method to the original FixMatch approach on two datasets with non-ImageNet-like properties. On both datasets, we can observe an increased accuracy. In the ablation studies, we show the positive impact of sharpening and investigate the influence of the amount of applied training during the follow-up training. It shows that different datasets require different degrees of augmentation. Finally, we do a quantitative analysis of the impact of single augmentation.

2 Related Work

2.1 Semi-Supervised Learning

Recently, many semi-supervised learning methods [1–3, 11, 15, 19, 21, 22] emerged implementing different algorithms to set new state-of-the-art results on a variety of challenges and datasets [6,10]. For this purpose Semi-Supervised Learning methods leverage unlabeled data to supplement usual supervised machine learning on labeled samples. This can be especially useful in cases where a huge number of unlabeled data is available but additional labeling exceeds existing resources or is plainly inconvenient. A method that can exploit unlabeled data and produce competitive results in the respective domain can be a big asset for many scientific fields. [20] evaluated a variety of Semi-Supervised Learning algorithms for robustness on datasets containing unlabeled images of classes not represented in the labeled fraction. Still, in most cases the evaluation of those methods [1–3,11,15,19,21,22] is done using well established datasets like ImageNet [6] which mainly include natural images in a common setting, in which the accumulation of data is comparatively easy in contrast to more domain-specific tasks which include more restrictive data.

Pseudo-labeling [12] is a simple and generally applicable method for Semi-Supervised Learning that enhances supervised training by additionally utilizing unlabeled samples. This is achieved by iteratively using the already trained network to predict future labels for unlabeled data. To do so the model assigns a probability value to all predictable classes which then is transferred into a pseudo label using a predefined threshold. The created pseudo labels can then be used as targets for a standard supervised loss function. In this sense, pseudo labeling has some similarities to self-training.

Consistency Regularization [9] is used by most state-of-the-art Semi-Supervised Learning methods and aims to increase the robustness of the trained model to perturbations in different image views of the same class. This usually is accomplished by minimizing the distance between two different instances of the same class or image. In visual terms, the goal is to separate data into clusters of their respective classes.

Recently many Semi-Supervised Learning methods [1–3,11,15,19,21,22] have been published and evaluated. One of the state-of-the-art Semi-Supervised Learning methods for image classification that has recently been published is FixMatch [19].

FixMatch [19] combines pseudo-labeling and consistency regularization in a quite simple yet effective approach. Parallel to conventional supervised training on the labeled fraction of the data, additional training is applied to the unlabeled data. For unlabeled samples, two views of the same image are created. One of the images is only transformed slightly (cropping and horizontal flipping), while the other is strongly augmented using RandAugment [5]. FixMatch refers to these views as weak and strong augmentation respectively. Next, the model predicts a class for the weakly augmented image. If the confidence of the prediction surpasses a certain threshold, the prediction is transformed into a one-hot pseudo-label. The resulting pseudo-label is then used as the target for the strongly augmented image. The FixMatch approach achieved state-of-the-art results on multiple benchmark datasets, however it was mainly evaluated on ImageNet [6], CIFAR-10 [10], CIFAR-100 [10], and SVHN [16].

2.2 Augmentation Learning

Most Semi-Supervised Learning methods rely heavily on a data augmentation pipeline. Many different approaches of augmentation have been proposed recently [2,5,13,14]. FixMatch relies on Randaugment [5] that applies randomly sampled operations from a pool of 15 augmentation operations (like rotation, shearing, and autocontrast). However, the augmentation method and the operations in the pool have been designed and tuned on ImageNet and similar datasets but might not be optimal for other domains.

Differential Automatic Data Augmentation (DADA) [13] is a method for augmentation learning. The method uses bi-Level optimization to deferentially optimize augmentation for supervised image classification on a certain dataset. An augmentation policy is learned during an additional augmentation learning phase prior to the actual model training. An augmentation policy consists of a set of sub-policies of two augmentation operations each. We extend the idea of DADA, which so far has only been applied in fully-supervised settings, and make it usable for the case of Semi-Supervised Learning .

3 Method

The main idea of the proposed approach is to learn augmentation policies using bi-level optimization in the first phase and use the learned policies as augmentation for the Semi-Supervised Learning method during a follow-up training in the second phase. Note that, while FixMatch is used as a reference, the overall architecture is independent of the semi-supervised learning framework and other methods could be used as well. Unlike DADA, we use the respective Semi-Supervised Learning architecture during the augmentation learning phase instead of a supervised one. We start by defining our definition of an augmentation policy before introducing the optimization problem of the augmentation learning phase.

3.1 Augmentation Policy

The goal of our system is to find an optimal augmentation policy, for a given dataset. Following Fast AutoAugment [14], we define an augmentation policy S as a set of N sub-policies s_i as described in Eq. 1.

$$S = \{s_1, s_2, s_3, ..., s_N\} \tag{1}$$

where N, denotes the total amount of sub-policies. Each sub-policy s_i consists of two operations O_1, O_2, with respective probabilities p_1, p_2 and magnitudes m_1, m_2. The two operations are applied successively. Each operation is applied

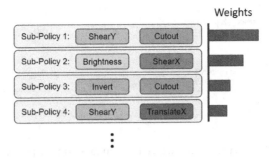

Fig. 1. Each sub-policy contains two operations. All sub-policies have a weight. The sub-policies are sampled by a weighted categorical distribution.

with its respective probability p_i and magnitude m_i. A Bernoulli experiment samples whether an operation is applied using the probability p_i. The magnitude of the operation is determined by m_i. Most operations are applied with a variable parameter such as rotation angle or intensity. All of these parameters are normalized to a scale from 0 to 1. The magnitude parameter m_i lies in the same range and determines the strength of the applied operation. For operations without variable parameters such as invert, the magnitude is simply ignored. Furthermore, each sub-policy is assigned a weight w, which represents the chance of the sub-policy being sampled. Including all components mentioned above, we define a sub-policy s_i in Eq. 2

$$s_i = ((O_{i,1},\ p_{i,1},\ m_{i,1}),\ (O_{i,2},\ p_{i,2},\ m_{i,2}),\ w_i) \qquad (2)$$

We use 15 different operations, leading to $N = 105$ different possible pairs of two operations which we use as sub-policies. Following DADA [13], the selection of sub-policies is modelled as sampling from a categorical distribution with probabilities according to w as visualized in Fig. 1. The application of operations is modeled as a Bernoulli experiment by the respective probability p_i. The search space is the set of all weights w, probabilities p, and magnitudes m in the augmentation policy S.

3.2 Optimization Problem

To find the optimal augmentation policy in the search space described above, we approach an optimization problem as described by DADA [13]. Our approach builds augmentation learning on top of FixMatch. Parallel to a regular training loop minimizing the loss of the FixMatch classification task, the augmentation training is performed. So, our training consists of two update steps. One to update the model and one to update the augmentation parameters. The two update steps are performed alternately. The FixMatch update step is performed just as described in Sect. 2.1. After each FixMatch update step, an update step for the augmentation training is applied. One augmentation update step is performed by minimizing a validation loss of a bi-level optimization problem. To

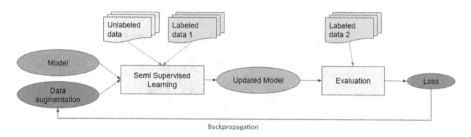

Fig. 2. Augmentation learning process: A Data augmentation policy (purple) is used to augment images for a Semi-Supervised Learning (FixMatch) update step. Instead of changing the original model (blue), a copy is created (green). All unlabeled data (light yellow) and a part of the labeled data (yellow) are used for the update step. The updated copy (green) is then evaluated using the second part of the labeled data (yellow) resulting in a loss term (red). Finally, the loss is backpropagated through the whole process to compute gradients for the augmentation parameters (purple). For the augmentation learning phase, this architecture is repeated in a training loop parallel to the regular FixMatch training, that updates the model (blue). (Color figure online)

do so, we copy the model, sample a sub-policy from a categorical distribution as described above, and perform an update step to the copied model according to the FixMatch loss. The updated copy of the model is then evaluated on an additional fraction of the labeled data, which is only reserved for this particular validation. The resulting validation loss is then differentiated all the way back to the augmentation parameters. A visualization of the augmentation learning process can be seen in Fig. 2 The gradient flow is estimated by the RELAX gradient estimator [7]. For more details see [13]. For our work, we chose to integrate DADA into FixMatch, but the approach will work for other Semi-Supervised Learning methods as well. Once the augmentation training phase is over, the resulting weights w are sharpened. Sharpening is done using the Softmax-function in Eq. 3.

$$w_i' = \frac{\exp(\frac{w_i}{T})}{\sum_{j=1}^{N} \exp(\frac{w_j}{T})} \ \forall i \in \{1, ..., N\} \tag{3}$$

The distribution of the weights can be controlled by varying the temperature parameter T. A high temperature makes the distribution more uniform, while a low temperature leads to a sharper distribution, s.t. the best sub-policies are used significantly more often than others. A visualization of the effect of sharpening can be seen in Fig. 3. During the follow-up learning phase, the learned augmentation is used for Fixmatch training. Unlike during the augmentation learning phase, the augmentations are no longer sampled batch-wise but image-wise, s.t. images in the same batch can have different augmentations. Furthermore, the augmentation is no longer limited to one sub-policy at a time. We thereby introduce a parameter n that denotes, how many augmentations are applied to each image.

Integrating DADA Augmentation Learning into FixMatch: For the augmentation training, the FixMatch architecture [19] was adapted to perform the additional augmentation learning step using bi-level optimization after each regular update step. Augmentation steps are performed as follows: For each unsupervised image, two views are created. One weakly augmented one and one strongly augmented one. For weak augmentation, we perform cropping and a random horizontal flip. To perform strong augmentation a single sub-policy is sampled for the whole batch. The resulting unsupervised loss is then used for the bi-level optimization as described above.

In parallel, the unsupervised images and an additional fraction of labeled images are used to update the model following the FixMatch method [19]. For the follow-up training, we apply FixMatch using the learned augmentation as strong augmentation replacing RandAugment [5] from the original approach.

4 Experiment

In this section, we introduce our experimental setup and discuss the performance of our approach. In the first step we generate baseline numbers for our datasets: EuroSAT [8] and sketch10 [17]. Here we use the standard augmentation methods introduced in the original papers respectively. In the second step, we run our FixMatch data augmentation search for each dataset to evaluate the baseline against our augmentation method. This chapter is structured as follows: In Sect. 4.1, we introduce our experimental setup and evaluation methods. In Sect. 4.2, the datasets for our experiments are introduced, before we compare our approach to state-of-the-art methods in Sect. 4.3. In Sect. 4.4 we'll further investigate our method with an ablation study consisting of quantitative parameter studies and an evaluation of single augmentation operations.

4.1 Implementation Details

Data Splitting: For all experiments, we used 80% of the data for training and 20% for testing. While we used all images in the training set, only a small fraction of labels was used. For our experiments, we used 10% of the training labels. The remaining images are considered unlabeled and the labels are dropped. During the augmentation learning phase, we split the labeled images into two partitions of equal size, leading to two labeled datasets containing 5% of the training data each. While one of the partitions was used as the labeled dataset for the respective Semi-Supervised Learning training, the other partition was used for validation in the bi-level optimization during augmentation steps. For the follow-up training, all labeled images (10% of the train set) were used for Semi-Supervised Learning training.

Augmentation Learning. For augmentation learning we adjust the setting from DADA for our Semi-Supervised case. We increase the number of trained epochs to 100 and use the dataset as described above. For the learning rate we used

$\eta_d = 3 \times 10^{-3}$ and the Adam optimizer. The parameters for the neural network are derived from the official DADA publication [13] and the batch size is 128. The probabilities p and magnitudes m are uniformly initialized with 0.5. Meaning that each operation is applied with a 50% chance and with medium magnitude.

Evaluation. All results are reported as average accuracy over all classes on a test set, that was not used for model training or policy search. We compare the proposed approach to the supervised baselines on the labeled images 10%, thus using only the labeled part for supervised training, as well as to the fully supervised baseline, which uses the full train set including the labels we dropped for the Semi-Supervised Learning experiments. These two can be seen as lower and upper bounds for our experiments. Additionally, we ran these two measures again with RandAugment, to make a fair comparison to the FixMatch algorithm, which uses RandAugment as well.

Network Specifications. For all experiments, we use ResNet-50 as the backbone network. We used a pre-trained architecture that was trained on ImageNet. According to the original FixMatch and DADA papers, we used a stochastic gradient descent (SGD) optimizer to update the model and an Adam optimizer to update the augmentation parameters.

4.2   Datasets

EuroSAT [8] is an image dataset containing satellite images of different land-scapes. The EuroSAT dataset is based on Sentinel-2-Satelite imagery covering 13 spectral bands. To have consistent image formats for better comparison of the augmentations, we choose to use the RGB dataset containing only three of the 13 original channels. The dataset contains 10 different classes with 2000 to 3000 images per class adding up to 27000 total images. Each class represents a certain kind of landscape, like *residential*, *pasture*, or *forest*. We've chosen to use EuroSAT, as its different classes are not recognized by recognizing objects but by environmental structures and properties.

Sketch10. We further derive the Sketch10 dataset as a subset from the original DomainNet dataset [17]. To this end, we only use those images of the dataset, that contain data in sketch style. The images are black and white images that contain sketches of 365 different classes. To keep a balanced distribution while at the same time providing enough data, the dataset was further reduced to the 10 largest classes. The reduced dataset contains a total of 6548 images among the 10 classes, with images per class ranging from 593 (*sleeping_bag*) to 729 (*square*). We propose the Sketch10 dataset as it significantly deviates from conventional object detection datasets, as the dataset contains high-resolution images with a very specific style and features.

4.3 Comparison to State-of-the-Art

In this section, we will compare our method of combining FixMatch's Semi-Supervised Learning training with DADA's approach of augmentation learning to the original approach FixMatch. We will start by evaluating the baselines using different augmentations, followed by the analysis for FixMatch. The FixMatch analysis begins with an evaluation of the original method to the supervised baselines, followed by a comparison to our method. The following analysis is based on the results in Table 1.

Supervised Baselines. We start by comparing the baselines using RandAugment to the baselines using weak augmentation. We can observe that for Sketch10 RandAugment performs better than weak augmentation. As both baselines (using 10% and 100% of data) show a significant improvement when using RandAugment. For EuroSAT, we can observe the opposite behavior, as weak augmentation performs significantly better than RandAugment. These results indicate, that not every augmentation technique does perform equally well for every dataset, but rather indicate the need for more targeted augmentation learning.

FixMatch VS FixMatch + DADA. Original FixMatch performs a significant improvement towards the lower bound baselines. For EuroSAT the accuracy is increased by 1.53% and 4.51%, compared to the weak and RandAugment baseline respectively. An even stronger improvement can be observed for Sketch10, where the baselines are outperformed by 5.45% (weak) and 4.11% (RandAugment). It further shows that our approach to combining FixMatch with DADA outperforms the original FixMatch in both datasets. For Sketch10 we achieve an improvement of 1.41% in classification accuracy towards the original method. For EuroSAT we could improve performance by 0.42%. To validate that the improvement is due to the proposed augmentation learning technique and not due to the way the augmentation is applied, we also compare to FixMatch using a random policy, which consists of a set of sub-policies just like our approach. The only difference is, that the weights are defined as uniform and all magnitudes and probabilities are 0.5. This is done to mimic parameters as they are before training. This way we ensure that the improvement is due to the learning phase.

4.4 Ablation and Analysis

Influence of sharpening Temperature. One technical contribution of this paper is the sharpening of the learned sub-policy weights after the augmentation training is finished. As described in Sect. 3.2, sharpening is performed using Softmax with a temperature parameter T. Without further sharpening, the weights vary only very little. With different temperatures T, we can control how much the weights deviate. Different levels of sharpness can be seen in Fig. 3. To investigate the influence of T we conduct a parameter study on both datasets. The results and a comparison to uniform sampling ($T = \infty$) can be seen in Table 2. We experimented temperature values ranging from 10^{-4} to 10^{-3}.

Table 1. Comparison of our approach to the original FixMatch and a version of our approach before training, s.t. the policy is not trained but uniformly random. Additionally, we compare our results with supervised baselines using FixMatch's weak augment and Randaugment respectively. Each accuracy was calculated as the average over three runs. The combination of FixMatch and DADA leads to state-of-the-art results for sketch10 and EuroSAT. The Table contains the average accuracy along three runs for each experiment

	Labels used	Sketch10	EuroSAT
Supervised baseline (weak augmentation)	10%	61.32	93.03
Supervised baseline (RandAugment)	10%	62.66	90.05
FixMatch (original)	10%	66.77	94.56
FixMatch + random policy	10%	67.43	94.81
FixMatch + DADA (ours)	10%	**68.18**	**94.98**
Fully supervised baseline (RandAugment)	100%	75.76	95.91
Fully supervised baseline (weak augmentation)	100%	74.03	97.09

Table 2. Parameter study on EuroSAT for the weight sharpening temperature T. The Table contains the average accuracy values over three runs following the FixMatch architecture using our learned augmentation. An infinite temperature ($T = \infty$) leads to a uniform selection of sub-policies. The results are additionally compared to the (unsharpened) original weights and RandAugment. For the runs on EuroSAT, we applied one sub-policy per image during training ($n = 1$). For Sketch10 we used $n = 4$.

T	$1e-4$	$2e-4$	$3e-4$	$4e-4$	$5e-4$	$6e-4$	$7e-4$	$8e-4$	$9e-4$	$1e-3$	∞	orig. w
EuroSAT	**94.98**	94.57	94.80	94.54	94.69	94.66	94.79	94.70	94.84	94.90	94.81	94.89
Sketch10	67.47	67.16	66.34	66.97	66.44	67.74	66.26	66.50	**68.18**	**68.18**	67.43	65.38

For both datasets, we observe an improvement of the sharpened results towards the original weights. The accuracy varies only very little for EuroSAT but we can still achieve an accuracy gain of 0.09%. For Sketch10, we can see a much bigger improvement, as sharpening increases classification accuracy by 2.80%. For EuroSAT, the best accuracy is achieved using a lower comparatively low temperature of $T = 1e - 4$. For Sketch10, we achieve best accuracy with higher temperatures of $T = 9e - 4$ and $T = 1e - 3$.

Quantitative Evaluation of the Number of Applied Sub-policies n. To explore the behavior of the performance of Fixmatch with harsher augmentation, we apply multiple sub-policies to each image during training. The results can be seen in Table 3. The results for both datasets show a clear trend, towards a sweet spot. On EuroSAT, we observe best accuracy with $n = 1$, while Sketch10 peaks at $n = 4$. This shows that depending on the dataset a different value for n is optimal which again indicates that augmentation policies can be dataset depended and that it might be desirable to adapt them individually.

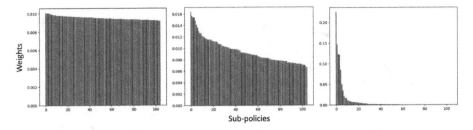

Fig. 3. Weight distribution among sub-policies: original (left), sharpened with $T = 10^{-3}$ (middle) and sharpened with $T = 10^{-4}$ (right). In the figures, each bar represents the weight of a single sub-policy. The sub-policies are ordered from left to right descending by weights. While the original distribution is close to uniform, the sharpened distributions become more selective with sharpening. This effect increases with a lower temperature.

Table 3. Parameter study of FixMatch for the number of applied sub-policies per image n. The table contains the average accuracy along three runs for each experiment. For the experiments, we used a Temperature of $T = 9e - 4$.

n	1	2	3	4
EuroSAT	**94.84**	94.31	94.16	94.12
Sketch10	66.85	67.29	65.56	**68.18**

Qualitative Evaluation of the Influence of Single Augmentation Operations. Our approach makes use of different augmentation operations by weighting them differently. This way some operations are applied more often, while others are applied less frequently. In Sect. 4 we've shown, that this leads to an increased accuracy among the tested datasets. To further investigate the influence of single operations we made an additional ablation study on the full Sketch dataset. For these experiments, we took each of our 15 augmentation operations and ran FixMatch training with only that one respective augmentation. So instead of sampling random augmentations from a pool, the same augmentation operation is applied to each image. We use the full Sketch dataset from DomainNet containing all 365 classes. The training process of the experiments can be observed in Fig. 4. In addition to the augmentations, we show two baseline experiments for comparison, a supervised baseline with weak augmentation s.t. we can see the improvement caused by the augmentation, as well as one experiment similar to the above but with an augmentation operation, that simply colors the whole image in black. This is supposed to work as a negative example of a bad augmentation, that is expected to mislead training and thus decrease performance. In Fig. 4 we can observe, that the bad augmentation (green) degrades accuracy compared to the supervised baseline (orange). On the contrary, none of our augmentation operations seems to be degrading training as all of them outperform the non-augmented baseline. This leads to the conclusion, that all

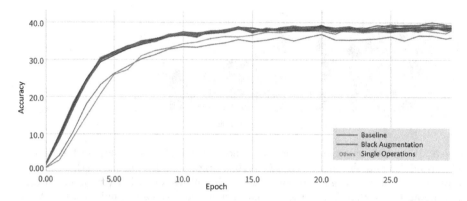

Fig. 4. Evaluation of single augmentation operations on Sketch10. Each line represents the accuracy during the first 40 training epochs. In orange, you can see the supervised baseline. The training with the bad augmentation (image set to black) is represented by the green line. Each of the other lines represents an experiment with one of the augmentation operations from our augmentation pool. A selection of the final accuracy values can be seen in Table 4 (Color figure online)

Table 4. Accuracy for FixMatch using only one augmentation operation. The table shows the accuracy for a selection of the operations as well as the accuracy for baseline and the purposely bad augmentation. These values refer to the curves in Fig. 4.

Operation	Baseline	Bad	Solarize	Invert	Cutout	Equalize	Color
Accuracy	38.70	36.88	39.53	38.95	38.90	40.07	38.65

augmentations can be applied to support training. In Table 4 we can observe that some augmentations score a higher accuracy than others. This indicates that even though all augmentations do increase accuracy, some operations have a greater effect than others. This supports the idea that all augmentations from the pool can be used but some should be applied more often than others.

5 Conclusion

In this work, we address the problem of learning augmentations in a Semi-Supervised Learning setup. While most augmentation methods are designed to perform well on ImageNet or similar datasets, we shift the focus towards more domain-specific datasets such as sketches and satellite images. We propose a novel method for Semi-Supervised Learning that trains specific data augmentation for a given dataset. We applied the approach to enhance FixMatch training. We've shown that our new method applies to different datasets and domains, to be precise satellite and sketch images, and has outperformed previous augmentation methods for those settings. Furthermore, we propose to add a sharpening step to the weights of the learned augmentation policy, to further improve the performance of the method and evaluated the effect of different sharpening temperatures in an ablation study. Additionally, we investigated the effect of an increased number of augmentation operations per image. Finally, we investigate the effect of single augmentations for training and find that all augmentations from our pool do improve FixMatch training, but some do more than others. We hope that the proposed method will make Semi-Supervised Learning more applicable to satellite or other domain-specific datasets.

References

1. Assran, M., et al.: Semi-supervised learning of visual features by non-parametrically predicting view assignments with support samples. arXiv preprint arXiv:2104.13963 (2021)
2. Berthelot, D., et al.: ReMixMatch: semi-supervised learning with distribution alignment and augmentation anchoring. arXiv preprint arXiv:1911.09785 (2019)
3. Berthelot, D., Carlini, N., Goodfellow, I., Papernot, N., Oliver, A., Raffel, C.: MixMatch: a holistic approach to semi-supervised learning. arXiv preprint arXiv:1905.02249 (2019)
4. Cubuk, E.D., Zoph, B., Mane, D., Vasudevan, V., Le, Q.V.: AutoAugment: Learning augmentation strategies from data. In: Proceedings of the IEEE/CVF Conference on Computer Vision and Pattern Recognition, pp. 113–123 (2019)
5. Cubuk, E.D., Zoph, B., Shlens, J., Le, Q.V.: RandAugment: practical automated data augmentation with a reduced search space. In: Proceedings of the IEEE/CVF Conference on Computer Vision and Pattern Recognition Workshops, pp. 702–703 (2020)
6. Deng, J., Dong, W., Socher, R., Li, L.J., Li, K., Fei-Fei, L.: ImageNet: a large-scale hierarchical image database. In: 2009 IEEE Conference on Computer Vision and Pattern Recognition, pp. 248–255. IEEE (2009)
7. Grathwohl, W., Choi, D., Wu, Y., Roeder, G., Duvenaud, D.: Backpropagation through the void: optimizing control variates for black-box gradient estimation. arXiv preprint arXiv:1711.00123 (2017)
8. Helber, P., Bischke, B., Dengel, A., Borth, D.: EuroSAT: a novel dataset and deep learning benchmark for land use and land cover classification (2017)
9. Hu, W., Miyato, T., Tokui, S., Matsumoto, E., Sugiyama, M.: Learning discrete representations via information maximizing self-augmented training. In: International Conference on Machine Learning, pp. 1558–1567. PMLR (2017)
10. Krizhevsky, A., Hinton, G., et al.: Learning multiple layers of features from tiny images (2009)
11. Kuo, C.-W., Ma, C.-Y., Huang, J.-B., Kira, Z.: FeatMatch: feature-based augmentation for semi-supervised learning. In: Vedaldi, A., Bischof, H., Brox, T., Frahm, J.-M. (eds.) ECCV 2020. LNCS, vol. 12363, pp. 479–495. Springer, Cham (2020). https://doi.org/10.1007/978-3-030-58523-5_28
12. Lee, D.H., et al.: Pseudo-label: the simple and efficient semi-supervised learning method for deep neural networks. In: Workshop on Challenges in Representation Learning, ICML, vol. 3, p. 896 (2013)
13. Li, Y., Hu, G., Wang, Y., Hospedales, T., Robertson, N.M., Yang, Y.: DADA: differentiable automatic data augmentation. arXiv preprint arXiv:2003.03780 (2020)
14. Lim, S., Kim, I., Kim, T., Kim, C., Kim, S.: Fast autoaugment. Adv. Neural. Inf. Process. Syst. **32**, 6665–6675 (2019)

15. Nassar, I., Herath, S., Abbasnejad, E., Buntine, W., Haffari, G.: All labels are not created equal: Enhancing semi-supervision via label grouping and co-training. In: Proceedings of the IEEE/CVF Conference on Computer Vision and Pattern Recognition, pp. 7241–7250 (2021)
16. Netzer, Y., Wang, T., Coates, A., Bissacco, A., Wu, B., Ng, A.Y.: Reading digits in natural images with unsupervised feature learning (2011)
17. Peng, X., Bai, Q., Xia, X., Huang, Z., Saenko, K., Wang, B.: Moment matching for multi-source domain adaptation. In: Proceedings of the IEEE International Conference on Computer Vision, pp. 1406–1415 (2019)
18. Shorten, C., Khoshgoftaar, T.M.: A survey on image data augmentation for deep learning. J. Big Data **6**(1), 1–48 (2019)
19. Sohn, K., et al.: FixMatch: simplifying semi-supervised learning with consistency and confidence. arXiv preprint arXiv:2001.07685 (2020)
20. Su, J.C., Cheng, Z., Maji, S.: A realistic evaluation of semi-supervised learning for fine-grained classification. In: Proceedings of the IEEE/CVF Conference on Computer Vision and Pattern Recognition, pp. 12966–12975 (2021)
21. Tian, Y., Sun, C., Poole, B., Krishnan, D., Schmid, C., Isola, P.: What makes for good views for contrastive learning? arXiv preprint arXiv:2005.10243 (2020)
22. Zhai, X., Oliver, A., Kolesnikov, A., Beyer, L.: S4l: Self-supervised semi-supervised learning. In: Proceedings of the IEEE/CVF International Conference on Computer Vision, pp. 1476–1485 (2019)

Interpretable Machine Learning

Multi-attribute Open Set Recognition

Piyapat Saranrittichai[1,2]([⊠]) [ID], Chaithanya Kumar Mummadi[2,3] [ID],
Claudia Blaiotta[1] [ID], Mauricio Munoz[1] [ID], and Volker Fischer[1] [ID]

[1] Bosch Center for Artificial Intelligence, Renningen, Germany
`Piyapat.Saranrittichai@de.bosch.com`
[2] University of Freiburg, Freiburg im Breisgau, Germany
[3] Bosch Center for Artificial Intelligence, Pittsburgh, USA

Abstract. Open Set Recognition (OSR) extends image classification
to an open-world setting, by simultaneously classifying known classes
and identifying unknown ones. While conventional OSR approaches can
detect Out-of-Distribution (OOD) samples, they cannot provide explanations indicating which underlying visual attribute(s) (e.g., shape, color
or background) cause a specific sample to be unknown. In this work, we
introduce a novel problem setup that generalizes conventional OSR to
a multi-attribute setting, where multiple visual attributes are simultaneously recognized. Here, OOD samples can be not only identified but
also categorized by their unknown attribute(s). We propose simple extensions of common OSR baselines to handle this novel scenario. We show
that these baselines are vulnerable to shortcuts when spurious correlations exist in the training dataset. This leads to poor OOD performance
which, according to our experiments, is mainly due to unintended cross-
attribute correlations of the predicted confidence scores. We provide an
empirical evidence showing that this behavior is consistent across different baselines on both synthetic and real world datasets.

Keywords: Open set recognition · Multi-task learning · Shortcut
learning

1 Introduction

In recent years, deep learning techniques have been applied to a variety of complex classification tasks with great success. However, the majority of these methods rely on the closed-set assumption, where all classes in the test data are *known*
during training. As a result, such methods are poorly suited to more realistic
scenarios where it is not possible to observe all classes during training. Open
Set Recognition (OSR) [23] extends the standard classification task to handle
unknown classes that are not included in the training set - that is, an OSR model
must discriminate known from unknown samples as well as classify known ones.

Supplementary Information The online version contains supplementary material
available at https://doi.org/10.1007/978-3-031-16788-1_7.

Previous research in the OSR domain has only considered a single classification task [3, 4, 13, 26, 30, 32], where a network takes an image as an input and produces a label prediction, possibly accompanied by a confidence score (to make a decision on whether the input belongs to a known or unknown class). Predicting a single label, however, is not sufficient in some real world applications. For example, a robot picking up a red shirt needs to recognize multiple attributes of an object, such as its shape ("shirt") and its color ("red").

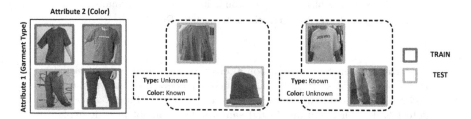

Fig. 1. Illustration of our multi-attribute Open Set Recognition. Dataset contains images with attribute annotations (e.g., garment type and color). Samples with some known attribute combinations are available during training. During inference, networks need to be able to handle images containing both known and unknown attribute values. In case of input with unknown attribute values, the networks have to identify which attributes are actually of unknown values. (Color figure online)

The task of predicting multiple attributes simultaneously is closely related to Compositional Zero-Shot Learning (CZSL) [2, 17, 19, 22], whose goal is to recognize unknown combinations of known attributes. However, one limitation of CZSL is that it assumes labels of input images to be already known. Therefore, when the model gets an input containing unknown attribute labels, it would incorrectly map them to known ones. In this work, we are interested in multi-attribute predictions, similar to CZSL, but we allow attributes of input images to be of unknown labels.

The scenario described above, can be cast as a multi-attribute OSR problem illustrated in Fig. 1. Given an image, the goal is to recognize multiple attributes (e.g., shape, color, background) at once. Additionally, if an attribute has an unknown value, the model should be able to identify it as such, irrespectively of whether the other attributes were seen or not before. We use the term *attribute* to denote a generic visual property of image's which can be either low-level (i.e., shape, color, etc.) or high-level (i.e., object type, background, etc.) depending on the target tasks. Please note that our work is conducted under the assumption that the available attributes in a task are semantically independent (cannot describe the same aspects of an image). For example, in an object recognition task, texture and material are not semantically independent attributes, since the material attribute also contain texture information.

Several OSR approaches can naturally be extended to this novel setting. However, additional challenges arise in the case that certain combinations of known attributes are not available during training. This is especially likely when the number of feasible combinations is large. In case of missing combinations, spurious correlations among attributes are introduced leading to shortcut learning [9]. Our setting enables analyzing the effect of shortcut learning on OSR. In contrast to previous works in the shortcut learning literature, which analyze the effect of shortcuts only the recognition of known classes, our setting extends the analysis to unknown classes. We will also demonstrate that the multi-attribute extensions of common OSR techniques are shortcut vulnerable consistently across different approaches and datasets.

The main contributions of this work are as follows: (1) We introduce the multi-attribute OSR setup, as a novel problem formulation promoting explainability. (2) We extend several OSR baselines to handle the multi-attribute setting. (3) We demonstrate, with extensive empirical analyses, on both synthetic and realistic datasets, that many state-of-the-art OSR methods are vulnerable to shortcut learning. Specifically, we found OSR performance to be inversely correlated to the strength of dataset biases.

2   Related Works

2.1   Open Set Recognition

Open-Set Recognition (OSR) is the problem of simultaneously classifying known samples and detecting unknown samples. OSR is conventionally a single-task problem, considering only one aspect of images (e.g., object type). With deep learning, the straightforward approach to solve OSR is Maximum Softmax Probability (MSP) applying softmax thresholding on the output of classification networks [20]. [3] shows that direct softmax thresholding does not minimize open space risk and proposes OpenMax as an alternative activation function that explicitly estimates the probability of a sample being unknown. [24] models prototypes of individual object types to detect unknown categories. Other approaches instead rely on generative models to improve OSR [13,21,25,27,32]. [8,20] generate synthetic unknown images to be used during training. [30] directly estimates the likelihood of a sample being of a known class using a flow-based model. [4,5] formulate constraints to maximize the difference between image features of known and unknown samples. Recently, [26] shows that network performance in OSR is heavily correlated with close-set accuracy and propose using Maximum Logit Score (MLS) for unknown class detection. These lines of work consider only object recognition but cannot recognize multiple attributes or infer which properties cause certain input images to be unknown. Some studies decompose feature space into multiple components based on image regions [12] or attributes [6] to improve performance on fine-grained datasets. Still, their final task is that of single-task OSR. On the other hand, we study a generalized version of the OSR problem, in which multiple attributes are recognized simultaneously.

2.2 Compositional Zero-Shot Learning

Compositional Zero-Shot Learning (CZSL) is the task of predicting both seen and unseen combinations of known attributes. VisProd is a naïve solution, which trains deep networks with cross-entropy losses to predict all attributes [19]. Recent works aim to model compatibility functions between attribute combinations and image features [2,16–19,22]. Our problem is closely related to CZSL as we also recognize multiple attributes at the same time. While CZSL assumes input images to have only known attribute values, we allow input images with unknown attribute values and would like to identify the unknown ones during inference.

2.3 Shortcut Learning

Shortcut Learning studies degradation of the recognition performance caused by spurious correlations [7,9]. [10] shows that real-world objects, in general, have shape-texture correlations and that deep networks trained with natural images tend to classify objects using the simpler visual clue, which is, in general, texture. [14] also shows that a trained model tends to extract information from visual features that are more linearly decodable. In contrast to most works on shortcut learning, which study its effects on the recognition of the known classes, we additionally study its effects on the recognition of the unknown classes.

3   Problem Formulation

In this work, we define *attributes* as semantically independent visual properties of an image. For each attribute, we aim to predict its value or to recognize it as unknown if the value was never seen during training.

Our task formulation can be formally defined as follows. A sample from the training set contains an image $I^i \in \mathcal{I}^{train}$ as well as its attribute annotation $\boldsymbol{y}^i = (a_1^i, a_2^i, \ldots, a_M^i) \in \mathcal{Y}^{train} = \mathcal{A}_1^k \times \mathcal{A}_2^k \times \ldots \times \mathcal{A}_M^k$ where M is the number of attributes and each $\mathcal{A}_j^k$ represents the set of all *attribute values* of the j-th attribute seen during training. The superscript k indicates that all attribute values available in the training set are of known values. On the other hand, a test sample can belong to either known or unknown values. In other words, $\mathcal{Y}^{test} = (\mathcal{A}_1^k \cup \mathcal{A}_1^u) \times (\mathcal{A}_2^k \cup \mathcal{A}_2^u) \times \ldots \times (\mathcal{A}_M^k \cup \mathcal{A}_M^u)$, where the superscript u represents ones containing unknown values.

Given the training set, our goal is to estimate a function $f(I) = (\hat{\boldsymbol{y}}, \hat{\boldsymbol{s}})$ that takes an image I from a test sample as an input and predicts attribute values $\hat{\boldsymbol{y}} \in \mathcal{Y}^{train}$ as well as attribute-wise confidence scores $\hat{\boldsymbol{s}} = (\hat{s}_1, \hat{s}_2, \ldots, \hat{s}_M)$. These confidence scores will be used to distinguish between known and unknown attribute values by thresholding. In our work, higher confidence score indicates higher likelihood for a sample to be of a known attribute value.

During training, some attribute combinations can be missing (see Fig. 5). On the other hand, any attribute combinations can be seen during testing, including the combinations containing unknown attribute values. We define the term *Open-Set OOD for* $\mathcal{A}_m$ (OOD_m^O) to represent a sample whose attribute values are partially unknown on the m-th attribute. Additional terms indicating samples with different categories of attribute combinations are defined in Fig. 2.

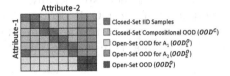

Fig. 2. Definitions of samples which can be found during inference. Samples with (dark or light) green colors represent samples whose attribute values are all *known*. These values can be either the seen combinations during training (dark green) or the unseen ones (light green). Yellow, blue and red boxes represent attribute combinations containing *unknown* attribute values. The yellow and blue boxes are partially unknown as only the values of attribute 1 (OOD_1^O) or attribute 2 (OOD_2^O) are unknown respectively. (Color figure online)

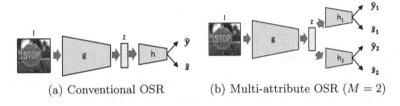

(a) Conventional OSR   (b) Multi-attribute OSR $(M = 2)$

Fig. 3. Illustration of generic architectures for single- and multi-attribute OSR.

4 Extension from Common OSR Approaches

For conventional single-task OSR, which is a special case of our setting where $M = 1$, model solves a single task and predicts one class label and one confidence score. These predictions are typically computed by a network combining a feature extractor (to compute intermediate representations) with a prediction head (to compute final predictions) as shown in Fig. 3(a). Given a feature extractor g and a prediction head h, the function f can be written as $f(I) = h(g(x))$, where $g(I) = z$ is the intermediate feature representation.

In this work, we study a simple generalization of single-task OSR methods, which is directly applicable to several state-of-the-art approaches. To extend a single-task model, we opt to use only a single feature extractor g similar to the case of conventional OSR. However, h is extended to have multiple heads $(h_1, h_2, \ldots, h_M)$ to support simultaneous prediction of multiple attributes. This extension can be seen in Fig. 3(b).

5   Experiments

In this section, we present a set of experiments and analysis to understand the behavior of different methods on multi-attribute OSR setting. We begin by describing our experimental setup and then present quantitative evaluation of various approaches on synthetic datasets. Additionally, we uncover a possible mechanism by which shortcuts can affect OSR performance, which relates to undesired correlation of confidence scores across attributes. Lastly, we show that our findings can also be observed in a more realistic dataset.

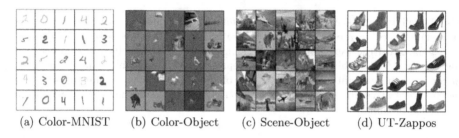

| (a) Color-MNIST | (b) Color-Object | (c) Scene-Object | (d) UT-Zappos |

Fig. 4. Images of example samples from datasets used in this work. (Color figure online)

5.1   Experiment Setup

In this subsection, details of our experiment setup will be described. In particular we will present the datasets, baselines and metrics used in our study.

Datasets. Datasets with multiple attribute annotations are required for multi-attribute OSR setting. Additionally, to enable shortcut analysis, we choose datasets where the available attributes have different complexity (i.e., in term of linear decodability as in [14]). In the presence of shortcuts, we expect neural networks to rely heavily on simpler but less robust visual clues. In this work, we consider datasets where two attributes are annotated ($M = 2$). The first attribute $\mathcal{A}_c$ is intended to be complex (e.g., shape, object type) while the second attribute $\mathcal{A}_s$ is intended to be simple (e.g., color, background). The datasets used in this work are as follows (example images are shown in Fig. 4):

- Color-MNIST: This dataset contains MNIST digits with different colors. We construct this dataset based on the DiagVib framework [7]. Attributes available in this dataset are digit shape and color.
- Color-Object: This dataset is inspired by [1] to simulate more realistic settings while full-control over dataset biases is still maintained. Each image sample contains an object from COCO [15] over a background of single color. Attributes available in this dataset are object type and background color respectively.

- Scene-Object: Similar to Color-Object, each image sample still contains a COCO object. However, instead of using color as background, scene images from [31] are used.
- UT-Zappos: This dataset contains images of shoes annotated with two attributes (shoe material and type) [28,29] which is commonly used as a CZSL benchmark.

We split datasets mentioned above so that some attribute values are kept unknown during training for OSR evaluation. Details of each dataset split will be presented in Appendix C.

Baselines. All baselines considered in this work comprise a feature extraction backbone (g) and multiple prediction heads ($h_1, h_2, \ldots, h_M$), as introduced in Sect. 4. The main difference among baselines lies in the modeling of loss functions and retrieval of confidence scores. Baselines considered in this work are:

- Maximum Softmax Probability (MSP) [20]: This standard baseline trains networks by minimizing a sum of cross-entropy losses across all prediction heads. The confidence score for each attribute is simply the maximum softmax value from its prediction head.
- OpenMax [3]: The training procedure of this baseline is similar to MSP. However, the final confidence score of each attribute will be calibrated to reduce probability of the predicted labels based on the distance between the estimated logit vector and its corresponding mean vector.
- ARPL [4]: This baseline trains the model so that feature representations of potential unknown samples are far away from the ones of known samples. The suffix +CS is appended when *confusing samples* are also generated and used for training.
- Maximum Logit Score (MLS) [26]: This baseline uses maximum logit value before softmax activation from each prediction head as the confidence score. This prevents certain information being discarded by softmax normalization.

Model architectures and hyperparameters used for each dataset will be presented in Appendix B.

Metrics. For the evaluation, we extend conventional OSR metrics for multi-task setting. In contrast to conventional OSR, we have multiple prediction heads so that the evaluation will be performed per head. We consider the average metrics over all heads to represent overall performance. Two main metrics adopted here are Open-Set Classification Rate (OSCR) and Area Under the Receiver Operating Characteristic (AUROC) similar to [4,26]. Quantitative results reported in this section are averaged across three different random seeds.

5.2 Shortcut Analysis in Multi-attribute OSR

In this section, we study effects of shortcut learning on synthetic datasets in which we can control the attribute combinations seen during training. A low

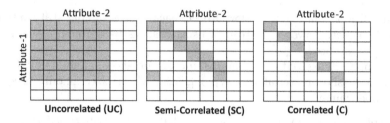

Fig. 5. Training dataset configurations. Each box represents an attribute combination whose yellow color indicates its presence during training. These three configurations provide different degrees of spurious correlations to simulate different shortcut opportunities. (Color figure online)

Table 1. Average OSCR (from all attributes) on Color-MNIST, Color-Object and Scene-Object.

Approach	Color-MNIST			Color-Object			Scene-Object		
	UC	SC	C	UC	SC	C	UC	SC	C
MSP	80.5	56.0	42.9	76.2	58.4	53.0	39.7	32.1	29.3
OpenMax	79.1	52.9	45.2	70.2	45.8	25.0	35.5	18.4	13.1
ARPL	80.8	54.0	49.2	77.3	54.4	36.0	42.5	34.5	29.9
ARPL+CS	78.7	52.7	49.9	77.6	53.9	38.5	44.7	34.8	28.3
MLS	76.5	44.5	36.0	74.9	57.0	51.6	40.4	32.2	29.4
MSP-D	80.0	58.3	46.4	75.0	61.7	52.4	42.9	35.5	28.8
OpenMax-D	76.8	49.1	43.8	75.2	48.5	22.6	38.6	16.6	12.2
ARPL-D	83.6	60.3	45.8	79.1	59.2	49.8	44.0	33.1	26.3

number of seen combinations can amplify the effects of shortcut learning. As illustrated in Fig. 5, we utilize three dataset configurations: (1) **Correlated (C)**: With this configuration, the number of seen combination is minimal. In other words, there is a one-to-one mapping between each available attribute. (2) **Semi-Correlated (SC)**: With this configuration, additional combinations are introduced so that a trained network has enough information to distinguish two visual attributes. The number of combinations in this configuration is two times higher than in the Correlated configuration. (3) **Uncorrelated (UC)**: All combinations are available.

We control dataset generation such that the number of samples are balanced across all attribute combinations. During testing, for each attribute, the number of the unknown attribute values is the same as the number of the known attribute values. In addition, the test combinations are also balanced so that the random chance of detecting an unknown attribute is 50% per attribute. More details of the splits are presented in Appendix C.

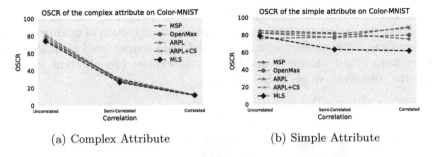

(a) Complex Attribute   (b) Simple Attribute

Fig. 6. Attribute-wise OSCR evaluation on Color-MNIST with different dataset configurations.

Table 1 shows OSCR across different approaches and dataset configurations (i.e., Uncorrelated (UC), semi-correlated (SC) and correlated (C)). We notice that, in uncorrelated cases, OSCR values are consistently the highest across all baselines and datasets. These values correspond to the ideal case that there is no dataset bias caused by spurious attribute correlations (low shortcut opportunities). In contrast, OSR performance degrades as soon as correlations are introduced, such as in the SC and C configurations. This suggests that attribute correlations in the SC and C cases can induce shortcut learning during training. Similar trends can also be observed with AUROC metrics (see Appendix A.2).

In order to investigate models's behavior in the presence of shortcut opportunities, we look at attribute-wise OSCR for the complex attribute ($\mathcal{A}_c$) and the simple attribute ($\mathcal{A}_s$). Figure 6 presents OSCR of $\mathcal{A}_c$ and $\mathcal{A}_s$ from different baselines on Color-MNIST dataset. According to the results in the Figure, spurious correlations do not have the same effects to both attributes. Specifically, the reduction of OSCR mainly occurs on $\mathcal{A}_c$ but not on $\mathcal{A}_s$ (For some baselines, OSCR values of $\mathcal{A}_s$ do not even reduce). A possible explanation of this behavior is that, during correlated training, a network tends to rely more heavily on the simple attribute compared to the complex one when both attributes are predictive of the model's target. Similar insights were reported by previous works on shortcut learning [9,14]. More evaluation details and discussions regarding to the attribute-wise evaluations will be presented in the Appendix A.1.

In addition to the baseline extension method described in Sect. 4, we also study another simple approach that simply duplicates the whole model for each attribute (represented with a -D appended after the approach names) resulting in models with two times many parameters (in the case of two attributes). According to the results in Table 1, the general trend of the performance degradation due to spurious correlations is still hold. Throughout this work, we opt to perform our analysis mainly based on the extension introduced in Sect. 4.

5.3 Effects of Shortcut on Confidence Scores

The results presented in the previous section indicate that spurious correlations can degrade multi-attribute OSR performance, as measured using common OSR metrics. Even though these metrics are useful for comparing models, they do not uncover the underlying mechanism by which the detection of unknown samples degrades. Since confidence scores are the main output used to distinguish between known and unknown samples, we will explore how shortcut learning affects the confidence scores in this section.

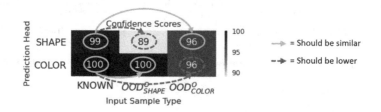

Fig. 7. Visualization of cross-attribute confidence scores

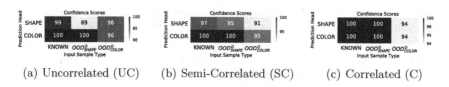

(a) Uncorrelated (UC)   (b) Semi-Correlated (SC)   (c) Correlated (C)

Fig. 8. Cross-attribute confidence scores of MSP on different configurations of the Color-MNIST dataset.

We will visualize the behavior of confidence scores as a heatmap $\mathcal{M}$ similar to Fig. 7. A value $\mathcal{M}_{ij}$ in the (i, j) cell is the average confidence score from the prediction head of the i-th attribute given input sample of type j ($1 =$ Known, $2 =$ Open-Set OOD for attribute 1 ($\mathcal{A}_c$), $3 =$ Open-Set OOD for attribute 2 ($\mathcal{A}_s$)). The ideal behaviour is that, if an input sample has a known attribute value for the attribute i, the confidence score of the i-th head should be similar to the case of known inputs (i.e., $\mathcal{M}_{11} \approx \mathcal{M}_{13}$ and $\mathcal{M}_{21} \approx \mathcal{M}_{22}$). On the other hand, if an input sample is unknown with respect to the i-attribute, the i-th confidence score should be lower (i.e., $\mathcal{M}_{11} > \mathcal{M}_{12}$ and $\mathcal{M}_{21} > \mathcal{M}_{23}$), in which case by thresholding the score, one can identify the unknown attribute value. Ideally, the confidence score of one attribute should not be impacted by the attribute value of another attribute. We called this property of the confidence score as *cross-attribute independence*.

We test the standard MSP baseline on uncorrelated, semi-correlated and correlated setting. The result of the Color-MNIST and Color-Object dataset shown in Fig. 8 and Fig. 9. Firstly, we notice that, in the uncorrelated case, confidence scores are more or less similar to the ideal behaviour mentioned above (e.g., see Fig. 8(a) and 9(a)). However, as the correlation is introduced, a cross-attribute

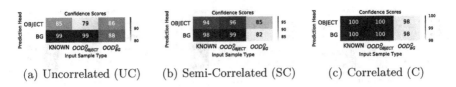

(a) Uncorrelated (UC)   (b) Semi-Correlated (SC)   (c) Correlated (C)

Fig. 9. Cross-attribute confidence scores of MSP on different configurations of Color-Object dataset.

dependency of the confidence scores can be observed. For example, considering the semi-correlated case in Fig. 9(b), confidence score of the first attribute (object type) drops when the second attribute (background) is unknown ($\mathcal{M}_{11} > \mathcal{M}_{13}$). This indicates unintended dependency between confidence score of the first attribute and the attribute value of the second attribute. In other words, the network incorrectly uses the information of second attribute to determine if the first attribute is unknown or not. This demonstrates one scenario that shortcut can affect the recognition performance of OOD. In addition, considering edge cases in which all attributes are correlated in Fig. 8(c) and 9(c), average confidence scores of the first attribute are unchanged regardless of whether actual attribute values are unknown or not (i.e., $\mathcal{M}_{11} = \mathcal{M}_{12}$). The network only use the information of the second attribute to detect the unknown of both attributes. This is an obvious sign of shortcuts similar to the semi-correlated case mentioned before.

5.4   Measuring Explainability for Unknown Samples

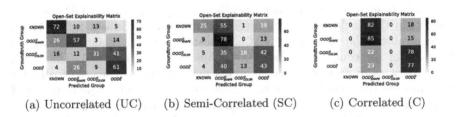

(a) Uncorrelated (UC)   (b) Semi-Correlated (SC)   (c) Correlated (C)

Fig. 10. Open-Set Explainability Matrix of MSP on different configurations of the Color-MNIST dataset.

As mentioned earlier, one benefit of our task is that, in contrast to conventional OSR or anomaly detection, models will be able to provide meaningful attribute-level explanations of why certain samples are identified as unknown. In other words, because models categorize each attribute separately as known or unknown, they can also explain which underlying attribute(s) are responsible for an input sample likely being unknown.

In this regard, we evaluate explainability using a confusion matrix $\mathcal{C}$, similarly to closed-set evaluation. However, instead of grouping samples by class labels,

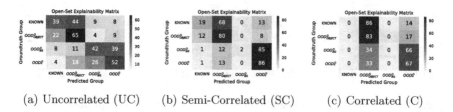

(a) Uncorrelated (UC)   (b) Semi-Correlated (SC)   (c) Correlated (C)

Fig. 11. Open-Set Explainability Matrix of MSP on different configurations of the Color-Object dataset.

we group samples based on whether they are known or unknown with respect to specific attributes. Each row and column index correspond to a type of sample, either known, Open-Set OOD for attribute 1, Open-Set OOD for attribute 2 or Open-Set OOD (refer to the definitions in Fig. 2). The horizontal and vertical axes correspond to prediction and ground truth respectively. A value in each cell indicates the percentage of samples from the ground truth group corresponded to the row index which the network predicts to the group corresponded to the column index. The sum of values in each row is normalized to 100. Ideally, we would like to get high values along the diagonal and low values on off-diagonal cells which indicates the prediction of the correct groups. It should be noted that, unlike previous experiments, the evaluation in this section needs thresholding to identify the unknowns. Here, we pick thresholds that maximize micro-F-Measure metric [11].

Results on the Color-MNIST and Color-Object datasets are shown in Figs. 10 and 11. In the uncorrelated case, we obtain high values along the diagonal, thus indicating good explainability of OOD samples (see Figs. 10(a) and 11(a)). Shortcuts do, as to be expected, degrade model's ability to explain an OOD outcome, as shown by the results in the semi-correlated and correlated cases. In Fig. 11(b), the high value in the off-diagonal cell C_{12} indicates poor performance to recognize unknown for the complex attribute (i.e., object type in this case). This result is consistent as in Sect. 5.3 since shortcuts make confidence scores of complex attributes less distinguishable for its own attribute. Recognition performance of the complex attribute is also poor even for the known attribute values, therefore, the optimal threshold get less reward from identifying a sample as the known. Thresholding is then likely to output more unknown predictions. This behaviour can be more clearly seen in the fully-correlated case (Figs. 10(c) and 11(c)), where complex attributes for all samples are identified as unknown. From all of our experiments, we can conclude that shortcuts affect performance to recognize OOD and explanability of the models.

5.5   Evaluation on a Realistic Dataset

In previous sections, we conducted experiments on well-controlled synthetic datasets and empirically shows effects of shortcut learning on multi-attribute OSR. In this section, we will demonstrate that our findings on synthetic datasets

Approach	$\mathcal{A}_c$	$\mathcal{A}_s$	$\bar{\mathcal{A}}$
MSP	45.3	67.7	56.5
OpenMax	45.2	68.3	56.8
ARPL	51.0	69.6	60.3
ARPL+CS	51.9	67.5	59.7
MLS	44.7	71.2	58.0

(a) AUROC evaluation

(b) Confidence scores

Fig. 12. Qualitative Evaluation on UT-Zappos (a) AUROC for material ($\mathcal{A}_c$), type ($\mathcal{A}_s$) predictions and their average ($\bar{\mathcal{A}}$) (b) Cross-attribute confidence scores of MSP.

can also be observed in realistic settings. In this regard, we use an open set split based on UT-Zappos dataset [28,29], a common dataset for CZSL. The dataset contains shoe images annotated with shoe materials and types. In the context of UT-Zappos, shoe material is relatively fine-grained compared to shoe type (as seen in Fig. 4(d)). Therefore, we consider shoe material as the complex attribute ($\mathcal{A}_c$) and shoe type as the simple attribute ($\mathcal{A}_s$).

Figure 12(a) shows AUROC on UT-Zappos from various baselines. The general trend follows synthetic scenarios that AUROC values tend to be lower for $\mathcal{A}_c$ and higher for $\mathcal{A}_s$. We also look at the cross-attribute confidence scores for MSP as in Fig. 12(b). According to the Figure, the scores are similar for the first and second column ($\mathcal{M}_{11} \approx \mathcal{M}_{12}$ and $\mathcal{M}_{21} \approx \mathcal{M}_{22}$) where shoe types are known, while the scores drop on the third column ($\mathcal{M}_{13}$ and $\mathcal{M}_{23}$) where shoe types are unknown. This indicates that shoe types are mainly determined the output of unknown detection even for the shoe material prediction head. In other words, models take $\mathcal{A}_s$ as shortcuts for unknown detection of $\mathcal{A}_c$ demonstrating the same observation as in the semi-correlated cases of Sect. 5.3. This shows that our findings are also generalized to realistic scenarios.

6   Conclusion

In this work, we generalize the single-task OSR to a multi-attribute OSR setup. This enables trained models to identify unknown properties of input images in an attribute-wise manner. We propose simple extensions of common OSR baselines for our task. These extended baselines are evaluated across multiple datasets. We found that these naïve extensions are shortcut vulnerable especially when higher degrees of attribute correlations are introduced in training sets. An investigation of how the models are affected by shortcuts is presented. We found that confidence scores predicted by the models are likely to be affected by unrelated attributes when spurious correlations are introduced. Lastly, we also evaluate the explainability of the models trained on our task. While the problem we investigated in this work remains open challenge in the domain of visual perception, we hope that it can inspire further researches in this direction.

References

1. Ahmed, F., Bengio, Y., van Seijen, H., Courville, A.: Systematic generalisation with group invariant predictions. In: International Conference on Learning Representations (2020)
2. Atzmon, Y., Kreuk, F., Shalit, U., Chechik, G.: A causal view of compositional zero-shot recognition. In: Larochelle, H., Ranzato, M., Hadsell, R., Balcan, M.F., Lin, H. (eds.) Advances in Neural Information Processing Systems, vol. 33, pp. 1462–1473. Curran Associates, Inc. (2020)
3. Bendale, A., Boult, T.E.: Towards open set deep networks. In: Proceedings of the IEEE Conference on Computer Vision and Pattern Recognition, pp. 1563–1572 (2016)
4. Chen, G., Peng, P., Wang, X., Tian, Y.: Adversarial reciprocal points learning for open set recognition. arXiv preprint arXiv:2103.00953 (2021)
5. Chen, G., et al.: Learning open set network with discriminative reciprocal points. In: Vedaldi, A., Bischof, H., Brox, T., Frahm, J.-M. (eds.) ECCV 2020. LNCS, vol. 12348, pp. 507–522. Springer, Cham (2020). https://doi.org/10.1007/978-3-030-58580-8_30
6. Du, S., Hong, C., Chen, Y., Cao, Z., Zhang, Z.: Class-attribute inconsistency learning for novelty detection. Pattern Recogn. **126**, 108582 (2022)
7. Eulig, E., et al.: Diagvib-6: a diagnostic benchmark suite for vision models in the presence of shortcut and generalization opportunities. In: Proceedings of the IEEE/CVF International Conference on Computer Vision, pp. 10655–10664 (2021)
8. Ge, Z., Demyanov, S., Chen, Z., Garnavi, R.: Generative openmax for multi-class open set classification. arXiv preprint arXiv:1707.07418 (2017)
9. Geirhos, R., et al.: Shortcut learning in deep neural networks. Nat. Mach. Intell. **2**(11), 665–673 (2020)
10. Geirhos, R., Rubisch, P., Michaelis, C., Bethge, M., Wichmann, F.A., Brendel, W.: ImageNet-trained CNNs are biased towards texture; increasing shape bias improves accuracy and robustness. In: ICLR (2018)
11. Geng, C., Huang, S.J., Chen, S.: Recent advances in open set recognition: a survey. IEEE Trans. Pattern Anal. Mach. Intell. **43**(10), 3614–3631 (2020)
12. Gillert, A., von Lukas, U.F.: Towards combined open set recognition and out-of-distribution detection for fine-grained classification. In: VISIGRAPP (5: VISAPP), pp. 225–233 (2021)
13. Guo, Y., Camporese, G., Yang, W., Sperduti, A., Ballan, L.: Conditional variational capsule network for open set recognition. arXiv preprint arXiv:2104.09159 (2021)
14. Hermann, K., Lampinen, A.: What shapes feature representations? exploring datasets, architectures, and training. In: NeurIPS, vol. 33, pp. 9995–10006. Curran Associates, Inc. (2020)
15. Lin, T.-Y., et al.: Microsoft COCO: common objects in context. In: Fleet, D., Pajdla, T., Schiele, B., Tuytelaars, T. (eds.) ECCV 2014. LNCS, vol. 8693, pp. 740–755. Springer, Cham (2014). https://doi.org/10.1007/978-3-319-10602-1_48
16. Mancini, M., Naeem, M.F., Xian, Y., Akata, Z.: Open world compositional zero-shot learning. In: Proceedings of the IEEE/CVF Conference on Computer Vision and Pattern Recognition, pp. 5222–5230 (2021)
17. Misra, I., Gupta, A., Hebert, M.: From red wine to red tomato: composition with context. In: Proceedings of the IEEE Conference on Computer Vision and Pattern Recognition, pp. 1792–1801 (2017)

18. Naeem, M.F., Xian, Y., Tombari, F., Akata, Z.: Learning graph embeddings for compositional zero-shot learning. In: Proceedings of the IEEE/CVF Conference on Computer Vision and Pattern Recognition, pp. 953–962 (2021)
19. Nagarajan, T., Grauman, K.: Attributes as operators: factorizing unseen attribute-object compositions. In: Proceedings of the European Conference on Computer Vision (ECCV), pp. 169–185 (2018)
20. Neal, L., Olson, M., Fern, X., Wong, W.K., Li, F.: Open set learning with counter-factual images. In: Proceedings of the European Conference on Computer Vision (ECCV), pp. 613–628 (2018)
21. Oza, P., Patel, V.M.: C2ae: class conditioned auto-encoder for open-set recognition. In: Proceedings of the IEEE/CVF Conference on Computer Vision and Pattern Recognition, pp. 2307–2316 (2019)
22. Purushwalkam, S., Nickel, M., Gupta, A., Ranzato, M.: Task-driven modular networks for zero-shot compositional learning. In: Proceedings of the IEEE/CVF International Conference on Computer Vision, pp. 3593–3602 (2019)
23. Scheirer, W.J., de Rezende Rocha, A., Sapkota, A., Boult, T.E.: Toward open set recognition. IEEE Trans. Pattern Anal. Mach. Intell. **35**(7), 1757–1772 (2013). https://doi.org/10.1109/TPAMI.2012.256
24. Shu, Y., Shi, Y., Wang, Y., Huang, T., Tian, Y.: P-ODN: prototype-based open deep network for open set recognition. Sci. Rep. **10**(1), 1–13 (2020)
25. Sun, X., Yang, Z., Zhang, C., Ling, K.V., Peng, G.: Conditional gaussian distribution learning for open set recognition. In: Proceedings of the IEEE/CVF Conference on Computer Vision and Pattern Recognition, pp. 13480–13489 (2020)
26. Vaze, S., Han, K., Vedaldi, A., Zisserman, A.: Open-set recognition: a good closed-set classifier is all you need. In: International Conference on Learning Representations (2021)
27. Yoshihashi, R., Shao, W., Kawakami, R., You, S., Iida, M., Naemura, T.: Classification-reconstruction learning for open-set recognition. In: Proceedings of the IEEE Conference on Computer Vision and Pattern Recognition, pp. 4016–4025 (2019)
28. Yu, A., Grauman, K.: Fine-grained visual comparisons with local learning. In: Proceedings of the IEEE Conference on Computer Vision and Pattern Recognition, pp. 192–199 (2014)
29. Yu, A., Grauman, K.: Semantic jitter: dense supervision for visual comparisons via synthetic images. In: Proceedings of the IEEE International Conference on Computer Vision, pp. 5570–5579 (2017)
30. Zhang, H., Li, A., Guo, J., Guo, Y.: Hybrid models for open set recognition. In: Vedaldi, A., Bischof, H., Brox, T., Frahm, J.-M. (eds.) ECCV 2020. LNCS, vol. 12348, pp. 102–117. Springer, Cham (2020). https://doi.org/10.1007/978-3-030-58580-8_7
31. Zhou, B., Lapedriza, A., Khosla, A., Oliva, A., Torralba, A.: Places: a 10 million image database for scene recognition. IEEE Trans. Pattern Anal. Mach. Intell. **40**(6), 1452–1464 (2017)
32. Zhou, D.W., Ye, H.J., Zhan, D.C.: Learning placeholders for open-set recognition. In: Proceedings of the IEEE/CVF Conference on Computer Vision and Pattern Recognition, pp. 4401–4410 (2021)

A Syntactic Pattern Recognition Based Approach to Online Anomaly Detection and Identification on Electric Motors

Kutalmış Coşkun$^{(\boxtimes)}$, Zeynep Kumralbaş , Hazel Çavuş , and Borahan Tümer

Faculty of Engineering, Marmara University, İstanbul, Turkey
{kutalmis.coskun,zeynep.kumralbas,
semiha.cavus,borahan.tumer}@marmara.edu.tr

Abstract. Online anomaly detection and identification is a major task of many Industry 4.0 applications. Electric motors, being one of the most crucial parts of many products, are subjected to end-of-line tests to pick up faulty ones before being mounted to other devices. With this study, we propose a Syntactic Pattern Recognition based approach to online anomaly detection and identification on electric motors. Utilizing Variable Order Markov Models and Probabilistic Suffix Trees, we apply both unsupervised and supervised approaches to cluster motor conditions and diagnose them. Besides being explainable, the diagnosis method we propose is completely online and suitable for parallel computing, which makes it a favorable method to use synchronously with a physical test system. We evaluate the proposed method on a benchmark dataset and on a case study, which is being worked on within the scope of a European Union funded research project on reliability.

Keywords: Syntactic Pattern Recognition · Variable Order Markov Models · Probabilistic Suffix Trees · Anomaly detection · Diagnosis

1 Introduction

Anomaly Detection (AD) and Anomaly IDentification (AID) are two sub-branches of Machine Learning (ML) which have been receiving a lot of attention since several decades, as these two related problems can find applicability in a wide spectrum of fields. AD is to reveal a possible deviation from a predefined normal functioning mode of a target system using a given set of time measurements or signals stemming from this target system. AID, on the other hand, is to recognize what anomaly, among several, of the target system the signal under analysis characterizes. Especially, the analysis of nonlinear signals in medical and industrial domains using ML methods for AD and AID that contribute a significant variety to classical signal processing techniques brought about this attention. Further, with the growing need for more accurate, dependable and economical methods for AD and AID in more complex systems, highly sophisticated techniques emerge based on a diversity of ML approaches.

B. Andres et al. (Eds.): DAGM GCPR 2022, LNCS 13485, pp. 116–132, 2022.
https://doi.org/10.1007/978-3-031-16788-1_8

Electric motors are major components of many highly developed systems in many domains, such as industrial production, transportation and household appliances to name a few. Reliability is an important aspect of electric motor production, since it is directly connected to the reliability of the system that the motor is installed in. End-of-line (EoL) tests are an important quality control (QC) step in motor production to detect faulty instances before they are used in other systems. In this respect, with the *Industry 4.0* principles, AD and AID in electric motors with ML approaches is a highly appealing task to enhance reliability, reduce costs and improve product quality.

Two distinct ML approaches that AD and AID methods fall within are the *decision-theoretic* and *syntactic* ones [12]. Decision theoretic methods assume that data under analysis are identically and independently distributed (IID) whereas methods classified into the syntactic approach exploit the temporal or spatial context dependence within data adopting Markovian paradigms. Building syntactic models of target systems for their behavior analysis is more complex than those in decision theoretic methods, whereas the syntactic methods are (a) more robust due to the two sequential stages of the syntactic approach where a possibly erroneous output of the first stage is tolerated and corrected in the second stage, (b) accurate enough to represent behavior of complex systems, (c) more capable of dealing with data scarcity, and finally (d) more explainable due to their tree or graph-like structures built upon meaningful contextual data.

The novelties and contributions of this study can be listed as follows:

- We provide a novel end-to-end framework for online classification of continuous time-series signals collected from electric motors.
- We utilize an unsupervised learning step before training condition models to reveal previously unknown (sub)classes of different reliability characteristics.
- We propose an online and efficient method to classify a test signal using the condition models and alphabet that are constructed priorly.

This paper is organized as follows. Section 2 discusses related studies and applications from the literature. Section 3 provides necessary background information about the methods and approaches that are mentioned in the paper. Section 4 involves the methodological information regarding the proposed approach. Section 5 reports and discusses experiment results. Finally, Sect. 6 finalizes the study with conclusions and possible future work.

2   Related Work

AD and AID applications on electric motors utilize conventional and advanced signal processing techniques to detect mechanical, electrical and environmental faults [15], which are generally bearing (45 %), stator/armature (35 %) and rotor (10 %) related [28]. Detection and identification of these faults are usually done using sensor readings collected from the motor during a test, which are generally vibration [18, 25, 33, 47], current [5, 30, 40, 48], power [14], acoustic noise (sound) [6, 9, 42], temperature [26] and thermograms [20].

Especially since the necessary hardware and software became more accessible, using Artificial Intelligence (AI) and ML approaches have been of substantial interest in many Industry 4.0 related applications. Regarding fault detection on electric motors, it is possible to classify ML approaches into two main categories, where (a) a list of (often statistical) features are prepared/automatically obtained from time-dependent measurements (usually current or vibration) then ML models are trained with these feature vectors and labels indicating fault status [10,14] and (b) ML models are trained directly on the time-series signals and then used to recognize faulty instances [5,7]. The latter approach, which the method this paper introduces is an example of, has an appealing aspect due to being more adaptable to different types of signals and applications.

For feature selection and extraction, Principal Component Analysis (PCA) and Independent Component Analysis (ICA) are effectively used [42]. Some ML algorithms previously used to classify faulty electric motors are Support Vector Machines (SVMs) [14] (sometimes accompanied by Genetic Algorithms (GAs) [29]), k-Nearest Neighbor (kNN) [10], Kernel Density Estimation (KDE) [11], decision trees [43], Self-Organizing Maps (SOMs) [35] and Artificial Neural Networks (ANNs) [2,22]. The review study in [21] provides a general list of ML approaches for various types of faults.

Among other approaches, Deep Learning (DL) is quite popular due to the minimal amount of expert knowledge necessary and the abundance of hardware and open-source implementations. Using a deep Convolutional Neural Network (CNN), FaultNet [27] achieved significant performance (95.27% accuracy) when applied directly on the raw signals from Case Western Reserve University (CWRU) bearing dataset and improved to 98.5% when additional 3 channels are introduced to incorporate more signal information. Using a series of deep Auto-Encoders (AEs), method proposed in [37] achieved 97.18% accuracy with automatically extracted features on the same dataset. Another study [38] using an adaptive Deep Belief Network (DBN) with dual-tree complex wavelet packet obtained 94.38% accuracy when applied directly on raw data and improved to 98.75% when manually selected extra 16 features are also fed to the model. Consequently, the state-of-the-art techniques achieve 97-100% accuracy figures on the benchmark dataset from CWRU. We also test the proposed method in CWRU bearing dataset and report the results in Sect. 5.1.

Syntactic Pattern Recognition (SPR) is an effective methodology (discussed more in detail in Sect. 3.1) to recognize patterns of varying complexity in signals where temporal dependence is important. It has been successfully applied to electrocardiogram (ECG) signals to detect arrhythmia [46], transmission lines to detect faults at power system waveforms [31] and process monitoring to extract important qualitative trends [32]. Variable Order Markov Models (VOMMs) have been used in various applications for prediction and classification [3]. More recently, an unsupervised approach that utilizes SPR with VOMMs has been shown to be quite successful at mode detection in Cyber-Physical Production Systems (CPPSs) [44]. We also utilize this approach before diagnosis as a preliminary step to observe the distribution of instances in the dataset.

3   Preliminaries

This section provides the background information about methods and approaches that are referred to throughout the study.

3.1   Syntactic Pattern Recognition

SPR is a paradigm which focuses on not only detecting a pattern (and hence classifying it) in some input signal, but also identifying the structural aspects of the pattern (and hence modeling it) which makes it unfit to other classes [12,13]. The approach in SPR involves describing patterns in a hierarchical (tree-like) structure, where simpler subpatterns are used as building blocks to describe more complex patterns. One important aspect of this technique is that, the subpatterns (or pattern primitives) themselves do not represent significant characteristics and are notably simpler than the target pattern, which makes them easily distinguishable in the signal.

A typical SPR application involves two fundamental sections: "lexical analysis" and "parsing". SPR is a powerful tool for sequential analysis where (i) in lexical analysis, the original (or properly preprocessed) time-series is chopped up into temporal patterns with no significant structure and each such pattern is replaced by a symbol from an alphabet generated a priori to reconstruct the original signal as sequence of alphabet symbols, and (ii) in parsing, the reconstructed sequence undergoes a syntactic analysis realized by a parser likewise built a priori and achieves a diagnosis about the target system. The two sections of SPR pass through three phases, where (i) in the first phase the primitive alphabet is constructed within lexical analysis by a diversity of clustering methods, (ii) in the second phase the training signals are reconstructed as sequences of alphabet symbols and the parsing tools are built in the lexical analysis and parsing, respectively and finally, (iii) in the third phase, an unknown or test signal is reconstructed as a series of symbols and the condition of the target system is diagnosed. This pipeline is summarized in Table 1.

Table 1. SPR phases and sections.

Phases	Lexical Analysis	Syntactic Recognition/Parsing
Phase 1	alphabet construction	-
Phase 2	training signal reconstruction	model learning
Phase 3	test signal reconstruction	diagnosis

The fault-tolerant aspect of SPR originates from the fact that the negative effect of a possible misrepresentation of a pattern in the original signal by a suboptimal alphabet symbol as the primary selection is suppressed in parsing through eventually that symbol ends up in a low probability while a better and hopefully optimal symbol has a higher selection probability.

3.2   Variable Order Markov Models

VOMMs extend Markov chains so that varying orders of dependencies are considered regarding the observed random variables [4]. This property makes VOMMs (a) efficient (since only significant conditional events are stored in the model), and (b) thanks to their flexibility, powerful (since the maximum order of dependence can be adjusted to fit different applications).

3.3   Probabilistic Suffix Trees

Probabilistic Suffix Tree (PST), first introduced in [34], is a data structure used to implement VOMMs. PST is an extension to Suffix Tree (ST), so that it reflects the probabilistic characteristics of the subsequences of the sequence that the PST is constructed from. A PST over an alphabet Σ is a rooted tree where each edge is associated with a symbol from Σ [3]. The unique sequence s of edge labels from the root to a node v defines the label of v. Each node in a PST also involves a probability vector for the corresponding next symbol probabilities. The subsequences and hence nodes in a PST are placed so that searching for probability $P(\sigma|s)$ in the tree, where $\sigma \in \Sigma$ and s is a sequence of symbols from Σ, is optimized. Namely, the subsequence s can be reached by following relevant edges from the root in $O(m)$ time, where m is the length of the subsequence s. Even if subsequence s does not exist in the tree, the search procedure terminates at the most relevant node.

While constructing PSTs, the complexity of the model is controlled via pruning parameters, which determine the maximum dependence level (L pruning) and the minimum number of occurrences of a subsequence to be included in the tree (t pruning). Depending on the construction approach, pruning can be done during or after tree construction.

4   Methodology

This section describes the proposed approach from a methodological aspect. Following the pipeline introduced in Sect. 3.1, we describe the consecutive steps of the proposed method in corresponding sections.

4.1   Lexical Analysis

Alphabet Construction. An alphabet is a set of representative time-series signals (i.e., primitives or subpatterns) to be used to reconstruct both training and test signals. To automatically obtain an alphabet from data, clustering methods are used. The expressivity of an alphabet is connected to the variety of primitives it contains. Therefore, to maximize the comprehensiveness of the alphabet, the input signal is decomposed into overlapping time-series fragments. These fragments are then subjected to clustering, after which each cluster representative becomes a primitive. The resulting clustering structure depends on

the parameters being used, which are selected using Davies-Bouldin (DB) score
[8]. The algorithm for alphabet construction is given in Algorithm 1.

Algorithm 1 Alphabet construction

Require: training set $\mathcal{X} = \{x_1, x_2, \dots\}$, overlap length k, fragment length l
1: **for all** $x \in \mathcal{X}$ **do**
2:      $i \leftarrow 0$, $L \leftarrow$ length of x
3:      **while** $i \leq (L - l)/k$ **do**
4:          add $x[ik : ik + l]$ to the fragment collection $\mathcal{F}$
5:          $i \leftarrow i + 1$
6:      **end while**
7: **end for**
8: cluster $\mathcal{F}$
9: $n \leftarrow 0$
10: **for all** cluster representative in clustering result **do**
11:      add cluster representative to alphabet Σ with ID n
12:      $n \leftarrow n + 1$
13: **end for**
14: **return** Σ

Signal Reconstruction. At this step, both training and test signals are reconstructed using the alphabet constructed earlier. Reconstruction is in principle
analogous to signal compression, which brings the trade-off between *compression ratio* and *reconstruction error*. While reconstructing a signal, it is essential
to preserve the significant structures that characterize different behaviors while
keeping the model complexity at a reasonable and workable level. Reconstruction of a raw signal is done by selecting the best primitive for each time-series
fragment that forms the signal. The algorithm for signal reconstruction is given
in Algorithm 2.

Algorithm 2 Signal Reconstruction

Require: input signal X, alphabet Σ
1: $E \leftarrow 0$
2: **for all** fragments in X **do**
3:      $e_{\min} \leftarrow +\infty$
4:      **for all** primitives in Σ **do**
5:          $e \leftarrow |\text{fragment} - \text{primitive}|$
6:          **if** $e < e_{\min}$ **then**
7:              $e_{\min} \leftarrow e$
8:              save primitive as best
9:          **end if**
10:      **end for**
11:      add ID of best primitive to reconstructed signal
12:      $E \leftarrow E + e_{\min}$
13: **end for**
14: **return** reconstructed signal, reconstruction error E

4.2 Model Learning

VOMMs are powerful mathematical tools to represent time-series signals with varying orders of time dependencies and PSTs are efficient data structures that can be used to implement VOMMs. In this regard, to learn behavior models, we construct PSTs from input signals.

PSTs are constructed so that the search complexity for finding a subsequence in the tree is optimized. Even if that particular subsequence does not exist in the tree, the search operation ends at the most relevant node. PST construction from a sequence is done in two phases, namely (i) *subsequence extraction*, where eligible subsequences are found and stored in a list along with the next symbol probability vectors and (ii) *tree construction*, where the subsequences are inserted to the tree. PSTs construction is explained in more detail in [36].

4.3 Unsupervised Condition Detection

Detecting conditions (or modes) without the need for correct labels is an appealing and equally challenging task. It is useful when (a) true labels for each sample do not exist, and (b) labels exist, but are not completely trusted. In this regard, an unsupervised analysis is useful to reveal previously unknown (sub)conditions, which can be utilized in supervised learning later by training different behavior models from the discovered subclasses.

Without labels, each instance in the dataset can be evaluated relative to other instances. Naturally, this necessitates a method to model and compare instances to eventually cluster them. To achieve this, each electric motor in the dataset is modeled with a VOMM (and hence with a PST). Then, utilizing the PST matching function given in [44] to obtain a matching cost between 0 and 1 for a given PST pair, we can generate a *distance matrix*, which involves the dissimilarity of each PST pair. This matrix is then used for clustering PSTs and mapping PSTs to an n-dimensional space with Multidimensional Scaling (MDS).

Obtaining condition clusters is in principle a way to classify the condition of a given test instance. However, due to high computational need of pairwise distancing, a more efficient diagnosis method is necessary.

4.4 Diagnosis

Diagnosis is where a label is assigned to a sequence of sensor measurements of a test motor using the previously constructed alphabet and condition models. For a given test signal, the first step is to reconstruct it using the available alphabet to obtain a discrete sequence of primitive IDs (symbols). Recall that this is done in an online manner. Then, the problem becomes finding the most relevant model to the test signal. We achieve this by calculating the conditional probability (conditioned at most to the level kept in the tree) of symbols in the reconstructed signal [36]. Since the multiplication of probabilities quickly approach zero, we follow the common convention and use the summation of log-probabilities. Again, this is done in an online manner, only with maximum conditionality long lag.

The resulting probability represents how likely it is to obtain the given test sequence if the tree is traversed. Since the goal is to find out the most fitting model to a given sequence, mentioned probabilities are obtained from all condition models, which in principle forms a probability distribution after normalization. The most probable tree then determines the label to be assigned to the test sequence. The algorithm is given in Algorithm 3.

Some advantages of such an assignment method are (a) each model is checked in an online manner, so the diagnosis runs simultaneously with the physical test system, (b) this process is highly parallelizable (each model could be evaluated completely separately in different processing units), and (c) the final probability distribution can be used to determine a confidence score about the assignment.

Algorithm 3 Online Time-Series Classification

Require: alphabet Σ, set of condition models $\mathbb{M}$, fragment length l, max order L
1: initialize queue Q of observations and empty vectors f, S
2: **while** Q is not empty **do**
3:     get observation o from Q and append to f
4:     **if** $|f| = l$ **then**
5:         predict f with Σ and get symbol s
6:         **for all** model m in $\mathbb{M}$ **do**
7:             predict $P(s|S)$ with m
8:         **end for**
9:         label input with model with maximum P
10:        append s to S
11:        **if** $|S| = L$ **then**
12:            remove oldest symbol from S
13:        **end if**
14:        empty f
15:     **end if**
16: **end while**
17: **return** label

4.5 Complexity

Constructing an alphabet from a set of time-series signals is essentially a clustering task, therefore the complexity of this step depends on the clustering approach being used. Reconstruction of a signal is done in $O(nk)$, where n is the number of fragments in the signal and k is the number of primitives in the alphabet. Model learning, namely constructing a PST from a discrete sequence of symbols, is done in $O(mL)$, where m is the sequence length and L is the maximum order of dependence allowed in the tree. Diagnosis of a test signal requires $O(nLM)$ for prediction with M condition models.

4.6 Explainability and Traceability

Inherent sophisticated and complex mechanisms of living organisms have been a tremendous source of inspiration for AI research. Methods mimicking or exploiting such mechanisms which still are not totally solved and still extensively studied usually fail to be interpretive or explainable even though the solutions they yield may outperform the solutions of other methods. This concept of *explainability* recently attracts attention [24] and a concept called Explainable AI (XAI) is extensively studied. XAI focuses, in addition to all aims targeted by regular AI methods, on methods that allow its user to completely understand how it attains the desired figures for the success defined objective. Explainability is essential for two reasons: (i) from a technical viewpoint a method that accomplishes to turn accurate results but has a weakness on revealing how it can manage to do this does not allow an experienced user to reuse it for another application with a possible modification of some level since the method is simply a black box for the user due to the method's missing explainability; (ii) from a sociological viewpoint a user trusts a method as much as the method has the user feel confident with the method and provides the user with the comfort of its use and change, if necessary, through the sufficient extent of its explainability.

Although it is a challenging task to measure the explainability of an AI algorithm or model, considering the methods we use in the proposed approach, we argue that it is significantly more explainable compared to black-box methods like DL and ANNs [23]. Combined with the principal approach of SPR about finding structural aspects of patterns that make them fit to the predicted class, the two main methods we use for lexical analysis and syntactic recognition, namely alphabet construction by clustering and learning models by constructing VOMMs using PSTs, are explainable considering the concepts of *transparency* and *causality* which are often used to describe explainability [16]. Decomposing signals into fragments and then applying clustering to obtain a primitive alphabet to be used in reconstruction of a signal, is subjectively easier to understand and is more *transparent* by design than approaches like AEs. Also, since the key idea behind VOMMs is that only the significant structures of varying complexities are kept in the model, it is possible to extract which key signal subpatterns are *causing* the decision made by the model. These significant structures, in principle, characterize the target pattern to be recognized and are themselves the justification of the diagnosis.

The practical advantage of the possibility of extracting the reason behind the diagnosis that the method makes is the ease of optimization, either by (a) changing the values of the parameters that the method uses and (b) improving the method itself through intermediate steps that are more suitable to the target application. Considering the explainable nature of the proposed method, this aspect is manifested throughout the SPR phases, while evaluating the comprehensiveness of the primitive alphabet and complexity of the condition models. Investigating the incorrect classifications that the method makes, the sufficiency of the extracted significant structures could be improved to characterize a certain type of fault by tuning the amount of detail to keep in VOMMs.

5   Experimental Evaluation

This section reports and discusses experimental evaluation results obtained on benchmark datasets and a case study.

5.1   CWRU Bearing Dataset

CWRU Bearing Dataset [1] is an open dataset that has become a standard reference to test new algorithms [41]. It provides vibration data recorded by accelerometers attached to the housing of electric motors with different bearing fault severity levels (fault diameter of 0.007, 0.014, 0.021 and 0.028 inches), fault locations (inner raceway, ball and outer raceway) and load conditions (0, 1, 2 and 3 horsepower) with a sampling rate of 12 kHz.

The dataset does not define or recommend a train/test split, however there are two major approaches, namely (i) forming train and test sets so that they contain all types of load conditions and (ii) training on data without load and testing on different load conditions. We prefer the latter approach since we believe that it is (a) more challenging since the models need to recognize signals from previously unseen conditions and (b) more realistic since motors usually experience changing amounts of load during operation.

For this dataset, an alphabet with $|\Sigma| = 120$ and primitive length $l_p = 10$ is constructed. From the signals in the training set, 12 condition models are trained, including the normal condition. PSTs for condition models are constructed with pruning parameters of $t = 100$ and $L = 3$. For each motor in the test set, 60 non-overlapping 200-long reconstructed signal parts are tested.

The confusion matrix obtained with the proposed method is given in Fig. 1a. From an AD perspective, all normal motors are classified as normal and all faulty motors are classified with a faulty condition. In this setting, namely AID by training on motors without load and testing on motors with load, the proposed method achieved 98.33% accuracy in a total of 2160 signal instances.

In Table 2, the performance of the state-of-the-art methods in terms of classification accuracy is listed. It should be noted that not all of the accuracy figures in Table 2 are obtained with the same train/test split approaches as previously described. This could be unjust to the proposed method as the scenario we test is more challenging, however we keep the table as given to demonstrate the capabilities of the SPR approach.

Moreover, we would also like to emphasize that the proposed method is significantly less complex and more explainable compared to state-of-the-art DL methods. Training of a condition model takes ≈ 0.3 seconds and diagnosis of an unknown signal takes ≈ 0.04 seconds respectively on a computer with 8 CPU cores and 16 GB of RAM. Also, we argue that the online and parallelizable nature of the diagnosis method we propose is another appealing aspect to be utilized in real-time test systems.

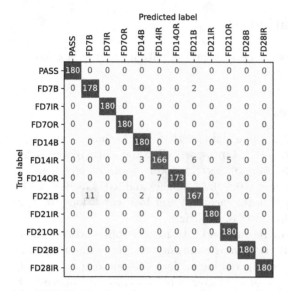

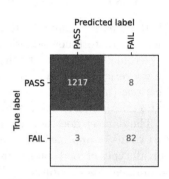

(a) CWRU Bearing Dataset result with 98.33 (2124/2160) accuracy.

(b) ATLAS dataset result with 0.9955 F_1 score.

Fig. 1. Confusion matrices from CWRU and ATLAS datasets.

Table 2. Performance of the proposed and state-of-the-art methods on CWRU bearing dataset.

Algorithm	Accuracy (%)
FaultNet [27] (with additional channels)	98.50
Proposed SPR based approach	98.33
Ensemble Deep Auto-Encoders [37]	97.18
Fault Diagnosis with DBN [45]	96.67
FaultNet [27] (on raw data)	95.27
Deep Wavelet Auto-Encoder with Extreme Learning Machine [17]	95.20
Stacked Residual Dilated CNN [49]	94.70
DBN with dual-tree complex wavelet packet [38]	94.37
Fault diagnosis using an optimization DBN [39]	88.20

5.2 Case Study: Electric Motor Reliability Tests in iRel40 Project

We also test the proposed approach on a custom dataset called ATLAS, which is collected within the scope of an European Union (EU) funded research project. This dataset includes current and vibration signals of 394 Brushless Direct Current (BLDC) motors. There are 367 healthy instances with code 11111, 16 faulty ones with code 00111, 3 faulty ones with code 00101, 1 faulty instance per code

10100, 10110, 10111 and 11101, and also 4 faulty instances with code 111110, which passed the automated current and vibration tests, but marked as faulty by the operator due to their sound during tests. The motors are tested without load at 9600 RPM with a sampling rate of 50 kHz. Labels are given to each motor by a semi-automated test system, which measures corresponding power in 5 different frequencies in the vibration signal. It takes each motor approximately 3 seconds to reach the steady-state, and the entire test takes 7 seconds.

The goal in this case study is to design an advanced AI-based detection system to detect faulty motors without causing any delay to the production. We first apply the unsupervised condition detection approach to find out different motor behaviors without using the labels. Then, we apply the supervised approach to diagnose motors using the condition models trained.

Unsupervised Condition Detection. Since the labels are obtained from a suboptimal test system, we first apply the unsupervised approach to reveal any subclasses and investigate if faulty instances remain distant from normal ones.

For this dataset, an alphabet with $|\Sigma| = 32$ and primitive length $l_p = 10$ is constructed. VOMMs with $t = 8$ and $L = 5$ are trained using 1-second-long current signals. For matching VOMMs, the matching function from [44] with $I = 0.5$ is used. In Fig. 2a, we show the representation of each VOMM in a 2-dimensional space, where the coordinates are obtained using MDS. As visible in Fig. 2a, healthy motors formed two main groups, which indicates existence of previously unknown subclasses. From the reliability point of view, we can argue that the cluster that is closer to faulty instances are more likely to fail as their signal characteristics are more similar to faulty ones. In Fig. 2b, VOMMs are clustered into 3 clusters using *k-medoids clustering* [19].

Supervised Diagnosis. After reconstruction using the same alphabet as described in the unsupervised approach, condition models are constructed with $t = 8$ and $L = 5$. Due to the limited amount of data for some fault classes, we construct models for the most frequent faults (00111 and 111110) and the normal condition (11111). We use multiple signal segments from each signal in the test set to maximize utilization of data. We apply 5-fold stratified cross-validation repeated 10 times to test on all portions of data. Also, to demonstrate the capability of our method about dealing with data scarcity, we use each single fold to train and remaining 4 folds to test. Since this is an AD task, we count assignments of faulty instances to any faulty condition model as correct. The confusion matrix from an example iteration is given in Fig. 1b. Overall, the proposed method achieved 0.9841 weighted average F_1 score.

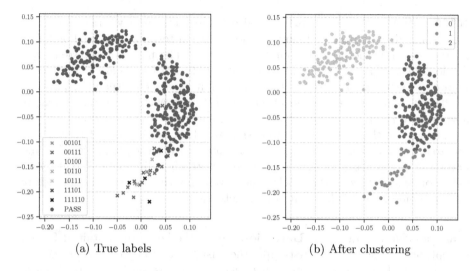

(a) True labels   (b) After clustering

Fig. 2. Scatter plot of motors. In (a), VOMMs are indicated according to true labels whereas in (b) according to the cluster they are assigned to.

6   Conclusion and Future Work

With this study, we introduced an SPR based online AD and AID method utilizing VOMMs that are implemented using PSTs. The diagnosis method we use works fully online (does not need the whole signal) and can be easily parallelized, which makes it a preferable method to be used simultaneously with a physical test system. Moreover, due to the key principle in SPR and the nature of the mathematical structure we use (VOMMs), we argue that our method is significantly more explainable and traceable compared to state-of-the-art DL methods. The results obtained in a benchmark dataset indicate the classification performance of our method is within the range of current state-of-the-art.

Evaluating the proposed method on other benchmark datasets and investigating robustness to noise are good future work ideas. Also, extending the proposed method so that it can work with multiple sources of data (e.g., data fusion at different levels) would be an important improvement.

Acknowledgments. This study is funded under project iRel40. iRel40 is a European co-funded innovation project that has been granted by the ECSEL Joint Undertaking (JU) under grant agreement No 876659. The funding of the project comes from the Horizon 2020 research programme and participating countries. National funding is provided by Germany, including the Free States of Saxony and Thuringia, Austria, Belgium, Finland, France, Italy, the Netherlands, Slovakia, Spain, Sweden, and Turkey. The document reflects only the author's view and the JU is not responsible for any use that may be made of the information it contains.

References

1. Bearing Data Center — Case School of Engineering — Case Western Reserve University. https://engineering.case.edu/bearingdatacenter (2021)
2. Bazan, G.H., Scalassara, P.R., Endo, W., Goedtel, A., Godoy, W.F., Palácios, R.H.C.: Stator fault analysis of three-phase induction motors using information measures and artificial neural networks. Electr. Power Syst. Res. **143**, 347–356 (2017). https://doi.org/10.1016/j.epsr.2016.09.031
3. Begleiter, R., El-Yaniv, R., Yona, G.: On Prediction Using Variable Order Markov Models. J. Artif. Intell. Res. **22**, 385–421 (2004). https://doi.org/10.1613/jair.1491
4. Buhlmann, P., Wyner, A.J.: Variable length Markov chains. Ann. Statist. **27**(2), 480-513 (1999). https://doi.org/10.1214/aos/1018031204
5. Chen, et al.: Novel data-driven approach based on capsule network for intelligent multi-fault detection in electric motors. IEEE Trans. Energy Convers. **36**(3), 2173–2184 (2021). https://doi.org/10.1109/TEC.2020.3046642
6. Choi, D.J., Han, J.H., Park, S.U., Hong, S.K.: Diagnosis of Electric Motor Using Acoustic noise Based on CNN. In: 2019 22nd International Conference on Electrical Machines and Systems (ICEMS), pp. 1–4 (2019). https://doi.org/10.1109/ICEMS.2019.8922130
7. Chuya-Sumba, J., Alonso-Valerdi, L.M., Ibarra-Zarate, D.I.: Deep-learning method based on 1D convolutional neural network for intelligent fault diagnosis of rotating machines. Appl. Sci. **12**(4), 2158 (2022). https://doi.org/10.3390/app12042158
8. Davies, D.L., Bouldin, D.W.: A Cluster Separation Measure. IEEE Trans. Pattern Anal. Mach. Intell. PAMI **1**(2), 224–227 (1979). https://doi.org/10.1109/TPAMI.1979.4766909
9. Delgado-Arredondo, P.A., Morinigo-Sotelo, D., Osornio-Rios, R.A., Avina-Cervantes, J.G., Rostro-Gonzalez, H., Romero-Troncoso, R.J.: Methodology for fault detection in induction motors via sound and vibration signals. Mech. Syst. Signal Process. **83**, 568–589 (2017). https://doi.org/10.1016/j.ymssp.2016.06.032
10. Egaji, O.A., Ekwevugbe, T., Griffiths, M.: A Data Mining based Approach for Electric Motor Anomaly Detection Applied on Vibration Data. In: 2020 Fourth World Conference on Smart Trends in Systems, Security and Sustainability (WorldS4), London, United Kingdom, pp. 330–334. IEEE (2020). https://doi.org/10.1109/WorldS450073.2020.9210318
11. Ferracuti, F., Giantomassi, A., Iarlori, S., Ippoliti, G., Longhi, S.: Electric motor defects diagnosis based on kernel density estimation and Kullback-Leibler divergence in quality control scenario. Eng. Appl. Artif. Intell. **44**, 25–32 (2015). https://doi.org/10.1016/j.engappai.2015.05.004
12. Fu, K.S.: Syntactic Methods in Pattern Recognition. Mathematics in Science and Engineering, Academic Press, New York (1974)
13. Fu, K.S., Keidel, W.D., Wolter, H. (eds.): Syntactic Pattern Recognition, Applications, Communication and Cybernetics, vol. 14. Springer, Heidelberg (1977). https://doi.org/10.1007/978-3-642-66438-0
14. Gou, X., Bian, C., Zeng, F., Xu, Q., Wang, W., Yang, S.: A Data-Driven Smart Fault Diagnosis Method for Electric Motor. In: 2018 IEEE International Conference on Software Quality, Reliability and Security Companion (QRS-C), pp. 250–257 (2018). https://doi.org/10.1109/QRS-C.2018.00053
15. Gundewar, S.K., Kane, P.V.: Condition monitoring and fault diagnosis of induction motor. J. Vib. Eng. Technol. **9**(4), 643–674 (2020). https://doi.org/10.1007/s42417-020-00253-y

16. Hagras, H.: Toward Human-Understandable. Explainable AI. Comput. **51**(9), 28–36 (2018). https://doi.org/10.1109/MC.2018.3620965
17. Haidong, S., Hongkai, J., Xingqiu, L., Shuaipeng, W.: Intelligent fault diagnosis of rolling bearing using deep wavelet auto-encoder with extreme learning machine. Knowl.-Based Syst. **140**, 1–14 (2018). https://doi.org/10.1016/j.knosys.2017.10.024
18. Junior, R.F.R., Areias, I.A.S., Campos, M.M., Teixeira, C.E., da Silva, L.E.B., Gomes, G.F.: Fault detection and diagnosis in electric motors using 1d convolutional neural networks with multi-channel vibration signals. Measurement **190**, 110759 (2022). https://doi.org/10.1016/j.measurement.2022.110759
19. Kaufman, L., Rousseeuw, P.J.: Partitioning around medoids (Program PAM). In: Wiley Series in Probability and Statistics, pp. 68–125. John Wiley & Sons Inc, Hoboken, NJ, USA (1990). https://doi.org/10.1002/9780470316801.ch2
20. Khanjani, M., Ezoji, M.: Electrical fault detection in three-phase induction motor using deep network-based features of thermograms. Measurement **173**, 108622 (2021). https://doi.org/10.1016/j.measurement.2020.108622
21. Kumar, P., Hati, A.S.: Review on machine learning algorithm based fault detection in induction motors. Arch. Comput. Methods Eng. **28**(3), 1929–1940 (2020). https://doi.org/10.1007/s11831-020-09446-w
22. Lashkari, N., Poshtan, J.: Detection and discrimination of stator interturn fault and unbalanced supply voltage fault in induction motor using neural network. In: The 6th Power Electronics, Drive Systems Technologies Conference (PEDSTC2015), pp. 275–280 (2015). https://doi.org/10.1109/PEDSTC.2015.7093287
23. Linardatos, P., Papastefanopoulos, V., Kotsiantis, S.: Explainable AI: a review of machine learning interpretability methods. Entropy **23**(1), 18 (2020). https://doi.org/10.3390/e23010018
24. Longo, L., Goebel, R., Lecue, F., Kieseberg, P., Holzinger, A.: Explainable artificial intelligence: concepts, applications, research challenges and visions. In: Holzinger, A., Kieseberg, P., Tjoa, A.M., Weippl, E. (eds.) CD-MAKE 2020. LNCS, vol. 12279, pp. 1–16. Springer, Cham (2020). https://doi.org/10.1007/978-3-030-57321-8_1
25. Lopez-Gutierrez, R., Rangel-Magdaleno, J.d.J., Morales-Perez, C.J., García-Perez, A.: Induction machine bearing fault detection using empirical wavelet transform. Shock Vibr. **2022**, 1–12 (2022). https://doi.org/10.1155/2022/6187912
26. Magadán, L., Suárez, F., Granda, J., García, D.: Low-cost real-time monitoring of electric motors for the Industry 4.0. Procedia Manufact. **42**, 393–398 (2020). https://doi.org/10.1016/j.promfg.2020.02.057
27. Magar, R., Ghule, L., Li, J., Zhao, Y., Farimani, A.B.: FaultNet: a deep convolutional neural network for bearing fault classification. IEEE Access **9**, 25189–25199 (2021). https://doi.org/10.1109/ACCESS.2021.3056944
28. Nandi, S., Toliyat, H., Li, X.: Condition monitoring and fault diagnosis of electrical motors—a review. IEEE Trans. Energy Convers. **20**(4), 719–729 (2005). https://doi.org/10.1109/TEC.2005.847955
29. Omoregbee, H.O., Heyns, P.S.: Fault classification of low-speed bearings based on support vector machine for regression and genetic algorithms using acoustic emission. J. Vibr. Eng. Technol. **7**(5), 455–464 (2019). https://doi.org/10.1007/s42417-019-00143-y
30. Park, Y., Kim, M.J.: Design of cost-effective auto-encoder for electric motor anomaly detection in resource constrained edge device. In: 2021 IEEE 3rd Eurasia Conference on IOT, Communication and Engineering (ECICE), pp. 241–246 (2021). https://doi.org/10.1109/ECICE52819.2021.9645739

31. Pavlatos, C., Vita, V., Dimopoulos, A.C., Ekonomou, L.: Transmission lines' fault detection using syntactic pattern recognition. Energy Syst. **10**(2), 299–320 (2018). https://doi.org/10.1007/s12667-018-0284-x

32. Rengaswamy, R., Venkatasubramanian, V.: A syntactic pattern-recognition approach for process monitoring and fault diagnosis. Eng. Appl. Artif. Intell. **8**(1), 35–51 (1995). https://doi.org/10.1016/0952-1976(94)00058-U

33. Ribeiro Junior, R.F., Areias, I.A.S., Gomes, G.F.: Fault detection and diagnosis using vibration signal analysis in frequency domain for electric motors considering different real fault types. Sens. Rev. **41**(3), 311–319 (2021). https://doi.org/10.1108/SR-02-2021-0052

34. Ron, D., Singer, Y., Tishby, N.: The power of amnesia: learning probabilistic automata with variable memory length. Mach. Learn. **25**(2–3), 117–149 (1997). https://doi.org/10.1007/BF00114008

35. Saucedo-Dorantes, J.J., Delgado-Prieto, M., Romero-Troncoso, R.D.J., Osornio-Rios, R.A.: Multiple-fault detection and identification scheme based on hierarchical self-organizing maps applied to an electric machine. Appl. Soft Comput. **81**, 105497 (2019). https://doi.org/10.1016/j.asoc.2019.105497

36. Schulz, M.H., Weese, D., Rausch, T., Döring, A., Reinert, K., Vingron, M.: Fast and adaptive variable order Markov chain construction. In: Crandall, K.A., Lagergren, J. (eds.) WABI 2008. LNCS, vol. 5251, pp. 306–317. Springer, Heidelberg (2008). https://doi.org/10.1007/978-3-540-87361-7_26

37. Shao, H., Jiang, H., Lin, Y., Li, X.: A novel method for intelligent fault diagnosis of rolling bearings using ensemble deep auto-encoders. Mech. Syst. Signal Process. **102**, 278–297 (2018). https://doi.org/10.1016/j.ymssp.2017.09.026

38. Shao, H., Jiang, H., Wang, F., Wang, Y.: Rolling bearing fault diagnosis using adaptive deep belief network with dual-tree complex wavelet packet. ISA Trans. **69**, 187–201 (2017). https://doi.org/10.1016/j.isatra.2017.03.017

39. Shao, H., Jiang, H., Zhang, X., Niu, M.: Rolling bearing fault diagnosis using an optimization deep belief network. Meas. Sci. Technol. **26**(11), 115002 (2015). https://doi.org/10.1088/0957-0233/26/11/115002

40. Shifat, T.A., Hur, J.W.: An effective stator fault diagnosis framework of BLDC motor based on vibration and current signals. IEEE Access **8**, 106968–106981 (2020). https://doi.org/10.1109/ACCESS.2020.3000856

41. Smith, W.A., Randall, R.B.: Rolling element bearing diagnostics using the case western reserve university data: a benchmark study. Mech. Syst. Signal Process. **64–65**, 100–131 (2015). https://doi.org/10.1016/j.ymssp.2015.04.021

42. Son, J., Kim, C., Jeong, M.: Unsupervised learning for anomaly detection of electric motors. Int. J. Precis. Eng. Manuf. **23**(4), 421–427 (2022). https://doi.org/10.1007/s12541-022-00635-0

43. Sun, W., Chen, J., Li, J.: Decision tree and PCA-based fault diagnosis of rotating machinery. Mech. Syst. Signal Process. **21**(3), 1300–1317 (2007). https://doi.org/10.1016/j.ymssp.2006.06.010

44. Sürmeli, B.G., Tümer, M.B.: Multivariate time series clustering and its application in industrial systems. Cybern. Syst. **51**(3), 315–334 (2020). https://doi.org/10.1080/01969722.2019.1691851

45. Tao, J., Liu, Y., Yang, D., Tang, F., Liu, C.: Fault diagnosis of rolling bearing using deep belief networks. In: Proceedings of the 2015 International Symposium on Material, Energy and Environment Engineering, Atlantis Press, Changsha City, China (2015). https://doi.org/10.2991/ism3e-15.2015.136

46. Tumer, M., Belfore, L., Ropella, K.: A syntactic methodology for automatic diagnosis by analysis of continuous time measurements using hierarchical signal representations. IEEE Tran. Syst. Man Cybern. Part B (Cybern.) **33**(6), 951–965 (2003). https://doi.org/10.1109/TSMCB.2002.804365
47. Ugwiri, M.A., Mpia, I., Lay-Ekuakille, A.: Vibrations for fault detection in electric machines. IEEE Instrum. Measur. Mag. **23**(1), 66–72 (2020). https://doi.org/10.1109/MIM.2020.8979527
48. Verma, A.K., Nagpal, S., Desai, A., Sudha, R.: An efficient neural-network model for real-time fault detection in industrial machine. Neural Comput. Appl. **33**(4), 1297–1310 (2020). https://doi.org/10.1007/s00521-020-05033-z
49. Zhuang, Z., Lv, H., Xu, J., Huang, Z., Qin, W.: A deep learning method for bearing fault diagnosis through stacked residual dilated convolutions. Appl. Sci. **9**(9), 1823 (2019). https://doi.org/10.3390/app9091823

Sparse Visual Counterfactual Explanations in Image Space

Valentyn Boreiko$^{(\boxtimes)}$, Maximilian Augustin, Francesco Croce, Philipp Berens, and Matthias Hein

University of Tübingen, Tübingen, Germany
valentyn.boreiko@uni-tuebingen.de

Abstract. Visual counterfactual explanations (VCEs) in image space are an important tool to understand decisions of image classifiers as they show under which changes of the image the decision of the classifier would change. Their generation in image space is challenging and requires robust models due to the problem of adversarial examples. Existing techniques to generate VCEs in image space suffer from spurious changes in the background. Our novel perturbation model for VCEs together with its efficient optimization via our novel Auto-Frank-Wolfe scheme yields sparse VCEs which lead to subtle changes specific for the target class. Moreover, we show that VCEs can be used to detect undesired behavior of ImageNet classifiers due to spurious features in the ImageNet dataset. Code is available under https://github.com/valentyn1boreiko/SVCEs_code.

Keywords: Interpretability · Adversarial robustness · Trustworthy AI

1 Introduction

The black-box nature of decisions made by neural networks is one of the main obstacles for the widespread use of machine learning in industry and science. It is likely that future regulatory steps will strengthen the "right for an explanation", which is currently already implemented in a weak form in the GDPR [63] and is included as "transparency of an AI system" in a draft for regulating AI of the European Union, at least concerning the use of AI in safety critical systems [12]. Apart from directly interpretable classifiers like linear models or decision trees, a variety of model-agnostic explanation techniques has been proposed: sensitivity based explanations [4], explanations based on feature attributions [3], saliency maps [21,54,55,57,64], Shapley additive explanations [38], and local fits of interpretable models [48], see [40] for a recent overview.

Another candidate are counterfactual explanations (CEs) introduced in [63] as a form of instance-specific explanations close to human reasoning [41]. Humans

---

Supplementary Information The online version contains supplementary material available at https://doi.org/10.1007/978-3-031-16788-1_9.

Original	AFW, $l_{1.5}$	APGD, l_2
cougar: 0.42	→cheetah: 0.99	→cheetah: 0.99

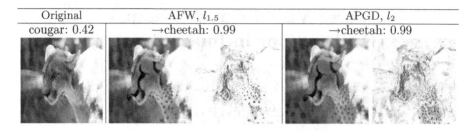

Fig. 1. VCEs for two different threat models. VCEs together with difference maps for the change "cougar ⟶ cheetah" for an adversarially robust ImageNet model [16,20]. Our novel $l_{1.5}$-VCEs yield more sparse changes which are mainly focused on the object compared to the previously considered l_2-VCEs [1,51].

often justify decisions by counterfactual reasoning: "I would have decided for X, if Y had been true". One of their biggest advantages in contrast to feature attribution and other mentioned above methods is that CEs [5,18,43,45,52,62,63] are actionable explanations [63] and thus are close to what the GDPR requires. Current approaches to generate CEs for classifier decisions can be summarized by answering the question: "What is the minimal change δ of the input x, so that the perturbed input $x + \delta$ is classified as the desired target class with sufficiently high confidence and is realistic?". From the developer's perspective, counterfactuals are interesting for debugging as they allow to detect spurious features which the classifier has picked up. We refer to [62] for a recent extensive overview on the literature of counterfactual explanations who note five criteria for CEs: i) **validity:** the changed input $x + \delta$ should have the desired target class, ii) **actionability:** the change δ should be possible to be realized by the human, iii) **sparsity:** the change δ should be sparse so that the change is interpretable for humans, iv) **realism:** the changed input $x + \delta$ should lie close to the data manifold, v) **causality:** CEs should maintain causal relations between features. Interestingly, [62] noted that most papers they reviewed just evaluate on tabular datasets or MNIST. The reason for this is that the process of generating CEs for high-dimensional image datasets (which we will refer to as visual counterfactual explanations, or VCEs for short) is very similar to that of generating adversarial examples [58] which just exploit non-robust features of the classifier and thus show no class-specific changes required for VCEs. Thus, realistic VCEs require either (adversarially) robust models as in [1,51] or that the images are implicitly restricted via the usage of a generative model [10,25,28,29,49,53]. Very recently visual counterfactuals based on generative models have been proposed [25,37,50] but no code has been released so far or it is restricted to MNIST. These methods require to specify the amount of "classifier guidance" which might be difficult to be choose as we discuss in App. F. For this reason, in this work we investigate the generation of VCEs directly in image space, instead of working in the latent space, and purely based on the classifier, thus showing its behavior without the influence of an auxiliary model. We make the following contributions: i) we show that the l_2-metric used for the generation of VCEs in [1,51] leads to changes all over the image (see Fig. 1) which are unrelated to the object. This is in particular true for ImageNet models; ii) we propose a new model for sparse VCEs based on the l_p-metric for $p = 1.5$. Since an efficient projection onto $l_{1.5}$-balls is not available, we develop a novel Auto-Frank-Wolfe (AFW) optimization scheme with an adaptive step-size for the generation of $l_{1.5}$-VCEs. The resulting VCEs are more sparse and "subtle" as confirmed by a user study; iii) we illustrate that VCEs are useful to detect spurious features in ImageNet classifiers, e.g., we detect the spurious feature "watermark" in the class granny smith due to a bias in the training set and show that our findings transfer to other ImageNet classifiers. This shows the utility of VCEs as a "debugging tool" for ML classifiers.

2 Visual Counterfactual Explanations (VCEs)

In this section, we first discuss the previously considered formulation of Visual Counterfactual Explanations (VCEs) of [1] in the image space and the required kind of (adversarial) robustness of the classifier. Then we discuss a novel perturbation model which overcomes the partially non-object-related changes of the VCEs proposed in [1]. For the optimization over this perturbation model we provide in Sect. 3 a novel adaptive Frank-Wolfe scheme.

We assume in the paper that the classifier, $f : \mathbb{R}^d \rightarrow \Delta_K$, where $\Delta_K := \{w \in \mathbb{R}^K_{\geq 0} | \sum_{i=1}^K w_i = 1\}$ is the probability simplex, outputs for every input x a probability distribution $\hat{p}_f(y|x)$ $(y \in \{1, \ldots, K\})$ over the classes. The l_p-distance on $\mathbb{R}^d$ is defined as: $\|x - y\|_p = \left(\sum_{i=1}^d |x_i - y_i|^p\right)^{\frac{1}{p}}$.

2.1 Formulation and Properties of VCEs

Counterfactual explanations for a given classifier are instance-wise explanations. Informally speaking, a visual counterfactual explanation for an input image x_0 is a new image $\hat{x}$ which is visually similar and as close as possible to a real image, but class-specific features have been changed such that the classifier now assigns to $\hat{x}$ a desired target class different from than one assigned to x_0 (counterfactual). In addition, it is often interesting which features appear if one aims to make the classifier maximally confident in its decision (same as for x_0).

VCEs via Constrained Optimization: In [63] (see also [43,62]) they suggest to determine counterfactuals by the following optimization problem:

$$\hat{x} = \underset{x \in \mathbb{R}^d}{\arg \min} \, L(k, f(x)) + \lambda \, d(x_0, x), \tag{1}$$

where L is a loss function, e.g. cross-entropy loss, $L(k, f(x)) = -\log \hat{p}_f(k|x)$, k is the desired target class and $d : \mathbb{R}^d \times \mathbb{R}^d \rightarrow \mathbb{R}$ a distance, measuring similarity of x_0 and $\hat{x}$. If the decision of the classifier for $\hat{x}$ changes to the target class k, then the counterfactual is "valid". The advantage of valid counterfactuals, compared to feature attribution methods or other instance-wise explanation techniques, is that the change $\hat{x} - x_0$ is actionable, in the sense that the user understands, how to influence and change the decision of the classifier. As λ has no direct interpretation, we employ the related and more interpretable objective of [1]

$$\underset{x \in [0,1]^d \cap B(x_0, \epsilon)}{\arg\max} \quad \log \hat{p}_f(k|x), \tag{2}$$

where $B(x_0, \epsilon) = \{x \in \mathbb{R}^d \mid d(x, x_0) \leq \epsilon\}$. The constraint, $x \in [0,1]^d$, is necessary as we want to generate valid images. The choice of the distance metric is crucial for the quality of the VCEs (see Sect. 2.3). The new free parameter ϵ can be interpreted as "perturbation budget" with respect to the chosen metric.

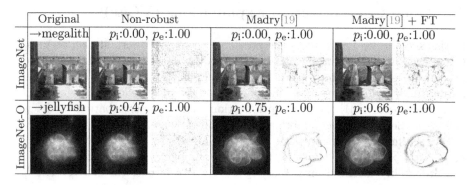

	Original	Non-robust	Madry[19]	Madry[19] + FT
ImageNet	→megalith	p_i:0.00, p_e:1.00	p_i:0.00, p_e:1.00	p_i:0.00, p_e:1.00
ImageNet-O	→jellyfish	p_i:0.47, p_e:1.00	p_i:0.75, p_e:1.00	p_i:0.66, p_e:1.00

Fig. 2. Dependence of $l_{1.5}$-VCEs on robustness of the model (for in- and out-of-distribution). VCEs for a non-robust ResNet50, a robust ResNet trained with l_2-Adversarial Training [19] and the same model finetuned for multiple norm robustness (Madry [19]+FT [16]). For the non-robust model, VCEs achieve high confidence without introducing any class-specific features or meaningful changes. For the robust models, VCEs only achieve high confidence by adding meaningful changes for the given target class (indicated by → in the original image). The multiple-norm robust model yields higher quality images than the original l_2-robust model.

VCEs and Robustness: It has been noted in [63] that counterfactuals generated via Eq. (1) are equivalent to targeted adversarial examples. In [63] this did not cause problems as they only handled very low-dimensional problems. In fact, adversarial attacks often maximize a surrogate loss, in this case the log-probability, to induce misclassification into the target class. However, adversarial attacks [39,58] on non-robust image classifiers typically show no class-specific changes, see Fig. 2. The standard method to increase robustness to adversarial attacks is adversarial training [39] based on projected gradient descent (PGD). Notably, [51,61] have observed that adversarially robust models have strong generative properties, which is closely related to the explainability of the classifier decisions. In Fig. 2 we show the VCEs for a robust ResNet50 [19] trained with adversarial training (Madry [19]) and the same model enhanced with multiple-norm finetuning [16] (Madry [19]+FT) and a non-robust model. The examples confirm that for meaningful VCE generation, a robust model is needed. Throughout the rest of the paper, we show VCEs for the robust Madry [19]+FT model. In the Appendix, we furthermore explore what kind of robustness is required for the VCE generation and how VCEs differ between robust models on both ImageNet and CIFAR10.

Table 1. ImageNet: Accuracy and $l_{1.5}$-, l_2-robust accuracy (RA) at $\epsilon_{1.5} = 12.5, \epsilon_2 = 2$ for the l_2-adv. robust model of Madry [19] and the fine-tuned Madry [19]+FT for multiple-norm robustness [16], and FID scores for $l_1, l_{1.5}$- and l_2-VCEs generated on in(ID)- and out-distribution(OD) images and their average. The Madry [19]+FT model achieves the best FID score for $l_{1.5}$-VCEs.

	Accuracies			FID scores (ID/OD/AVG)		
	Acc.	l_2-RA	$l_{1.5}$-RA	l_1-VCE, $\epsilon = 400$	$l_{1.5}$-VCE, $\epsilon = 50$	l_2-VCE, $\epsilon = 12$
Madry[19]	57.9	45.7	37.4	13.6/41.6/27.6	**8.4/24.3/16.4**	**8.4/22.8/15.6**
[19] +FT	57.5	44.6	40.1	9.6/35.7/22.6	**6.9/22.6/14.8**	7.9/23.1/15.5

Properties of VCEs: Following [43,62], we aim to achieve the following main properties for our VCEs: i) **validity:** from Eq. (2), one sees that, for a given perturbation budget, we find the VCE with maximum probability $\hat{p}_f(k|\hat{x})$ in the target class k for f; ii) **sparsity:** $\hat{x}$ should be visually similar to x_0 and only contain sparse changes which is exactly the reason for our considered distance metric, see Sect. 2.3; iii) **realism:** $\hat{x}$ should lie on the data manifold and look like a real image. For qualitatitve results we show examples of VCEs and for quantitative analysis we use the Frechet Inception Distance (FID) [32] both on VCEs generated from in-distribution test set, and from out-distribution samples, see Sect. 2.2, and a user-study in Sect. 2.3.

We stress that our primary goal is to explain the inner workings of a given classifier and not necessarily to generate the best looking images. We demonstrate in Sect. 4 that our VCEs can be successfully used to reveal undesired behavior of ImageNet classifiers due to biases in the ImageNet dataset.

2.2   Generation and evaluation of VCEs

We generate VCEs by approximately solving the non-convex problem Eq. (2) with a small computational bugdet. We thus use the efficient APGD [14] (only available for l_1, l_2 and l_∞) or our adaptive Frank-Wolfe scheme AFW (see Sect. 3). For both we use a budget of 5 random restarts each with 75 iterations. Typical deep learning classifiers are not calibrated, that is their decisions are either over- or underconfident [26]. We calibrate them using temperature rescaling by minimizing the expected calibration error (ECE) on a holdout validation set, so that confidence values are comparable, see App. D.1.

For the quantitative evaluation of the image quality of VCEs produced by different methods and classifiers, we use several metrics. First, FID scores [32] by

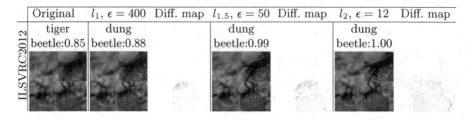

Fig. 3. ImageNet: l_p**-VCEs** for $p \in \{1, 1.5, 2\}$. l_p-VCEs into correct class for a misclassified Image of class "dung beetle". for the multiple-norm adversarially robust model Madry [19]+FT. l_1-VCEs are too sparse and introduce artefacts and l_2-VCEs change the background. Our $l_{1.5}$-VCEs are sparse and object-related (see difference maps right from the respective l_p-VCEs).

generating 10.000 VCEs from the test set for the in-distribution (ID) evaluation where the target class is the second most likely class computed by using an ensemble of all classifiers used in the comparison, see Fig. 15 (top) in App. B. An evaluation using FID scores on the in-distribution test (FID ID) set only is in our setting problematic, as methods with no (or minimal) change would get the best FID-score. Thus, we also use VCEs generated from out-of-distribution images (ImagetNet-A and ImageNet-O [31]) where the target label corresponds to the decision of an ensemble with all classifiers used in the comparison, see Fig. 15 (bottom) in App. B. As out-of-distribution images are not part of the data distribution, non-trivial changes are required to turn them into images of the in-distribution. Thus methods with almost no change will suffer here from large FID scores as the images are far from the in-distribution. In our experience from the qualitative inspection of the images, the average (AVG) of FID-scores on in-distribution (FID ID) and out-of-distribution images (FID OD) reflects best the realism and quality of the VCEs. Note that our FID scores cannot be directly compared to the ones of generative models as VCEs are not based on sampling. We just use the FID scores as a quantitative way to compare the different classifiers and perturbation models for VCEs. Moreover, we evaluate the utility of l_p-VCEs in a user study in Sect. 2.3.

2.3 Sparse VCEs via the $l_{1.5}$-metric

The perturbation budget of VCEs in Eq. (2), in particular the chosen distance metric, is crucial for the generation of realistic VCEs. It might seem natural to use for l_2-adversarially robust models also the l_2-metric for the perturbation budget of the VCEs. However, as we show in Fig. 1 and Fig. 3, the problem of the l_2-budget is that one typically gets non-sparse changes over the full image which are not centered on the object. Aiming at sparse VCEs it seems like the l_1-metric might be well-suited as it is known to lead to sparse changes. However, as one can see in Fig. 3, the changes are in fact extremely sparse and often show color artefacts: *e.g.* for the dung beetle, single pixels are changed to non-natural extreme colors. As a compromise between l_1 (too sparse) and l_2 (non-sparse),

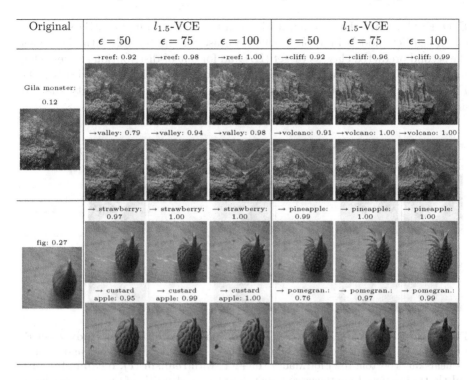

Fig. 4. ImageNet: $l_{1.5}$-VCEs. (First two rows) $l_{1.5}$-VCEs for Madry [19]+FT with varying radii for a misclassified image of class "coral reef" for the target classes: "coral reef", "cliff", "valley" and "volcano" (same wordnet category "geological formation"). (Second two rows) $l_{1.5}$-VCEs for Madry [19]+FT with varying radii for an image of class "fig" for the target classes: "strawberry", "pineapple", "custard apple", and 'pomegranate' (same wordnet category "edible fruit"). The changes are sparse and subtle for radius 50 and get more pronounced for larger budgets.

we propose to use the $l_{1.5}$-metric for the perturbation model in Eq. (2). In Fig. 1 and Fig. 3, for ImageNet the changes of $l_{1.5}$-VCEs are sparse and localized on the object. For the generation of the FID scores for $l_{1.5}$-VCEs, we used $\epsilon = 50$ for ImageNet. Apart from the better FID-scores of $l_{1.5}$-VCEs we quantify in Table 16 in App. B for ImageNet the concentration of the changes on the actual object using the pixel-wise segmentations of ImageNet test images in [22].

We found the chosen radii to work well for most images. However, for visualizing the VCEs to a user, the best option is to let the user see how the changes evolve as one changes the radius in an interactive fashion. Rather subtle changes with a small budget are already sufficient for some images, whereas for other images larger budgets are necessary due to a significant change of color or shape. As such an interactive process cannot be shown, we provide panels with different radii of the perturbation model in Fig. 4 and the Appendix.

FID Evaluation: For a quantitative evaluation, we compute FID scores for our ImageNet models in Table 1, where we use for the ImageNet validation set the second predicted class as target (ID) and for out-of-distribution images (OD) from ImageNet-O/ImageNet-A we generate the VCE for the predicted class. The FID scores indicate that $l_{1.5}$-VCEs have higher **realism** and **sparsity** than l_1- and l_2-VCEs, on both in- and out-of-distribution images.

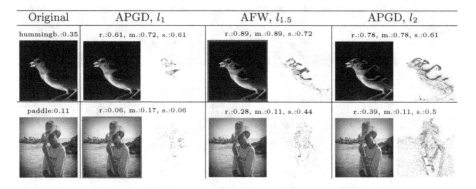

Fig. 5. Best (blue) and worst (red) rated images from the user study. l_p-VCEs for $p \in \{1, 1.5, 2\}$ for the change "hummingbird → brambling" (top row) and "paddle → bearskin" (bottom row) for Madry [19]+FT, with **realism (r)**, **meaningful (m)**, **subtle (s)** fractions from the user study (r:0.61 means that 61% of the users considered this image to be realistic).

User Study: We perform a user study (18 participants) to compare $l_{1.5}$-, l_1-, and l_2-VCEs (the Madry [19]+FT model on ImageNet is used). For each target image (94 in total), we show l_p-VCEs for $p \in \{1, 1.5, 2\}$, to the users, who can choose which ones satisfy the following properties (none or multiple answers are allowed): i) **realism**, ii) "meaningful features in the target class are introduced" (**meaningful**), iii) "subtle, yet understandable changes are introduced" (**subtle**). The percentages for l_1-, $l_{1.5}$-, and l_2-VCEs are: **realism** - 23.5%, **38.2%**, 33.8%; **meaningful** - 37.5%, 63.1%, **64.0%**; **subtle** - 34.7%, **49.1%**, 41.5%. While the difference of $l_{1.5}$-VCEs compared to l_2-VCEs is small for meaningfulness, $l_{1.5}$-VCEs are considered more subtle and realistic. In Fig. 5, we show the best and worst rated images from the user study. Note that for the worst one, the changes into the target class "bearskin" are not achievable in the given budget and thus all methods fail to produce meaningful images.

Details about the User Study: Participants are researchers in machine learning (volunteers) not working on VCEs themselves and neither being exposed to the generated images or compared methods before. The p-values, using the two-sample two-sided binomial test, for the best and next best methods are: 0.02 for

realism of $l_{1.5}$ vs l_2, 0.6 for **meaningful** of l_2 vs $l_{1.5}$, and $5.3 \cdot 10^{-5}$ for **subtle** of $l_{1.5}$ vs l_2, that is $l_{1.5}$ outperforms statistically significantly l_2 in realism/subtle (significance level 0.05).

3 Auto-Frank-Wolfe for l_p-VCEs

For deep models, the optimization problem for l_p-VCEs

$$\max_{x \in B_p(x_0, \epsilon) \cap [0,1]^d} \log \hat{p}(y|x), \tag{3}$$

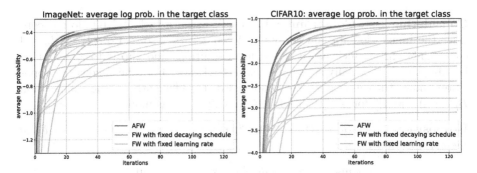

Fig. 6. Comparison of our adaptive Frank-Wolfe scheme (AFW) vs non-adaptive FW. We plot avg. log probability of the $l_{1.5}$-VCEs (ImageNet: $\epsilon = 50$, CIFAR10: $\epsilon = 6$) with the second predicted class as target for ImageNet (left) and CIFAR10 (right). Our novel AFW (blue curve) is adaptive to the budget, without any need for additional hyperparameter tuning. We show the result of AFW for a budget of 25, 75 and 125. We observe that it matches the best or is better than FW with fixed learning rate (red) or various decaying stepsize schemes (green) for the given number of iterations for both datasets. (Color figure online)

is non-convex and related to targeted adversarial attacks, for which AutoPGD (APGD) [14] has been shown to be very effective. APGD requires projections onto l_p-balls which are available either in closed form for l_2 and l_∞ or can be computed efficiently for l_1. However, for $p \notin \{1, 2, \infty\}$, there is no such projection available and one cannot use APGD. Thus, in order to generate l_p-VCEs for $p > 1$, we propose an adaptive version of the Frank-Wolfe (FW) algorithm [34,42], which we call Auto-Frank-Wolfe (AFW). FW has the advantage that it is projection-free and thus allows to use more complex constraint sets. In particular, we can use arbitrary l_p norm balls for $p > 1$.

Auto-Frank-Wolfe: At each iteration k, FW maximizes the first-order Taylor expansion at the iterate x^k of the objective in the feasible set, i.e.

$$s^k = \operatorname*{arg\,max}_{s \in B_p(x_0, \epsilon) \cap [0,1]^d} \left\langle s, \nabla_{x^k} \log \hat{p}(y|x^k) \right\rangle, \tag{4}$$

and the next iterate is the convex combination

$$x^{k+1} = (1 - \gamma^k)x^k + \gamma^k s^k. \tag{5}$$

The choice of the learning rate $\gamma^k \in (0,1)$ is crucial for the success of the algorithm: in the context of adversarial attacks, [11] use a fixed value γ_0 for every k, while [60,66] decrease it as $\frac{\gamma_0}{\gamma_0+k}$. In both cases the schedule is agnostic of the total budget of iterations, and γ_0 needs to be tuned. Thus, we propose to use an adaptive scheme for choosing γ^k at each iteration as $\gamma^k = \frac{M}{2+\sqrt{k}}$ where $M \leq 2$ is adapted during the optimization. This yields our AFW attack which automatically adapts to different budgets (details of AFW in App. C.1).

Considering Box-Constraints: Prior FW-based attacks [11,60] do not consider the image domain constraints $[0,1]^d$ but rather solve Eq. (4) for l_p-ball constraints only (which has a closed form solution) and clip it to $[0,1]^d$. This is suboptimal, especially when p is close to 1, see [15]. The following proposition shows that it is possible to solve Eq. (4) efficiently in the intersection $B_p(x_0, \epsilon) \cap [0,1]^d$ for $p > 1$ (proof in App. C.2, $p = 1$ is more simple, see [15],).

Proposition 1. *Let $w \in \mathbb{R}^d$, $x \in [0,1]^d$, $\epsilon > 0$ and $p > 1$. The solution δ^* of the optimization problem*

$$\underset{\delta \in \mathbb{R}^d}{\arg\max} \langle w, \delta \rangle \quad s.th. \ \|\delta\|_p \leq \epsilon, \ x + \delta \in [0,1]^d \tag{6}$$

is given, with the convention $\operatorname{sign} 0 = 0$, by

$$\delta_i^* = \min\left\{ \gamma_i, \left(\frac{|w_i|}{p\mu^*} \right)^{\frac{1}{p-1}} \right\} \operatorname{sign} w_i, \quad i = 1, \ldots, d,$$

where $\gamma_i = \max\{-x_i \operatorname{sign} w_i, (1 - x_i) \operatorname{sign} w_i\}$ and $\mu^* > 0$ can be computed in $O(d \log d)$ time.

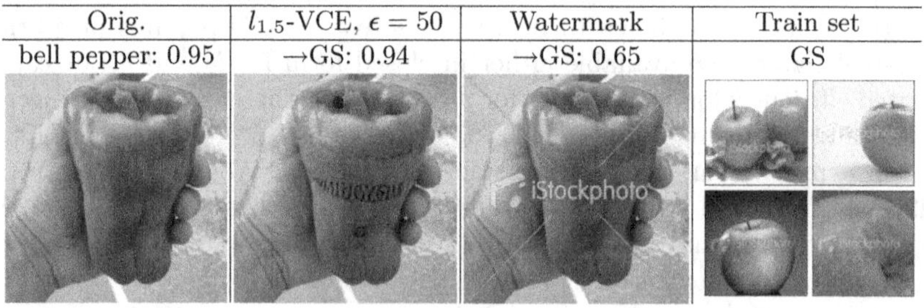

Orig.	$l_{1.5}$-VCE, $\epsilon = 50$	Watermark	Train set
bell pepper: 0.95	→GS: 0.94	→GS: 0.65	GS

Fig. 7. Spurious feature: watermark. The $l_{1.5}$-VCE with target class "granny smith" (GS) for Madry [19]+FT shows that the model has associated a spurious "text" feature with this class. This is likely due to "iStockphoto" watermarked images in its training set (right). Adding the watermark changes the decision of the classifier to GS.

Experiments: To evaluate the effectiveness of AFW, we compare its performance when optimizing Eq. (3) in the $l_{1.5}$-ball of radius 50. We use different budgets of $25, 75, 125$ iterations (75 is used for generating all VCEs), and test a variety of fixed parameters for the FW attacks of [11] ($\gamma_0 \in \{0.1, 0.2, ..., 0.9\}$ as constant stepsize and $\gamma_0 \in \{1, 5, ..., 25, 50, 75, 100\}$ and $M \in \{2, ...\}$ for stepsize decaying with k). Figure 6 shows that AFW achieves the maximal objective (log probability of the target class) for 75 and is second best for the budget of 25 and 125 iterations. Thus AFW adapts to the given budget and outperforms FW with fixed stepsize schemes. In App. C.3, we provide additional experiments.

4   Finding Spurious Features with $l_{1.5}$-VCEs

Neural networks are excellent feature extractors and very good at finding correlations in the data. This makes them susceptible to learn spurious features which are not task-related [7,9,23,33,67], to the extent that the actual object is not recognized, *e.g.* a cow on a beach is not recognized without the appearance of the spurious feature "pasture/grass" [6,56]. We show how VCEs can be used for finding such spurious features. While an automatic pipeline is beyond the scope of this paper, we believe that this can be done with minimal human supervision.

Failure A, Watermark Text as Spurious Feature for "Granny Smith": We detected this failure when creating VCEs for the target class "granny smith". We consistently observed text-like features on the generated $l_{1.5}$-VCEs which are obviously not related to this class. In Fig. 7 we illustrate the $l_{1.5}$-VCE for an image from the class "bell pepper". More examples are in App. E.1. Since almost none of the "granny smith" training images contains text, we came up with the hypothesis that the reason is a high percentage of watermarked images in the training set. Manual inspection showed that 90 out of 1300 training images contain a watermark, out of which 53 contain the one of "iStockphoto" (see the rightmost image in Fig. 7). While watermarked images appear in several classes in ImageNet, this significant fraction of one type of watermark in the training set seems to only be present in the class "granny smith". We tested this hypothesis by simulating the watermark of "iStockphoto" on the test set, for an example see the second image from the right in Fig. 7 and App. E.1 for more details. In Table 2 we show that adding the "iStockphoto"-watermark has a negative influence on top-1 accuracy not only for the adv. robust model Madry [19]+FT but also other non-robust models. The reason is that this particular watermark contains features (lines) which are characteristic for classes such as bow, safety pin, reel. However, even though the "iStockphoto"-watermark contains no characteristic features of "granny smith", adding the watermark leads to significantly worse precision of the granny smith class (basically an increase in false positives while false negatives stay the same). Interestingly, even an accurate model such as NS-B7 [65] shows this effect although trained using the much larger non-public JFT-300M dataset, suggesting that JFT-300M contains these artefacts as well.

Failure B, Cages as Spurious Feature for "White Shark": The next failure was detected using $l_{1.5}$-VCEs for the shark classes where very frequently grid-like structures appear - but only for VCEs with target class "white shark" not for "tiger shark" or "hammerhead". A typical situation is shown in Fig. 8, where the original image is from class "coral reef". The VCE for "tiger shark" shows a shark coming from the left whereas the VCE for "white shark" shows just a grid-like structure, see App. E.2 for more such VCEs. An inspection of the "white shark" training set reveals that many of the images contain parts of cages protecting the photographing diver, see the rightmost image in Fig. 8 for an illustration. The model has picked up on this feature as a fairly dominant one for white sharks, which is clearly spurious and undesirable. Interestingly, the VCEs allow us to find such artefacts even without images of white-sharks which is an advantage over saliency or feature attribution methods.

Table 2. We show top-1 accuracy for the test set, and precision/recall for the class "granny smith" (GS) on the test set before and after adding the "iStockphoto"-watermark. Note that the watermark has a quite significant impact on accuracy and in particular on the precision of GS (more false positives), which confirms our hypothesis on the bias induced by the GS training set.

	Original			W. Watermark		
Model	Top-1	GS vs Rest		Top-1	GS vs Rest	
	Acc.	Prec.	Rec.	Acc.	Prec.	Rec.
Madry [19]+FT	57.5	61.1	73.3	50.4	43.8	70.0
ResNet50 [19]	76.0	90.3	93.3	62.3	53.2	83.3
NS-Eff. B7 [65]	86.6	90.3	93.3	84.1	68.3	93.3

Orig.	$l_{1.5}$-VCE, $\epsilon = 100$		Train set
coral reef: 0.58	→t. shark: 0.96	→w. shark: 0.99	white shark

Fig. 8. Spurious feature: cage. The $l_{1.5}$-VCE for an image from class coral reef with target "tiger shark" shows a tiger shark, but with target "white shark" grid-like structures as spurious feature. The training set of white shark (right) contains many images with cages.

5   Discussion and Limitations

We have shown that our $l_{1.5}$-VCEs are sparse and do subtle changes located on the object of interest even for ImageNet resolution. We have shown that $l_{1.5}$-VCEs are a useful debugging tool for detecting spurious features which the classifier has picked up. Not all VCEs are meaningful which can have different reasons: i) the perturbation budget is too small to be able to change to more distinct classes, ii) the model has not picked up the right features, or iii) VCEs show spurious features, as discussed in Sect. 4. However, these "limitations" just reflect that our classifiers are not yet perfect and are not a failure of VCEs. In the future it will be interesting to generate an automatic pipeline for the detection of spurious features with minimal human supervision.

Acknowledgement. M.H., P.B., and V.B. acknowledge support by the the DFG Excellence Cluster Machine Learning - New Perspectives for Science, EXC 2064/1, Project number 390727645.

References

1. Augustin, M., Meinke, A., Hein, M.: Adversarial robustness on in- and out-distribution improves explainability. In: Vedaldi, A., Bischof, H., Brox, T., Frahm, J.-M. (eds.) ECCV 2020. LNCS, vol. 12371, pp. 228–245. Springer, Cham (2020). https://doi.org/10.1007/978-3-030-58574-7_14
2. Avrahami, O., Lischinski, D., Fried, O.: Blended diffusion for text-driven editing of natural images (2021)
3. Bach, S., Binder, A., Gregoire Montavon, F.K., Müller, K.R., Samek, W.: On pixel-wise explanations for non-linear classifier decisions by layer-wise relevance propagation. PLoS ONE **10**(7), e0130140 (2015)
4. Baehrens, D., Schroeter, T., Harmeling, S., Kawanabe, M., Hansen, K., Müller, K.R.: How to explain individual classification decisions. J. Mach. Learn. Res. (JMLR) **11**, 1803–1831 (2010)
5. Barocas, S., Selbst, A.D., Raghavan, M.: The hidden assumptions behind counterfactual explanations and principal reasons. In: FACCT, pp. 80–89 (2020)
6. Beery, S., Van Horn, G., Perona, P.: Recognition in terra incognita. In: Ferrari, V., Hebert, M., Sminchisescu, C., Weiss, Y. (eds.) ECCV 2018. LNCS, vol. 11220, pp. 472–489. Springer, Cham (2018). https://doi.org/10.1007/978-3-030-01270-0_28
7. Brendel, W., Bethge, M.: Approximating CNNs with bag-of-local-features models works surprisingly well on imageNet. In: ICLR (2019)
8. Carmon, Y., Raghunathan, A., Schmidt, L., Duchi, J.C., Liang, P.: Unlabeled data improves adversarial robustness. In: NeurIPS (2019)
9. Carter, S., Armstrong, Z., Schubert, L., Johnson, I., Olah, C.: Exploring neural networks with activation atlases. Distill (2019)
10. Chang, C.H., Creager, E., Goldenberg, A., Duvenaud, D.: Explaining image classifiers by counterfactual generation. In: ICLR (2019)
11. Chen, J., Yi, J., Gu, Q.: A Frank-Wolfe framework for efficient and effective adversarial attacks. In: AAAI (2019)
12. Commission, E.: Regulation for laying down harmonised rules on AI. European Commission (2021). https://eur-lex.europa.eu/legal-content/EN/TXT/PDF/?uri=CELEX:52021PC0206&from=EN

13. Croce, F., et al.: Robustbench: a standardized adversarial robustness benchmark. In: NeurIPS Track on Benchmark and Datasets (2021)
14. Croce, F., Hein, M.: Reliable evaluation of adversarial robustness with an ensemble of diverse parameter-free attacks. In: ICML (2020)
15. Croce, F., Hein, M.: Mind the box: l_1-APGD for sparse adversarial attacks on image classifiers. In: ICML (2021)
16. Croce, F., Hein, M.: Adversarial robustness against multiple l_p-threat models at the price of one and how to quickly fine-tune robust models to another threat model. In: ICML (2022)
17. Dhariwal, P., Nichol, A.: Diffusion models beat GANs on image synthesis. arXiv preprint arXiv:2105.05233 (2021)
18. Dhurandhar, A., et al.: Explanations based on the missing: towards contrastive explanations with pertinent negatives. In: NeurIPS (2018)
19. Engstrom, L., Ilyas, A., Salman, H., Santurkar, S., Tsipras, D.: Robustness (python library) (2019). https://github.com/MadryLab/robustness
20. Engstrom, L., Ilyas, A., Santurkar, S., Tsipras, D., Tran, B., Madry, A.: Adversarial robustness as a prior for learned representations (2019)
21. Etmann, C., Lunz, S., Maass, P., Schönlieb, C.B.: On the connection between adversarial robustness and saliency map interpretability. In: ICML (2019)
22. Gao, S., Li, Z.Y., Yang, M.H., Cheng, M.M., Han, J., Torr, P.: Large-scale unsupervised semantic segmentation. arXiv preprint arXiv:2106.03149 (2021)
23. Goh, G., et al.: Multimodal neurons in artificial neural networks. Distill (2021)
24. Gowal, S., Qin, C., Uesato, J., Mann, T., Kohli, P.: Uncovering the limits of adversarial training against norm-bounded adversarial examples. arXiv preprint arXiv:2010.03593v2 (2020)
25. Goyal, Y., Wu, Z., Ernst, J., Batra, D., Parikh, D., Lee, S.: Counterfactual visual explanations. In: ICML (2019)
26. Guo, C., Pleiss, G., Sun, Y., Weinberger, K.Q.: On calibration of modern neural networks. In: ICML (2017)
27. He, K., Zhang, X., Ren, S., Sun, J.: Identity mappings in deep residual networks. In: ECCV (2016)
28. Hendricks, L.A., Akata, Z., Rohrbach, M., Donahue, J., Schiele, B., Darrell, T.: Generating visual explanations. In: ECCV (2016)
29. Hendricks, L.A., Hu, R., Darrell, T., Akata, Z.: Grounding visual explanations. In: ECCV (2018)
30. Hendrycks, D., Mu, N., Cubuk, E.D., Zoph, B., Gilmer, J., Lakshminarayanan, B.: AugMix: a simple data processing method to improve robustness and uncertainty. In: ICLR (2020)
31. Hendrycks, D., Zhao, K., Basart, S., Steinhardt, J., Song, D.: Natural adversarial examples. In: CVPR (2021)
32. Heusel, M., Ramsauer, H., Unterthiner, T., Nessler, B., Hochreiter, S.: GANs trained by a two time-scale update rule converge to a local nash equilibrium. In: NeurIPS (2017)
33. Hohman, F., Park, H., Robinson, C., Chau, D.H.: Summit: scaling deep learning interpretability by visualizing activation and attribution summarizations. IEEE Trans. Vis. Comput. Graph. (TVCG) **26**(1), 1096–1106 (2020). https://doi.org/10.1109/tvcg.2019.2934659
34. Jaggi, M.: Revisiting Frank-Wolfe: projection-free sparse convex optimization. In: ICML (2013)
35. Kolesnikov, A., et al.: Big transfer (bit): general visual representation learning. In: ECCV (2020)

36. Laidlaw, C., Singla, S., Feizi, S.: Perceptual adversarial robustness: defense against unseen threat models. In: ICLR (2021)
37. Lang, O., et al.: Explaining in style: training a GAN to explain a classifier in stylespace. arXiv preprint arXiv:2104.13369 (2021)
38. Lundberg, S.M., Lee, S.I.: A unified approach to interpreting model predictions. In: NeurIPS (2017)
39. Madry, A., Makelov, A., Schmidt, L., Tsipras, D., Vladu, A.: Towards deep learning models resistant to adversarial attacks. In: ICLR (2018)
40. Marcinkevičs, R., Vogt, J.E.: Interpretability and explainability: a machine learning zoo mini-tour. arXiv:2012.01805 (2020)
41. Miller, T.: Explanation in artificial intelligence: insights from the social sciences. Artif. Intell. **267**, 1–38 (2019)
42. Moraru, V.: An algorithm for solving quadratic programming problems. Comput. Sci. J. Moldova **5**(2), 14 (1997)
43. Mothilal, R.K., Sharma, A., Tan, C.: Explaining machine learning classifiers through diverse counterfactual explanations. In: FAccT (2020)
44. Nichol, A., et al.: Glide: towards photorealistic image generation and editing with text-guided diffusion models (2021)
45. Pawlowski, N., Coelho de Castro, D., Glocker, B.: Deep structural causal models for tractable counterfactual inference. In: NeurIPS (2020)
46. Radford, A., et al.: Learning transferable visual models from natural language supervision. In: ICML (2021)
47. Recht, B., Roelofs, R., Schmidt, L., Shankar, V.: Do CIFAR-10 classifiers generalize to CIFAR-10? arXiv preprint arXiv:1806.00451 (2018)
48. Ribeiro, M.T., Singh, S., Guestrin, C.: "why should i trust you?": explaining the predictions of any classifier. In: KDD, pp. 1135–1144 (2016)
49. Samangouei, P., Saeedi, A., Nakagawa, L., Silberman, N.: ExplainGAN: model explanation via decision boundary crossing transformations. In: Ferrari, V., Hebert, M., Sminchisescu, C., Weiss, Y. (eds.) ECCV 2018. LNCS, vol. 11214, pp. 681–696. Springer, Cham (2018). https://doi.org/10.1007/978-3-030-01249-6_41
50. Sanchez, P., Tsaftaris, S.A.: Diffusion causal models for counterfactual estimation. In: First Conference on Causal Learning and Reasoning (2022)
51. Santurkar, S., Tsipras, D., Tran, B., Ilyas, A., Engstrom, L., Madry, A.: Image synthesis with a single (robust) classifier. In: NeurIPS (2019)
52. Schut, L., et al.: Generating interpretable counterfactual explanations by implicit minimisation of epistemic and aleatoric uncertainties. In: AISTATS (2021)
53. Schutte, K., Moindrot, O., Hérent, P., Schiratti, J.B., Jégou, S.: Using styleGAN for visual interpretability of deep learning models on medical images. In: NeurIPS Workshop "Medical Imaging Meets NeurIPS" (2020)
54. Selvaraju, R.R., Cogswell, M., Das, A., Vedantam, R., Parikh, D., Batra, D.: Grad-cam: visual explanations from deep networks via gradient-based localization. Int. J. Comput. Vision **128**(2), 336–359 (2019)
55. Simonyan, K., Vedaldi, A., Zisserman, A.: Deep inside convolutional networks: visualising image classification models and saliency maps. In: ICLR (2014)
56. Singla, S., Nushi, B., Shah, S., Kamar, E., Horvitz, E.: Understanding failures of deep networks via robust feature extraction. In: CVPR (2021)
57. Srinivas, S., Fleuret, F.: Full-gradient representation for neural network visualization. In: NeurIPS (2019)
58. Szegedy, C., et al.: Intriguing properties of neural networks. In: ICLR, pp. 2503–2511 (2014)

59. Torralba, A., Fergus, R., Freeman, W.T.: 80 million tiny images: a large data set for nonparametric object and scene recognition. IEEE PAMI **30**(11), 1958–1970 (2008)
60. Tsiligkaridis, T., Roberts, J.: Understanding frank-wolfe adversarial training. In: CVPR (2022)
61. Tsipras, D., Santurkar, S., Engstrom, L., Turner, A., Madry, A.: Robustness may be at odds with accuracy. In: ICLR (2019)
62. Verma, S., Dickerson, J.P., Hines, K.: Counterfactual explanations for machine learning: a review. arXiv preprint, arXiv:2010.10596 (2020)
63. Wachter, S., Mittelstadt, B., Russell, C.: Counterfactual explanations without opening the black box: automated decisions and the GDPR. Harvard J. Law Technol. **31**, 841–887 (2018)
64. Wang, Z., Wang, H., Ramkumar, S., Fredrikson, M., Mardziel, P., Datta, A.: Smoothed geometry for robust attribution. In: NeurIPS (2020)
65. Xie, Q., Luong, M.T., Hovy, E., Le, Q.V.: Self-training with noisy student improves imagenet classification. In: CVPR (2020)
66. Yu, Y., Zhang, X., Schuurmans, D.: Generalized conditional gradient for sparse estimation. J. Mach. Learn. Res. **18**(144), 1–46 (2017)
67. Zech, J.R., Badgeley, M.A., Liu, M., Costa, A.B., Titano, J.J., Oermann, E.K.: Confounding variables can degrade generalization performance of radiological deep learning models. arXiv preprint arXiv:1807.00431 (2018)

Low-Level Vision and Computational Photography

Blind Single Image Super-Resolution via Iterated Shared Prior Learning

Thomas Pinetz[1,3(✉)], Erich Kobler[4], Thomas Pock[2], and Alexander Effland[1]

[1] Institute of Applied Mathematics, University of Bonn, Bonn, Germany
{pinetz,effland}@iam.uni-bonn.de
[2] Institute of Computer Graphics and Vision, Graz University of Technology, Graz, Austria
pock@tugraz.at
[3] Austrian Institute of Technology, Vision, Automation and Control, Vienna, Austria
[4] Johannes Kepler University Linz, Institute of Computer Graphics, Linz, Austria
erich.kobler@jku.at

Abstract. In this paper, we adapt shared prior learning for blind single image super-resolution (SISR). From a variational perspective, we are aiming at minimizing an energy functional consisting of a learned data fidelity term and a data-driven prior, where the learnable parameters are computed in a mean-field optimal control problem. In the associated loss functional, we combine a supervised loss evaluated on synthesized observations and an unsupervised Wasserstein loss for real observations, in which local statistics of images with different resolutions are compared. In shared prior learning, only the parameters of the prior are shared among both loss functions. The kernel estimate is updated iteratively after each step of shared prior learning. In numerous numerical experiments, we achieve state-of-the-art results for blind SISR with a low number of learnable parameters and small training sets to account for real applications.

1 Introduction

Single image super-resolution (SISR) is the problem of retrieving a high-resolution image from a low-resolution observation, which is often additionally degraded by noise. If the downsampling kernel is unknown, then this problem is known as *blind* SISR. Driven by the progress in deep learning throughout recent years, the demand for SISR in real-world applications has risen, e.g. in medical imaging [10], microscopy [29], and satellite imagery [28].

Recent deep learning approaches for non-blind SISR encompass the very deep residual channel attention network [37], wide activation networks [34], neural texture transfer [38], the end-to-end trainable unfolding network [35], the content-adaptive resampler [30], or the densely residual Laplacian network [2]. In all these methods, convolutional neural networks with sophisticated design patterns including additional residual blocks, residual connections, larger receptive fields due to wider activation or attention are primarily exploited to retrieve the high-frequency information and fine pattern structures that are lost during downsampling.

Supplementary Information The online version contains supplementary material available at https://doi.org/10.1007/978-3-031-16788-1_10.

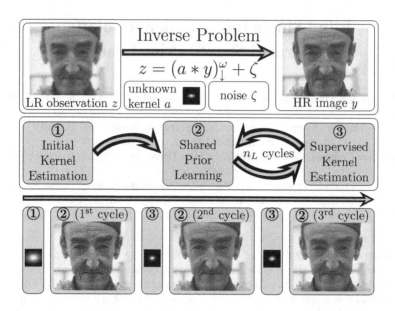

Fig. 1. Inverse problem for blind SISR (top), building blocks of proposed method (middle), restored kernels & images (bottom).

Besides the issues related to *non-blind* SISR, the accuracy of the restored images in *blind* SISR tremendously depends on the quality of the estimated kernel as observed in KernelGAN [3]. Here, the parameters of the generator network of a generative adversarial network are optimized such that the discriminator network cannot distinguish between the patch distributions of the generated and the original low-resolution images. In [19], two separate networks for kernel estimation and image reconstruction are alternated, which are trained via an unfolding in an end-to-end fashion giving rise to a mutual dependency of the learnable parameters. Gu et al. [11] advocated learning the unknown isotropic kernel iteratively, i.e. after each kernel estimation the high-resolution images are generated by a super-resolution network using spatial feature transform. This iterative kernel estimation scheme is similar to our method introduced below. For a comprehensive overview of recent deep-learning-based approaches for SISR, we refer the reader to [33].

Frequently, blind SISR is cast as an ill-posed inverse problem. In the associated forward model, an unknown kernel is applied to the high-resolution image, which is subsequently downsampled and possibly further degraded by additive noise (see Fig 1 (top)). In a variational setting of this inverse problem, an energy functional commonly composed of a data fidelity term and a prior (regularizer) is minimized, in which the former enforces data consistency and the latter enhances interfacial structures and sharpens the solution. Here, the associated minimizer is an approximation of the high-resolution ground truth image.

In numerical experiments, the proper choice of the regularizer has proven to be crucial for high-quality results. Classical hand-crafted regularizers including the total variation [26] or the total generalized variation [5] are outperformed by learned regularizers with improved statistical modeling of natural images, which has already been anticipated more than two decades ago [40]. Common choices for learned regularizers include the Fields of Experts regularizer [25], or the deep denoiser prior [36].

In this paper, we integrate the data-driven total deep variation (TDV) regularizer [16,17] representing a deep multi-scale convolutional neural network into the variational approach. Apart from the low-resolution observations possibly degraded by noise, we require a high-resolution *unrelated* dataset with uncorrupted real images. We emphasize that our approach is primarily designed for *blind* SISR, the high-resolution dataset is unexceptionally utilized to learn natural image statistics. The proposed method encompasses three steps: the initial kernel estimation, shared prior learning, and a supervised kernel estimation, where both latter steps are alternated in n_L cycles (see Fig 1 (middle)).

① Initially, the kernel is estimated solely based on a comparison of distributions of the low-resolution observations with the downsampled high-resolution dataset in the patch-based Wasserstein distance.

② In this step, we advocate an energy functional composed of a squared ℓ^2-data fidelity term with learned scaling and the data-driven TDV regularizer as a prior. The energy is minimized using a time discretization of the gradient flow of the energy, where the terminal state defines the restored image. All learnable parameters are computed in a mean-field optimal control problem. The associated loss functional comprises two parts: a supervised loss functional only evaluated on the high-resolution dataset and the patch-based Wasserstein loss functional, in which both the high-resolution dataset and the observations are incorporated. We emphasize that only the learnable parameters of the prior are *shared* among both loss functionals, which gives rise to the name *shared prior learning*.

③ Then, the kernel estimate is updated by comparing the restored images to the low-resolution observations.

To suppress artifacts and promote regularity of the kernels, all estimated kernels are represented as a linear combination of Gabor filters to reduce dimensionality following the paradigm *regularization by discretization* [12]. We emphasize that already a small number of Gabor filters suffices to ensure an excellent approximation quality of most real-world kernels including Gaussian, motion, and blur kernels.

In this paper, we deliberately exploit small networks with less than 500 000 learnable parameters and only utilize small training sets since in many real world applications including microscopy or medical imaging only small datasets are available, which prevents the use of deep networks.

The main contributions of this work are as follows:

– We propose a novel scheme for blind SISR based on shared prior learning and iterative kernel estimation.
– Our method is also applicable in the one-shot case for a single degraded image.
– We achieve state-of-the-art results for blind SISR.
– Interestingly, the proposed *blind* method is almost on par with state-of-the-art *non-blind* methods, although our approach facilitates several orders of magnitude less parameters than most competing methods.

Shared prior learning has recently been introduced in [23] for general image reconstruction problems. The main novelty of this work compared to [23] is the application to *blind* SISR, in which the downsampling operator in the inverse problem is unknown. In particular, we here do *not* require any ground truth data for training and we propose a completely novel way to estimate the unknown kernels in the space of Gabor filters. Moreover, by integrating multiple bins into our method we can simultaneously estimate different kernels at the same time.

2   Preliminaries

In this section, we briefly recall two necessary concepts required for this paper: the discrete Wasserstein distance and Gabor filters.

2.1   Discrete Wasserstein Distance

Next, we briefly recall the (discrete) Wasserstein distance and refer the reader to the literature [22,27,31] for further details. Intuitively, the Wasserstein distance quantifies the minimum cost to transform one measure into another given a predefined cost function. We consider the collection of points $v = (v_1, \ldots, v_N)$, $v_i \in \mathbb{R}^n$, which defines the *discrete measure* $\mu[v]$ as $\mu[v](S) := \frac{1}{N} \sum_{i=1}^{N} \delta_{v_i}(S)$ for $S \subset \mathbb{R}^n$, where $\delta_{v_i}(S)$ is 1 if $v_i \in S$ and 0 otherwise. Given a second collection of points $w = (w_1, \ldots, w_N)$, $w_i \in \mathbb{R}^n$, the *cost matrix* $C_p[v, w] \in \mathbb{R}^{N \times N}$ for $p \geq 1$ is defined as $(C_p[v, w])_{i,j} := \|v_i - w_j\|_p$ with $\|\cdot\|_p$ denoting the usual ℓ^p-norm. Following [27, Chapter 6.4], the *discrete Wasserstein distance* with cost matrix $C_p[v, w]$ reads as

$$\mathbf{W}_p(\mu[v], \mu[w]) := \inf_{P \in (\mathbb{R}_0^+)^{N \times N}} \{\operatorname{tr}((C_p[v, w])^\top P) : P^\top \mathbf{1}_N = \tfrac{1}{N} \mathbf{1}_N, P\mathbf{1}_N = \tfrac{1}{N} \mathbf{1}_N\}, \tag{1}$$

where tr denotes the trace of the matrix, $A^\top$ refers to the transpose of A, and $\mathbf{1}_N$ is the all-ones vector in $\mathbb{R}^N$.

In this work, we evaluate the Wasserstein distance on the coefficients of the discrete cosine transform rather than directly on images. We remark that the use of the discrete cosine transform for image feature extraction has been well studied and analyzed by Mumford et al. [14,18,21]. To extract features from images, we incorporate the discrete cosine transform-II (DCT-II) [6] (further choices of feature extraction operators have been discussed in [23]). We highlight that we focus on the comparison of local features in SISR, that is why the DCT coefficients are extracted patchwise. Thus, the linear DCT operator is a mapping $\mathrm{DCT} : \mathbb{R}^n \to (\mathbb{R}^{n_{\mathrm{patch}}^2 - 1})^N$, which splits each input image into N overlapping square patches of size n_{patch}^2 and assigns DCT coefficients to each patch. Note that the first coefficient is neglected to obtain a mean-invariant representation of patches.

Throughout this paper, we only consider the patch-based discrete Wasserstein distance for $p = 1$ evaluated on DCT coefficients of image patches giving rise to the definition

$$\widetilde{\mathbf{W}}(v, w) := \mathbf{W}_1(\mu[\mathrm{DCT}[v]], \mu[\mathrm{DCT}[w]]). \tag{2}$$

The optimization in Eq. (2) is performed using a proximal version of the classical Sinkhorn algorithm (see supplementary material), in which a Bregman divergence on the entropy is added [4,32]. This choice has numerically proven to be superior compared with the classical Sinkhorn algorithm.

2.2 Kernel Representation Using Gabor Filters

Throughout this work, each unknown downsampling kernel $a \in \mathbb{R}^{n_a \times n_a}$ of size $n_a \times n_a$ is approximated by an estimated kernel $\widehat{a} \in \mathbb{R}^{n_a \times n_a}$, which is represented by a linear combination of n_G Gabor filters. Gabor filters are primarily used for two reasons: dimensionality reduction and promotion of intrinsic regularization by discretization [12]. Each Gabor filter G_{ξ_i}, $i = 1, \ldots, n_G$, is described by 8 parameters $\xi_i = (\xi_i^{\text{fac}}, \xi_i^{\text{rot}}, \xi_i^x, \xi_i^y, \xi_i^{\text{aniso}}, \xi_i^{\text{std}}, \xi_i^{\text{wave}}, \xi_i^{\text{offset}}) \in \mathbb{R}^8$, and is defined as

$$G_{\xi_i}(x,y) = \xi_i^{\text{fac}} \exp\left(-\frac{\widetilde{x}^2 + (\xi_i^{\text{aniso}})^2 \widetilde{y}}{2(\xi_i^{\text{std}})^2}\right) \cos(2\pi \xi_i^{\text{wave}} \widetilde{x} + \xi_i^{\text{offset}}) \tag{3}$$

for $x, y \in \mathbb{R}$, where the rotated coordinates are given by

$$\begin{pmatrix} \widetilde{x} \\ \widetilde{y} \end{pmatrix} = \begin{pmatrix} \cos(\xi_i^{\text{rot}}) & \sin(\xi_i^{\text{rot}}) \\ -\sin(\xi_i^{\text{rot}}) & \cos(\xi_i^{\text{rot}}) \end{pmatrix} \begin{pmatrix} x \\ y \end{pmatrix} + \begin{pmatrix} \xi_i^x \\ \xi_i^y \end{pmatrix}. \tag{4}$$

We denote the entity of all parameters comprising the Gabor filters by $\xi = (\xi_i)_{i=1}^{n_G} \in \mathbb{R}^{8n_G}$. To highlight the dependency of the estimated kernel on ξ, we write $\widehat{a}_\xi$, which yields for $s, t = 1, \ldots, n_a$ representing an $n_a \times n_a$ grid $\widehat{a}_\xi(s,t) = \sum_{i=1}^{n_G} G_{\xi_i}(s,t)$. Note that most Gaussian, motion, and blur kernels can already be represented with a high accuracy by a very low number of Gabor filters.

3 Proposed Method

In this section, we elaborate on the proposed method for blind SISR. As a starting point, we cast blind SISR as a linear inverse problem. To this end, we consider an uncorrupted high-resolution (HR) image y with C color channels and a resolution of $n_w \times n_h$, which implies $y \in \mathbb{R}^{n_w \times n_h \times C}$. In blind SISR, the image is degraded by an unknown kernel a of size $n_a \times n_a$, which is realized by a convolution of each channel separately. Subsequently, the image is downscaled by a known factor $\omega \geq 2$ using a convolution with stride ω. Frequently, the downscaled image is additionally deteriorated by additive noise $\zeta \in \mathbb{R}^{(n_w/\omega) \times (n_h/\omega) \times C}$ with expectation $\mathbb{E}[\zeta] = 0$ and variance σ^2. Hence, the resulting low-resolution (LR) observation $z \in \mathbb{R}^{(n_w/\omega) \times (n_h/\omega) \times C}$ is related to y via

$$z = (a * y)_{\downarrow}^{\omega} + \zeta. \tag{5}$$

Here, $(\cdot)_{\downarrow}^{\omega}$ denotes the downsampling operator realized by a convolution with stride ω, and $*$ is the channel-wise convolution operator.

For training, we consider low-resolution observations categorized in B disjoint bins $\text{BIN}_1, \ldots, \text{BIN}_B$, where each LR observation z of a distinct bin BIN_b, $b = 1, \ldots, B$, is corrupted by exactly the same unknown kernel a_b of size $n_a \times n_a$. We denote by

$\mathcal{T}_b^{\mathrm{LR}}$ the distribution describing the entity of observations in BIN_b. Further, we assume that the associated ground truth images y are unknown with the same unknown noise distribution among all bins such that the forward model Eq. (5) still applies. Note that the case $B = 1$, in which only a single kernel has to be estimated, and bins with a single image are admissible. Since our approach is based on the comparison of local image statistics by means of the Wasserstein distance, we additionally require a dataset of noise-free/uncorrupted high-resolution reference image patches $p \in \mathbb{R}^{n_w \times n_h \times C}$ with the distribution $\mathcal{T}^{\mathrm{HR}}$, which are *unrelated* to the low-resolution observations. This dataset should be visually similar to the actual dataset of interest.

At its core, our proposed method encompasses three substeps, where ② and ③ are alternated in n_L cycles:

① initial kernel estimation,
② shared prior learning,
③ supervised kernel estimation.

Initial guesses for the unknown kernels are estimated from local image statistics in ①. In shared prior learning ②, the learnable control parameters of the image reconstruction algorithm given the current estimated kernels are computed. The reconstructed images of the previous step ② are integrated as approximate ground truth images in a supervised learning problem in ③ to update the kernel estimates. In both ① and ③, the kernel is represented as a linear combination of Gabor kernels introduced in Subsect. 2.2. Depending on the number n_G of Gabor kernels, only the low-frequency components of the actual kernel are properly estimated while the high-frequency components are neglected.

3.1 Initial Kernel Estimation

In the first step, we approximate the unknown kernel a_b of each bin BIN_b, $b = 1, \ldots, B$, by $\widehat{a}_{\xi_b}$ with $\xi_b \in \mathbb{R}^{8n_G}$ (see Subsect. 2.2). The parameters ξ_b of the initial kernel $\widehat{a}_{\xi_b}$ are estimated such that in average the observed LR observations z taken from BIN_b are close to the downsampled HR patches $(\widehat{a}_{\xi_b} * p)_{\downarrow}^{\omega}$, where p varies in the collection of reference patches $\mathcal{T}^{\mathrm{HR}}$. Since no ground truth images are available for training, we incorporate Eq. (2) to compare the statistics on the level of DCT features using the Wasserstein distance. Hence, the parameters ξ_b are retrieved from

$$\xi_b \in \underset{\xi \in \mathbb{R}^{8n_G}}{\operatorname{argmin}} \, \mathbb{E}_{\substack{z \sim \mathcal{T}_b^{\mathrm{LR}} \\ p \sim \mathcal{T}^{\mathrm{HR}}}} \left[\widetilde{\mathbf{W}}(z, (\widehat{a}_\xi * p)_{\downarrow}^{\omega}) \right]. \tag{6}$$

We remark that the Wasserstein distance is translation-invariant w.r.t. the blur kernel. Therefore, we fix the center for all Gabor filters to the center pixel of the kernel.

3.2 Shared Prior Learning

In the second step, we apply shared prior learning to retrieve high-resolution images from (possibly corrupted) low-resolution observations, where we roughly follow the approach in [23]. The loss functional in shared prior learning is a convex combination of a supervised loss functional and an unsupervised patch-based Wasserstein loss functional. The former loss functional quantifies the average distance of HR reference images and restored downsampled observations, which are synthesized from the HR images using estimated kernels. In the latter functional, the patch statistics of the reconstructed LR observations and HR reference images are compared. The control parameters of the regularizer (prior) are *shared* among both loss functionals. We highlight that all kernels ξ_b remain unchanged in this step, which are either taken from ① (if this step is executed for the first time) or from ③.

In detail, the goal of this step is the computation of an approximation $x \in \mathbb{R}^{n_w \times n_h \times C}$ of the ground truth image y from a LR observation z related via Eq. (5), for which we use the known approximations $\hat{a}_{\xi_b}$ of a_b for $b = 1, \ldots, B$. Initially, we cast the reconstruction subtask as a variational problem, in which a squared ℓ^2-data fidelity term enforces data consistency of $(\hat{a}_{\xi_b} * x)^\omega_\downarrow$ and z. This problem is known to be ill-posed, which necessitates the inclusion of a regularizer for x. Throughout this paper, we exclusively use the data-driven *total deep variation (TDV)* regularizer $\mathcal{R}$ [16,17], which depends on x and learned parameters $\theta \in \Theta$ with Θ representing a compact parameter set. TDV is a multi-scale convolutional neural network consisting of three subsequent U-Net like blocks [24] with additional residual and skip connections (for further details see supplementary material). Hence, the variational problem reads as

$$x \in \operatorname*{argmin}_{\tilde{x} \in \mathbb{R}^{n_w \times n_h \times C}} \frac{\lambda}{2} \|(\hat{a}_{\xi_b} * \tilde{x})^\omega_\downarrow - z\|_2^2 + \mathcal{R}(\tilde{x}, \theta) \tag{7}$$

for a scaling parameter $\lambda > 0$. Following [9,16], a semi-implicit time discretization of the gradient flow of Eq. (7) with $S \in \mathbb{N}$ iteration steps yields the recursion scheme

$$x_{s+1} = x_s - \frac{\lambda}{S}\overline{\hat{a}_{\xi_b}} * ((\hat{a}_{\xi_b} * x_{s+1})^\omega_\downarrow - z)^\omega_\uparrow - \frac{1}{S}\nabla_1 \mathcal{R}(x_s, \theta) \tag{8}$$

for $s = 0, \ldots, S - 1$. Here, $\overline{\hat{a}_{\xi_b}}$ denotes the transposed convolution and $(\cdot)^\omega_\uparrow$ refers to upsampling with scale ω, which is exactly the adjoint operator of $(\cdot)^\omega_\downarrow$. In this case, x_S defines the output image. To allow for an improved data-driven scaling of both the data fidelity term and the regularizer in Eq. (8), we advocate *learnable* scaling parameters $T^{\text{dat}}, T^{\text{reg}} > 0$ instead of $\frac{\lambda}{S}$ and $\frac{1}{S}$, which implies

$$x_{s+1} = x_s - T^{\text{dat}}\overline{\hat{a}_{\xi_b}} * ((\hat{a}_{\xi_b} * x_{s+1})^\omega_\downarrow - z)^\omega_\uparrow - T^{\text{reg}}\nabla_1 \mathcal{R}(x_s, \theta). \tag{9}$$

Since a semi-implicit scheme can equivalently be expressed using the proximal operator [7], we can rewrite Eq. (9) as

$$x_{s+1} = \operatorname{prox}_{T^{\text{dat}}, \xi_b}\left(x_s + T^{\text{dat}}\overline{\hat{a}_{\xi_b}} * (z)^\omega_\uparrow - T^{\text{reg}}\nabla_1 \mathcal{R}(x_s, \theta)\right). \tag{10}$$

Following [39], $\operatorname{prox}_{T^{\text{dat}}, \xi_b}$ has the closed-form solution

$$T^{\text{dat}}\mathcal{F}^{-1}\left(\mathcal{F}(x) - \overline{\mathcal{F}(\hat{a}_{\xi_b})} \odot (r(\hat{a}_{\xi_b}, x))_\Uparrow\right), \tag{11}$$

where r is defined as

$$r(a, x) = (\mathcal{F}(a) \odot \mathcal{F}(x))_\Downarrow \oslash \left((\mathcal{F}(a) \odot \overline{\mathcal{F}(a)})_\Downarrow + \frac{1}{T^{\text{dat}}}\mathbf{1}\right). \tag{12}$$

Here, $\odot$ and $\oslash$ denote elementwise multiplication and division, $\mathcal{F}$ is the Fourier operator with periodic boundary conditions, $\overline{\mathcal{F}(\cdot)}$ denotes complex conjugation of the Fourier coefficients and $\mathbf{1}$ is the all-one vector. The downsampling operator $(\cdot)_{\Downarrow}$ in Fourier space is realized by averaging $\omega \times \omega$ blocks and the upsampling operator $(\cdot)_{\Uparrow}$ is its adjoint operator (i.e. the transpose of the matrix representing downsampling). Finally, we denote by $x(z, \mathbb{T}, \theta, \xi)$ the value of the terminal step x_S in Eq. (9) using $z, \mathbb{T}, \theta, \xi$ with $\mathbb{T} = (T^{\mathrm{dat}}, T^{\mathrm{reg}})$. Note that Eq. (9) can be derived using a time-continuous gradient flow formulation of Eq. (7) with a proper rescaling argument [9].

The control parameters $\mathbb{T}$ and θ are derived in a mean-field optimal control problem [8], which combines the supervised and the unsupervised loss functional. Here, $\mathbb{T}$ is estimated for each loss functional individually, while θ is shared among both.

The loss functional in the *supervised* loss is given by

$$\mathcal{J}^{\mathrm{Su}}(\mathbb{T}, \theta, \xi) := \mathbb{E}_{p \sim T^{\mathrm{HR}}}[\ell(p, x((\widehat{a}_\xi * p)^\omega_{\downarrow}, \mathbb{T}, \theta, \xi))] \tag{13}$$

for $\ell(x) = \sqrt{\|x\|_1^2 + \epsilon^2}$. Throughout all experiments, we use the regularization parameter $\epsilon = 10^{-3}$. In Eq. (13), images p from the HR reference distribution T^{HR} are randomly drawn and downsampled via $(\widehat{a}_\xi * p)^\omega_{\downarrow}$. Then, control parameters are computed such that the mean distance of p and the terminal state of the gradient flow $x((\widehat{a}_\xi * p)^\omega_{\downarrow}, \mathbb{T}, \theta, \xi)$ associated with the downsampled image $(\widehat{a}_\xi * p)^\omega_{\downarrow}$ is minimized. We emphasize that in the supervised loss functional only the HR dataset T^{HR} is included.

The LR observations are integrated into the mean-field optimal control problem only via the subsequent unsupervised loss functional. The core idea of this loss functional is the local comparison of image statistics of HR patches $p \sim T^{\mathrm{HR}}$ with output images $x(z, \mathbb{T}, \theta, \xi)$ associated with given LR observations $z \sim T^{\mathrm{LR}}_b$. To this end, we employ the patch-based Wasserstein distance in the DCT feature space Eq. (2), in which the local image statistics in the DCT feature space are compared. Thus, the loss functional in the *unsupervised* loss reads as

$$\mathcal{J}^{\mathrm{Un}}_b(\mathbb{T}, \theta, \xi) := \mathbb{E}_{\substack{z \sim T^{\mathrm{LR}}_b \\ p \sim T^{\mathrm{HR}}}}[\widetilde{\mathbf{W}}(p, x(z, \mathbb{T}, \theta, \xi))]. \tag{14}$$

We stress the dependency on BIN_b in this loss functional.

The loss ℓ appearing in Eq. (13) is a common metric for image comparison, which leads to impressive results if the kernel a_b is known [35]. However, an inaccurate kernel estimation dramatically deteriorates the performance for the reconstruction of the LR observations. On the contrary, the unsupervised loss functional Eq. (14) compares the local statistics of the high-resolution patches and the restored LR observations in terms of the Wasserstein distance, and is by design less prone to inaccurate kernel estimates. A pure inclusion of this loss functional frequently results in blurry restored images without fine texture patterns. The loss functional in shared prior learning is a convex combination of both aforementioned loss functionals, in which the parameter θ of the regularizer is shared among both. Thereby, shared prior learning takes advantage of the performance of the supervised loss, while at the same time adapting to the LR observations. In summary, the loss functional reads as

$$\inf_{\substack{\theta \in \Theta \\ (\mathbb{T}_b^{\mathrm{Su}}, \mathbb{T}_b^{\mathrm{Un}}) \in (\mathbb{R}^+)^2 \times (\mathbb{R}^+)^2}} \left\{ \sum_{b=1}^{B} \alpha \mathcal{J}^{\mathrm{Su}}(\mathbb{T}_b^{\mathrm{Su}}, \theta, \xi_b) + (1 - \alpha) \mathcal{J}_b^{\mathrm{Un}}(\mathbb{T}_b^{\mathrm{Un}}, \theta, \xi_b) \right\} \quad (15)$$

for a constant balance parameter $\alpha \in [0, 1]$. We highlight that *no ground truth data for the* LR *observations are required*. For ③, only the control parameters $\mathbb{T}^{\mathrm{Un}}, \theta$ of the unsupervised subproblem are used.

3.3 Supervised Kernel Estimation

In the final step, we update the kernel parameters $\xi_1, \ldots, \xi_B$ for each bin in a supervised fashion using the control parameters $\mathbb{T}_b^{\mathrm{Un}}$ and θ of Eq. (15). To this end, we randomly draw LR observations z, which are subsequently restored using our proposed algorithm with the control parameters of the previous step (including ξ_b). Then, the restored image is degraded by convolution and downsampling yielding $(\widehat{a}_{\widetilde{\xi}} * x(z, \mathbb{T}_b^{\mathrm{Un}}, \theta, \xi_b))_{\downarrow}^{\omega}$, which is subsequently compared to z in terms of the squared ℓ^2-norm with $\widetilde{\xi}$ denoting the optimization variable. Hence, the updated kernel ξ_b^{new} for BIN_b is derived from

$$\xi_b^{\mathrm{new}} \in \underset{\widetilde{\xi} \in \mathbb{R}^{8 n_G}}{\mathrm{argmin}} \, \mathbb{E}_{z \sim \mathcal{T}_b^{\mathrm{LR}}} \tfrac{1}{2} \| (\widehat{a}_{\widetilde{\xi}} * x(z, \mathbb{T}_b^{\mathrm{Un}}, \theta, \xi_b^{\mathrm{old}}))_{\downarrow}^{\omega} - z \|_2^2. \quad (16)$$

We highlight that we employ the estimated kernel of the previous step ξ_b^{old} for the restored image $x(z, \mathbb{T}_b^{\mathrm{Un}}, \theta, \xi_b^{\mathrm{old}})$ to enhance numerical stability in the optimization.

4 Experimental Results for Blind SISR

We present experimental results for our proposed method for general and one-shot (i.e. one bin BIN_b with a single image) *blind* SISR. The code will be released after paper acceptance.

In all experiments, we use a batch size of 10 and an image patch size of 70×70. We set $S = 20$, $\alpha = 0.99$ and $n_L = 3$. The initial image always coincides with bicubic upsampling. To avoid bad local minima, we reinitialize θ with random Gaussian noise [13] and $\mathbb{T}_b^{\mathrm{Su}} = \mathbb{T}_b^{\mathrm{Un}} = (1, 0.01)$ before shared prior learning. All kernels have a size of $n_a = 25$. If not specified otherwise, we set $n_G = 1$.

For the computation of the Wasserstein distance, 50 iterations of the Sinkhorn-type [23] algorithm are performed with regularization parameter set to 1. The patches for the DCT operator have a size of $n_{\mathrm{patch}} = 6$ and are computed in the Y-channel of the YCbCr color space, the corresponding number of patches $N = 3610$ is implied by the number of overlapping patches in 10 images of size 70×70.

To compute the control parameters in Eqs. (6), (15) and (16), we utilize the ADAM optimizer [15] with a learning rate of 10^{-2} (for ① and ③) and $4 \cdot 10^{-4}$ (for ②), and momentum variables $\beta_1 = 0.5$ and $\beta_2 = 0.9$, where we employ 10 000 iterations for ① and 5 000 iterations for ② and ③. In the final cycle, we employ 20 000 iterations to compute the control parameters for ②.

In all experiments, the high-resolution patch dataset defining $\mathcal{T}^{\text{HR}}$ is the BSD400 dataset [20]. The PSNR score is evaluated in the RGB color channel following the benchmark [35], for which ω pixels are removed from each side.

4.1 SISR with Multiple Bins

In the first experiment, we consider $B = 8$ bins, each comprised of 100 successive images taken from the DIV2K training dataset [1]. All images of a distinct bin are downsampled by Gaussian kernels a_b, which are isotropic for $b = 1, \ldots, 4$ and anisotropic for $b = 5, \ldots, 8$. This benchmark has been introduced in [35] for *non-blind* SISR, and we stress that we compare our *blind* results with the respective *non-blind* SISR scores of the competing methods, i.e. we never use any ground truth kernels nor ground truth images for training. The BSD68 dataset is used for validation.

Figure 2 (left) depicts all considered kernels after each estimation for $\omega = 3$ (for $\omega \in \{2, 4\}$ we refer to the supplementary material). Again, the initial estimation (second row) only indicates the precise angle of inclination and substantially differs from the ground truth kernels (first row). However, already after the first supervised kernel estimation in ③ there is hardly any visual difference between the estimations and the ground truth kernels. The right plot visualizes the ℓ^2-distance of the estimated and the ground truth kernels after each update step for each color-coded bin. We emphasize that the curves are monotonically decreasing.

In Fig. 3, a visual comparison of the proposed method with bicubic upsampling, KernelGAN [3], and USRNet [35] for $\omega = 2$ (first row) and $\omega = 4$ (second row) is conducted. As a result, the quality of the high-resolution output images generated with our method is slightly inferior to the competing *non-blind* USRNet, but clearly superior to the competing blind methods. Likewise, Fig. 4 contains an analogous comparison for $\omega = 3$. We highlight that KernelGAN is only applicable for $\omega \in \{2, 4\}$, that is why we use the results for $\omega = 2$.

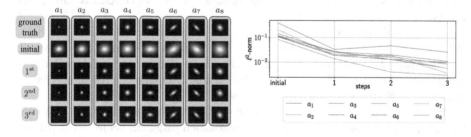

Fig. 2. Left: Ground truth kernels (first row), initial kernel via ① (second row), first to third kernel estimations via ③ for scale $\omega = 3$ (third to fifth row). Right: ℓ^2-distance of estimated and ground truth kernels after each update step.

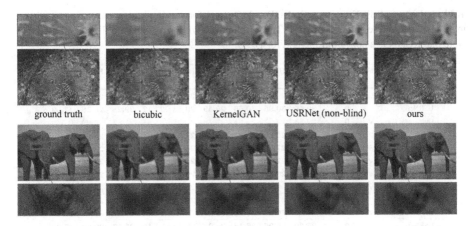

Fig. 3. From left to right: ground truth images, bicubic upsampling, KernelGAN, non-blind USR-Net and our method for $\omega = 2$ (first row) and $\omega = 4$ (second row). The magnification factor of the zoom is 6.

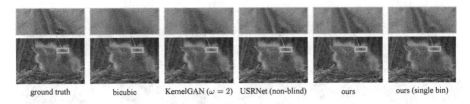

Fig. 4. From left to right: ground truth image, bicubic upsampling, KernelGAN, non-blind USR-Net, our method learned with all bins simultaneously, our method (single bin) for $\omega = 3$. Note that KernelGAN is applied for $\omega = 2$. The magnification factor of the zoom is 6.

A quantitative assessment of the PSNR scores for all bins, all scale factors, all noise instances and all methods is provided in Table 1. We note that ZSSR [3] is *non-blind* and an upper bound for the PSNR score of KernelGAN. Since we are strictly better than ZSSR (apart from one distinct bin), we did not report all values of KernelGAN. In summary, our method is only slightly inferior to *non-blind* USRNet, but clearly outperforms ZSSR, RCAN [37] and IKC [11]. We stress that our method exhibits an impressively low number of parameters (less than 5% of competing methods). Moreover, we could not incorporate the recently proposed method DAN [19] due to differences in the down-sampling procedure, which makes a fair comparison impossible.

4.2 One-Shot SISR

Next, we present a less computationally demanding inference method for one-shot SISR (single image in a single bin, i.e. $B = 1$). The parameters of the network are initialized with the computed parameters for $\omega = 4$ in the previous section. Contrary to the scheme introduced above, only the unsupervised loss functional is considered for optimization (i.e. $\alpha = 0$) and we perform 100 ADAM iterations in each cycle. In particular, only $\mathbb{T}_b^{\text{Un}}$ is optimized in step ②, the parameters θ remain unchanged.

Table 1. List of all PSNR scores (in RGB color space) for varying scales and various methods in all bins (noise-free and noisy cases). The best non-blind/blind score is highlighted in blue/red. Note that RCAN is a *non-blind* method for BIN_2.

scale	method	blind	noise σ	BIN_1	BIN_2	BIN_3	BIN_4	BIN_5	BIN_6	BIN_7	BIN_8	# parameter $(\cdot 10^6)$
2	ZSSR		0	29.44	29.48	28.57	27.42	27.15	26.81	27.09	26.25	n.a
	USRNet		0	30.55	30.96	30.56	29.49	29.13	29.12	29.28	28.28	17.02
	Ours	✓	0	29.18	29.52	28.81	27.79	27.61	27.51	27.51	26.95	0.5
3	ZSSR		0	25.13	25.80	25.94	25.77	25.61	25.23	25.68	25.41	n.a
	USRNet		0	27.16	27.76	27.90	27.88	27.71	27.68	27.74	27.57	17.02
	RCAN	✓	0	24.93	27.30	25.79	24.61	24.57	24.38	24.55	23.74	16.00
	Ours	✓	0	26.15	26.38	26.66	26.53	26.46	25.52	25.90	26.32	0.5
	Ours (single bin)	✓	0	26.34	26.83	26.73	27.34	26.44	26.39	26.21	26.92	0.5
	USRNet		2.55	26.99	27.40	27.23	26.78	26.55	26.60	26.72	26.14	17.02
	ours	✓	2.55	25.85	26.38	26.11	25.41	25.04	24.92	25.34	24.42	0.5
4	USRNet		0	25.30	25.96	26.18	26.29	26.20	26.15	26.17	26.30	17.02
	RCAN	✓	0	22.68	25.31	25.59	24.63	24.37	24.23	24.43	23.74	16
	IKC	✓	0	22.69	25.26	25.63	25.21	24.71	24.20	24.39	24.77	8
	Ours	✓	0	24.20	25.10	25.64	25.83	25.48	24.72	25.13	25.78	0.5

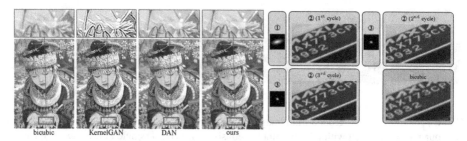

Fig. 5. Left: Comparison of one-shot SISR methods for $\omega = 4$. Right: Results of all cycles for one-shot SISR for an image taken from [35] compared to bicubic upsampling ($\omega = 4$).

Figure 5 (left) contains a visual comparison of our method with bicubic upsampling and KernelGAN for $\omega = 4$ applied to a cartoon from [35], for which no ground truth image exists. Compared to bicubic upsampling, our method clearly retrieves fine details and patterns and retains the cartoonish look. For KernelGAN, we used the best result out of 5, which, however, still exhibits clearly visible artifacts.

In Fig. 5 (right), all images and kernel estimates generated by the proposed technique for $n_L = 3$ and $\omega = 4$ are compared with bicubic upsampling, for which the observation is taken from [35]. Here, the choice $n_G = 3$ (used in the final cycle) turns out to be numerically superior to $n_G = 1$. Interestingly, the computed output images and kernels in the second and third cycle are visually nearly indistinguishable showing that the method already converged.

Note that KernelGAN is not applicable due to the limited observation size. We remark that the mean squared ℓ^2-distance between the downsampled reconstruction using the estimated kernel and the observation is $9.5 \cdot 10^{-8}$, which is impressively low.

5   Conclusions

We introduced a framework for blind SISR based on shared prior learning, in which local image statistics are compared by means of the Wasserstein distance. The unknown kernels are represented by Gabor filters and learned after each application of shared prior learning. In several numerical experiments, we have demonstrated that the kernel estimation is visually accurate even for highly anisotropic kernels. Moreover, for inexact kernel estimates, our proposed method can reliably reconstruct the high-resolution images due to the inclusion of the Wasserstein distance. Small imperfections of the high-resolution images are subsequently removed by the total deep variation regularizer. We emphasize that in many cases we achieve a similar quality with our *blind* method compared to state-of-the-art *non-blind* approaches. Finally, our approach can even be applied as an inference method, which was nicely demonstrated in the case of one-shot SISR.

Funding. This work was supported by the German Research Foundation under Germany's Excellence Strategy - EXC-2047/1 – 390685813 and – EXC2151 – 390873048.

References

1. Agustsson, E., Timofte, R.: NTIRE 2017 challenge on single image super-resolution: dataset and study. In: CVPR (2017)
2. Anwar, S., Barnes, N.: Densely residual Laplacian super-resolution. IEEE Trans. Pattern Anal. Mach. Intell. (2020). https://doi.org/10.1109/TPAMI.2020.3021088
3. Bell-Kligler, S., Shocher, A., Irani, M.: Blind super-resolution kernel estimation using an internal-GAN. In: NIPS, pp. 284–293 (2019)
4. Benamou, J.D., Carlier, G., Cuturi, M., Nenna, L., Peyré, G.: Iterative Bregman projections for regularized transportation problems. SIAM J. Sci. Comput. **37**(2), 1111–1138 (2015). https://doi.org/10.1137/141000439
5. Bredies, K., Kunisch, K., Pock, T.: Total generalized variation. SIAM J. Imaging Sci. **3**(3), 492–526 (2010). https://doi.org/10.1137/090769521
6. Britanak, V., Yip, P.C., Rao, K.: Discrete Cosine and Sine Transforms. Academic Press (2006). https://doi.org/10.1016/b978-012373624-6/50003-5
7. Chambolle, A., Pock, T.: An introduction to continuous optimization for imaging. Acta Numer. **25**, 161–319 (2016)
8. E, W., Han, J., Li, Q.: A mean-field optimal control formulation of deep learning. Res. Math. Sci. **6**(1), 10 (2019). https://doi.org/10.1007/s40687-018-0172-y
9. Effland, A., Kobler, E., Kunisch, K., Pock, T.: Variational networks: an optimal control approach to early stopping variational methods for image restoration. J. Math. Imaging Vision **62**(3), 396–416 (2020). https://doi.org/10.1007/s10851-019-00926-8
10. Greenspan, H.: Super-resolution in medical imaging. Comput. J. **52**(1), 43–63 (2008). https://doi.org/10.1093/comjnl/bxm075
11. Gu, J., Lu, H., Zuo, W., Dong, C.: Blind super-resolution with iterative kernel correction. In: CVPR (2019)
12. Hämarik, U., Kaltenbacher, B., Kangro, U., Resmerita, E.: Regularization by discretization in Banach spaces. Inverse Prob. **32**(3), 035004 (2016). https://doi.org/10.1088/0266-5611/32/3/035004

13. He, K., Zhang, X., Ren, S., Sun, J.: Delving deep into rectifiers: surpassing human-level performance on imageNet classification. In: ICCV, pp. 1026–1034 (2015). https://doi.org/10.1109/ICCV.2015.123

14. Huang, J., Mumford, D.: Statistics of natural images and models. In: CVPR, vol. 1, pp. 541–547 (1999). https://doi.org/10.1109/CVPR.1999.786990

15. Kingma, D.P., Ba, J.L.: ADAM: a method for stochastic optimization. In: ICLR (2015)

16. Kobler, E., Effland, A., Kunisch, K., Pock, T.: Total deep variation for linear inverse problems. In: CVPR (2020)

17. Kobler, E., Effland, A., Kunisch, K., Pock, T.: Total deep variation: a stable regularizer for inverse problems. IEEE Trans. Pattern Anal. Mach. Intell. (2021). https://doi.org/10.1109/TPAMI.2021.3124086

18. Lee, A.B., Pedersen, K.S., Mumford, D.: The nonlinear statistics of high-contrast patches in natural images. Int. J. Comput. Vis. **54**, 83–103 (2003). https://doi.org/10.1023/A:1023705401078

19. Luo, Z., Huang, Y., Li, S., Wang, L., Tan, T.: Unfolding the alternating optimization for blind super resolution. In: Advances in Neural Information Processing Systems 33 (2020)

20. Martin, D., Fowlkes, C., Tal, D., Malik, J.: A database of human segmented natural images and its application to evaluating segmentation algorithms and measuring ecological statistics. In: ICCV, vol. 2, pp. 416–423 (2001)

21. Mumford, D., Gidas, B.: Stochastic models for generic images. Quart. Appl. Math. **59**(1), 85–111 (2001). https://doi.org/10.1090/qam/1811096

22. Peyré, G., Cuturi, M.: Computational optimal transport: with applications to data science. In: Now Foundations and Trends (2019). https://doi.org/10.1561/2200000073

23. Pinetz, T., Kobler, E., Pock, T., Effland, A.: Shared prior learning of energy-based models for image reconstruction. SIAM J. Imaging Sci. **14**(4), 1706–1748 (2021). https://doi.org/10.1137/20M1380016

24. Ronneberger, O., Fischer, P., Brox, T.: U-Net: convolutional networks for biomedical image segmentation. In: Navab, N., Hornegger, J., Wells, W.M., Frangi, A.F. (eds.) MICCAI 2015. LNCS, vol. 9351, pp. 234–241. Springer, Cham (2015). https://doi.org/10.1007/978-3-319-24574-4_28

25. Roth, S., Black, M.J.: Fields of experts. Int. J. Comput. Vis. **82**(2), 205–229 (2009). https://doi.org/10.1007/s11263-008-0197-6

26. Rudin, L.I., Osher, S., Fatemi, E.: Nonlinear total variation based noise removal algorithms. Phys. D **60**(1–4), 259–268 (1992). https://doi.org/10.1016/0167-2789(92)90242-F

27. Santambrogio, F.: Optimal Transport for Applied Mathematicians. PNDETA, vol. 87. Springer, Cham (2015). https://doi.org/10.1007/978-3-319-20828-2

28. Shermeyer, J., Van Etten, A.: The effects of super-resolution on object detection performance in satellite imagery. In: CVPR (2019)

29. Stockert, J.C., Castro, A.B.: Fluorescence Microscopy In Life Sciences. Bentham Science Publishers (2017)

30. Sun, W., Chen, Z.: Learned image downscaling for upscaling using content adaptive resampler. IEEE Trans. Image Process. **29**, 4027–4040 (2020). https://doi.org/10.1109/TIP.2020.2970248

31. Villani, C.: Optimal transport: old and new. Springer, Heidelberg (2009). https://doi.org/10.1007/978-3-540-71050-9

32. Xie, Y., Wang, X., Wang, R., Zha, H.: A fast proximal point method for computing exact Wasserstein distance. In: UAI (2019)

33. Yang, W., Zhang, X., Tian, Y., Wang, W., Xue, J.H., Liao, Q.: Deep learning for single image super-resolution: a brief review. IEEE Trans. Multimedia **21**(12), 3106–3121 (2019). https://doi.org/10.1109/TMM.2019.2919431

34. Yu, J., Fan, Y., Huang, T.: Wide activation for efficient image and video super-resolution. In: BMVC (2019)
35. Zhang, K., Van Gool, L., Timofte, R.: Deep unfolding network for image super-resolution. In: CVPR (2020)
36. Zhang, K., Zuo, W., Gu, S., Zhang, L.: Learning deep CNN denoiser prior for image restoration. In: CVPR (2017)
37. Zhang, Y., Li, K., Li, K., Wang, L., Zhong, B., Fu, Y.: Image super-resolution using very deepresidual channel attention networks. In: ECCV (2018)
38. Zhang, Z., Wang, Z., Lin, Z., Qi, H.: Image super-resolution by neural texture transfer. In: CVPR (2019)
39. Zhao, N., Wei, Q., Basarab, A., Dobigeon, N., Kouamé, D., Tourneret, J.Y.: Fast single image super-resolution using a new analytical solution for $\ell_2 - \ell_2$ problems. IEEE Trans. Image Process. **25**(8), 3683–3697 (2016)
40. Zhu, S.C., Wu, Y., Mumford, D.: Filters, random fields and maximum entropy (FRAME): towards a unified theory for texture modeling. Int. J. Comput. Vis. **27**(2), 107–126 (1998). https://doi.org/10.1023/A:1007925832420

A Bhattacharyya Coefficient-Based Framework for Noise Model-Aware Random Walker Image Segmentation

Dominik Drees[1]ⓘ, Florian Eilers[1]ⓘ, Ang Bian[2]ⓘ, and Xiaoyi Jiang[1(✉)]ⓘ

[1] Faculty of Mathematics and Computer Science, University of Münster, Münster, Germany
xjiang@uni-muenster.de
[2] College of Computer Science, Sichuan University, Chengdu, China

Abstract. One well established method of interactive image segmentation is the random walker algorithm. Considerable research on this family of segmentation methods has been continuously conducted in recent years with numerous applications. These methods are common in using a simple Gaussian weight function which depends on a parameter that strongly influences the segmentation performance. In this work we propose a general framework of deriving weight functions based on probabilistic modeling. This framework can be concretized to cope with virtually any parametric noise model. It eliminates the critical parameter and thus avoids time-consuming parameter search. We derive the specific weight functions for common noise types and show their superior performance on synthetic data as well as different biomedical image data (MRI images from the NYU fastMRI dataset, larvae images acquired with the FIM technique). Our framework could also be used in multiple other applications, e.g., the graph cut algorithm and its extensions.

Keywords: Random walker · Image segmentation · Pixel similarity measure · Noise models

1 Introduction

Interactive image segmentation aims to segment the objects of interest with minimal user input. Despite the remarkable performance achieved by deep learning techniques, interactive segmentation approaches remain attractive. Supervised learning methods require accurate ground truth pixel-level training data, which

---

D. Drees and F. Eilers—These authors contributed equally to this work.

Supplementary Information The online version contains supplementary material available at https://doi.org/10.1007/978-3-031-16788-1_11.

is often expensive and tedious to produce – a problem which interactive image segmentation algorithms (as sophisticated labeling tools) help to mitigate. Supervised learning methods also tend to perform poorly on unseen object classes. Furthermore, in application fields like biomedicine one may also be confronted with the problem of prohibitively small data sets. Therefore, considerable research on interactive segmentation has been continuously conducted in recent years [28,50,52,55].

Random walker is one of the most popular interactive segmentation families [51] since its inception in Grady's seminal work [19]. This method models a 2D or higher dimensional image as a graph and achieves a multi-region segmentation by calculating probabilities that each pixel is connected to the user provided class-specific seed pixels (seeds). Considerable recent developments have been reported for this family of segmentation methods [12,15,20,24,42,49] and numerous applications of random walker segmentation can be found in the literature [10,18,33,44]. In particular, it plays an important role in biomedical imaging. For instance, the recent platform Biomedisa for biomedical image segmentation [31] is fully based on random walker.

Besides user provided seeds, random walker also requires a well-defined weight function for mapping the image information to a graph. Grady [19] used the simple Gaussian weight function, chosen for empirical reasons, which has become common practice and has also been adopted by the recent developments of random walker segmentation [12,15,20,24,42,49]. However, Bian et al. [4,5] showed that the optimal choice for its configurable parameter β highly influences the segmentation performance and depends on the image conditions. The optimal value varies even within rather homogeneous datasets and different regions of the same image. Instead of the simple definition, we propose in this work a general framework of deriving weight functions based on probabilistic modeling. This framework can be concretized to cope with virtually any parametric noise model. This approach avoids the critical parameter. While previous methods on alternative weight functions work for specific noise models (additive Gaussian noise [4] and multiplicative speckle noise [5]), solutions for other noise models and in particular multi-channel images and noise are yet missing. Our work extends the application spectrum of adaptive random walker methods to many domains (e.g., biomedical imaging, remote sensing), where imaging modalities with different noise models are of high importance.

In summary, with this work we *contribute* the following: 1) A general framework for deriving pixel similarity measures for a given noise model and its utilization as a weight function (Sect. 3). 2) Derivations of weight functions for specific noise models using the framework, in particular for Poisson and multivariate Gaussian noise (Sect. 4). 3) Demonstration of on-par or superior performance compared to state of the art (Sect. 5). 4) An implementation of the presented work as an easy-to-use and open source python package available online[1].

---

[1] https://zivgitlab.uni-muenster.de/ag-pria/rw-noise-model.

2   Related Work

There is very little work on weight function for random walker image segmentation. Even most of the recent developments are based on the standard definition. The variant in [45] includes a spatial term (difference of two neighbors) into the weight function that has a minor influence. Freedman [17] proposes a weight function based on per-class density in LUV color space estimated from the colors of seed pixels. As a consequence, semantically different regions in the image are expected to have distinct colors, which is likely not compatible with many (single channel) biomedical images. Cerrone et al. [8] propose a random walker based method with an end-to-end learned weight function. While very noteworthy and interesting theoretically, the need for labeled training data (60% of all available data in their evaluation) drastically reduces the usefulness of this method in practice as this is in direct conflict with the use as a labeling tool itself.

There are two major works we consider as direct prior work for noise model incorporation into random walker weight functions [4,5]. In [4] additive Gaussian noise with constant global variance is assumed and the PDF of the estimated local means' difference is applied as an adaptive weight function. In [5], the signal-dependent local Gaussian model with variable regional variances is assumed for the multiplicative speckle noise (with additive Gaussian noise and Loupas noise as special cases). A statistical T-test based weight function is proposed.

Integration of prior knowledge from the application field in general has been studied for image denoising [13] and motion analysis [14], but also for noise model-guided image segmentation in particular. In [11,32] it is shown that the noise type has an impact in active contours based image segmentation. The authors incorporate knowledge of the underlying noise model in an external energy to improve the results. A number of variational approaches have utilized knowledge about the underlying noise. This is done either by specifically designed data fidelity terms (e.g., for additive and multiplicative noise [2], Poisson noise, additive Gaussian noise and multiplicative speckle noise [9]) or variational frameworks [41,46] with concretization to particular noise models. Our work follows the general strategy of the latter approach and develops such a general framework for random walker segmentation.

3   Framework

As discussed in the introduction, random walker segmentation as introduced by Grady [19] is highly dependent on the choice of its parameter β. In this section we present the general idea of the framework for random walker weight functions (independent of a concrete noise model) that is independent of such parameter usage. After a brief introduction to random walker segmentation this includes the formulation of the weight function and a model for sampling concrete image pixels from the neighborhood of an edge that will be used to define the weight.

3.1 Random Walker Segmentation

An image is defined as an undirected graph $G(V, E)$, where V is the set of nodes corresponding to pixels and E is the set of weighted edges connecting adjacent nodes. The random walker algorithm assigns each unmarked node a per-class probability, corresponding to the probability that a random walker starting in a marked seed reaches this node first. The class with the highest probability is assigned to the node. By partitioning the nodes into V_M (marked seed nodes) and V_U (unmarked nodes), the probabilities $P(V_U)$ for one class can be solved as a combinatorial Dirichlet problem with boundary conditions:

$$P(V_U) = -(L_U)^{-1} B^T P(V_M); \quad \text{with components from } L = \begin{bmatrix} L_M & B \\ B^T & L_U \end{bmatrix} \quad (1)$$

where L is the Laplacian matrix with $L_{\mathcal{X}\mathcal{Y}}$, $\mathcal{X} \neq \mathcal{Y}$, equal to weight $-w_{\mathcal{X}\mathcal{Y}}$ for each edge, $\sum_{\mathcal{Y}} w_{\mathcal{X}\mathcal{Y}}$ for diagonal elements $L_{\mathcal{X}\mathcal{X}}$, and 0 otherwise. A Gaussian weight function (with x/y being the intensity in $\mathcal{X}/\mathcal{Y}$): $w_{\mathcal{X}\mathcal{Y}} = \exp(-\beta(x - y)^2)$ measuring pixel intensity difference with parameter β is applied. The probabilities $P(V_M)$ are set to 1 for the seeds of a particular label and 0 for the rest. This procedure is repeated for each label to obtain the corresponding probabilities $P(V_U)$. Finally, each unmarked node from V_U receives the label with the highest probability among all labels.

3.2 Weight Function

In general, the edge weight function $w_{\mathcal{X}\mathcal{Y}}$ should express a similarity of the two adjacent pixels $\mathcal{X}$ and $\mathcal{Y}$. For this we model the value of a pixel $\mathcal{X}$ as a probability distribution $p(x|\kappa_{\mathcal{X}})$ with parameters $\kappa_{\mathcal{X}}$. The actual pixel values in an image are thus assumed to be drawn from the (per-pixel) distribution. Let X and Y be multi-sets of n samples each, drawn from the distributions of the adjacent pixels $\mathcal{X}$ and $\mathcal{Y}$. We assume $|X|$ to be sufficiently big to estimate $\kappa_{\mathcal{X}}$, which can be ensured by increasing the size of X, see next section. Since we only have one sample per pixel (i.e., the *actual* image value) we assume that pixels in the *neighborhood* are from the same distribution. This assumption is also made in previous work [4,5]. Subsect. 3.3 is concerned with the construction of these neighborhoods. We can estimate the distribution of the parameters $\kappa_{\mathcal{X}}$ given X (and $\kappa_{\mathcal{Y}}$ given Y accordingly) via Bayesian estimation:

$$p(\kappa_{\mathcal{X}}|X) = \frac{p(X|\kappa_{\mathcal{X}})p(\kappa_{\mathcal{X}})}{\int_{P_\kappa} p(X|\kappa)p(\kappa)d\kappa} = \frac{p(\kappa_{\mathcal{X}})\prod_{x \in X} p(x|\kappa_{\mathcal{X}})}{\int_{P_\kappa} p(\kappa)\prod_{x \in X} p(x|\kappa)d\kappa} = \frac{\prod_{x \in X} p(x|\kappa_{\mathcal{X}})}{\int_{P_\kappa} \prod_{x \in X} p(x|\kappa)d\kappa} \quad (2)$$

Here, we first applied Bayes' theorem and then used the fact that all samples in X are independent. In the last step we assumed that κ is uniformly distributed in P_κ, i.e., we assume no further prior knowledge about its distribution within P_κ. This common assumption simplifies the calculations, however, in specific use cases prior knowledge could be incorporated by assuming another (non-uniform) distribution within P_κ. In this form, $p(\kappa_\mathcal{X}|X)$ is easy to apply to many noise models since it only depends on the PDF $p(x|\kappa)$. Given X and Y, we can then define $w_{\mathcal{X}\mathcal{Y}} := S(p(\cdot|X), p(\cdot|Y))$ using a similarity measure S between probability distributions. In this paper, we use the Bhattacharyya coefficient [3] $BC(p(\cdot), q(\cdot)) = \int_P \sqrt{p(r)q(r)}dr$, which is a closed form similarity measure of probability distributions based on their PDF. As illustrated in Fig. 1 it is 0 for non-overlapping PDFs and increases with the amount of overlap up to a value of 1. It thus enables graphical interpretation of the weight function and it is easily applicable to any noise model that has a PDF. Using Eq. 2 it allows for simplifications:

$$
\begin{aligned}
w_{\mathcal{X}\mathcal{Y}} = BC(p(\cdot|X), p(\cdot|Y)) &= \int_{P_\kappa} \sqrt{p(\kappa|X)p(\kappa|Y)}d\kappa \\
&= \int_{P_\kappa} \sqrt{\frac{\prod_{x\in X} p(x|\kappa) \prod_{y\in Y} p(y|\kappa)}{\int_{P_\kappa} \prod_{x\in X} p(x|\tilde\kappa)d\tilde\kappa \int_{P_\kappa} \prod_{y\in Y} p(y|\tilde\kappa)d\tilde\kappa}} d\kappa \\
&= \frac{\int_{P_\kappa} \sqrt{\prod_{x\in X} p(x|\kappa) \prod_{y\in Y} p(y|\kappa)}d\kappa}{\sqrt{\int_{P_\kappa} \prod_{x\in X} p(x|\kappa)d\kappa \int_{P_\kappa} \prod_{y\in Y} p(y|\kappa)d\kappa}}
\end{aligned}
\tag{3}
$$

The final result is only dependent on the pixel-value PDF of the noise model. The integrals in the numerator and denominator are quite similar and can be solved in similar fashion in practice (see Sect. 4).

3.3   Neighborhood

In this section we describe how to determine a fitting *neighborhood* as needed in Subsect. 3.2. In [5] Bian et al. proposes a variation of a well proven (e.g., [53]) optimal neighborhood selection schema which we also adopt here: To determine the optimal neighborhood of $\mathcal{X}$, let $X^1, \ldots, X^{(2k+1)^2}$ be the $(2k+1)^2$ quadratic neighborhoods including $\mathcal{X}$. The optimal neighborhood can now be found as the neighborhood that maximizes the probability of having sampled the pixel value x of $\mathcal{X}$. Formally, this is described as:

$$
X = \operatorname*{argmax}_{N\in\{X^1,\ldots,X^{(2k+1)^2}\}} p(x|N),
\tag{4}
$$

where $p(\cdot|N)$ is the PDF of the assumed noise model with parameters estimated from the pixel intensities in N. It should be noted that the neighborhoods X and Y of pixels $\mathcal{X}$ and $\mathcal{Y}$ can overlap. In order to ensure statistical independence of samples in X and Y, pixels in the overlap have to be assigned to either X or Y. In [5] it is proposed to assign pixels from the overlap based on the Euclidean distance to one of the center pixels. However, this ultimately leads to a non-symmetric weight function. Instead, we sort and divide using the difference of the Euclidean distances to *both* center pixels, which results in a dividing line orthogonal to the graph edge (see Fig. 2). Ties are resolved deterministically.

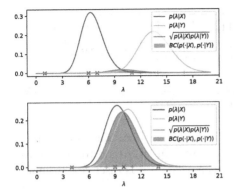

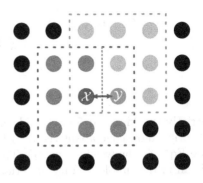

Fig. 1. Illustration of the behavior of the Bhattacharyya coefficient as a similarity measure for weight function applied to two measurement sets under Poisson noise.

Fig. 2. Solve overlap of neighborhoods by sorting and dividing by difference of Euclidean distance to both pixels. Pixels $\mathcal{X}$, $\mathcal{Y}$ are to be compared, blue/red dashed lines show respective selected neighborhoods. (Color figure online)

4 Application to Concrete Noise Models

In this section we apply the framework presented in Sect. 3 to three noise models relevant to various imaging modalities and obtain closed form solutions. We choose Poisson noise as it occurs in many imaging procedures used in biology [40, 47], as well as Gaussian noise - with two different configurations: fixed variance over the whole image and variable variance per image region - which is common in many images including medically relevant techniques like MRI and CT. For Poisson noise this is the first derivation of a noise model specific weight function for random walker, whereas the two versions of Gaussian noise model have been considered in [4,5], respectively. See supplementary material for derivations in more detail.

4.1 Poisson Noise

In this subsection we assume an image that is affected by Poisson noise (also called "shot noise"), which occurs, for example, as an effect of photon or electron counting in imaging systems (e.g., fluorescence microscopy [47], positron emission tomography [43], low dose CT [29]). In this model the measured pixel values $x, y \in \mathbb{N}$ are drawn from a Poisson distribution with unknown parameter $\kappa = \lambda$, which corresponds to the true pixel value. We assume the prior distribution of λ to be uniform in $P = (0, a)$ for some sufficiently large value a. For convenience, we define $\tilde{X} = \sum_{x \in X} x$ and $\tilde{Y} = \sum_{y \in Y} y$. Then, using Eq. 3, we obtain:

$$w_{XY} = BC(p(\cdot|X), p(\cdot|Y)) = \frac{\sqrt{\int_P \prod_{x \in X} \frac{e^{-\lambda}\lambda^x}{x!} \prod_{y \in Y} \frac{e^{-\lambda}\lambda^y}{y!} d\lambda}}{\sqrt{\int_P \prod_{x \in X} \frac{e^{-\lambda}\lambda^x}{x!} d\lambda \int_P \prod_{y \in Y} \frac{e^{-\lambda}\lambda^y}{y!} d\lambda}}$$

$$= \frac{\Gamma(\frac{\tilde{X}+\tilde{Y}}{2}+1)}{\sqrt{\Gamma(\tilde{X}+1)\Gamma(\tilde{Y}+1)}} \tag{5}$$

Strictly speaking, Eq. 5 only holds asymptotically for $a \to \infty$. Since we assume no prior knowledge about the distribution of λ, we can let a tend to infinity to use Eq. 5 as the weight function. The convergence of Eq. 5 is discussed in more detail in the supplementary materials.

4.2 Multivariate Gaussian Noise with Constant Covariance

In this subsection we assume an m-channel image with concrete pixel values $x, y \in \mathbb{R}^m$. The true image values are perturbed by additive Gaussian noise and are thus modeled by a Gaussian PDF with (unknown) parameter $\kappa = \mu \in \mathbb{R}^m$, which also corresponds to the true pixel value. The covariance matrix C is assumed to be constant and known for the whole image. In practice, C can be estimated from a small number of samples from the image [6]. This noise model applies, for example, in complex valued MRI images [22]. Further, we assume that μ is priorly uniformly distributed in $P = (-a, a)^m$ for some sufficiently large value a. It should be noted that the special case $m = 1$ is the setting that is assumed in prior work [4]. Starting from Eq. 2 we obtain:

$$p(\mu|X) = \frac{\prod_{x \in X} \frac{1}{\sqrt{(2\pi)^m \det(C)}} \exp(-\frac{1}{2}(x-\mu)^T C^{-1}(x-\mu))}{\int_P \prod_{x \in X} \frac{1}{\sqrt{(2\pi)^m \det(C)}} \exp(-\frac{1}{2}(x-\tilde{\mu})^T C^{-1}(x-\tilde{\mu}))d\tilde{\mu}}$$

$$= \frac{\exp(-\frac{1}{2}\sum_{x \in X}(x-\mu)^T C^{-1}(x-\mu))}{\int_P \exp(-\frac{1}{2}\sum_{x \in X}(x-\tilde{\mu})^T C^{-1}(x-\tilde{\mu}))d\tilde{\mu}}$$

$$= \frac{1}{\sqrt{(2\pi)^m \det(\frac{C}{n})}} \exp\left(-\frac{1}{2}(\mu - \sum_{x \in X}\frac{x}{n})^T \left(\frac{C}{n}\right)^{-1}(\mu - \sum_{x \in X}\frac{x}{n})\right) \tag{6}$$

Similar to Eq. 5, this equation only holds asymptotically for $a \to \infty$, but we can choose a large enough for arbitrary precision. Equation 6 shows that $p(\mu|X)$ is simply the density function of a normal distribution with mean $\sum_{x \in X}\frac{x}{n} =: \bar{X}$ and covariance matrix $\frac{C}{n}$ (and $p(\mu|Y)$ accordingly). As shown in [37] the Bhattacharyya coefficient is then:

$$w_{XY} = BC(p(\cdot|X), p(\cdot|Y)) \propto \exp\left(-\frac{1}{8}(\bar{X}-\bar{Y})^T \left(\frac{C}{n}\right)^{-1}(\bar{X}-\bar{Y})\right) \tag{7}$$

4.3   Gaussian Noise with Signal-Dependent Variance

In this subsection we assume additive Gaussian noise on single channel images where, however, σ^2 differs between image regions (in contrast to Subsect. 4.2 which assumes a global, constant $C = \sigma^2$ for m = 1). Thus, pixel values are modeled by $x = \mu_{\chi} + \mathcal{N}(0, \sigma_{\chi}^2)$. A special case is Loupas noise, where $\sigma_{\chi}^2 = \mu_{\chi}\sigma^2$ for some fixed (global) σ^2. It applies, for example, to speckled SAR and medical ultrasound images [5,46] Thus, we have to estimate μ and σ^2 simultaneously and set κ from Eq. 3 to be (μ, σ^2).

To solve Eq. 3 we set $P_a := (0, a) \times (-a, a)$ (again, a sufficiently large) and assume the prior distribution of (μ, σ^2) to be uniform. We then have to calculate the integrals in the enumerator and denominator of Eq. 3, which can be reformulated to a similar form and then can be calculated analogously:

$$\int_P \left(\frac{1}{\sqrt{2\pi\sigma^2}}\right)^n \exp\left(-\frac{1}{2\sigma^2}\sum_{x \in X}(x - \mu)^2\right) d(\mu, \sigma^2)$$

$$= \frac{1}{\sqrt{n}}\left(\frac{1}{2\pi}\right)^{n-1}\Gamma\left(\frac{n-3}{2}\right)\left(\frac{1}{4n}\sum_{x_1,x_2 \in X}(x_1 - x_2)^2\right)^{\frac{-n+3}{2}} \quad (8)$$

$$\int_P \left(\frac{1}{\sqrt{2\pi\sigma^2}}\right)^n \exp\left(-\frac{1}{4\sigma^2}\sum_{z \in X \cup Y}(z - \mu)^2\right) d(\mu, \sigma^2)$$

$$= \frac{1}{\sqrt{n}}\left(\frac{1}{2\pi}\right)^{n-1}\Gamma\left(\frac{n-3}{2}\right)\left(\frac{1}{16n}\sum_{z_1,z_2 \in X \cup Y}(z_1 - z_2)^2\right)^{\frac{-n+3}{2}} \quad (9)$$

Inserting these equations into Eq. 3 and canceling the fraction yields:

$$w_{\chi y} = BC(p(\cdot|X), p(\cdot|Y)) = \left(4\frac{\sqrt{\sum_{x_1,x_2 \in X}(x_1 - x_2)^2 \sum_{y_1,y_2 \in Y}(y_1 - y_2)^2}}{\sum_{z_1,z_2 \in X \cup Y}(z_1 - z_2)^2}\right)^{\frac{n-3}{2}}$$

$$= \left(\frac{\sqrt{Var(X)Var(Y)}}{Var(X \cup Y)}\right)^{\frac{n-3}{2}} \quad (10)$$

5   Experimental Results

We conduct three experiments to compare our suitable methods with Grady [19] and the noise model based approaches of Bian et al. [4,5]: We demonstrate differences in seed propagation on synthetic data under different noise conditions and report results on real world image data (FIM [40] and MRI [26]). To compare to Grady [19], we use two approaches: 1) We search for the on average best β over the whole dataset. This mimics the behavior of a user determining a "good" value for β initially on a some images. 2) We also report the results where β is tuned optimally for every single image and label configuration, which is unrealistic, but serves as a performance upper bound. Since the overall quality of all segmentation algorithms is already quite high our improvements are relatively minor. However, we want to stress that these experiments are supposed to 1) show that performance is (at least) retained when comparing to the baseline [19] while completely avoiding the parameter search and 2) make noise model based approaches applicable to more than just 1D-Gaussian noise [4,5].

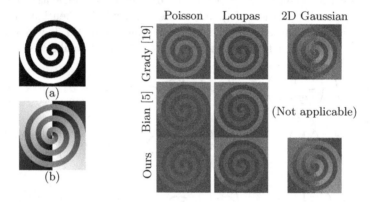

Fig. 3. Illustration of behavior on spiral synthetic data with mediocre noise level ($\lambda_0/\lambda_1 = 32/64$, $\sigma = 0.2$ (Loupas), $\sigma = 0.3$ (Gaussian)). (a) Ground truth image for all cases; (b) Phase of the uncorrupted 2D vector-valued image, discontinuities are due to phase wraps, the magnitude was set to be constant at 1.

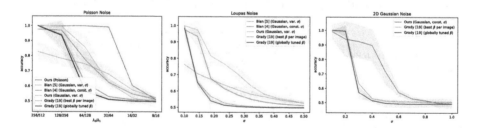

Fig. 4. Accuracy of applicable methods on synthetic image for Poisson/Loupas/2D Gaussian noise (left/center/right). Lines show mean, shadows show standard deviation.

5.1   Results on Synthetic Data

To evaluate how class probabilities propagate from an initial seed under noisy conditions, we follow Grady's idea [19] and generate a spiral structure, see Fig. 3.

For scalar images, the two regions simply differ in intensity. For the (2D) vector-valued image the two regions correspond to vector fields defining a flow into and out of the spiral, respectively. The magnitude of all vectors is unity. For both regions, one seed is placed at the central start of the spiral. In a total of three noise scenarios, the base images are perturbed by Poisson and Loupas noise (scalar) as well as uncorrelated, symmetric 2D-multivariate Gaussian noise (vector image) which can also be interpreted as complex Gaussian noise as it would be present in MRI images. For each of the three scenarios, applicable weight functions are applied and 100 realizations of the random noise for each noise type and each noise level were evaluated. For Poisson noise, we modulate the noise level by decreasing the mean intensity of the two image regions (λ_0, λ_1) from (256, 512) to (8, 16), which reduces the signal-to-noise ratio. For Loupas noise, the region intensity were set to 0.1 and 1 and σ varied between 0.1 and 0.5. For the vector images the uncorrelated, symmetric 2D-multivariate Gaussian noise σ was set in $[0, 1]$. Figure 3 examplarily shows the results on images with intermediate noise levels, while Fig. 4 shows quantitative results. Accuracy is a suitable measure in this scenario since the two classes are of equal size.

All three scenarios show that our method with the suitable noise model leads to superior performance, which gets beat substantially only in one scenario ([19] for low level of multivariate Gaussian noise). This however still has the drawback of having to choose the correct parameter β and it drops off at a noise level of roughly $\sigma = 0.3$. For Poisson noise, the hardest competitors are [5] and our method for variable Gaussian noise, which is unsurprising, since Poisson noise can be approximated by Gaussian noise with signal-dependent σ. [5] also works well for strong Loupas noise, which is also the noise model it was designed for, however still falls short to the proposed method at all noise levels.

5.2 Results on Real World Data

For the following real world data evaluation we employ an automatic incremental seed placement strategy [34]: Initially, all connected components of individual classes are assigned a first seed point at their center. Then, based on an intermediate result of the method to be evaluated, additional seeds are placed for the class with the worst Dice score in the largest misclassified region. This allows observation of 1) mean segmentation quality for a given number of seeds and 2) the required number of seeds to achieve a specific quality. Quality measurement for the following multi-class problems is done using the Variation of Information (VOI) [35] and Adapted Rand Error (ARAND). Both produce good results even in the presence of class imbalance. VOI measures the mutual information of the two multi-class segmentations with 0 describing full agreement and higher scores increasing disagreement. ARAND is defined as one minus the Adjusted Rand Index (ARI) [39], which measures if pixel pairs are labeled accordingly in the segmentations. It is normalized to be 0 for random and 1 for perfectly matching segmentations, meaning ARI < 0 ($\Rightarrow$ ARAND > 1) is possible for worse-than-random segmentations. As an intuitive explanation, consider that a doubling of one minus the (non-adjusted) Rand Index (RI) describes a doubling of mislabeled pixels. For ARAND the effect is similar, but scores are adjusted for class imbalance. The scores in the examples in Fig. 6 and Fig. 7 are given to further build intuition.

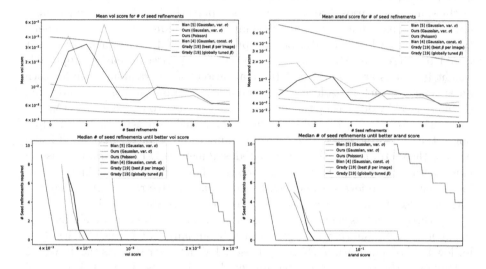

Fig. 5. FIM Larvae dataset experiments: Mean VOI/ARAND scores after placing n additional seeds (top) and median number of additional seeds required to achieve a specific VOI/ARAND score (bottom). Seeds were set as explained in Subsect. 5.2.

FIM Larvae Images. The FIM larvae dataset consists of 21 images of Drosophila Melanogaster larvae acquired by the FIM technique [40] where Poisson noise can be assumed. The hand labeled ground truth masks consist of the background and up to five foreground classes: one per larva. The images and corresponding ground truth masks are available online[2].

The results in Fig. 5 show that the proposed weight function under the Poisson model outperforms all competitor methods. Notably, it shows better scores without additional seeds than other methods achieve even with up to 10 additional seeds (see bottom row). Other weight functions tend to either undersegment (Grady [19], Bian et al. [5]) or over-segment (ours with variable variance Gaussian model) the larvae (see example in Fig. 6).

FastMRI Dataset. Image data for this dataset were obtained from the NYU fastMRI Initiative database [26,54] (publicly available at: fastmri.med.nyu.edu), where a listing of NYU fastMRI investigators, which provided data but did not contribute to the work in any other way, can also be found. The complex valued k-space single coil knee data was converted into the complex image space by inverse Fourier transform. 100 images were hand labeled into four classes: upper bone, lower bone, knee tissue, and background. The resulting complex image

---

[2] https://uni-muenster.sciebo.de/s/DK9F0f6p5ppsWXC.

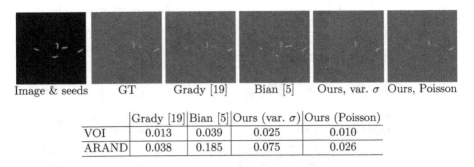

Image & seeds   GT   Grady [19]   Bian [5]   Ours, var. σ Ours, Poisson

	Grady [19]	Bian [5]	Ours (var. σ)	Ours (Poisson)
VOI	0.013	0.039	0.025	0.010
ARAND	0.038	0.185	0.075	0.026

Fig. 6. Qualitative results of FIM Larvae dataset experiments with initial seeds and class maps overlaid on top of the original image. Quantitative results for the shown images are reported in table. For Grady the best β for this image was selected.

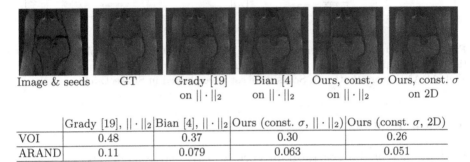

Image & seeds   GT   Grady [19] on $\|\cdot\|_2$ Bian [4] on $\|\cdot\|_2$ Ours, const. σ on $\|\cdot\|_2$ Ours, const. σ on 2D

	Grady [19], $\|\cdot\|_2$	Bian [4], $\|\cdot\|_2$	Ours (const. σ, $\|\cdot\|_2$)	Ours (const. σ, 2D)
VOI	0.48	0.37	0.30	0.26
ARAND	0.11	0.079	0.063	0.051

Fig. 7. Qualitative results of fastMRI dataset experiments with ten additional seeds and class maps overlaid on top of the original image. Quantitative results for the shown images are reported in table. For Grady the best β for this image was selected.

(isomorphic to 2D vector image) can be processed as-is by Grady's method and the proposed weight function for the multivariate Gaussian case. Bian's methods, that only operate on scalar value images, are applied to the magnitude images.

Overall, the mean scores imply that in this specific case the proposed method for the appropriate image model (2D Gaussian noise) performs roughly on par with competing methods by Bian et al. [4,5] operating on the magnitude image (Fig. 8), which suggests that the practice of approximating the Rician distribution in MRI magnitude images with a Gaussian [1] works well in practice. Notably, our method benefits from the 2D information compared to the magnitude-variant, while Grady's method benefits only in some cases and performs considerably worse overall.

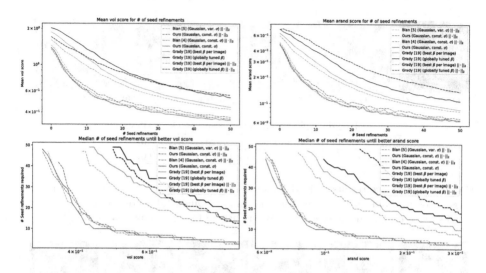

Fig. 8. fastMRI dataset experiments: Mean VOI/ARAND scores after placing n additional seeds (top) and median number of additional seeds required to achieve a specific VOI/ARAND score (bottom). Seeds were set as explained in Subsect. 5.2.

6   Conclusion

We have presented a general framework to derive noise model specific weight functions for random walker segmentation. Under the assumption of a known noise model, our framework enables the derivation of a weight function based on the Bhattacharyya coefficient, which takes the pixel distribution into account and is thus robust against noise. We have derived the specific weight functions for Poisson and Gaussian noise with global and region-specific variance and show their suitability in the segmentation of synthetic as well as real world data.

Our method may further be applied to other domains by computing the explicit weight functions in Eq. 3. Examples include magnitude images with Rician noise [1], raw images of digital imaging sensors with Poissonian-Gaussian noise [16], SAR images with speckle noise modeled by Gamma, Weibull or Fisher distributions [30,48]. Additionally, extensions of the random walker algorithm (e.g. random walker with restarts [20,25], non-local random walker [49]) can easily be incorporated into our framework. Applications beyond segmentation could also benefit from the improved weight function, such as random walker for visual tracking [27], target detection [38], and saliency detection [23].

Since the main contribution of this work is the definition and derivation of a similarity measure for pixel values in the presence of noise, this similarity measure and the related Hellinger distance function [21] can be used in other methods, e.g. graph cut algorithm [7], live wire segmentation [36] and extensions.

Acknowledgements. We thank qubeto GmbH and Julian Bigge for providing the FIM larvae images and Jiaqi Zhang for her support with data annotations. This work was partially funded by the Deutsche Forschungsgemeinschaft (DFG) – CRC 1450 – 431460824. Florian Eilers is a member of CiM-IMPRS, the joint graduate school of the Cells-in-Motion Interfaculty Centre, University of Münster, Germany and the International Max Planck Research School - Molecular Biomedicine, Münster, Germany.

References

1. Aja-Fernández, S., Vegas-Sánchez-Ferrero, G.: Statistical Analysis of Noise in MRI - Modeling, Filtering and Estimation. Springer, Cham (2016). https://doi.org/10.1007/978-3-319-39934-8

2. Ali, H., Rada, L., Badshah, N.: Image segmentation for intensity inhomogeneity in presence of high noise. IEEE Trans. Image Process. **27**(8), 3729–3738 (2018)

3. Bhattacharyya, A.: On a measure of divergence between two multinomial populations. Sankhyā Indian J. Stat. 401–406 (1946)

4. Bian, A., Jiang, X.: Statistical modeling based adaptive parameter setting for random walk segmentation. In: Blanc-Talon, J., Distante, C., Philips, W., Popescu, D., Scheunders, P. (eds.) ACIVS 2016. LNCS, vol. 10016, pp. 698–710. Springer, Cham (2016). https://doi.org/10.1007/978-3-319-48680-2_61

5. Bian, A., Jiang, X.: T-test based adaptive random walk segmentation under multiplicative speckle noise model. In: Chen, C.-S., Lu, J., Ma, K.-K. (eds.) ACCV 2016, Part II. LNCS, vol. 10117, pp. 570–582. Springer, Cham (2017). https://doi.org/10.1007/978-3-319-54427-4_41

6. Bibby, J.M., Mardia, K.V., Kent, J.T.: Multivariate Analysis. Academic Press, London (1979)

7. Boykov, Y., Jolly, M.-P.: Interactive organ segmentation using graph cuts. In: Delp, S.L., DiGoia, A.M., Jaramaz, B. (eds.) MICCAI 2000. LNCS, vol. 1935, pp. 276–286. Springer, Heidelberg (2000). https://doi.org/10.1007/978-3-540-40899-4_28

8. Cerrone, L., Zeilmann, A., Hamprecht, F.A.: End-to-end learned random walker for seeded image segmentation. In: Proceedings of the of CVPR, pp. 12559–12568 (2019)

9. Chen, Q., He, C.: Variational segmentation model for images with intensity inhomogeneity and poisson noise. EURASIP J. Image Video Process. **2013**(1), 1–11 (2013)

10. Cheng, D.C., Chi, J.H., Yang, S.N., Liu, S.H.: Organ contouring for lung cancer patients with a seed generation scheme and random walks. Sensors **20**(17), 4823 (2020)

11. Chesnaud, C., Refregier, P., Boulet, V.: Statistical region snake-based segmentation adapted to different physical noise models. IEEE Trans. PAMI **21**(11), 1145–1157 (1999)

12. Cui, B., Xie, X., Ma, X., Ren, G., Ma, Y.: Superpixel-based extended random walker for hyperspectral image classification. IEEE Trans. Geosci. Remote Sens. **56**(6), 3233–3243 (2018)

13. Darbon, J., Meng, T., Resmerita, E.: On Hamilton-Jacobi PDEs and image denoising models with certain nonadditive noise. J. Math. Imaging Vis. **64**(4), 408–441 (2022)

14. Dawood, M., Gigengack, F., Jiang, X., Schäfers, K.: A mass conservation-based optical flow method for cardiac motion correction in 3D-PET. Med. Phys. **40**(1), 012505 (2013)

15. Drees, D., Eilers, F., Jiang, X.: Hierarchical random walker segmentation for large volumetric biomedical images. IEEE Trans. Image Process. **31**, 4431–4446 (2022)
16. Foi, A., Trimeche, M., Katkovnik, V., Egiazarian, K.: Practical Poissonian-Gaussian noise modeling and fitting for single-image raw-data. IEEE Trans. Image Process. **17**(10), 1737–1754 (2008)
17. Freedman, D.: An improved image graph for semi-automatic segmentation. SIViP **6**(4), 533–545 (2012)
18. Gerlein-Safdi, C., Ruf, C.S.: A CYGNSS-based algorithm for the detection of inland waterbodies. Geophys. Res. Lett. **46**(21), 12065–12072 (2019)
19. Grady, L.: Random walks for image segmentation. IEEE Trans. PAMI **28**(11), 1768–1783 (2006)
20. Ham, B., Min, D., Sohn, K.: A generalized random walk with restart and its application in depth up-sampling and interactive segmentation. IEEE Trans. Image Process. **22**(7), 2574–2588 (2013)
21. Hellinger, E.: Neue Begründung der Theorie quadratischer Formen von unendlichvielen Veränderlichen. J. für die reine und angewandte Mathematik **1909**(136), 210–271 (1909)
22. Henkelman, R.M.: Measurement of signal intensities in the presence of noise in MR images. Med. Phys. **12**(2), 232–233 (1985)
23. Jian, M., et al.: Saliency detection based on background seeds by object proposals and extended random walk. J. Vis. Commun. Image Represent. **57**, 202–211 (2018)
24. Kang, X., Zhu, L., Ming, A.: Dynamic random walk for superpixel segmentation. IEEE Trans. Image Process. **29**, 3871–3884 (2020)
25. Kim, T.H., Lee, K.M., Lee, S.U.: Generative image segmentation using random walks with restart. In: Forsyth, D., Torr, P., Zisserman, A. (eds.) ECCV 2008. LNCS, vol. 5304, pp. 264–275. Springer, Heidelberg (2008). https://doi.org/10.1007/978-3-540-88690-7_20
26. Knoll, F., et al.: fastMRI: a publicly available raw k-space and DICOM dataset of knee images for accelerated MR image reconstruction using machine learning. Radiol. Artif. Intell. **2**(1), e190007 (2020)
27. Li, X., Han, Z., Wang, L., Lu, H.: Visual tracking via random walks on graph model. IEEE Trans. Cybernet. **46**(9), 2144–2155 (2015)
28. Li, Z., Chen, Q., Koltun, V.: Interactive image segmentation with latent diversity. In: Proceedings of CVPR, pp. 577–585 (2018)
29. Lu, H., Hsiao, I.T., Li, X., Liang, Z.: Noise properties of low-dose CT projections and noise treatment by scale transformations. In: IEEE Nuclear Science Symposium Conference Record (Cat. No.01CH37310), vol. 3, pp. 1662–1666 (2001)
30. Luo, S., Sarabandi, K., Tong, L., Guo, S.: An improved fuzzy region competition-based framework for the multiphase segmentation of SAR images. IEEE Trans. Geosci. Remote Sens. **58**(4), 2457–2470 (2020)
31. Lösel, P.D., et al.: Introducing biomedisa as an open-source online platform for biomedical image segmentation. Nat. Commun. **11**, 5577 (2020)
32. Martin, P., Réfrégier, P., Goudail, F., Guérault, F.: Influence of the noise model on level set active contour segmentation. IEEE Trans. PAMI **26**(6), 799–803 (2004)
33. Mathewlynn, S., Collins, S.: Volume and vascularity: using ultrasound to unlock the secrets of the first trimester placenta. Placenta **84**, 32–36 (2019)
34. McGuinness, K., O'Connor, N.E.: Toward automated evaluation of interactive segmentation. Comput. Vis. Image Underst. **115**(6), 868–884 (2011)
35. Meilă, M.: Comparing clusterings by the variation of information. In: Schölkopf, B., Warmuth, M.K. (eds.) COLT-Kernel 2003. LNCS (LNAI), vol. 2777, pp. 173–187. Springer, Heidelberg (2003). https://doi.org/10.1007/978-3-540-45167-9_14

36. Mortensen, E.N., Morse, B., Barrett, W., Udupa, J.: Adaptive boundary detection using "live-wire" two-dimensional dynamic programming. Comput. Cardiol., 635 (1992)

37. Nielsen, F., Boltz, S.: The Burbea-Rao and Bhattacharyya centroids. IEEE Trans. Inf. Theory **57**(8), 5455–5466 (2011)

38. Qin, Y., Bruzzone, L., Gao, C., Li, B.: Infrared small target detection based on facet kernel and random walker. IEEE Trans. Geosci. Remote Sens. **57**(9), 7104–7118 (2019)

39. Rand, W.M.: Objective criteria for the evaluation of clustering methods. J. Am. Stat. Assoc. **66**(336), 846–850 (1971)

40. Risse, B., et al.: FIM, a novel FTIR-based imaging method for high throughput locomotion analysis. PLoS ONE **8**(1), e53963 (2013)

41. Sawatzky, A., Tenbrinck, D., Jiang, X., Burger, M.: A variational framework for region-based segmentation incorporating physical noise models. J. Math. Imaging Vis. **47**(3), 179–209 (2013)

42. Shen, J., Du, Y., Wang, W., Li, X.: Lazy random walks for superpixel segmentation. IEEE Trans. Image Process. **23**(4), 1451–1462 (2014)

43. Shepp, L.A., Vardi, Y.: Maximum likelihood reconstruction for emission tomography. IEEE Trans. Med. Imag. **1**(2), 113–122 (1982)

44. Shi, Z., et al.: Many is better than one: an integration of multiple simple strategies for accurate lung segmentation in CT images. Biomed. Res. Int. **2016**, 1480423 (2016)

45. Sinop, A.K., Grady, L.: A seeded image segmentation framework unifying graph cuts and random walker which yields a new algorithm. In: Proceedings of ICCV, pp. 1–8 (2007)

46. Tenbrinck, D., Jiang, X.: Image segmentation with arbitrary noise models by solving minimal surface problems. Pattern Recogn. **48**(11), 3293–3309 (2015)

47. Vonesch, C., Aguet, F., Vonesch, J.L., Unser, M.: The colored revolution of bioimaging. IEEE Signal Process. Mag. **23**(3), 20–31 (2006)

48. Wang, F., Wu, Y., Li, M., Zhang, P., Zhang, Q.: Adaptive hybrid conditional random field model for SAR image segmentation. IEEE Trans. Geosci. Remote Sens. **55**(1), 537–550 (2017)

49. Wang, L., Li, M., Fang, X., Nappi, M., Wan, S.: Improving random walker segmentation using a nonlocal bipartite graph. Biomed. Signal Process. Control **71**, 103154 (2022)

50. Wang, T., Qi, S., Yang, J., Ji, Z., Sun, Q., Ge, Q.: Interactive image segmentation based on label pair diffusion. IEEE Trans. Industr. Inform. **17**(1), 135–146 (2021)

51. Wang, Z., Guo, L., Wang, S., Chen, L., Wang, H.: Review of random walk in image processing. Arch. Comput. Methods Eng. **26**, 17–34 (2019)

52. Xu, J., et al.: Scribble-supervised semantic segmentation inference. In: Proceedings of ICCV, pp. 15354–15363 (2021)

53. Yokoya, N., Levine, M.D.: Range image segmentation based on differential geometry: a hybrid approach. IEEE Trans. PAMI **11**(6), 643–649 (1989)

54. Zbontar, J., et al.: fastMRI: an open dataset and benchmarks for accelerated MRI. arXiv:1811.08839 (2018)

55. Zhang, S., Liew, J.H., Wei, Y., Wei, S., Zhao, Y.: Interactive object segmentation with inside-outside guidance. In: Proceedings of CVPR, pp. 12231–12241 (2020)

Optimizing Edge Detection for Image Segmentation with Multicut Penalties

Steffen Jung[1]([⊠])[ID], Sebastian Ziegler[2], Amirhossein Kardoost[2][ID],
and Margret Keuper[1,3][ID]

[1] Max Planck Institute for Informatics, Saarland Informatics Campus, Saarbrücken,
Germany
steffen.jung@mpi-inf.mpg.de
[2] University of Mannheim, Mannheim, Germany
[3] University of Siegen, Siegen, Germany

Abstract. The Minimum Cost Multicut Problem (MP) is a popular
way for obtaining a graph decomposition by optimizing binary edge
labels over edge costs. While the formulation of a MP from independently estimated costs per edge is highly flexible and intuitive, solving
the MP is NP-hard and time-expensive. As a remedy, recent work proposed to predict edge probabilities with awareness of potential conflicts
by incorporating cycle constraints in the prediction process. We argue
that such formulation, while providing a first step towards end-to-end
learnable edge weights, is suboptimal, since it is built upon a loose relaxation of the MP. We therefore propose an adaptive CRF that allows to
progressively consider more violated constraints and, in consequence, to
issue solutions with higher validity. Experiments on the BSDS500 benchmark for natural image segmentation as well as on electron microscopic
recordings show that our approach yields more precise edge detection
and image segmentation.

1 Introduction

Image Segmentation is the task of partitioning an image into multiple disjoint
components such that each component is a meaningful part of the image. While
there are many different approaches for image segmentation [6], formulations
based on the Minimum Cost Multicut Problem (MP) [15,18], also called Correlation Clustering [9], were very successful in the past [3,10,23,31]. In this
formulation, the number of components is unknown beforehand and no bias is
assumed in terms of component sizes. The resulting segmentation is only determined by an input graph [31] built upon image pixels or superpixels, for which
edge features can be generated by an edge detector such as Convolutional Neural
Networks (CNNs) that predict edge probabilities (see Fig. 1 for examples).

A feasible solution to the MP decomposes the graph into disjoint subgraphs
via a *binary* edge labeling. The decomposition is enforced by cycle consistency
constraints in general graphs. If a path exists between two nodes where the direct
edge between both is cut, then this constraint is violated. [42] introduced relaxed

B. Andres et al. (Eds.): DAGM GCPR 2022, LNCS 13485, pp. 182–197, 2022.
https://doi.org/10.1007/978-3-031-16788-1_12

(a) Original Image   (b) RCF   (c) RCF-basic-CRF (d) RCF-adaptive-CRF

Fig. 1. (a) Example BSDS500 [7] test image, (b) the edge map produced with the RCF edge detector [37], (c) the edge map by RCF-CRF using the basic CRF (our result), and (d) the edge map from RCF-CRF using our adaptive CRF (our result). The adaptive CRF promotes closed contours and removes trailing edges.

cycle constraints, i.e. constraints evaluated on non-binary network predictions, as higher-order potentials in a Conditional Random Field (CRF) to allow for end-to-end training of graph-based human pose estimation. By doing so, cycle constraint violations become a supervision signal for pose tracking. We transfer this approach to image segmentation, where such constraints enforce that object contours are closed. Yet, we observe that optimizing non-binary network predictions instead of binary edge labels only leads to few additionally closed contours. This is consistent with prior works on linear program multicut solvers which show that relaxations of the cycle constraints to non-binary edge labels are too loose in practice [23]. In the CRF formulation, we propose to alleviate this issue by enforcing "more binary" (i.e. closer to 0 or 1) edge predictions that lead to less violated cycle constraints after discretization. Our contributions are twofold. We are the first to address learnable boundary driven image segmentation using multicut constraints. To this end, we combine a CRF with the neural edge detection model Richer Convolutional Features (RCF) by [37] to design an end-to-end trainable architecture that inputs the original image and produces a graph with learnable edge probabilities optimized by the CRF. Secondly, we propose an approach that progressively uses "closer to binary" boundary estimates in the optimization of the CRF model by [42] and thus resolves progressively more boundary conflicts. In consequence, the end-to-end trained network yields more and more certain predictions throughout the training process while reducing the number of violated constraints. We show that this approach yields improved results for edge detection and segmentation on the BSDS500 benchmark [7] and on neuronal structures [8]. An example result is given in Fig. 1. Compared to the plain RCF model as well as to the RCF with the CRF by [42], our approach issues cleaner, less cluttered edge maps with closed contours.

2   Related Work

In the following, we first review the related work on edge detection and minimum cost multicuts in the context of image segmentation.

Edge detection in the context of image segmentation is usually based on learning-driven approaches to learn to discriminate between object boundaries and other sources of brightness change such as textures. Structured random forests have been employed in [19]. [45] proposed a CNN-based approach called holistically nested edge detection (HED) that leverages multiple edge map resolutions. Similarly, [33] propose an end-to-end CNN for low-, mid- and high-level vision tasks such as boundary detection, semantic segmentation, region proposal generation, and object detection in a single network based on multi-scale learning. Convolutional oriented boundaries (COB) [38] compute multiscale oriented contours and region hierarchies in a single forward pass. Such boundary orientations are needed as input along with the edge maps to compute hierarchical image segmentations in frameworks such as MCG [5,40] or gpb-owt-ucm [7]. In [20], a bi-directional cascade network (BDCN) is proposed for edge detection of objects in different scales, where individual layers of a CNN model are trained by labeled edges at a specific scale. Similarly, to address the edge detection in multiple scales and aspect ratios, [37] provide an edge detector using richer convolutional features (RCF) by exploiting multiscale and multilevel information of objects. Although BDCN provides slightly better edge detection accuracy on the BSDS dataset [7], we base our approach on the RCF edge detection framework because of its more generic training procedure.

The multicut approach has been extensively used for image and motion segmentation, for example in [1,4,7,10,23,25,26,29–31,36]. Due to the NP-hardness of the MP, segmentation has often been addressed on pre-defined superpixels [3,10,23,24]. While [25] utilize multicuts as a method for discretizing a grid graph defined on the image pixels, where the local connectivity of the edges define the join/cut decisions and the nodes represent the image pixels, [31] proposed long-range terms in the objective function of the multicut problem defined on the pixel grid. An iterative fusion algorithm for the MP has been proposed in [10] to decompose the graph. [4] propose a graphical model for probabilistic image segmentation and globally optimal inference on the objective function with higher orders. A similar higher order approach is proposed also in [24,32] for image segmentation. [22] introduce a general solver for multicut problems based on graph convolutional neural networks and [28] extend the heuristic from [31] to facilitate the estimation of uncertainties.

3   Learning of Edge Weights for Graph Decompositions

3.1   Cycle Constraints in the Multicut Problem

The MP is based on a graph $G = (V, E)$, where every pixel (or superpixel) is represented by an individual node or vertex $v \in V$. Edges $e \in E$ encode whether two pixels belong to the same component or not. The goal is to assign every node to a cluster by labeling the edges between all nodes as either "cut" or "join" in an optimal way based on real-valued edge costs c_e, where positive edge costs are attractive and negative edge costs are repulsive. One of the main advantages of this approach is that the number of components is not fixed beforehand, contrary to other clustering algorithms, and is determined by the input graph instead. Since the number of segments in an image cannot be foreseen, the MP is a well-suited approach. The MP can be formulated as integer linear program [15, 18] with objective function $c : E \to \mathbb{R}$ as follows:

$$\min_{y \in \{0,1\}^E} \sum_{e \in E} c_e y_e \qquad (1)$$

subject to

$$\forall C \in cc(G) \forall e \in C : y_e \leq \sum_{e' \in C \setminus \{e\}} y_{e'}, \qquad (2)$$

where y_e is the binary labeling of an edge e that can be either 0 (join) or 1 (cut), and $cc(G)$ represents the set of all chordless cycles in the graph. If the cycle inequality constraint in Eq. (2) is satisfied, the MP solution results in a decomposition of the graph and therefore in a segmentation of the image. Informally, cycle inequality constraints ensure that there cannot be exactly one cut edge in any chordless cycle. However, computing an exact solution is not tractable in many cases due to the NP-hardness of the problem. Relaxing the integrality constraints such that $y \in [0,1]^E$ can improve tractability, however, valid edge label configurations are not guaranteed in this case. An example can be seen in Fig. 2, where node B is supposed to be in the same component as A and C, however, A and C are considered to be in different components. Infeasible solutions have to be repaired in order to obtain a meaningful segmentation of the input image. This can be achieved by using heuristics like in [11, 27, 31, 39].

3.2   Incorporating Cycle Constraints into a CRF

To improve the validity of relaxed solutions, [42] reformulate the MP as an end-to-end trainable CRF based on a formulation as Recurrent Neural Network (RNN) by [46]. By doing so, they are able to impose costs for violations of cycle inequality constraints during training. This is accomplished by first transforming the MP into a binary cubic problem, considering all triangles in the graph:

$$\min_{y \in \{0,1\}^E} \sum_{e \in E} c_e y_e + \gamma \sum_{\{u,v,w\} \in \binom{V}{3}} (y_{uv} \overline{y}_{vw} \overline{y}_{uw} + \overline{y}_{uv} y_{vw} \overline{y}_{uw} + \overline{y}_{uv} \overline{y}_{vw} y_{uw}). \qquad (3)$$

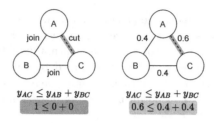

Fig. 2. Invalid solution to the Multicut Problem. (left) Covered by cycle inequality constraints given the integer solution. (right) Not covered given a relaxed solution that results in (left) when rounded.

This formulation moves cycle inequalities into the objective function by incurring a large cost γ whenever there is an invalid edge label configuration like $(cut, join, join)$ in a clique (as shown in Fig. 2 – all other orders implied). The binary cubic problem is then transformed to a CRF by defining a random field over the edge variables $y = (y_1, y_2, ..., y_{|E|})$, which is conditioned on the image I. The cycle inequality constraints are incorporated in the form of higher-order potentials as they always consider three edge variables. The combination of unary and third-order potentials yields the following energy function building the CRF:

$$E(y|I) = \sum_i \psi_i^U(y_i) + \sum_c \psi_c^{Cycle}(y_c) \qquad (4)$$

The energy $E(y|I)$ is the sum of the unary potentials and the higher-order potentials. For the latter [42] used pattern-based potentials proposed by [34]: $\psi_c^{Cycle}(y_c) = \gamma_{y_c}$ if $y_c \in P_c$, γ_{max} otherwise. P_c represents the set of all valid edge label configurations, which are $(join, join, join)$, $(join, cut, cut)$, and (cut, cut, cut). The invalid edge label configuration is $(cut, join, join)$. The potential assigns a high cost γ_{max} to an invalid labeling and a low cost γ_{y_c} to a valid labeling.

Such CRFs can be made end-to-end trainable using Mean-Field Updates, as proposed by [46]. This approach computes an auxiliary distribution Q over y such as to minimize the Kullback-Leibler Divergence (KL-Divergence) [16,17] between Q and the true posterior distribution of y. This step of optimizing $Q(y_i)$ instead of y_i can be interpreted as relaxation. Instead of considering violated constraints on binary edge variables (see Eq. (1)), we optimize probabilities of y_i taking a certain label l and optimize $Q(y_i = l)$ which admits values in the interval $[0, 1]$.

[46] reformulate the update steps as individual CNN layers and then repeat this stack multiple times in order to compute multiple mean-field iterations. The repetition of the CNN layer stack is treated equally to an RNN and remains fully trainable via backpropagation. [44] extends this idea by incorporating higher-order potentials in the form of pattern-based potentials and co-occurrence potentials. For the CRF by [42] the corresponding update rule becomes:

$$Q_i^t(y_i = l) = \frac{1}{Z_i} exp\left\{ -\sum_{c \in C} \left(\overbrace{\sum_{p \in P_{c|y_i=l}} \left(\prod_{j \in c, j \neq i} Q_j^{t-1}(y_j = p_j) \right) \gamma_p}^{\text{valid labeling case gets low costs}} \right. \right.$$

$$\left. \left. + \gamma_{max} \underbrace{\left(1 - \left(\sum_{p \in P_{c|y_i=l}} \left(\prod_{j \in c, j \neq i} Q_j^{t-1}(y_j = p_j) \right) \right) \right)}_{\text{inverse of the valid labeling case gets high costs}} \right) \right\},$$

$$(5)$$

where $Q_i^t(y_i = l) \in [0,1]$ is the Q value of one edge variable at mean-field iteration t with fixed edge label l (either *cut* or *join*). $P_{c|y_i=l}$ represents the set of valid edge label configurations according to Eq. (2), where the considered edge label l is fixed. Looking at the case where $y_i = 1$ (*cut*), possible valid configurations are $(y_i,0,1)$, $(y_i,1,0)$, and $(y_i,1,1)$. For all valid labelings the other two variables $y_{j \neq i}$ in clique c are taken into account. Their multiplied label probabilities from iteration $t-1$ for every valid label set, are summed and then multiplied with the cost for valid labelings γ_p. The inverse of the previous result is then multiplied with γ_{max}. Taking the inverse is equal to computing the same as in the valid case but with all possible invalid labelings for the considered edge variable. The results of all cliques C, which the variable y_i is part of, are summed. The updated $Q(y_i = l)$ are projected onto $[0, 1]$ using softmax. Costs γ_p and γ_{max} are considered as trainable parameters, and the update rule is differentiable with regard to the input $Q(y_i = l)$ (a network estimate of the likelihood of y_i taking label l) and the cost parameters. Since non-binary values for $Q(y_i = l)$ are optimized, invalid configurations are assigned lower costs when they become uncertain, i.e., as $Q(y_i = l) \to 0.5$.

3.3 Cooling Mean-Field Updates

There have been various attempts to tighten the relaxation of the MP. For example [43] incorporate odd-wheel inequalities and [24] use additional terminal cycle constraints. While these approaches can achieve tighter solution bounds, they involve constraints defined on a larger number of edges. A formulation of such constraints in the context of higher-order CRFs, requiring at least an order of 4, is intractable. Therefore, we choose an alternative, more straight forward approach – we push the network predictions $Q(y)$, which we interpret as relaxed edge labels, progressively closer to 0 or 1 in the mean-field update by introducing a cooling scheme. This not only issues solutions closer to the integer solution, but also provides a better training signal to the CRF, where cycle constraints penalize non-valid solutions more consistently. For this, we substitute $Q_i^{t-1}(y_i = p_j)$ in Eq. (5) by $\phi\left(Q_j^{t-1}(y_j = p_j), k \right)$, where ϕ is the newly introduced function modifying a probability q as follows:

$$\phi(q, k) = \begin{cases} 1 - (1 - q)^k & \text{if } q >= 0.5 \\ q^k & \text{otherwise.} \end{cases} \tag{6}$$

Here, k is an exponent that can be adapted during training, and q is the edge probability. This function pushes values larger or equal to 0.5 closer to 1 and values below 0.5 closer to 0. Using this transformation in the mean-field iterations reduces the integrality gap and therefore enforces the MP cycle constraints more strictly. This effect is amplified the larger the exponent k becomes.

Choosing a large k from the start hampers network training as the edge detection parameters would need to adapt too drastically for close-to-binary edges. We thus aim at adapting k throughout the training process such as to first penalize violated cycle constraints on the most confident network predictions and progressive addressing violated constraints on less confident (i.e. "less binary") estimates. We therefore propose a cooling schedule, which defines criteria upon which the parameter k is increased, as follows:

$$k = \begin{cases} k + 0.05 & \text{if } N(C_{inv}) < a \\ k & \text{otherwise,} \end{cases} \tag{7}$$

where $N(C_{inv})$ is the average number of invalid cycles (that do not adhere to the cycle inequality constraints) across all images and the hyperparameter a is the number of allowed cycle constraint violations before increasing the exponent k. The exponent therefore is increased after every epoch in which the number of invalid (relaxed) cycles has been decreased below the threshold a.

Leveraging the mean-field update for image segmentation requires an edge detection network that provides values for the CRF potentials. A possible learning-based approach that provides high quality edge estimates is the RCF [37] architecture. In practice, the edge detection network is first pre-trained until convergence, and then fine-tuned with the CRF. Parameter k is initialized as 1 and updated using Eq. (7) during training.

4   Richer Convolutional Features - CRF

The Richer Convolutional Features (RCF) architecture for edge detection has been recently developed by [37]. Their main idea is based on Holistically-nested edge detection (HED) [45], where an image classification architecture like VGG16 [41] is divided into five stages. Each stage produces a side output. These side outputs are trained with an individual loss function and combined by a weighted fusion layer that learns to combine them. In contrast to HED, which only considers the last convolutional layer from each stage, the RCF architecture uses all layer information. Hence, the features used become "richer". Every side output is transformed via sigmoid activation, creating edge probability maps.

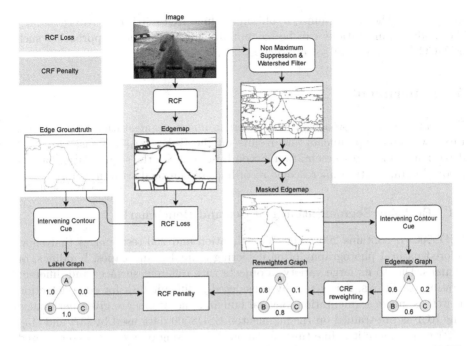

Fig. 3. The RCF-CRF training process is depicted, where blue highlights the RCF loss and purple highlights the additional CRF penalty. (Color figure online)

RCF-CRF Architecture. Figure 3 shows the full proposed architecture where the CRF is combined with the RCF to optimize for consistent boundary predictions. In a first step edge maps Pb from the input image are computed by the RCF, applying the RCF Loss during training. To apply the CRF Penalty, we then need to efficiently generate a pixel-graph that represents boundaries as edge weights. For every pixel, edges of the 8-connectivity are inserted for all distances in the range of 2 to 8 pixels yielding a significant amount of cycles. For efficient weight computation, we compute Watershed boundaries on the non-maximum suppressed RCF output of the pretrained RCF model *once*. We can use those to mask subsequent RCF predictions and efficiently retrieve graph weights as they are updated by the network. As edge weights, we consider the Intervening Contour Cue (ICC) [35] which computes the probability of an edge between pixels i and j to be cut as $W_{i,j} = max(Pb(x)_{x \in L_{i,j}})$, where x is an image coordinate, $Pb(x)$ is the edge probability at x and $L_{i,j}$ indicates the set of all coordinates on the line between i and j including themselves. From the Watershed masks, potential locations of the maximum can be pre-computed for efficiency.

Edge ground truth labels are created on the fly similar to the ICC by checking if there is an edge on the line between two pixels in the ground truth edge probability map to determine their cut/join label. The RCF loss is based on the cross entropy used in the original RCF [37], which ignores controversial edge points that have been annotated as an edge by less than half of the annotators but at least one. They are summed to obtain the final RCF-CRF loss. After training, the model segmentations can be computed using hierarchical approaches such as MCG [5] or multicut solvers such as [31].

5   Experiments

We evaluate our approach in two different image segmentation applications. First, we show experiments and results on the BSDS500 [7] dataset for edge detection and image segmentation. Second, we consider the segmentation of biomedical data, electron microscopic recordings of neuronal structures [8].

5.1   Berkeley Segmentation Dataset and Benchmark

BSDS500 [7] contains 200 train, 100 validation and 200 test images that show colored natural photography often depicting animals, landscapes, buildings, or humans. Due to its large variety in objects with different surfaces and different lighting conditions, it is generally considered a difficult task for edge detection as well as image segmentation. Several human annotations are given per image. The RCF is pre-trained on the augmented BSDS500 data used by [37] and [45]. After convergence it is fine-tuned with our CRF using only the non-augmented BSDS images to reduce training time. We evaluate the impact of fine-tuning the CRF in different training settings. These are: (Baseline RCF) further training of the RCF without CRF, (Baseline CRF) fine-tuning the RCF network without cooling scheme, and (Adaptive CRF) fine-tuning with cooling scheme. Additionally, we consider two settings where we enforce more binary solutions by introducing temperature decay in the softmax [21] that is applied after each mean field iteration. Here, we consider two cases: (Softmax Linear) where we decay the temperature by 0.05 after each epoch, and (Softmax Adaptive), where we consider the same adaption process as in Eq. (7).

Invalid Cycles. Figure 4(b) depicts the number of violated cycle inequalities during fine-tuning of the RCF network in different settings. There, it can be seen that Baseline CRF is able to reduce the number of violations rapidly to around 500 invalid cycles per image on average. During training, it constantly stays at this level and does not significantly change anymore. Due to this observation we set parameter a in the cooling scheme of Adaptive CRF and softmax temperature decay to 500. When training Adaptive CRF with this parameter setting, the number of violations further decreases to zero. The impact of reduced uncertainty can furthermore be seen when looking at the number of invalid cycles after rounding edge probabilities to binary edge labels. As Fig. 4(c) shows, only the settings Adaptive CRF and Softmax Linear are able to reduce the number of invalid cycles after rounding. However, Softmax Linear is not able to reduce the number of violations before rounding in contrast to Adaptive CRF. This indicates that the cooling scheme of Adaptive CRF provides a better training signal for the RCF, which is also confirmed considering RCF training loss depicted

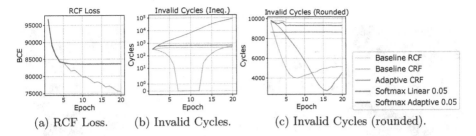

(a) RCF Loss.   (b) Invalid Cycles.   (c) Invalid Cycles (rounded).

Fig. 4. (a) Training progress in terms of RCF loss when training in different settings. Only Adaptive CRF is able to reduce the RCF loss further, while all other settings provide insufficient training signal to further improve on the basic RCF model. (b) Number of invalid cycle inequalities during training. Adaptive CRF significantly outperforms all other training settings. (c) Number of invalid cycle inequalities after rounding the solution during training. Adaptive CRF and Softmax CRF are able to improve on baselines significantly.

in Fig. 4(a). Only Adaptive CRF is able to provide sufficiently strong training signals such that the RCF network can further decrease its training loss. Interestingly, the number of invalid rounded cycles as well as constraint violations start increasing again after some training iterations for the adaptive CRF. This shows the trade-off between the RCF loss and the penalization by the CRF.

Edge Detection. Table 1 shows evaluation scores on the BSDS500 test set. The F-measure at the optimal dataset scale (ODS) and the optimal image scale (OIS) as well as the Average Precision (AP) are reported. The multiscale version (MS) is computed similar to [37] with scales 0.5, 1.0 and 1.5. Adaptive CRF achieves significant improvements in terms of ODS and OIS to all other training settings. The respective precision recall curves are given in the Appendix. AP decreases slightly with the CRF models, which is expected since the CRF removes uncertain edges that do not form closed components and therefore affects the high recall regime. A qualitative example is shown in Fig. 5 and in the Appendix.

Image Segmentation. To obtain a hierarchical segmentation using the predicted edge maps we compute MCG [5] based Ultrametric Contour Maps (UCM) [7] that generate hierarchical segmentations based on different edge probability thresholds. Edge orientations needed for MCG were computed using the standard filter operations. In contrast to [37] we do not use the COB framework but use pure MCG segmentations to allow for a more direct assessment of the proposed approach. Results for all training settings are reported in Table 1. Again, the Adaptive CRF models outperforms all other models in ODS, while AP is only slightly affected. Multi-scale (MS) information additionally improves results.

Figure 6 depicts the segmentation PR curves comparing the RCF based methods to other standard models. Similar to the edge map evaluation (see Appendix) the curves are steeper for the CRF based model compared with the plain RCF, thereby following the bias of human annotations, i.e., approaching the green

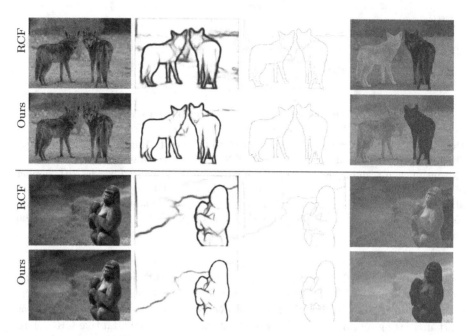

Fig. 5. Example BSDS500 [7] test images. Top row depicts the original image, edgemaps, UCMs, and segmentations of the baseline RCF model. Bottom row depicts the respective images for our Adaptive CRF model. The edge map optimized with Adaptive CRF is less cluttered and accurately localizes the contours. (Color figure online)

Table 1. Edge Detection and Segmentation results on the BSDS500 test set. All RCFs are based on VGG16. Results reported for Baseline RCF are computed for a model trained by us and are slightly worse than the scores reported in [37].

Models	Edge Detection			Segmentation		
	ODS	OIS	AP	ODS	OIS	AP
Baseline RCF	0.811	0.827	0.815	0.803	0.829	0.832
Baseline RCF (MS)	0.812	0.830	**0.836**	0.808	0.832	**0.849**
Baseline CRF (ours)	0.810	0.827	0.815	0.804	0.828	0.831
Baseline CRF (MS) (ours)	0.812	0.831	**0.836**	0.808	0.831	**0.849**
Softmax Linear (ours)	0.810	0.826	0.815	0.803	0.829	0.831
Softmax Linear (MS) (ours)	0.812	0.831	**0.836**	0.808	0.831	**0.849**
Adaptive CRF (ours)	0.815	0.830	0.812	0.808	0.830	0.828
Adaptive CRF (MS) (ours)	**0.817**	**0.835**	0.833	**0.813**	**0.834**	0.847

marker in Fig. 6. Depending on when the curves start to tilt the corresponding F-measure can be slightly lower as it is the case for the basic CRF. Adaptive CRF, however, also yields a considerably higher F-score improving over the baseline from 0.808 to 0.813. This result shows that employing cycle information is generally beneficial to estimate closed boundaries.

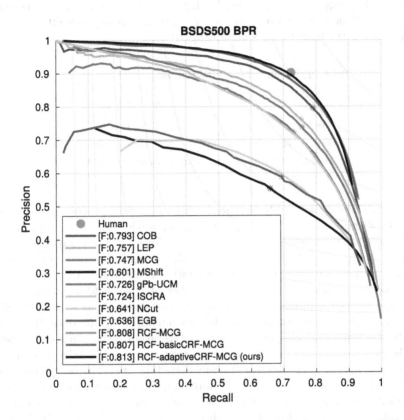

Fig. 6. Precision recall curves for segmentation on the BSDS500 test set. The proposed RCF with Adaptive CRF yields the highest ODS score and operates at a higher precision level than other models.

5.2 Neuronal Structure Segmentation

Next, we conduct experiments on the segmentation of neuronal structures [8]. The data was obtained from a serial section Transmission Electron Microscopy dataset of the Drosophila first instar larva ventral nerve cord [13,14]. This technique captures images of the Drosophila brain with a volume of $2 \times 2 \times 1.5\mu$ and a resolution of $4 \times 4 \times 50\,nm/pixel$. The volumes are anisotropic, i.e. while the x- and y-directions have a high resolution the z-direction has a rather low resolution [8]. Both, training and test set consist of a stack of 30 consecutive grayscale images. The goal of the challenge is to produce a binary map that corresponds to the membranes of cells in the image.

[12] have applied a multicut approach to this application. Their pipeline first produced an edge map from the original images by using either a cascaded random forest or a CNN. In order to reduce the complexity they aggregated individual pixels to superpixels by using the distance transform watershed technique [2]. Based on these superpixels they solve the multicut and the lifted multicut problem using the fusion moves algorithm [10].

Table 2. Results of the ISBI challenge on the test set.

Models	V^{Rand}	V^{Info}
Baseline [12]	0.9753	0.9874
Basic-CRF-optimized (ours)	0.9784	**0.9889**
Adaptive-CRF-optimized (ours)	**0.9808**	0.9887

In this context, we apply Adaptive CRF as a post-processing method to an existing graph without training the underlying edge detection. Edge weights for the test set are computed using a random forest in the simple (not lifted) multicut pipeline from [12] and define a graph. We optimize these graph weights with the proposed approach and subsequently decompose the graph using the fusion move algorithm as in [12]. The number of mean-field iterations was set to 20 and for the adaptive CRF the update threshold a was set to 100. Since the CRF is not trained but used only for optimizing the graph once, the update threshold is evaluated after every mean-field iteration rather than every epoch.

The graph obtained from [12] for the test set contained 74 485 cycles in total. Before applying the CRF, 61 099 of them violated the cycle inequality constraints and 38 283 cycles were invalid after rounding. Afterwards, both cycle counts were close to zero. Table 2 contains the results obtained for the not-modified edge weights (Baseline), the edge weights optimized with Baseline CRF and the edge weights optimized with Adaptive CRF. For evaluation we also refer to the ISBI challenge [8] that indicates two measures: the foreground-restricted Rand Scoring after border thinning V^{Rand} and the foreground-restricted Information Theoretic Scoring after border thinning V^{Info}. Both CRF models were able to improve the segmentation result in both evaluation metrics. While the differences in V^{Info}-score are rather small, Adaptive CRF increased the V^{Rand}-score by 0.005 compared to the baseline. Taking into account that the baseline is already very close to human performance, this is a very good result. Comparing the two CRF models it can be seen that the V^{Info}-score is almost the same for both approaches. In terms of V^{Rand}-score, Adaptive CRF improves stronger over the baseline than Baseline CRF. Overall, this experiment shows that applying the CRF is beneficial for image segmentation even without training the edge extraction. Accordingly, our approach can be applied even as a post-processing step without increasing training time.

6 Conclusion

We introduce an adaptive higher-order CRF that can be optimized jointly with an edge detection network and encourages edge maps that comply with the cycle constraints from the Minimum Cost Multicut Problem. Combining the CRF with the RCF model [37] for edge detection yields much sharper edge maps and promotes closed contours on BSDS500. PR curves show that the CRF based model yields steeper curves having a higher precision level. Similarly, the resulting segmentations show that the approach is able to generate more accurate and valid solutions. Moreover, the CRF can be used as post-processing to optimize a graph for cycle constraints as shown on the electron microscopy data. It has shown considerable improvement in the evaluation metrics without increasing training time.

References

1. Abbas, A., Swoboda, P.: Combinatorial optimization for panoptic segmentation: a fully differentiable approach. Adv. Neural. Inf. Process. Syst. **34**, 15635–15649 (2021)
2. Acharjya, P., Sinha, A., Sarkar, S., Dey, S., Ghosh, S.: A new approach of watershed algorithm using distance transform applied to image segmentation. Int. J. Innov. Res. Comput. Commun. Eng. **1**(2), 185–189 (2013)
3. Andres, B., et al.: Segmenting planar superpixel adjacency graphs w.r.t. non-planar superpixel affinity graphs. In: EMMCVPR (2013)
4. Andres, B., Kappes, J.H., Beier, T., Köthe, U., Hamprecht, F.A.: Probabilistic image segmentation with closedness constraints. In: ICCV (2011)
5. Arbeláez, P., Pont-Tuset, J., Barron, J., Marques, F., Malik, J.: Multiscale combinatorial grouping. In: Computer Vision and Pattern Recognition (2014)
6. Arbelaez, P., Maire, M., Fowlkes, C., Malik, J.: From contours to regions: an empirical evaluation. In: 2009 IEEE Conference on Computer Vision and Pattern Recognition, pp. 2294–2301. IEEE (2009)
7. Arbelaez, P., Maire, M., Fowlkes, C., Malik, J.: Contour detection and hierarchical image segmentation. IEEE Trans. Pattern Anal. Mach. Intell. **33**(5), 898–916 (2010)
8. Arganda-Carreras, I., et al.: Crowdsourcing the creation of image segmentation algorithms for connectomics. Front. Neuroanat. **9**, 142 (2015)
9. Bansal, N., Blum, A., Chawla, S.: Correlation clustering. Mach. Learn. **56**, 89–113 (2004). https://doi.org/10.1023/B:MACH.0000033116.57574.95
10. Beier, T., Hamprecht, F.A., Kappes, J.H.: Fusion moves for correlation clustering. In: Proceedings of the IEEE Conference on Computer Vision and Pattern Recognition, pp. 3507–3516 (2015)
11. Beier, T., Kroeger, T., Kappes, J.H., Kothe, U., Hamprecht, F.A.: Cut, glue & cut: a fast, approximate solver for multicut partitioning. In: Proceedings of the IEEE Conference on Computer Vision and Pattern Recognition, pp. 73–80 (2014)
12. Beier, T., et al.: Multicut brings automated neurite segmentation closer to human performance. Nat. Methods **14**(2), 101–102 (2017)
13. Cardona, A., et al.: An integrated micro-and macroarchitectural analysis of the drosophila brain by computer-assisted serial section electron microscopy. PLoS Biol. **8**(10), e1000502 (2010)

14. Cardona, A., et al.: Trakem2 software for neural circuit reconstruction. PLoS ONE **7**(6), e38011 (2012)
15. Chopra, S., Rao, M.R.: The partition problem. Math. Program. **59**(1–3), 87–115 (1993)
16. Csiszár, I.: I-divergence geometry of probability distributions and minimization problems. Ann. Prob. **3**, 146–158 (1975)
17. Csiszár, I., Katona, G.O., Tardos, G. (eds.): Entropy, search, complexity. Springer, Heidelberg (2007). DOIurl10.1007/978-3-540-32777-6
18. Deza, M., Laurent, M., Weismantel, R.: Geometry of cuts and metrics. Math. Methods Oper. Res.-ZOR **46**(3), 282–283 (1997)
19. Dollár, P., Zitnick, C.L.: Structured forests for fast edge detection. In: ICCV (2013)
20. He, J., Zhang, S., Yang, M., Shan, Y., Huang, T.: BDCN: bi-directional cascade network for perceptual edge detection. IEEE Transactions on Pattern Analysis and Machine Intelligence (2020). https://doi.org/10.1109/TPAMI.2020.3007074
21. Hinton, G., Vinyals, O., Dean, J.: Distilling the knowledge in a neural network (2015)
22. Jung, S., Keuper, M.: learning to solve minimum cost multicuts efficiently using edge-weighted graph convolutional neural networks. arXiv preprint arXiv:2204.01366 (2022)
23. Kappes, J.H., Speth, M., Andres, B., Reinelt, G., Schnörr, C.: Globally optimal image partitioning by multicuts. In: EMMCVPR (2011)
24. Kappes, J.H., Speth, M., Reinelt, G., Schnörr, C.: Higher-order segmentation via multicuts. CoRR abs/1305.6387 (2013). http://arxiv.org/abs/1305.6387
25. Kappes, J.H., Swoboda, P., Savchynskyy, B., Hazan, T., Schnörr, C.: Probabilistic correlation clustering and image partitioning using perturbed multicuts. In: SSVM (2015)
26. Kardoost, A., Ho, K., Ochs, P., Keuper, M.: Self-supervised sparse to dense motion segmentation. In: Proceedings of the Asian Conference on Computer Vision (ACCV) (2020)
27. Kardoost, A., Keuper, M.: Solving minimum cost lifted multicut problems by node agglomeration. In: Jawahar, C.V., Li, H., Mori, G., Schindler, K. (eds.) ACCV 2018. LNCS, vol. 11364, pp. 74–89. Springer, Cham (2019). https://doi.org/10.1007/978-3-030-20870-7_5
28. Kardoost, A., Keuper, M.: Uncertainty in minimum cost multicuts for image and motion segmentation. In: de Campos, C., Maathuis, M.H. (eds.) Proceedings of the Thirty-Seventh Conference on Uncertainty in Artificial Intelligence. Proceedings of Machine Learning Research, 27–30 Jul 2021, vol. 161, pp. 2029–2038. PMLR (2021)
29. Keuper, M.: Higher-order minimum cost lifted multicuts for motion segmentation. In: Proceedings of the IEEE International Conference on Computer Vision (ICCV) (2017)
30. Keuper, M., Andres, B., Brox, T.: Motion trajectory segmentation via minimum cost multicuts. In: Proceedings of the IEEE International Conference on Computer Vision (ICCV) (2015)
31. Keuper, M., Levinkov, E., Bonneel, N., Lavoué, G., Brox, T., Andres, B.: Efficient decomposition of image and mesh graphs by lifted multicuts. In: Proceedings of the IEEE International Conference on Computer Vision, pp. 1751–1759 (2015)
32. Kim, S., Yoo, C.D., Nowozin, S.: Image segmentation using higher-order correlation clustering. IEEE TPAMI **36**(9), 1761–1774 (2014)

33. Kokkinos, I.: Ubernet: Training a universal convolutional neural network for low-, mid-, and high-level vision using diverse datasets and limited memory. In: Proceedings of the IEEE Conference on Computer Vision and Pattern Recognition (CVPR) (2017)
34. Komodakis, N., Paragios, N.: Beyond pairwise energies: efficient optimization for higher-order MRFs. In: 2009 IEEE Conference on Computer Vision and Pattern Recognition, pp. 2985–2992. IEEE (2009)
35. Leung, T., Malik, J.: Contour continuity in region based image segmentation. In: Burkhardt, H., Neumann, B. (eds.) ECCV 1998. LNCS, vol. 1406, pp. 544–559. Springer, Heidelberg (1998). https://doi.org/10.1007/BFb0055689
36. Levinkov, E., Kardoost, A., Andres, B., Keuper, M.: Higher-order multicuts for geometric model fitting and motion segmentation. IEEE Trans. Pattern Anal. Mach. Intell. (2022). https://doi.org/10.1109/TPAMI.2022.3148795
37. Liu, Y., et al.: Richer convolutional features for edge detection. IEEE Trans. Pattern Anal. Mach. Intell. (TPAMI) 41(8), 1939–1946 (2019)
38. Maninis, K.-K., Pont-Tuset, J., Arbeláez, P., Van Gool, L.: Convolutional oriented boundaries. In: Leibe, B., Matas, J., Sebe, N., Welling, M. (eds.) ECCV 2016. LNCS, vol. 9905, pp. 580–596. Springer, Cham (2016). https://doi.org/10.1007/978-3-319-46448-0_35
39. Pape, C., Beier, T., Li, P., Jain, V., Bock, D.D., Kreshuk, A.: Solving large multicut problems for connectomics via domain decomposition. In: Proceedings of the IEEE International Conference on Computer Vision Workshops, pp. 1–10 (2017)
40. Pont-Tuset, J., Arbeláez, P., Barron, J., Marques, F., Malik, J.: Multiscale combinatorial grouping for image segmentation and object proposal generation. arXiv:1503.00848 (2015)
41. Simonyan, K., Zisserman, A.: Very deep convolutional networks for large-scale image recognition. arXiv preprint arXiv:1409.1556 (2014)
42. Song, J., Andres, B., Black, M.J., Hilliges, O., Tang, S.: End-to-end learning for graph decomposition. In: Proceedings of the IEEE International Conference on Computer Vision, pp. 10093–10102 (2019)
43. Swoboda, P., Andres, B.: A message passing algorithm for the minimum cost multicut problem. In: Proceedings of the IEEE Conference on Computer Vision and Pattern Recognition, pp. 1617–1626 (2017)
44. Vineet, V., Warrell, J., Torr, P.H.: Filter-based mean-field inference for random fields with higher-order terms and product label-spaces. Int. J. Comput. Vision 110(3), 290–307 (2014)
45. Xie, S., Tu, Z.: Holistically-nested edge detection. In: Proceedings of the IEEE International Conference on Computer Vision, pp. 1395–1403 (2015)
46. Zheng, S., et al.: Conditional random fields as recurrent neural networks. In: Proceedings of the IEEE International Conference on Computer Vision, pp. 1529–1537 (2015)

Hyperspectral Demosaicing of Snapshot Camera Images Using Deep Learning

Eric L. Wisotzky[1,2]([✉]) [iD], Charul Daudkane[1], Anna Hilsmann[1] [iD],
and Peter Eisert[1,2] [iD]

[1] Computer Vision and Graphics, Fraunhofer Heinrich Hertz Institute,
Berlin, Germany
`eric.wisotzky@hhi.fraunhofer.de`
[2] Visual Computing, Institut für Informatik, Humboldt-University, Berlin, Germany

Abstract. Spectral imaging technologies have rapidly evolved during
the past decades. The recent development of single-camera-one-shot techniques for hyperspectral imaging allows multiple spectral bands to be
captured simultaneously (3×3, 4×4 or 5×5 mosaic), opening up a wide
range of applications. Examples include intraoperative imaging, agricultural field inspection and food quality assessment. To capture images
across a wide spectrum range, i.e. to achieve high spectral resolution, the
sensor design sacrifices spatial resolution. With increasing mosaic size,
this effect becomes increasingly detrimental. Furthermore, demosaicing
is challenging. Without incorporating edge, shape, and object information during interpolation, chromatic artifacts are likely to appear in the
obtained images. Recent approaches use neural networks for demosaicing, enabling direct information extraction from image data. However,
obtaining training data for these approaches poses a challenge as well.
This work proposes a parallel neural network based demosaicing procedure trained on a new ground truth dataset captured in a controlled environment by a hyperspectral snapshot camera with a 4×4 mosaic pattern.
The dataset is a combination of real captured scenes with images from
publicly available data adapted to the 4×4 mosaic pattern. To obtain real
world ground-truth data, we performed multiple camera captures with
1-pixel shifts in order to compose the entire data cube. Experiments show
that the proposed network outperforms state-of-art networks.

Keywords: Sensor array and multichannel signal processing · Deep
learning · Biomedical imaging techniques · Image analysis

1 Introduction

Spectral imaging technologies have rapidly evolved during the past decades.
The light captured by the camera sensor contains information across a wide
range of the electromagnetic spectrum, which can potentially be used to identify the texture and the material/molecular composition of any given object of
interest. Hyperspectral sensors with up to 150 or even 256 spectral channels

© The Author(s), under exclusive license to Springer Nature Switzerland AG 2022
B. Andres et al. (Eds.): DAGM GCPR 2022, LNCS 13485, pp. 198–212, 2022.
https://doi.org/10.1007/978-3-031-16788-1_13

within and outside the visible spectral range have been developed in the last few years for various applications within health care [3,22], industrial imaging [29] or agriculture [15,25]. However, current acquisition methods for such devices (as filter-wheels [36], line-scanning [27]) have decisive disadvantages, trading the acquisition of hyperspectral images (HSI) with high costs or long acquisition times. Alternative approaches are Multi Spectral Filter Arrays (MSFA) based on spectral masking on pixel-level using a single sensor plane similar to the Bayer pattern for single chip RGB cameras [1]. This single-camera-one-shot (mosaic snapshot) technique allows multiple spectral bands to be captured simultaneously in a simple and compact system. The captured image data is defined by its moxel (mosaic element) corresponding to the occurring filter pattern and stored in a hypercube representation with three dimensions, two spatial (width and height) and one spectral (wavelength λ). The simplest example is similar to the Bayer pattern, with one green filter element being replaced by another filter resulting in a 2×2 pattern [12]. These systems can be extended to 3×3, 4×4, 5×5 or even non-quadratic 2×3 mosaic patterns for recording wavelengths in near-ultraviolet, visible and near-infrared spectral range. However, a mosaic pattern is always a compromise between spatial and spectral resolution, as with increasing mosaic size (for higher spectral resolution) the spatial resolution decreases. This spectral-spatial trade-off can be resolved through interpolation or prediction of the missing spectral values, such that the final HSI exhibits higher resolution (spatial and spectral). Techniques for spectral reconstruction include bilinear and nonlinear filtering methods and are referred to as demosaicing.

Typically, demosaicing is achieved by interpolation based on the information from neighboring pixels. Traditional algorithms such as bilinear, bicubic interpolation are popular choices in the field of image processing, where missing pixels are calculated from their neighborhood. Further, interpolation methods based on image fusion have been proposed, where spatial-resolution is enhanced through fusion with Pseudo Panchromatic Images (PPI), statistics based fusion techniques, e.g. Maximum a posteriori (MAP) estimation, stochastic mixing model [7,8,11], and dictionary-based fusion techniques, e.g. spectral and spatial dictionary based methods [2,39,40]. Fusion based methods usually require the availability of a guiding image with higher spatial resolution, which is difficult to obtain in many scenarios. Demosaicing by interpolation based techniques, both traditional as well as fusion-based, is easy to achieve, however, these methods suffer from color artifacts and lead to lower spatial resolution. Especially at edges, they do not take into account the spectral correlations between adjacent bands as well as due to crosstalk. This results in spectral distortions in the demosaiced image, especially for increasing mosaic filter size.

Alternatively, deep neural networks can be trained to account for scene information as well as correlations between individual spectral bands. Demosaicing using convolutional neural networks (CNN) for images with 2×2 Bayer pattern was first proposed in [32] and [9]. In recent years, CNN based color image super resolution (SR) has gained popularity. Examples of such networks include SRCNN [6], DCSCN [37] and EDSR [21]. Due to their success, these networks have been extended to HSI super resolution [20]. The underlining aspect of all CNN based HSI demosaicing networks is the utilization of spatial and spectral context from the data during training. However, the need of high quality ground truth data leads to challenges. In such a dataset, each pixel should contain the entire spectral information, which is difficult to acquire in a natural environment.

The contribution of this work is as follows. We present a new ground-truth dataset acquired and generated using a shifting unit to achieve a 1-pixel movement on the camera side in order to obtain a full resolution image for all color channels. Further, we propose a new demosaicing network and compare it to three relevant network architectures, performing demosaicing on a dataset combining captured and publicly available data.

The remainder of this paper is as follows. The next chapter gives an overview on related publications relevant for this work. Section 3 describes the proposed network architecture, before Sect. 4 explains the acquisition of the ground truth data. Section 5 introduces training and evaluation parameters. Section 6 describes experiments and results, followed by a thorough discussion and conclusion.

2   Related Work

In the last years, several HSI demosaicing algorithms have been presented. Some methods require presence of a dominant-band (as in the Bayer pattern) [26], but of more interest are methods without such explicit assumptions designed for mosaic pattern having no redundant band [28].

Dijkstra et al. [5] proposed a similarity maximization network for HSI demosaicing, inspired by single image SR. This network learns to reconstruct a downsampled HSI by upscaling via deconvolutional layers. The network results are presented for a 4×4 mosaic pattern and the demosaiced HSI showed high spatial and spectral resolution. Habtegebrial et al. [10] use residual blocks to learn the mapping between low and high resolution HSI, inspired by the HCNN+ architecture [30]. These two networks use 2D convolutions in order to learn the spectral-spatial correlations. An important characteristic of HSI is the correlation between adjacent spectral bands which are not taken into account when using 2D convolutional based networks. These correlations can be incorporated by using 3D convolutional networks. Mei et al. [23] proposed one of the first 3D CNNs for hyperspectral image SR addressing both the spatial context between neighboring pixels as well as the spectral correlation between adjacent bands of the image. A more effective way to learn the spatial and spectral correlations is through a mixed 2D/3D convolutional network, as proposed in [19].

One major challenge for the task of snapshot mosaic HSI demosaicing using neural networks is the lack of real world ground truth data. Publicly available real world datasets, such as CAVE [38] or HyTexiLa [16], were recorded either using a push-broom technique or by spatio-spectral-line scans. Hence, the data has different characteristics than snapshot mosaic data (e.g., missing cross talk) and can therefore not be used to adequately train a robust network for demosaicing. One alternative is a downsampling strategy from captured snapshot mosaic data as presented in [5]. However, simple downsampling leads to differences in distances of adjacent pixels, which affects the network results.

3   Network Architecture

We propose a new neural network architecture to generate a full-spectrum hypercube (dimension $[L \times W \times H]$) with L wavelength bands from a captured mosaic image (dimension $[1 \times W \times H]$), represented as a low resolution or sparse hypercube. Here, W and H correspond to the spatial width and height of the image and L represents the spectral resolution. In this work, a snapshot mosaic camera with a 4×4 pattern, i.e. $L = 16$ bands, is used as shown in Fig. 1.

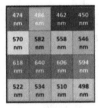

Fig. 1. 4×4 filter pattern with 16 wavelengths

The building blocks of our demosaicing network (Fig. 2a) are a feature extraction layer along with a feature addition (*FeatureAdd*) block and two deconvolution (*deconv*) layers. The feature extraction layer of the network is split into two parallel parts: (1) a mosaic to cube converter (M2C) implemented by a convolutional layer (*conv*) and (2) feature extraction using four residual blocks (*Resblocks*). These two paths learn the spatial spectral correlations from different representations of the input mosaic image. The input to the M2C is a 2D mosaic image MI_{2D} of dimension $[1, W, H]$, while the input to the *Resblocks* is a 3D cube representation C_{M2C} of dimension $[L, W/\sqrt{L}, H/\sqrt{L}]$ created by resampling the one channel input image as follows:

$$C_{M2C}(x, y, z) = MI_{2D}(u, v), \qquad (1)$$

with

$$u = x \cdot \sqrt{L} + z \bmod \sqrt{L}, \qquad (2)$$

$$v = y \cdot \sqrt{L} + z \operatorname{div} \sqrt{L}, \qquad (3)$$

where u, v correspond to the 2D mosaic pixel coordinate, x, y, z correspond to the 3D multispectral voxel coordinate and $\sqrt{L}$ is the dimension of the mosaic pattern; in our case $\sqrt{L} = 4$. The operation div describes integer division. The M2C composed of a convolutional layer is defined as

$$C_{nn}(x, y, z) = MI_{2D} \otimes_4 \mathcal{G}_{16}^{4 \times 4}, \qquad (4)$$

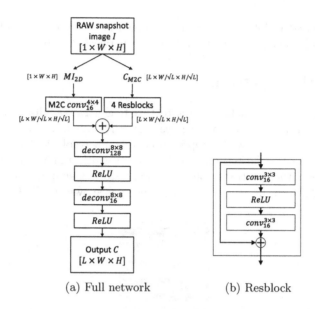

(a) Full network   (b) Resblock

Fig. 2. (a) Architecture of the hyperspectral demosaicing network. (b) Architecture of the resnet block. The full network includes four consecutive resnet blocks. The resnet block is build up of two convolutional layers holding 16 convolutional filters with size 3×3 each. These two layers are separated by a ReLU activation function.

where $\otimes$ and $\mathcal{G}$ represent the convolutional operator with stride of 4, equal to mosaic size, and the set of 16 filters with a size of 4×4 respectively. The features of C_{M2C} are extracted by four consecutive residual blocks, where a single block consists of two convolutional layers separated by a rectified linear unit (ReLU) activation function and interconnected through skip connection avoiding the problem of vanishing gradients [13]. In addition, the ReLU function clips values below zero as negative spectral responses cannot exist. Each convolutional layer uses a filter of dimension 3×3 with stride and padding of 1, see Fig. 2b. Finally, a ReLU activation function is applied to the obtained feature map and the resulting feature map is passed onto the next residual block as input.

The extracted features are of the same size and concatenated in the FeatureAdd block. The combined feature map is passed to two upsampling layers, which upsample by a factor of $4 \times 4 = 16$ to produce a fully defined hyperspectral cube of dimension $[L, W, H]$ in a non-linear fashion. The first deconv layer determines the capacity of the network with 128 filters, while the second layer has the same amount of filters as the number of required spectral bands

$$O(C) = \Phi(\Phi(C_{add} \oslash_2 \mathcal{F}_{128}^{8 \times 8}) \oslash_2 \mathcal{F}_{16}^{8 \times 8}), \tag{5}$$

where $\oslash$ and $\mathcal{F}$ represent the deconvolutional operators with stride of 2 and the filter sets with a size of 8×8 respectively. The ReLU activation function Φ after each *deconv* layer accounts for non-linearity in the interpolation process.

4   Data Acquisition

In order to train the network with real ground truth images, we created a customized dataset from publicly available as well as new self-recorded ground truth data.

A HSI captured with a 4×4 mosaic pattern contains information for 1 out of 16 wavelength bands in each pixel only. For training the demosaicing algorithm, ground-truth data is necessary such that for each pixel, full spectral information exists across all 16 wavelength bands. Hence, we captured an unprecedented new HSI dataset, providing accurate ground truth upsampling information. We capture in an controlled environment with a Ximea snapshot 4×4-VIS camera using an IMEC CMOS sensor. The sensor resolution is 2048×1088 px, with an active area of 2048×1024 px and the 4×4 mosaic filter pattern captures 16 wavelength bands in the spectral range from 463 nm to 638 nm.

For the generation of the ground-truth information, we captured 16 images with precise pixel-wise shifting, meandering along the 4×4 mosaic pattern for each scene, using a computer-controlled shifting unit. To achieve accurate 1-pixel shifts, the camera was calibrated and the scene-camera distance was measured. After acquiring the $4 \times 4 = 16$ images, a full resolution image with $L = 16$ wavelengths was created by resampling the image stack. At each position, we captured and averaged several images to decrease the influence of sensor noise. In order to account for illumination differences and work with reflectance intensity, all captured images were corrected using a white reference image according to [34]. Further, snapshot mosaic images contain spectral crosstalk, which influences the reflectance behavior [35]. To learn this behavior during demosaicing, the ground-truth data was crosstalk corrected in addition to white reference correction, while the training and test input data were white reference corrected only.

We captured a total of twelve scenes, six with a color chart and two of each showing different vegetables, different meats, as well as a combination of vegetables and meats, see Fig. 3. It is important to note, that a correct 1-pixel shift can only be achieved for the focus plane and points in front or behind that plane will always show slightly divergent pixel shifts of $(1\text{-px}\pm\epsilon)$. For this reason, we added a flat color chart to half of the entire dataset and filtered the remaining images with a Gaussian filter with $\sigma = 1.5$ to smooth the present shifting error.

In addition, to increase the dataset, our captured data was combined with synthetic images generated from the publicly available CAVE dataset [38]. The CAVE dataset has 32 reflectance images of real-world objects. In total 18 images of the CAVE data sections 'skin and hair', 'food and drinks', 'real and fake' as well as 'stuff' were added to our dataset by interpolating the needed spectral bands and building up a simulated mosaic pattern representation of each scene. The entire dataset will be available upon publication.

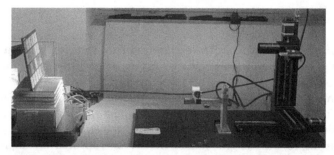

(a) Experimental setup with a color chart as captured object

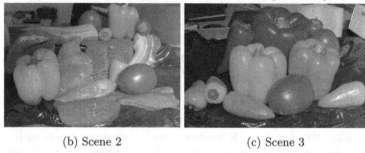

(b) Scene 2   (c) Scene 3

Fig. 3. (a) Experimental setup for recording hyperspectral images using a computer-controlled shifting unit, allowing exact 1-px shifts of the camera. Examples for two captured scenes containing (b) a combination of vegetables and meat and (c) different types of vegetables. (Color figure online)

5   Training and Network Evaluation Metrics

During training, we used image patches of size $[1 \times 100 \times 100] = [16 \times 25 \times 25]$ as input for the network. We split the dataset into a training set with 1000 patches of eleven captured images and 17 images of the CAVE data as well as a test set including 75 patches of each of the two datasets. We used the ADAM optimizer with an adaptive learning rate strategy and an initial learning rate of 0.001 [17]. The learning rate was reduced after each epoch until a value of 0.0001 was reached, using at least 30k epochs. A batch size of 20 was used for updating the weights during the network training. The M2C block was initialized with uniform random weight. The loss function for calculating the difference between the ground truth and the predicted full-spectrum hyperspectral cube is defined by the mean squared error (MSE)

$$MSE(o,p) = \frac{1}{N} \sum_{i=0}^{N} |o_i - p_i|^2, \tag{6}$$

where o is the ground truth and p is the predicted value.

6 Experiments and Results

For quantitative analysis, we use the structural similarity index (SSIM), measuring the similarity between spectral cubes [33] from predicted and ground-truth data as well as the peak signal to noise ratio (PSNR) [14]. Both, SSIM and PSNR are calculated individually for each spectral channel and averaged over all channels for the test images.

We compare the results of our proposed network to two state-of-the-art demosaicing approaches DCCNN [5] and DeepCND [10]. Further, we analyze the resulting images visually and, to show the usability of our work, we visually analyze intraoperative snapshot images acquired during a parotidectomy.

6.1 Quantitative Results

All networks, our proposed network as well as the two reference networks, were trained on the created dataset and the networks learned to predict a full spectral cube of dimension $[16 \times 100 \times 100]$ from the input mosaic image of dimension $[1 \times 100 \times 100]$. As the quality of the results depends on the number of filters in the first deconvolutional layer, with best results reported between 32 and 256 filters [5], we trained two versions of our as well as the DCCNN [5] network using 32 and 128 filters in the first deconvolutional layer. Table 1 reports the SSIM and PSNR results of our network and the DCCNN using 32 and 128 filters, respectively. Using 32 filters and 1000 images as well as 30k epochs for training, the DCCNN network shows results comparable to the initial results reported in Dijkstra et al. [5]. Our proposed network outperforms the reference network approximately by 2% using the same parameter and training set, see Table 1. Further, the results show that using 128 filters yields better results as with 32 filters as recommended by Dijkstra et al. [5]. Therefore, for further analysis, we have used 128 filters in the first *deconv* layer for the other experiments.

Table 1. SSIM and PSNR results of our proposed network and the DCCNN [5] using 32 and 128 filters.

# of filters networks	32		128		
	SSIM	PSNR	SSIM	PSNR	Epochs
DCCNN [5]	0.755	40.05	0.825	41.54	30k
Ours	0.776	40.50	0.836	42.11	30k
Ours	0.784	40.95	0.841	42.63	40k

Table 2. PSNR results of all analyzed demosaicing methods.

Networks	PSNR [dB]
Ours	43.06
DeepCND [10]	42.38
DCCNN [5]	41.54
2D-3D-Net [4]	41.33
Intensity Difference [24]	40.43
Bilinear Interpolation	40.23
Bicubic Interpolation	39.20

In addition, we noticed that with 30k epochs, the training error was still decreasing for our network, while it converged for the reference networks. Therefore, the quality of our results increases further when using up to 40k epochs during training. The final results, shown in Table 2, present the PSNR at lowest training loss showing that our model outperforms the two reference networks as well as traditional interpolation methods by approximately 1 dB (compared to DeepCND [10]) to 4 dB (compared to bicubic interpolation).

6.2 Qualitative Results

In the following, we visually analyze of differences between individual result images. This qualitative analysis includes a spectral signature analysis, analyzing the spectral behavior of the predicted hyperspectral cube across all 16 wavelengths. Additionally, we provide a visual comparison for the single spectral bands as well as calculated RGB image of the predicted hyperspectral cube. Figure 4 shows full-resolution RGB images (ground truth image and demosaiced result with our approach) of one example image in our captured dataset (dimension of 1024 × 2048 pixels). The RGB images have been calculated using the CIE

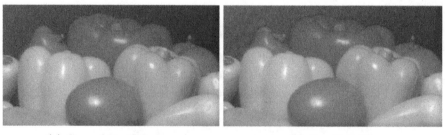

(a) Ground Truth Image   (b) Our Network

Fig. 4. RGB representation of one captured HSI scene as (a) high resolution ground truth image and (b) demosaiced images using our network.

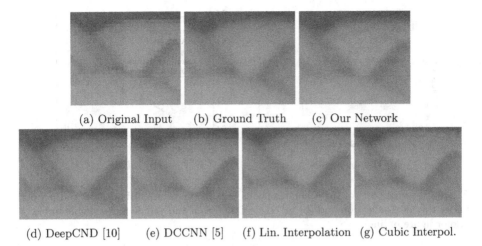

(a) Original Input   (b) Ground Truth   (c) Our Network

(d) DeepCND [10]   (e) DCCNN [5]   (f) Lin. Interpolation   (g) Cubic Interpol.

Fig. 5. RGB representation of a crop of Fig. 4 (center of the right image half). Our result is most similar to the ground truth, while traditional interpolation shows color artifacts at the edges. (Color figure online)

color matching functions [31] with standard illuminant D65. Note, that the calculated RGB images show missing red components, since the snapshot camera is only sensitive up to 638 nm and thus information is missing in the red channel of the RGB images.

Figure 5 shows enlarged cutouts of the scene depicted in Fig. 4 for the ground truth images as well as the input image and demosaiced versions of our network as well as linear and bilinear interpolation and the reference demosaicing networks. Compared to the original input image, our demosaiced result shows more structure while maintaining edges and color. In the reference networks the mosaic pattern is visible over the entire demosaiced image, c.f. Fig. 5(d) and (e). This effect is drastically reduced by our approach, where this artifact only slightly appears especially around specular reflections as well as some homogeneous but noisy regions, which are not perfectly in focus, c.f. Fig. 5(c). Classical linear and cubic interpolation increase noise present in the input images, while single-pixel information is lost resulting in not correctly reconstructed edges. For the interpolation-based results, color artifacts appear around the edges (Fig. 5(f) and (g)) due to wrong spectral demosaicing. On the other hand, all neural network approaches learned to denoise the image as well as to correct the crosstalk.

Figure 6 plots the spectral signatures of two example regions in the image for all compared demosaicing approaches. For homogeneous regions, the spectral signatures of all analyzed methods are close to that of the ground truth image region, c.f. Fig. 6(a). For edges, the spectral signature produced by our network almost completely follows that of the ground truth, followed closely by DeepCND [10] and then DCCNN [5], while the classical interpolation methods are not able to reconstruct similar characteristics of the spectral curves, resulting in wrong color appearance in the RGB images.

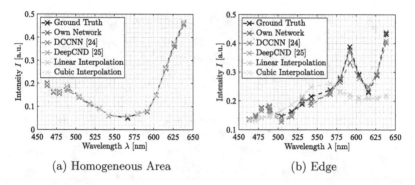

Fig. 6. Spectral plots of (a) a homogeneous area of the centered backmost red pepper under the total reflection and (b) an edge of the green and yellow parts visible in Fig. 5 (Color figure online).

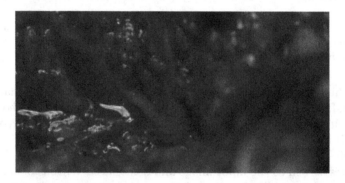

Fig. 7. RGB representation of a captured surgical scene using the 4 × 4 snapshot camera and demosaiced with our network.

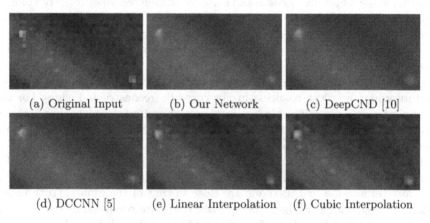

Fig. 8. RGB represenation of a crop of Fig. 7 (image center). (Color figure online)

6.3   Intraoperative Image Demosaicing

We also applied our approach to intraoperative image data, as HSI can be used in intraoperative settings in order to differentiate between different tissue types [35] or to extract vital information [18,27]. Figure 7 shows an example of a demosaiced image acquired intraoperatively. Our network is able to demosaic the original input and perform denoising as well as crosstalk correction at the same time, while the overall texture and color appearance is preserved. In the overall impression, all visual analyses from the test data are confirmed, c.f. Fig. 8.

7   Discussion and Conclusion

In this work, we propose a neural network architecture for hyperspectral demosaicing for snapshot 4×4 mosaic cameras. Additionally, we present a new unprecendened ground-truth dataset of real scenes for training, acquired with a sensor shifting unit and pixel reordering strategy. This dataset is combined with synthetic data generated from the CAVE [38] dataset. The performance of the network is evaluated using SSIM and PSNR scores and compared to traditional interpolation methods as well as to two demosaicing networks [5,10]. The results show that our proposed network with parallel feature extraction outperforms the reference networks with nearly 2% and 0.4% increase in SSIM score and 1.05 dB and 0.6 dB increase in PSNR. The scores of the classical interpolation methods are lowest as no spectral-spatial correlations are taken into consideration during demosaicing, through which they fail to preserve the spectral signature. This behavior visually emerges at edges. All network-based approaches are able to preserve the spectral signatures.

In detail, the results show that increasing the number of filters allows the network to learn more features (e.g., spatial-spectral correlations and edges) resulting in improved demosaicing. The improved performance for our network can be attributed to the feature addition layer, which combines the features from the M2C layer and the deep features extracted through the four residual blocks from the hand-crafted M2C input. This indicates that the upsampling performed on extracted feature maps (from four residual blocks) might yield better spatial-spectral resolution in the full spectrum mosaic cube. Currently, our network is only designed for 4×4 mosaic pattern but similar architectures are possible for 3×3 or 5×5 patterns through adaptions at the deconvolutional layers.

Visual inspection of the results show a slight presence of the 4×4 mosaic pattern in the demosaiced images, due to the challenge of creating a real world dataset using the 1-pixel shifting of a captured 3D scene. This 1-pixel shifting is dependent on the distance between camera and object, while the 3D nature of the scene did not allow an exact 1-pixel shift for the entire scene leaving a shadowing mosaic pattern as artifact. One approach to decrease or overcome this problem would be to use synthetic data, which would be completely aligned to (specific) mosaic snapshot cameras. We assume that this will further improve the results, since demosaicing results are heavily dependent on the quality of the full spectrum hyperspectral data available for training.

Acknowledgment. This work was funded by the German Federal Ministry of Education and Research (BMBF) under Grant No. 16SV8061 (MultiARC) and the German Federal Ministry for Economic Affairs and Climate Action (BMWi) under Grant No. 01MK21003 (NaLamKI). Only tissue that has been exposed during normal surgical treatment has been scanned additionally with our described camera. This procedure has been approved by Charité–Universitätsmedizin Berlin, Germany.

References

1. Bayer, B.: Color imaging array us patent 3 971 065 (1976)
2. Bendoumi, M.A., He, M., Mei, S.: Hyperspectral image resolution enhancement using high-resolution multispectral image based on spectral unmixing. IEEE Trans. Geosci. Remote Sens. **52**(10), 6574–6583 (2014)
3. Calin, M.A., Parasca, S.V., Savastru, D., Manea, D.: Hyperspectral imaging in the medical field: present and future. Appl. Spectrosc. Rev. **49**(6), 435–447 (2014)
4. Daudkhane, C.: Hyperspectral demosaicing of snapshot camera images using deep learning. Master's thesis, Technical University Berlin (2021)
5. Dijkstra, K., van de Loosdrecht, J., Schomaker, L.R.B., Wiering, M.A.: Hyperspectral demosaicking and crosstalk correction using deep learning. Mach. Vision Appl. **30**(1), 1–21 (2018). https://doi.org/10.1007/s00138-018-0965-4
6. Dong, C., Loy, C.C., He, K., Tang, X.: Learning a deep convolutional network for image super-resolution. In: Fleet, D., Pajdla, T., Schiele, B., Tuytelaars, T. (eds.) ECCV 2014. LNCS, vol. 8692, pp. 184–199. Springer, Cham (2014). https://doi.org/10.1007/978-3-319-10593-2_13
7. Eismann, M.T., Hardie, R.C.: Application of the stochastic mixing model to hyperspectral resolution enhancement. IEEE Trans. Geosci. Remote Sens. **42**(9), 1924–1933 (2004)
8. Eismann, M.T., Hardie, R.C.: Hyperspectral resolution enhancement using high-resolution multispectral imagery with arbitrary response functions. IEEE Trans. Geosci. Remote Sens. **43**(3), 455–465 (2005)
9. Gharbi, M., Chaurasia, G., Paris, S., Durand, F.: Deep joint demosaicking and denoising. ACM Trans. Graph. (TOG) **35**(6), 1–12 (2016)
10. Habtegebrial, T.A., Reis, G., Stricker, D.: Deep convolutional networks for snapshot hypercpectral demosaicking. In: 2019 10th Workshop on Hyperspectral Imaging and Signal Processing: Evolution in Remote Sensing (WHISPERS), pp. 1–5. IEEE (2019)
11. Hardie, R.C., Eismann, M.T., Wilson, G.L.: Map estimation for hyperspectral image resolution enhancement using an auxiliary sensor. IEEE Trans. Image Process. **13**(9), 1174–1184 (2004)
12. Hershey, J., Zhang, Z.: Multispectral digital camera employing both visible light and non-visible light sensing on a single image sensor. uS Patent 7,460,160 (2008)
13. Hochreiter, S.: The vanishing gradient problem during learning recurrent neural nets and problem solutions. Int. J. Uncertainty Fuzziness Knowl.-Based Syst. **6**(02), 107–116 (1998)
14. Hore, A., Ziou, D.: Image quality metrics: PSNR vs. SSIM. In: 2010 20th International Conference on Pattern Recognition, pp. 2366–2369. IEEE (2010)
15. Jung, A., Kardeván, P., Tőkei, L.: Hyperspectral technology in vegetation analysis. Progr. Agric. Eng. Sci. **2**(1), 95–117 (2006)

16. Khan, H.A., Mihoubi, S., Mathon, B., Thomas, J.B., Hardeberg, J.Y.: Hytexila: high resolution visible and near infrared hyperspectral texture images. Sensors **18**(7), 2045 (2018)

17. Kingma, D.P., Ba, J.: Adam: a method for stochastic optimization. arXiv preprint arXiv:1412.6980 (2014)

18. Kossack, B., Wisotzky, E., Eisert, P., Schraven, S.P., Globke, B., Hilsmann, A.: Perfusion assessment via local remote photoplethysmography (rppg). In: Proceedings of the IEEE/CVF Conference on Computer Vision and Pattern Recognition (CVPR) Workshops, pp. 2192–2201 (2022)

19. Li, Q., Wang, Q., Li, X.: Mixed 2D/3D convolutional network for hyperspectral image super-resolution. Remote Sens. **12**(10), 1660 (2020)

20. Li, Y., Zhang, L., Dingl, C., Wei, W., Zhang, Y.: Single hyperspectral image super-resolution with grouped deep recursive residual network. In: 2018 IEEE Fourth International Conference on Multimedia Big Data (BigMM), pp. 1–4. IEEE (2018)

21. Lim, B., Son, S., Kim, H., Nah, S., Mu Lee, K.: Enhanced deep residual networks for single image super-resolution. In: Proceedings of the IEEE Conference on Computer Vision and Pattern Recognition Workshops, pp. 136–144 (2017)

22. Lu, G., Fei, B.: Medical hyperspectral imaging: a review. J. Biomed. Opt. **19**(1), 10901 (2014). https://doi.org/10.1117/1.JBO.19.1.010901

23. Mei, S., Yuan, X., Ji, J., Zhang, Y., Wan, S., Du, Q.: Hyperspectral image spatial super-resolution via 3D full convolutional neural network. Remote Sens. **9**(11), 1139 (2017)

24. Mihoubi, S., Losson, O., Mathon, B., Macaire, L.: Multispectral demosaicing using intensity-based spectral correlation. In: International Conference on Image Processing Theory, Tools and Applications (IPTA), vol. 5, pp. 461–466. IEEE (2015). https://doi.org/10.1109/IPTA.2015.7367188, http://ieeexplore.ieee.org/document/7367188/

25. Moghadam, P., Ward, D., Goan, E., Jayawardena, S., Sikka, P., Hernandez, E.: Plant disease detection using hyperspectral imaging. In: 2017 International Conference on Digital Image Computing: Techniques and Applications (DICTA), pp. 1–8. IEEE (2017)

26. Monno, Y., Tanaka, M., Okutomi, M.: Multispectral demosaicking using guided filter. In: Digital Photography VIII, vol. 8299, p. 82990O. International Society for Optics and Photonics (2012)

27. Mühle, R., Markgraf, W., Hilsmann, A., Malberg, H., Eisert, P., Wisotzky, E.L.: Comparison of different spectral cameras for image-guided organ transplantation. J. Biomed. Opt. **26**(7), 076007 (2021). https://doi.org/10.1117/1.JBO.26.7.076007

28. Ogawa, S., et al.: Demosaicking method for multispectral images based on spatial gradient and inter-channel correlation. In: Mansouri, A., Nouboud, F., Chalifour, A., Mammass, D., Meunier, J., ElMoataz, A. (eds.) ICISP 2016. LNCS, vol. 9680, pp. 157–166. Springer, Cham (2016). https://doi.org/10.1007/978-3-319-33618-3_17

29. Shafri, H.Z., Taherzadeh, E., Mansor, S., Ashurov, R.: Hyperspectral remote sensing of urban areas: an overview of techniques and applications. Res. J. Appl. Sci. Eng. Technol. **4**(11), 1557–1565 (2012)

30. Shi, Z., Chen, C., Xiong, Z., Liu, D., Wu, F.: Hscnn+: advanced CNN-based hyperspectral recovery from RGB images. In: Proceedings of the IEEE Conference on Computer Vision and Pattern Recognition Workshops, pp. 939–947 (2018)

31. Stockman, A.: Cone fundamentals and CIE standards. Curr. Opin. Behav. Sci. **30**, 87–93 (2019)

32. Wang, Y.Q.: A multilayer neural network for image demosaicking. In: 2014 IEEE International Conference on Image Processing (ICIP), pp. 1852–1856. IEEE (2014)
33. Wang, Z., Bovik, A.C., Sheikh, H.R., Simoncelli, E.P.: Image quality assessment: from error visibility to structural similarity. IEEE Trans. Image Process. **13**(4), 600–612 (2004)
34. Wisotzky, E.L., et al.: Validation of two techniques for intraoperative hyperspectral human tissue determination. In: Proceedings of SPIE, vol. 10951, p. 109511Z (2019). https://doi.org/10.1117/12.2512811
35. Wisotzky, E.L., Kossack, B., Uecker, F.C., Arens, P., Hilsmann, A., Eisert, P.: Validation of two techniques for intraoperative hyperspectral human tissue determination. J. Med. Imaging **7**(6) (2020). https://doi.org/10.1117/1.JMI.7.6.065001
36. Wisotzky, E.L., Uecker, F.C., Arens, P., Dommerich, S., Hilsmann, A., Eisert, P.: Intraoperative hyperspectral determination of human tissue properties. J. Biomed. Opt. **23**(9), 1–8 (2018). https://doi.org/10.1117/1.JBO.23.9.091409
37. Yamanaka, J., Kuwashima, S., Kurita, T.: Fast and accurate image super resolution by deep cnn with skip connection and network in network. In: Liu, D., Xie, S., Li, Y., Zhao, D., El-Alfy, E.S. (eds.) ICONIP 2017, vol. 10635, pp. 217–225. Springer, Heidelberg (2017). https://doi.org/10.1007/978-3-319-70096-0_23
38. Yasuma, F., Mitsunaga, T., Iso, D., Nayar, S.K.: Generalized assorted pixel camera: postcapture control of resolution, dynamic range, and spectrum. IEEE Trans. Image Process. **19**(9), 2241–2253 (2010)
39. Yokoya, N., Yairi, T., Iwasaki, A.: Coupled nonnegative matrix factorization unmixing for hyperspectral and multispectral data fusion. IEEE Trans. Geosci. Remote Sens. **50**(2), 528–537 (2011)
40. Zhang, Y.: Spatial resolution enhancement of hyperspectral image based on the combination of spectral mixing model and observation model. In: Image and Signal Processing for Remote Sensing XX, vol. 9244, p. 924405. International Society for Optics and Photonics (2014)

Motion, Pose Estimation and Tracking

SF2SE3: Clustering Scene Flow into SE(3)-Motions via Proposal and Selection

Leonhard Sommer[(✉)], Philipp Schröppel, and Thomas Brox

University of Freiburg, Freiburg im Breisgau, Germany
{sommerl,schroepp,brox}@cs.uni-freiburg.de
https://lmb.informatik.uni-freiburg.de

Abstract. We propose SF2SE3, a novel approach to estimate scene dynamics in form of a segmentation into independently moving rigid objects and their $SE(3)$-motions. SF2SE3 operates on two consecutive stereo or RGB-D images. First, noisy scene flow is obtained by application of existing optical flow and depth estimation algorithms. SF2SE3 then iteratively (1) samples pixel sets to compute $SE(3)$-motion proposals, and (2) selects the best $SE(3)$-motion proposal with respect to a maximum coverage formulation. Finally, objects are formed by assigning pixels uniquely to the selected $SE(3)$-motions based on consistency with the input scene flow and spatial proximity.

The main novelties are a more informed strategy for the sampling of motion proposals and a maximum coverage formulation for the proposal selection. We conduct evaluations on multiple datasets regarding application of SF2SE3 for scene flow estimation, object segmentation and visual odometry. SF2SE3 performs on par with the state of the art for scene flow estimation and is more accurate for segmentation and odometry.

Keywords: Low-level vision and optical flow · Clustering · Pose estimation · Segmentation · Scene understanding · 3D vision and stereo

1 Introduction

Knowledge about dynamically moving objects is valuable for many intelligent systems. This is the case for systems that take a passive role as in augmented reality or are capable of acting as in robot navigation and object manipulation.

In this work, we propose a novel approach for this task that we term Scene-Flow-To-$SE(3)$ (SF2SE3). SF2SE3 estimates scene dynamics in form of a segmentation of the scene into independently moving objects and the $SE(3)$-motion for each object. SF2SE3 operates on two consecutive stereo or RGB-D images. First, off-the-shelf optical flow and disparity estimation algorithms are applied

Supplementary Information The online version contains supplementary material available at https://doi.org/10.1007/978-3-031-16788-1_14.

Fig. 1. Overview of SF2SE3: Optical flow and disparity are estimated with off-the-shelf networks and combined to an initial scene flow estimate. The resulting scene flow is noisy due to inaccurate estimations and due to occlusions (center image). SF2SE3 optimizes a set of objects with corresponding $SE(3)$-motions and an assignment from pixels to objects such that the initial scene flow is best covered with a minimal number of objects. Finally, an improved scene flow estimate can be derived from the object segmentation and $SE(3)$-motions, as shown in the last image. Furthermore, SF2SE3 obtains the camera egomotion by determining the $SE(3)$-motion of the background.

to obtain optical flow between the two timesteps and depth maps for each timestep. The predictions are combined to obtain scene flow. Note that the obtained scene flow is noisy, especially in case of occlusions. SF2SE3 then iteratively (1) samples pixel sets to compute $SE(3)$-motion proposals, and (2) selects the best $SE(3)$-motion proposal with respect to a maximum coverage formulation. Finally, objects are created for the selected $SE(3)$-motions by grouping pixels based on concistency of the input scene flow with the object $SE(3)$-motion. Further, SF2SE3 derives scene flow and the camera egomotion from the segmentation and $SE(3)$-motions. The described pipeline is illustrated in Fig 1.

Regarding related work, SF2SE3 is most similar to ACOSF [12] in that it approaches the problem as iteratively finding $SE(3)$-motion proposals and optimizing an assignment of pixels to the proposals. However, SF2SE3 introduces several improvements. Firstly, instead of randomly accumulating clusters that serve to estimate $SE(3)$-motion proposals, we propose a more informed strategy that exploits a rigidity constraint, *i.e.* forms clusters from points that have fixed 3D distances. Secondly, we propose a coverage problem formulation for selecting the best motion proposal such that (a) the input scene flow of all data points is best covered, and (b) irrelevant or similar $SE(3)$-motions are prohibited. The iterative process ends when no proposal fulfills the side-constraints from (b), whereas ACOSF iteratively selects a fixed number of $SE(3)$-motions.

We evaluate SF2SE3 and compare to state-of-the-art approaches for multiple tasks and datasets: we evaluate scene flow estimation on the KITTI [17] and FlyingThings3D [16] datasets, moving object segmentation on FlyingThings3D, and visual odometry on FlyingThings3D, KITTI and TUM RGB-D [19]. We use the state-of-the-art approaches CamLiFlow [13], RAFT-3D [22], RigidMask [30] and ACOSF as strong baselines for the comparison. CamLiFlow, RAFT-3D and RigidMask are currently the best approaches on the KITTI leaderboard and ACOSF is the most similar baseline to SF2SE3.

Compared to RAFT-3D, SF2SE3 obtains similar scene flow outlier rates on KITTI (-0.45%) and FlythingThings3D ($+0.47\%$). However, the advantage is additional output information in form of the object segmentation as opposed to pixel-wise motions.

Compared to RigidMask, the scene flow outlier rate of SF2SE3 is slightly worse on KITTI (+0.43%) but significantly better on FlyingThings3D (−6.76%), which is due to assumptions about blob-like object shapes within RigidMask. Regarding object segmentation, SF2SE3 achieves higher accuracy than Rigid-Mask on FlyingThings3D (+2.59%).

Compared to ACOSF, SF2SE3 decreases the scene flow outlier rate on KITTI (−2.58%). Further, the runtime is decrease from 5 min to 2.84 s.

On all evaluated dynamic sequences of the TUM and Bonn RGB-D dataset, SF2SE3 achieves, compared to the two-frame based solutions RigidMask and VO-SF, the best performance.

To summarize, SF2SE3 is useful to retrieve a compressed representation of scene dynamics in form of an accurate segmentation of moving rigid objects, their corresponding $SE(3)$-motions, and the camera egomotion.

2   Related Work

In the literature, different models for the scene dynamics between two frames exist: (1) non-rigid models estimate pointwise scene flow or $SE(3)$-transformations, and (2) object-rigid models try to cluster the scene into rigid objects and estimate one $SE(3)$-transformation per object. Regarding the output, all models allow to derive pointwise 3D motion. Object-rigid models additionally provide a segmentation of the scene into independently moving objects. Furthermore, if an object is detected as static background, odometry information can be derived.

Our work falls in the object-rigid model category, but we compare to strong baselines from both categories. In the following, we give an overview of related works that estimate scene dynamics with such models.

2.1   Non-rigid Models

Non-rigid models make no assumptions about rigidity and estimate the motion of each point in the scene individually as scene flow or $SE(3)$-transformations.

The pioneering work of Vedula *et al.* [24] introduced the notion of scene flow and proposed algorithms for computing scene flow from optical flow depending on additional surface information.

Following that, multiple works built on the variational formulation for optical flow estimation from Horn and Schunk [5] and adapted it for scene flow estimation [1,6,9,23,25,28].

With the success of deep learning on classification tasks and with the availability of large synthetic datasets like Sintel [3] and FlyingThings3D [16], deep learning models for the estimation of pointwise scene dynamics have been proposed [7,11,14,18,22,29]. In particular, in this work, we compare with RAFT-3D [22], which estimates pixel-wise $SE(3)$-motions from RGB-D images. RAFT-3D iteratively estimates scene flow residuals and a soft grouping of pixels with similar 3D motion. In each iteration, the residuals and the soft grouping are used to optimize pixel-wise $SE(3)$-motions such that the scene flow residuals for the respective pixel and for grouped pixels are minimized.

2.2 Object-Rigid Models

Object-rigid models segment the scene into a set of rigid objects and estimate a $SE(3)$-transformation for each object. The advantages compared to non-rigid models are a more compressed representation of information, and the availability of the object segmentation. The disadvantage is that scene dynamics cannot be correctly represented in case that the rigidity assumption is violated.

Classical approaches in this category are PRSM [26,27] and OSF [17], which split the scene into rigid planes based on a superpixelization and assign $SE(3)$-motions to each plane. MC-Flow [10] estimates scene flow from RGB-D images by optimizing a set of clusters with corresponding $SE(3)$-motions and a soft assignment of pixels to the clusters. A follow-up work [8] splits the clusters into static background and dynamic objects and estimates odometry and dynamic object motion separately.

An early learned object-rigid approach is ISF [2], which builds on OSF but employs deep networks that estimate an instance segmentation and object coordinates for each instance. The later approach DRISF [15] employs deep networks to estimate optical flow, disparity and instance segmentation and then optimizes a $SE(3)$-motion per instance such that is consistent with the other quantities.

In this work, we compare to the more recent learned approaches ACOSF [12] and RigidMask [30]. ACOSF takes a similar approach as OSF but employs deep networks to estimate optical flow and disparity. RigidMask employs deep networks to estimate depth and optical flow and to segment static background and dynamic rigid objects. Based on the segmentation, $SE(3)$ motions are fit for the camera egomotion and the motion of all objects. A key difference between RigidMask and our approach is that RigidMask represents objects with polar coordinates, which is problematic for objects with complex structures. In contrast, our approach takes no assumptions about object shapes.

3 Approach

In the following, we describe the proposed SF2SE3 approach. SF2SE3 takes two RGB-D images from consecutive timestamps τ_1 and τ_2 and the associated optical flow as input. While the optical flow is retrieved with RAFT [21], the depth is retrieved with a depth camera or LEAStereo [4] in the case of a stereo camera. Using the first RGB-D image as reference image, the corresponding depth at τ_2 is obtained by backward warping the second depth image according to the optical flow. Further, occlusions are estimated by applying an absolute limit on the optical flow forward-backward inconsistency [20]. The depth is indicated as unreliable in case of invalid measurements and additionally for the depth at τ_2 in case of temporal occlusions. SF2SE3 then operates on the set $\mathcal{D}$ of all image points of the reference image:

$$\mathcal{D} = \{\, D_i = (\underbrace{x_i, y_i, z_i, \overbrace{p_i^{\tau_1}, p_i^{\tau_2}, r_i^{\tau_1}}^{motion}, u_i, v_i, d_i, r_i^{\tau_2}}_{spatial})\,\}, \tag{1}$$

where each image point D consists of its pixel coordinates (x, y), its depth z at τ_1, its 3D points (p^{τ_1}, p^{τ_2}), its optical flow (u, v), its warped disparity d at τ_2 and its depth reliability indications r^{τ_1} and r^{τ_2}.

The objective then is to estimate a collection of objects $\mathcal{O}$ where each object O consists of a point cloud $\mathcal{P}$ and a $SE(3)$-motion (R, t):

$$\mathcal{O} = \{\, O_k = (\ \underbrace{\mathcal{P}_k}_{spatial}\ , \overbrace{R_k, t_k}^{motion})\,\}. \tag{2}$$

3.1 Algorithm Outline

SF2SE3 aims to estimate objects $\mathcal{O}$ which explain or rather cover the down-sampled image points $\mathcal{D}$. To quantify the coverage of an image point D by an object O, we introduce a motion inlier model $P_I^{motion}(D, O)$ and a spatial inlier model $P_I^{spatial}(D, O)$. These models are described in detail in Sect. 3.2. Based upon these models, objects $\mathcal{O}$ are retrieved iteratively, see Fig. 2.

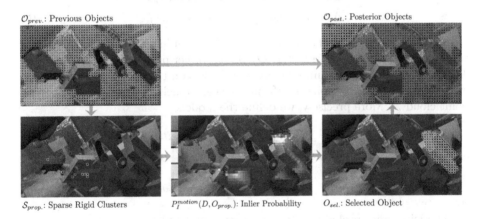

$\mathcal{O}_{prev.}$: Previous Objects $\mathcal{O}_{post.}$: Posterior Objects

$\mathcal{S}_{prop.}$: Sparse Rigid Clusters $P_I^{motion}(D, O_{prop.})$: Inlier Probability $O_{sel.}$: Selected Object

Fig. 2. Cycle of Single Object Estimation: SF2SE3 estimates objects $\mathcal{O}$ iteratively. All image points which are not covered by any previous objects $\mathcal{O}_{prev.}$, and which depth is reliable, are accumulated to obtain sparse rigid clustered $\mathcal{S}_{prop.}$. This is described in Sect. 3.3. Fitting an $SE(3)$-motion to each cluster results in the proposed objects $\mathcal{O}_{prop.}$ which do not contain a spatial model. Based on the inlier probabilities for the proposed and the previous objects, $P_I^{motion}(D, O_{prop.})$ and $P_I(D, O_{prev.})$, the one object is selected which maximizes the coverage objective. The coverage problem is described in Sect. 3.4. After selecting a single object $O_{sel.}$, the image points which are covered based on the motion model $P_I^{motion}(D, O_{sel})$ are forming the point cloud which serves from then on as spatial model. Further, the selected object is split into multiple objects by splitting the point cloud into multiple spatially connected point clouds. This is not illustrated in the diagram for the sake of clarity. In case no proposed object has a sufficiently high coverage, the iterative process ends.

Finally, based on the obtained rigid objects $\mathcal{O}$, SF2SE3 derives odometry, segmentation and scene flow, which is described in Sect. 3.5. For this, one object is determined as background and each image point is assigned to one object based on the likelihood $f(D|O)$, which is introduced in Sect. 3.2.

For further implementation details, including parameter settings, we publish the source code at https://www.github.com/lmb-freiburg/sf2se3.

3.2 Consensus Models

To quantify the motion consensus between the scene flow of a data point and the $SE(3)$-motion of an object, we define a motion inlier probability $P_I^{motion}(D, O)$ and likelihood $f^{motion}(D|O)$. These are defined by separately imposing Gaussian models on the deviation of the data point's optical flow in x- and y-direction and the disparity d of the second time point from the respective projections π_u, π_v, π_d of the forward transformed 3D point p^{τ_1} according to the object's rotation R and translation t. Formally, this can be written as

$$\Delta u = u - \pi_u(Rp^{\tau_1} + t) \sim \mathcal{N}(0, \sigma_u^2) \tag{3}$$

$$\Delta v = v - \pi_v(Rp^{\tau_1} + t) \sim \mathcal{N}(0, \sigma_v^2) \tag{4}$$

$$\Delta d = d - \pi_d(Rp^{\tau_1} + t) \sim \mathcal{N}(0, \sigma_d^2). \tag{5}$$

Spatial proximity of the data point and the object's point cloud is measured with the likelihood $f^{spatial}(D|O)$ and the inlier probability $P_I^{spatial}(D, O)$. Therefore, we separately impose Gaussian models on the x-, y-, and z-deviation of the data point's 3D point p^{τ_1} from its nearest neighbor inside the object's point cloud $\mathcal{P}$. More precisely, we define the models

$$\Delta x = x - x^{NN} \sim \mathcal{N}(0, \sigma_{geo-2D}^2) \tag{6}$$

$$\Delta y = y - y^{NN} \sim \mathcal{N}(0, \sigma_{geo-2D}^2) \tag{7}$$

$$\Delta z_{rel} = \frac{z - z^{NN}}{\frac{z+z^{NN}}{2}} \sim \mathcal{N}(0, \sigma_{geo-depth-rel}^2). \tag{8}$$

The joint inlier probability for the spatial model yields

$$P_I^{spat.}(D, O) = \begin{cases} P_{I,Gauss.}(\Delta x)P_{I,Gauss.}(\Delta y)P_{I,Gauss.}(\Delta z_{rel}) & , r^{\tau_1} = 1 \\ P_{I,Gauss.}(\Delta x)P_{I,Gauss.}(\Delta y) & , r^{\tau_1} = 0 \end{cases}, \tag{9}$$

likewise the spatial likelihood $f^{spatial}(D|O)$ is calculated. Details for the calculation of the Gaussian inlier probability $P_{I,Gauss.}$ are provided in the Supplementary.

Regarding the motion model, the joint inlier probability yields

$$P_I^{mot.}(D, O) = \begin{cases} P_{I,Gauss.}(\Delta u)P_{I,Gauss.}(\Delta v)P_{I,Gauss.}(\Delta d) & , r^{\tau_1} = 1, r^{\tau_2} = 1 \\ P_{I,Gauss.}(\Delta u)P_{I,Gauss.}(\Delta v) & , r^{\tau_1} = 1, r^{\tau_2} = 0 \\ 1 & , else, \end{cases} \tag{10}$$

the same applies for the motion likelihood $f^{motion}(D|O)$.

Joining the motion and the spatial model, under the assumption of independence, results in

$$f(D|O) = f^{spatial}(D|O)f^{motion}(D|O) \tag{11}$$

$$P_I(D,O) = P_I^{spatial}(D,O)P_I^{motion}(D,O). \tag{12}$$

3.3   Proposals via Rigidity Constraint

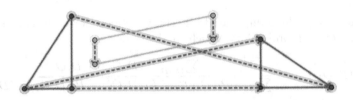

Fig. 3. Rigidity: Points of the same color are rigid, which means that the distance between each pair remains constant despite the movement. Two accumulated points are already sufficient to calculate new $SE(3)$-motion proposals.

Each proposed object is found by fitting an $SE(3)$-motion to a cluster of scene flow points which fulfill the rigidity constraint, see Fig. 3. For each pair of points (p_i, p_j) it must hold

$$\left|\, \left\|p_i^{T_2} - p_j^{T_2}\right\| - \left\|p_i^{T_1} - p_j^{T_1}\right\|\, \right| < \delta_{rigid-dev-max}. \tag{13}$$

Clusters are instantiated by single scene flow points, which are sampled uniformly. Further points are iteratively added while preserving rigidity. Even though two points are already sufficient to estimate a $SE(3)$-motion, additional points serve robustness against noise.

3.4   Selection via Coverage Problem

Having obtained the $SE(3)$-motion proposals $\mathcal{O}_{prop.}$, we select the one which covers the most scene flow points which are not sufficiently covered by previous objects $\mathcal{O}_{prev.}$. Coverage is measured for the proposed objects with the motion model $P_I^{motion}(D,O)$. For previously selected objects, the spatial model is available in form of a point cloud. This allows us to use the joint model $P_I(D,O)$, consisting of motion and spatial model. Formally, we define the objective as

$$\max_{O \in \mathcal{O}_{prop.}} \frac{1}{|\mathcal{D}|} \sum_{D \in \mathcal{D}} \max \left[P_I^{motion}(D,O), \max_{\tilde{O} \in \mathcal{O}_{prev.}} P_I(D,\tilde{O}) \right]. \tag{14}$$

Separating the previous coverage results in

$$\max_{O \in \mathcal{O}_{prop.}} P_{contribute}(\mathcal{D}, O, \mathcal{O}_{prev.}) + \frac{1}{|\mathcal{D}|} \sum_{D_i \in \mathcal{D}} \max_{\tilde{O} \in \mathcal{O}_{prev.}} P_I(D, \tilde{O})), \quad (15)$$

with the contribution probability $P_{contribute}(\mathcal{D}, O, \mathcal{O}_{prev.})$ defined as

$$P_{contribute}(\mathcal{D}, O, \mathcal{O}_{prev.}) = \frac{1}{|\mathcal{D}|} \sum_{D \in \mathcal{D}} \max \left[P_I^{motion}(D, O) - \max_{\tilde{O} \in \mathcal{O}_{prev.}} P_I(D, \tilde{O}), 0 \right]. \quad (16)$$

To exclude irrelevant objects, we impose for each object a minimum contribution probability.

Moreover, to exclude duplicated objects, we impose for each pair of objects a maximum overlap probability, which we define as

$$P_{overlap}(\mathcal{D}, O_1, O_2) = \frac{\sum_{D \in \mathcal{D}} P_I(D, O_1) P_I(D, O_2)}{\sum_{D \in \mathcal{D}} P_I(D, O_1) + P_I(D, O_2) - P_I(D, O_1) P_I(D, O_2)}. \quad (17)$$

This overlap probability constitutes an extension of the intersection-over-union metric for soft assignments, e.g., probabilities.

Taken together, we formulate the optimization problem as

$$\max_{O \subseteq \mathcal{O}_{prop.}} P_{contrib.}(\mathcal{D}, O, \mathcal{O}_{prev.}) \quad (18a)$$

$$\text{subject to } P_{contrib.}(\mathcal{D}, O, \mathcal{O}_{prev.}) \geq \delta_{contrib.-min} \quad (18b)$$

$$P_{overlap}(\mathcal{D}, O, \mathcal{O}_{prev.}) \leq \delta_{overlap-max} \quad \forall O_{prev.} \in \mathcal{O}_{prev.} \quad (18c)$$

An example for the calculation of contribution as well as overlap probability is provided in Fig. 4.

Automatically the algorithm ends when the contribution probability falls below the minimum requirement.

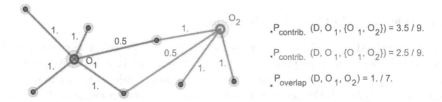

Fig. 4. Contribution and Overlap Probability for two Objects: The edge weights equal the inlier probabilities $P_I(D, O)$, a missing edge indicates $P_I(D, O) = 0$. Corresponding probabilities for contribution of each object and the overlap probability of both objects are calculated on the right side.

3.5 Deduction of Odometry, Image Segmentation, and Scene Flow

For estimating the odometry we determine the dynamic rigid object that equals the background. Assuming that the background equals the largest object, we choose the one that yields the largest contribution probability

$$O_{background} = \arg\max_{O \in \mathcal{O}} P_{contribute}(\mathcal{D}, O, \mathcal{O}). \tag{19}$$

Based on the maximum likelihood, we assign each pixel from the high-resolution image to one of the objects

$$\phi_{D,O} = \begin{cases} 1 & , \arg\max_{O_k} f(D|O_k) = O \\ 0 \end{cases}. \tag{20}$$

Given the object assignment the scene flow s can be retrieved for each 3D point p^{τ_1} as

$$s = Rp^{\tau_1} + t - p^{\tau_1}. \tag{21}$$

4 Results

We compare the performance of our method against the state of the art regarding scene flow, segmentation, odometry, and runtime (Fig. 5).

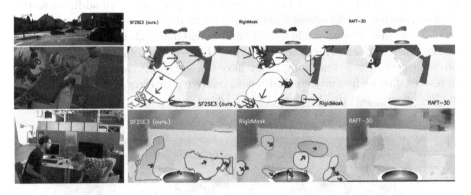

Fig. 5. Qualitative results of our approach, RigidMask, and Raft-3D (left to right) on KITTI-2015, FlyingThings3D, and TUM RGB-D (top to bottom). The scene flow is color coded for the x- and z-directions, as indicated by the color wheel. The edges of the object segmentation are highlighted and the motions of object centroids are indicated with arrows. The odometry is indicated with an arrow starting from the center of the color wheel. Note that RAFT-3D estimates no segmentation and odometry.

Table 1. Listed are the outlier percentages for disparities at both timestamps, optical flow, and scene flow. An outlier for optical flow and disparity implies a deviation from the ground truth of > 3 pxl absolutely and > 5% relatively. An outlier for scene flow implies an outlier for either disparity or optical flow.

Method	Dataset	D1 out. [%]	D2 out. [%]	OF out. [%]	SF out. [%]
ACOSF [12]	KITTI - test	3.58	5.31	5.79	7.90
DRISF [15]	KITTI - test	2.55	4.04	4.73	6.31
RigidMask [30]	KITTI - test	1.89	3.23	3.50	4.89
RAFT-3D [22]	KITTI - test	1.81	3.67	4.29	5.77
CamLiFlow [13]	KITTI - test	1.81	2.95	3.10	**4.43**
SF2SE3 (ours.)	KITTI - test	1.65	3.11	4.11	5.32
Warped Scene Flow	FT3D - test	2.35	16.19	9.43	19.09
RigidMask	FT3D - test	2.35	6.98	15.42	15.49
RAFT-3D	FT3D - test	2.35	4.40	8.47	**8.26**
SF2SE3 (ours.)	FT3D - test	2.35	4.86	8.76	8.73

Scene Flow. To evaluate the performance of estimating scene flow, we measure the outlier percentages of disparity, optical flow and scene flow, in the same way as the KITTI-2015 benchmark [17]. The results for KITTI-2015 and FlyingThings3D are listed in Table 1.

Segmentation. For the segmentation evaluation, we retrieve a one-to-one matching between predicted and ground truth objects with the Hungarian method and report the accuracy, *i.e.* the ratio of correctly assigned pixels. In addition to the accuracy, we report the average number of extracted objects per frame.

In Table 2 the results are listed for the FlyingThings3D dataset. The original ground truth segmentation can not be directly used, as it splits the background into multiple objects even though they have the same $SE(3)$-motion (Fig. 6 left). To resolve this, we fuse objects that have a relative pose error, as defined in Eq. 24 and 25, below a certain threshold (Fig. 6 right).

Fig. 6. Based on the segmentation of objects from the FlyingThings3D dataset, illustrated on the left side, the segmentation for evaluation, shown on the right side, is retrieved. To achieve this, we fuse objects with similar $SE(3)$-motion.

Table 2. Results for segmenting frames into moving objects. Metrics are the segmentation accuracy and the average objects count in each frame.

Method	Dataset	Segmentation acc. [%]	Objects count [#]
RigidMask	FT3D - test	80.71	16.32
SF2SE3 (ours.)	FT3D - test	**83.30**	7.04

Odometry. We evaluate the odometry with the relative pose error, which has a translational part RPE_{transl} and a rotational part RPE_{rot}. These are computed from the relative transformation T_{rel} between the ground truth transformation $^{t_1}\hat{T}_{t_0}$ and the estimated transformation $^{t_1}T_{t_0}$, which is defined as follows:

$$T_{rel} = {}^{t_1}\hat{T}_{t_0}^{-1} \, {}^{t_1}T_{t_0} \tag{22}$$

$$T_{rel} = \begin{bmatrix} R_{rel} & t_{rel} \\ 0 & 1 \end{bmatrix}. \tag{23}$$

The translational and rotational relative pose errors RPE_{transl} and RPE_{rot} are computed as follows:

$$RPE_{transl} = \frac{\|t_{rel}\|}{t_1 - t_0} \text{ in } \frac{m}{s} \tag{24}$$

$$RPE_{rot} = \frac{\|w(R_{rel})\|}{t_1 - t_0} \frac{360}{2\pi} \text{ in } \frac{deg}{s}, \tag{25}$$

with $w(R_{rel})$ being the axis-angle representation of the rotation. We report the results on FlyingThings3D and TUM RGB-D in Table 3.

Table 3. Results for odometry estimation on FlyingThings3D and TUM RGB-D using the translation and rotational relative pose errors RPE_{transl} and RPE_{rot}.

Method	Dataset	RPE transl. [m/s]	RPE rot. [deg/s]
Static	FT3D - test	0.364	2.472
RigidMask	FT3D - test	0.082	0.174
SF2SE3 (ours.)	FT3D - test	**0.025**	**0.099**
Static	TUM FR3	0.156	18.167
RigidMask	TUM FR3	0.281	4.345
SF2SE3 (ours.)	TUM FR3	**0.090**	**3.535**

Runtime. We report average runtimes of SF2SE3 and the baselines in Table 4. The runtimes were measured on a single Nvidia GeForce RTX 2080Ti.

Table 4. Runtimes for different approaches on FlyingThings3D, KITTI-2015, and TUM RGB-D. If depth and optical flow are estimated separately and the runtime is known, it is listed. Runtimes in red are from the original authors on different hardware.

Method	Dataset	Depth [s]	Optical flow [s]	Total [s]
ACOSF	KITTI - test	–	–	300.00
DRISF	KITTI - test	–	–	0.75
RigidMask	KITTI - test	1.46	–	4.90
RAFT-3D	KITTI - test	1.44	–	2.73
CAMLiFlow	KITTI - test	–	–	1.20
SF2SE3 (ours.)	KITTI - test	1.43	0.42	2.84
RigidMask	FT3D - test	1.60	–	8.54
RAFT-3D	FT3D - test	1.58	–	2.92
SF2SE3 (ours.)	FT3D – test	1.58	0.40	3.79
RigidMask	TUM FR3	0.23	–	2.34
RAFT-3D	TUM FR3	0.23	–	1.15
SF2SE3 (ours.)	TUM FR3	0.23	0.36	2.29

5   Discussion

Our method performs on par with state-of-the-art methods of the KITTI-2015 scene flow benchmark, achieving a scene flow outlier rate similar to RigidMask (+0.43%), CamLiFlow (+0.89%) and RAFT-3D (−0.45%). Further, on FlyingThings3D it achieves similar scene flow performance as the pointwise method RAFT-3D (−0.47%) and outperforms RigidMask significantly (−6.76%) while also achieving an higher segmentation accuracy (+2.59%). In contrast to Rigid-Mask and others, our method generalizes better because supervision is only applied for estimating optical flow and depth. Therefore, we detect the pedestrians in Fig. 7.

Fig. 7. Segmenting pedestrians on KITTI-2015: ground truth, estimate from SF2SE3, estimate from RigidMask (left to right). In contrast to RigidMask, the proposed SF2SE3 approach detects the pedestrians (marked with white bounding boxes) because it is not visually fine-tuned for cars. This problem of RigidMask is not reflected in the quantitative results because ground truth is missing for these points.

Moreover, our representation does not geometrically restrict object shapes. Thus, we are able to fit objects with complex shapes, as shown in Fig. 8.

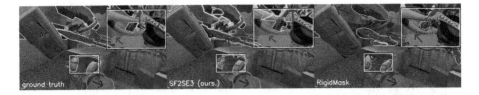

Fig. 8. Segmenting objects with complex shapes on FlyingThings3D: ground truth, estimate from SF2SE3, estimate from RigidMask (left to right). RigidMask over-segments the semi-circular shaped headphones on the bottom and misses the headphones on the right (marked with white bounding boxes).

Compared to ACOSF, which is the most accurate method in scene flow on KITTI-2015 that estimates segmentation and takes no assumptions about object shapes, our method reduces the scene flow outlier percentage by (-2.58%) and the runtime from 300 s to 2.84 s. Furthermore, we expect ACOSF to perform even worse in case of more objects, e.g. in FlyingThings3D, as it uses random sampling for retrieving initial $SE(3)$-motions and assumes a fixed number of objects.

6   Conclusion

We have proposed SF2SE3: a novel method that builds on top of state-of-the-art optical flow and disparity networks to estimate scene flow, segmentation, and odometry. In our evaluation on KITTI-2015, FlyingThings3D and TUM RGB-D, SF2SE3 shows better performance than the state of the art in segmentation and odometry, while achieving comparative results for scene flow estimation.

Acknowledgment. The research leading to these results is funded by the German Federal Ministry for Economic Affairs and Climate Action within the project "KI Delta Learning" (Förderkennzeichen 19A19013N). The authors would like to thank the consortium for the successful cooperation.

References

1. Basha, T., Moses, Y., Kiryati, N.: Multi-view scene flow estimation: a view centered variational approach. In: 2010 IEEE Computer Society Conference on Computer Vision and Pattern Recognition, pp. 1506–1513 (2010). https://doi.org/10.1109/CVPR.2010.5539791
2. Behl, A., Hosseini Jafari, O., Karthik Mustikovela, S., Abu Alhaija, H., Rother, C., Geiger, A.: Bounding boxes, segmentations and object coordinates: How important is recognition for 3D scene flow estimation in autonomous driving scenarios? In: Proceedings of the IEEE International Conference on Computer Vision, pp. 2574–2583 (2017)

3. Butler, D.J., Wulff, J., Stanley, G.B., Black, M.J.: A naturalistic open source movie for optical flow evaluation. In: Fitzgibbon, A., Lazebnik, S., Perona, P., Sato, Y., Schmid, C. (eds.) ECCV 2012. LNCS, vol. 7577, pp. 611–625. Springer, Heidelberg (2012). https://doi.org/10.1007/978-3-642-33783-3_44

4. Cheng, X., et al.: Hierarchical neural architecture search for deep stereo matching. arXiv preprint arXiv:2010.13501 (2020)

5. Horn, B.K., Schunck, B.G.: Determining optical flow. Artif. Intell. **17**(1–3), 185–203 (1981)

6. Huguet, F., Devernay, F.: A variational method for scene flow estimation from stereo sequences. In: 2007 IEEE 11th International Conference on Computer Vision, pp. 1–7. IEEE (2007)

7. Hur, J., Roth, S.: Self-supervised monocular scene flow estimation. In: Proceedings of the IEEE/CVF Conference on Computer Vision and Pattern Recognition, pp. 7396–7405 (2020)

8. Jaimez, M., Kerl, C., Gonzalez-Jimenez, J., Cremers, D.: Fast odometry and scene flow from rgb-d cameras based on geometric clustering. In: 2017 IEEE International Conference on Robotics and Automation (ICRA), pp. 3992–3999. IEEE (2017)

9. Jaimez, M., Souiai, M., Gonzalez-Jimenez, J., Cremers, D.: A primal-dual framework for real-time dense RGB-D scene flow. In: 2015 IEEE International Conference on Robotics and Automation (ICRA), pp. 98–104. IEEE (2015)

10. Jaimez, M., Souiai, M., Stückler, J., Gonzalez-Jimenez, J., Cremers, D.: Motion cooperation: Smooth piece-wise rigid scene flow from rgb-d images. In: 2015 International Conference on 3D Vision, pp. 64–72. IEEE (2015)

11. Jiang, H., Sun, D., Jampani, V., Lv, Z., Learned-Miller, E., Kautz, J.: Sense: a shared encoder network for scene-flow estimation. In: Proceedings of the IEEE/CVF International Conference on Computer Vision, pp. 3195–3204 (2019)

12. Li, C., Ma, H., Liao, Q.: Two-stage adaptive object scene flow using hybrid CNN-CRF model. In: 2020 25th International Conference on Pattern Recognition (ICPR), pp. 3876–3883. IEEE (2021)

13. Liu, H., Lu, T., Xu, Y., Liu, J., Li, W., Chen, L.: Camliflow: bidirectional camera-lidar fusion for joint optical flow and scene flow estimation. arXiv preprint arXiv:2111.10502 (2021)

14. Liu, X., Qi, C.R., Guibas, L.J.: Flownet3d: learning scene flow in 3D point clouds. In: Proceedings of the IEEE/CVF Conference on Computer Vision and Pattern Recognition, pp. 529–537 (2019)

15. Ma, W.C., Wang, S., Hu, R., Xiong, Y., Urtasun, R.: Deep rigid instance scene flow. In: Proceedings of the IEEE/CVF Conference on Computer Vision and Pattern Recognition, pp. 3614–3622 (2019)

16. Mayer, N., et al.: A large dataset to train convolutional networks for disparity, optical flow, and scene flow estimation. In: Proceedings of the IEEE Conference on Computer Vision and Pattern Recognition, pp. 4040–4048 (2016)

17. Menze, M., Geiger, A.: Object scene flow for autonomous vehicles. In: Proceedings of the IEEE Conference on Computer Vision and Pattern Recognition, pp. 3061–3070 (2015)

18. Schuster, R., Unger, C., Stricker, D.: A deep temporal fusion framework for scene flow using a learnable motion model and occlusions. In: Proceedings of the IEEE/CVF Winter Conference on Applications of Computer Vision, pp. 247–255 (2021)

19. Sturm, J., Engelhard, N., Endres, F., Burgard, W., Cremers, D.: A benchmark for the evaluation of rgb-d slam systems. In: 2012 IEEE/RSJ International Conference on Intelligent Robots and Systems, pp. 573–580. IEEE (2012)

20. Sundaram, N., Brox, T., Keutzer, K.: Dense point trajectories by GPU-accelerated large displacement optical flow. In: Daniilidis, K., Maragos, P., Paragios, N. (eds.) ECCV 2010. LNCS, vol. 6311, pp. 438–451. Springer, Heidelberg (2010). https://doi.org/10.1007/978-3-642-15549-9_32

21. Teed, Z., Deng, J.: RAFT: recurrent all-pairs field transforms for optical flow. In: Vedaldi, A., Bischof, H., Brox, T., Frahm, J.-M. (eds.) ECCV 2020. LNCS, vol. 12347, pp. 402–419. Springer, Cham (2020). https://doi.org/10.1007/978-3-030-58536-5_24

22. Teed, Z., Deng, J.: Raft-3D: scene flow using rigid-motion embeddings. In: Proceedings of the IEEE/CVF Conference on Computer Vision and Pattern Recognition, pp. 8375–8384 (2021)

23. Valgaerts, L., Bruhn, A., Zimmer, H., Weickert, J., Stoll, C., Theobalt, C.: Joint estimation of motion, structure and geometry from stereo sequences. In: Daniilidis, K., Maragos, P., Paragios, N. (eds.) ECCV 2010. LNCS, vol. 6314, pp. 568–581. Springer, Heidelberg (2010). https://doi.org/10.1007/978-3-642-15561-1_41

24. Vedula, S., Baker, S., Rander, P., Collins, R., Kanade, T.: Three-dimensional scene flow. In: Proceedings of the Seventh IEEE International Conference on Computer Vision, vol. 2, pp. 722–729. IEEE (1999)

25. Vogel, C., Schindler, K., Roth, S.: 3D scene flow estimation with a rigid motion prior. In: 2011 International Conference on Computer Vision, pp. 1291–1298. IEEE (2011)

26. Vogel, C., Schindler, K., Roth, S.: Piecewise rigid scene flow. In: Proceedings of the IEEE International Conference on Computer Vision, pp. 1377–1384 (2013)

27. Vogel, C., Schindler, K., Roth, S.: 3D scene flow estimation with a piecewise rigid scene model. Int. J. Comput. Vision 115(1), 1–28 (2015)

28. Wedel, A., Rabe, C., Vaudrey, T., Brox, T., Franke, U., Cremers, D.: Efficient dense scene flow from sparse or dense stereo data. In: Forsyth, D., Torr, P., Zisserman, A. (eds.) ECCV 2008. LNCS, vol. 5302, pp. 739–751. Springer, Heidelberg (2008). https://doi.org/10.1007/978-3-540-88682-2_56

29. Yang, G., Ramanan, D.: Upgrading optical flow to 3D scene flow through optical expansion. In: Proceedings of the IEEE/CVF Conference on Computer Vision and Pattern Recognition, pp. 1334–1343 (2020)

30. Yang, G., Ramanan, D.: Learning to segment rigid motions from two frames. In: Proceedings of the IEEE/CVF Conference on Computer Vision and Pattern Recognition, pp. 1266–1275 (2021)

Improving Unsupervised Label Propagation for Pose Tracking and Video Object Segmentation

Urs Waldmann[1,2(✉)] ⓘ, Jannik Bamberger[1], Ole Johannsen[1] ⓘ,
Oliver Deussen[1,2] ⓘ, and Bastian Goldlücke[1,2] ⓘ

[1] Department of Computer and Information Science, University of Konstanz,
Konstanz, Germany
urs.waldmann@uni-konstanz.de
[2] Centre for the Advanced Study of Collective Behaviour, University of Konstanz,
Konstanz, Germany

Abstract. Label propagation is a challenging task in computer vision with many applications. One approach is to learn representations of visual correspondence. In this paper, we study recent works on label propagation based on correspondence, carefully evaluate the effect of various aspects of their implementation, and improve upon various details. Our pipeline assembled from these best practices outperforms the previous state of the art in terms of $PCK_{0.1}$ on the JHMDB dataset by 6.5%. We also propose a novel joint framework for tracking and keypoint propagation, which in contrast to the core pipeline is applicable to tracking small objects and obtains results that substantially exceed the performance of the core pipeline. Finally, for VOS, we extend the core pipeline to a fully unsupervised one by initializing the first frame with the self-attention layer from DINO. Our pipeline for VOS runs online and can handle static objects. It outperforms unsupervised frameworks with these characteristics.

Keywords: Label propagation · Unsupervised · Pose tracking · VOS

1 Introduction

Learning representations of visual and temporal correspondence is a fundamental task in computer vision. It has many applications ranging from depth estimation [16] and optical flow [2,4,12] to segmentation and tracking [38,40,50]. Many

We acknowledge funding by the Deutsche Forschungsgemeinschaft (DFG, German Research Foundation) under Germany's Excellence Strategy - EXC 2117 - 422037984. The authors also thank Hemal Naik, Nagy Máté, Fumihiro Kano and Iain D. Couzin for providing the real-world pigeon data.

Supplementary Information The online version contains supplementary material available at https://doi.org/10.1007/978-3-031-16788-1_15.

B. Andres et al. (Eds.): DAGM GCPR 2022, LNCS 13485, pp. 230–245, 2022.
https://doi.org/10.1007/978-3-031-16788-1_15

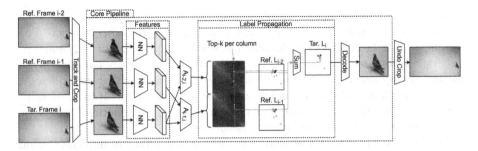

Fig. 1. *Overview of the joint tracking and label propagation pipeline, showing pigeon keypoint tracking as an example.* The core pipeline of our method uses deep neural network features to compute affinity matrices between a target frame and one or multiple reference frames. Labels for the target frame are computed by propagating the reference labels based on the combined affinity matrices. Finally, the predicted labels are decoded to coordinate values. The proposed extended pipeline shown outside the dashed box is necessary for tracking small objects. Here, an object tracker is used to locate the object of interest in each frame. This allows us to crop a region around the object and perform keypoint propagation at a much higher resolution, after which we undo the coordinate transform of the cropping for the decoded keypoints.

methods have been developed that can be split into two main categories [26], according to whether they learn correspondence on a pixel level [1,44,48,51,57] or a coarser level, i.e. region or object-based [12,27,30,43]. Recent approaches show that the two tasks can be modeled together with a single transformation operation [26,52].

The first networks learning representations for visual correspondence were trained in a supervised manner [4,11,12,39,42,46,49] and have some limitations. In particular, they do not generalize well to real-world scenes when trained on synthetic data, or rely on human annotations. That is why subsequently methods with less supervision have been preferred. Most of them are self-supervised or weakly supervised [13,22,23,26,29,52], and also reason at various levels of visual correspondence.

We focus on the notion of visual correspondence in tracking since it plays a key role in many applications, ranging from autonomous driving [6] to biology [15]. Categories of tracking differ in which kind of information is tracked throughout the frames. In Visual Object Tracking (VOT) [21], the typical aim is to track just the position or bounding box of an object throughout a video, given the location in the first frame. In contrast, Video Object Segmentation (VOS) [37] aims for a more fine-grained tracking, where we track segmentation masks on the pixel-level instead of bounding boxes. Somewhere in between, there is pose keypoint propagation, which tracks keypoints or a skeleton of an object. All of these tracking tasks can be subsumed within the framework of label propagation [48], on which we focus in this work.

Many recent state-of-the-art approaches for unsupervised label propagation employ similar methodology, in particular correspondence-based representation learning [3,13,22,23,26,52]. During inference, they also tend to do something similar at the core, and compute a pixel-to-pixel affinity (similarity score) between adjacent frames, using this affinity function to propagate the label function. The computation of the affinity is predominantly based on top-k (cf. Sect. 3.2) and context frames (long-term vs. short-term, cf. Sect. 3.2). Further key parameters are feature, affinity and label normalization. Although using a similar methodology, the actual implementations of label propagation are quite different in the details. At the same time, these details are often not discussed at great length in the papers, as they can be found in the accompanying source code.

However, in experiments we find that these minor details in implementation can indeed have a very big impact on the performance, and that there are further improvements to be made which also contribute to a better accuracy. We therefore believe that a study of the effects of the details, in conjunction with a discussion on the best choice for particular implementations, can be a quite useful contribution.

Contributions. First, we present a pipeline for label propagation based on visual correspondence, which is built by carefully evaluating and selecting best practices, and improving upon previous work in important implementation details. This way, we outperform state of the art pipelines in terms of Percentage of Correct Keypoints ($PCK_{0.1}$) on the JHMDB [14] dataset by at least 6.5% in pose tracking. Second, we extend the pipeline to a joint tracking and keypoint propagation framework. This allows us to perform pose tracking for a novel data set for pigeons, which plays a role in our biological research on collective behaviour, and where the objects to be tracked are small compared to the frame size. With the proposed technique, we obtain excellent performance in pose tracking, exceeding the performance for humans (JHMDB) and substantially surpassing the core pipeline. Finally, for VOS, we present a pipeline which is fully unsupervised, initializing the first frame with the self-attention layer from DINO [3] that is trained without supervision. Here, if we disregard non-interactive post-processing, we outperform other unsupervised methods that do not rely on motion segmentation, which limits the method to moving objects. Both dataset and our code are publicly available at https://urs-waldmann.github.io/improving-unsupervised-label-propagation/.

2   Related Work

Unsupervised Label Propagation. Unsupervised label propagation has been studied extensively in recent years, for example to overcome the need for annotated training data. The key idea in Wang et al. [52] is to train with UDT-like [50] cycles, i.e. tracking backward and forward along a cycle in time. The inconsistency between start and end point serves as the loss function. The authors also demand cycle-consistency of a static track by forcing the tracker to relocate the next patch in each successive frame. To overcome momentary occlusions and ease learning in case of sudden changes in object pose, they also implement skip-cycles and learn from shorter cycles when the full cycle is too difficult. Lai and Xie [23] extend a framework [48] where tracking emerges automatically by learning the target colors for a gray-scale input frame. The authors add channel-wise dropout and color jitter to the input. Li et al. [26] show that enforcing cycle-consistency is equivalent to regularizing the affinity to be orthogonal, i.e. they encourage every pixel to fall into the same location after one cycle of forward and backward tracking. Lai et al. [22] augment the architecture with a long- and short-term memory component to remember older frames: a two-step attention mechanism first coarsely searches for candidate windows and then computes the fine-grained matching. This ROI-based affinity computation additionally saves memory and computational overhead. Jabri et al. [13] use a Graph Neural Network [8,47] to learn representations of visual and temporal correspondence. The authors demand cycle-consistency for a walk on a space-time graph that is constructed from a video, where nodes are image patches and edges are only between neigh-bouring nodes. They include also edge dropout [41] and test-time adaptation. i.e. the model can be improved for correspondence by fine-tuning the representation at test time on new videos. In contrast to us, they need to manually initialize the mask of the first frame. Caron et al. [3] follow the experimental protocol in [13], but use different features. Our core pipeline is similar to UVC [26] but includes some improvements from STC [13] and CycleTime [52]. Further, we include new improvements to the keypoint label creation, add frame upscaling and object tracking [50] to improve the keypoint accuracy.

Video Object Segmentation. Yang et al. in [53] introduce an architecture where they exploit motion, using only optical flow as input, and train it without any manual supervision. They use L2 loss between input and reconstructed flow, pixel-wise entropy regularisation on inferred masks, multi-step flow I from multiple time steps as objects may be static for some frames, i.e. $\{I_{t\to t+n_1}, I_{t\to t+n_2}\}$, $n_1, n_2 \in \{-2, -1, 1, 2\}$, and a consistency loss. Yang et al. in [55] present an adversarial contextual model to detect moving objects in images. Their approach exploits classical region-based variational segmentation in addition to modern deep learning-based self-supervision. The authors encourage temporal consistency on the final masks and apply a CRF-based [20] post-processing on them.

In contrast to both works [53,55] we use an architecture based on correspondence that does not require object motion and can handle also objects which are static for longer time intervals. We are also able to propagate both masks and keypoints, while they can only propagate masks. In addition, we initialize the first frame with the self-attention layer from DINO [3] that is trained without supervision, so we do not depend on human annotation at all. Furthermore, in contrast to [55], our framework runs online, while they make use of offline post-processing.

3   Label Propagation

3.1   General Task

Label propagation is the task of propagating a number l of one or more label functions in a semantically plausible way trough a video. Given an initial set of label functions $L_1 \in [0,1]^{h \times w \times l}$ and a video $V = \{I_i | i \in 1, \ldots, N\}$ with frames

$I_i \in \mathcal{C}^{H \times W}$ in color space $\mathcal{C}$, the goal is to predict a new set of label functions $L_i \in [0,1]^{h \times w \times l}, i \geq 2$ for each subsequent frame in the video. Note that label functions are typically given at a lower resolution than the input images to match the feature extractor.

The common approach to this problem is based on training a feature extractor $\mathcal{F} : \mathcal{C}^{H \times W} \to \mathbb{R}^{h \times w \times d}$. It has to create location-aware features, i.e. there needs to be a spatial pixel-to-feature correspondence. The feature extractor is then used to compute pixel-wise frame-to-frame affinities which represent the semantic similarity, the larger, the stronger the semantic similarity. Let $F_i := \mathcal{F}(I_i)$ be the feature map for frame i and $\bar{F}_i \in \mathbb{R}^{hw \times d}$ be the linearized feature representation, where each row is a feature vector corresponding to one spatial location in the feature map. Then the affinity between frames I_i and I_j is given by $A_{i,j} = \bar{F}_i \bar{F}_j^T \in \mathbb{R}^{hw \times hw}$. Each entry in this affinity map corresponds to the semantic similarity of a pixel in frame I_i and another pixel in frame I_j.

To propagate a label function L_{i-1} by one frame – i.e. predicting L_i – the affinity matrix $A_{i-1,i}$ is computed. This allows us to compute the pixels of L_i from the correspondence $\hat{p}$ with highest affinity,

$$L_i = L_{i-1}\big(c(\hat{p})\big) \text{ with } \hat{p}(x,y) = \underset{q \in \{1,\dots hw\}}{\operatorname{argmax}} \big\{ A_{i-1,i}\big(q, c^{-1}(x,y)\big) \big\}. \quad (1)$$

Here, $c : \{1,\dots,hw\} \to \{1,\dots,h\} \times \{1,\dots,w\}$ is a coordinate translation function that maps the linearized coordinates in $\bar{F}$ to the corresponding spatial coordinates in F.

Choice of Feature Extractor. The feature extraction is an integral building block of label propagation. In this work we are not concerned with different strategies to build and train the feature extraction network, but look at the inference pipeline used for label propagation, so no new networks were trained. We use a ResNet18 [10] trained with the methodology of Li et al. [26] for pose tracking. Even though this method is no longer state of the art, we show that minor improvements to the inference pipeline can make the method competitive again. For our fully unsupervised segment propagation experiments, we rely on a vision transformer [18] trained with DINO [3]. In line with [3,13,26], we found that L_2 normalization of each feature vector is beneficial for the tracking performance (cf. 'No Feature Normalization' vs. 'Baseline' in Table 1).

3.2 Common Extensions

The general approach to label propagation is conceptually sound, but has some difficulties in the real world. Real-world data is noisy, the feature extractors are not able to compute exact semantic similarities and the compute resources are limited. Therefore, a myriad of extensions and modifications to the simple label propagation are made, which are different across methods. In our work, we analyze various implementations of current label propagation methods and notice that they tend to implement the same functionality in slightly different ways. We took this as an opportunity to look at the performance implications of such differences. This allows us to combine the best choice for each subtask to obtain higher-quality results than each method individually.

Affinity Top-K and Normalization. In Eq. (1) we have used the location of the maximum to select the propagated value. In theory, this is the optimal choice, but the noisy nature of the implementation can lead to outliers in the affinity matrix. To mitigate the impact of a single outlier, it is common [13, 22, 23, 26, 52] to select more than one similar location and aggregate the corresponding label function values. The aggregation of values differs from method to method. CycleTime [52] applies a softmax function to the affinity matrix columns and then aggregates the top k values with a weighted sum. The affinity scores act as the weights. In contrast, STC [13] selects the top k values first and then applies the softmax function afterwards. Further, UVC [26] and STC [13] have a temperature parameter in their softmax implementation that helps to sharpen or soften the output distribution. Many methods [3, 26] also apply a network-specific transformation to the affinity values. Our implementation uses a top-k-based implementation with network-specific transformations for UVC and DINO. We perform the normalization after applying top-k, using softmax for UVC and a simple normalization for DINO. We found that these combinations work best for the respective networks. Results of ablation experiments concerning the number of reference locations k (top-k also compared against a pure argmax approach) and the normalization are shown in Table 1.

Local Affinity. Another measure to prevent implausible solutions is the use of local affinity [13, 23, 26]. An object in a video can only travel a limited distance between frames. The actual number of pixels depends on parameters like movement speed, camera motion and frame rate. Assumptions about the maximum displacement of an object between frames allow us to consider only a fixed-size neighborhood around each location for propagation. The benefits of this approach are two-fold. For one, the restriction to plausible movements in the image prevents some undesired solutions that would lead to discontinuities in the predicted label functions. This restriction leads to better results (cf. Table 1). Secondly, a consistent local neighborhood implementation brings potential for large performance improvements and memory reduction. Because only a small area around each pixel is required, the affinity matrix does not have to be computed entirely, and the memory requirement exhibits a linear instead of a quadratic growth in the number of pixels.

Context Frames. Videos commonly contain frames of varying quality, thus it proves beneficial to use more than one reference frame at once. In this work we compared two approaches to using such context frames: First, we analyzed the results of individual propagation from each context frame and subsequent aggregation of the individual results. Secondly, we analyzed the joint propagation from all context frames at once, cf. Fig. 1. The first approach is used by [23, 26, 52] and simply averages the label function results of each context frame. The joint propagation used by [3, 13] treats the affinity matrices of each context frame as one big matrix with columns containing positions in all context frames. The propagation is then performed by selecting the top-k values from the columns of this joint affinity matrix. This joint approach allows to skip bad frames altogether and instead select more values from higher-quality frames. We found that the second approach works substantially better (cf. 'Batched Label Propagation' vs. 'Baseline' in Table 1). The context frames we use are the first frame and a fixed number of directly preceding frames (cf. Figs. 1 and 2 and Tables 2 and 3 in our supplemental material). Using the first frame as context is advisable as the label functions for this frame are given. Hence, they are correct all the time which helps to avoid drift during longer tracking.

4   Applications and Case Studies

The generic way of formulating label propagation enables the propagation of various kinds of information through a video with a single framework. Examples include masks, keypoints and textures. Here, we take a look at mask and keypoint propagation. For each of these tasks, we have certain information in our problem domain $\mathbb{P}$, which we have to map to our label propagation framework. Thus, we have to define an encoding function $E : \mathbb{P} \to [0, 1]^{h \times w \times l}$ and a decoder $D : [0, 1]^{h \times w \times l} \to \mathbb{P}$. Definitions of our encoders and decoders with their implementation details are in Sect. 1 of our supplemental material.

4.1   Pose Tracking

We implement our encoding and decoding functions for the pose tracking core pipeline (cf. dashed box in Fig. 1) in such a way that the keypoints are computed with sub-pixel precision (cf. Sect. 1.1 in our supplementary).

We also contribute a new finding related to the sub-pixel precision requirement of keypoint encoding and decoding. Somewhat surprisingly, we found that upsampling of the input frames before processing is actually of substantial benefit. Although this does not add any additional information, the increase in spatial resolution of the feature map reduces the precision loss during encoding and decoding and leads to an overall gain in performance (cf. 'Image Scale 320' vs. 'Baseline' in Table 1). In consequence, our final proposed pipeline includes this step.

4.2   Joint Tracking and Keypoint Propagation

Inspired by our particular use case of pigeons (cf. Fig. 4), we first track the object using [50] and then propagate the keypoints on the cropped images (cf. Sect. 4.1). This is our novel joint tracking and keypoint propagation framework (cf. Fig. 1). Details are provided in Sect. 1 in the supplementary material. We use this novel joint tracking and keypoint propagation pipeline only for pose tracking, not VOS.

4.3   Unsupervised Zero-Shot VOS

Encoding a set of $j = 1, \ldots, n$ masks $M_i^j \in \{0, 1\}^{H \times W}$ for unsupervised VOS is relatively simple [22,23,26,52]. Details on this and our unsupervised mask initialization can be found in Sect. 1.3 in our supplemental material.

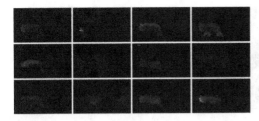

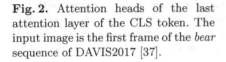

Fig. 2. Attention heads of the last attention layer of the CLS token. The input image is the first frame of the *bear* sequence of DAVIS2017 [37].

Fig. 3. Ground truth mask (left), input frame (middle) and predicted mask (right) for the *bear*, *dog-agility* and *drift-straight* sequences of DAVIS2017.

Unsupervised Mask Initialization. Caron et al. [3] found that their unsupervised training method DINO results in a vision transformer with semantically relevant attention (cf. Fig. 1 in [3]). We use this finding together with the learned attention layer to perform fully unsupervised object segmentation. Note that so far, the only human intervention in our tracking pipeline is the initialization in the first frame. To get rid of it, we generate a mask prediction for the first frame from the last attention layer of the CLS token. Some of the attention heads focus on background objects (e.g. Fig. 2 second row, second and fourth image). Further, we observe that the attention heads seldom focus on the entire object, and are more likely to select a single feature of the object of interest. Hence, we employ a heuristic to select attention heads that are important by computing the median value per attention head and discarding all masks with a median value below a fixed quantile. The reasoning behind this selection is that attention focused on the background is spread out more than attention focusing on a single feature or object. Therefore, the median value is below average.

Next, we follow the steps of Caron et al. [3] to select pixel locations per attention head.

One disadvantage of the attention is that it is rather coarse. Thus, we improve the mask quality by performing CRF-based refinement which fits the mask prediction to the input image. These mask refinement steps are similar to the postprocessing steps performed by some other label propagation methods [29,55].

Note that this approach only works for a single object, and can fail for objects that occupy only a small area of the image. This is due to the nature of our attention selection mechanism, where we combine multiple attention heads. Another caveat is the heuristic-based nature of this approach. Ideally, we would find a way to perform the attention head selection automatically. Still, the method shows that the use of attention for mask initialization already gives promising results as shown in Fig. 3.

Real-world dataset	$PCK_{0.1}$	$PCK_{0.2}$
Core pipeline	7.5%	25.1%
Joint pipeline	81.0%	97.5%
Synthetic dataset	$PCK_{0.1}$	$PCK_{0.2}$
Core pipeline	0.4%	1.0%
Joint pipeline	65.7%	89.1%

Fig. 4. *Results for pigeon tracking, showing the last frame of the sequence with the tracked keypoints. Left image*: crop of the real-world sequence. *Right image*: crop of the synthetic dataset. *Table*: comparison of the results for the core pipeline (Sect. 4.1) and the proposed joint tracking and keypoint propagation pipeline introduced in Sect. 4.2.

5 Experiments

In this section we present ablation studies and discuss results of our applications and case studies. For more ablation studies, additional qualitative and quantitative results, we refer to Sects. 2–4 respectively in our supplemental material.

5.1 Ablation Studies

Table 1. *Ablation study of joint tracking and keypoint propagation on the JHMDB test set.* We measure performance as the percentage of correct keypoints (PCK) [56]. Keypoints are correct if the distance to the corresponding ground truth keypoint relative to the object size falls within a threshold α. Our implementation of PCK is equivalent to the one used by UVC [26], using 60% of the bounding box diagonal as the baseline radius ($\alpha = 1.0$). PCK is shown at thresholds $\alpha = 0.1$ and $\alpha = 0.2$, while Δ_α denotes the absolute difference to the baseline configuration which includes all improvements.

	$PCK_{0.1}$	$\Delta_{0.1}$	$PCK_{0.2}$	$\Delta_{0.2}$
Baseline	65.8	–	84.2	–
No Feature Normalization	64.0	−1.8	82.5	−1.7
Affinity Top-1 (ArgMax)	59.8	−6.0	80.8	−3.4
Affinity Top-5	65.0	−0.8	83.8	−0.4
No Affinity Normalization	65.3	−0.5	83.9	−0.3
Affinity Softmax-Normalization	65.2	−0.6	83.8	−0.4
Unrestricted Local Affinity	65.6	−0.2	83.9	−0.3
Batched Label Propagation	61.6	−4.2	80.5	−3.7
No Subpixel-Accurate Labels	65.5	−0.3	84.0	−0.2
Image Scale 320	63.2	−2.6	82.1	−2.1

Pose Tracking. For our pose tracking framework, we perform various ablation experiments to ensure that our pose tracking pipeline works as intended, and analyze the impact of the different components and improvements in the implementation. The baseline configuration of the pipeline is specified in Sect. 4. The

Table 2. *Ablation study for different types of mask initialization.* Performance is measured as IoU using the first mask of DAVIS2016 as ground truth. Delta shows absolute difference to the baseline mask initialization.

Ablation	mean	Δ	median	Δ
Baseline	50.8	–	54.7	–
No med. pre-filter	49.1	−1.7	51.7	−3.0
No mask refinement	41.1	−9.7	38.3	−16.4
No med. post-filter	49.9	−0.9	53.9	−0.8

majority of experiments are summarized in Table 1. Besides the listed results, we also experimented with various local affinity sizes. The optimal size for our configuration is 12. Further, we looked at the influence of the number of similar locations to aggregate for label propagation (cf. affinity top-k, Sect. 3.2). Here, we found that increasing or decreasing the baseline value of 20 by 5 corresponds to a performance loss of roughly 0.2% $PCK_{0.1}$.

Unsupervised Mask Initialization. The baseline configuration is described in Sect. 4. All results using unsupervised mask initialization use the ViT_b/8 model trained with DINO [3]. We evaluate the performance of the mask initialization on its own by comparing our mask prediction and the ground truth mask of frames from the DAVIS2016 [35] dataset. The quality of the mask prediction is computed as the intersection over union (IoU) of the binary masks. Table 2 shows how the performance changes in response to the removal of mask refinement or one of the median filtering steps. Removal of the mask refinement step altogether leads to the biggest drop in performance. Intuitively, this makes sense, as we combine multiple coarse attention masks, thus the refinement can capture a lot of the details in the image. Mask refinement also requires most of the initialization time, thus we chose the number of iterations as 10 to strike a balance between result quality and speed. Going from 1 to 10 iterations improves the results by 5.2% but increasing the iterations further, up to 50, only gives an additional 0.5% while requiring significantly more time. For both the quantile and mass percentage, we found that changes from the baseline in either direction reduce the performance. Increases as well as decreases by 0.05 reduce the mean and median performance by values ranging from 0.5% to 6.9%. This trend continues for larger changes as well. Reducing the spatial resolution or transformer network size have a major negative impact on the performance. Using ViT_b/16 or ViT_s/8 decrease the mean IoU by 5.0% and by 11.9% respectively.

5.2   Label Propagation

Pose Tracking. We show that our modifications to the label propagation pipeline can achieve substantial improvements in tracking accuracy. Quantitative results on JHMDB [14] are given in Table 3 where 15 human keypoints are

Table 3. *Results for pose tracking on the JHMDB test set. Ours denotes just the core pipeline, while Ours + tracking includes joint tracking and keypoint propagation introduced in Sec. 4.2. Values are given in PCK at thresholds 0.1 and 0.2, respectively.*

	ClrPtr [48]	SIFTflow [27]	CycleTime [52]	mgPFF [19]	CorrFlow [23]	UVC [26]	STC [13]	Ours	Ours + trk	Supervised [54]
$PCK_{0.1}$	45.2	49.0	57.7	58.4	58.5	58.6	59.3	63.9	**65.8**	68.7
$PCK_{0.2}$	69.6	68.6	78.5	78.1	78.8	79.8	**84.9**	82.8	84.2	92.1

tracked. In terms of $PCK_{0.1}$, we achieve an improvement of 7.2% over UVC [26] and 6.5% over STC [13], respectively, the latter being the current state-of-the-art at the time of writing. However, for the less precise $PCK_{0.2}$, we outperform UVC but are behind STC. Since we use the exact network weights as UVC, it is possible that switching to the same feature extraction network as STC might make a difference here. We leave testing this hypothesis to future work.

Pigeon Keypoint Tracking. We use a newly created dataset with video material showing a pigeon. Seven keypoints located at the head, shoulders and tail are annotated. Frames have a resolution of 1080×1920 pixels and the pigeon occupies a region of roughly 200×150 pixels on average. A real-world video of 326 frames and a synthetically generated sequence (for details cf. our supplementary) with 949 frames form the dataset. Figure 4 shows results on these sequences. Clearly, with our tracking modification (cf. Sect. 4.2) our method can achieve a similar magnitude of performance as JHMDB whereas the core pipeline is not capable to handle such a scenario.

Fig. 5. *Qualitative results on DAVIS2016val with zero-shot inference. The shown sequences are blackswan, bmx-trees, breakdance and dance-twirl, listed from top to bottom. The first frame shows the mask initialization result. The following frames were sampled over the entire video length maintaining even spacing in between.*

Table 4. *Results for VOS on zero-shot DAVIS2016val. Supervision* refers to the the use of human annotations during training. Methods are considered unsupervised if no training is performed or no human annotations are used. Weak supervision refers to the use of human annotations without pixel-precision, e.g. bounding boxes or class labels. A method is considered *online*, if it processes videos as a stream of frames instead of using them all at once. The results have to be produced immediately, before the next frame is used. *Post-processing* refers to refinement steps after the actual segmentation, such as temporal smoothing or averaging of an ensemble of evaluation runs. Such techniques could be applied to other methods as well and they typically operate offline. *"Motion only"* marks methods that perform motion segmentation. These methods only work for moving objects, which limits their applicability. The results for methods other than our own are collected from the official DAVIS2016 results page [36] and the respective papers. For CIS [55], AMD [28] and 3DC-Seg [31], some measures were not reported, hence they are missing in the table. ∗: Results are available with a few frames delay.

Method	Online	Post-processing	Motion only	$\mathcal{J}\&\mathcal{F}_m$	$\mathcal{J}_m$	$\mathcal{J}_r$	$\mathcal{F}_m$	$\mathcal{F}_r$
Unsupervised								
MGR [34]	×	×	✓	44.0	48.9	44.7	39.1	28.6
KEY [24]	×	✓	×	46.3	49.8	59.1	42.7	37.5
MSG [32]	×	×	×	52.1	53.3	61.6	50.8	60.0
NLC [7]	×	✓	✓	53.7	55.1	55.8	52.3	51.9
FST [33]	×	✓	×	53.5	55.8	64.9	51.1	51.6
MuG [29]	×	✓	×	54.8	58.0	65.3	51.5	53.2
AMD [28]	✓	×	✓	–	57.8	–	–	–
CIS [55]	✓	×	✓	–	59.2	–	–	–
Ours	✓	×	×	59.8	61.6	71.3	58.0	63.3
MoGr [53]	✓	×	✓	64.7	68.3	79.5	61.1	72.1
CIS + pp [55]	×	✓	✓	–	71.5	–	–	–
Weakly supervised								
COSEG [45]	×	✓	×	51.1	52.8	50.0	49.3	52.7
MuG [29]	×	✓	×	58.7	61.2	74.5	56.1	62.1
Fully supervised								
FSEG [5]	✓	×	×	68.0	70.7	83.5	65.3	73.8
ARP [17]	×	×	×	73.4	76.2	91.1	70.6	83.5
MATNet [58]	✓	✓	×	81.6	82.4	94.5	80.7	90.2
3DC-Seg [31]	✓∗	×	×	84.5	84.3	–	84.7	–

Table 5. *Z-VOS results on SegTrackV2.* The Z-VOS inference treats the dataset as a single-object dataset, i.e. all individual object masks are merged into one object. †: These methods use either offline post-processing or rely on some component with supervised training.

	MoGr [53]	CIS [55]	FST [33]	AMD [28]	SAGE [9]	Ours	MoGr†	CIS+pp†	NLC†[7]
$\mathcal{J}_m$	37.8	45.6	47.8	57.0	57.6	58.4	58.6	62.0	67.2

Unsupervised Zero-Shot VOS. Single-object Z-VOS results can be found in Tables 4 and 5 for DAVIS2016 and SegTrackV2 [25] respectively. On DAVIS2016, only motion segmentation methods (CIS [55] and MoGr [53]) achieve better performance. Motion segmentation has the disadvantage that static, non-moving objects cannot be segmented, whereas our method can also detect such objects. Incidentally, DAVIS2016 and SegTrackV2 contains only objects in motion, thus posing no problem for motion segmentation methods. Further, CIS uses extensive post-processing including an ensemble of models, temporal smoothing, and refinement with a CRF. Yang et al. [53] argument that a fair comparison should not use such post-processing, since it reduces real-world use of the methods. If we consider the results of CIS without the post-processing ($\mathcal{J}_m = 59.2$), our method surpasses this result by 2.4%. Some other methods also apply post-processing, as noted in Table 4. Additionally, some of the methods listed in the *unsupervised* section actually use some supervised components. NLC relies on supervised boundary detection and MoGr uses supervised optical flow to achieve the listed results. Compared to MoGr with unsupervised flow, we surpass their result of $\mathcal{J}_m = 53.2$ [53] by 8.4%. Qualitative single-object Z-VOS results on DAVIS2016val are in Fig. 5.

Qualitative results of fully unsupervised mask initialization instead are shown in Fig. 3 and the first column in Fig. 5. We can observe that our method has difficulties selecting a good mask for objects that appear at a very small scale, but for larger objects the results look visually good.

Inference Speed. A rigorous evaluation of the inference speed is impossible without similar implementations and data captured on identical hardware. This is out of scope for our work, but we give a rough expected performance in the supplemental material.

6   Conclusions

In this work, we perfom a careful study of the state-of-the-art in correspondence-based label propagation methods and present a pipeline composed of the best practices and with improvements in various implementation details. For pose tracking, the proposed pipeline outperforms previous state of the art in terms of $PCK_{0.1}$ on the JHMDB dataset by at least 6.5%, more precisely, 59.3% in [13] vs. 65.8% for our method. In addition, we propose a joint tracking and keypoint propagation framework which allows to accurately propagate keypoints in our new dataset for tracking of pigeons, which is not possible with the standard pipeline. Finally, for video object segmentation, we extend our pipeline to a truly unsupervised one by initializing the first frame with the self-attention layer from DINO that is trained with no supervision. Our method is online and can compete with state of the art pipelines. Note that while [53] achieves a higher score among the unsupervised pipelines, their framework (and others) is based on optical flow and does not work for static objects. Furthermore, while [55] can achieve a higher score with their post-processing framework, it is computationally intensive and could be applied to any of the methods.

References

1. Bertinetto, L., Valmadre, J., Henriques, J.F., Vedaldi, A., Torr, P.H.S.: Fully-convolutional siamese networks for object tracking. In: Hua, G., Jégou, H. (eds.) ECCV 2016. LNCS, vol. 9914, pp. 850–865. Springer, Cham (2016). https://doi.org/10.1007/978-3-319-48881-3_56
2. Brox, T., Bruhn, A., Papenberg, N., Weickert, J.: High accuracy optical flow estimation based on a theory for warping. In: Pajdla, T., Matas, J. (eds.) ECCV 2004. LNCS, vol. 3024, pp. 25–36. Springer, Heidelberg (2004). https://doi.org/10.1007/978-3-540-24673-2_3
3. Caron, M., et al.: Emerging properties in self-supervised vision transformers. In: ICCV (2021)
4. Dosovitskiy, A., et al.: Flownet: learning optical flow with convolutional networks. In: ICCV (2015)
5. Dutt Jain, S., Xiong, B., Grauman, K.: FusionSeg: learning to combine motion and appearance for fully automatic segmentation of generic objects in videos. In: CVPR, pp. 3664–3673 (2017)
6. Ess, A., Schindler, K., Leibe, B., Gool, L.V.: Object detection and tracking for autonomous navigation in dynamic environments. Int. J. Rob. Res. 29(14), 1707–1725 (2010)
7. Faktor, A., Irani, M.: Video segmentation by non-local consensus voting. In: BMVC (2014)
8. Hamilton, W.L., Ying, R., Leskovec, J.: Inductive representation learning on large graphs. In: Proceedings of the 31st International Conference on Neural Information Processing Systems, NIPS 2017, pp. 1025–1035 (2017)
9. Hamilton, W.L., Ying, R., Leskovec, J.: Inductive representation learning on large graphs. In: NeurIPS, pp. 1025–1035 (2017)
10. He, K., Zhang, X., Ren, S., Sun, J.: Deep residual learning for image recognition. In: CVPR, pp. 770–778 (2016)
11. Held, D., Thrun, S., Savarese, S.: Learning to track at 100 FPS with deep regression networks. In: Leibe, B., Matas, J., Sebe, N., Welling, M. (eds.) ECCV 2016. LNCS, vol. 9905, pp. 749–765. Springer, Cham (2016). https://doi.org/10.1007/978-3-319-46448-0_45
12. Ilg, E., Mayer, N., Saikia, T., Keuper, M., Dosovitskiy, A., Brox, T.: Flownet 2.0: evolution of optical flow estimation with deep networks. In: CVPR (2017)
13. Jabri, A., Owens, A., Efros, A.: Space-time correspondence as a contrastive random walk. In: NeurIPS, pp. 19545–19560 (2020)
14. Jhuang, H., Gall, J., Zuffi, S., Schmid, C., Black, M.J.: Towards understanding action recognition. In: ICCV (2013)
15. Kays, R., Crofoot, M.C., Jetz, W., Wikelski, M.: Terrestrial animal tracking as an eye on life and planet. Science 348(6240), aaa2478 (2015)
16. Kendall, A., et al.: End-to-end learning of geometry and context for deep stereo regression. In: ICCV (2017)
17. Koh, Y.J., Kim, C.S.: Primary object segmentation in videos based on region augmentation and reduction. In: CVPR, pp. 7417–7425 (2017)
18. Kolesnikov, A., Dosovitskiy, A., et al.: An image is worth 16×16 words: transformers for image recognition at scale. In: ICLR (2021)
19. Kong, S., Fowlkes, C.: Multigrid predictive filter flow for unsupervised learning on videos. arXiv preprint arXiv:1904.01693 (2019)

20. Krähenbühl, P., Koltun, V.: Efficient inference in fully connected CRFs with gaussian edge potentials. In: NeurIPS (2011)
21. Kristan, M., et al.: A novel performance evaluation methodology for single-target trackers. IEEE TPAMI **38**(11), 2137–2155 (2016)
22. Lai, Z., Lu, E., Xie, W.: Mast: a memory-augmented self-supervised tracker. In: CVPR (2020)
23. Lai, Z., Xie, W.: Self-supervised learning for video correspondence flow. In: BMVC (2019)
24. Lee, Y.J., Kim, J., Grauman, K.: Key-segments for video object segmentation. In: ICCV, pp. 1995–2002 (2011)
25. Li, F., Kim, T., Humayun, A., Tsai, D., Rehg, J.M.: Video segmentation by tracking many figure-ground segments. In: ICCV, pp. 2192–2199 (2013)
26. Li, X., Liu, S., De Mello, S., Wang, X., Kautz, J., Yang, M.H.: Joint-task self-supervised learning for temporal correspondence. In: NeurIPS (2019)
27. Liu, C., Yuen, J., Torralba, A.: Sift flow: dense correspondence across scenes and its applications. IEEE TPAMI **33**(5), 978–994 (2011)
28. Liu, R., Wu, Z., Yu, S., Lin, S.: The emergence of objectness: learning zero-shot segmentation from videos. In: NeurIPS, vol. 34 (2021)
29. Lu, X., Wang, W., Shen, J., Tai, Y.W., Crandall, D.J., Hoi, S.C.H.: Learning video object segmentation from unlabeled videos. In: CVPR (2020)
30. Lucas, B.D., Kanade, T.: An iterative image registration technique with an application to stereo vision. In: DARPA Image Understanding Workshop, pp. 121–130 (1981)
31. Mahadevan, S., Athar, A., Ošep, A., Hennen, S., Leal-Taixé, L., Leibe, B.: Making a case for 3D convolutions for object segmentation in videos. In: BMVC (2020)
32. Ochs, P., Brox, T.: Object segmentation in video: a hierarchical variational approach for turning point trajectories into dense regions. In: ICCV, pp. 1583–1590 (2011)
33. Papazoglou, A., Ferrari, V.: Fast object segmentation in unconstrained video. In: ICCV, pp. 1777–1784 (2013)
34. Pathak, D., Girshick, R., Dollár, P., Darrell, T., Hariharan, B.: Learning features by watching objects move. In: CVPR, pp. 2701–2710 (2017)
35. Perazzi, F., Pont-Tuset, J., McWilliams, B., Van Gool, L., Gross, M., Sorkine-Hornung, A.: A benchmark dataset and evaluation methodology for video object segmentation. In: CVPR (2016)
36. Perazzi, F., Pont-Tuset, J., McWilliams, B., Van Gool, L., Gross, M., Sorkine-Hornung, A.: Official davis 2016 results list (2016). https://davischallenge.org/davis2016/soa_compare.html
37. Pont-Tuset, J., Perazzi, F., Caelles, S., Sorkine-Hornung, A., Arbeláez, P., Gool, L.V.: Davis challenge on video object segmentation 2017 (2017). https://davischallenge.org/challenge2017/index.html
38. Rafi, U., Doering, A., Leibe, B., Gall, J.: Self-supervised keypoint correspondences for multi-person pose estimation and tracking in videos. In: Vedaldi, A., Bischof, H., Brox, T., Frahm, J.-M. (eds.) ECCV 2020. LNCS, vol. 12365, pp. 36–52. Springer, Cham (2020). https://doi.org/10.1007/978-3-030-58565-5_3
39. Ranjan, A., Black, M.J.: Optical flow estimation using a spatial pyramid network. In: CVPR (2017)
40. Smith, S., Brady, J.: Asset-2: real-time motion segmentation and shape tracking. IEEE TPAMI **17**(8), 814–820 (1995)

41. Srivastava, N., Hinton, G., Krizhevsky, A., Sutskever, I., Salakhutdinov, R.: Dropout: a simple way to prevent neural networks from overfitting. J. Mach. Learn. Res. **15**(56), 1929–1958 (2014)
42. Sun, D., Yang, X., Liu, M.Y., Kautz, J.: Pwc-net: CNNs for optical flow using pyramid, warping, and cost volume. In: CVPR (2018)
43. Tao, R., Gavves, E., Smeulders, A.W.: Siamese instance search for tracking. In: CVPR (2016)
44. Thomee, B., et al.: Yfcc100m: the new data in multimedia research. Commun. ACM **59**(2), 64–73 (2016)
45. Tsai, Y.-H., Zhong, G., Yang, M.-H.: Semantic co-segmentation in videos. In: Leibe, B., Matas, J., Sebe, N., Welling, M. (eds.) ECCV 2016. LNCS, vol. 9908, pp. 760–775. Springer, Cham (2016). https://doi.org/10.1007/978-3-319-46493-0_46
46. Valmadre, J., Bertinetto, L., Henriques, J., Vedaldi, A., Torr, P.H.S.: End-to-end representation learning for correlation filter based tracking. In: CVPR (2017)
47. Veličković, P., Cucurull, G., Casanova, A., Romero, A., Liò, P., Bengio, Y.: Graph attention networks. In: ICLR (2018)
48. Vondrick, C., Shrivastava, A., Fathi, A., Guadarrama, S., Murphy, K.: Tracking emerges by colorizing videos. In: ECCV (2018)
49. Wang, N., Yeung, D.Y.: Learning a deep compact image representation for visual tracking. In: NeurIPS, vol. 26 (2013)
50. Wang, N., Zhou, W., Song, Y., Ma, C., Liu, W., Li, H.: Unsupervised deep representation learning for real-time tracking. IJCV **129**, 400–418 (2021)
51. Wang, Q., Zhang, L., Bertinetto, L., Hu, W., Torr, P.H.: Fast online object tracking and segmentation: a unifying approach. In: CVPR (2019)
52. Wang, X., Jabri, A., Efros, A.A.: Learning correspondence from the cycle-consistency of time. In: CVPR (2019)
53. Yang, C., Lamdouar, H., Lu, E., Zisserman, A., Xie, W.: Self-supervised video object segmentation by motion grouping. In: ICCV, pp. 7177–7188 (2021)
54. Yang, L., Wang, Y., Xiong, X., Yang, J., Katsaggelos, A.K.: Efficient video object segmentation via network modulation. In: CVPR (2018)
55. Yang, Y., Loquercio, A., Scaramuzza, D., Soatto, S.: Unsupervised moving object detection via contextual information separation. In: CVPR, pp. 879–888 (2019)
56. Yang, Y., Ramanan, D.: Articulated human detection with flexible mixtures of parts. IEEE TPAMI **35**, 2878–2890 (2012)
57. Zhou, Q., Liang, X., Gong, K., Lin, L.: Adaptive temporal encoding network for video instance-level human parsing. In: ACM MM, p. 1527–1535 (2018)
58. Zhou, T., Wang, S., Zhou, Y., Yao, Y., Li, J., Shao, L.: Motion-attentive transition for zero-shot video object segmentation. In: AAAI, pp. 13066–13073 (2020)

D-InLoc++: Indoor Localization in Dynamic Environments

Martina Dubenova[1,2](✉) ⓘ, Anna Zderadickova[1,2] ⓘ, Ondrej Kafka[1,2] ⓘ,
Tomas Pajdla[1,2] ⓘ, and Michal Polic[1,2] ⓘ

[1] CIIRC - Czech Institute of Informatics, Robotics and Cybernetics,
Czech Technical University in Prague, Prague, Czech Republic
`dubenma1@fel.cvut.cz`
[2] Visual Recognition Group, Faculty of Electrical Engineering,
Czech Technical University in Prague, Prague, Czech Republic

Abstract. Most state-of-the-art localization algorithms rely on robust relative pose estimation and geometry verification to obtain moving object agnostic camera poses in complex indoor environments. However, this approach is prone to mistakes if a scene contains repetitive structures, e.g., desks, tables, boxes, or moving people. We show that the movable objects incorporate non-negligible localization error and present a new straightforward method to predict the six-degree-of-freedom (6DoF) pose more robustly. We equipped the localization pipeline InLoc with real-time instance segmentation network YOLACT++. The masks of dynamic objects are employed in the relative pose estimation step and in the final sorting of camera pose proposal. At first, we filter out the matches laying on masks of the dynamic objects. Second, we skip the comparison of query and synthetic images on the area related to the moving object. This procedure leads to a more robust localization. Lastly, we describe and improve the mistakes caused by gradient-based comparison between synthetic and query images and publish a new pipeline for simulation of environments with movable objects from the Matterport scans. All the codes are available on https://github.com/dubenma/D-InLocpp.

Keywords: Visual localization · Dynamic environments · Robot navigation

1 Introduction

Accurate camera pose is required for many applications, such as self-driving cars [10], navigation of mobile robots [13], or augmented reality [57]. The global navigation satellite systems (GNSS) provide camera position within 4.9m for GPS [47] and 4m for Galileo [7] while camera rotation remains unknown. The accuracy of localization from Wi-Fi [37], or Bluetooth [33], based on the signal strength varies a lot depending on the number and distance from signal broadcasters. Moreover, these methods provide the camera position only. The

© The Author(s), under exclusive license to Springer Nature Switzerland AG 2022
B. Andres et al. (Eds.): DAGM GCPR 2022, LNCS 13485, pp. 246–261, 2022.
https://doi.org/10.1007/978-3-031-16788-1_16

inertial measurement unit (IMU) allows camera pose tracking but cannot be employed for 6DoF localization. The last and most popular approach is visual localization, i.e., estimation of camera pose (i.e., position and orientation) given an RGB image.

Visual localization [22,43,51] is a challenging task since even small changes in camera pose lead to significant 3D mapping or navigation errors. In addition, the indoor environment is often repetitive [55]. Moreover, many plain walls, windows, or mirrors do not provide helpful information for localization. Another challenge is that the environment is only rarely static and often contains a lot of movable objects.

The main goal of this paper is to improve the visual localization so that it becomes more robust in dynamic environments, i.e., environments with moving objects. The motivation for this step is that moving objects often lead to significant changes in the scene, which make the localization algorithm work inaccurately. Also, dynamic environments are more common in the real world, making this improvement even more critical. We demonstrate a new method by improving the state-of-the-art localization pipeline InLoc [51].

2 Related Work

The recently published localization pipelines show remarkable performance in indoor spaces and urban environments [22,43,45]. The recent state-of-the-art algorithms follow a common scheme:

- **Image retrieval** step describes query image by feature vector and finds the most similar images in the database [8,21,38,39].
- **Relative pose** step finds local correspondences [17,18,27,31,40,49] between the query image and the k most similar images selected in the image retrieval step. Furthermore, the correspondences are verified by a robust model estimator [11,12,15,16,44,50,53,58] using a suitable relative pose solver [20,24,25].
- **Absolute pose** step constructs 2D-3D correspondences from 2D-2D correspondences found in previous step. The correspondences are calculated for t database images with the most inliers. Further, an absolute pose solver [28] in a robust model estimator provides a camera pose proposals.
- **Pose correction** step optimizes [22,29,56] the camera pose proposals.
- **Pose selection** step evaluates the camera pose proposals by photometric consistency and selects the most fitting candidate [6,9,30].

The last two steps are not included in run-time methods, e.g., [43]. Recently published localization algorithms focus on improving specific modules while the general scheme remains the same.

The images are usually described by NetVLAD [8] but several extensions, e.g., GeM [38], AP-GeM [39] and i-GeM [21] were published. Relative pose estimation has experienced the largest evolution in recent years [23].

Key point detectors evolved from handcrafted, e.g., SIFT [31], to the learned ones, e.g., SuperPoint [17], D2-Net [18], R2D2 [40], LoFTR [49] or a Key.Net [27] paired with HardNet or SOSNet descriptors. The matching can start by Context Networks (CNe) [50,58] to pre-filter the outliers followed by RANSAC based (Lo-RANCAS [15], DEGNSAC [16], GC-RANSAC [11], MAGSASC++ [12] or Deep-MAGSAC [53]) or neural-network based (e.g., SuperGlue [44]) matches verifier. There are also the end-to-end detectors + matchers, e.g., Sparse-NCNet [41] or Patch2Pix [59]. Moreover, a list of relative pose solvers employed in the scope of RANSAC-based algorithm, e.g., H4P [20], E5P [24], F7P [20] or F10e [25], is available. Each combination of listed relative pose algorithms lead to different camera pose accuracy and robustness. The most common among learned key-point detectors is the SuperPoint [17] and the matching algorithm is the Super-Glue [44]. As far as we know, the latest approaches for detection and matching of keypoints [23,27,53] were not published in a localization pipeline yet.

The absolute pose step estimates the camera pose by robust model estimator (usually the Lo-RANSAC [15]). The constraints on a camera define the minimal solver used, e.g., P3P, P4Pf [28] or PnP [20].

The pose correction step optimizes previously estimated camera poses. The optimization requires additional time to run and improves the results mainly in sparsely mapped indoor environments with texture-less areas, e.g., in the InLoc [51] dataset. Therefore, it is employed mainly for offline indoor localization. The Pixel-Perfect-SfM [29] adjusts keypoints by featuremetric refinement followed by the featuremetric Bundle Adjustment (BA) [56]. The PCLoc [22] generates "artificial images" close to the camera pose proposal composed of reprojected feature points. Further, the relative and absolute pose step runs again to calculate camera pose from generated artificial image. As far as we know, the combination of both mentioned methods was not published yet.

The last step of this standard scheme is the photometric verification of the camera pose proposals. The online algorithms, e.g., the Hierarchical Localization [43], do select the camera pose with the most inliers after the absolute pose estimation step. The photometric verification requires a 3D model of the environment and appears beneficial in indoor spaces [51]. The idea is to render synthetic images for the t camera pose proposals and compare them by pixel-wise patch descriptors, e.g., DenseRootSIFT [9,30], with the query image. The rendering can be done either by standard software as Pyrender [6] (implemented on InLoc), or Neural Rerendering in the Wild [34], or the NeRF in the Wild [34] to obtain realistically looking synthetic images. As far as we know, the NeRF-based approaches were not published in a localization pipeline yet.

As mentioned in the previous paragraph, the map format plays an important role. The photometric verification cannot run if the 3D model of the environment is unknown. The paper Torii et al. [54] shows that more database images in the map lead to more accurate and robust localization. In the case of dynamic environment, the map can be composed by [36,42].

The last direction of the research focuses on localization from a sequence of images. Having a set of pictures with known poses in the local coordinate system and the 2D-3D correspondences, we can utilize the generalized absolute pose solver, e.g., gp3p or gp4ps [26], to get the global pose of the sequence of images.

The 2D keypoints are converted to 3D rays and aligned with 3D points from the map by Euclidean transformation. This approach was published in Stenborg et al. [48].

Generally, there exists a number of extensions [23,25,29,34,53] that can be used to improve individual modules of the state-of-the-art localization [19]. However, we would like to avoid mechanical replacement of particular methods and open new unexplored yet important topics. As far as we know, the scenes with movable objects were not addressed in detail yet. Our contributions are:

- the evaluation of localization accuracy in the environment with movable objects
- implementation of D-InLoc++ that is robust against the mismatches caused by movable objects
- new approach to comparing the synthetic and query images
- automated pipeline for testing the localization w.r.t. movable objects

The rest of the paper is organized as follows. The following section describes the moving object filtering during the localization process. Further on, we show the challenges related to the usage of DenseRootSIFT and propose a new solution for comparing synthetic and query images. The fifth section describes a new pipeline for generating synthetic datasets with movable objects. The last section evaluates dynamic object filtering on the published datasets.

3   Dynamic Object Filtering

We propose a simple yet effective approach to dealing with movable objects. The pseudocode of the algorithm is shown in Algorithm 1. Let us assume that we have a static map realized as in the InLoc dataset [51]. The map consists of N RGB-D images $\mathcal{I} = \{I_1, \ldots, I_N\}$ with known camera poses $\mathcal{P}_i = \{R_i, t_i\}$, i.e., the rotation $R_i \in \mathbb{R}^{3\times3}$ and translation $t_i \in \mathbb{R}^3$. Without loss of generality, we assume no radial distortion and images are captured by the same camera. The camera intrinsic parameters are the focal length $f \in \mathbb{R}$ and principal point $p \in \mathbb{R}^2$. The depth images in the map are converted into mesh $\mathcal{M}_\mathcal{I}$ by the Truncated Signed Distance Function (TSDF) algorithm. The set of M query images is denoted by $\mathcal{Q} = \{Q_1, \ldots, Q_M\}$. If the same camera does not capture the query images and the database images in the map, the resolution is adjusted in advance. Let us assume that the query images $\mathcal{Q}$ already match the resolution of images $\mathcal{I}$ in the database.

At first we add a preprocessing step, i.e., we extend the map with the correspondences between the pairs of database images. The database images are described by feature vectors (e.g., by NetVLAD) and keypoints (e.g., by Super-Point). For the top k closest database images (computed as dot product between feature vectors) are found tentative matches (e.g., by SuperGlue). Next, we verify the tentative matches by relative pose constrains extracted from known camera poses.

Algorithm 1. The pseudo-code of D-InLoc++

1: **Inputs:** set of query images $\mathcal{Q}$; map: RGB-D images $\mathcal{I}$ and camera poses $\mathcal{P}_{\mathcal{I}}$; epipolar error threshold $\mathcal{T}$, min. mask size γ, moving object criterion threshold δ
2: **Outputs:** camera poses $\mathcal{P}_{\mathcal{Q}}$ for query images $\mathcal{Q}$;
3:
4: **Pre-process the map (offline):**
5: Mesh $\mathcal{M}_{\mathcal{I}} \leftarrow \text{TSDF}(\mathcal{I}, \mathcal{P}_{\mathcal{I}})$;
6: Keypoints $\boldsymbol{u}^{(\mathcal{I})}$, Visibility ids set $\mathcal{Y}_{\mathcal{I}}$, Points $\boldsymbol{X}_{\mathcal{I}} \leftarrow \text{sparse\_reconstruction}(\mathcal{I}, \mathcal{P}_{\mathcal{I}})$
7: Masks $\boldsymbol{S}_{\mathcal{I}}, \mathcal{D}_{\mathcal{I}}, \mathcal{U}_{\mathcal{I}} \leftarrow \text{instance\_segmentation}(\mathcal{I})$
8: Masks $\boldsymbol{S}_{\mathcal{I}}, \mathcal{U}_{\mathcal{I}} \leftarrow \text{reassign\_small\_masks}(\gamma, \boldsymbol{S}_{\mathcal{I}}, \mathcal{U}_{\mathcal{I}})$
9:
10: **Localize query images (online):**
11: $\mathcal{P}_{\mathcal{Q}} \leftarrow []$
12: **for each** $Q_j \in \mathcal{Q}$ **do**
13:     Masks $\mathcal{S}_{Q_j}, \mathcal{D}_{Q_j}, \mathcal{U}_{Q_j} \leftarrow \text{instance\_segmentation}(Q_j)$
14:     Masks $\mathcal{S}_{Q_j}, \mathcal{U}_{Q_j} \leftarrow \text{reassign\_small\_masks}(\gamma, \mathcal{S}_{Q_j}, \mathcal{U}_{Q_j})$
15:     $\boldsymbol{u}^{(Q_j)} \leftarrow \text{compute\_keypoints}(Q_j)$
16:     $\{T_1, \ldots, T_k\} \in \mathcal{I} \leftarrow \text{find\_closest\_images}(k, Q_j, \mathcal{I})$
17:     $P_{Q_j} \leftarrow []$
18:     $L_{Q_j} \leftarrow []$
19:     **for each** $T \in \{T_1, \ldots, T_k\}$ **do**
20:         $\mathcal{Y}_{Q_j,T} \leftarrow \text{find\_correspondences\_2D3D}(\text{compute\_matches}(\boldsymbol{u}^{(Q_j)}, \boldsymbol{u}^{(T)}, \mathcal{D}_{(T_i)}, \mathcal{D}_{(Q_i)}), \mathcal{Y}_{\mathcal{I}})$
21:         $\beta_T \leftarrow \text{calculate\_moving\_object\_criteria}((\mathcal{Y}_{Q_j,T} \cup \mathcal{Y}_{\mathcal{I}}), \boldsymbol{u}^{(Q_j)}, \mathcal{U}_T)$
22:         $\beta_{Q_j} \leftarrow \text{calculate\_moving\_object\_criteria}((\mathcal{Y}_{Q_j,T} \cup \mathcal{Y}_{\mathcal{I}}), \boldsymbol{u}^{(Q_j)}, \mathcal{U}_{Q_j})$
23:         $\mathcal{S}_T^*, \mathcal{D}_T^* \leftarrow \text{reassign\_unknown\_masks}(\mathcal{S}_T, \mathcal{D}_T, \mathcal{U}_T, (\beta_T < \delta))$
24:         $\mathcal{S}_{Q_j}^*, \mathcal{D}_{Q_j}^* \leftarrow \text{reassign\_unknown\_masks}(\mathcal{S}_{Q_j}, \mathcal{D}_{Q_j}, \mathcal{U}_{Q_j}, (\beta_{Q_j} < \delta))$
25:         $\mathcal{Y}_{Q_j,T}^* \leftarrow \text{filter\_moving\_objects\_matches}(\mathcal{Y}_{Q_j,T}, \mathcal{D}_T^*, \mathcal{D}_{Q_j}^*)$
26:         $\mathcal{P}_{Q_j,T}, \mathcal{Y}_{Q_j,T}^+ \leftarrow \text{estimate\_absolute\_pose}((\boldsymbol{u}^{\mathcal{I}} \cup \boldsymbol{u}^{(Q_j)}), \boldsymbol{X}_{\mathcal{I}}, \mathcal{Y}_{Q_j,T}^*)$
27:         $L_{Q_j} \leftarrow [L_{Q_j}, \text{count\_number\_of\_inliers}(\mathcal{Y}_{Q_j,T}^+)]$
28:         $P_{Q_j} \leftarrow [P_{Q_j}, \mathcal{P}_{Q_j,T}]$
29:     **end for**
30:     $\bar{\mathcal{P}}_{Q_j} \leftarrow \text{sort\_poses\_descending}(L_{Q_j}, P_{Q_j})$
31:     $\bar{L}_{Q_j} \leftarrow []$
32:     **for each** $p \in \{1, \ldots, l\}$ **do**
33:         $\bar{Q}_{j,p} \leftarrow \text{render\_image}(\bar{\mathcal{P}}_{Q,p}, \mathcal{M}_{\mathcal{I}})$
34:         $\bar{L}_{Q_j} \leftarrow [\bar{L}_{Q_j}, \text{compare\_synth\_and\_query\_image}(\bar{Q}_{j,p}, Q_j)]$
35:     **end for**
36:     $\tilde{\mathcal{P}}_{Q_j} \leftarrow \text{sort\_poses\_ascending}(\bar{L}_{Q_j}, \bar{\mathcal{P}}_{Q_j})$
37:     $\mathcal{P}_{\mathcal{Q}} \leftarrow [\mathcal{P}_{\mathcal{Q}}, \tilde{\mathcal{P}}_{Q_j,1}]$
38: **end for**
39: **return** $\mathcal{P}_{\mathcal{Q}}$;

Let us define the calibration matrix K and camera center $\boldsymbol{C}_i$ as

$$K = \begin{bmatrix} f & 0 & p_1 \\ 0 & f & p_2 \\ 0 & 0 & 1 \end{bmatrix} \quad and \quad \boldsymbol{C}_i = -R_i^\top t. \tag{1}$$

We assume the Fundamental matrix F to equal

$$F = K^{-\top}R_2[C_2 - C_1]_\times R_1^\top K^{-1}, \tag{2}$$

and epipolar constrains for keypoint $\begin{bmatrix} u_1^{(i)} & u_2^{(i)} & 1 \end{bmatrix}^\top$ in the i-th and $\begin{bmatrix} u_1^{(j)} & u_2^{(j)} & 1 \end{bmatrix}^\top$ in the j-th image:

$$\begin{bmatrix} u_1^{(j)} & u_2^{(j)} & 1 \end{bmatrix} F \begin{bmatrix} u_1^{(i)} \\ u_2^{(i)} \\ 1 \end{bmatrix} < \mathcal{T}. \tag{3}$$

The value $\mathcal{T}$ represents the threshold. If the Eq. 3 holds, the correspondence $\{u^{(i)}, u^{(j)}\}$ is assumed to be correct (i.e., inlier) and stored in the map. All keypoints detected on database images are called $u^{(\mathcal{I})}$. The map is further extended with points $\mathcal{X}_\mathcal{I}$ and the index set $(i,j) \in \mathcal{Y}_\mathcal{I}$ storing the information that j-th point $X_j \in \mathbb{R}^3$ is visible in i-th image I_i. This step is done by the function sparse_reconstruction($\mathcal{I},\mathcal{P}_\mathcal{I}$) on line 6 in the pseudocode of Algorithm 1.

Further, in the case of moving objects in the map, we run the instance segmentation on database images $\mathcal{I}$ to have the object masks in advance. This method separates the background from possibly movable instances of the objects. We assume three classes of objects, the static one $\mathcal{C}_S$, dynamic (moving) one $\mathcal{C}_D$ and movable (unknown) $\mathcal{C}_U$. Related masks in the image i are called $\mathcal{S}_i$, $\mathcal{D}_i$, and $\mathcal{U}_i$. The background is an example of static class $\mathcal{C}_S$. People and cars are an example of $\mathcal{C}_D$ and the rest of objects where we cannot decide in advance is in $\mathcal{C}_U$.

The online localization process starts with segmentation of the images $\mathcal{Q}$ by a real-time instance segmentation (e.g., the YOLACT++). We assume the same classes for the objects as for the database images. The masks for single query image Q_j are called $\mathcal{S}_{Q_j}$ for static, $\mathcal{D}_{Q_j}$ for dynamic, and $\mathcal{U}_{Q_j}$ for movable objects. The image retrieval module extracts the feature vectors and finds the k most similar images $\{T_1, \ldots, T_k\}$ in the database, function find_closest_images(k, Q_j, $\mathcal{I}$). Next, the algorithm calculates keypoints $u^{(Q_j)}$, matches, and 2D-3D correspondences $\mathcal{Y}_{Q_j,T}$ between Q_j and the database image T. All the keypoints laying inside $\mathcal{D}_T$ and $\mathcal{D}_{Q_j}$ masks are not assumed for computation of matches. Next, we propose a simple criterion to decide which image areas out of $\mathcal{U}_T$ and $\mathcal{U}_{Q_j}$ will be utilised further. At first, we check the instance segmentation masks and all that are small enough, i.e., smaller than γ, are reassigned to $\mathcal{S}_T$ or $\mathcal{S}_{Q_j}$. For the rest of object masks in $\mathcal{U}_T$ and $\mathcal{U}_{Q_j}$ we calculate

$$\beta_{T_s} = g(u_{T_s}) - num\_px(u_{T_s}) \tag{4}$$

where g gives the number of observations with tracks of length ≥ 3 and a correspondence in Q_j that are laying in s-th object mask $u_{T_s} \in \mathcal{U}_T$. The vector for all the masks is called β_T for T image and β_{Q_j} for Q_j image. In other words, we count the number of observations that have our query image in the track, and the track has a length larger than three, i.e., the point in 3D is visible in

Fig. 1. The images from left to right correspond to: the query image, the first and the second most similar synthetic images sorted by the DenseRootSIFT criterion. It can be seen that a completely wrong image has a better score because the gradient of the background is almost identical to the gradient of the wall and pillar.

more than two views. Such tracks should appear if the object is static. Large masks should contain more tracks fulfilling this condition. The num_px function counts the number of pixels in some object mask, e.g., u_{T_s}. All the object masks with $\beta_T > \delta$ are reassigned to $\mathcal{S}_T$ and $\beta_{Q_j} > \delta$ to $\mathcal{S}_{Q_j}$. Remaining masks are reassigned to $\mathcal{D}_T$ or $\mathcal{D}_{Q_j}$. This step creates masks $\mathcal{S}_T^*$, $\mathcal{S}_{Q_j}^*$ for each pair of query-database images. Only the keypoints and matches found in $\mathcal{S}_T^*$, $\mathcal{S}_{Q_j}^*$ are utilised in the next absolute pose estimation module.

Further, the algorithm follows the standard localization scheme, see Sect. 2. The absolute pose module estimates the camera pose in the global coordinate system. The pose correction module is skipped in our reference algorithm InLoc [51], and we do not assume it either. The last module of this scheme is related to pose selection out of the proposals, and we discuss it in the following section.

4   Image Selection Step

This step of the localization process selects the most appropriate pose among all the proposals and, therefore, directly influences the results of the rest of the pipeline. The standard approach to comparing the synthetic and real images starts with applying a path descriptor (e.g., the DenseRootSIFT) to all the patches in both images. This provides a feature vector that describes the surrounding area of each pixel. Then a median of the norms of related feature vector differences is taken. Smaller values indicate greater similarity. This approach is used in many algorithms, such as [22,51], for photometric comparison of a pair of images.

However, this approach leads to several issues, as can be seen in Fig. 1. The first issue is that the gradient-based comparison of images does not take into account the colors. For example, the flat white walls have almost zero error w.r.t. the background of the synthetic image. This is caused by lack of gradient on both areas. If the indoor space consists of textureless corridors or rooms, the poses looking outside the mapped area have a small error and may be selected. Second, this approach does not consider movable objects and assumes the same weight for all the pixels. An example of such objects can be people, chairs, doors, and other equipment that is usually not static w.r.t. the walls, pillars, etc.

Because the starting position for the image selection step is several images, for which similarity is to be pair-wisely compared, the first considered approach was to use some already published learnable methods for relative pose estimation. Various approaches also utilizing convolutional neural networks (CNN) for this task were examined in [46]. Remarkable results regarding this issue were achieved in [14]. However, in our case, we found it too narrowly focused on pose estimation. So for our task, we opted for a more general approach similar to the one adopted in [35]. Therefore, the foundation of our method is a CNN used as an image encoder, EfficientNet [52]. This part of our method is a representational part, i.e., it outputs a vector representation of what is in the images. This part is then followed by a regression part - a fully connected layer.

To be more specific, the algorithm itself works as follows. Input is a set of the top k proposed images $\mathcal{I}_k \subseteq \mathcal{I}$ and query image $Q_i \in \mathcal{Q}$.

Inputs to our network are then all k pairs of images (Q_i, I_j), where $I_j \in \mathcal{I}_k$. If rescaling is needed, both Q_i and all I_j are reshaped to fit the CNN input dimensions. Then instance segmentation masks and masks of the moving objects in query image allow to select compared areas, by setting the pixels to white.

These pairs are then sequentially processed by the representational part, producing feature vectors $f_i, f_j \in \mathbb{R}^{1280 \times l_1 \times l_2}$. These are then fed into the regression part and output score $s \in \mathbb{R}$.

The value of s was trained to represent a measure of similarity of the images. The ground truth values (targets) from the training dataset were computed as $min(1, (\theta + 10t)/50)$, the result of which is a value for each training pair ranging in the interval from 0 to 1. The formula provides a value of 1 for everything that exceeds the threshold of similarity, that is $\theta + 10t = 50$, where θ is the angular difference between the two images and t distance between camera positions $t_i, t_j \in \mathbb{R}^3$ computed as

$$\theta = \arccos\left(\frac{1}{2}(\text{trace}(R) - 1)\right), \ t = |t_i - t_j|, \tag{5}$$

where $R \in \mathbb{R}^{3 \times 3}$ is a rotation matrix representing rotation between cameras corresponding to Q_i and I_j, and $t_i, t_j \in \mathbb{R}^3$ are vectors of camera positions. The parameter 10 in the mentioned formula was empirically set to balance the range of values θ and t.

Finally, the comparison of our CNN-based approach (combined with Dense-RootSIFT - the CNN serves as guidance for DSIFT as to which images to consider) with other methods is in the Fig. 5. These results were obtained on 180 query images and show the percentage of the cases when the chosen image pose was within the thresholds shown in the figure.

5   Dynamic Dataset Generation

Most of the current localization datasets [2] include entities such as people, doors, and chairs that are seldom static. However, the masks of stationary and moving objects are missing because manual labeling is time-consuming. We propose a new pipeline that takes as input standard mapping technology with additional models of movable objects. Our method generates camera poses and the RGB-D images with masks of movable objects.

We chose the services provided by Matterport [3] as the scanning technology of indoor spaces. To create the 3D model of the environment, the customer can use a user-friendly application and a reasonably expensive scanner. The scanner captures 360 °C RGB-D images aligned to a single coordinate system. However, these scans are not directly available as the RGB-D panoramic images. We provide the script for downloading camera poses from the Matterport API endpoint. Further, Matterport API provides six square pictures of the panoramic image projected onto the shape of a cube. These images follow the global coordinate system, and we projected them back into panoramic images by cube2sphere [1] library. Each panoramic image is projected into 36 RGB perspective images. These images are called cutouts [51]. The related depth images are obtained by rendering the mesh in the AI Habitat [32] simulator.

In this way, we acquire a dataset representing a scene without any moving objects. The simplest way to add moving objects to queries is by adding artificial textures of the moving objects in the query images.

To have consistent data for the localization of RGB-D image sequences, we propose to add the movable objects directly into the 3D model of the environment to preserve the geometry. AI Habitat renders the depth, semantic masks, and RGB images. However, the RGB cutouts channels have higher quality than rendered images. Therefore, the script replaces any image data outside the masks of movable objects with original cutouts projected from panoramic images. An example of such an image can be seen in Fig. 3.

Published codes simplify the creation of datasets with movable objects and speed up further development.

6   Experimental Evaluation

This section compares the original localization pipeline and the adjusted method by robust filtering of movable objects. A new dynamic localization dataset generator produced all the data utilized here.

6.1   Composition of Test Datasets

As far as we know, datasets with ground truth semantic masks for movable and static objects were not published yet [19]. We provide such a dataset. We recorded a real environment, i.e., the Hospital space. An example of reconstructed space is in Fig. 2. For recording, we used the device the Matterport Pro 3D Camera [4]. We aimed to have around 1.5 m between the camera locations and cover the whole space during the capturing. The Hospital space contains 116 scans. It resulted in 696 images of skyboxes, i.e., images projected into cube faces, provided by Matterport API. These images have a resolution

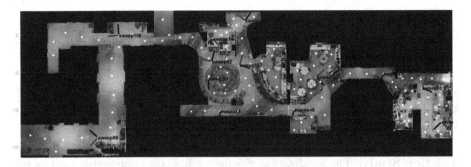

Fig. 2. The visualization of the Hospital space. Purple dots show the positions of Matterport scans that are in Matterport terminology referred to as sweeps. The sweeps that are used to generate query images are highlighted by showing their coordinate systems.

of 2048×2048 pixels. We used them to compose 116 panoramic images with a resolution of 8192×4096 pixels. Next, we downloaded the dense reconstruction model. To generate the cutouts, we adopted the same strategy as presented in InLoc [51], i.e., generated 36 images out of one panoramic image using a sampling of 30 °C in yaw and ±30 °C in pitch angles. This gave us 4176 cutouts in total. To project the panoramic images into the perspective ones, we have chosen the HoloLens photometric camera intrinsic parameters, i.e., the focal length $f = 1034$, principal point $p = [672, 378]$ and images resolution 1344×756 pixels. Anyone can adjust these parameters in the dataset generation pipeline.

Further, we randomly added objects inside the reconstructed area. We manually checked if the object collided with any other meshes and moved such objects to a new location. The rendering of the mesh with moving objects is implemented in AI Habitat and takes about 0.35 s/image on a personal laptop. AI Habitat requires the input in the .glb format. The script employs obj2gltf [5] library for the conversion of all the models (i.e., objects, and the environment). The AI Habitat generates the synthetic images and masks for static and movable objects in a way that they correspond to each cutout. In the case of dynamic datasets, the rendered texture of moving objects replaces related areas in the cutouts of query images. The resulting image can be seen in Fig. 3. The database images do not contain any moving objects.

Generally, we created two datasets: static and dynamic. The dataset without any dynamic objects is called a static dataset. The dynamic dataset has the objects placed on the ground with the average area of the objects masking 20.63% of the whole query image for ground truth masks and 13.09% from proposed instance segmentation. We used 15 of the Matterport scans to generate query images that all face only the horizontal direction to simulate a camera on a robot, i.e., 180 queries for the Hospital scene. The rest of the images is utilized for creating the localization map.

6.2   Evaluation

The main part of this paper is to show the influence of movable objects appearing in the localization dataset. We compared four main scenarios, i.e., running

1. original Inloc,
2. improvement with neural network (InLoc++),
3. improvement with filtering of matches (D-InLoc),
4. improvement with combination of 2) and 3) (D-InLoc++).

Ablation Study. The localization pipelines follow common steps, such as relative and absolute pose estimation. These algorithms are, in general, prone to errors. A common issue is that a subset of outliers is marked as inliers. The pose is then optimized to minimize the error w.r.t. the outliers. Let us show an example of how the semantic masks work on a query image (see Fig. 3).

Fig. 3. The example of the query image and masks. The top left image is a query image without any moving objects. The top right image is a dynamic query with added objects. The bottom left image shows the ground truth masks of the added objects. The bottom right image shows the result of our instance segmentation using YOLACT.

The relative pose correspondences are filtered according to YOLACT masks (Fig. 3) because of laying on movable objects. It can be seen that a significant part of the correspondences would distort the relative pose estimation step and allow further propagation of mismatches. The image selection step (i.e., the EfficientNet B3 + fully connected layer projection head outputting one number) was trained using 20k image pairs, with 5% employed as test set and the rest as the training set; Adam optimizer with learning rate 0.0001; MSE loss; batch size of 16 (Fig. 4).

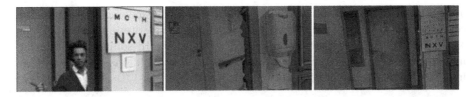

Fig. 4. The query image at left and its corresponding rendered synthetic images. The center image shows the best pose candidate using DSIFT only. The right one is using a combination of DSIFT and CNN.

Quantitative Evaluation. This part shows the performance of the localization with and without filtering moving objects. Our map Dynamic Broca gathers 3636 RGB-D images with known camera poses. We further assume a set of 180 query images. The dataset has 20.63% of the mean query images occupied by moving objects. The details about the dataset are in Sect. 6.1.

The comparison is shown in Fig. 5. In our experiments, we assumed YOLACT classes *background*, *TV* and *refrigerator* as static and the class *person* as dynamic

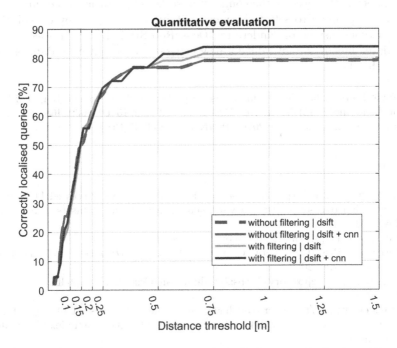

Fig. 5. The comparison of original InLoc (blue dashed), InLoc++ (red), D-InLoc (yellow) and D-InLoc++ (purple) on Dynamic Broca dataset. The rotation error threshold is 10% degrees. We show the localization improvement on images with moving objects occupancy of more than 30% of the image. The filtering of moving objects (D-InLoc++) improves the overall localization accuracy in comparison with original InLoc algorithm. (Color figure online)

object classes. It leads to the 86.9% accuracy of the moving objects masks compared to ground truth masks. The moving object criterion threshold was $\delta = 10^{-9}$. We can see that the proposed straightforward solution for filtering moving objects improves the localization on the dynamic dataset and is further improved with the use of convolutional neural network.

7   Conclusion

This paper opens the essential and not fully explored topic of movable object filtering in the scope of visual localization. We publish a new simple algorithm that detects moving objects based on the query and database images' track lengths and instance segmentation masks. The instance segmentation masks are categorized into moving and static classes and utilized to avoid the propagation of the outliers through the localization process. Mainly, the propagation of the outliers that are close to correct matches and influences the accuracy of camera poses. The results show non-negligible improvement, i.e., we reach approximately 7% more camera poses within the threshold of 1m for a dataset where movable objects occupy 20.63% of query images. The second contribution of this paper is that we list the common mistakes of gradient-based image comparison and propose to select the most suitable camera pose by convolutional neural network instead of handcrafted DenseRootSIFT. Lastly, to speed up this area's development, we introduce a new generator of localization datasets with moving objects.

Acknowledgements. This research was supported by the European Regional Development Fund under IMPACT No. CZ.02.1.01/0.0/0.0/15 003/0000468, EU H2020 ARtwin No. 856994, and EU H2020 SPRING No. 871245 Projects.

References

1. cube2sphere 0.2.1. https://pypi.org/project/cube2sphere/. Accessed 11 May 2022
2. Localization datasets. https://www.visuallocalization.net/datasets/. Accessed 31 May 2022
3. Matterport. https://matterport.com/. Accessed 20 May 2022
4. Mattreport Pro 3D Camera. https://matterport.com/cameras/pro2-3D-camera. Accessed 20 May 2022
5. obj2gltf github repository. https://github.com/CesiumGS/obj2gltf. Accessed 20 May 2022
6. Pyrender. https://pyrender.readthedocs.io/en/latest/. Accessed 14 May 2022
7. Agency, E.S.: Galileo (2021). https://gssc.esa.int/navipedia/index.php/Galileo_Performances
8. Arandjelovic, R., Gronat, P., Torii, A., Pajdla, T., Sivic, J.: Netvlad: CNN architecture for weakly supervised place recognition. In: Proceedings of the IEEE Conference on Computer Vision and Pattern Recognition, pp. 5297–5307 (2016)
9. Arandjelović, R., Zisserman, A.: Three things everyone should know to improve object retrieval. In: 2012 IEEE Conference on Computer Vision and Pattern Recognition, pp. 2911–2918. IEEE (2012)

10. Badue, C., et al.: Self-driving cars: a survey. Expert Syst. Appl. **165**, 113816 (2021)
11. Barath, D., Matas, J.: Graph-cut ransac. In: Proceedings of the IEEE Conference on Computer Vision and Pattern Recognition, pp. 6733–6741 (2018)
12. Barath, D., Noskova, J., Ivashechkin, M., Matas, J.: Magsac++, a fast, reliable and accurate robust estimator. In: Proceedings of the IEEE/CVF Conference on Computer Vision and Pattern Recognition, pp. 1304–1312 (2020)
13. Bonin-Font, F., Ortiz, A., Oliver, G.: Visual navigation for mobile robots: a survey. J. Intell. Rob. Syst. **53**(3), 263–296 (2008)
14. Chen, K., Snavely, N., Makadia, A.: Wide-baseline relative camera pose estimation with directional learning. In: Proceedings of the IEEE/CVF Conference on Computer Vision and Pattern Recognition, pp. 3258–3268 (2021)
15. Chum, O., Matas, J., Kittler, J.: Locally optimized RANSAC. In: Michaelis, B., Krell, G. (eds.) DAGM 2003. LNCS, vol. 2781, pp. 236–243. Springer, Heidelberg (2003). https://doi.org/10.1007/978-3-540-45243-0_31
16. Chum, O., Werner, T., Matas, J.: Two-view geometry estimation unaffected by a dominant plane. In: 2005 IEEE Computer Society Conference on Computer Vision and Pattern Recognition (CVPR 2005), vol. 1, pp. 772–779. IEEE (2005)
17. DeTone, D., Malisiewicz, T., Rabinovich, A.: Superpoint: self-supervised interest point detection and description. In: Proceedings of the IEEE Conference on Computer Vision and Pattern Recognition Workshops, pp. 224–236 (2018)
18. Dusmanu, M., et al.: D2-net: a trainable CNN for joint description and detection of local features. In: Proceedings of the IEEE/CVF Conference on Computer Vision and Pattern Recognition, pp. 8092–8101 (2019)
19. Hammarstrand, L., et al.: Workshop on long-term visual localization under changing conditions (2020). https://www.visuallocalization.net/workshop/eccv/2020/
20. Hartley, R., Zisserman, A.: Multiple View Geometry in Computer Vision. Cambridge University Press, Cambridge (2003)
21. Hyeon, J., et al.: Kr-net: a dependable visual kidnap recovery network for indoor spaces. In: 2020 IEEE/RSJ International Conference on Intelligent Robots and Systems (IROS), pp. 8527–8533. IEEE (2020)
22. Hyeon, J., Kim, J., Doh, N.: Pose correction for highly accurate visual localization in large-scale indoor spaces. In: Proceedings of the IEEE/CVF International Conference on Computer Vision, pp. 15974–15983 (2021)
23. Jin, Y.: Image matching across wide baselines: from paper to practice. Int. J. Comput. Vision **129**(2), 517–547 (2021)
24. Kukelova, Z., Bujnak, M., Pajdla, T.: Polynomial eigenvalue solutions to the 5-pt and 6-pt relative pose problems. In: BMVC, vol. 2, p. 2008 (2008)
25. Kukelova, Z., Heller, J., Bujnak, M., Fitzgibbon, A., Pajdla, T.: Efficient solution to the epipolar geometry for radially distorted cameras. In: Proceedings of the IEEE International Conference on Computer Vision, pp. 2309–2317 (2015)
26. Kukelova, Z., Heller, J., Fitzgibbon, A.: Efficient intersection of three quadrics and applications in computer vision. In: Proceedings of the IEEE Conference on Computer Vision and Pattern Recognition, pp. 1799–1808 (2016)
27. Laguna, A.B., Mikolajczyk, K.: Key. net: keypoint detection by handcrafted and learned CNN filters revisited. IEEE Trans. Pattern Anal. Mach. Intell. (2022)
28. Larsson, V., Kukelova, Z., Zheng, Y.: Making minimal solvers for absolute pose estimation compact and robust. In: Proceedings of the IEEE International Conference on Computer Vision, pp. 2316–2324 (2017)
29. Lindenberger, P., Sarlin, P.E., Larsson, V., Pollefeys, M.: Pixel-perfect structure-from-motion with featuremetric refinement. In: Proceedings of the IEEE/CVF International Conference on Computer Vision, pp. 5987–5997 (2021)

30. Liu, C., Yuen, J., Torralba, A.: Sift flow: dense correspondence across scenes and its applications. IEEE Trans. Pattern Anal. Mach. Intelligence **33**(5), 978–994 (2010)
31. Lowe, D.G.: Distinctive image features from scale-invariant keypoints. Int. J. Comput. Vision **60**(2), 91–110 (2004)
32. Savva*, M., et al.: Habitat: a platform for embodied AI research. In: Proceedings of the IEEE/CVF International Conference on Computer Vision (ICCV) (2019)
33. Marcel, J.: Bluetooth technology is getting precise with positioning systems (2019). https://www.bluetooth.com/blog/bluetooth-positioning-systems/
34. Martin-Brualla, R., Radwan, N., Sajjadi, M.S., Barron, J.T., Dosovitskiy, A., Duckworth, D.: NeRF in the wild: neural radiance fields for unconstrained photo collections. In: Proceedings of the IEEE/CVF Conference on Computer Vision and Pattern Recognition, pp. 7210–7219 (2021)
35. Melekhov, I., Ylioinas, J., Kannala, J., Rahtu, E.: Relative camera pose estimation using convolutional neural networks. In: Blanc-Talon, J., Penne, R., Philips, W., Popescu, D., Scheunders, P. (eds.) ACIVS 2017. LNCS, vol. 10617, pp. 675–687. Springer, Cham (2017). https://doi.org/10.1007/978-3-319-70353-4_57
36. Palazzolo, E., Behley, J., Lottes, P., Giguere, P., Stachniss, C.: Refusion: 3D reconstruction in dynamic environments for RGB-D cameras exploiting residuals. In: 2019 IEEE/RSJ International Conference on Intelligent Robots and Systems (IROS), pp. 7855–7862. IEEE (2019)
37. Pourhomayoun, M., Fowler, M.: Improving wlan-based indoor mobile positioning using sparsity. In: 2012 Conference Record of the Forty Sixth Asilomar Conference on Signals, Systems and Computers (ASILOMAR), pp. 1393–1396 (2012). https://doi.org/10.1109/ACSSC.2012.6489254
38. Radenović, F., Tolias, G., Chum, O.: Fine-tuning CNN image retrieval with no human annotation. IEEE Trans. Pattern Anal. Mach. Intell. **41**(7), 1655–1668 (2018)
39. Revaud, J., Almazán, J., Rezende, R.S., Souza, C.R.D.: Learning with average precision: training image retrieval with a listwise loss. In: Proceedings of the IEEE/CVF International Conference on Computer Vision, pp. 5107–5116 (2019)
40. Revaud, J., et al.: R2d2: repeatable and reliable detector and descriptor. arXiv preprint arXiv:1906.06195 (2019)
41. Rocco, I., Arandjelović, R., Sivic, J.: Efficient neighbourhood consensus networks via submanifold sparse convolutions. In: Vedaldi, A., Bischof, H., Brox, T., Frahm, J.-M. (eds.) ECCV 2020. LNCS, vol. 12354, pp. 605–621. Springer, Cham (2020). https://doi.org/10.1007/978-3-030-58545-7_35
42. Runz, M., Buffier, M., Agapito, L.: Maskfusion: real-time recognition, tracking and reconstruction of multiple moving objects. In: 2018 IEEE International Symposium on Mixed and Augmented Reality (ISMAR), pp. 10–20. IEEE (2018)
43. Sarlin, P.E., Cadena, C., Siegwart, R., Dymczyk, M.: From coarse to fine: robust hierarchical localization at large scale (2019)
44. Sarlin, P.E., DeTone, D., Malisiewicz, T., Rabinovich, A.: Superglue: learning feature matching with graph neural networks. In: Proceedings of the IEEE/CVF Conference on Computer Vision and Pattern Recognition, pp. 4938–4947 (2020)
45. Sarlin, P.E., et al.: Back to the feature: learning robust camera localization from pixels to pose. In: Proceedings of the IEEE/CVF Conference on Computer Vision and Pattern Recognition, pp. 3247–3257 (2021)
46. Shavit, Y., Ferens, R.: Introduction to camera pose estimation with deep learning. arXiv preprint arXiv:1907.05272 (2019)
47. for Space-Based Positioning Navigation, N.C.O., Timing: GPS accuracy (2022). https://www.gps.gov/systems/gps/performance/accuracy/

48. Stenborg, E., Sattler, T., Hammarstrand, L.: Using image sequences for long-term visual localization. In: 2020 International Conference on 3D Vision (3DV), pp. 938–948. IEEE (2020)
49. Sun, J., Shen, Z., Wang, Y., Bao, H., Zhou, X.: LoFTR: detector-free local feature matching with transformers. In: Proceedings of the IEEE/CVF Conference on Computer Vision and Pattern Recognition, pp. 8922–8931 (2021)
50. Sun, W., Jiang, W., Trulls, E., Tagliasacchi, A., Yi, K.M.: ACNE: attentive context normalization for robust permutation-equivariant learning. In: Proceedings of the IEEE/CVF Conference on Computer Vision and Pattern Recognition, pp. 11286–11295 (2020)
51. Taira, H., et al.: Inloc: indoor visual localization with dense matching and view synthesis. CoRR abs/1803.10368 (2018). https://arxiv.org/abs/1803.10368
52. Tan, M., Le, Q.: Efficientnet: rethinking model scaling for convolutional neural networks. In: International Conference on Machine Learning, pp. 6105–6114. PMLR (2019)
53. Tong, W., Matas, J., Barath, D.: Deep magsac++. arXiv preprint arXiv:2111.14093 (2021)
54. Torii, A., Arandjelovic, R., Sivic, J., Okutomi, M., Pajdla, T.: 24/7 place recognition by view synthesis. In: Proceedings of the IEEE Conference on Computer Vision and Pattern Recognition, pp. 1808–1817 (2015)
55. Torii, A., Sivic, J., Pajdla, T., Okutomi, M.: Visual place recognition with repetitive structures. In: Proceedings of the IEEE Conference on Computer Vision and Pattern Recognition, pp. 883–890 (2013)
56. Triggs, B., McLauchlan, P.F., Hartley, R.I., Fitzgibbon, A.W.: Bundle adjustment—a modern synthesis. In: Triggs, B., Zisserman, A., Szeliski, R. (eds.) IWVA 1999. LNCS, vol. 1883, pp. 298–372. Springer, Heidelberg (2000). https://doi.org/10.1007/3-540-44480-7_21
57. Vidal-Balea, A., et al.: Analysis, design and practical validation of an augmented reality teaching system based on microsoft hololens 2 and edge computing. Eng. Proc. **2**, 52 (2020)
58. Yi, K.M., Trulls, E., Ono, Y., Lepetit, V., Salzmann, M., Fua, P.: Learning to find good correspondences. In: Proceedings of the IEEE Conference on Computer Vision and Pattern Recognition, pp. 2666–2674 (2018)
59. Zhou, Q., Sattler, T., Leal-Taixe, L.: Patch2pix: epipolar-guided pixel-level correspondences. In: Proceedings of the IEEE/CVF Conference on Computer Vision and Pattern Recognition, pp. 4669–4678 (2021)

Global Hierarchical Attention for 3D
Point Cloud Analysis

Dan Jia$^{(\boxtimes)}$, Alexander Hermans , and Bastian Leibe

Visual Computing Institute, RWTH Aachen University, Aachen, Germany
{jia,hermans,leibe}@vision.rwth-aachen.de

Abstract. We propose a new attention mechanism, called Global Hierarchical Attention (GHA), for 3D point cloud analysis. GHA approximates the regular global dot-product attention via a series of coarsening and interpolation operations over multiple hierarchy levels. The advantage of GHA is two-fold. First, it has linear complexity with respect to the number of points, enabling the processing of large point clouds. Second, GHA inherently possesses the inductive bias to focus on spatially close points, while retaining the global connectivity among all points. Combined with a feedforward network, GHA can be inserted into many existing network architectures. We experiment with multiple baseline networks and show that adding GHA consistently improves performance across different tasks and datasets. For the task of semantic segmentation, GHA gives a +1.7% mIoU increase to the MinkowskiEngine baseline on ScanNet. For the 3D object detection task, GHA improves the CenterPoint baseline by +0.5% mAP on the nuScenes dataset, and the 3DETR baseline by +2.1% mAP_{25} and +1.5% mAP_{50} on ScanNet.

1 Introduction

Recent years have witnessed a significant increase in interest for point cloud analysis [8,33,45], which is fundamental in many applications. Due to the lack of an inherent order in the point cloud representation, methods that aim to directly process a point cloud need to have permutation invariance [33]. Attention mechanisms, being a set to set operation (which is permutation invariant), are an interesting candidate for this task. Originally introduced for language tasks, attention-based transformers have recently shown great success in a range of computer vision tasks [3,4,12,24]. Several recent works have applied transformer models to 3D tasks, including classification [16], detection [25,27–29], and segmentation [30,66], and have obtained promising results.

There are two major challenges when applying attention to point clouds. Firstly, the required memory quickly grows out of bounds for large point clouds, due to the quadratic space complexity of the attention matrix. Secondly, the global receptive field of an attention layer allows the network to easily overfit

---

Supplementary Information The online version contains supplementary material available at https://doi.org/10.1007/978-3-031-16788-1_17.

B. Andres et al. (Eds.): DAGM GCPR 2022, LNCS 13485, pp. 262–277, 2022.
https://doi.org/10.1007/978-3-031-16788-1_17

to distracting long range information, instead of focusing on local neighborhoods, which provide important geometric information [9,36,62]. To solve these two problems, existing point cloud methods often resort to computing attention only within a local neighborhood (*local attention*), and channel global information either through customized multi-scale architectures [29,66] or via modeling interactions between point clusters [29].

In this work we propose a novel attention mechanism, called *Global Hierarchical Attention* (GHA), which natively addresses the aforementioned two challenges. The memory consumption of GHA scales linearly with respect to the number of points, a significant reduction to the regular quadratic attention. In addition, GHA by design embodies the inductive bias that encourages the network to focus more on local neighbors, while retaining a global receptive field.

The core of GHA is a series of hierarchical levels, connected using *coarsening* and *interpolation* operations. Given an input point cloud, the coarsening operation is used to construct hierarchies with different levels of details. Within each hierarchy level, local attention is computed, and the results from all levels are collated via the interpolation operation. The output of GHA can be computed without needing to reconstruct the memory-intensive attention matrix, and it approximates the output of regular attention, while giving more emphasis to the nearby points. Our method is inspired by the recent H-Transformer-1D [69], which produces an efficient hierarchical approximation of the attention matrix for 1D (language) sequences, but due to its reliance on the existence of a 1D order, it cannot be directly applied to point clouds.

We propose two realizations of GHA, compatible with either raw or voxelized point clouds. We design an add-on module based on GHA that can be easily inserted into an existing network. We experiment with various baseline networks on both 3D object detection and segmentation tasks. Our experiments show that GHA brings a consistent improvement to a range of point cloud networks and tasks, including +1.7% mIoU on ScanNet segmentation for the MinkowskiEngine [8], +0.5% mAP on nuScenes detection for CenterPoint [60], and +2.1% mAP_{25} and +1.5% mAP_{50} on ScanNet detection for 3DETR.

2 Related Work

Point Cloud Analysis. Existing architectures for analyzing point clouds fall into several categories. Projection-based methods [18,21,41,43] process the point clouds by projecting them onto 2D grids and applying 2D CNNs to the obtained image. Voxel-based approaches [8,15,22,37,68] use 3D (sparse) CNNs on the voxelized point cloud. In addition, there are methods that do not rely on discretization and operate directly on point clouds, via PointNet [34], continuous convolutions [26,45,51,54], or graph neural networks [17,19,20,23,47,50,65]. Recent works [13,16,25,28–30,66] have attempted to adapt transformers and attention mechanisms [46] for point cloud processing, encouraged by their recent success in language and vision tasks.

Attention for Point Clouds. Several works have used attention mechanisms for point clouds. Group-free Transformer [25] is an object detection framework that uses a PointNet++ [34] backbone to generate initial bounding box proposals, and a stack of self and cross-attention layers for proposal refinement. Pointformer [29] is another detection network which builds a multi-scale backbone network via a series of customized local and global attention mechanisms. VoTr [27] proposed to replace the sparse voxel convolution in the SECOND detector [56] with local and dilated attention and obtained good detection results. These works rely on specially crafted attention mechanisms and network architectures. 3DETR [28] is the first work that uses a standard end-to-end transformer architecture for object detection, following the framework laid out by the image-based DETR object detector [3]. In addition to detection, attention mechanisms have also been used on tasks like analyzing point cloud videos [13], registration [49], or normal estimation [16].

Two works have aimed at designing attention-based networks specifically for different point cloud tasks. Zhao *et al.* [66] proposed Point Transformer, a multi-scale U-net architecture with local attention computed among k-nearest-neighbors. It was shown to perform well for shape classification on Model-Net40 [52], object part segmentation on ShapeNet [59], and semantic segmentation on S3DIS [1]. Fast Point Transformer [30] modified the Point Transformer architecture to operate on voxels for improved speed and performance.

Similar to these [30,66], GHA is intended as a general-purpose method that can be applied to a wide range of tasks. However, our focus lies on the attention mechanism itself, rather than the network architecture. We conduct experiments by augmenting existing well-known networks with several attention layers, and compare the performance between networks using different types of attention (*e.g.* GHA, local, or regular). Excluding architecture design enables us to draw conclusions on the attention mechanism itself from comparative experiments.

Efficient Transformers. A large body of works exists in the NLP community that aims to reduce the memory consumption of the attention mechanism (*e.g.* [7,44,48,61,69]). The most relevant to our work is that of Zhu and Soricut [69], which proposed a hierarchical attention mechanism to approximate the full attention matrix with linear space complexity. As they exploit the fixed order of a 1D sequence to represent the attention matrix in a matrix block hierarchy, their exact formulation does not readily generalize to higher dimensions. In this work, we extend this idea to point cloud analysis and propose the GHA mechanism that can work with both 3D point clouds and voxels.

In the vision community, most methods resort to computing attention only within local windows [24,66] to reduce the memory consumption and rely on architectural level design to channel long-range information. Compared to these methods, GHA has the advantage of having a global field of view, without imposing additional constraints on the network architecture. As such, GHA can easily be integrated into a whole range of existing networks.

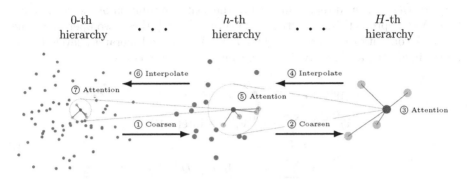

Fig. 1. The operations of **one GHA layer** (not a complete network). The operation order is shown with circled numbers. See Sec. 3.2 for a detailed explanation.

3   Global Hierarchical Attention (GHA)

3.1   Background: Dot-Product Attention

Given the query, key, and value matrices Q, K, $V \in \mathbb{R}^{N \times d}$, the output $Z \in \mathbb{R}^{N \times d}$ of a regular scaled dot-product attention [46] is defined as: $Z = \text{softmax}(\frac{QK^T}{\sqrt{d}})V$, where Q, K, V represents the token queries, keys, values stacked as rows of the matrices, N is the number of tokens, and d is the dimension of the embedding space. This equation can be expressed in a more compact matrix form: $Z = D^{-1}AV$ with $A = e^S$, $S_{ij} = \frac{Q_iK_j^T}{\sqrt{d}}$, $D = \text{diag}(A \cdot \mathbf{1}_N)$, $\mathbf{1}_N = [1, 1, \ldots, 1]^T$. $S_{i,j}$ represents the unnormalized cosine similarity between the i-th query and the j-th key embedding. The normalized attention matrix $D^{-1}A$ has $O(n^2)$ space complexity, making it memory intensive for large numbers of tokens.

3.2   GHA for Point Cloud Analysis

Computing full attention on the raw point cloud is in general not feasible, due to the large number of points in a scene. We propose a global hierarchical attention mechanism, which approximates the full attention while significantly reducing the memory consumption. The core of GHA is a series of hierarchical levels, augmented with three key ingredients: the *coarsening* operation and the *interpolation* operation that connect tokens between two hierarchies, and the *neighborhood topology* that connects tokens within a single hierarchy (Fig. 1).

Specifically, starting from $\tilde{Q}^{(0)} = Q$ (and identically for K and V), the coarsening operation

$$\tilde{Q}^{(h+1)} = \text{Coarsen}(\tilde{Q}^{(h)}, \mathcal{T}^{(h)}) \tag{1}$$

recursively computes a (down-sampled) representation for each hierarchy level by averaging points via a defined neighborhood topology $\mathcal{T}^{(h)}$ (until all remaining points belong to a single neighborhood), and the interpolation operation

$$\tilde{Y}^{(h)} = \text{Interp}(\tilde{Y}^{(h+1)}) \tag{2}$$

expands the coarsened representation to the spatial resolution of the level above (here $Y^{(h)}$ represents any arbitrary embedding). With these two operation, one can first compute the coarsened $\tilde{Q}^{(h)}$, $\tilde{K}^{(h)}$, $\tilde{V}^{(h)}$ for all hierarchy levels h and approximate the attention weighted output Z via the recursion

$$\tilde{A}_{ij}^{(h)} = e^{\tilde{S}_{ij}^{(h)}} = e^{\frac{\tilde{Q}_i^{(h)}(\tilde{K}_i^{(h)})^T}{\sqrt{d}}}$$

$$\tilde{Y}_i^{(h)} = \sum_{j \in \mathcal{T}_i^{(h)}} \tilde{A}_{ij}^{(h)} \tilde{V}_j^{(h)} + \mathrm{Interp}(\tilde{Y}^{(h+1)})_i$$

$$\tilde{D}_i^{(h)} = \sum_{j \in \mathcal{T}_i^{(h)}} \tilde{A}_{ij}^{(h)} + \mathrm{Interp}(\tilde{D}^{(h+1)})_i \tag{3}$$

$$Z \approx \tilde{Z} = \mathrm{diag}(\tilde{D}^{(0)})^{-1} \tilde{Y}^{(0)}.$$

This procedure is summarized in Algorithm 1. Note that here, the attention at each level is only computed within the local neighborhood $\mathcal{T}$. For N points, the memory cost is proportional to $\sum_{h=0}^{H} \frac{1}{k^h} Nk = \frac{1-k^{-(H+1)}}{1-k^{-1}} Nk = \frac{k^{H+1}-1}{k^{H-1}(k-1)} N$ with $H = log_k N$ level of hierarchies. The sum of this series approaches $\frac{k^2}{k-1} N$ with $H \to \infty$, showing the complexity of GHA is upper bounded by a linear function. This linear complexity makes it possible to process large-scale point clouds.

The procedure outlined in Eqs. 1–3 assigns higher attention weights for closer points (see supplementary for an example). Thus, GHA natively embodies the inductive bias to focus more on local neighborhoods while retaining the global connectivity. In this light, local attention as in [30,66] can be viewed as a special case of GHA which truncates all hierarchy below the initial input level.

Algorithm 1. GHA for Point Cloud Analysis

Input: $Q, K, V \in \mathbb{R}^{N \times d}$

Output: $\tilde{Z} \approx \mathrm{softmax}(\frac{QK^T}{\sqrt{d}})V$

  $\tilde{Q}^{(0)}, \tilde{K}^{(0)}, \tilde{V}^{(0)} \leftarrow Q, K, V$ ▷ Coarsening

  for h in $(0, \ldots, H-1)$ **do**

    compute $\tilde{Q}^{(h+1)}$, $\tilde{K}^{(h+1)}$, $\tilde{V}^{(h+1)}$ via Eqn. 1

  end for

  $\tilde{Y}^{(H)}, \tilde{D}^{(H)} \leftarrow 0, 0$ ▷ Interpolation

  for h in $(H-1, \ldots, 0)$ **do**

    compute $\tilde{Y}^{(h)}, \tilde{D}^{(h)}$ via Eqn. 3

  end for

  $\tilde{Z} \leftarrow \mathrm{diag}(\tilde{D}^{(0)})^{-1} \tilde{Y}^{(0)}$

In order to apply GHA to both point-based and voxel-based methods, we propose two flavors of GHA. Taking a voxelized point cloud as input, **Voxel-GHA** uses average pooling as the coarsen operation, unpooling as the interpolation operation, and the local kernel window as the neighborhood topology

$\mathcal{T}$. These operations can be efficiently accomplished using existing sparse convolution libraries [8,55]. **Point-GHA** operates directly on the raw point clouds instead. It uses *kNN* as the neighborhood topology, and conducts coarsening via farthest point sampling $\tilde{Q}^{(h+1)} = \text{Sample}_{(h)}(\frac{1}{K}\sum_{j\in T_i^{(h)}} \tilde{Q}^{(h)})$, and interpolation based on nearest neighbor interpolation $\tilde{Y}^{(h)} = \text{NN}(\tilde{Y}^{(h+1)})$. Having to compute *kNN* neighborhoods and perform sampling means Point-GHA has some computational overhead compared to its voxel-based counterpart. In a block composed of multiple GHA layers, the sampling and *kNN* neighborhood computation only needs to be done once and can be shared between all layers, amortizing this overhead.

3.3 GHA Block

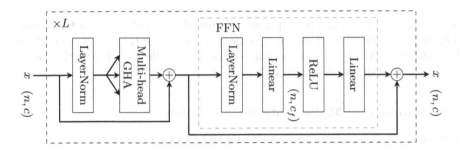

Fig. 2. In our GHA block the attention and FFN are repeated L times. n is the number of points/voxels and c/c_f are the feature dimensionalities. (Position embeddings are omitted.)

Following Vaswani *et al.* [46], we combine GHA with a feedforward network (FFN) into a GHA layer and stack a total of L layers within a GHA Block as shown in Fig. 2. The input to a block consists of n tokens with a dimensionality of c, which we keep throughout the block, apart from the dimensionality c_f that is used between the two linear layers of the FFN. We apply dropout during training, with probability 0.1 in the attention layer, and 0.3 in the FFN layers.

In order to give the network spatial information, we compute random Fourier mappings [42] $\gamma(\mathbf{p}) = [cos(2\pi\mathbf{b}_1^T\mathbf{p}), sin(2\pi\mathbf{b}_1^T\mathbf{p}), \cdots, cos(2\pi\mathbf{b}_m^T\mathbf{p}), sin(2\pi\mathbf{b}_m^T\mathbf{p})]^T$ and use them as positional embedding when computing attention ($\mathbf{p} \in \mathbb{R}^3$ and $\mathbf{b}_i \sim \mathcal{N}(0,1)$ are sampled at initialization). Our method uses positional embeddings based on relative positions $\mathbf{y}_i = \sum_j \mathbf{q}_i^T(\mathbf{k}_j + \gamma(\mathbf{p}_i - \mathbf{p}_j))\mathbf{v}_j$, but we also conduct ablation on using absolute positions $\mathbf{y}_i = \sum_j(\mathbf{q}_i + \gamma(\mathbf{p}_i))^T(\mathbf{k}_j + \gamma(\mathbf{p}_j))\mathbf{v}_j$.

4   Evaluation

Our evaluation can be split into three main parts. We first evaluate Voxel-GHA for the task of 3D semantic segmentation and secondly for 3D object detection. In

Table 1. 3D semantic segmentation performance (mIoU) on ScanNet validation set using original or cleaned labels.

Method	Original		Clean [58]	
	5 cm	2 cm	5 cm	2 cm
ME-UNet18	67.8	72.6	68.4	73.2
+ local attention	69.0	**73.3**	69.6	**73.8**
+ local attention ($L = 8$)	68.8	–	69.3	–
+ GHA	**69.6**	72.8	**70.2**	73.4
ME-UNet34	68.3	72.9	69.0	73.7
+ local attention	68.6	**73.6**	69.0	**74.6**
+ local attention ($L = 8$)	69.1	–	69.7	–
+ GHA	**70.0**	73.5	**70.3**	74.1

both cases we extend different sparse CNN based approaches with a GHA block and evaluate how this affects their performance. In the third part we evaluate how Point-GHA can serve as a replacement for vanilla global attention in the recent 3DETR object detection approach [28].

4.1   Voxel-GHA: 3D Semantic Segmentation

Dataset. We conduct our experiment on the challenging ScanNet dataset [11]. It contains 3D reconstructions of indoor rooms collected using RGB-D scanners and points are labeled with 20 semantic classes. We follow the official training, validation, and test split (1201, 312, and 100 scans).

Setting. We use two MinkUNet [8] architectures as baselines, the smaller ME-UNet18 and the bigger ME-UNet34, and test them on two voxel sizes, 2 cm and 5 cm. Both networks are based on ResNet encoders (18 and 34 layers, respectively) and a symmetric decoder. We insert $L = 6$ GHA layers ($c = 256, c_f = 128$, 8 heads) to the decoder branch after the convolution block at 2× voxel stride (at 4× voxel stride for 2 cm experiments, in order to roughly match the number of voxels in the attention layer). On average, this resulted in 5-12k voxels per frame as input for the attention, a number for which computing multiple layers of full global attention is generally infeasible. We use a $3 \times 3 \times 3$ local window for the neighborhood in GHA (which we apply for all of our experiments). See supplementary for details on the training.

Main Results. In Table 1 we present the mean intersection-over-union (mIoU) between the predicted and labeled masks on the ScanNet validation set (see supplementary for per-class performance). In addition to the official annotation, we also report an evaluation done using the cleaned validation labels from [58]. Compared to the CNN only baseline, GHA gives a clear improvement across all network models and voxel sizes. The performance gap is especially visible for the coarser 5 cm voxels, where GHA improves the baseline by 1.7% mIoU. At finer voxel sizes, however, we see that the improvement of GHA is small, only

RGB   MinkUNet   GHA   Ground truth

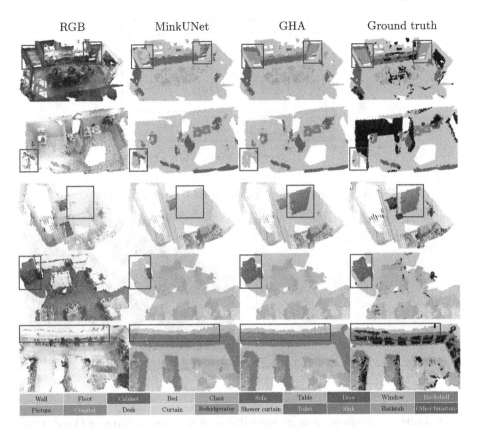

| Wall | Floor | Cabinet | Bed | Chair | Sofa | Table | Door | Window | Bookshelf |
| Picture | Counter | Desk | Curtain | Refridgerator | Shower curtain | Toilet | Sink | Bathtub | Other furniture |

Fig. 3. Qualitative semantic segmentation results on the ScanNet validation set. Predictions with GHA show clear improvement in the marked regions, where semantic labels are ambiguous judging from local geometry and color information alone. This improvement highlights the benefit of long-range information.

0.2% mIoU, for the weaker ME-UNet18 backbone. We speculate that, at this fine scale, a smaller backbone may not be strong enough to extract rich features that can support the global fitting of GHA. The results using cleaned validation labels are in general higher, but the trend matches that observed using original labels, suggesting that the networks do not have special behavior with respect to labeling noise.

In addition, we conduct ablation studies by replacing GHA with local attention. Since local attention consumes less memory than GHA, to have a fair comparison, we also experiment with a bigger model composed of eight layers, which surpasses memory consumption of GHA. With 5 cm voxels, using the same memory, GHA outperforms local attention by 0.8% mIoU. This shows the benefit of having a global field of view. However, with 2 cm voxels, local attention outperforms GHA. This may suggest that, depending on the resolution and the capacity of the feature extractor, limiting field of view can be beneficial to the overall performance, and prompts further architecture level investigation. Figure 3 shows some qualitative results. The predictions of GHA are significantly better on the regions

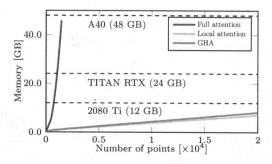

Fig. 4. Training memory measured for 6 attention layers.

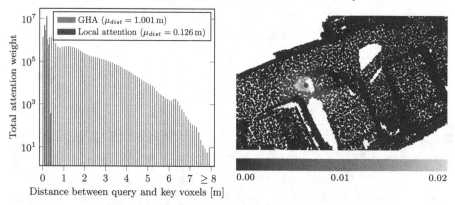

Fig. 5. Left: The distribution of attention distances for both the GHA and local attention. Local attention is incapable of attending to voxels beyond a fixed threshold, whereas GHA can and does indeed attend globally. Notice, however, the logarithmic y-axis. **Right:** The attention heatmap of a **randomly initialized** GHA layer (source point marked with •). Closer points tend to have higher weights. Both figures show the locality bias of GHA.

where the semantic labels are ambiguous based on local geometry and color information alone, showing the advantage of including non-local information for inference. Figure 4 shows the memory consumption of one forward and backward pass for different attention types. GHA has linear space complexity, similar to that of local attention, while having a global field of view. The memory consumption of full attention is prohibitively expensive. Training the ME-18 network (5 cm) takes 34 h for GHA and 27.5 h for local attention, both using a single A40 GPU. For inference on ScanNet, GHA averaged 5.6 and 3.7 FPS for 5 and 2 cm voxels (local attention has 12.9 and 6.5 FPS). The inference speed can be improved with a cuda-optimized indexing implementation and in-place aggregation.

Figure 5 (Left) shows the distribution of attention at different distances. While local attention only attends within a local neighborhood, GHA has a global receptive field, and can attend to all regions in the scene. In addition, GHA has the inductive bias to place an emphasis on nearby points, leading to the skewed pattern in the attention histogram. Figure 5 (Right) shows the attention of a randomly

Table 2. Influence of different factors on the ScanNet validation set performance.

# Layers	mIoU	Embedding	Relative	mIoU	Attention type	mIoU
2	68.3	None		69.0	Cosine [30]	68.8
4	68.6	Learnable	✗	69.3	Vector [66]	71.2
6	70.0	Fourier	✗	69.4	Dot-product [46]	70.0
8	69.5	Fourier	✓	70.0		

initialized GHA layer as a heatmap. Its inductive bias can clearly be seen, as close points tend to receive higher weights, even without being trained.

Additional Experiments. We conduct experiments evaluating several design choices. These experiments are done on ScanNet using the ME-UNet34 model with 5 cm voxels, and the results are presented in Table 2.

Number of Layers. Experiments on different numbers of layers show that, with sufficient network depth, GHA outperforms the baseline or the local attention variants. We attribute this superior performance to its global receptive field, which channels information beyond a local neighborhood.

Positional Embedding. We experiment with different types of positional embedding, including the learned embedding via a two-layer MLP. Results show that random Fourier mapping with relative positions gives the best performance while requiring no additional parameters.

Attention Type. In addition to the standard scaled dot-product attention [46], cosine-similarity-based attention [30] and full vector attention [64] have also been used in transformer architectures for point clouds. The full vector attention gives a 1.2% mIoU performance increase, at the cost of increased memory requirements and parameter counts (training batch size needs to be halved). We use the regular dot-product attention to stay consistent with most existing research.

Local Window vs. kNN Neighbors. Our method uses $3 \times 3 \times 3$ local windows as the neighborhood $\mathcal{T}$ in Eq. 3. As an alternative, we can use a *kNN*-neighborhood ($k = 27$), resulting in on-par performance (69.9% mIoU). We opt for the faster local window-based neighborhood, which in addition has the advantage of being robust against varying point densities.

4.2 Voxel-GHA: 3D Object Detection

Dataset. We conduct our experiments using the *KITTI* [14] and the *nuScenes* dataset [2], both are collected using cars equipped with LiDAR sensors driving on the city streets. The KITTI dataset contains 7,481 LiDAR scans for training and 7,518 for testing. We follow prior work [68] and divide the training split into 3,712 samples for training and 3,769 for validation. The nuScenes dataset is bigger and more challenging, containing 1,000 sequences (380,000 scans), divided into 700/150/150 sequences for training, validation, and testing. The KITTI dataset is annotated with bounding boxes for three classes, whereas the nuScenes dataset is annotated with ten classes.

Setting. We use implementations from the MMDetection3D library [10] for the next set of our experiments. For the KITTI dataset, we experiment with

Table 3. 3D object detection performance (mAP) on the KITTI validation set for (E)asy, (M)oderate, and (H)ard objects. [†]: numbers taken from [10].

Table 4. 3D object detection performance on nuScenes validation set.

Method	Car			Cyclist			Pedestrian		
	E	M	H	E	M	H	E	M	H
VoxelNet [68]	82.0	65.5	62.9	67.2	47.7	45.1	57.9	53.4	48.9
SECOND [56]	87.4	76.5	69.1	–	–	–	–	–	–
F-PointNet [32]	83.8	70.9	63.7	–	–	–	–	–	–
PointRCNN [39]	89.1	78.7	78.2	**93.5**	**74.2**	**70.7**	65.8	59.6	52.8
MVF[†] [67]	88.6	77.7	75.1	80.9	61.9	59.5	61.3	55.7	50.9
Part-A^2 [40]	89.5	79.5	78.5	88.3	73.1	70.2	**70.4**	**63.9**	**57.5**
PV-RCNN [38]	**92.6**	**84.8**	**82.7**	–	–	–	–	–	–
3DSSD [57]	89.7	79.5	78.7	–	–	–	–	–	–
SECOND	88.6	77.6	**74.8**	80.4	66.7	63.1	61.5	55.5	50.1
+ LA	**89.0**	77.8	74.5	76.8	61.7	59.7	60.2	53.2	49.2
+ LA ($L = 6$)	88.0	77.5	74.4	77.7	64.2	60.1	63.5	55.8	51.2
+ GHA	88.8	**77.8**	74.6	**81.7**	**67.8**	**63.9**	**64.0**	**56.1**	**51.2**

Method	mAP	NDS
PointPillars [21]	28.2	46.8
3DSSD [57]	42.6	56.4
CenterPoint [60]	**56.4**	**64.8**
SASA [5]	45.0	61.0
CenterPoint (10 cm)	56.2	64.4
+ LA	**56.8**	**64.8**
+ LA ($L = 6$)	**56.8**	64.7
+ GHA	56.7	64.7
CenterPoint (7.5 cm)	57.3	65.2
+ LA	57.7	65.6
+ LA ($L = 6$)	OOM	
+ GHA	**57.9**	**65.7**

augmenting the SECOND detector [56] with GHA. The SECOND detector uses a sparse voxel-based backbone to encode point cloud features, which are then flattened into a dense 2D feature map and passed into a standard detection head for bounding box regression. We add $L = 4$ GHA layers ($c = 64, c_f = 128$, 4 heads) at the end of the sparse voxel encoder and leave the rest of the network unchanged (the dimension of GHA layers is chosen to match the encoder output).

For the nuScenes dataset, we experiment with the state-of-the-art Center-Point detector [60] which combines a VoxelNet [68] backbone and a center-based object detection head. Similar to the KITTI experiment, we add $L = 4$ GHA layers ($c = 128, c_f = 256$, 8 heads) at the end of the backbone. We experiment with two voxel sizes, 10 cm and 7.5 cm. To reduce the training time, we load a pre-trained model from [10], and fine-tune the network end-to-end for three epochs (the pre-trained model was trained for 20 epochs).

Results. In Table 3 we report the performance of the retrained SECOND detector with and without GHA, along with several other methods for comparison, and in Table 4 we report detection mAP and NDS (nuScenes detection score) on nuScene dataset. In all experiment cases, GHA matches or outperforms the baseline results. On the KITTI dataset, the benefit is especially visible on the smaller cyclist and pedestrian classes (1.1% and 0.6% mAP increase respectively for the moderate setting). On the nuScenes dataset, fine-tuning with GHA for only 3 epochs consistently brings a 0.5% mAP and 0.3% NDS improvement for both voxel sizes. See supplementary for qualitative results.

4.3 Point-GHA: 3D Object Detection

Dataset. To evaluate point-based GHA for object detection, we experiment on ScanNet detection dataset [11], which contains 1,513 indoor scans with annotated bounding boxes, split into 1,201 scenes for training and 312 for validation. Following prior works [6,31,53,63], we report the mean average precision, specifically mAP_{25} and mAP_{50}, computed at a 0.25 and 0.5 IoU threshold respectively.

Table 5. 3D object detection performance on the ScanNet validation set.

Method	mAP$_{25}$	mAP$_{50}$
VoteNet [31]	60.4	37.5
MLCVNet [35]	64.7	42.1
BRNet [6]	66.1	50.9
H3DNet [63]	67.2	48.1
VENet [53]	67.7	–
GroupFree3D [24]	**69.1**	**52.8**
3DETR [28]	62.7	37.5
3DETR-m [28]	**65.0**	**47.0**
GHA-3DETR	64.3	45.6
GHA-3DETR-p	65.4	46.1
GHA-3DETR-p (4096)	**67.1**	**48.5**

Table 6. 3DETR performance with different encoder self-attention or *kNN* neighborhood sizes.

Attention	mAP$_{25}$	mAP$_{50}$
Regular	62.7	37.5
Local	63.1	43.9
BigBird [61]	63.4	43.4
GHA	**64.3**	**45.6**

kNN size	mAP$_{25}$	mAP$_{50}$
$k = 2$	64.1	42.9
$k = 4$	64.1	43.6
$k = 6$	**64.3**	**45.6**
$k = 8$	63.4	43.2
$k = 10$	62.6	44.3
$k = 20$	61.7	41.1

Setting. We experiment with the 3DETR network proposed by Misra *et al.* [28]. 3DETR follows a transformer encoder-decoder architecture. From the input point cloud, 3DETR first samples 2048 points and extracts their neighboring features via a single set aggregation operation, as introduced by Qi *et al.* in their PointNet++ [34]. These points are then processed with a transformer encoder composed of multiple self-attention layers. During the decoding stage, 3DETR samples a set of query points and projects them into the embedding space (*object queries*), and through a stack of self and cross-attention, decodes each of the object queries into bounding boxes.

To evaluate Point-GHA, we replace 3DETR's encoder self-attention with Point-GHA ($k = 6$ for the *kNN* neighborhood), leaving all other network components unchanged. We refer to this network as 3DETR-GHA. In addition, Misra *et al.* experimented with masking of attention between points further than a threshold, and obtained improved results. This version, called 3DETR-m, also includes an intermediate pooling layer. Since GHA inherently has the inductive bias to focus on local neighborhoods, we do not need to apply distance-based masking. Rather, we experiment with adding the intermediate pooling layer, and refer to this version as 3DETR-GHA-p. Finally, with the benefit of the reduced memory consumption of GHA, we experiment with a bigger model by including more points (4096) into the encoder.

Results. In Table 5 we present the main experiment result. Compared to the 3DETR baseline, our GHA-3DETR obtains an improvement of 1.6% on mAP$_{25}$ and 8.1% on mAP$_{50}$. Compared to the masking 3DETR-m, our GHA-3DETR-p achieves similar performance. When including more points, GHA-3DETR-p gives an mAP$_{25}$ and mAP$_{50}$ improvement of 2.1% and 1.5% respectively, coming closer to state-of-the-art performance.

In Table 6 we present an ablation study, where we replace the self-attention in 3DETR with different attention mechanisms. Compared to the regular attention (used in 3DETR), local attention achieved improved results, especially for

mAP_{50}, despite not having a global field of view. This demonstrates the value of focusing on local neighbors. GHA outperforms local attention, thanks to the additional access to global information acquired from its hierarchical design. We additionally implement a variant of BigBird [61] to work with point clouds (it was originally proposed for language tasks), which augments local attention with several tokens that have global connectivity (*global attention*), and randomly activate a small number of non-local attentions (*random sparse attention*). GHA outperforms our BigBird implementation. Even though both methods have global connectivity and have linear memory complexity, GHA additionally embodies the inductive bias to focus on local information, to which we attribute its better performance. In Table 6 we also present a study on the effect of the *kNN* neighborhood size, and the result shows that GHA is robust to a wide range *k*, consistently outperforming its counterpart using regular attention.

5 Conclusion

In this paper we have proposed Global Hierarchical Attention (GHA) for point cloud analysis. Its inductive bias towards nearby points, its global field of view, as well as its linear space complexity, make it a promising mechanism for processing large point clouds. Extensive experiments on both detection and segmentation show that adding GHA to an existing network gives consistent improvements over the baseline network. Moreover, ablation studies replacing GHA with other types of attention have demonstrated its advantage.

The overall positive results point to future research directions. The GHA mechanism can in principle be applied to image-domain tasks as well, which we have not experimented with so far. In addition, it would be interesting to explore new architectures with GHA, beyond plugging it into existing networks.

Acknowledgements. This project was funded by the BMBF project 6GEM (16KISK036K) and the ERC Consolidator Grant DeeVise (ERC-2017-COG-773161). We thank Jonas Schult, Markus Knoche, Ali Athar, and Christian Schmidt for helpful discussions.

References

1. Armeni, I., et al.: 3d semantic parsing of large-scale indoor spaces. In: CVPR (2016)
2. Caesar, H., et al.: nuScenes: a multimodal dataset for autonomous driving. In: CVPR (2020)
3. Carion, N., Massa, F., Synnaeve, G., Usunier, N., Kirillov, A., Zagoruyko, S.: End-to-end object detection with transformers. In: Vedaldi, A., Bischof, H., Brox, T., Frahm, J.-M. (eds.) ECCV 2020. LNCS, vol. 12346, pp. 213–229. Springer, Cham (2020). https://doi.org/10.1007/978-3-030-58452-8_13
4. Caron, M.: Emerging properties in self-supervised vision transformers. In: ICCV (2021)
5. Chen, C., Chen, Z., Zhang, J., Tao, D.: SASA: semantics-augmented set abstraction for point-based 3D object detection. In: AAAI (2022)

6. Cheng, B., Sheng, L., Shi, S., Yang, M., Xu, D.: Back-tracing representative points for voting-based 3D object detection in point clouds. In: CVPR (2021)
7. Choromanski, K., et al.: Rethinking attention with performers. In: ICLR (2020)
8. Choy, C., Gwak, J., Savarese, S.: 4D Spatio-Temporal ConvNets: Minkowski convolutional neural networks. In: CVPR (2019)
9. Choy, C., Park, J., Koltun, V.: Fully convolutional geometric features. In: ICCV (2019)
10. Contributors, M.: MMDetection3D: OpenMMLab next-generation platform for general 3D object detection (2020). https://github.com/open-mmlab/mmdetection3d
11. Dai, A., Chang, A.X., Savva, M., Halber, M., Funkhouser, T., Nießner, M.: ScanNet: Richly-annotated 3D Reconstructions of Indoor Scenes. In: CVPR (2017)
12. Dosovitskiy, A., et al.: An image is worth 16x16 words: transformers for image recognition at scale. In: ICLR (2021)
13. Fan, H., Yang, L., Kankanhalli, M.: Point 4D transformer networks for spatio-temporal modeling in point cloud videos. In: CVPR (2021)
14. Geiger, A., Lenz, P., Stiller, C., Urtasun, R.: Vision meets robotics: the KITTI dataset. IJRR **32**(11), 1231–1237 (2013)
15. Graham, B., Engelcke, M., van der Maaten, L.: 3D semantic segmentation with submanifold sparse convolutional networks. In: CVPR (2018)
16. Guo, M.-H., Cai, J.-X., Liu, Z.-N., Mu, T.-J., Martin, R.R., Hu, S.-M.: PCT: point cloud transformer. Comput. Visual Media **7**(2), 187–199 (2021). https://doi.org/10.1007/s41095-021-0229-5
17. Jiang, L., Zhao, H., Liu, S., Shen, X., Fu, C.W., Jia, J.: Hierarchical point-edge interaction network for point cloud semantic segmentation. In: ICCV (2019)
18. Kanezaki, A., Matsushita, Y., Nishida, Y.: RotationNet for joint object categorization and unsupervised pose estimation from multi-view images. PAMI 43 (2021)
19. Landrieu, L., Boussaha, M.: Point cloud oversegmentation with graph-structured deep metric learning. In: CVPR (2019)
20. Landrieu, L., Simonovsky, M.: Large-scale point cloud semantic segmentation with superpoint graphs. In: CVPR (2018)
21. Lang, A.H., Vora, S., Caesar, H., Zhou, L., Yang, J., Beijbom, O.: PointPillars: fast encoders for object detection from point clouds. In: CVPR (2019)
22. Li, Y., Bu, R., Sun, M., Wu, W., Di, X., Chen, B.: PointCNN: convolution on X-transformed points. In: NeurIPS (2018)
23. Li, G., et al.: Deepgcns: Making gcns go as deep as cnns. PAMI (2021)
24. Liu, Z., et al.: Swin transformer: hierarchical vision transformer using shifted windows. In: ICCV (2021)
25. Liu, Z., Zhang, Z., Cao, Y., Hu, H., Tong, X.: Group-free 3D object detection via transformers. In: ICCV (2021)
26. Mao, J., Wang, X., Li, H.: Interpolated convolutional networks for 3D point cloud understanding. In: ICCV (2019)
27. Mao, J., et al.: Voxel transformer for 3D object detection. In: ICCV (2021)
28. Misra, I., Girdhar, R., Joulin, A.: An end-to-end transformer model for 3D object detection. In: ICCV (2021)
29. Pan, X., Xia, Z., Song, S., Li, L.E., Huang, G.: 3D object detection with point-former. In: CVPR (2021)
30. Park, C., Jeong, Y., Cho, M., Park, J.: Fast point transformer. arXiv:2112.04702 (2021)
31. Qi, C.R., Litany, O., He, K., Guibas, L.J.: Deep hough voting for 3D object detection in point clouds. In: ICCV (2019)

32. Qi, C.R., Liu, W., Wu, C., Su, H., Guibas, L.J.: Frustum PointNets for 3D object detection from RGB-D data. In: CVPR (2018)
33. Qi, C.R., Su, H., Mo, K., Guibas, L.J.: PointNet: deep learning on point sets for 3D classification and segmentation. In: CVPR (2017)
34. Qi, C.R., Yi, L., Su, H., Guibas, L.J.: PointNet++: deep hierarchical feature learning on point sets in a metric space. In: NeurIPS (2017)
35. Qian, X., et al.: MLCVNet: multi-level context VoteNet for 3D object detection. In: CVPR (2020)
36. Raghu, M., Unterthiner, T., Kornblith, S., Zhang, C., Dosovitskiy, A.: Do Vision Transformers See Like Convolutional Neural Networks? arXiv:2108.08810 (2021)
37. Riegler, G., Ulusoy, A.O., Geiger, A.: OctNet: learning deep 3D representations at high resolutions. In: CVPR (2017)
38. Shi, S., Guo, C., Jiang, L., Wang, Z., Shi, J., Wang, X., Li, H.: PV-RCNN: point-voxel feature set abstraction for 3D object detection. In: CVPR (2020)
39. Shi, S., Wang, X., Li, H.: PointRCNN: 3D object proposal generation and detection from point cloud. In: CVPR (2019)
40. Shi, S., Wang, Z., Shi, J., Wang, X., Li, H.: From points to parts: 3D object detection from point cloud with part-aware and part-aggregation network. PAMI (2020)
41. Su, H., et al.: SPLATNet: sparse lattice networks for point cloud processing. In: CVPR (2018)
42. Tancik, M., et al.: Fourier features let networks learn high frequency functions in low dimensional domains. In: NeurIPS (2020)
43. Tatarchenko, M., Park, J., Koltun, V., Zhou, Q.Y.: Tangent convolutions for dense prediction in 3D. In: CVPR (2018)
44. Tay, Y., Dehghani, M., Bahri, D., Metzler, D.: Efficient transformers: a survey. arXiv:2009.06732 (2020)
45. Thomas, H., Qi, C., Deschaud, J.E., Marcotegui, B., Goulette, F., Guibas, L.: KPConv: flexible and deformable convolution for point clouds. In: ICCV (2019)
46. Vaswani, A., et al.: Attention is all you need. In: NeurIPS (2017)
47. Wang, L., Huang, Y., Hou, Y., Zhang, S., Shan, J.: Graph attention convolution for point cloud semantic segmentation. In: CVPR (2019)
48. Wang, S., Li, B.Z., Khabsa, M., Fang, H., Ma, H.: Linformer: self-attention with linear complexity. arXiv:2006.04768 (2020)
49. Wang, Y., Solomon, J.M.: Deep closest point: learning representations for point cloud registration. In: ICCV (2019)
50. Wang, Y., Sun, Y., Liu, Z., Sarma, S.E., Bronstein, M.M., Solomon, J.M.: Dynamic graph CNN for learning on point clouds. ACM Trans. Graphics **38**(5) (2019). https://doi.org/10.1145/3326362
51. Wu, W., Qi, Z., Fuxin, L.: PointConv: deep convolutional networks on 3D point clouds. In: CVPR (2019)
52. Wu, Z., et al.: 3D ShapeNets: a deep representation for volumetric shapes. In: CVPR (2015)
53. Xie, Q., et al.: VENet: voting enhancement network for 3D object detection. In: ICCV (2021)
54. Xu, Y., Fan, T., Xu, M., Zeng, L., Qiao, Yu.: SpiderCNN: deep learning on point sets with parameterized convolutional filters. In: Ferrari, V., Hebert, M., Sminchisescu, C., Weiss, Y. (eds.) ECCV 2018. LNCS, vol. 11212, pp. 90–105. Springer, Cham (2018). https://doi.org/10.1007/978-3-030-01237-3_6
55. Yan, Y.: SpConv: Spatially Sparse Convolution Library. https://github.com/traveller59/spconv. Accessed 04 Mar 2022

56. Yan, Y., Yuxing Mao, B.L.: SECOND: Sparsely Embedded Convolutional Detection. Sensors (2018)
57. Yang, Z., Sun, Y., Liu, S., Jia, J.: 3DSSD: point-based 3D single stage object detector. In: CVPR (2020)
58. Ye, S., Chen, D., Han, S., Liao, J.: Learning with noisy labels for robust point cloud segmentation. In: ICCV (2021)
59. Yi, L., et al.: A scalable active framework for region annotation in 3D shape collections. ACM Trans. Graphics **35** (2016)
60. Yin, T., Zhou, X., Krähenbühl, P.: Center-based 3D object detection and tracking. In: CVPR (2021)
61. Zaheer, M., et al.: Big bird: transformers for longer sequences. In: NeurIPS (2020)
62. Zeng, A., Song, S., Nießner, M., Fisher, M., Xiao, J., Funkhouser, T.: 3DMatch: learning local geometric descriptors from RGB-D reconstructions. In: CVPR (2017)
63. Zhang, Z., Sun, B., Yang, H., Huang, Q.: H3DNet: 3D object detection using hybrid geometric primitives. In: Vedaldi, A., Bischof, H., Brox, T., Frahm, J.-M. (eds.) ECCV 2020. LNCS, vol. 12357, pp. 311–329. Springer, Cham (2020). https://doi.org/10.1007/978-3-030-58610-2_19
64. Zhao, H., Jia, J., Koltun, V.: Exploring self-attention for image recognition. In: CVPR (2020)
65. Zhao, H., Jiang, L., Fu, C.W., Jia, J.: PointWeb: enhancing local neighborhood features for point cloud processing. In: CVPR (2019)
66. Zhao, H., Jiang, L., Jia, J., Torr, P.H., Koltun, V.: Point transformer. In: ICCV (2021)
67. Zhou, Y., et al.: End-to-end multi-view fusion for 3D object detection in LiDAR point clouds. In: CoRL (2019)
68. Zhou, Y., Tuzel, O.: VoxelNet: end-to-end learning for point cloud based 3D object detection. In: CVPR (2017)
69. Zhu, Z., Soricut, R.: H-Transformer-1D: fast one-dimensional hierarchical attention for sequences. In: ACL (2021)

3D Vision and Stereo

InterCap: Joint Markerless 3D Tracking of Humans and Objects in Interaction

Yinghao Huang[1][(✉)], Omid Taheri[1], Michael J. Black[1], and Dimitrios Tzionas[2]

[1] Max Planck Institute for Intelligent Systems, Tübingen, Germany
{yhuang2,otaheri,black}@tue.mpg.de
[2] University of Amsterdam, Amsterdam, The Netherlands
d.tzionas@uva.nl

Abstract. Humans constantly interact with daily objects to accomplish tasks. To understand such interactions, computers need to reconstruct these from cameras observing whole-body interaction with scenes. This is challenging due to occlusion between the body and objects, motion blur, depth/scale ambiguities, and the low image resolution of hands and graspable object parts. To make the problem tractable, the community focuses either on interacting hands, ignoring the body, or on interacting bodies, ignoring hands. The GRAB dataset addresses dexterous whole-body interaction but uses marker-based MoCap and lacks images, while BEHAVE captures video of body-object interaction but lacks hand detail. We address the limitations of prior work with InterCap, a novel method that reconstructs interacting whole-bodies and objects from multi-view RGB-D data, using the parametric whole-body model SMPL-X and known object meshes. To tackle the above challenges, Inter-Cap uses two key observations: (i) Contact between the hand and object can be used to improve the pose estimation of both. (ii) Azure Kinect sensors allow us to set up a simple multi-view RGB-D capture system that minimizes the effect of occlusion while providing reasonable inter-camera synchronization. With this method we capture the InterCap dataset, which contains 10 subjects (5 males and 5 females) interacting with 10 objects of various sizes and affordances, including contact with the hands or feet. In total, InterCap has 223 RGB-D videos, resulting in 67,357 multi-view frames, each containing 6 RGB-D images. Our method provides pseudo ground-truth body meshes and objects for each video frame. Our InterCap method and dataset fill an important gap in the literature and support many research directions. Our data and code are available for research purposes at https://intercap.is.tue.mpg.de.

1 Introduction

A long-standing goal of Computer Vision is to understand human actions from videos. Given a video people effortlessly figure out what objects exist in it,

Supplementary Information The online version contains supplementary material available at https://doi.org/10.1007/978-3-031-16788-1_18.

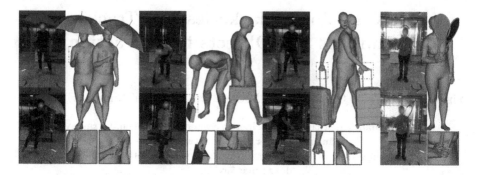

Fig. 1. Humans interact with objects to accomplish tasks. To understand such interactions we need the tools to reconstruct them from whole-body videos in 4D, i.e., as 3D meshes in motion. Existing methods struggle, due to the strong occlusions, motion blur, and low-resolution of hands and object structures in such videos. Moreover, they mostly focus on the main body, ignoring the hands and objects. We develop InterCap, a novel method that reconstructs plausible interacting whole-body and object meshes from multi-view RGB-D videos, using contact constraints to account for strong ambiguities. With this we capture the rich InterCap dataset of 223 RGB-D videos (67,357 multi-view frames, with 6 Azure Kinects) containing 10 subjects (5 fe-/males) interacting with 10 objects of various sizes and affordances; note the hand-object grasps.

the spatial layout of objects, and the pose of humans. Moreover, they deeply understand the depicted action. What is the subject doing? Why are they doing this? What is their goal? How do they achieve this? To empower computers with the ability to infer such abstract concepts from pixels, we need to capture rich datasets and to devise appropriate algorithms.

Since humans live in a 3D world, their physical actions involve interacting with objects. Think of how many times per day one goes to the kitchen, grabs a cup of water, and drinks from it. This involves contacting the floor with the feet, contacting the cup with the hand, moving the hand and cup together while maintaining contact, and drinking while the mouth contacts the cup. Thus, to understand human actions, it is necessary to reason in 3D about humans and objects *jointly*.

There is significant prior work on estimating 3D humans without taking into account objects [4] and estimating 3D objects without taking into account humans [68]. There is even recent work on inserting bodies into 3D scenes such that their interactions appear realistic [16,30,65]. But there is little work on estimating 3D humans interacting with scenes and moving objects, in which the human-scene/object contact is explicitly modeled and exploited. To study this problem, we need a dataset of videos with rich human-object interactions and reliable 3D ground truth.

PROX [15] takes a step in this direction by estimating the 3D body in a known 3D scene. The scene mesh provides information that helps resolve pose ambiguities commonly encountered when a single camera is used. However, PROX involves only coarse interactions of bodies, static scenes with no moving objects, and no dexterous fingers. The recent BEHAVE dataset [3] uses multi-view RGB-D data to capture humans interacting with objects but does not include detailed hand pose or fine hand-object contact. Finally, the GRAB dataset [54] captures the kind of detailed hand-object and whole-body-object interaction that we seek but is captured using marker-based MoCap and, hence, lacks images paired with the ground-truth scene.

We argue that what is needed is a new dataset of RGB videos containing natural human-object interaction in which the whole body is tracked reliably, the hand pose is captured, objects are also tracked, and the hand-object contact is realistic; see Fig. 1. This is challenging and requires technical innovation to create. To that end, we design a system that uses multiple RGB-D sensors that are spatially calibrated and temporally synchronized. To this data we fit the SMPL-X body model, which has articulated hands, by extending the PROX [15] method to use multi-view data and grasping hand-pose priors. We also track the 3D objects with which the person interacts. The objects used in this work are representative of items one finds in daily life. We obtain accurate 3D models for each object with a handheld Artec scanner. Altogether we collect 223 sequences (67,357 multi-view frames), with 10 subjects interacting with 10 objects.

The problem, however, is that separately estimating the body and objects is not sufficient to ensure accurate 3D body-object contact. Consequently, a key innovation of this work is to estimate these *jointly*, while exploiting information about *contact*. Objects do not move independently, so, when they move, it means the body is in contact. We define likely contact regions on objects and on the body. Then, given frames with known likely contacts, we enforce contact between the body and the object when estimating the body and object poses. The resulting method produces natural body poses, hand poses, and object poses. Uniquely, it provides detailed pseudo ground-truth contact information between the whole body and objects in RGB video.

In summary, our major contributions are as follows: (1) We develop a novel Motion Capture method utilizing multiple RGB-D cameras. It is relatively lightweight and flexible, yet accurate enough, thus suitable for data capture of daily scenarios. (2) We extend previous work on fitting SMPL-X to images to fit it to multi-view RGB-D data while taking into account body-object contact. (3) We capture a novel dataset that contains whole-body human motions and interaction with objects, as well as multi-view RGB-D imagery. Our data and code are available at https://intercap.is.tue.mpg.de.

2 Related Work

There is a large literature on estimating 3D human pose and shape from images or videos [4,7,25,29,37,41,44,57]. Here we focus on the work most closely related to ours, particularly as it concerns, or enables, capturing human-object interaction.

MoCap from Multi-view Videos and IMUs. Markerless MoCap from multi-view videos [8,22,31] is widely studied and commercial solutions exist (e.g., Theia Markerless). Compared with traditional marker-based MoCap, markerless offers advantages of convenience, applicability in outdoor environments, non-intrusiveness, and greater flexibility. However, traditional MoCap methods, both marker-based and markerless, focus on extracting a 3D skeleton. This is useful for biomechanics but our goal is to reason about body-scene contact. To enable that, we need to capture the body surface.

Various 3D human representations have been proposed, with recent work focused on learning a parametric mesh-based model of body shape from large-scale collections of 3D scans [2,33,42–44,50,59]. Here we use the SMPL-X model [44] because it contains fully articulated hands, which are critical for reasoning about object manipulation. The body parameters are often estimated by fitting the 3D generative model to various 2D cues like landmarks detected by Convolutional Neural Networks [6,39,58] or silhouettes [1,47,60]. Though effective, these monocular video-based methods suffer from depth ambiguity and occlusions. To address this issue, researchers have proposed to combine IMUs with videos to obtain better and more robust results [36,45].

Many methods estimate 3D bodies from multi-view images but focus on skeletons and not 3D bodies [9,10,19,24,46,55,66]. Recent work addresses 3D body shape estimation from multiple views [11,22,67]. Most related to our work are two recent datasets. The RICH dataset [21], fits SMPL-X bodies to multi-view RGB videos taken both indoors and outdoors. The method uses a detailed 3D scan of the scene and models the contact between the body and the world. RICH does not include any object motion; the scenes are completely rigid. In contrast, BEHAVE [3] contains SMPL bodies interacting with 3D objects that move. We go beyond that work, however, to integrate novel contact constraints and to capture hand pose, which is critical for human-object interaction. Additionally, BEHAVE focuses on large objects like boxes and chairs, whereas we have a wider range of object sizes, including smaller objects like cups.

Human-Object Interaction. There has been a lot of work on modeling or analyzing human-object interactions [3,13,14,18,26,40,48,56,61]. A detailed discussion is out of the scope of this work. Here, we focus on modeling and analyzing human-object interaction in 3D space. Most existing work, however, only focuses on estimating hand pose [14,17,18,49], ignoring the strong relationship between body motion, hand motion, and object motion. Recent work considers whole-body motion. For example, the GRAB [54] dataset provides detailed object motion and whole-body motion in a parametric body format (SMPL-X). Unfortunately, it is based on MoCap and does not include video. Here our focus is on tracking the whole-body motion, object motion, and the detailed hand-object contact to provide ground-truth 3D information in RGB video.

Joint Modeling of Humans and Scenes. There is some prior work addressing human-object contact in both static images and video. For example, PHOSA estimates a 3D body and a 3D object with plausible interaction from a single RGB image [63]. Our focus here, however, is on dynamic scenes. Motivated by the observation that natural human motions always happen inside 3D scenes, researchers have proposed to model human motion jointly with the surrounding environment [5,15,51,62]. In PROX [15] the contact between humans and scenes is explicitly used to resolve ambiguities in pose estimation. The approach avoids bodies interpenetrating scenes while encouraging contact between the scene and nearby body parts. Prior work also tries to infer the most plausible position and pose of humans given the 3D scene [16,30,65]. Most recently, MOVER [62] estimates the 3D scene and the 3D human directly from a static monocular video in which a person interacts with the scene. While the 3D scene is ambiguous and the human motion is ambiguous, by exploiting contact, the method resolves many ambiguities, improving the estimates of both the scene and the person. Unfortunately, this assumes a static scene and does not model hand-object manipulation.

Datasets. Traditionally, MoCap is performed using marker-based systems inside lab environments. To capture object interaction and contact, one approach uses MoSh [32] to fit a SMPL or SMPL-X body to the markers [35]. An advanced version of this is used for GRAB [54]. Such approaches lack synchronized RGB video. The HumanEva [52] and Human3.6M [23] datasets combine multi-camera RGB video capture with synchronized ground-truth 3D skeletons from marker-based MoCap. These datasets lack ground-truth 3D body meshes, are captured in a lab setting, and do not contain human-object manipulation. 3DPW [36] is the first in-the-wild dataset that jointly features natural human appearance in video and accurate 3D pose. This dataset does not track objects or label human-object interaction. PiGraphs [51] and PROX [15] provide both 3D scenes and human motions but are relatively inaccurate, relying on a single RGB-D camera. This makes these datasets ill-suited as evaluation benchmarks. The recent RICH dataset [21] addresses many of these issues with indoor and outdoor scenes, accurate multi-view capture of SMPL-X, 3D scene scans, and human-scene contact. It is not appropriate for our task, however, as it does not include object manipulation.

An alternative approach is the one of GTA-IM [5] and SAIL-VOS [20], which generate human-scene interaction data using either 3D graphics or 2D videos. They feature high-accuracy ground truth but lack visual realism. In summary, we believe that a 3D human-object interaction dataset needs to have accurate hand poses to be useful, since hands are how people most often interact with objects. We compare our InterCap dataset with other ones in Table 1.

Table 1. Dataset statistics. Comparison of our InterCap dataset to existing datasets.

Name	# of Seq.	Natural Appear.	Moving Objects	Accurate Motion	With Image	Artic Hands
HumanEva [52]	56	✓	✗	✓	✓	✗
Human3.6M [23]	165	✓	✗	✓	✓	✗
AMASS [35]	11265	✓	✗	✓	✗	✗
GRAB [54]	1334	✓	✓	✓	✗	✓
3DPW [36]	60	✓	✗	✓	✓	✗
GTA-IM [5]	119	✗	✗	✓	✓	✗
SAIL-VOS [20]	201	✗	✗	✗	✗	✗
PiGraphs [51]	63	✓	✗	✓	✓	✗
PROX [15]	20	✓	✗	✗	✓	✗
RICH [21]	142	✓	✗	✓	✓	✗
BEHAVE [3]	321	✓	✓	✓	✓	✗
InterCap (ours)	223	✓	✓	✓	✓	✓

3   InterCap Method

Our core goal is to accurately estimate the human and object motion throughout a video. Our markerless motion capture method is built on top of the PROX-D method of Hassan et al. [15]. To improve the body tracking accuracy we extend this method to use multiple RGB-D cameras; here we use the latest Azure Kinect cameras. The motivation is that multiple cameras observing the body from different angles give more information about the human and object motion. Moreover, commodity RGB-D cameras are much more flexible to deploy out of controlled lab scenarios than more specialized devices.

The key technical challenge lies in accurately estimating the 3D pose and translation of the objects while a person interacts with them. In this work we focus on 10 variously sized rigid objects common in daily life, such as cups and chairs. Being rigid does not make the tracking of the objects trivial because of the occlusion by the body and hands. While there is a rich literature on 6 DoF object pose estimation, much of it ignores hand-object interaction. Recent work in this direction is promising but still focuses on scenarios that are significantly simpler than ours, cf. [53].

Similar to previous work on hand and object pose estimation [14] from RGB-D videos, in this work we assume that the 3D meshes of the objects are known in advance. To this end, we first gather the 3D models of these objects from the Internet whenever possible and scan the remaining objects ourselves. To fit the known object models to image data, we first preform semantic segmentation, find the corresponding object regions in all camera views, and fit the 3D mesh to the segmented object contours via differentiable rendering. Since heavy occlusion between humans and objects in some views may make the segmentation results unreliable, aggregating segmentation from all views boosts the object tracking performance.

In the steps above, both the subject and object are treated separately and processing is per frame, with no temporal smoothness or contact constraint applied. This produces jittery motions and heavy penetration between objects and the body. Making matters worse, our human pose estimation exploits OpenPose for 2D keypoint detection, which struggles when the object occludes the body or the hands interact with it. To mitigate this issue and still get reasonable body, hand and object pose in these challenging cases, we manually annotate the frames where the body or the hand is in contact with the object, as well as the body, hand and object vertices that are most likely to be in contact. This manual annotation can be tedious; automatic detection of contact is an open problem and is left for future work. We then explicitly encourage the labeled body and hand vertices to be in contact with the labeled object vertices. We find that this straightforward idea works well in practice. More details are described in the following.

3.1   Multi-Kinect Setup

We use 6 Azure Kinects to track the human and object together, deployed in a "ring" layout in an office; see Sup. Mat. Multiple RGB-D cameras provide a good balance between body tracking accuracy and applicability to real scenarios, compared with costly professional MoCap systems like Vicon, or cheap and convenient but not-so-accurate monocular RGB cameras. Moreover, this approach does not require applying any markers, making the images natural. Intrinsic camera parameters are provided by the manufacturer. Extrinsic camera parameters are obtained via camera calibration with Azure Kinect's API [38]. However, these can be a bit noisy, as non-neighbouring cameras in a sparse "ring" layout don't observe the calibration board well at the same time. Thus, we manually refine in MeshLab the extrinsics by comparing the point clouds for neighbouring cameras for several iterations. The hardware synchronization of Azure Kinects is empirically reasonable. Given the calibration information, we choose one camera's 3D coordinate frame as the global frame and transform the point clouds from the other frames into the global frame, which is where we fit the SMPL-X and object models.

3.2   Sequential Object-Only Tracking

Object Segmentation. To track an object during interaction, we need reliable visual cues about it to compare with the 3D object model. To this end, we perform semantic segmentation by applying PointRend [28] to the whole image. We then extract the object instances that correspond to the categories of our objects; for examples see Sup. Mat. We assume that the subject interacts with a single object. Note that, in contrast to previous approaches where the objects occupy a large portion of the image [14,15,40,56], in our case the entire body is visible, thus, the object takes up a small part of the image and is often occluded by the body and hands; our setting is much more challenging. We observe that PointRend works reasonably well for large objects like chairs, even with heavy occlusion between the object and the human, while for small objects, like a bottle or a cup, it struggles significantly due to occlusion.

In extreme cases, it is possible for the object to not be detected in most of the views. But even when the segmentation is good, the class label for the objects may be wrong. To resolve this, we take two steps: (1) For every frame, we detect all possible object segmentation candidates and their labels. This step takes place offline and only once. (2) During the object tracking phase, for each view, we compare the rendering of the tracked object from the ith frame with all the detected segmentation candidates for the $(i+1)^{\text{th}}$ frame, and preserve only the candidate with the largest overlap ratio. This render-compare-and-preserve operation takes place iteratively during tracking.

Object Tracking. Given object masks via semantic segmentation over the whole sequence, we track the object by fitting its model to observations via differentiable rendering [27,34]. This is similar to past work for hand-object tracking [14]. We assume that the object is rigid and its mesh is given. The configuration of the rigid object in the tth frame is specified via a 6D rotation and translation vector ξ. For initialization, we manually obtain the configuration of the object for the first frame by matching the object mesh into the measured point clouds. Let R_S and R_D be functions that render a synthetic mask and depth image for the tracked 3D object mesh, M. Let also $S = \{S_\nu\}$ be the "observed" object masks and $D = \{D_\nu\}$ be corresponding depth values for the current frame, where ν is the camera view. Then, we minimize:

$$E_O(\xi; S, D) = \sum_{\text{view } \nu} \lambda_{segm} \|(R_S(\xi, M, \nu) - S_\nu) * S_\nu\|_F^2 \qquad (1)$$
$$+ \lambda_{depth} \|(R_D(\xi, M, \nu) - D_\nu) * S_\nu\|_F^2,$$

where the two terms compute how well the rendered object mask and depth image match the detected mask and observed depth; the $*$ is an element-wise multiplication, and $\|.\|_F$ the Frobenius norm; λ_{segm} and λ_{depth} are steering weights set empirically. For simplicity, we assume that transformations from the master to other camera frames are encoded in the rendering functions R_S, R_D; we do not denote these explicitly here.

3.3 Sequential Human-Only Tracking

We estimate body shape and pose over the whole sequence from multi-view RGB-D videos in a frame-wise manner. This is similar in spirit with the PROX-D method [15], but, in our case, there is no 3D scene constraint and multiple cameras are used. The human pose and shape are optimized independently in each frame. We use the SMPL-X [44] model to represent the 3D human body. SMPL-X is a function that returns a water-tight mesh given parameters for shape, β, pose, θ, facial expression, ψ, and translation, γ. We follow the common practice of using a 10-dimensional space for shape, β, and a 32-dimensional latent space in VPoser [44] to represent body pose, θ.

We minimize the loss defined below. For each frame we essentially extend the major loss terms used in PROX [15] to multiple views:

$$E_B(\beta, \theta, \psi, \gamma; K, J_{est}) = E_J + \lambda_D E_D + \lambda_{\theta_b} E_{\theta_b} + \lambda_{\theta_h} E_{\theta_h} + \lambda_{\theta_f} E_{\theta_f} \qquad (2)$$
$$+ \lambda_\alpha E_\alpha + \lambda_\beta E_\beta + \lambda_\varepsilon E_\varepsilon + \lambda_P E_P,$$

where E_β, E_{θ_b}, E_{θ_h}, E_{θ_f}, E_ε are prior loss terms for body shape, body pose, hand pose, facial pose and expressions. Also, E_α is a prior for extreme elbow and knee bending. For detailed definitions of these terms see [15]. E_J is a 2D keypoint re-projection loss:

$$E_J(\beta, \theta, \gamma; K, J_{\text{est}}) = \sum_{\text{view } \nu} \sum_{\text{joint } i} k_i^\nu w_i^\nu \rho_J \left(\Pi_K^\nu \left(R_{\theta\gamma}(J(\beta)_i) \right) - J_{est,i}^\nu \right), \qquad (3)$$

where $\theta = \{\theta_b, \theta_h, \theta_f\}$, ν and i iterate through views and joints, k_i^ν and w_i^ν are the per-joint weight and detection confidence, ρ_J is a robust Geman-McClure error function [12], Π_K^ν is the projection function with K camera parameters,

Fig. 2. The objects of our InterCap dataset. **Left:** Color photos. **Right:** Annotations for object areas that are likely to come in contact during interaction, shown in red. (Color figure online)

$R_{\theta\gamma}(J(\beta)_i)$ are the posed 3D joints of SMPL-X, and $J^\nu_{est,i}$ the detected 2D joints. The term E_D is:

$$E_D(\beta, \theta, \gamma; K) = \sum_{view\ \nu} \sum_{p \in P^\nu} \min_{v \in V^\nu_b} \|v - p\|, \tag{4}$$

where P^ν is Azure Kinect's segmented point cloud for the νth view, and V^ν_b are SMPL-X vertices that are visible in this view. This term measures how far the estimated body mesh is from the combined point clouds, so that we minimize this discrepancy. Note that, unlike PROX, we have multiple point clouds from all views, i.e., our E_D is a multi-view extension of PROX's [15] loss. For each view we dynamically compute the visible body vertices, and "compare" them against the segmented point cloud for that view.

Finally, the term $E_\mathcal{P}$ penalizes self-interpenetration of the SMPL-X body mesh; see PROX [15] for a more detailed and formal definition of this:

$$E_\mathcal{P}(\theta, \beta, \gamma) = E_{\mathcal{P}_{self}}(\theta, \beta). \tag{5}$$

3.4   Joint Human-Object Tracking over All Frames

We treat the result of the above optimization as initialization for refinement via *joint* optimization of the body and the object *over all frames*, subject to *contact* constraints.

For this we fix the body shape parameters, β, as the mean body shape computed over all frames from the first stage, as done in [22]. Then, we jointly optimize the object pose and translation, ξ, body pose, θ, and body translation, γ, over all frames. We add a temporal smoothness loss to reduce jitter for both the human and the object. We also penalize the   body-object interpenetration, as done in PROX [15]. A key difference is that in PROX the scene is static, while here the object is free to move.

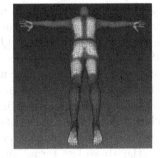

Fig. 3. Annotation of likely body contact areas (red color). (Color figure online)

To enforce contact, we annotate the body areas that are most likely to be in contact with the objects and, for each object, we label vertices most likely to be contacted. These annotations are shown in Fig. 3 and Fig. 2-right, respectively, in red. We also annotate frame sub-sequences where the body is in contact with objects, and enforce contact between them explicitly to get reasonable tracking even when there is heavy interaction and occlusion between hands and objects. Such interactions prove to be challenging for state-of-the-art 2D joint detectors, e.g., OpenPose, especially for hands.

Formally, we perform global optimization over all T frames, and minimize a loss, E, that is composed of an object fitting loss, E_O, a body fitting loss, E_B, a motion smoothness prior [64] loss, E_S, and a loss penalizing object acceleration, E_A. We also use a ground support loss, E_G, that encourages the human and the object to be above the ground plane, i.e., to not penetrate it. Last, we use a body-object contact loss, E_C, that attaches the body to the object for frames with contact. The loss E is defined as:

$$
\begin{aligned}
E = & \frac{1}{T} \sum_{\text{frame } t} \left[E_O(\Xi_t; \mathcal{S}_t, \mathcal{D}_t) + E_B(\beta^*, \Theta_t, \Psi_t, \Gamma_t; \mathcal{J}_{est}) \right] \\
& + \frac{1}{T} \sum_{\text{frame } t} \left[E_{\mathcal{P}}(\Theta_t, \beta^*, \Gamma_t) + E_C(\beta^*, \Theta_t, \Psi_t, \Gamma_t, \Xi_t, M) \right] \\
& + \frac{\lambda_{\mathcal{G}}}{T} \sum_{\text{frame } t} \left[E_{\mathcal{G}}(\beta^*, \Theta_t, \Psi_t, \Gamma_t) + E_{\mathcal{G}'}(\Xi_t, M) \right] \\
& + \frac{\lambda_{\mathcal{Q}}}{T} \sum_{\text{frame } t} \left[Q_t * E_C(\beta^*, \Theta_t, \Psi_t, M', \Xi_t) \right] \\
& \qquad + \lambda_S E_S(\Theta, \Psi, \Gamma, A; \beta^*, T) \\
& \qquad + \lambda_A E_A(\Xi, T, M),
\end{aligned}
\tag{6}
$$

where E_O comes from Eq. 1 and E_B from Eq. 2, and both go through all views ν, while $E_{\mathcal{P}}$ comes from Eq. 5. For all frames $t = \{1, \dots, T\}$ of a sequence, $\Theta = \{\theta_t\}$, $\Psi = \{\psi_t\}$, $\Gamma = \{\gamma_t\}$, are the body poses, facial expressions and translations, $\Xi = \{\xi_t\}$ is the object rotations and translations, $\mathcal{S} = \{S_t\}$ and $\mathcal{D} = \{D_t\}$ are masks and depth patches, and $\mathcal{J}_{est} = \{J_{est,t}\}$ are detected 2D keypoints. M is the object mesh, and β^* the mean body shape. E_C encourages body-object contact for frames in contact, which are indicated by the manually annotated binary vectors $Q = \{Q_t\}$, $t = \{1, \dots, T\}$; Q_t is set to 1 if in the tth frame any body part (e.g., hand, foot, thighs) is in contact with the object, and set to 0 otherwise. The motion smoothness loss E_S penalizes abrupt position changes for body vertices, and the vertex acceleration loss E_A encourages smooth object trajectories. We estimate the ground plane surface by fitting a plane to chosen floor points in the observed point clouds. The terms $E_{\mathcal{G}}$ and $E_{\mathcal{G}'}$ measure whether the body and object penetrate the ground, respectively. For more details on the above loss terms, please see Sup. Mat. Finally, the parameters $\lambda_{\mathcal{G}}$, $\lambda_{\mathcal{Q}}$, λ_S, and λ_A are steering weights that are set empirically.

4   InterCap Dataset

We use the proposed InterCap algorithm (Sect. 3) to capture the InterCap dataset, which uniquely features whole-body interactions with objects in multi-view RGB-D videos.

Fig. 4. Samples from our InterCap dataset, drawn from four sequences with different subjects and objects. The estimated 3D object and SMPL-X human meshes have plausible contacts that agree with the input images. Best viewed zoomed in.

Data-Capture Protocol. We use 10 everyday objects, shown in Fig. 2-left, that vary in size and "afford" different interactions with the body, hands or feet; we focus mainly on hand-object interactions. We recruit 10 subjects (5 males and 5 females) that are between 25–40 years old. The subjects are recorded while interacting with 7 or more objects, according to their time availability. Subjects are instructed to interact with objects as naturally as possible. However, they are asked to avoid very fast interactions that cause severe motion blur (Azure Kinect supports only up to 30 FPS), or misalignment between the RGB and depth images for each Kinect (due to technicalities of RGB-D sensors). We capture up to 3 sequences per object depending on object shape and functionality, and by picking an interaction intent from the list below, as in GRAB [54]:

- **"Pass"**: The subject passes the object on to another imaginary person standing on their left/right side; a graspable area needs to be free for the other person to grasp.
- **"Check"**: The subject inspects visually the object from several viewpoints by first picking it up and then manipulating it with their hands to see several sides of it.
- **"Use"**: The subject uses the object in a natural way that "agrees" with the object's affordances and functionality for everyday tasks.

We also capture each subject performing a freestyle interaction of their choice. All subjects gave informed written consent to publicly share their data for research.

4D Reconstruction. Our InterCap method (Sect. 3) takes as input multi-view RGB-D videos and outputs 4D meshes for the human and object, i.e., 3D meshes over time. Humans are represented as SMPL-X meshes [44], while object meshes are acquired with an Artec hand-held scanner. Some dataset frames along with

Fig. 5. Contact heatmaps for each object (across all subjects) and the human body (across all objects and subjects). Contact likelihood is color-coded; high likelihood is shown with red, and low with blue. Color-coding is normalized separately for each object, the body, and each hand.

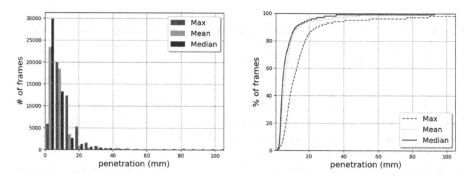

Fig. 6. Statistics of human-object mesh penetration for all InterCap sequences. **Left:** The number of frames (Y-axis) with a certain penetration depth (X-axis). **Right:** The percentage of frames (Y-axis) with a penetration depth below a threshold (X-axis). In the legend, "Max", "Mean" and "Median" refer to three ways of reporting the penetration for each frame, i.e., taking the maximum, mean and median value of the penetration depth of all vertices, respectively. (Color figure online)

the reconstructed meshes are shown in Fig. 1 and Fig. 4; see also the video on our website. Reconstructions look natural, with plausible contact between the human and the object.

Dataset Statistics. InterCap has 223 RGB-D videos with a total of 67,357 multi-view frames (6 RGB-D images each). For a comparison with other datasets, see Table 1.

5   Experiments

Contact Heatmaps. Figure 5-left shows contact heatmaps on each object, across all subjects. We follow the protocol of GRAB [54], which uses a proximity metric on reconstructed human and object meshes. First, we compute per-frame binary contact maps by thresholding (at 4.5 mm) the distances from each body vertex to the closest object surface point. Then, we integrate these

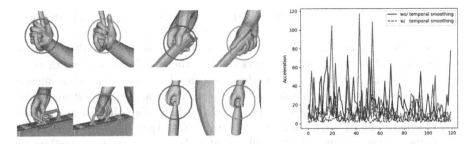

Fig. 7. Left: Qualitative ablation of our contact term. Each pair of images shows results wo/ (red) and w/ (green) the contact term. Encouraging contact results in more natural hand poses and hand-object grasps. **Right:** Acceleration of a random vertex w/ (dashed line) and wo/ (solid line) temporal smoothing for 3 sequences (shown with different color) over the first 120 frames. Dashed lines (w/ temporal smoothing) correspond to lower acceleration, i.e., less jitter. (Color figure online)

maps over time (and subjects) to get "heatmaps" encoding contact likelihood. InterCap reconstructs human and object meshes accurately enough so that contact heatmaps agree with object affordances, e.g., the handle of the suitcase, umbrella and tennis racquet are likely to be grasped, the upper skateboard surface is likely to be contacted by the foot, and the upper stool surface by the buttocks.

Figure 5-right shows heatmaps on the body, computed across all subjects and objects. Heatmaps show that most of InterCap's interactions involve mainly the right hand. Contact on the palm looks realistic, and is concentrated on the fingers and MCP joints. The "false" contact on the dorsal side is attributed to our challenging camera setup and interaction scenarios, as well as some reconstruction jitter.

Penetration. We evaluate the penetration between human and object meshes for all sequences of our dataset. We follow the protocol of GRAB et al. [54]; we first find the "contact frames" for which there is at least minimal human-object contact, and then report statistics for these. In Fig. 6-left we show the distribution of penetrations, i.e., the number of "contact frames" (Y axis) with a certain mesh penetration depth (X axis). In Fig. 6-right we show the cumulative distribution of penetration, i.e., the percentage of "contact frames" (Y axis) for which mesh penetration is below a threshold (X axis). Roughly 60% of "contact frames" have ≤ 5 mm, 80% ≤ 7 mm, and 98% ≤ 20 mm mean penetration. The average penetration depth over all "contact frames" is 7.2 mm.

Fitting Accuracy. For every frame, we compute the distance from each mesh vertex to the closest point-cloud (PCL) point; for each human or object mesh we take into account only the respective PCL area obtained with PointRend [28] segmentation. The mean vertex-to-PCL distance is 20.29 mm for the body, and 18.50 mm for objects. In comparison, PROX-D [15], our base method, achieves an error of 13.02 mm for the body. This is expected since PROX-D is free to change the body shape to fit each individual frame, while our method estimates a single body shape for the whole sequence. SMPLify-X [44] achieves an mean error of 79.54 mm, for VIBE the mean error is 55.59 mm, while ExPose gets an mean error of 71.78 mm. These numbers validate the effectiveness of our method for body tracking. Note that these methods are based on monocular RGB images only, so there is not enough information for them to accurately estimate the global position of the 3D body meshes. Thus we first align the output meshes with the point clouds, then compute the error. Note that the error is bounded from below for two reasons: (1) it is influenced by factory-design imperfections in the synchronization of Azure Kinects, and (2) some vertices reflect body/object areas that are occluded during interaction and their closest PCL point is a wrong correspondence. Despite this, InterCap empirically estimates reasonable bodies, hands and objects in interaction, as reflected in the contact heatmaps and penetration metrics discussed above.

Ablation of Contact Term. Fig. 7-left shows results with-/out our term that encourages body-object contact; visualization "zooms" into hand-object grasps. We see that encouraging contact yields more natural hand poses and fewer inter-penetrations. This is backed up by the contact heatmaps and penetration metrics discussed above.

Ablation of Temporal Smoothing Term. Fig. 7-right shows results with-/out our temporal smoothing term. Each solid line shows the acceleration of a randomly chosen vertex without the temporal smoothness term; we show 3 different motions. The dashed lines of the same color show the same motions with the smoothness term; these are clearly smoother. We empirically find that the learned motion prior of Zhang et al. [64] produces a more natural motion than handcrafted ones [22].

Discussion on Jitter. Despite the smoothing, some jitter is still inevitable. We attribute this to two factors: (1) OpenPose and Mask-RCNN are empirically relatively sensitive to occlusions and illumination (e.g., reflections, shadows, poor lighting); the data terms for fitting 3D models depend on these. (2) Azure Kinects have a reasonable synchronization, yet there is still a small delay among cameras to avoid depth-camera interference; the point cloud "gathered" across views is a bit "patchy" as information pieces have a small time difference. The jitter is more intense for hands relatively to the body, due to their low image resolution, motion blur, and coarse point clouds. Despite these challenges, InterCap is a good step towards capturing everyday whole-body interactions with commodity hardware. Future work will study advanced motion priors.

6   Discussion

Here we focus on whole-body human interaction with everyday rigid objects. We present a novel method, called InterCap, that reconstructs such interactions from multi-view full-body videos, including natural hand poses and contact with objects. With this method, we capture the novel InterCap dataset, with a variety of people interacting with several common objects. The dataset contains reconstructed 3D meshes for the whole body and the object over time (i.e., 4D meshes), as well as plausible contacts between them. In contrast to most previous work, our method uses no special devices like optical markers or IMUs, but only several consumer-level RGB-D cameras. Our setup is lightweight and has the potential to be used in daily scenarios. Our method estimates reasonable hand poses even when there is heavy occlusion between hands and the object. In future work, we plan to study interactions with smaller objects and dexterous manipulation. Our data and code are available at https://intercap.is.tue.mpg. de.

Acknowledgements. We thank Chun-Hao Paul Huang, Hongwei Yi, Jiaxiang Shang, as well as Mohamed Hassan for helpful discussion about technical details. We thank Taylor McConnell, Galina Henz, Marku Höschle, Senya Polikovsky, Matvey Safroshkin and Tsvetelina Alexiadis for the data collection and data cleaning. We thank all the participants of our experiments. We also thank Benjamin Pellkofer for the IT and website support.

The authors thank the International Max Planck Research School for Intelligent Systems (IMPRS-IS) for supporting OT. This work was supported by the German Federal Ministry of Education and Research (BMBF): Tübingen AI Center, FKZ: 01IS18039B.

Conflict of Interest. Disclosure: https://files.is.tue.mpg.de/black/CoI_GCPR_2022. txt.

References

1. Alldieck, T., Magnor, M., Xu, W., Theobalt, C., Pons-Moll, G.: Video based reconstruction of 3D people models. In: Computer Vision and Pattern Recognition (CVPR), pp. 8387–8397 (2018)
2. Anguelov, D., Srinivasan, P., Koller, D., Thrun, S., Rodgers, J., Davis, J.: SCAPE: shape completion and animation of people. Trans. Graph. (TOG) **24**(3), 408–416 (2005)
3. Bhatnagar, B.L., Xie, X., Petrov, I.A., Sminchisescu, C., Theobalt, C., Pons-Moll, G.: BEHAVE: Dataset and method for tracking human object interactions. In: Computer Vision and Pattern Recognition (CVPR), pp. 15935–15946 (2022)
4. Bogo, F., Kanazawa, A., Lassner, C., Gehler, P., Romero, J., Black, M.J.: Keep It SMPL: automatic estimation of 3D human pose and shape from a single image. In: Leibe, B., Matas, J., Sebe, N., Welling, M. (eds.) ECCV 2016. LNCS, vol. 9909, pp. 561–578. Springer, Cham (2016). https://doi.org/10.1007/978-3-319-46454-1_34
5. Cao, Z., Gao, H., Mangalam, K., Cai, Q.-Z., Vo, M., Malik, J.: Long-term human motion prediction with scene context. In: Vedaldi, A., Bischof, H., Brox, T., Frahm, J.-M. (eds.) ECCV 2020. LNCS, vol. 12346, pp. 387–404. Springer, Cham (2020). https://doi.org/10.1007/978-3-030-58452-8_23
6. Cao, Z., Hidalgo, G., Simon, T., Wei, S.E., Sheikh, Y.: OpenPose: realtime multiperson 2D pose estimation using part affinity fields. Trans. Pattern Anal. Mach. Intell. (TPAMI) **43**(1), 172–186 (2019)

7. Choutas, V., Pavlakos, G., Bolkart, T., Tzionas, D., Black, M.J.: Monocular expressive body regression through body-driven attention. In: Vedaldi, A., Bischof, H., Brox, T., Frahm, J.-M. (eds.) ECCV 2020. LNCS, vol. 12355, pp. 20–40. Springer, Cham (2020). https://doi.org/10.1007/978-3-030-58607-2_2

8. De Aguiar, E., Stoll, C., Theobalt, C., Ahmed, N., Seidel, H.P., Thrun, S.: Performance capture from sparse multi-view video. Trans. Graph. (TOG) **27**(3), 1–10 (2008)

9. Dong, J., Fang, Q., Jiang, W., Yang, Y., Huang, Q., Bao, H., Zhou, X.: Fast and robust multi-person 3D pose estimation and tracking from multiple views. Trans. Pattern Anal. Mach. Intell. (TPAMI) **14**(8), 1–12 (2021)

10. Dong, J., Jiang, W., Huang, Q., Bao, H., Zhou, X.: Fast and robust multi-person 3D pose estimation from multiple views. In: Computer Vision and Pattern Recognition (CVPR), pp. 7792–7801 (2019)

11. Dong, Z., Song, J., Chen, X., Guo, C., Hilliges, O.: Shape-aware multi-person pose estimation from multi-view images. In: International Conference on Computer Vision (ICCV), pp. 11158–11168 (2021)

12. Geman, S., McClure, D.E.: Statistical methods for tomographic image reconstruction. In: Proceedings of the 46th Session of the International Statistical Institute, Bulletin of the ISI, vol. 52 (1987)

13. Hamer, H., Schindler, K., Koller-Meier, E., Van Gool, L.: Tracking a hand manipulating an object. In: International Conference on Computer Vision (ICCV), pp. 1475–1482 (2009)

14. Hampali, S., Rad, M., Oberweger, M., Lepetit, V.: HOnnotate: a method for 3D annotation of hand and object poses. In: Computer Vision and Pattern Recognition (CVPR), pp. 3193–3203 (2020)

15. Hassan, M., Choutas, V., Tzionas, D., Black, M.J.: Resolving 3D human pose ambiguities with 3D scene constrains. In: International Conference on Computer Vision (ICCV), pp. 2282–2292 (2019)

16. Hassan, M., Ghosh, P., Tesch, J., Tzionas, D., Black, M.J.: Populating 3D scenes by learning human-scene interaction. In: Computer Vision and Pattern Recognition (CVPR), pp. 14708–14718 (2021)

17. Hasson, Y., Tekin, B., Bogo, F., Laptev, I., Pollefeys, M., Schmid, C.: Leveraging photometric consistency over time for sparsely supervised hand-object reconstruction. In: Computer Vision and Pattern Recognition (CVPR), pp. 568–577 (2020)

18. Hasson, Y., Varol, G., Tzionas, D., Kalevatykh, I., Black, M.J., Laptev, I., Schmid, C.: Learning joint reconstruction of hands and manipulated objects. In: Computer Vision and Pattern Recognition (CVPR), pp. 11807–11816 (2019)

19. He, Y., Yan, R., Fragkiadaki, K., Yu, S.I.: Epipolar transformers. In: Computer Vision and Pattern Recognition (CVPR), pp. 7776–7785 (2020)

20. Hu, Y.T., Chen, H.S., Hui, K., Huang, J.B., Schwing, A.G.: SAIL-VOS: semantic amodal instance level video object segmentation - a synthetic dataset and baselines. In: Computer Vision and Pattern Recognition (CVPR), pp. 3105–3115 (2019)

21. Huang, C.H.P., et al.: Capturing and inferring dense full-body human-scene contact. In: Computer Vision and Pattern Recognition (CVPR), pp. 13274–13285 (2022)

22. Huang, Y., et al.: Towards accurate marker-less human shape and pose estimation over time. In: International Conference on 3D Vision (3DV), pp. 421–430 (2017)

23. Ionescu, C., Papava, D., Olaru, V., Sminchisescu, C.: Human3.6M: large scale datasets and predictive methods for 3D human sensing in natural environments. Trans. Pattern Anal. Mach. Intell. (TPAMI) **36**(7), 1325–1339 (2014)

24. Iskakov, K., Burkov, E., Lempitsky, V., Malkov, Y.: Learnable triangulation of human pose. In: International Conference on Computer Vision (ICCV), pp. 7717–7726 (2019)
25. Kanazawa, A., Black, M.J., Jacobs, D.W., Malik, J.: End-to-end recovery of human shape and pose. In: Computer Vision and Pattern Recognition (CVPR), pp. 7122–7131 (2018)
26. Karunratanakul, K., Yang, J., Zhang, Y., Black, M.J., Muandet, K., Tang, S.: Grasping field: learning implicit representations for human grasps. In: International Conference on 3D Vision (3DV), pp. 333–344 (2020)
27. Kato, H., Ushiku, Y., Harada, T.: Neural 3D mesh renderer. In: Computer Vision and Pattern Recognition (CVPR), pp. 3907–3916 (2018)
28. Kirillov, A., Wu, Y., He, K., Girshick, R.: PointRend: image segmentation as rendering. In: Computer Vision and Pattern Recognition (CVPR), pp. 9799–9808 (2020)
29. Kocabas, M., Athanasiou, N., Black, M.J.: VIBE: video inference for human body pose and shape estimation. In: Computer Vision and Pattern Recognition (CVPR), pp. 5252–5262 (2020)
30. Li, X., Liu, S., Kim, K., Wang, X., Yang, M., Kautz, J.: Putting humans in a scene: learning affordance in 3D indoor environments. In: Computer Vision and Pattern Recognition (CVPR), pp. 12368–12376 (2019)
31. Liu, Y., Stoll, C., Gall, J., Seidel, H.P., Theobalt, C.: Markerless motion capture of interacting characters using multi-view image segmentation. In: Computer Vision and Pattern Recognition (CVPR), pp. 1249–1256 (2011)
32. Loper, M., Mahmood, N., Black, M.J.: MoSh: motion and shape capture from sparse markers. Trans. Graph. (TOG) **33**(6), 1–13 (2014)
33. Loper, M., Mahmood, N., Romero, J., Pons-Moll, G., Black, M.J.: SMPL: a skinned multi-person linear model. Trans. Graph. (TOG) **34**(6), 248:1–248:16 (2015)
34. Loper, M.M., Black, M.J.: OpenDR: an approximate differentiable renderer. In: Fleet, D., Pajdla, T., Schiele, B., Tuytelaars, T. (eds.) ECCV 2014. LNCS, vol. 8695, pp. 154–169. Springer, Cham (2014). https://doi.org/10.1007/978-3-319-10584-0_11
35. Mahmood, N., Ghorbani, N., F. Troje, N., Pons-Moll, G., Black, M.J.: AMASS: archive of motion capture as surface shapes. In: International Conference on Computer Vision (ICCV), pp. 5441–5450 (2019)
36. von Marcard, T., Henschel, R., Black, M.J., Rosenhahn, B., Pons-Moll, G.: Recovering accurate 3D human pose in the wild using IMUs and a moving camera. In: Ferrari, V., Hebert, M., Sminchisescu, C., Weiss, Y. (eds.) ECCV 2018. LNCS, vol. 11214, pp. 614–631. Springer, Cham (2018). https://doi.org/10.1007/978-3-030-01249-6_37
37. Mehta, D., et al.: VNect: real-time 3D human pose estimation with a single RGB camera. Trans. Graph. (TOG) **36**(4), 44:1–44:14 (2017)
38. Microsoft: Azure Kinect SDK (K4A) (2022). https://github.com/microsoft/Azure-Kinect-Sensor-SDK
39. Newell, A., Yang, K., Deng, J.: Stacked hourglass networks for human pose estimation. In: Leibe, B., Matas, J., Sebe, N., Welling, M. (eds.) ECCV 2016. LNCS, vol. 9912, pp. 483–499. Springer, Cham (2016). https://doi.org/10.1007/978-3-319-46484-8_29
40. Oikonomidis, I., Kyriazis, N., Argyros, A.A.: Full DOF tracking of a hand interacting with an object by modeling occlusions and physical constraints. In: International Conference on Computer Vision (ICCV), pp. 2088–2095 (2011)

41. Omran, M., Lassner, C., Pons-Moll, G., Gehler, P., Schiele, B.: Neural body fitting: unifying deep learning and model based human pose and shape estimation. In: International Conference on 3D Vision (3DV), pp. 484–494 (2018)

42. Osman, A.A.A., Bolkart, T., Tzionas, D., Black, M.J.: SUPR: a sparse unified part-based human body model. In: European Conference on Computer Vision (ECCV) (2022)

43. Osman, A.A.A., Bolkart, T., Black, M.J.: STAR: sparse trained articulated human body regressor. In: Vedaldi, A., Bischof, H., Brox, T., Frahm, J.-M. (eds.) ECCV 2020. LNCS, vol. 12351, pp. 598–613. Springer, Cham (2020). https://doi.org/10.1007/978-3-030-58539-6_36

44. Pavlakos, G., et al.: Expressive body capture: 3D hands, face, and body from a single image. In: Computer Vision and Pattern Recognition (CVPR), pp. 10975–10985 (2019)

45. Pons-Moll, G., Baak, A., Helten, T., Müller, M., Seidel, H.P., Rosenhahn, B.: Multisensor-fusion for 3D full-body human motion capture. In: Computer Vision and Pattern Recognition (CVPR), pp. 663–670 (2010)

46. Qiu, H., Wang, C., Wang, J., Wang, N., Zeng, W.: Cross view fusion for 3D human pose estimation. In: International Conference on Computer Vision (ICCV), pp. 4341–4350 (2019)

47. Rhodin, H., Robertini, N., Casas, D., Richardt, C., Seidel, H.-P., Theobalt, C.: General automatic human shape and motion capture using volumetric contour cues. In: Leibe, B., Matas, J., Sebe, N., Welling, M. (eds.) ECCV 2016. LNCS, vol. 9909, pp. 509–526. Springer, Cham (2016). https://doi.org/10.1007/978-3-319-46454-1_31

48. Rogez, G., III, J.S.S., Ramanan, D.: Understanding everyday hands in action from RGB-D images. In: International Conference on Computer Vision (ICCV), pp. 3889–3897 (2015)

49. Romero, J., Kjellström, H., Kragic, D.: Hands in action: Real-time 3D reconstruction of hands in interaction with objects. In: International Conference on Robotics and Automation (ICRA), pp. 458–463 (2010)

50. Romero, J., Tzionas, D., Black, M.J.: Embodied hands: Modeling and capturing hands and bodies together. Trans. Graph. (TOG) 36(6), 245:1–245:17 (2017)

51. Savva, M., Chang, A.X., Hanrahan, P., Fisher, M., Nießner, M.: PiGraphs: Learning interaction snapshots from observations. Trans. Graph. (TOG) 35(4), 139:1–139:12 (2016)

52. Sigal, L., Balan, A., Black, M.J.: HumanEva: Synchronized video and motion capture dataset and baseline algorithm for evaluation of articulated human motion. Int. J. Comput. Vision (IJCV) 87(1–2), 4–27 (2010)

53. Sun, J., Wang, Z., Zhang, S., He, X., Zhao, H., Zhang, G., Zhou, X.: OnePose: one-shot object pose estimation without CAD models. In: CVPR, pp. 6825–6834 (2022)

54. Taheri, O., Ghorbani, N., Black, M.J., Tzionas, D.: GRAB: a dataset of whole-body human grasping of objects. In: Vedaldi, A., Bischof, H., Brox, T., Frahm, J.-M. (eds.) ECCV 2020. LNCS, vol. 12349, pp. 581–600. Springer, Cham (2020). https://doi.org/10.1007/978-3-030-58548-8_34

55. Tu, H., Wang, C., Zeng, W.: VoxelPose: towards multi-camera 3d human pose estimation in wild environment. In: Vedaldi, A., Bischof, H., Brox, T., Frahm, J.-M. (eds.) ECCV 2020. LNCS, vol. 12346, pp. 197–212. Springer, Cham (2020). https://doi.org/10.1007/978-3-030-58452-8_12

56. Tzionas, D., Ballan, L., Srikantha, A., Aponte, P., Pollefeys, M., Gall, J.: Capturing hands in action using discriminative salient points and physics simulation. Int. J. Comput. Vis. (IJCV) **118**(2), 172–193 (2016)
57. Varol, G., Laptev, I., Schmid, C.: Long-term temporal convolutions for action recognition. Trans. Pattern Anal. Mach. Intell. (TPAMI) **40**(6), 1510–1517 (2017)
58. Wei, S.E., Ramakrishna, V., Kanade, T., Sheikh, Y.: Convolutional pose machines. In: Computer Vision and Pattern Recognition (CVPR), pp. 4724–4732 (2016)
59. Xu, H., Bazavan, E.G., Zanfir, A., Freeman, W.T., Sukthankar, R., Sminchisescu, C.: GHUM & GHUML: generative 3D human shape and articulated pose models. In: Computer Vision and Pattern Recognition (CVPR), pp. 6183–6192 (2020)
60. Xu, W., Chatterjee, A., Zollhöfer, M., Rhodin, H., Mehta, D., Seidel, H.P., Theobalt, C.: MonoPerfCap: human performance capture from monocular video. Trans. Graph. (TOG) **37**(2), 1–15 (2018)
61. Yao, B., Fei-Fei, L.: Modeling mutual context of object and human pose in human-object interaction activities. In: Computer Vision and Pattern Recognition (CVPR), pp. 17–24 (2010)
62. Yi, H., et al.: Human-aware object placement for visual environment reconstruction. In: Computer Vision and Pattern Recognition (CVPR), pp. 3959–3970 (2022)
63. Zhang, J.Y., Pepose, S., Joo, H., Ramanan, D., Malik, J., Kanazawa, A.: Perceiving 3D human-object spatial arrangements from a single image in the wild. In: European Conference on Computer Vision (ECCV) (2020)
64. Zhang, S., Zhang, Y., Bogo, F., Pollefeys, M., Tang, S.: Learning motion priors for 4D human body capture in 3D scenes. In: Computer Vision and Pattern Recognition (CVPR), pp. 11323–11333 (2021)
65. Zhang, Y., Hassan, M., Neumann, H., Black, M.J., Tang, S.: Generating 3D people in scenes without people. In: Computer Vision and Pattern Recognition (CVPR), pp. 6193–6203 (2020)
66. Zhang, Y., An, L., Yu, T., Li, X., Li, K., Liu, Y.: 4D association graph for realtime multi-person motion capture using multiple video cameras. In: Computer Vision and Pattern Recognition (CVPR), pp. 1321–1330 (2020)
67. Zhang, Y., Li, Z., An, L., Li, M., Yu, T., Liu, Y.: Light-weight multi-person total capture using sparse multi-view cameras. In: International Conference on Computer Vision (ICCV), pp. 5560–5569 (2021)
68. Zollhöfer, M.: State of the art on 3D reconstruction with RGB-D cameras. Comput. Graph. Forum (CGF) **37**(2), 625–652 (2018)

Online Marker-Free Extrinsic Camera Calibration Using Person Keypoint Detections

Bastian Pätzold$^{(\boxtimes)}$, Simon Bultmann , and Sven Behnke

University of Bonn, Institute for Computer Science VI, Autonomous Intelligent
Systems, Friedrich-Hirzebruch-Allee 8, 53115 Bonn, Germany
{paetzold,bultmann,behnke}@ais.uni-bonn.de
https://www.ais.uni-bonn.de

Abstract. Calibration of multi-camera systems, i.e. determining the relative poses between the cameras, is a prerequisite for many tasks in computer vision and robotics. Camera calibration is typically achieved using offline methods that use checkerboard calibration targets. These methods, however, often are cumbersome and lengthy, considering that a new calibration is required each time any camera pose changes. In this work, we propose a novel, marker-free online method for the extrinsic calibration of multiple smart edge sensors, relying solely on 2D human keypoint detections that are computed locally on the sensor boards from RGB camera images. Our method assumes the intrinsic camera parameters to be known and requires priming with a rough initial estimate of the camera poses. The person keypoint detections from multiple views are received at a central backend where they are synchronized, filtered, and assigned to person hypotheses. We use these person hypotheses to repeatedly solve optimization problems in the form of factor graphs. Given suitable observations of one or multiple persons traversing the scene, the estimated camera poses converge towards a coherent extrinsic calibration within a few minutes. We evaluate our approach in real-world settings and show that the calibration with our method achieves lower reprojection errors compared to a reference calibration generated by an offline method using a traditional calibration target.

Keywords: Camera calibration · Human pose estimation · Factor graphs

This work was funded by grant BE 2556/16-2 (Research Unit FOR 2535 Anticipating Human Behavior) of the German Research Foundation (DFG).

Supplementary Information The online version contains supplementary material available at https://doi.org/10.1007/978-3-031-16788-1_19.

B. Andres et al. (Eds.): DAGM GCPR 2022, LNCS 13485, pp. 300–316, 2022.
https://doi.org/10.1007/978-3-031-16788-1_19

1 Introduction

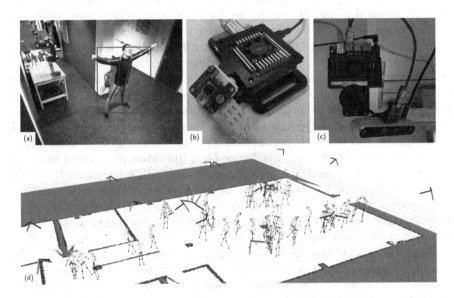

Fig. 1. Extrinsic camera calibration using person keypoint detections (a) computed locally on different smart edge sensors: (b) based on a Google EdgeTPU Dev Board [12] and (c) based on an Nvidia Jetson Xavier NX Developer Kit [26]. 2D keypoints from multiple views are synchronized, filtered, and assigned to 3D person hypotheses (d) on a central backend. Observations are accumulated over time and a factor graph optimization is solved to obtain the optimal camera poses (coordinate systems in (d), with the blues axis being the view direction). (Color figure online)

Sensor calibration is an essential prerequisite for most intelligent systems, as they combine data from numerous sensors to perceive a scene. To successfully interpret and fuse the measurements of multiple sensors, they need to be transformed into a common coordinate frame. This requires the sensor poses in a common reference frame—their extrinsic calibration. An imprecise calibration can lead to degradation in performance and can possibly cause critical safety issues.

For multiple reasons, the task of camera calibration is an inherently difficult one to solve [25]: First, the calibration parameters change over time, by normal usage, e.g. due to vibration, thermal expansion, or moving parts. Therefore, it is not sufficient to calibrate the parameters only once during the construction of the system. Instead, calibration must be performed repeatedly throughout its lifetime. Second, the calibration parameters cannot be measured directly with sufficient precision; they must be inferred from the data captured by the considered cameras. Typically, the calibration is performed by actively deploying a calibration target of known correspondences in front of the cameras, e.g. a checkerboard pattern [34]. However, this requires expertise and might be perceived as cumbersome and lengthy when it has to be applied repeatedly for a large multi-camera system. Further challenges for inferring calibration parameters from image data involve accounting for noisy measurements and collecting a sufficient amount of data points spread over the entirety of the image planes.

In this work, we develop a novel, marker-free method for calibrating the extrinsic parameters of a network of static smart edge sensors, where each sensor runs inference for 2D human pose estimation. In particular, we infer the relative poses between the cameras of the deployed smart edge sensor boards in real time using the person keypoint detections transmitted by the sensors [3], as illustrated in Fig. 1. 2D keypoints from multiple views are synchronized, filtered, and assigned to 3D person hypotheses on a central backend, where observations are accumulated over time and a factor graph optimization [8] is solved to obtain the optimal camera poses. The method can handle multiple persons in the scene, as well as arbitrary occlusions, e.g. from tables or pillars. We assume the intrinsic parameters of the cameras to be known and a rough initial estimate of the extrinsic calibration to be available, which can easily be obtained, e.g. from a floor plan or by tape measure.

Our proposed method alleviates many of the issues mentioned above: No specific calibration target is required; it suffices for one or several persons to walk through the scene. The method handles data association between multiple observed persons and their unknown dimensions. We propose an efficient online algorithm that optimizes the camera poses on-the-fly, giving direct feedback on success and when enough data has been captured. The calibration procedure thus can be repeated easily to account for parameter change over time, without expert knowledge. Furthermore, person keypoints can be detected from a significantly larger range of viewing angles (e.g. front, back, or side-view) than the pattern of a classical checkerboard calibration target, which is well detected only from a frontal view. This facilitates the collection of a sufficient amount of corresponding data points visible in multiple cameras that well constrain the factor graph optimization, further reducing the time required for calibration.

We evaluate the proposed approach in real-world settings and show that the calibration obtained with our method achieves better results in terms of reprojection errors in the targeted application domain of 3D multi-person pose estimation, compared to a reference calibration generated by an offline method using a traditional calibration target. We make our implementation publicly available[1].

2   Related Work

Camera Calibration. Traditional methods for camera calibration are based on using artificial image features, so-called *fiducials*. Their common idea is to deploy a calibration target with known correspondences in the overlapping field of view

---

[1] https://github.com/AIS-Bonn/ExtrCamCalib_PersonKeypoints.

(FoV) of the considered cameras. Zhang [34] utilizes a checkerboard pattern on a planar surface to perform intrinsic calibration of single cameras. The *kalibr* toolkit [28] uses a planar grid of *AprilTags* [27] to perform offline extrinsic and intrinsic calibration of multiple cameras, which allows to fully resolve the target's orientation towards the cameras and is robust against occlusions. We apply this method to obtain a reference calibration for evaluating our work.

Reinke et al. [29] propose an offline method for finding the relative poses between a set of (two) cameras and the base frame of a quadruped robot. They use a fiducial marker mounted on the end-effector of a limb as the calibration target. The camera poses are resolved using a *factor graph* [8], modeling kinematic constraints between the marker frame and the base frame together with the visual constraints. We take up the idea of using factor graphs to model the calibration constraints in our work.

To cope with the issues of traditional approaches, methods for camera calibration have been proposed that do not extract fiducial features from calibration targets but use naturally occurring features instead. Komorowski et al. [18] extract SIFT features [23] and find correspondences between multiple views using RANSAC [11]. They use segmentation to remove dynamic objects and validate their approach on stereo vision datasets. Their method is targeted towards one or a few small-baseline stereo cameras and offline processing of a small batch of images. Bhardwaj et al. [1] calibrate traffic cameras by extracting vehicle instances via deep neural networks (DNNs) and matching them to a database of popular car models. The extracted features and known dimensions of the car models are then used to formulate a PnP problem [11]. They assume a planar ground surface in the vicinity of the cars and process results offline.

A variety of methods considering surveillance scenarios use pedestrians as calibration targets. Lv et al. [24] track head & feet detections of a single pedestrian walking on a planar surface during the leg-crossing phases to perform offline extrinsic calibration of a single camera based on the geometric properties of vanishing points. Following a tracking approach, they resolve the corresponding intrinsic parameters based on Zhang [34]. Hödlmoser et al. [16] use a similar approach as [24], but expand the method to calibrate a camera network from pairwise relative calibrations. The absolute scale of the camera network is resolved by manually specifying the height of the walking person. Liu et al. [21] require a moderately crowded scene to perform online intrinsic and extrinsic calibration of a single camera by assuming strong prior knowledge regarding the height distribution of the observed pedestrians. The approach is based on computing vanishing points using RANSAC. In [22] they expand their method by introducing a joint calibration for a network of cameras based on the Direct Linear Transform [14]. Henning et al. [15] jointly optimize the trajectory of a monocular camera and a human body mesh by formulating an optimization problem in the form of a factor graph. They apply a human motion model to constrain sequential body postures and to resolve scale.

Guan et al. [13,31] detect head & feet keypoints for each observable pedestrian and perform pairwise triangulation assuming an average height for all visible persons in the image pair. They then compute the calibration offline, using RANSAC, followed by a gradient descent-based refinement scheme. Their resulting calibration is only defined up to an unknown scale factor, which must be resolved manually. The method assumes the center lines between all pedestrians to be parallel, in other words, all persons are assumed to stand upright during the calibration, whereas other poses, e.g. sitting persons, are not supported. Our method, in contrast, extracts up to 17 keypoints per person [20] using convolutional neural networks (CNNs) and assumes neither the dimensions or height of the persons, nor their pose or orientation towards the cameras to be known. As for the unknown dimensions of the persons, the scale of our calibration is also ambiguous up to a single scale factor. To address this issue, we force the scale of the initial estimate of the extrinsic calibration to be maintained throughout the calibration procedure.

Human Pose Estimation. Human pose estimation refers to the task of detecting anatomical keypoints of persons on images. Early works use manually designed feature extractors like HOG-descriptors [6] or pictorial structures [9,10]. In recent years, approaches using CNNs have become popular and yield impressive results. Two well-known state-of-the-art and publicly available methods for human pose estimation are *OpenPose* [5] and *AlphaPose* [19]. Both methods estimate the poses of multiple persons simultaneously and in real time.

2D keypoint detections from multiple, calibrated camera views can be fused to obtain 3D human poses. We consider a network of smart edge sensors, introduced by Bultmann et al. [3,4], performing 3D human pose estimation in real time. Each smart edge sensor performs 2D human pose estimation, processing the image data locally on the sensor boards and transmitting only the obtained keypoint data. A central backend fuses the data received by the sensors to perform 3D human pose estimation via direct triangulation, and a semantic feedback loop is implemented to improve the 2D pose estimation on the sensor boards by incorporating global context information.

We adopt the smart edge sensor network [3] for our work, using the 2D person keypoints detected by the sensors as calibration features and aim to improve and facilitate the camera calibration required for this application scenario.

3   Method

Our method uses the image streams of a multi-camera system $\mathcal{S}_N$ with $N > 1$ projective cameras $\mathcal{C}_i$, $i \in [0 .. N-1]$, to extract and maximize knowledge about the relative poses between all cameras in real-time, i.e. finding the translation $\mathbf{t}_{ij} \in \mathbb{R}^3$ and rotation $\mathbf{R}_{ij} \in \mathcal{SO}(3) \subset \mathbb{R}^{3 \times 3}$ between all camera pairs ij, where the pose of the optical center of $\mathcal{C}_i$ is defined by

$$\mathbf{C}_i = \begin{pmatrix} \mathbf{R}_i & \mathbf{t}_i \\ \mathbf{0} & 1 \end{pmatrix} \in \mathcal{SE}(3) . \tag{1}$$

We call this the *extrinsic calibration* of the multi-camera system $\mathcal{S}_N$. Without loss of generality, we chose the first camera $\mathcal{C}_0$ to be the origin of the global

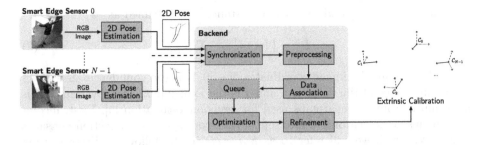

Fig. 2. Proposed pipeline for extrinsic camera calibration using smart edge sensors and person keypoint detections. Images are analyzed locally on the sensor boards. Keypoint detections are transmitted to the backend where multiple views are fused to construct and solve optimization problems using factor graphs. A queue decouples the preprocessing and optimization stages.

reference frame and set $\mathbf{C}_0 = \mathbf{I}_{4\times4}$. In its local coordinate system, the view direction of each camera is the z-axis.

Figure 2 gives an overview of our proposed pipeline. Each camera stream is fed into a person keypoint detector on the connected inference accelerator [3]. We refer to the unity of camera and detector as a *smart edge sensor*. The keypoint detections are transmitted to a central backend where they are time-synchronized and processed further. The clocks of sensors and backend are software-synchronized via NTP and each keypoint detection message includes a timestamp representing the capture time of the corresponding image.

The *preprocessing* stage removes redundant and noisy detections after which *data association* is performed, where correspondences between person detections from multiple views are established. Corresponding person detections are fused to form a person hypothesis and attached to a queue, which serves to decouple the preprocessing stage from the rest of the pipeline. The *optimization* stage continuously reads from this queue, selects several person hypotheses, and uses them to construct and solve an optimization problem in the form of a factor graph [8]. The *refinement* stage updates the current estimate of the extrinsic calibration by smoothing the intermediate results generated by the optimization and compensates for scaling drift w.r.t. the initialization. As prerequisites for our method, we assume the intrinsic parameters of the cameras to be known and a rough initial estimate of the extrinsic calibration to be available, e.g. by tape measure or from a floor plan. The FoVs of all cameras must overlap in such a way that S_N forms a connected graph.

3.1 Preprocessing

The backend receives N person keypoint detection streams and synchronizes and preprocesses them such that they can be used for optimization. Each keypoint detection $\mathcal{D}_j^p$ is associated to a person instance p and defined as

$$\mathcal{D}_j^p = \{ (u, v)^\mathsf{T}, c, \mathbf{\Sigma} \}, \tag{2}$$

where $(u, v)^\mathsf{T}$ are the image coordinates, $c \in [0, 1]$ is the confidence, $\mathbf{\Sigma} \in \mathbb{R}^{2 \times 2}$ is the covariance of the detection, and j is the joint index. The covariance $\mathbf{\Sigma}$ is determined from the heatmaps used for keypoint estimation [3]. First, incoming streams are synchronized into sets of time-corresponding detection messages of size N, which we will refer to as *framesets* in the following. Preprocessing then rejects false, noisy, redundant, and low-quality detections, passing through only detections that are considered accurate and suitable for contributing to improving the extrinsic calibration. For this, we check different conditions for each frameset, which address the number of detections per sensor, the timestamps associated to each sensor, or the confidence value of each detection. In particular, we reject all framesets where the maximum span or standard deviation of timestamps exceeds a threshold and consider only joint detections with a minimum confidence of 0.6. We further require the hip and shoulder detections of each person to be valid, which is necessary for robust data association. After filtering, we use the distortion coefficients of each camera to undistort the coordinates of all valid detections using the *OpenCV* library [2].

3.2 Data Association

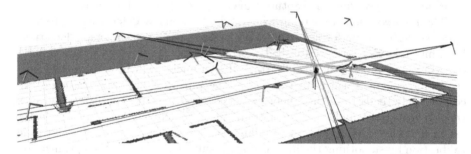

Fig. 3. Data Association: 3D back-projection rays embedded in the global coordinate system for the joint detections of one person (black), the corresponding reduction to line segments after applying depth estimation (green), and the center of mass of the corresponding person hypothesis (black). 3D human pose estimation according to [3] shown for illustration purposes only. (Color figure online)

In the data association step, we find correspondences between detections from different sensors based on the current estimate of the multi-view geometry of the camera network, which can still be inaccurate. First, we back-project each 2D detection $\mathcal{D}$ into 3D, obtaining a ray $\mathbf{p}_\mathcal{D}$ with undetermined depth originating at the optical center of the respective camera. Next, we reduce each ray $\mathbf{p}_\mathcal{D}$ to a line segment l_D by estimating the interval $[z_{min}, z_{max}]$ in which the depth z of each detection $\mathcal{D}$ lies, as illustrated in Fig. 3. For the depth interval estimation, we assume a minimum and maximum torso height and width for the detected persons, derived by a specified minimum and maximum person height to be expected during calibration. The four torso keypoints (shoulders and hips) empirically are the most stable and least occluded ones, and the physical distances between them can be assumed constant for a person due to the human anatomy, independent of the pose. The respective measured distance, however, depends on the persons' orientation towards the cameras. Here, we assume worst-case orientations, leading to larger depth intervals. In summary, we do not require persons to always stand upright but support arbitrary poses and orientations towards the cameras instead. Specifying a short person height interval leads to a more constrained search space during data association, accommodating for an inaccurate initial estimate of the extrinsic calibration or a crowded scene. A wider interval, however, yields equal results in common scenarios, while supporting small and tall persons as calibration targets alike. Depth estimation is the only component in the pipeline, where human anatomy is exploited.

To find the correspondences between person detections from multiple views, we deploy an iterative greedy search method similar to the approach of Tanke et al. [30], using the distances between the previously estimated line segments as data association cost. We define the distance of two line segments l_1, l_2 as the Closest Point-distance described by Wirtz et al. [33]:

$$d_{\text{closestpoint}}(l_1, l_2) = \min\left(d_\perp(l_1, l_2), d_\perp(l_2, l_1)\right). \tag{3}$$

To further improve the robustness of the approach, as the extrinsic calibration is not precisely known, we iterate over all person detections, sorted in ascending depth order, utilizing the depth estimation $(z_{min} + z_{max})/2$ of each person detection. This exploits the fact that near person detections have a relatively short interval $[z_{min}, z_{max}]$ and, thus, a more constrained localization in 3D space. Lastly, we compute the *center of mass* for each person hypothesis, which serves to give a rough localization of each person hypothesis in 3D space, by averaging the center points of the line segments of all assigned torso keypoints.

The data association stage outputs a list of person hypotheses that have been observed by at least two different cameras, which will be used to construct a factor graph optimization problem in the following.

3.3 Factor Graph Optimization

The optimization stage processes the person hypotheses obtained through data association to extract knowledge about the extrinsic calibration of the utilized multi-camera system. To this end, we construct a factor graph [7] encoding projective constraints, based on a selection of person hypotheses, as well as prior knowledge on the camera poses w.r.t. the initial estimate of the extrinsic calibration or the results of previous optimization cycles.

The optimal selection of person hypotheses used in an optimization cycle is determined by a selection algorithm from all available hypotheses, ensuring an optimal spatial and temporal distribution of the observations, to obtain a well-constrained optimization problem while also maintaining a reasonable degree of entropy between selections over consecutive optimization cycles. For this, we generate a random permutation of the indices of all available person hypotheses, which is biased towards selecting newer hypotheses first. Selecting newer hypotheses with higher probability is advantageous, as their data association and center of mass are estimated more reliably, given that the extrinsic calibration improves over time. Additionally, we ensure a minimum spacing between all selected person hypotheses, w.r.t. to their center of mass, by only including the next person hypothesis within the permutation if its distance towards all previously selected person hypotheses is above a spacing threshold $s = 0.2\,\mathrm{m}$.

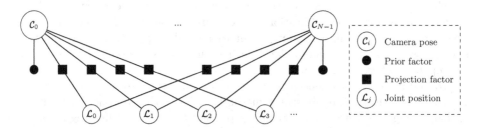

Fig. 4. Factor graph with camera variable nodes for the camera poses $\mathcal{C}_i$ and landmark variable nodes for the 3D person joint positions $\mathcal{L}_j$. Camera and landmark nodes can be connected via binary projection factors to constrain the reprojection error of a person keypoint detection. Each landmark node must be connected to at least two projection factors for allowing triangulation. All camera nodes are connected to a unary prior factor that encodes the initial uncertainty of the camera pose.

For each optimization cycle t, we construct a factor graph $\mathcal{G}_t$ by using a selection of person hypotheses $\mathcal{H}_t$. A factor graph is a bipartite graph consisting of *variable nodes* and *factor nodes* [8]. Variable nodes represent the unknown random variables of the optimization problem, i.e. the 3D joint positions of the person hypotheses in $\mathcal{H}_t$ (*landmark nodes*) and the considered camera poses of the multi-camera system $\mathcal{S}_N$ (*camera nodes*). Factor nodes constrain the variable nodes by encoding the available knowledge about the underlying distribution of the considered random variables. In particular, this refers to the obtained observations contained in $\mathcal{H}_t$ as well as the resulting camera poses from previous optimization cycles. Each factor node uses a Gaussian noise model that reflects the confidence in the constraint it represents. The constructed factor graph is illustrated in Fig. 4. We equip every camera node $\mathcal{C}_i^t$ with a unary prior factor, encoding prior knowledge about the camera pose and its uncertainty, and use binary projection factors connecting camera nodes to landmark nodes to encode observation constraints based on person keypoint detections. Projection factors calculate the reprojection error for a 2D detection w.r.t. the corresponding camera pose and landmark position using the known intrinsic parameters

$\mathbf{K}_i$. Camera nodes are initialized with the current estimate for the extrinsic calibration (for $t = 0$, we use the initial estimate and for $t > 0$, we resue the result of the previous time step). Landmark nodes are initialized by triangulation of the 2D observations using the latest camera geometry estimate [14]. Note, that we perform triangulation in every optimization cycle, even when using a person hypothesis that was already utilized in a previous optimization cycle. Hence, the triangulation results are updated based on the current estimate of the extrinsic calibration. We solve each factor graph $\mathcal{G}_t$ for the most likely camera poses by applying a Levenberg-Marquardt optimization scheme, provided by the GTSAM framework [7]. A successful optimization yields a new candidate for the extrinsic calibration of $\mathcal{S}_N$. We forward this candidate to the refinement stage where the current estimate of the extrinsic calibration will be updated based on this candidate. The updated estimate for the extrinsic calibration will then be used for constructing and initializing the factor graph in the next optimization cycle.

3.4   Camera Pose Refinement

After each successful optimization, we obtain new candidates $\hat{\mathcal{C}}_i^t$ for the extrinsic calibration of a subset of cameras $i \subseteq \mathcal{S}_N$ that were constrained by the factor graph $\mathcal{G}_t$. We smooth between the previous state and the new measurement using a Kalman filter to obtain the current estimate of the extrinsic calibration $\mathcal{C}_i^t$. As each optimization cycle contains only a limited number of observations in the factor graph to enable real-time operation, smoothing prevents overconfidence towards a specific set of observations and improves the convergence behavior. We update the previous estimate with the result of the factor graph optimization using the marginalized uncertainty from the optimized factor graph as measurement noise. Between optimization cycles, we add a constant process noise to each predicted camera pose uncertainty, enabling convergence over longer time horizons. Finally, we prevent scaling drift of the updated extrinsic calibration by applying the scaling factor that minimizes the distance towards the initial estimate of the extrinsic calibration according to Umeyama's method [32].

4   Evaluation

We evaluate the proposed method in challenging real-world settings in our lab, a large room with an area of $\sim$240 m^2 and a height of 3.2 m. As the room is partly a robotics workshop and partly a desk-based workspace, it is densely filled with different objects and furniture, which can cause false detections and occlusion. The cameras are distributed throughout the room as illustrated in Fig. 5 at similar heights of around 2.6 m. We deploy 20 smart edge sensors, 16 of which are based on the Google EdgeTPU, and 4 are based on the Nvidia Jetson Xavier NX (cf. Fig. 1). Both sensor types provide person keypoint detections in identical format and will be treated in the same way during the experiments.

For evaluation, we apply our pipeline to recordings of one and two persons (1.96 m & 1.70 m) crossing the room and generating detections in all cameras

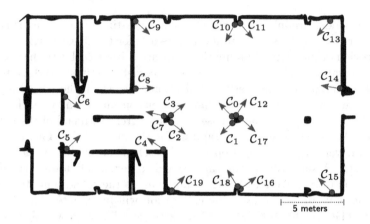

Fig. 5. Sketched floor plan with camera poses for the evaluation experiments.

over ~180 s. We repeat the experiment 10 times with different initializations and compare our results towards a reference calibration obtained by applying the kalibr toolkit [28]. We apply an initial error of 0.25 m and 10° in a random direction w.r.t. the reference calibration for all cameras C_i for $i > 0$ and use default parameters provided in the linked repository. We empirically verified that errors of this order of magnitude are easily attainable via manual initialization utilizing a floor plan, height measurements, and RGB images from all cameras.

Table 1. Statistics of the position and orientation error towards the reference calibration averaged over 10 repetitions of the experiment.

Error	1 Person				2 Persons			
	Avg.	Std.	Min.	Max.	Avg.	Std.	Min.	Max.
Position	0.053 m	0.030 m	0.011 m	0.119 m	0.052 m	0.030 m	0.017 m	0.122 m
Orientation	0.390°	0.184°	0.120°	0.891°	0.436°	0.177°	0.154°	0.818°

Table 1 shows the statistics of the final position and orientation error distributions towards the reference calibration averaged over all repetitions of the experiments with one or two persons present in the scene, respectively. The position error is obtained by rigid alignment of the calibration result towards the reference according to Umeyama's method [32] without rescaling. The orientation error is computed as the angle between two orientations via the shortest arc [17]. We do not observe a significant difference in the final result between calibrating with one or two persons. However, convergence is faster in the two-person case, as all cameras provide detections earlier in the procedure.

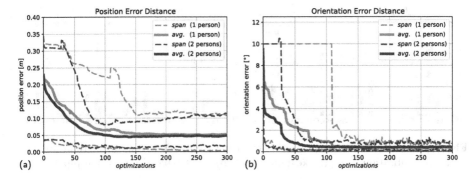

Fig. 6. Evolution of mean and min–max span of (a) position and (b) orientation error towards the reference calibration. Convergence is faster when observing multiple persons.

Figure 6 shows the evolution of the error over time for one exemplary repetition of the resp. experiment with one or two persons. The majority of the convergence takes place in the first ∼50 optimization cycles or ∼35 s and after ∼100 optimizations, the camera poses and errors remain stable in the two-person experiment. With only a single person, convergence is slower. Observations from all cameras are obtained after ∼110 optimization cycles and it takes ∼150 iterations for the poses to remain stable.

Table 2 shows the final position error for different initialization errors with two persons. Convergence remains stable for initial errors up to 35 cm and 15° but becomes less reliable for larger errors. In particular, the likelihood of the camera poses being stuck in a local minimum consistent with queued person hypotheses containing false data association increases with larger initialization errors, as the accuracy of the data association relies on the geometry of the provided initialization.

Table 2. Position error towards the reference calibration for different initial errors.

Initial Error	0.10 m, 5°	0.25 m, 10°	0.35 m, 15°	0.50 m, 20°	0.75 m, 20°
Final Error	0.050 m	0.052 m	0.067 m	0.118 m	0.214 m
Std.	0.003 m	0.030 m	0.011 m	0.073 m	0.164 m

Additionally, we compare reprojection errors, measured using two different evaluation pipelines, using the calibration obtained from our experiments with two persons. The first evaluation processes keypoint detections for 3D human pose estimation [3] and matches the domain in which our calibration was obtained. Here, we use a distinct recording unseen during the calibration. The second pipeline uses a sequence of multi-view images of the AprilTag grid used to obtain the reference calibration [28] and, thus, matches its data domain. In general, the keypoint-based evaluation is biased towards our keypoint-based calibration method, while the AprilTag evaluation is biased towards the reference calibration.

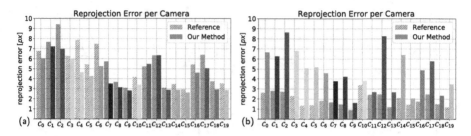

Fig. 7. Comparison of the reprojection error per camera between our method and the reference calibration using (a) keypoint- and (b) marker-based evaluation pipelines.

Figure 7 shows the reprojection error per camera for both evaluation pipelines and Table 3 reports the averaged reprojection error. For the keypoint-based evaluation, we observe that our calibration achieves lower reprojection errors for all but two cameras. For the marker-based evaluation, our calibration achieves similar reprojection errors as for the keypoint-based pipeline, while the reprojection errors of the reference calibration are significantly lower. Our flexible, marker-free method achieves lower reprojection errors for the envisaged application of 3D multi-person pose estimation and still achieves a coherent result when evaluating with a traditional calibration target. The difference in accuracy for the second evaluation is mainly due to our method being marker-free using features from persons of unknown dimensions for calibration, while the reference method knows the exact scale of the calibration (and evaluation) target. Also, the noise in the joint detections may be larger than for the tag detections.

The averaged reprojection error per joint group for the keypoint-based evaluation is shown in Table 4. Our method achieves lower reprojection errors in all categories. The reprojection error is larger for faster-moving joints like ankles and wrists, while it is smaller for more stable joints. This can be explained by limitations in the synchronization within framesets.

It is worth noting that the measured reprojection error does not exclusively originate from the provided extrinsic calibration, but also from other factors, e.g. the intrinsic camera calibration, or the approach for detection, data association, and triangulation.

Table 3. Comparison of the average reprojection error of our method and the reference calibration for keypoint- and AprilTag-based evaluations, averaged over 10 repetitions.

Calibration	Keypoints	AprilTag Grid
Reference	4.57px	**1.95px**
Our Method	**4.01px**	5.00px

Table 4. Comparison of the reprojection errors per joint group between our method and the reference calibration averaged over 10 repetitions of the experiment.

Calibration	Head	Hips	Knees	Ankles	Shlds	Elbows	Wrists
Reference	4.02px	5.10px	4.83px	5.88px	3.61px	4.29px	5.14px
Our Method	**3.55px**	**4.28px**	**4.20px**	**5.27px**	**3.21px**	**3.75px**	**4.55px**

5 Conclusion

In this work, we developed a marker-free online method for extrinsic camera calibration in a scene observed by multiple smart edge sensors, relying solely on person keypoint detections. The keypoint detections are fused into 3D person hypotheses at a central backend by synchronization, filtering, and data association. Factor graph optimization problems are repeatedly solved to estimate the camera poses constrained by the observations. Knowledge about the camera poses obtained through the optimization of one factor graph is used during the construction of the next factor graph, enabling the accumulation of knowledge and the convergence of all cameras towards an accurate pose. Lastly, the convergence behavior is improved by a refinement scheme based on a Kalman filter.

Our method is designed to be robust against false or sparse sets of detections and occlusions, and is free of many typical assumptions of similar methods: It does not require a specific calibration target, can cope with and exploit the detections of multiple persons simultaneously, and handles arbitrary person poses. We evaluate the proposed method in a series of experiments and compare our calibration results to a reference calibration obtained by an offline calibration method based on traditional calibration targets. We show that our calibration results are more accurate than the reference calibration by reliably achieving lower reprojection errors in a 3D multi-person pose estimation pipeline used as application scenario. Not only provides our method a quick and easy-to-use calibration utility, but it also achieves state-of-the-art accuracy.

The limitations of our method are mainly related to scaling ambiguity and data association: The scale of the initial estimate of the extrinsic calibration is maintained throughout the calibration procedure. It inherently cannot resolve the scale in case the initial estimate is biased or inaccurate, as the dimensions of the persons used as calibration targets are unknown. Data association could be improved for inaccurate initial estimates of the extrinsic calibration by using visual re-id descriptors. We assume the intrisic camera calibration to be known. Our method could be extended by including intrinsic camera parameters in the optimization. Finally, our method could be extended by also using additional environment features for calibration.

References

1. Bhardwaj, R., Tummala, G.K., Ramalingam, G., Ramjee, R., Sinha, P.: Auto-Calib: automatic traffic camera calibration at scale. ACM Trans. Sensor Networks (TOSN) **14**(3–4), 1–27 (2018). https://doi.org/10.1145/3199667
2. Bradski, G.: The OpenCV Library. Dr. Dobb's Journal of Software Tools (2000)
3. Bultmann, S., Behnke, S.: Real-time multi-view 3D human pose estimation using semantic feedback to smart edge sensors. In: Robotics: Science and Systems XVII (RSS) (2021). https://doi.org/10.15607/rss.2021.xvii.040
4. Bultmann, S., Behnke, S.: 3D semantic scene perception using distributed smart edge sensors. In: IEEE International Conference on Intelligent Autonomous Systems (IAS) (2022). https://doi.org/10.48550/ARXIV.2205.01460
5. Cao, Z., Hidalgo, G., Simon, T., Wei, S.E., Sheikh, Y.: OpenPose: realtime multi-person 2D pose estimation using part affinity fields. IEEE Trans. Pattern Anal. Mach. Intell. (PAMI) **43**(1), 172–186 (2021). https://doi.org/10.1109/TPAMI.2019.2929257
6. Dalal, N., Triggs, B.: Histograms of oriented gradients for human detection. In: IEEE Computer Society Conference on Computer Vision and Pattern Recognition (CVPR), vol. 1, p. 886–893 (2005). https://doi.org/10.1109/CVPR.2005.177
7. Dellaert, F.: Factor graphs and GTSAM: a hands-on introduction. Tech. Rep. GT-RIM-CP&R-2012-002, Georgia Institute of Technology (2012). https://research.cc.gatech.edu/borg/sites/edu.borg/files/downloads/gtsam.pdf
8. Dellaert, F., Kaess, M.: Factor graphs for robot perception. Found. Trends Robot. (FNT) **6**(1–2), 1–139 (2017). https://doi.org/10.1561/2300000043
9. Felzenszwalb, P.F., Huttenlocher, D.P.: Pictorial structures for object recognition. Int. J. Comput. Vis. (IJCV) **61**(1), 55–79 (2005). https://doi.org/10.1023/B:VISI.0000042934.15159.49
10. Fischler, M., Elschlager, R.: The representation and matching of pictorial structures. IEEE Trans. Comput. **C-22**(1), 67–92 (1973). https://doi.org/10.1109/T-C.1973.223602
11. Fischler, M.A., Bolles, R.C.: Random sample consensus: a paradigm for model fitting with applications to image analysis and automated cartography. Commun. ACM **24**(6), 381–395 (1981). https://doi.org/10.1145/358669.358692
12. Google: EdgeTPU dev board (2020). https://coral.ai/docs/dev-board/datasheet. Accessed 25 Mar 2022
13. Guan, J., Deboeverie, F., Slembrouck, M., Van Haerenborgh, D., Van Cauwelaert, D., Veelaert, P., Philips, W.: Extrinsic calibration of camera networks based on pedestrians. Sensors **16**(5) (2016). https://doi.org/10.3390/s16050654
14. Hartley, R., Zisserman, A.: Multiple View Geometry in Computer Vision, 2nd edn. Cambridge University Press, USA (2003)
15. Henning, D., Laidlow, T., Leutenegger, S.: BodySLAM: joint camera localisation, mapping, and human motion tracking. In: European Conference on Computer Vision (ECCV) (2022). https://doi.org/10.48550/ARXIV.2205.02301
16. Hödlmoser, M., Kampel, M.: Multiple camera self-calibration and 3D reconstruction using pedestrians. In: International Symposium on Visual Computing (ISVC) (2010). https://doi.org/10.1007/978-3-642-17274-8_1
17. Huynh, D.Q.: Metrics for 3D rotations: comparison and analysis. J. Math. Imaging Vis. **35**(2), 155–164 (2009)

18. Komorowski, J., Rokita, P.: Extrinsic camera calibration method and its performance evaluation. In: Bolc, L., Tadeusiewicz, R., Chmielewski, L.J., Wojciechowski, K. (eds.) ICCVG 2012. LNCS, vol. 7594, pp. 129–138. Springer, Heidelberg (2012). https://doi.org/10.1007/978-3-642-33564-8_16

19. Li, J., Wang, C., Zhu, H., Mao, Y., Fang, H.S., Lu, C.: CrowdPose: efficient crowded scenes pose estimation and a new benchmark. In: IEEE/CVF Conference on Computer Vision and Pattern Recognition (CVPR), pp. 10855–10864 (2019). https://doi.org/10.1109/CVPR.2019.01112

20. Lin, T.Y., et al.: Microsoft COCO: common objects in context. In: European Conference on Computer Vision (ECCV), pp. 740–755 (2014). https://doi.org/10.1007/978-3-319-10602

21. Liu, J., Collins, R.T., Liu, Y.: Surveillance camera autocalibration based on pedestrian height distributions. In: British Machine Vision Conference (BMVC), p. 144 (2011). https://doi.org/10.5244/C.25

22. Liu, J., Collins, R.T., Liu, Y.: Robust autocalibration for a surveillance camera network. In: IEEE Workshop on Applications of Computer Vision (WACV), pp. 433–440 (2013). https://doi.org/10.1109/WACV.2013.6475051

23. Lowe, D.: Object recognition from local scale-invariant features. In: IEEE International Conference on Computer Vision (ICCV), vol. 2, pp. 1150–1157 (1999). https://doi.org/10.1109/ICCV.1999.790410

24. Lv, F., Zhao, T., Nevatia, R.: Camera calibration from video of a walking human. IEEE Trans. Pattern Anal. Mach. Intell. (PAMI) 28(9), 1513–1518 (2006). https://doi.org/10.1109/TPAMI.2006.178

25. Maye, J., Furgale, P., Siegwart, R.: Self-supervised calibration for robotic systems. In: IEEE Intelligent Vehicles Symposium (IV), pp. 473–480 (2013). https://doi.org/10.1109/IVS.2013.6629513

26. NVIDIA: Nvidia Jetson Xavier NX Developer Kit (2020). https://developer.nvidia.com/embedded/jetson-xavier-nx-devkit. Accessed25 Mar 2022

27. Olson, E.: AprilTag: a robust and flexible visual fiducial system. In: IEEE International Conference on Robotics and Automation (ICRA), pp. 3400–3407 (2011). https://doi.org/10.1109/ICRA.2011.5979561

28. Rehder, J., Nikolic, J., Schneider, T., Hinzmann, T., Siegwart, R.: Extending kalibr: calibrating the extrinsics of multiple IMUs and of individual axes. In: IEEE International Conference on Robotics and Automation (ICRA), pp. 4304–4311 (2016). https://doi.org/10.1109/ICRA.2016.7487628

29. Reinke, A., Camurri, M., Semini, C.: A factor graph approach to multi-camera extrinsic calibration on legged robots. In: IEEE International Conference on Robotic Computing (IRC), pp. 391–394 (2019). https://doi.org/10.1109/IRC.2019.00071

30. Tanke, J., Gall, J.: Iterative greedy matching for 3D human pose tracking from multiple views. In: DAGM German Conference on Pattern Recognition (GCPR) (2019). https://doi.org/10.1007/978-3-030-33676-9_38

31. Truong, A.M., Philips, W., Guan, J., Deligiannis, N., Abrahamyan, L.: Automatic extrinsic calibration of camera networks based on pedestrians. In: IEEE International Conference on Distributed Smart Cameras (ICDSC) (2019). https://doi.org/10.1145/3349801.3349802

32. Umeyama, S.: Least-squares estimation of transformation parameters between two point patterns. IEEE Trans. Pattern Anal. Mach. Intell. (PAMI) 13(04), 376–380 (1991). https://doi.org/10.1109/34.88573

33. Wirtz, S., Paulus, D.: Evaluation of established line segment distance functions. Pattern Recogn. Image Anal. **26**(2), 354–359 (2016). https://doi.org/10.1134/S1054661816020267
34. Zhang, Z.: A flexible new technique for camera calibration. IEEE Trans. Pattern Anal. Mach. Intell. (PAMI) **22**(11), 1330–1334 (2000). https://doi.org/10.1109/34.888718

NeuralMeshing: Differentiable Meshing of Implicit Neural Representations

Mathias Vetsch[1], Sandro Lombardi[1(✉)], Marc Pollefeys[1,2],
and Martin R. Oswald[1,3]

[1] Department of Computer Science, ETH Zurich, Zürich, Switzerland
{mathias.vetsch,sandro.lombardi,marc.pollefeys,
martin.oswald}@inf.ethz.ch
[2] Mixed Reality and AI Zurich Lab, Microsoft, Zürich, Switzerland
[3] University of Amsterdam, Amsterdam, Netherlands

Abstract. The generation of triangle meshes from point clouds, *i.e.* meshing, is a core task in computer graphics and computer vision. Traditional techniques directly construct a surface mesh using local decision heuristics, while some recent methods based on neural implicit representations try to leverage data-driven approaches for this meshing process. However, it is challenging to define a learnable representation for triangle meshes of unknown topology and size and for this reason, neural implicit representations rely on non-differentiable post-processing in order to extract the final triangle mesh. In this work, we propose a novel differentiable meshing algorithm for extracting surface meshes from neural implicit representations. Our method produces the mesh in an iterative fashion, which makes it applicable to shapes of various scales and adaptive to the local curvature of the shape. Furthermore, our method produces meshes with regular tessellation patterns and fewer triangle faces compared to existing methods. Experiments demonstrate the comparable reconstruction performance and favorable mesh properties over baselines.

Keywords: Meshing · Deep learning

1 Introduction

Meshing of 3D point clouds has been studied extensively. Traditional methods either employ direct approaches based on local neighborhood properties [1–4,9, 21,22] or use an implicit volumetric representation as an intermediary step [11, 23,28,31–34,36,39,44,50,54]. While early works perform poorly on noisy real-world input or exhibit high computational demands, follow-up methods have addressed several of these shortcoming [10,40,55,61].

Supplementary Information The online version contains supplementary material available at https://doi.org/10.1007/978-3-031-16788-1_20.

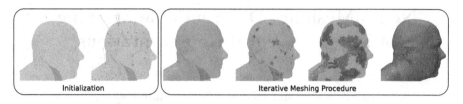

Fig. 1. NeuralMeshing. We propose a novel meshing algorithm specifically designed for neural implicit representations (NIRs). Starting from an initial set of randomly placed seed triangles on the zero level set of the implicit neural representation, NeuralMeshing iteratively expands the triangles into all directions until the full zero level set is covered

In recent years, neural implicit representations (NIRs) [15,41,43,46] have been used to improve upon traditional implicit-based representations by storing the implicit function within a deep neural network. Follow-up approaches based on these have addressed various issues, *e.g.*, concerning scalability [12,30,48], quality [20,52,53] or processing of raw data [5,6,24]. However, such methods still rely on an isosurface extraction method like marching cubes [36,39] in order to generate the final triangle mesh, usually resulting in unnecessarily high-resolution triangle meshes. Furthermore, those post-processing steps are often not differentiable, prohibiting end-to-end training of networks.

In this paper, we propose NeuralMeshing (Fig. 1), a novel data-driven approach for directly predicting a triangle-mesh from a NIR. NeuralMeshing aims to close the gap of a differentiable meshing approach specifically designed for the usage with NIRs. Starting from a seed of initially placed triangles, NeuralMeshing iteratively extends triangles at boundary edges by predicting new vertex locations given local geometry information like curvature, SDF and surface normals through queries on the underlying implicit representation. This allows to adaptively place bigger triangles at surface areas with lower curvature, *i.e.*flat surface patches, and smaller triangles at areas with high curvature. The main contributions of this paper can be summarized as follows: (**1**) We propose NeuralMeshing, a novel data-driven meshing approach for NIRs. Our method iteratively predicts new triangles based on local surface information from the implicit representation. (**2**) Extensive experiments show that NeuralMeshing better approximates the surface of NIRs while using considerably fewer triangles than commonly used iso-surface extraction methods [36].

2   Related Work

Traditional Deterministic Reconstruction Methods.   Early works on shape reconstruction from points have proposed deterministic approaches using alpha shapes [21,22], Delaunay triangulation [9] or ball-pivoting [7]. Such methods make local decisions to directly triangulate the given input point cloud. Later works focused on extracting the surface as the crust of a Voronoi diagram [1–4].

However, these methods do not well handle noise or outliers and thus perform poorly on real-world data, creating noisy and incomplete output meshes.

Traditional Implicit Reconstruction Approaches. In contrast to triangulation methods, implicit-based approaches try to represent the surface as an implicit function. The pioneering work of Hoppe *et al.* [28] introduced a method for creating a piecewise smooth surface through implicit modeling of a distance field. An alternative approach relies on radial basis function methods [11] which try to fit implicit functions to a surface. Another line of work focuses on extracting the iso-surface from signed distance function values (SDF) of a volumetric grid, the most prominent known as the marching cubes algorithm [36,39]. There has been a plethora of follow-up work [31,50,54], improving upon marching cubes. Moving least-squares (MLS) [23,34,44] based techniques locally reconstruct the surface with local functions approximating the SDF in the local neighborhood. Poisson surface reconstruction [32,33] reconstructs surfaces from oriented points via energy optimization. While these methods are able to close larger surface holes they come with high computational demands.

Neural Implicit Representations. Recently, neural implicit representations are used as an alternative representation for surface reconstruction. Pioneering works [15,41,43,46] use coordinate-based deep networks in order to learn a continuous SDF or occupancy function. While the early works have been limited to objects and low levels of details, follow-up approaches have extended the representations to scenes of larger scale [12,17,30,38,42,48], proposed learning on raw data [5,6,18,24], improved details [53] or improved upon the training scheme [20,52]. In order to obtain the final mesh, all these methods rely on extracting the surface via an iso-surface extraction approach like marching cubes [39].

Data-Driven Direct Meshing Approaches. Recent works have started to adopt deep learning-based approaches for triangulation and meshing of shapes. Early approaches used deep networks in order to warp 2D patches onto the point cloud [25,59]. Such parametric approaches often lead to undesirable holes and overlapping patches. Some works proposed to utilize grids, *e.g.* to predict a signed distance field using random forests [35], to deform and fit a shape [60] or to extract the surface via a differentiable marching cubes algorithms [37]. However, they come with high computational resource demands. BSP-Net [14] and CvxNet [19] both build upon the idea of predicting a set of hyperplanes for creating convex shapes as building blocks of the final shape. The triangulation is extracted through a non-differentiable post-processing step involving convex hull computations in the dual domain. However, the number of planes is fixed which limits the reconstruction to objects of smaller scale. Another line of work deforms and fits a template mesh to the input point cloud [27,45,57,58]. However, the topology of the reconstructed shape is usually fixed to the topology of the provided template mesh. Recently, PointTriNet [51] proposed to directly predict the connectivity of the given input point cloud. In an iterative procedure, triangle candidates are first proposed and then classified for their suitability to be part of the final mesh. While the method is local and differentiable, the resulting meshes often include holes. Similarly, Rakotosaona *et al.* [49] model the problem of triangulation locally by predicting a logarithmic map which allows triangulation in 2D using non-differentiable Delaunay triangulation. Finally, some recent work focus on using the neural implicit representation as the core representation for differentiable meshing or learning [16,26,47]. Neural Marching Cubes [16] implements a data-driven approach to improve the mesh quality at sharp edges by defining a learnable representation to differentiate between the topological configurations of marching cubes. They introduce additional vertices inside cells of the underlying grid and predict the offset of these vertices. However, they use a 3D ResNet and rely on discretized inputs, limiting the resolution and making it less memory efficient. In contrast, our method operates in continuous space and therefore on arbitrary resolutions. DeepMesh [26] uses a trick, *i.e.*, an additional forward pass on all mesh vertex locations for computing gradients with respect to an underlying implicit representation without the need to make the meshing differentiable. They use a non-differentiable marching cubes algorithm to generate the output and define loss functions directly on the obtained mesh. The recent work by Peng *et al.* [47] instead proposes a new shape representation based on a differentiable Poisson solver. Contrary to those two works, we aim to directly create a triangle mesh from the underlying neural implicit representation.

3   Method

NeuralMeshing takes as input an oriented point cloud $\mathbf{P} = \{(\mathbf{p}_i, \mathbf{n}_i) \mid \mathbf{p}_i \in \mathbb{R}^3, \mathbf{n}_i \in \mathbb{R}^3\}_{i=1}^N$. Our goal is to compute a surface mesh $\mathcal{M} = (\mathbf{V}, \mathbf{F})$ defined as a set of vertices $\mathbf{V} = \{\mathbf{v}_i \in \mathbb{R}^3\}$ and a set of triangular faces $\mathbf{F}$ in order to approximate the surface of a shape. In a first step, we employ a modified neural implicit representation $\mathcal{S}$ in order to learn a continuous SDF field approximating the shape's surface. In a second step, we use the neural representation as input for our meshing algorithm in order to extract an explicit representation $\mathcal{M}$ of the surface. In order to effectively predict new triangles, our neural representation $\mathcal{S}$ uses an extra branch in addition to the existing SDF branch, which outputs curvature information. Please refer to Fig. 2 for an overview of our method.

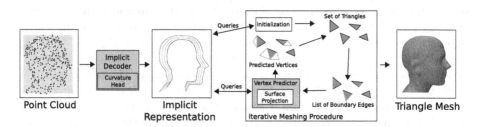

Fig. 2. Overview. Given an input point cloud $\mathbf{P}$ (left), we use a neural implicit representation with added curvature head $\mathcal{S}$ (middle) to extract a continuous SDF field. After placing a set of random triangles on the zero level set of $\mathcal{S}$, NeuralMeshing then queries $\mathcal{S}$ in order to predict a triangular mesh $\mathcal{M}$ (right) in an iterative fashion. Red blocks denote trainable MLPs (Color figure online)

3.1 Modified Neural Implicit Representation

Ideally, we aim for small triangles where the curvature is high and larger triangles at low curvature. To account for this, we extend the neural implicit representation $\mathcal{S}$ with curvature information. In order to learn a NIR, we follow Gropp *et al.* [24] and use implicit geometric regularization (IGR) for network training.

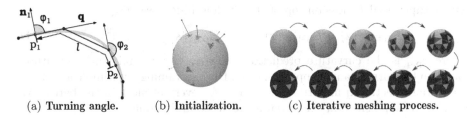

(a) **Turning angle.**   (b) **Initialization.**   (c) **Iterative meshing process.**

Fig. 3. Meshing procedure. (a) We employ the turning angle for approximating the curvature, *i.e.*, the signed angle between the tangential lines, defined by query point $\mathbf{p}_1$ and the target point $\mathbf{p}_2$, respectively. (b) NeuralMeshing first randomly places points in space (blue points), which are then projected to the zero surface of $\mathcal{S}$. The resulting projections (red points) serve as the initialization locations for new surface triangles. (c) Based on the implicit shape (orange sphere), a set of initialization triangles (light blue) is placed on the surface of the object. In an iterative fashion, new faces (green triangles) are added at boundary edges of the existing faces (blue triangles) until the mesh is complete (Color figure online)

Curvature Information. Our method grows the mesh seeds by generating new triangles in orthogonal direction of unprocessed boundary edges. For generating new vertices close to the implicit surface, we are interested in the curvature only along that particular direction, *i.e.*, normal curvature, which we found to provide more meaningful information than aggregated curvature measures, *e.g.*, mean or gauss curvature. The problem of measuring normal curvature on a surface in 3D can be reduced to a line on a 2D-plane, defined by a query point $\mathbf{p}_1$, its corresponding surface normal $\mathbf{n}_1$ and a query direction vector $\mathbf{q}$. To this end, we employ the turning angle for approximating the curvature, *i.e.*, the signed angle between the tangential lines, defined by query point $\mathbf{p}_1$ and the target point $\mathbf{p}_2$, respectively. For our case, $\mathbf{p}_2$ is computed by following the geodesic path on the discrete mesh along $\mathbf{q}$ until a fixed distance l has been covered, as illustrated in Fig. 3a. We define $\phi_1 = \frac{\pi}{2}$ as the angle between the tangential line and the surface normal at $\mathbf{p}_1$, and ϕ_2 as the angle between the tangential line at $\mathbf{p}_2$ and the surface normal $\mathbf{n}_1$ at $\mathbf{p}_1$. The turning angle is then computed as $\kappa_{\mathbf{p}_1,\mathbf{q}} = \phi_2 - \phi_1 = \phi_2 - \pi/2$. The resulting value is positive for surfaces bending away from the surface normal $\mathbf{n}_1$, negative for surfaces bending towards the surface normal $\mathbf{n}_1$ and zero for flat surfaces. Furthermore, the distance l determines the scale of detected curvatures and is fixed to 0.005 for all of our experiments. Although just an approximation of curvature, we found the turning angle to be a good indicator for predicting the amount of surface bending.

Directed Curvature Head. We extend the neural implicit representation of IGR [24] with an additional directed curvature head in order to predict the curvature $\kappa_{\mathbf{p},\mathbf{q}}$ of a surface point $\mathbf{p}$ along the tangential direction $\mathbf{q}$. The extended signed distance function $(s_{\mathbf{p}}, \kappa_{\mathbf{p},\mathbf{q}}) = f_\kappa((\mathbf{p}, \mathbf{q}); \theta; \mathbf{z})$ returns a tuple of signed distance and normal curvature at point $\mathbf{p}$. We make the curvature query optional, such that the extended decoder can be queried for signed distance values only. We use the same training losses as in IGR [24]. We train the curvature head with a supervised L_2 loss on top of the existing IGR losses $\mathcal{L}_{\mathrm{IGR}}$:

$$\mathcal{L}_{\mathrm{Total}}(\theta; \mathbf{z}) = \mathcal{L}_{\mathrm{IGR}}(\theta; \mathbf{z}) + \lambda_{\mathrm{Curv}}\mathbb{E}_{\mathbf{p},\mathbf{q}}(\|\kappa_{\mathbf{p},\mathbf{q}} - \kappa_{\mathrm{GT}}\|_2^2), \qquad (1)$$

where $\kappa_{\mathbf{p},\mathbf{q}}$ is the curvature prediction and κ_{GT} the ground truth curvature, based on the turning angle approximation. During training, we sample a surface-tangential direction $\mathbf{q}$ uniformly at random for every element in the batch. We refer to the supplementary material for architectural details.

3.2   Iterative Meshing Procedure

The input to our *iterative meshing module* are the predictions of our modified implicit representation $\mathcal{S}$. The resolution of the output mesh $\mathcal{M} = (\mathbf{V}, \mathbf{F})$ is defined by the default equilateral triangle with circumradius r_d which is provided as an input parameter. In an initial step, random faces are placed along the surface defined by $\mathcal{S}$. Further processing then iteratively extends existing triangles by inserting new faces along boundary edges until completion of the mesh, as shown in Fig. 3c. In order to keep track of boundary edges, we employ a halfedge data structure, which provides efficient operations for boundary edge access, vertex insertion and face insertion. To find vertices in a local region quickly, we use an additional k-d tree to keep track of mesh vertices.

Initialization. As visualized in Fig. 3b, the set of initial triangles $\{T_i\}^I$ is computed by first sampling a set of I points uniformly at random within the bounding box of the point cloud $\mathbf{P}$. This set of points is then projected onto the surface using the gradient $\nabla_{\mathbf{p}}f(\mathbf{p}; \mathbf{z})$ of the SDF prediction. For each projected point, we construct an equilateral triangle on the tangential plane with circumradius r_d and random location of vertices. We enforce a minimum euclidean distances $d_{\mathrm{min}} = 3r_d$ to be present between all projected points in order to avoid overlapping triangles. We use a k-d tree data structure to query candidates within a radius d_{min} efficiently and filter out overlapping triangles. As the underlying implicit representation $\mathcal{S}$ might exhibit inaccuracies, *e.g.*, far from the surface, we employ a simple heuristic in order to accurately place the initialization triangles. We perform the surface projection P times for $k \times I$ points, each time bringing the initial random samples closer to the surface, similar to Chibane *et al.* [18]. Finally, we choose random I non-overlapping points as initialization locations for the triangles.

Iterative Face Insertion. Given the initial set of triangles $\{T_i\}^I$, our iterative meshing module proceeds to iteratively select boundary edges, *i.e.*, edges of existing triangles which only have one connected face, and predict new vertices until no boundary edges are left. The process can be accelerated by computing batches of vertex insertions. To this end, the vertex predictions are computed batchwise on the GPU. As batch processing introduces the risk of inserting overlapping triangles, we employ two simple strategies: **(1)** Only boundary edges with distances between their mid-points greater than a certain threshold are processed in the same batch and **(2)** we filter overlapping face insertion candidates before adding the faces to the mesh. This procedure ensures that no overlapping triangles are inserted, given a reasonable threshold. Since the sampling of non-overlapping boundary edges reduces the number of available boundary edges, we use a simplified procedure in practice where we apply a minimum threshold of $3r_d$ between the boundary edge centers. Although this reduces the number of collisions, the absence of overlaps is not guaranteed. We apply a final overlap check in order to reject candidates with small distances between triangle centers.

3.3   Merging Surface Patches

Naively inserting new faces for every boundary edge leads to overlapping surface patches. Therefore, we employ a deterministic procedure for merging such faces. Prior to creating the triangle proposed by the vertex prediction, we replace it by the existing vertex closest to the center **m** of the boundary edge, provided the vertical distance is below a threshold $t_v = \frac{r_d}{2}$ and the prospective new triangle does not overlap with an existing triangle.

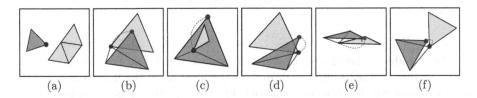

$$\begin{array}{cccccc} \text{(a)} & \text{(b)} & \text{(c)} & \text{(d)} & \text{(e)} & \text{(f)} \end{array}$$

Fig. 4. Triangle-overlap scenarios during merging. Prior to inserting a prospective new triangle (green), a series of checks is performed, measuring the overlap with existing triangles (blue). In overlap cases, the prospective vertex (green) is replaced with the existing vertex (blue). (a) No overlap. (b) Predicted vertex inside existing triangle. (c) Existing triangle inside predicted triangle. (d) Triangle edge overlap. (e) No overlap, but close vertical proximity of triangles. (f) No overlap, but close proximity of vertices (Color figure online)

In order to decide whether two triangles overlap, we distinguish between several scenarios illustrated in Fig. 4. For the most frequent case 4a where no overlap occurs, the prediction is not replaced. Case Fig. 4b handles geometric intersections between the predicted vertex and the existing triangle, while Fig. 4c addresses the case where an existing triangle is completely contained in the prospective new triangle. In both cases, the predicted vertex is projected onto the triangle plane followed by a simple inside-outside test. Since vertex projection is not sufficient in all cases, we additionally perform edge intersection tests (Fig. 4d) and compare the vertical distance between triangle planes (Fig. 4e). Finally, we consider vertices in close proximity to the prediction to be overlapping, as shown in Fig. 4f. Please refer to the supplementary material for more details.

3.4   Vertex Prediction

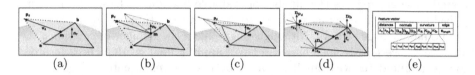

| (a) | (b) | (c) | (d) | (e) |

Fig. 5. Vertex prediction and Feature embedding. In order to predict vertex $\mathbf{p}_d$, we parameterize the prediction with 2 of the available 3 degrees of freedom, *i.e.*, the angle r_{ER} around the boundary edge (b) and the height r_{LS} of the prospective triangle (c). Note that we omit the angle around the face normal of the triangle adjacent to the boundary edge (green) for practical reasons. By default, the predictor returns the default vector $\mathbf{v}_d$, extending the surface along the same plane as defined by the boundary edge and the corresponding triangle, shown in (a). Input to the predictor is a 22-dimensional feature vector conditioned on the given boundary edge (d+e). It contains the SDF values, the gradients of the SDF values and the curvature predictions from our modified implicit representation $\mathcal{S}$ at the three vertices of the default triangle, *i.e.*, boundary edge end points $\mathbf{a}$ and $\mathbf{b}$, and the vertex at the default location $\mathbf{v}_d$. Best viewed digitally (Color figure online)

We introduce a novel *vertex prediction module* which takes a boundary edge and a feature vector as input and predicts the location of the next vertex based on local geometry information. The output of the predictor is a 2-dimensional vector $\mathbf{r} = \begin{bmatrix} r_{LS} & r_{ER} \end{bmatrix}$. As demonstrated in Fig. 5, both target a separate degree of freedom for transforming the default prediction $\mathbf{v}_d$ at the center of the boundary edge $\mathbf{m}$. Note that we define $\mathbf{v}_d$ such that it is orthogonal to the boundary edge and the face normal $\mathbf{n}_F$ and incidentally defines the height of the predicted triangle. The first component denotes the *boundary edge rotation*, *i.e.* the angle $r_{ER} \in \left[-\frac{\pi}{2}, \frac{\pi}{2} \right]$ defining the rotation around the boundary edge (Fig. 5b). The *length scaling* factor $r_{LS} \in [-1, 1]$ scales the length of the default vector $\mathbf{v}_d$. Negative values decrease the vector length whereas positive values increase its length. Note that we intentionally only predict two out of 3 DoF, *i.e.*, we omit the rotation around the face normal $\mathbf{n}_F$ belonging to the face of the boundary edge, since we found no performance improvement in incorporating the 3rd DoF.

Feature Embedding. To effectively predict accurate vertex locations, we provide the predictor with a feature embedding containing information about the local geometry. Figure 5e depicts the used feature vector. We consider the 3 points defined by the default triangle, *i.e.*, the vertex at the default location $\mathbf{v}_d$

and the two boundary edge end points, $\mathbf{a}$ and $\mathbf{b}$. For each of these 3 points, we query the implicit representation $\mathcal{S}$ for SDF values ($s_{\mathbf{p_d}}$, $s_{\mathbf{a}}$ and $s_{\mathbf{b}}$), SDF gradients or normals ($\mathbf{n_{p_d}}$, $\mathbf{n_a}$ and $\mathbf{n_b}$) and directional curvature values ($\kappa_{\mathbf{p_d}}$, $\kappa_{\mathbf{a}}$ and $\kappa_{\mathbf{b}}$) (Fig. 5d). In practice, we use multiple directional curvature queries for each query point. Additionally, we feed the length of the boundary edge $e_{\text{length}} = \|\mathbf{a} - \mathbf{b}\|_2$ into the feature vector. Note that the feature embedding can be made invariant to rotation and translation. Prior to inference, we therefore transform the normals into a local coordinate system with the boundary edge center $\mathbf{m}$ as its origin. The network predictions can be readily applied within the world coordinate system to obtain the new vertex $\mathbf{p_d}$. In order to reduce prediction errors, we apply surface projection once as a post-processing step in the same way as performed during the initialization phase.

Loss Functions. We introduce a surface distance loss $\mathcal{L}_{\text{SD}} = |s_{\mathbf{p_d}}|$, in order to penalize any deviation from the zero value for the SDF $s_{\mathbf{p_d}}$ of the predicted vertex $\mathbf{p_d}$. To encourage the network to predict triangles with default size r_d, we additionally define a length regularization loss $\mathcal{L}_{\text{LR}} = |r_{\text{LS}}|$ which prevents prediction of degenerate triangles close to the boundary edge and competes with the surface distance loss. Based on the surface mapping procedure, applied as a post-processing step, we can compute the ground truth turning angle ϕ_{GT}, located at the boundary edge. Therefore, the boundary edge rotation loss $\mathcal{L}_{\text{ER}} = |r_{\text{ER}} - \phi_{\text{GT}}|$ encourages the network to predict vertices close to the surface and penalize the predicted boundary angle r_{ER}. The final loss then consists of a weighted sum of those loss terms, $i.e.$, $\mathcal{L}_{\text{Total}} = \lambda_{\text{SD}}\mathcal{L}_{\text{SD}} + \lambda_{\text{ER}}\mathcal{L}_{\text{ER}} + \lambda_{\text{LR}}\mathcal{L}_{\text{LR}}$.

4 Evaluation

For the experiments, we use a subset of the D-Faust [8] dataset, containing high-resolution scans of humans in different poses and corresponding triangle meshes, which we use as ground truth (GT) reference. We train, validate and test on 512, 64 and 32 poses respectively, sampled randomly from the subset used in IGR [24]. To further evaluate our capability of dealing with sharp corners and edges, we evaluate on a selected subset of shapes, belonging to the *file cabinet* category of the ShapeNet [13] dataset. We use 147 models for training, 32 for validation and 32 for testing and preprocess the models with ManifoldPlus [29].

4.1 Reconstruction Quality

Reconstruction Error. We evaluate the reconstruction error of the produced triangle meshes with the Chamfer-L1 distance in Table 1. The Chamfer distance is reported in two directions, $i.e.$, from the prediction to the ground truth and the implicit representation, respectively, and vice versa. We report both, the distance to the ground truth mesh and the distance to the respective implicit representation, since there is a discrepancy between both, introducing an additional error

Table 1. Reconstruction error on D-Faust [8]. We report the distances of closest point pairs between the generated meshes and the ground truth (GT) or the implicit representation (IGR) respectively. The distances are evaluated at 20k randomly sampled surface points. For the implicit representation the sampled GT points are projected to the zero level set of the implicit representation

from to		Generated mesh GT[1e-4]↓	IGR[1e-4]↓	GT Generated Mesh[1e-4]↓	IGR	Bidirectional GT[1e-4]↓	IGR[1e-4]↓
Ours	$r_d = 0.02$	83.221	14.691	25.434	16.405	54.328	15.548
	$r_d = 0.01$	58.686	4.950	20.859	8.264	39.772	6.607
	$r_d = 0.005$	44.768	**1.096**	19.994	**5.643**	32.381	**3.370**
MC [36]	$res = 128$	90.298	68.332	78.490	76.412	84.394	72.372
	$res = 256$	60.221	34.591	43.419	39.869	51.820	37.230
	$res = 512$	46.340	17.380	27.767	21.997	37.053	19.689
PointTriNet GT [51]		**6.552**	16.626	**7.634**	17.495	**7.093**	17.061
PointTriNet IGR [51]		38.156	5.519	23.758	12.747	30.957	9.133
PSR [32]		38.764	2.3667	19.086	4.444	28.925	3.405
DSE [49]		43.021	5.5607	22.892	11.612	32.957	8.586

in the reported numbers. We compare our method to the SotA method Point-TriNet [51], however, since PointTriNet directly operates on point clouds sampled from the ground truth mesh, the reported error appears lower than methods working directly on implicit representations. We therefore evaluate PointTriNet on both, points sampled on the ground truth mesh, and points generated from the implicit representation by first sampling surface points on the ground truth mesh and projecting them to the zero level set of the implicit representation. We further compare our method to a version of marching cubes [36] implemented by scikit-image [56], which we evaluate on three different resolutions. In the same manner, we evaluate our method for three different triangle sizes r_d. Finally, we compare to PSR [32] from Open3D (depth=10), and DSE [49], with the author-provided model. On the highest resolution, our method outperforms all baselines, when measured on the implicit representation, while yielding comparable results on the medium resolution. Compared to marching cubes, our method improves on every comparable level of resolution. For evaluations on the ground truth mesh, NeuralMeshing also outperforms marching cubes. PointTriNet evaluated on the ground truth sampled points shows comparatively better numbers, which is expected because of the error introduced by the underlying implicit representation.

Reconstruction Accuracy and Completeness. We report further quantitative results in Table 2. Specifically, we report the accuracy, completeness and the F-score for 3 different inlier thresholds, evaluated on both implicit surface representation and ground truth mesh. The accuracy is computed as the ratio of inlier points, *i.e.*sampled points on the predicted mesh which are within inlier distance of the ground truth mesh, and total number of sampled points. The completeness is computed similarly in the opposite direction. Our method again outperforms marching cubes on implicit surface evaluations while PointTriNet

Table 2. Reconstruction accuracy and completeness on D-Faust [8] (top) and ShapeNet [13] (bottom). We report accuracy, completeness and F1-score for 3 different inlier thresholds when evaluated on the implicit representation or the ground truth mesh respectively

IGR/GT		$d_{inlier} = 0.001(0.05\%)$			$d_{inlier} = 0.005(0.25\%)$			$d_{inlier} = 0.01(0.5\%)$		
		Acc. ↑	Com. ↑	F1 ↑	Acc. ↑	Com. ↑	F1 ↑	Acc. ↑	Com. ↑	F1 ↑
Ours	$r_d = 0.02$	0.406/0.136	0.535/0.317	0.453/0.180	0.620/0.339	0.839/0.793	0.700/0.447	0.660/0.369	0.863/0.851	0.732/0.484
	$r_d = 0.01$	**0.975**/0.479	0.787/0.393	0.870/0.431	**1.000**/0.953	0.830/0.802	0.906/0.870	**1.000**/0.982	0.851/0.845	0.919/0.907
	$r_d = 0.005$	0.971/0.452	**0.968**/0.475	**0.969**/0.463	0.989/0.898	**0.985**/0.947	**0.987**/0.922	0.999/0.932	0.988/0.979	0.993/0.954
MC [36]	$res = 128$	0.072/0.068	0.067/0.067	0.069/0.068	0.362/0.346	0.339/0.341	0.350/0.343	0.763/0.724	0.720/0.713	0.741/0.718
	$res = 256$	0.140/0.133	0.133/0.134	0.136/0.134	0.756/0.689	0.723/0.694	0.739/0.691	**1.000**/0.947	0.986/0.965	0.993/0.956
	$res = 512$	0.279/0.262	0.268/0.266	0.274/0.264	**1.000**/0.893	0.983/0.913	0.991/0.902	**1.000**/0.955	0.987/0.976	**0.994**/**0.965**
PointTriNet [51] GT		0.445/**0.831**	0.425/**0.811**	0.435/**0.811**	0.957/**0.990**	0.947/**0.982**	0.952/**0.986**	0.990/**0.997**	**0.991**/**0.998**	0.991/0.997
PointTriNet [51] IGR		0.849/0.430	0.777/0.407	0.811/0.418	0.998/0.922	0.965/0.924	0.981/0.923	1.000/0.959	0.984/0.973	0.992/0.966

IGR/GT		$d_{inlier} = 0.001(0.05\%)$			$d_{inlier} = 0.005(0.25\%)$			$d_{inlier} = 0.01(0.5\%)$		
		Acc. ↑	Com. ↑	F1 ↑	Acc. ↑	Com. ↑	F1 ↑	Acc. ↑	Com. ↑	F1 ↑
Ours	$r_d = 0.02$	0.848/0.630	0.807/0.613	0.826/0.620	0.902/0.778	0.850/0.758	0.874/0.766	0.936/0.815	0.871/0.792	0.901/0.801
	$r_d = 0.01$	0.982/0.706	0.852/0.620	0.911/0.659	0.999/0.855	0.876/0.755	0.933/0.801	**1.000**/0.874	0.884/0.775	0.937/0.820
	$r_d = 0.005$	**0.981**/0.719	**0.881**/0.656	**0.927**/0.685	0.998/0.857	**0.903**/0.783	**0.947** / 0.817	**1.000**/0.874	0.909/0.803	0.951/0.836
MC [36]	$res = 128$	0.007/0.013	0.004/0.011	0.004/0.012	0.206/0.174	0.163/0.144	0.181/0.158	0.635/0.624	0.524/0.529	0.573/0.572
	$res = 256$	0.008/0.013	0.005/0.010	0.006/0.011	0.633/0.576	0.538/0.495	0.581/0.532	**1.000**/0.922	0.872/0.806	0.931/0.859
	$res = 512$	0.084/0.055	0.070/0.046	0.075/0.050	**1.000**/0.863	0.873/0.753	0.932/0.803	**1.000**/0.907	0.880/0.796	0.935/0.847
PointTriNet [51] GT		0.667/**0.928**	0.615/**0.845**	0.640/**0.884**	0.889/**0.980**	0.859/**0.935**	0.873/**0.957**	0.920/**0.997**	0.917/**0.980**	0.918/**0.988**
PointTriNet [51] IGR		0.945/0.605	0.807/0.512	0.870/0.554	0.984/0.877	0.884/0.782	0.931/0.826	0.997/0.896	**0.924**/0.822	**0.959**/0.857

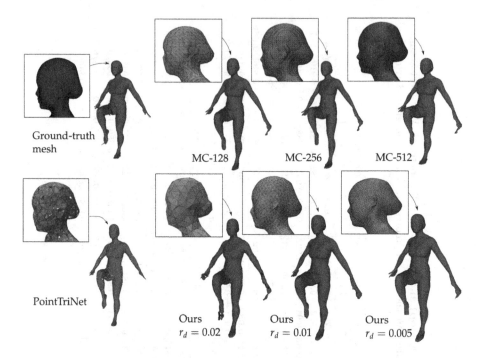

Fig. 6. Qualitative results. Result meshes of various baselines from a single sample. The level of detail reconstructed on the face heavily depends on the resolution and method. IGR artifacts were manually removed. Best viewed digitally

performs better when evaluated on the ground truth mesh, presumably because of reconstruction errors inherent in the implicit surface representation.

Qualitative Results. Figure 6 shows the meshes of all methods on one example. NeuralMeshing yields well behaved triangle meshes with regularly shaped and sized triangles, reconstructing high-level details in accordance to the chosen triangle size r_d. While marching cubes on comparable resolution levels reconstructs a similar level of detail, their generated triangle sizes cannot become bigger than the underlying voxel size. PointTriNet reconstructs the full shape with some level of detail but introduces many visible holes and overlapping faces.

4.2   Triangle Mesh Properties

In this section, we evaluate several mesh properties and triangle metrics.

Mesh Metrics. To demonstrate the capability of producing detail-preserving, low-memory triangle meshes, we report typical mesh metrics in Table 3, *i.e.*, number of triangles, number of vertices and the average triangle area. We also list the inference time for speed comparisons. Our method produces less but bigger triangles than marching cubes for comparable levels of detail.

Table 3. Mesh metrics. We report number of faces (#F), number of vertices (#V), the average triangle area and the run-time in seconds. Where appropriate, values are scaled for better readability. PointTriNet roughly generated similarily sized meshes as NeuralMeshing with $r_d = 0.02$. Likewise, marching cubes with a resolution of 128 produces comparably sized meshes as ours with $r_d = 0.01$

		$F_{[1e3]}$	$V_{[1e3]}$	$Area_{[1e6]}$	$Time_{[s]}$
Ours	$r_d = 0.02$	4.93	2.52	381.28	14.28
	$r_d = 0.01$	41.73	20.97	42.82	226.64
	$r_d = 0.005$	81.95	41.13	22.27	182.47
MC [36]	$res = 128$	21.15	10.60	83.59	3.42
	$res = 256$	86.26	43.19	20.95	23.42
	$res = 512$	347.55	173.91	5.24	187.29
PointTriNet GT [51]		18.88	10.00	88.51	1530.35
PointTriNet IGR [51]		18.93	10.00	90.03	1862.27

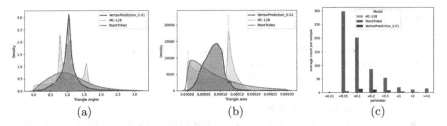

Fig. 7. Distribution analysis. We compare the distribution of triangle angles in radians (a), triangle areas (b) and average number of holes (c) between our method, PointTriNet [51] and marching cubes [36] on the D-Faust [8] dataset

Distribution of Face Area, Triangle Angles and Holes. To demonstrate the regularity of the generated faces, Fig. 7a shows the angle distribution observed in generated meshes of each method. Compared to marching cubes and PointTriNet, our method produces triangle angles closer to the equilateral triangle, containing very few triangles with tiny angles. Figure 7b provides similar insights by comparing the triangle area distribution. It can be observed that our method produces more similarly sized faces while still allowing some variation in order to adapt to more complex surface patches. In Fig. 7c, we plot the number of holes vs. the hole size and compare it with both baselines, illustrating that the vast majority of holes produced by NeuralMeshing are very small. We refer to the supplementary material for more quantitative metrics and ablation studies.

Limitations. NeuralMeshing does not guarantee watertightness, but typically produces meshes with fewer holes than comparable methods. Sharp edges are sometimes problematic which we attribute to the performance of the prediction network. Like marching cubes, NeuralMeshing does not provide a manifoldness guarantee. However, our mesh growing strategy can effectively avoid the insertion of non-manifold edges, while marching cubes requires expensive post-processing.

5 Conclusion

We introduced NeuralMeshing, a novel meshing algorithm for neural implicit representations. We exploit curvature information learned as part of the neural implicit representation in order to guide the predictions of new triangles. Our iterative, curvature-based processing of boundary edges allows us to generate triangle sizes in accordance to the underlying curvature, yielding preferable mesh properties. Experiments demonstrate that NeuralMeshing outperforms existing meshing algorithms, producing meshes with lower triangle counts.

Acknowledgments. This work has been supported by Innosuisse funding (Grant No. 100.567 IP-ICT).

References

1. Amenta, N., Bern, M.: Surface reconstruction by voronoi filtering. Discrete Comput. Geometry **22**, 481–504 (1999)
2. Amenta, N., Bern, M., Kamvysselis, M.: A new voronoi-based surface reconstruction algorithm. In: Proceedings of the 25th Annual Conference on Computer Graphics and Interactive Techniques (1998)
3. Amenta, N., Choi, S., Kolluri, R.K.: The power crust. In: Proceedings of the Sixth ACM Symposium on Solid Modeling and Applications (2001)
4. Amenta, N., Choi, S., Kolluri, R.K.: The power crust, unions of balls, and the medial axis transform. Comput. Geom. **19**, 127–153 (2001)
5. Atzmon, M., Lipman, Y.: SAL: sign agnostic learning of shapes from raw data. In: Proceedings of the IEEE/CVF Conference on Computer Vision and Pattern Recognition (2020)
6. Atzmon, M., Lipman, Y.: SALD: sign agnostic learning with derivatives. In: International Conference on Learning Representations (2020)
7. Bernardini, F., Mittleman, J., Rushmeier, H., Silva, C., Taubin, G.: The ball-pivoting algorithm for surface reconstruction. IEEE Trans. Visual Comput. Graphics **5**, 349–359 (1999)
8. Bogo, F., Romero, J., Pons-Moll, G., Black, M.J.: Dynamic FAUST: registering human bodies in motion. In: 2017 IEEE Conference on Computer Vision and Pattern Recognition (CVPR) (2017)
9. Boissonnat, J.D.: Geometric structures for three-dimensional shape representation. ACM Trans. Graph. (TOG) **3**, 266–286 (1984)
10. Boltcheva, D., Lévy, B.: Surface reconstruction by computing restricted Voronoi cells in parallel. Comput. Aided Des. **90**, 123–134 (2017)
11. Carr, J.C., et al.: Reconstruction and representation of 3D objects with radial basis functions. In: Proceedings of the 28th Annual Conference on Computer Graphics and Interactive Techniques (2001)

12. Chabra, R., Lenssen, J.E., Ilg, E., Schmidt, T., Straub, J., Lovegrove, S., New-combe, R.: Deep local shapes: learning local SDF priors for detailed 3D reconstruction. In: Vedaldi, A., Bischof, H., Brox, T., Frahm, J.-M. (eds.) ECCV 2020. LNCS, vol. 12374, pp. 608–625. Springer, Cham (2020). https://doi.org/10.1007/978-3-030-58526-6_36
13. Chang, A.X., et al.: ShapeNet: an information-rich 3D model repository. Tech. Rep. arXiv:1512.03012 [cs.GR], Stanford University – Princeton University – Toyota Technological Institute at Chicago (2015)
14. Chen, Z., Tagliasacchi, A., Zhang, H.: BSP-Net: generating compact meshes via binary space partitioning. In: Proceedings of the IEEE/CVF Conference on Computer Vision and Pattern Recognition (2020)
15. Chen, Z., Zhang, H.: Learning implicit fields for generative shape modeling. In: Proceedings of the IEEE Conference on Computer Vision and Pattern Recognition (2018)
16. Chen, Z., Zhang, H.: Neural Marching Cubes. arXiv:2106.11272 [cs] (2021)
17. Chibane, J., Alldieck, T., Pons-Moll, G.: Implicit functions in feature space for 3D shape reconstruction and completion. In: Proceedings of the IEEE/CVF Conference on Computer Vision and Pattern Recognition (2020)
18. Chibane, J., Mir, M.A., Pons-Moll, G.: Neural unsigned distance fields for implicit function learning. Adv. Neural. Inf. Process. Syst. **33**, 21638–21652 (2020)
19. Deng, B., Genova, K., Yazdani, S., Bouaziz, S., Hinton, G., Tagliasacchi, A.: CvxNet: learnable convex decomposition. In: Proceedings of the IEEE/CVF Conference on Computer Vision and Pattern Recognition (2020)
20. Duan, Y., Zhu, H., Wang, H., Yi, L., Nevatia, R., Guibas, L.J.: Curriculum DeepSDF. In: Vedaldi, A., Bischof, H., Brox, T., Frahm, J.-M. (eds.) ECCV 2020. LNCS, vol. 12353, pp. 51–67. Springer, Cham (2020). https://doi.org/10.1007/978-3-030-58598-3_4
21. Edelsbrunner, H., Kirkpatrick, D., Seidel, R.: On the shape of a set of points in the plane. IEEE Trans. Inf. Theory **29**, 551–559 (1983)
22. Edelsbrunner, H., Mücke, E.P.: Three-dimensional alpha shapes. ACM Trans. Graph. **13**, 43–72 (1994)
23. Fleishman, S., Cohen-Or, D., Silva, C.T.: Robust moving least-squares fitting with sharp features. ACM Trans. Graph. **24**, 544–552 (2005)
24. Gropp, A., Yariv, L., Haim, N., Atzmon, M., Lipman, Y.: Implicit Geometric Regularization for Learning Shapes. arXiv:2002.10099 [cs, stat] (2020)
25. Groueix, T., Fisher, M., Kim, V.G., Russell, B.C., Aubry, M.: A Papier-Mâché Approach to Learning 3D Surface Generation. In: Proceedings of the IEEE Conference on Computer Vision and Pattern Recognition (2018)
26. Guillard, B., et al.: DeepMesh: Differentiable Iso-Surface Extraction. arXiv:2106.11795 [cs] (2021)
27. Hanocka, R., Metzer, G., Giryes, R., Cohen-Or, D.: Point2Mesh: a self-prior for deformable meshes. ACM Trans. Graph. **39** (2020)
28. Hoppe, H., DeRose, T., Duchamp, T., McDonald, J., Stuetzle, W.: Surface reconstruction from unorganized points. In: Proceedings of the 19th Annual Conference on Computer Graphics and Interactive Techniques (1992)
29. Huang, J., Zhou, Y., Guibas, L.: Manifoldplus: a robust and scalable watertight manifold surface generation method for triangle soups. arXiv preprint arXiv:2005.11621 (2020)
30. Jiang, C.M., Sud, A., Makadia, A., Huang, J., Niessner, M., Funkhouser, T.: Local implicit grid representations for 3D scenes. In: Proceedings of the IEEE/CVF Conference on Computer Vision and Pattern Recognition (2020)

31. Ju, T., Losasso, F., Schaefer, S., Warren, J.: Dual contouring of hermite data. In: Proceedings of the 29th Annual Conference on Computer Graphics and Interactive Techniques (2002)

32. Kazhdan, M., Bolitho, M., Hoppe, H.: Poisson surface reconstruction. In: Proceedings of the Fourth Eurographics Symposium on Geometry Processing (2006)

33. Kazhdan, M., Hoppe, H.: Screened poisson surface reconstruction. ACM Trans. Graph. **32**, 29:1–29:13 (2013)

34. Kolluri, R.: Provably good moving least squares. ACM Trans. Algorithms **4**, 18:1–18:25 (2008)

35. Ladický, L., Saurer, O., Jeong, S., Maninchedda, F., Pollefeys, M.: From point clouds to mesh using regression. In: 2017 IEEE International Conference on Computer Vision (ICCV) (2017)

36. Lewiner, T., Lopes, H., Vieira, A.W., Tavares, G.: Efficient implementation of marching cubes' cases with topological guarantees. J. Graph. Tools **8**, 1–15 (2003)

37. Liao, Y., Donné, S., Geiger, A.: Deep marching cubes: learning explicit surface representations. In: Proceedings of the IEEE Conference on Computer Vision and Pattern Recognition (2018)

38. Lombardi, S., Oswald, M.R., Pollefeys, M.: Scalable point cloud-based reconstruction with local implicit functions. In: 2020 International Conference on 3D Vision (3DV) (2020)

39. Lorensen, W.E., Cline, H.E.: Marching cubes: a high resolution 3d surface construction algorithm. In: Proceedings of the 14th Annual Conference on Computer Graphics and Interactive Techniques (1987)

40. Lv, C., Lin, W., Zhao, B.: Voxel structure-based mesh reconstruction from a 3D point cloud. IEEE Trans. Multimedia **24**, 1815–1829 (2022)

41. Mescheder, L., Oechsle, M., Niemeyer, M., Nowozin, S., Geiger, A.: Occupancy networks: learning 3D reconstruction in function space. In: Proceedings of the IEEE/CVF Conference on Computer Vision and Pattern Recognition (2019)

42. Mi, Z., Luo, Y., Tao, W.: SSRNet: Scalable 3D Surface Reconstruction Network. arXiv:1911.07401 [cs] (2020)

43. Michalkiewicz, M., Pontes, J.K., Jack, D., Baktashmotlagh, M., Eriksson, A.: Deep level sets: implicit surface representations for 3D shape inference. arXiv:1901.06802 [cs] (2019)

44. Öztireli, A.C., Guennebaud, G., Gross, M.: Feature preserving point set surfaces based on non-linear kernel regression. Comput. Graph. Forum **28**, 493–501 (2009)

45. Pan, J., Han, X., Chen, W., Tang, J., Jia, K.: Deep mesh reconstruction from single RGB images via topology modification networks. In: Proceedings of the IEEE/CVF International Conference on Computer Vision (2019)

46. Park, J.J., Florence, P., Straub, J., Newcombe, R., Lovegrove, S.: DeepSDF: learning continuous signed distance functions for shape representation. In: Proceedings of the IEEE Conference on Computer Vision and Pattern Recognition (2019)

47. Peng, S., Jiang, C.M., Liao, Y., Niemeyer, M., Pollefeys, M., Geiger, A.: Shape as points: a differentiable poisson solver. arXiv:2106.03452 [cs] (2021)

48. Peng, S., Niemeyer, M., Mescheder, L., Pollefeys, M., Geiger, A.: Convolutional occupancy networks. In: Vedaldi, A., Bischof, H., Brox, T., Frahm, J.-M. (eds.) ECCV 2020. LNCS, vol. 12348, pp. 523–540. Springer, Cham (2020). https://doi.org/10.1007/978-3-030-58580-8_31

49. Rakotosaona, M.J., Guerrero, P., Aigerman, N., Mitra, N.J., Ovsjanikov, M.: Learning delaunay surface elements for mesh reconstruction. In: Proceedings of the IEEE/CVF Conference on Computer Vision and Pattern Recognition (2021)

50. Schaefer, S., Warren, J.: Dual marching cubes: primal contouring of dual grids. In: 12th Pacific Conference on Computer Graphics and Applications, 2004. PG 2004. Proceedings (2004)

51. Sharp, N., Ovsjanikov, M.: PointTriNet: learned triangulation of 3D point sets. In: Vedaldi, A., Bischof, H., Brox, T., Frahm, J.-M. (eds.) ECCV 2020. LNCS, vol. 12368, pp. 762–778. Springer, Cham (2020). https://doi.org/10.1007/978-3-030-58592-1_45

52. Sitzmann, V., Chan, E., Tucker, R., Snavely, N., Wetzstein, G.: MetaSDF: meta-learning signed distance functions. In: Advances in Neural Information Processing Systems (2020)

53. Sitzmann, V., Martel, J., Bergman, A., Lindell, D., Wetzstein, G.: Implicit neural representations with periodic activation functions. In: Advances in Neural Information Processing Systems (2020)

54. Taubin, G.: Smooth signed distance surface reconstruction and applications. In: Progress in Pattern Recognition, Image Analysis, Computer Vision, and Applications (2012)

55. Thayyil, S.B., Yadav, S.K., Polthier, K., Muthuganapathy, R.: Local Delaunay-based high fidelity surface reconstruction from 3D point sets. Comput. Aided Geometr. Des. **86**, 101973 (2021)

56. van der Walt, S., et al.: The scikit-image contributors: scikit-image: image processing in Python. PeerJ **2**, e453 (2014). https://doi.org/10.7717/peerj.453. https://doi.org/10.7717/peerj.453

57. Wang, N., Zhang, Y., Li, Z., Fu, Y., Liu, W., Jiang, Y.G.: Pixel2Mesh: generating 3D mesh models from single RGB images. In: Proceedings of the European Conference on Computer Vision (ECCV) (2018)

58. Wen, C., Zhang, Y., Li, Z., Fu, Y.: Pixel2Mesh++: multi-view 3D mesh generation via deformation. In: Proceedings of the IEEE/CVF International Conference on Computer Vision (2019)

59. Williams, F., Schneider, T., Silva, C., Zorin, D., Bruna, J., Panozzo, D.: Deep geometric prior for surface reconstruction. In: Proceedings of the IEEE/CVF Conference on Computer Vision and Pattern Recognition (2019)

60. Yang, Y., Feng, C., Shen, Y., Tian, D.: FoldingNet: point cloud auto-encoder via deep grid deformation. In: Proceedings of the IEEE Conference on Computer Vision and Pattern Recognition (2018)

61. Zhong, S., Zhong, Z., Hua, J.: Surface reconstruction by parallel and unified particle-based resampling from point clouds. Comput. Aided Geometr. Des. **71**, 43–62 (2019)

Detection and Recognition

Image-Based Detection of Structural Defects Using Hierarchical Multi-scale Attention

Christian Benz$^{(\boxtimes)}$ and Volker Rodehorst

Bauhaus-Universität, Weimar, Germany
{christian.benz,volker.rodehorst}@uni-weimar.de

Abstract. With improving acquisition technologies, the inspection and monitoring of structures has become a field of application for deep learning. While other research focuses on the design of neural network architectures, this work points out the applicability of transfer learning for detecting cracks and other structural defects. Being a high-performer on the Cityscapes benchmark, *hierarchical multi-scale attention* [43] also renders suitable for transfer learning in the domain of structural defects. Using the joint scales of 0.25, 0.5, and 1.0, the approach achieves 92% mean intersection-over-union on the test set. The effectiveness of multi-scale attention is demonstrated for class demarcation on large scales and class determination on lower scales. Furthermore, a *line-based tolerant intersection-over-union* metric is introduced for more robust benchmarking in the field of crack detection. The dataset of 743 images covering *crack, spalling, corrosion, efflorescence, vegetation,* and *control point* is unprecedented in terms of quantity and realism.

Keywords: Deep learning · Structural defects · Crack detection · Hierarchical multi-scale attention

1 Introduction

The field of structural health monitoring (SHM) deals with the regular inspection and assessment of engineering structures, such as bridges, to ensure their safe use. With the ongoing digitalization in SHM, the amount and quality of imagery of critical infrastructure is successively growing. Automated image-based detection of structural defects can substantially support the human decision makers in assessing the operationality of a structure. An appropriate set of images can serve several purposes, including the 3D reconstruction and maintenance of a digital twin of the structure. Furthermore, high-quality imagery can effectively be used for non-destructive SHM. One informative surface property for condition assessment is the formation of cracks. Other defects, however, also provide substantial insights, defects such as spalling, corrosion, efflorescence, and vegetation. Furthermore, for purposes of georeferencing, control points constitute another worthwhile class for automated detection.

© The Author(s), under exclusive license to Springer Nature Switzerland AG 2022
B. Andres et al. (Eds.): DAGM GCPR 2022, LNCS 13485, pp. 337–353, 2022.
https://doi.org/10.1007/978-3-031-16788-1_21

Unlike other work in the domain, that dedicates to the design of suitable artificial neural network architectures, the here presented work applies transfer learning. For that purpose, a high-ranking approach in the Cityscapes benchmark [10] with accessible code is used, the hierarchical multi-scale attention (HMA) approach by [43]. The effectiveness of HMA for semantic segmentation of structural defects is demonstrated and the role of multi-scale attention further investigated. For all classes except spalling, larger scales seem to draw more attention towards class demarcation, while smaller scales rather engage in content determination.

The plausible evaluation of detection performance is key to advancements in the field. The appropriateness of area-based metrics, such as F_1 score and intersection-over-union (IoU), for crack detection are debatable. Cracks can conceptually rather be considered as lines, thus, the here introduced metric of line-based tolerant IoU can support more robust benchmarking.

The contributions of this work are fourfold: (1) The creation of a dataset[1] that is unprecedented with respect to realism and classes. (2) A demonstration of the applicability of transfer learning to a state-of-the-art semantic segmentation approach for the domain of structural defects[2]. (3) An analysis of the role of attention in multi-scale fusion of different classes. And (4) the presentation of the line-based tolerant IoU evaluation metric that is more appropriate for crack segmentation.

2   Related Work

The related work covers the detection of structural defects resp. anomalies, which include cracks, and the field of transfer learning.

2.1   Anomaly Detection

In recent years, the emergence and utilization of data-driven methods in image processing as well as the potential impact in SHM has fueled the research activity in image-based anomaly detection. In the context of structural health monitoring, the term *anomaly* refers to irregularities in the structure that potentially impede its functionality. Here it is interchangeably used with (*structural*) *defects*.

Cracks form one prominent class of defects. Due to the high relevance for SHM, the attention on visual crack detection has steadily been growing [32]. Especially approaches based on convolutional neural networks (CNN) have had a large impact on the field of image-based object detection [11,22,26,41,42] and are increasingly used for crack detection. Image classification is one conceptual approach to crack detection, where each patch of the image receives a positive or negative response. [13] provides a comparatively large dataset, SDNET, and e.g. [12,37,48] propose image classification-based CNNs for crack detection. With

---

[1] The dataset is available at https://github.com/ben-z-original/s2ds.
[2] Code is available at https://github.com/ben-z-original/detectionhma..

the introduction of fully-convolutional neural networks (FCN) [31], semantic segmentation – producing dense, pixelwise predictions – have become the natural approach for many applications, including crack detection: The more precise localization facilitates further geometric analysis such as crack width estimation, cf. [3].

Among the fully-convolutional approaches to crack detection are [15,29,30, 45,46,54]. [30] propose a network topology based on U-NET [40] and demonstrate its superiority over a simpler FCN design. U-NET makes use of skip connections between encoder and decoder to convey information from earlier stages to later stages of the model. Conceptually similar but more elaborated topologies are used by [29,54], who independently introduce a separate fusion stage: Skip connections do not map from encoder to decoder, but to a separate fusion module. This module, a cascade of convolutional layers, is fed from different scales of encoder and decoder and, through upsampling and fusion, derives a prediction.

With transformer approaches gaining more relevance in visual applications [6,14,51], they have also been explored for crack detection. [28] extend the Seg-Net approach [2] by self-attention modules in order to exploit long-range dependencies of cracks. While the convolutional mechanism is meant to capture fine details of thin cracks, the attention module is designed to form a continuous crack representation.

Providing substantial insights into the health of a structure, the image-based detection of structural defects, other than cracks, has also gained attention. Classification-based detectors for corrosion and spalling are proposed, by e.g. [1,17,18,34,39], while others [16,23–25,33] choose segmentation approaches at pixel-level. [16,25] for instance, use, investigate, and show the applicability of the U-NET for corrosion detection, even though inconsistently outperformed by the FCN. [33] create a synthetic dataset and achieve IoUs of roughly 40% for exposed reinforcement bar (similar to corrosion) and concrete damage on a very small real-world test set. Concrete damage and its severity are also targeted by [36], who use a bounding box-based detection approach to localize defects. Being also applied by [7], the bounding box approach, however, appears inappropriate for less compact defects such as cracks. [38] use mold, stain, and deterioration as classes and retrain VGG [41] for classification.

2.2 Transfer Learning

While most of the related work engages in designing a network architecture, customized for anomaly detection, transfer learning is rather exceptionally applied. Transfer learning refers to a learning process, where the learner must perform multiple different, but related tasks [20]. In the context of artificial neural networks, it typically refers to a change in targets, such as the visual categories to be classified. The underlying assumption is that different targets share low-level features and, thus, can mutually benefit. The effectiveness of transfer learning has been demonstrated for various tasks, including domain adaptation and learning from little data.

The success of transfer learning being one reason for most of the deep learning libraries to provide a model zoo, a collection of established deep learning models, such as [8,9,22]. The DeepLab approach [8,9] uses an encoder-decoder design and atrous spatial pyramid pooling (ASPP), to efficiently extend the receptive field. An effective source for performance comparison is provided through benchmarking challenges such as Cityscapes [10], KITTI [19], COCO [27], or ADE20K [52]. At the time of experimentation, hierarchical multi-scale attention (HMA) [43] was the best performing model in the Cityscapes semantic segmentation challenge with accessible code. It was, thus, considered to be a powerful approach for a domain adaptation to structural defects through transfer learning.

3   Data

Even though growing, the number of publicly available datasets for structural defects is rather limited. For cracks a number of datasets are available, such as [13,29,53,54]. They differ in annotation style (image-, line-, segmentwise), represented surfaces (asphalt, concrete, stone, etc.), and level of difficulty (presence of crack-resembling artifacts). Datasets for structural defects other than cracks are less common or incomplete, e.g. [4,35]. Potential reasons are low accessibility of defects on structures, vagueness of defect boundaries, high variance of surfaces and structures, high annotation effort (involving experts), and commercially induced reluctance to data publication. Due to lack of data, [33] created a synthetic dataset.

Table 1. Overview of the structural defects dataset (S2DS).

Class	Training			Validation			Test		
	Images	Pixels	Area	Images	Pixels	Area	Images	Pixels	Area
Background	556	519.9 M	88.1 %	87	83.8 M	91.9 %	93	87.7 M	90.0 %
Crack	180	0.6 M	0.1 %	25	0.1 M	0.1 %	27	0.1 M	0.1 %
Spalling	151	39.2 M	6.6 %	23	3.3 M	3.6 %	20	4.2 M	4.3 %
Corrosion	209	8.8 M	1.5 %	36	0.5 M	0.6 %	38	0.9 M	0.9 %
Efflorescence	96	4.6 M	0.8 %	13	0.6 M	0.7 %	17	1.5 M	1.5 %
Vegetation	97	15.7 M	2.7 %	16	2.7 M	2.9 %	18	2.9 M	2.9 %
Control point	70	1.5 M	0.3 %	9	0.2 M	0.2 %	10	0.2 M	0.3 %
Total	563	590.35 M	100 %	87	91.23 M	100 %	93	97.52 M	100 %

Scarcity and inappropriateness of the available datasets rendered necessary the creation of a suitable dataset, the *structural defect dataset*, S2DS. For that purpose, 743 patches of size 1024×1024 px were extracted from 8,435 images taken by structural inspectors at real inspection sites. The images were acquired with various different camera platforms, such as DSLR cameras, mobile phones, or drones (UAS). The quality and resolution of many of the images were insufficient for usage due to invisibility of defects or severe blur. A considerable number of selected patches, however, still vary in quality, i.e. in sharpness, lighting conditions, and color constancy. The images were selected and labeled by one trained computer scientist. For highest diligence and accuracy in labeling finest cracks, the scaling and blending options in the available annotation tools were too limited. These limitations and the comparatively low number of images rendered GIMP a suitable tool for annotation. Table 1 provides an overview of the dataset. Figure 3 and 4 in the results section convey a visual impression of the dataset. The dataset was manually split into subsets of 75% for training, 12% for validation, and 13% for testing. In order to get a realistic assessment given proper image material, only images with a fair chance of recognition made their way into the test set. For the other subsets, however, images with blurry, poorly resolved, or hardly visible defects were considered to enrich the yet relatively small training set. Due to the nature of the classes, the dataset is highly unbalanced with respect to the number of pixels and area per class. The imbalance in the number images is due to the imagery provided by structural inspectors: the prevalence of cracks, spalling, and corrosion as well as their major relevance for structure inspection, lead to higher amounts of image material of these classes. The imbalance in the number of pixels indicates the global underrepresentation of the crack class, which is, furthermore, confirmed by the relative occupation in terms of area.

The selected portfolio of classes contains crack, spalling, corrosion, efflorescence, vegetation, and control point: *cracks* represent linear fractures in the material, *spalling* refers to a material detachment from the surface, *corrosion* denotes the rust formation by oxidizing metal parts, *efflorescence* are depositions of dissolved chemicals on the structure's surface, *vegetation* refers to surficial plant growth, and *control points* are geodetic fiducial markers for georeferencing. Control points do not form a class of structural defects. They are, however, substantial for georeferencing and SHM and, thus, are included and, for simplicity, referred to as structural defects in this work.

4   Hierarchical Multi-scale Attention

At the time of experimentation HMA [43], was the highest ranked approach with publicly accessible code in the pixel-level semantic segmentation benchmark of Cityscapes [10]. It has recently been surpassed by [5], who introduce a structured boundary-aware loss. Applying this loss to HMA, an improvement of 0.5% points was achieved on the benchmark. As of May 2022, HMA occupies the second place of approaches with published code and the tenth place in the overall competition. It, thus, can still be considered a state-of-the-art approach to semantic segmentation.

CNNs often struggle with the detection of objects that occur in various sizes [44]. To incorporate multiple scales, HMA proposes a dynamic combination of results from different scales based on simultaneously generated attention maps. The attention maps are contrastively learned based on two scales only. For inference, however, the number of scales can be arbitrarily chosen.

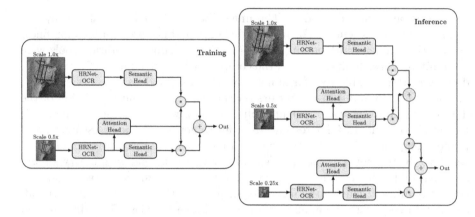

Fig. 1. Hierarchical multi-scale attention (HMA). Based on [43].

Figure 1 provides a high-level overview on the training and inference procedure. During training, the input image passes through the backbone (HRNet-OCR) [47] and the head for semantic segmentation in two different scales. On the smaller scale, the image additionally runs through the attention head. The attention head returns high values for image regions that obtain high attention for the given scale. For low-attention regions the results from the other scale gain higher relevance.

A recursive application of contrastive attention allows for arbitrarily many scales in inference, cf. Fig. 1 (bottom). The results from the two larger scales are merged, weighted by the pixel-wise attention. These weighted results are again weighted and fused based on the attention maps from the next scale. The scales shown in Fig. 1 represent the scales actually used for training and inference for structural defects.

HMA uses the HRNet-OCR [47] as backbone, where OCR refers to object-contextual representations. [47] splits the image into regions, for which a region representation is computed by aggregation of pixel representations. Based on the relation of pixels and regions, an object-contextual representation is derived, that augments the pixel's representation. Each pixel, thereby, obtains more information about its context.

The fully-convolutional head used for semantic segmentation consists of $(3 \times 3$ conv$) \to ($BN$) \to ($ReLU$) \to (3 \times 3$ conv$) \to ($BN$) \to ($ReLU$) \to (1 \times 1$ conv$)$ [43]. The attention head is, apart from the number of outputs, structurally equivalent to the semantic head. Furthermore, there is an auxiliary semantic head docking to HRNet, before OCR (not shown in Fig. 1).

HMA uses the *region mutual information* (RMI) loss introduced by [50], where $\mathcal{L}_{all}$ composes of a cross-entropy component $\mathcal{L}_{ce}$ and a component representing mutual information (MI) resp. I_l:

$$\mathcal{L}_{\text{all}}(y,p) = \lambda \mathcal{L}_{\text{ce}} + (1-\lambda)\frac{1}{B}\sum_{b=1}^{B}\sum_{c=1}^{C}(-I_l^{b,c}(\mathbf{Y};\mathbf{P})) \tag{1}$$

$$I_l(\mathbf{Y};\mathbf{P}) = -\frac{1}{2}\log(\det(\mathbf{\Sigma}_{\mathbf{Y}|\mathbf{P}})). \tag{2}$$

λ represents the weighting factor, B the number of batches, C the number of classes. Based on the assumption that pixels do not show local independence, the neighborhood around the pixel is incorporated into the MI computation: $\mathbf{Y}$ and $\mathbf{P}$ form matrices of the ground truth and predictions around the pixel. Equation 2 shows the calculation of RMI by taking the negative log of the determinant of the covariance matrix of $\mathbf{Y}$ and $\mathbf{P}$. A higher pixel-wise correlation in the region leads to larger determinants, increasing I_l and decreasing the MI component in Eq. 1.

During training, data augmentation was used to compensate for the comparatively low amount of data. Scaling, rotation, and shifting are applied to 80% of the samples during training. The images are cropped, if needed, and 20% of the samples obtain 3×3 Gaussian blur. The sampling of patches during training is controlled, such that at 50% of the patches contain defects while the other half does not. Furthermore, boundary tolerance is used in order to account for annotation inaccuracies and uncertainties at class boundaries.

5 Results

In the following, the relevant metrics are introduced, the performance of HMA for different scales is investigated, the attention maps are analyzed, and, finally, benchmarking for crack detection is performed.

5.1 Metrics

Intersection-over-union (aka IoU or Jaccard index) forms the standard evaluation measure for semantic segmentation as applied in benchmarks such as Cityscapes [10] or ADE20K [52]. For evaluating crack segmentation, other measures have been proposed, such as ODS, optimal dataset scale, and OIS, optimal image scale, cf. [28,45,54]. Both metrics compute the F1 score, ODS conditioned by the optimal threshold over the entire dataset and IDS for each individual image being optimally thresholded.

Neither IoU nor ODS and OIS appear to be ideal metrics for the assessment of crack detection. Both are sensitive towards the area occupied by a crack, favoring wider compared to more narrow cracks. They consider all pixels, including those at the crack boundary, where class membership is regularly uncertain. As a consequence, an approach is proposed that abstracts from area and takes into

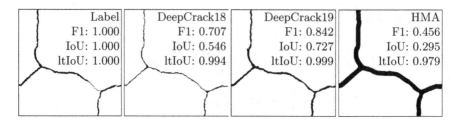

Fig. 2. Evaluation metrics applied on predictions of different approaches. A tolerance of 4 px is used for ltIoU.

account the line-like structure of cracks. For that purpose, the true positives (TP), the false negatives (FN), and the false positives (FP) are computed by:

$$\text{TP} = S(T) \bigcap \left[S(P) \oplus C(\theta) \right] \tag{3}$$

$$\text{FP} = S(P) \setminus \left[S(P) \bigcap \left[S(T) \oplus C(\theta) \right] \right] \tag{4}$$

$$\text{FN} = S(T) \setminus \left[S(T) \bigcap \left[S(P) \oplus C(\theta) \right] \right] = S(T) \setminus \text{TP} \tag{5}$$

T refers to the binary image that represents the ground truth, P to the binary image of predictions, $S(\cdot)$ a skeletonization or thinning method – such as [21,49] – that transforms areas into lines resp. medial axes. Furthermore, C is a circular morphological element with diameter θ that is used for dilation operation $\oplus$. The diameter θ represents the applied tolerance around the medial axis of each, ground truth and prediction. The *line-based tolerant intersection-over-union* metric is defined as ltIoU = $\frac{TP}{TP+FP+FN}$ using TP, FP, and FN from above.

Figure 2 shows three different predictions for a crack patch, DeepCrack18 [54], DeepCrack19 [29], and the here presented HMA [43]. The top left shows the label. The robustness of ltIoU towards the width of prediction is demonstrated by the relatively stable, close to perfect value of ltIoU, while F1 and IoU vary distinctively. Note that ltIoU is inappropriate if the results from crack segmentation also serve crack width estimation.

5.2 Scales

For assessing the performance of the HMA with respect to all classes, the standard IoU is used. Table 2 shows the IoU for each class conditioned by the scales used for inference. Generally, the inclusion of more scales leads to higher mean IoU, even though the combination of [0.25, 1.0] produces decent results as well. Seemingly, the scale 0.25 contributes to a better detection of the efflorescence. Unlike for the original HMA – which uses [0.5, 1.0, 2.0] for semantic segmentation of street sceneries – including scale 2.0 does not have a positive impact on performance. An explanation might be that the larger scale does not add information, especially not to the detection of fine structures and boundaries.

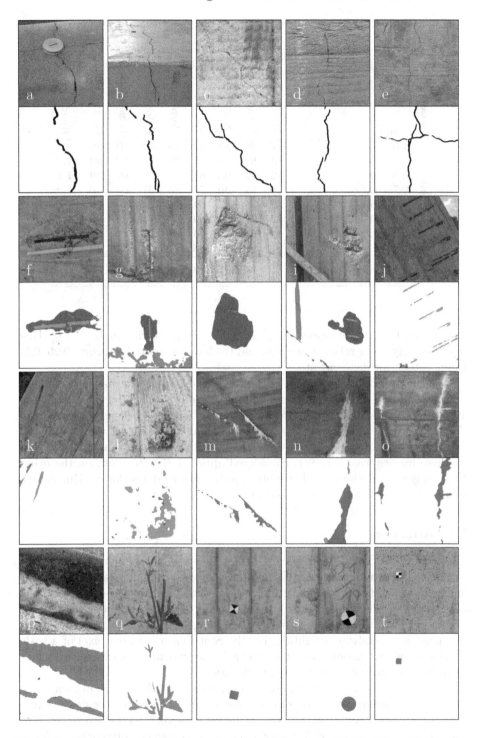

Fig. 3. Qualitative results of HMA on the test set. Classes: crack (black), spalling (red), corrosion (orange), efflorescence (blue), vegetation (green), and control point (purple). (Color figure online)

Table 2. Effects of different scales of HMA on the S2DS dataset.

Dataset	Scales	Mean IoU	Background	Crack	Spalling	Corrosion	Efflorescence	Vegetation	Control Point	Runtime (rel.)
						Intersection-over-Union [%]				
Validation	[1.0]	77	96	89	69	79	34	70	**99**	*1.0*
	[0.25, 1.0]	86	**98**	88	80	**90**	74	72	**99**	*1.3*
	[0.5, 1.0]	82	97	**90**	81	87	53	69	**99**	*1.2*
	[0.75, 1.0]	78	96	**90**	74	85	31	69	**99**	*1.3*
	[1.0, 1.5]	75	96	87	64	77	34	70	**99**	*1.6*
	[0.5, 1.0, 2.0]	82	97	86	80	87	53	69	**99**	*2.1*
	[0.25, 0.5, 1.0]	**87**	**98**	87	83	**90**	**76**	72	**99**	*1.4*
	[0.25, 0.5, 0.75, 1.0]	**87**	**98**	87	**84**	**90**	**76**	72	**99**	*1.6*
Test	[0.25, 0.5, 1.0]	92	99	91	91	88	90	87	100	–

The overall best combinations are [0.25, 0.5, 1.0] and [0.25, 0.5, 0.75, 1.0]. Due to the slightly lower relative runtime, and the lower memory footprint, [0.25, 0.5, 1.0] is chosen for deployment.

When applied to the test set, Table 2, the overall performance as well as the performance on each class individually improves. This behavior, which is atypical for artificial neural networks, is caused by the higher quality of data in the test set. Due to lack of data, the training and validation set were populated with images of lower quality, in order to hopefully benefit training. Detection on these images was, however, considered optional. The test set, on the other hand, only contains images where detection is considered mandatory. Qualitative results on the test set are presented in Fig. 3.

5.3 Attention

Fig. 4 illustrates how – mediated by attention – the three different scales contribute to the overall prediction. The top row of each example displays the input image alongside the fused prediction. Below, the attention maps (left) and the corresponding predictions (right) are shown for the three different scales 0.25, 0.5, and 1.0. The attention maps result from a pixelwise softmax across the scales and provide a pixelwise weighting, i.e. the contribution of each pixel of a scale for the overall prediction. Brighter regions in the attention maps refer to higher attention and darker regions to lower attention.

It can be observed that for all classes, despite spalling, the highest scale (1.0×) shows strong activation of attention around the defect. The defect itself, however, obtains lower attention. On the lowest scale (0.25×) the reverse applies: while the vicinity of the defect shows darker areas which correspond to lower

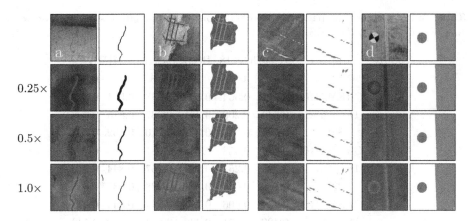

Fig. 4. Attention maps for multiple scales. The input image is displayed in the upper left; right beside the fused prediction. Below the per-scale attention maps are shown with corresponding predictions. Classes: crack (black), spalling (red), corrosion (orange), efflorescence (blue), vegetation (green), and control point (purple). (Color figure online)

attention, higher attention is paid to the defect itself. This observation applies to crack, corrosion, and efflorescence, whereas control point and vegetation show a similar pattern with less activation on the low scale.

A potential interpretation for this observation is that the highest scales are responsible to determine the point of transition from defect to background for accurate boundary demarcation. Lower scales, on the other hand, possibly rather determine the content of the defect. While the shape of boundary is arbitrary for all defects other than crack and control point, the intensity and color can be characteristic: crack is relatively dark, efflorescence relatively whitish, corrosion has a brownish and vegetation a greenish hue. It is conceivable that these color-related aspects receive more considerations on lower scales.

Contrasting the above observation, spalling seems to show reverse behavior. Lower scales show higher activation in the vicinity and lower activation at the defect itself. On higher scales, the attention at the location of the defect is, however, higher than for other classes. Since the detachment of material causes an edgy and peaky texture in the spalling, it can be conjectured that those relevant details vanish or blur on lower scales. Thus, these features require attention on the highest scale for spalling classification.

5.4 Benchmark

No benchmark is yet available for structural defects as represented in the S2DS dataset. S2DS is rather intended to form a first such benchmark. Certainly, more data need to be acquired and made available to the public, in order to obtain better generalizing models. For crack detection, however, datasets and approaches are available for benchmarking. As pointed out above, IoU does not

Table 3. Performance comparison with other approaches and datasets for crack detection. F1 conforms to the ODS metric.

Tol [px]	Dataset	DeepCrack18		DeepCrack19		HMA	
		F1	ltIoU	F1	ltIoU	F1	ltIoU
0	CRKWH100	0.721	0.564	0.559	0.388	0.521	0.353
	DeepCrack	0.344	0.208	0.881	0.787	0.815	0.688
	S2DS	0.080	0.041	0.347	0.210	0.862	0.758
2	CRKWH100	0.920	0.853	0.735	0.581	0.628	0.458
	DeepCrack	0.405	0.254	0.923	0.857	0.844	0.730
	S2DS	0.156	0.084	0.384	0.238	0.937	0.881
4	CRKWH100	0.951	0.906	0.781	0.641	0.644	0.475
	DeepCrack	0.427	0.271	0.938	0.884	0.856	0.749
	S2DS	0.162	0.088	0.402	0.252	0.949	0.903
8	CRKWH100	0.965	0.932	0.826	0.703	0.659	0.491
	DeepCrack	0.448	0.288	0.952	0.908	0.870	0.769
	S2DS	0.166	0.090	0.430	0.274	0.960	0.922
16	CRKWH100	0.972	0.945	0.873	0.775	0.680	0.516
	DeepCrack	0.474	0.310	0.962	0.928	0.884	0.793
	S2DS	0.170	0.093	0.476	0.312	0.967	0.936
32	CRKWH100	0.976	0.954	0.915	0.844	0.718	0.560
	DeepCrack	0.518	0.349	0.972	0.946	0.901	0.819
	S2DS	0.176	0.096	0.538	0.368	0.972	0.946

appear to be a proper metric, which therefore is replaced by ltIoU for the given evaluation.

Table 3 shows three approaches, DeepCrack18 [54], DeepCrack19 [29], and the here presented HMA [43] applied to three datasets, CRKWH100 [54], Deep-Crack [29], and the presented S2DS. The publication of code has not yet become standard practice in crack detection. DeepCrack18 [54] and DeepCrack19 [29], however, are prominent approaches with working code and are used by others for benchmarking, e.g. [28]. CRKWH100 [54] and DeepCrack [29] are the accompanying datasets and regularly serve for benchmarking. The CRKWH100 contains thin pavement cracks, DeepCrack covers various types of cracks, and S2DS mainly represents cracks in concrete walls. Six levels of tolerance for the positioning of the medial axis are investigated.

Generally, F1 and ltIoU improve with higher tolerance. Even though at tolerance level 16 and 32 px saturation effects can be observed, i.e. more tolerance does not lead to distinctively better performance. This point can be considered the currently best possible performance of the classifier. All approaches perform best on the datasets created in their context. There are, however, differences with respect to the generalization capabilities. While DeepCrack18 shows at most mediocre performance on datasets other than CRKWH100, the performance of HMA also deteriorates on the other data, but less severely. On CRKWH100, the HMA regularly shows activation for the spalling class. This confusion might be rooted in the occasional textural similarity of pavement and spalling. It, however, raises the question, if pavement crack detection and spalling detection can be reasonably represented in a single approach. Based on the benchmarking results can be stated that a domain gap exists, particularly with respect to pavement cracks, which, though, might be bridgeable even with HMA.

6 Conclusion

In the context of this work, a dataset was created for multi-class classification of several structural defects. This dataset is unprecedented in quantity and quality and is intended to form a first benchmarking dataset in the domain. While other researchers focus on the design of suitable artificial neural network architectures, it is demonstrated that by means of transfer learning on the state-of-the-art approach of hierarchical multi-scale attention [43] a decent performance can be achieved. Network design can, however, be appropriate if a relatively small, application-tailored model is required, e.g. for deployment in an embedded platform on a UAS.

Furthermore, the investigation of attention revealed the relevance of large scales for demarcating class boundaries. Smaller scales, on the other hand, show higher activation directly at the defect, which led to the conjecture, that they contribute to determining the proper class. Justifications for spalling not conforming to this pattern was given by the high degree of details in the textural pattern only perceivable on larger scales.

It is claimed, that standard evaluation metrics, such as F1 and IoU, are not appropriate for evaluating crack segmentation. The measures conceptually evaluate the overlap of areas. Cracks are, however, rather line-like structures and, thus, require other metrics for plausible comparison. For that purpose, the ltIoU was introduced, which reduces a prediction to a medial axis and assesses the intersection and union of medial axes of ground truth and prediction given a certain positional tolerance. Note that the measure is, however, unsuited if the predictions are directly used for crack width estimation. By means of ltIoU an intra-domain gap could be observed in benchmarking: the performance of crack detection very much depends on the data available during training. This holds for the background, e.g. pavement being mistaken for spalling, or distractive artifacts, such as concrete texture falsely classified as cracks. To come up with a general approach to crack detection covering various different surfaces and crack types remains an open challenge.

Acknowledgment. The authors would like to thank *DB Netz AG* and *Leonhardt, Andrä und Partner* (LAP) for providing numerous images as well as their consent to publication. Without them this work would have been impossible.

References

1. Atha, D.J., Jahanshahi, M.R.: Evaluation of deep learning approaches based on convolutional neural networks for corrosion detection. Struct. Health Monit. **17**(5), 1110–1128 (2018)
2. Badrinarayanan, V., Kendall, A., Cipolla, R.: Segnet: a deep convolutional encoder-decoder architecture for image segmentation. IEEE Trans. Pattern Anal. Mach. Intell. **39**(12), 2481–2495 (2017)
3. Benz, C., Rodehorst, V.: Model-based crack width estimation using rectangle transform. In: 17th International Conference on Machine Vision and Applications (MVA), pp. 1–5. IEEE (2021)
4. Bianchi, E., Abbott, A.L., Tokekar, P., Hebdon, M.: Coco-bridge: structural detail data set for bridge inspections. J. Comput. Civil Eng. **35**(3), 04021003 (2021)
5. Borse, S., Wang, Y., Zhang, Y., Porikli, F.: Inverseform: a loss function for structured boundary-aware segmentation. In: Proceedings of the IEEE/CVF Conference on Computer Vision and Pattern Recognition, pp. 5901–5911 (2021)
6. Carion, N., Massa, F., Synnaeve, G., Usunier, N., Kirillov, A., Zagoruyko, S.: End-to-end object detection with transformers. In: Vedaldi, A., Bischof, H., Brox, T., Frahm, J.-M. (eds.) ECCV 2020. LNCS, vol. 12346, pp. 213–229. Springer, Cham (2020). https://doi.org/10.1007/978-3-030-58452-8_13
7. Cha, Y.J., Choi, W., Suh, G., Mahmoudkhani, S., Büyüköztürk, O.: Autonomous structural visual inspection using region-based deep learning for detecting multiple damage types. Comput.-Aided Civil Infrastruct. Eng. **33**(9), 731–747 (2018)
8. Chen, L.C., Papandreou, G., Kokkinos, I., Murphy, K., Yuille, A.L.: Deeplab: semantic image segmentation with deep convolutional nets, atrous convolution, and fully connected crfs. IEEE Trans. Pattern Anal. Mach. Intell. **40**(4), 834–848 (2017)
9. Chen, L.C., Papandreou, G., Schroff, F., Adam, H.: Rethinking atrous convolution for semantic image segmentation. arXiv preprint arXiv:1706.05587 (2017)
10. Cordts, M., et al.: The cityscapes dataset for semantic urban scene understanding. In: Proceedings of the IEEE Conference on Computer Vision and Pattern Recognition, pp. 3213–3223 (2016)
11. Deng, J., Dong, W., Socher, R., Li, L.J., Li, K., Fei-Fei, L.: Imagenet: a large-scale hierarchical image database. In: IEEE Conference on Computer Vision and Pattern Recognition, pp. 248–255. IEEE (2009)
12. Dorafshan, S., Thomas, R.J., Maguire, M.: Comparison of deep convolutional neural networks and edge detectors for image-based crack detection in concrete. Constr. Build. Mater. **186**, 1031–1045 (2018)
13. Dorafshan, S., Thomas, R.J., Maguire, M.: Sdnet 2018: an annotated image dataset for non-contact concrete crack detection using deep convolutional neural networks. Data Brief **21**, 1664–1668 (2018)
14. Dosovitskiy, A., et al.: An image is worth 16×16 words: transformers for image recognition at scale. arXiv preprint arXiv:2010.11929 (2020)
15. Dung, C.V., et al.: Autonomous concrete crack detection using deep fully convolutional neural network. Autom. Constr. **99**, 52–58 (2019)
16. Duy, L.D., Anh, N.T., Son, N.T., Tung, N.V., Duong, N.B., Khan, M.H.R.: Deep learning in semantic segmentation of rust in images. In: Proceedings of the 9th International Conference on Software and Computer Applications, pp. 129–132 (2020)

17. Forkan, A.R.M., et al.: Corrdetector: a framework for structural corrosion detection from drone images using ensemble deep learning. arXiv preprint arXiv:2102.04686 (2021)

18. Gao, Y., Mosalam, K.M.: Deep transfer learning for image-based structural damage recognition. Comput.-Aided Civil Infrastruct. Eng. **33**(9), 748–768 (2018)

19. Geiger, A., Lenz, P., Urtasun, R.: Are we ready for autonomous driving? the kitti vision benchmark suite. In: IEEE Conference on Computer Vision and Pattern Recognition, pp. 3354–3361. IEEE (2012)

20. Goodfellow, I., Bengio, Y., Courville, A.: Deep Learning. MIT press, Cambridge (2016)

21. Guo, Z., Hall, R.W.: Parallel thinning with two-subiteration algorithms. Commun. ACM **32**(3), 359–373 (1989)

22. He, K., Zhang, X., Ren, S., Sun, J.: Deep residual learning for image recognition. In: Proceedings of the IEEE Conference on Computer Vision and Pattern Recognition, pp. 770–778 (2016)

23. Hoskere, V., Narazaki, Y., Hoang, T., Spencer Jr, B.: Vision-based structural inspection using multiscale deep convolutional neural networks. arXiv preprint arXiv:1805.01055 (2018)

24. Hoskere, V., Narazaki, Y., Hoang, T.A., Spencer, B., Jr.: Madnet: multi-task semantic segmentation of multiple types of structural materials and damage in images of civil infrastructure. J. Civil Struct Health Monit **10**, 757–773 (2020)

25. Katsamenis, I., Protopapadakis, E., Doulamis, A., Doulamis, N., Voulodimos, A.: Pixel-Level corrosion detection on metal constructions by fusion of deep learning semantic and contour segmentation. In: Bebis, G., et al. (eds.) ISVC 2020. LNCS, vol. 12509, pp. 160–169. Springer, Cham (2020). https://doi.org/10.1007/978-3-030-64556-4_13

26. Krizhevsky, A., Sutskever, I., Hinton, G.E.: Imagenet classification with deep convolutional neural networks. Adv. Neural Inf. Process. Syst. **25**, 1097–1105 (2012)

27. Lin, T.-Y., et al.: Microsoft COCO: common objects in context. In: Fleet, D., Pajdla, T., Schiele, B., Tuytelaars, T. (eds.) ECCV 2014. LNCS, vol. 8693, pp. 740–755. Springer, Cham (2014). https://doi.org/10.1007/978-3-319-10602-1_48

28. Liu, H., Miao, X., Mertz, C., Xu, C., Kong, H.: Crackformer: transformer network for fine-grained crack detection. In: Proceedings of the IEEE/CVF International Conference on Computer Vision, pp. 3783–3792 (2021)

29. Liu, Y., Yao, J., Lu, X., Xie, R., Li, L.: Deepcrack: a deep hierarchical feature learning architecture for crack segmentation. Neurocomputing **338**, 139–153 (2019)

30. Liu, Z., Cao, Y., Wang, Y., Wang, W.: Computer vision-based concrete crack detection using u-net fully convolutional networks. Autom. Constr. **104**, 129–139 (2019)

31. Long, J., Shelhamer, E., Darrell, T.: Fully convolutional networks for semantic segmentation. In: Proceedings of the IEEE Conference on Computer Vision and pattern recognition, pp. 3431–3440 (2015)

32. Mohan, A., Poobal, S.: Crack detection using image processing: a critical review and analysis. Alexandria Eng. J. **57**(2), 787–798 (2018)

33. Narazaki, Y., Hoskere, V., Yoshida, K., Spencer, B.F., Fujino, Y.: Synthetic environments for vision-based structural condition assessment of Japanese high-speed railway viaducts. Mech. Syst. Signal Process. **160**, 107850 (2021)

34. Ortiz, A., Bonnin-Pascual, F., Garcia-Fidalgo, E., et al.: Vision-based corrosion detection assisted by a micro-aerial vehicle in a vessel inspection application. Sensors **16**(12), 2118 (2016)

35. Ortiz, A., Bonnin-Pascual, F., Garcia-Fidalgo, E., Company, J.P.: Visual inspection of vessels by means of a micro-aerial vehicle: an artificial neural network approach for corrosion detection. In: Robot 2015: Second Iberian Robotics Conference. AISC, vol. 418, pp. 223–234. Springer, Cham (2016). https://doi.org/10.1007/978-3-319-27149-1_18

36. Pan, X., Yang, T.: Postdisaster image-based damage detection and repair cost estimation of reinforced concrete buildings using dual convolutional neural networks. Comput.-Aided Civil Infrastruct. Eng. **35**(5), 495–510 (2020)

37. Pauly, L., Hogg, D., Fuentes, R., Peel, H.: Deeper networks for pavement crack detection. In: Proceedings of the 34th ISARC, pp. 479–485. IAARC (2017)

38. Perez, H., Tah, J.H., Mosavi, A.: Deep learning for detecting building defects using convolutional neural networks. Sensors **19**(16), 3556 (2019)

39. Petricca, L., Moss, T., Figueroa, G., Broen, S.: Corrosion detection using AI: a comparison of standard computer vision techniques and deep learning model. In: Proceedings of the Sixth International Conference on Computer Science, Engineering and Information Technology, vol. 91, p. 99 (2016)

40. Ronneberger, O., Fischer, P., Brox, T.: U-net: convolutional networks for biomedical image segmentation. In: Navab, N., Hornegger, J., Wells, W.M., Frangi, A.F. (eds.) MICCAI 2015. LNCS, vol. 9351, pp. 234–241. Springer, Cham (2015). https://doi.org/10.1007/978-3-319-24574-4_28

41. Simonyan, K., Zisserman, A.: Very deep convolutional networks for large-scale image recognition. arXiv preprint arXiv:1409.1556 (2014)

42. Szegedy, C., et al.: Going deeper with convolutions. In: Proceedings of the IEEE Conference on Computer Vision and pattern recognition, pp. 1–9 (2015)

43. Tao, A., Sapra, K., Catanzaro, B.: Hierarchical multi-scale attention for semantic segmentation. arXiv preprint arXiv:2005.10821 (2020)

44. Xu, Y., Xiao, T., Zhang, J., Yang, K., Zhang, Z.: Scale-invariant convolutional neural networks. arXiv preprint arXiv:1411.6369 (2014)

45. Yang, F., Zhang, L., Yu, S., Prokhorov, D., Mei, X., Ling, H.: Feature pyramid and hierarchical boosting network for pavement crack detection. IEEE Trans. Intell. Transp. Syst. **21**(4), 1525–1535 (2019)

46. Yang, X., Li, H., Yu, Y., Luo, X., Huang, T., Yang, X.: Automatic pixel-level crack detection and measurement using fully convolutional network. Comput.-Aided Civil Infrastruct. Eng. **33**(12), 1090–1109 (2018)

47. Yuan, Y., Chen, X., Wang, J.: Object-contextual representations for semantic segmentation. In: Vedaldi, A., Bischof, H., Brox, T., Frahm, J.-M. (eds.) ECCV 2020. LNCS, vol. 12351, pp. 173–190. Springer, Cham (2020). https://doi.org/10.1007/978-3-030-58539-6_11

48. Zhang, L., Yang, F., Zhang, Y.D., Zhu, Y.J.: Road crack detection using deep convolutional neural network. In: IEEE International Conference on Image Processing (ICIP), pp. 3708–3712. IEEE (2016)

49. Zhang, T.Y., Suen, C.Y.: A fast parallel algorithm for thinning digital patterns. Commun. ACM **27**(3), 236–239 (1984)

50. Zhao, S., Wang, Y., Yang, Z., Cai, D.: Region mutual information loss for semantic segmentation. arXiv preprint arXiv:1910.12037 (2019)

51. Zheng, S., et al.: Rethinking semantic segmentation from a sequence-to-sequence perspective with transformers. In: Proceedings of the IEEE/CVF Conference on Computer Vision and Pattern Recognition, pp. 6881–6890 (2021)

52. Zhou, B., et al.: Semantic understanding of scenes through the ade20k dataset. Int. J. Comput. Vision **127**(3), 302–321 (2019)

53. Zou, Q., Cao, Y., Li, Q., Mao, Q., Wang, S.: Cracktree: automatic crack detection from pavement images. Pattern Recogn. Lett. **33**(3), 227–238 (2012)
54. Zou, Q., Zhang, Z., Li, Q., Qi, X., Wang, Q., Wang, S.: Deepcrack: learning hierarchical convolutional features for crack detection. IEEE Trans. Image Process. **28**(3), 1498–1512 (2018)

A Dataset for Analysing Complex Document Layouts in the Digital Humanities and Its Evaluation with Krippendorff's Alpha

David Tschirschwitz$^{(\boxtimes)}$ ⓘ, Franziska Klemstein ⓘ, Benno Stein ⓘ, and Volker Rodehorst ⓘ

Bauhaus-Universität, Weimar, Germany
david.tschirschwitz@uni-weimar.de

Abstract. We introduce a new research resource in the form of a high-quality, domain-specific dataset for analysing the document layout of historical documents. The dataset provides an instance segmentation ground truth with 19 classes based on historical layout structures that stem (a) from the publication production process and the respective genres (life sciences, architecture, art, decorative arts, etc.) and, (b) from selected text registers (such as monograph, trade journal, illustrated magazine). Altogether, the dataset contains more than 52,000 instances annotated by experts. A baseline has been tested with the well-known Mask R-CNN and compared to the state-of-the-art model VSR [55]. Inspired by evaluation practices from the field of Natural Language Processing (NLP), we have developed a new method for evaluating annotation consistency. Our method is based on Krippendorff's alpha (K-α), a statistic for quantifying the so-called "inter-annotator-agreement". In particular, we propose an adaptation of K-α that treats annotations as a multipartite graph for assessing the agreement of a variable number of annotators. The method is adjustable with regard to evaluation strictness, and it can be used in 2D or 3D as well as for a variety of tasks such as semantic segmentation, instance segmentation, and 3D point cloud segmentation.

Keywords: Document layout analysis · Digital humanities · Instance segmentation · Inter-annotator-agreement

1 Introduction

Research in the digital humanities requires experts to interpret large corpora and to be able to search these corpora for specific information. Existing tools and analysis methods in digital humanities focus on digitized text, while visual content in the form of images is often neglected. In "The visual digital turn" by Wevers et al. [51] this bias is explained by the availability of Optical Character

B. Andres et al. (Eds.): DAGM GCPR 2022, LNCS 13485, pp. 354–374, 2022.
https://doi.org/10.1007/978-3-031-16788-1_22

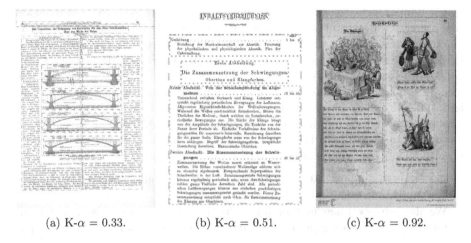

(a) K-α = 0.33.   (b) K-α = 0.51.   (c) K-α = 0.92.

Fig. 1. Comparing images with different K-α values. Dashed lines marks annotator A and dotted lines signifies annotator B. The colors indicate matching (green), missed (blue) or class wise disagreed (red) annotations. (Color figure online)

Recognition (OCR) and other powerful tools for the analysis of text. However, to get a "holistic understanding" of a document, images have to be included into the analysis as well. To extract structured data, an understanding of the document layout is necessary: Knowing the document layout allows precise extraction of layout elements (e.g., images, equations, editorial notes) and to handle them in a suitable manner depending on the type of information they contain [38]. Moreover, layout information is a useful preprocessing step for image processing and related recognition tasks in a document understanding system [13,16,47].

Several commercial tools do exist to execute document layout analysis, such as Kofax OmniPage [30], Abbyy FineReader [6] or PRImA Aletheia [14,43]. Additionally, large public datasets like PubLayNet [56] or DocBank [35] can be used to train highly-accurate data-driven methods like deep neural networks for document layout analysis. For historical data, datasets like HJDataset [49] or IMPACT [42] are available. While all of these approaches work to some degree for the digital humanities domain, the selection of layout elements in these datasets is often not designed to identify specific artistic elements in the layout (e.g., decorations or frames). This makes it impossible to capture specific historical production processes as well as the importance of the publication as an artistic medium.

In order to address these issues we created a high-quality dataset for document layout analysis with fine-grained annotations, including instance segmentation level ground truth data (see Fig. 1). The dataset intends to serve the community as a resource to further test and enhance methods running on historical document layout analysis. As our benchmarking shows, state-of-the-art models [55] designed for contemporary literature document layout analysis fall short compared to well established generic approaches [23] for instance segmentation. Since the creation process of the dataset had very specific requirements by the domain experts, we also introduce a new method to evaluate annotation consistency. Our method is an adaptation of Krippendorff's alpha [22,33] (K-α) for computer vision, a statistical measurement, which is commonly used in Natural Language Processing (NLP) and other Machine Learning (ML) subfields [39]. Our comprehensive, stage-less and customizable method can be used in multiple scenarios. Such as, the annotation consistency evaluation on a subset of a finalized dataset to describe the quality, on the entire dataset to provide feedback if disagreements between annotators occur which allows filtering or correction of low quality annotations or the identification of specific hard examples. Our work makes two key contributions:

- A new high-quality historical document layout analysis dataset with over 52,000 instances and a benchmark on our dataset.
- We also propose a new method for evaluating annotation consistency in computer vision, extending K-α by treating annotations as a multipartite graph.

2   Related Work

State-of-the-art techniques rely on data-driven deep learning techniques. Two general approaches to analyse the layout seem generally feasible. For born-digital documents which contain embedded text that can be used as input data, models like BERT [17] or LayoutLM [54] have been used with great success. On the other hand, models like Faster R-CNN [44] or Mask R-CNN [23] can be utilized using the visual cues. As a hybrid solution models can also use both aspects like the current best performing layout model VSR [55]. Various public datasets exist to train and benchmark these models like PubLayNet [56], DocBank [35] or IMPACT [42]. Using models that rely on text-based ground truth is problematic for historical none-digital-born documents, since they are often missing ground truth texts. OCR methods can be used to obtain the text, however, while these OCR results are often highly accurate, some errors are still occurring and these are passed to models that use text as input data. Manually creating ground truth text data for a historical dataset to use them in addition to the image for training, does not seem viable, since during inference no textual ground truth would be available as well. This could be considered a limiting factor for using models like BERT, LayoutLM or VSR on historical documents.

During the selection of documents that are part of the annotated dataset, a categorization to cover the presumably different types of layouts is necessary. Kise [31] provides a breakdown of the different layout types into several subcategories, namely, rectangular, Manhattan, non-Manhatten and two types of overlapping layouts (further called arbitrary complex [10]). By considering these layout types during data selection of documents to be annotated, a possible wider range of practice relevant cases were covered during training, that then can be beneficial for inference. While these layout types can give an orientation on how challenging different layouts might be, it is not given that learning one of these layout-types allows transfer to other documents of the same layout type. Our dataset contains three of these layout types (rectangular, Manhattan, and non-Manhattan), but while some of the historical sources tend to be hybrids, this creates another complexity. For this reason, we have added further layout components in addition to the typical ones such as text blocks, illustrations and tables.

Evaluating annotation consistency in computer vision is often done with the same metrics that are used for evaluating model performance like mean Average Precision (mAP) or the F_1 score. Many datasets rely entirely on the manual [37] or automated annotation pipeline [35,56] and no extra quality assurance step is taken, while in some cases a small sample of the dataset is double annotated and evaluated with such above mentioned metrics [21]. In the creation process of datasets in other domains (ML and NLP), agreements between annotators are calculated with statistical measurements like K-α [22,33] or Cohen's kappa [15]. Reasons to make the extra effort for these additional annotations are [7]:

- Validating and improving the annotation guideline and existing annotations.
- Identifying difficult cases or ambiguities.
- Assessment of the interpretation of the annotating data within the guideline range.
- Comparing annotator speed and accuracy.

Current approaches [41,46] for evaluating the inter-annotator agreement in computer vision rely on pixel-level comparison, that views the image as a long list of entries and then compares them to use them with the regular procedure of inter-annotator-agreement calculation. While this method can work for balanced datasets in some cases, it neglects criteria like the number of instances or at what point annotators really meant the same entity and did not just by chance overlapped in the same region. To remedy the above-mentioned limitations, we propose an adaptation of K-α, by interpreting annotations as a graph and rely on the Intersection over Union (IoU) in the first step of our calculation step. Thanks to the variety of different IoU versions, our method is flexible and universal applicable in the entire computer vision domain.

3   Evaluation Annotation Consistency

3.1   Data Quality Metric

To calculate K-α a multi-step procedure is applied, which is outlined in Fig. 2. As a result of this calculation a single α value is reported which measures the inter-annotator-agreement, where $\alpha = 1$ is a perfect agreement, $\alpha = 0$ means there is no agreement and values < 0 indicate a disagreement. The general form of K-α is $\alpha = 1 - \frac{D_o}{D_e}$, where D_o is the observed disagreement and D_e is the expected disagreement, going further we will explain the calculation of α for nominal data.

Assuming there are Ω annotators, where the first annotator is Ω_A, with a set of annotations $a = \{a_i\}_{i=1}^N$ and the second annotator is Ω_B with its own set of annotations $b = \{b_i\}_{j=1}^M$. Each such annotation a_i and b_i contains an arbitrary

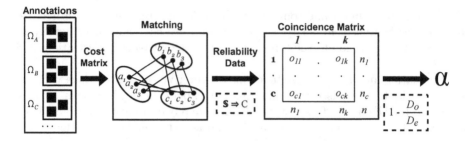

Fig. 2. Outline of the calculation process.

shape $\mathbb{S} \subseteq \mathbb{R}^n$ that is defined as A or B respectively. These shapes can be either in 2D or 3D space and the IoU is calculated with the following equation:

$$IoU(A, B) = \frac{|A \cap B|}{|A \cup B|} \qquad (1)$$

In order to match all the entries of Ω_A and Ω_B, a cost matrix is created with the following cost function:

$$C(i, j) = 1 - IoU(a_i, b_j) \qquad (2)$$

The two sets are viewed as a bipartite graph and can therefore be matched via the Hungarian algorithm. This requires $N = M$, for which the smaller set is padded with $\varnothing$ so that $N = M$. Finding the permutation matrix X is done by optimizing $argmin \sum_{i=1}^{N} \sum_{j=1}^{M} C_{i,j} X_{i,j}$. While an optimal solution exists for a bipartite graph ($|\Omega| = 2$), a multipartite graph, which exists if $|\Omega| > 2$, an optimal solution cannot necessarily be found since the problem is considered APX-complete [8,27]. However, for most cases $N = M$ is sufficiently small, so it can be assumed that an optimal solution can be found with a simple greedy matching between $|\Omega| > 2$. After matching, the obtained reliability data can be organized in a matrix. Instead of the shapes $\mathbb{S}$ now the classes contained in each annotation are used.

From the reliability data a coincidence matrix is calculated which contains the values $o_{ck} = \sum_u \frac{\text{Number of c-k pairs in unit } u}{m_u - 1}$, where m_u is the number of observers m for unit u. Further, we can calculate $n_c = \sum_k o_{ck}$ and $n = \sum_c n_c$. This allows calculation of α for nominal data using the following equation:

$$\alpha = 1 - \frac{D_o}{D_e} = \frac{(n-1)\sum_c o_{cc} - \sum_c n_c(n_c - 1)}{n(n-1) - \sum_c n_c(n_c - 1)} \qquad (3)$$

To discourage annotators from missing entries, the $\varnothing$ is replaced by a filler class instead of a "cannot code" or "no data available" entry like in the canonical Krippendorff alpha version. This leads to worse agreement scores if one annotator missed an entry that others found. A calculation example is attached in Appendix 1. Our code for calculating K-α on COCO[1] formatted data can be found here, https://github.com/Madave94/KrippendorffAlphaComputerVision.

---

[1] Format defintion: https://cocodataset.org/#format-data.

3.2 Method Properties

No Pipeline. Human annotated datasets often rely on multi-stage annotation pipelines [21,37]. For example, the COCO dataset uses a pipeline where the first three steps are category labeling, instance spotting and instance segmentation. This requires to a certain degree that the first stage (category labeling) is finished before the second stage (instance spotting) can start. This however, is not required when using the here presented adaptation of K-α. Since there are no stages in the annotation process, annotators can annotate independent from each other and annotations can be extended even after the initial dataset was finished (e.g., active learning). The process can only be considered stage-less within each annotation iteration and after creation of a final guideline.

Cherry-Picking Annotations. Besides determining the quality of annotations K-α allows the evaluation of rater vitality [39]. This evaluation is a way of measuring how well a single annotator compares to the entire annotator group. It is defined as:

$$v_i = \alpha_\Omega - \alpha_{\Omega \setminus \Omega_i} \tag{4}$$

In case the annotator performs better than the rest of the group, the value will be positive, while the value is negative if the annotator performs worse than the group. With the help of this measurement, annotators with inconsistent quality can be excluded from the annotation process or the final dataset.

Shape and Dimension Independence. Since the IoU is used as an evaluation metric, the entire annotation consistency evaluation method is dimension independent and can be used in 2D or 3D space. Furthermore, it can be used to evaluate annotations created to solve different tasks like semantic segmentation, object detection or instance segmentation. It is also easy to adapt for specific use cases such as action detection where the Generalized Intersection over Union (GIoU) [45] could be used.

Customizability. Different task, might have more-or-less strict annotation requirements or allow more ambiguity. In order to adapt which annotations are accepted, the α threshold can be increased, which would require a higher agreement between annotators for an image to be accepted. Further, if a larger overlap between annotations is necessary the IoU threshold could be increased, so that only more overlapping areas are considered to be matching. To allow more ambiguity, K-α can be used in the canonical form that does not penalize missing data as much by including a default value that provides no reliability data instead of a filler class as described above. Lastly, adoptions could be made by including the classes during calculation of the cost function [12] and allow a more "trustful" matching. Some adaptation examples can be found in Appendix 1.

Precise Guideline Requirement. A challenging part of any annotation process is the exact formulation of the annotation guideline. This process gets more difficult for more complex data. There are domains like medicine or civil engineering that require expert knowledge to formulate and annotate the data. While for simpler classes a pipeline approach might be more accessible, since for each stage only a single step needs to be finished, for more complex tasks, the context often matters and only a more holistic approach will yield success. Our method is more suited for complex tasks, where during the guideline definition, domain experts and data scientists are in an iterative process of further and further refining the exact annotation guideline.

Additional Annotations. Manual annotated data are expensive to obtain. On the other hand, it is also necessary to ensure sufficient quality of the ground truth data. Other datasets would often rely entirely on their annotation pipeline, either manual [37] or automated [35,56] without further quality evaluation. A better approach is to take a sample of the dataset by double annotating a subset [21] to evaluate the quality of the dataset. By using the here presented method, it is possible to evaluate such an annotation subset, however we see the application on more complex data that might contain some ambiguity or requires very strict quality control. An open question regarding these multi-per-image available annotations would be, if anything useful can be yielded by using them for training. A possible approach would be to use the annotations with some kind of a probability map similar to distillation learning [26].

4 TexBiG Dataset

4.1 Dataset Design

Due to the numerous digitization projects in the past decades, fundamental archival holdings and (historical) publications have been transferred into digital collections, which are thus highly relevant for research in the humanities. Although numerous digital collections from different disciplines are available, these have so far often only been the starting point for the analysis of one specific domain or just a few layout classes, e.g. images of newspapers [51] or headlines and visual content [34]. The analysis of the complexity of the entire layout of an investigation domain as well as the comparison between different domains has been missing so far.

The aim of creating the dataset is to be able to analyse the intersections and differences between various domains of investigation in the period from 1880 to 1930 concerning their layout and their respective text-image relation. The starting point for this analysis is the Virtual Laboratory [1], which is a collection of sources on the history of experimental life sciences for the period 1830 to about 1930. As part of the dataset creation process, this corpus of texts on the history of nature and science was expanded to include artistic, applied arts, and humorous-satirical text sources.

We made this selection because a search for new values can be observed in various areas of life and society in the late 19th century. This search is reflected, among other things, in an increased interest of artists in technology, industry and life sciences [18]. This interest culminated at the beginning of the 20th century in various social reform movements around the world, with a great impact on developments in technology, science, also politics [9,40]. The sources we have selected are exemplary for their respective research domains. They were selected concerning their significance and relevance for the domain in the time frame investigated.

For the analysis of genre- and media-specific layout structures of historical documents, instance segmentation is necessary because it recognizes objects in images along with their associated shape, as well as very fine structures. This is of particular importance to us because layouts change significantly over time. For example, there are frames and decorations on the pages or even drawings that need to be recognized in a shape-specific way, partly because they vary greatly between the domains of investigation, but also because they converge over time. The need for this is evident in the artistic-experimental works, which are characterized by a high degree of innovative layout design. Particularly in the course of the 1920s, there is an effort to break up the two-dimensionality of the book by disrupting clear layout structures [32]. In addition, new pictorial elements, such as the symbol of the arrow, are invented, which then develop out of the artistic-experimental domain and only a little later find application in other domains, especially in sciences, as well [20].

The documents we selected come from different genres and domains with a range of production processes and vary in page count (see: Table 1, for further information on the sources, see: Appendix 2).

Table 1. Document selection and layout type

Name	Layout	Pages	Domain	Year
"Pädagogisches Skizzenbuch" [29]	Non-Manhatten	61	Art	1925
"Zeitschrift für Physiologie und Psychologie der Sinnesorgane" [4]	Manhatten	493	Life Sciences	1907
"Lehre von den Tonempfindungen" [25]	Manhatten	658	Life Sciences	1863
"Das Kunstgewerbe" [5]	Mixed type	454	Applied Arts	1890–1892
"Fliegende Blätter" [2]	Mixed type	196	Satiric	1844–1845
"Centralblatt der Bauverwaltung" [3]	Mixed type	395	Architecture	1881

4.2 Dataset Construction

Creation of the dataset was done by a selected group of annotators, all with extended knowledge of the application domain. An initial guideline was developed by the organizers and presented to these annotators. After creation of the guideline each iteration of the annotation process can be considered stage-less, since each iteration does only require a single processing step by each annotator. According to the guideline, annotators started ground truthing the dataset. On the way to the final dataset, at multiple points, the preliminary dataset was evaluated on K-α and trained on intermediate models. These evaluations and results of the model served as an orientation to further modify and refine the annotation guideline. Annotators that got assigned a set of documents, did work the entire annotation process on these annotations, no reassignments were made in between iterations.

After all pages have been annotated, multiple correction iterations were done. In these correction iterations annotators would only receive information about which pages had a low agreement or disagreement, we set K-α < 0.8 as the threshold for pages to be reviewed. During the last iterations of the annotation process we decided to apply a stricter criterion to find overlooked annotations, which is easily adjustable with our K-α method.

A principal that we applied to our annotation process, is that annotators would generally not be allowed to view the annotations of their cross-annotators (annotators assigned to the same document image). However, for guideline re-evaluation purpose and solving of possible annotation ambiguities, selected annotations have been reviewed by the entire annotator group. We assume that it is more aspirational that annotators only rely on the guideline as their reference and do not discuss unclear cases with each other. In the best case this leads to a more and more refined guideline. Hence, the designed annotation guideline can later be reused for dataset extension.

For the annotation process, we used the computer vision annotation tool (CVAT) [48]. Besides our annotations we will also publish the annotation guideline as a supplement. The dataset and guideline can be found at https://doi. org/10.5281/zenodo.6885144.

4.3   Dataset Analysis

Figure 3 shows several comparisons with PubLayNet [56] and DocBank [35] to get an idea about characteristics and properties of our dataset.

Unsurprisingly, there is an unbalance in the dataset as shown in Fig. 3a as it is often the case in document analysis. This is further increased by research relevant classes like advertisements, logos, or frames. Due to the larger number of classes, the number of categories found per page as shown in Fig. 3b is also significantly larger than in other datasets. Reasons for this are due to; many classes that are "auxiliary" to the main text body like headers, footers and decorations. On the other hand, the total number of instances per document page appears slightly lower than in PubLayNet and a bit higher than in DocBank as depicted in Fig. 3c. Lastly, TexBiG contains more large regions > 40% of the document page compared to the benchmarked datasets, these details can be found in Fig. 3d. In Table 2 the split of the dataset is shown. A split 70-15-15 for train, validation and test respectively subset was chosen. Some prior information is included in the split since data are divided according to the different layout types so that each layout type is roughly represented the same in each subset.

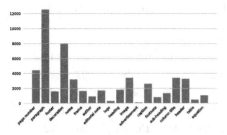

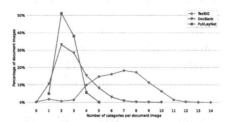

(a) Number of instances for each category. It shows the class in-balance of more often occurring classes like paragraph or decoration compared to authors or tables in the application domain data.

(b) Comparison of the average number of classes appearing per document page. It shows the more fine-grained class definition in the TexBiG dataset compared to datasets on contemporary literature.

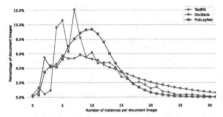

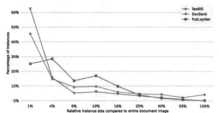

(c) The number of instances per document page shows that some classes that are split into multiple instances are combined in the TexBiG dataset, according to the requirements of the domain experts.

(d) Relative size of instances compared to the document page size. It shows that the TexBiG dataset contains a higher number of larger classes compared to other datasets.

Fig. 3. Dataset statistics.

4.4 Dataset Quality Evaluation

In this section the method previously explained is applied to evaluate the quality of the dataset. While technically values of K-α could be between -1 and $+1$, our dataset contains exactly one data point with a value of 0 and none below 0. While we think that someone might only want to use a subset of high-quality data for training and testing purposes, we release the entire dataset and leave the decision to researchers using our dataset to opt by themselves on whichever subset they use. In Fig. 4, a quality comparison of the data is shown, starting with a sorting into different quality regiments in Fig. 4a. The two Figs. 4b and 4c show a comparison between K-α and the F_1 score, both using an IoU of 0.5. It illustrates two things. First, with more document images containing more instances and classes the agreement decreases, which implies that the data gets more complex. Comparing α with F_1 shows that α is a more critical metric since the values are lower and more spread along the y axis, hence allowing a more differentiated evaluation. Three example images in Fig. 1 show how document

Table 2. Semantic structure statistic of training, validation and test sets in TexBiG.

Split	Train		Validation		Test		All	
Advertisement	61	0.17%	10	0.12%	18	0.23%	89	0.17%
Author	623	1.72%	142	1.72%	142	1.81%	907	1.73%
Caption	1816	5.01%	408	4.94%	360	4.58%	2584	4.93%
Column title	2341	6.45%	504	6.11%	547	6.97%	3392	6.48%
Decoration	5413	14.93%	1335	16.18%	1247	15.88%	7995	15.27%
Editorial note	1206	3.33%	265	3.21%	221	2.81%	1692	3.23%
Equation	764	2.11%	163	1.98%	119	1.52%	1046	2.0%
Footer	1093	3.01%	244	2.96%	244	3.11%	1581	3.02%
Footnote	544	1.5%	125	1.51%	120	1.53%	789	1.51%
Frame	1132	3.12%	237	2.87%	265	3.37%	1634	3.12%
Header	2267	6.25%	479	5.81%	507	6.46%	3253	6.21%
Heading	1224	3.37%	334	4.05%	234	2.98%	1792	3.42%
Image	2339	6.45%	536	6.5%	508	6.47%	3383	6.46%
Logo	218	0.6%	46	0.56%	34	0.43%	298	0.57%
Noise	2225	6.13%	466	5.65%	471	6.0%	3162	6.04%
Page number	3072	8.47%	655	7.94%	689	8.77%	4416	8.43%
Paragraph	8633	23.8%	2030	24.6%	1887	24.03%	12550	23.96%
Sub-heading	955	2.63%	207	2.51%	168	2.14%	1330	2.54%
Table	342	0.94%	65	0.79%	72	0.92%	479	0.91%
Total	36268	69.24%	8251	15.75%	7853	14.99%	52372	100.0%

images look if they contain a very high, high or low agreement. For visualization purpose we only used document images with a maximum of two annotators.

4.5 Benchmarking

As our baseline approach we use Mask R-CNN [23] with the Detectron2 [52] framework. After some hyper-parameter tuning, we found that the model worked best on our dataset with a ResNet50 [24] backbone, a feature pyramid network with 3×3 convolutions (FPN) [36] and weights from a model trained on Pub-LayNet[2]. The results can be found in Table 3 and the model is compared with the current state-of-the-art model VSR [55] for document layout analysis.

While VSR showed significant improvements on DocBank or PubLayNet, the results on our dataset are not as impressive. We tried a multitude of configurations to improve our results including changes to the ResNeXt-101 [53] backbone to a ResNeXt-50 backbone, switching BERT's [17] weights from the

---

[2] Weights: https://github.com/hpanwar08/detectron2.

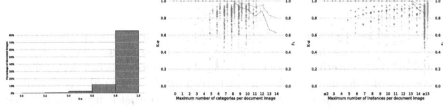

(a) Overall quality distribution.

(b) Quality distribution by number of different classes per page.

(c) Quality distribution by number of different instances per page.

Fig. 4. Dataset quality evaluation. In Figure b and c the F_1 score (orange) is compared with K-α (blue), with the line showing the median. (Color figure online)

Table 3. Benchmark results on TexBiG comparing Mask R-CNN and VSR for object detection and instance segmentation. Extended version in Appendix 3.

Task	Bounding box		Mask	
Model	Mask R-CNN	VSR	Mask R-CNN	VSR
mAP	73.18	75.90	65.43	65.80
mAP_{50}	85.12	87.80	80.31	82.60

English version[3] to a German version[4] and using both pre-trained models the authors provide. Even after an extended hyper-parameter search, we could only exceed the results that Mask R-CNN achieves slightly. We assume that there are multiple underlying issues, related to different properties of historical document layout analysis data.

Firstly, there is no existing ground truth text, we used Tesseract [28] to generate the text that was then used by the model to analyse the layout. We have to assume that the OCR is not perfect, hence the errors then propagate into the network and cause inconsistencies in the training data that do not exist for the plain layout data. This is an issue not specific to our dataset since none-born-digital documents do not have a perfect textual representation, which means that models using this kind of information need to deal with inherently noisy or slightly faulty data. Furthermore, the pre-trained models are trained on English data, while our data is mainly in German, we, therefore, could assume that the semantic backbone branch of VSR is not as applicable with the German word embeddings as with the English ones. This would mean that Mask R-CNN has a significant advantage since it has a reasonable weight initialization from transfer learning. The code to our VSR implementation can be found at https://github.com/Madave94/VSR-TexBiG-Dataset.

---

[3] Weights: https://huggingface.co/bert-base-uncased.

[4] Weights: https://huggingface.co/dbmdz/bert-base-german-uncased.

5   Conclusion

We have introduced a stage-less evaluation method to create high-quality annotations for data. The method can be generally applied in computer vision including 2D and 3D data, covering a variety of tasks. The method was developed during the creation of a domain-specific dataset (which will be made publicly available) that provides the community with a research resource that can be used for the development and design of new architectures and methods. When the dataset was benchmarked on a state-of-the-art model, it has shown that there is a gap between models, which were developed on contemporary layout analysis datasets and their application to historical documents. Lastly, with the current state of the dataset, models trained on it can already become a research tool that can be useful for researchers in digital humanities.

Acknowledgments. This work was supported by the Thuringian Ministry for Economy, Science and Digital Society/Thüringer Aufbaubank (TMWWDG/TAB). In addition, the following persons should be mentioned, without whom the project would not have been feasible: Sascha Breithaupt, Johannes Hess, Henrik Leisdon, Josephine Tiede and Ina Tscherner. Lastly, we would like to thank Christian Benz and Jan Frederick Eick for their in-depth discussion and feedback and in particular Henning Schmidgen.

Appendix 1

In this part some example calculations for K-α are illustrated. It shows different forms of how the metric can be adapted. As a helpful resource for further understanding we recommend reading [33]. There are two aspects that we assume will affect most adaptation possibilities: the creation of the cost matrix, which would change the creation of the reliability data and the handling of missing data when calculating K-α.

Figure 5 is used as an example and the resulting reliability matrix after the graph matching would look as shown in the matrix below. For this matching a IoU threshold of 0.5 is used and the normal matching is used.

	Unit 1	Unit 2	Unit 3	Unit 4	Unit 5
Ω_A	a_1	a_2	a_3	a_4	$\varnothing$
Ω_B	b_1	b_2	b_3	b_4	$\varnothing$
Ω_C	$\varnothing$	c_2	c_3	c_4	c_1

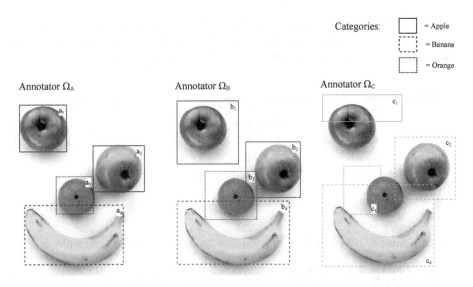

Fig. 5. Three annotator visual examples of matching with $IoU > 0.5$ threshold. Image source: https://commons.wikimedia.org/wiki/File:Smile_at_a_stranger.jpg

Strict Matching, Don't Allow Missing Data

After the reliability data is calculated all values a_n, b_m and c_p are replaces with their classes and for this case which doesn't allow missing data ∅ is replaced with the filler class 0. Hence, the matrix would look as follow:

	Unit 1	Unit 2	Unit 3	Unit 4	Unit 5
Ω_A	1	1	3	2	0
Ω_B	1	1	3	2	0
Ω_C	0	2	3	2	1

From here K-α is calculated the regular way, by first creating the coincidence matrix. Unit 1 contains $3(3-1) = 6$ pairs, 2 matching **1–1** pairs, 2 mismatching **1–0** pairs and 2 mismatching **0–1** pairs, it contributes $\frac{2}{3-1} = 1$ to the $o_{1,1}$ cell, $\frac{2}{3-1} = 1$ to the $o_{1,0}$ cell and $\frac{2}{3-1} = 1$ to $o_{0,1}$ cell. Unit 2 contains $\frac{3}{3-1} = 6$ pairs, 2 matching **1–1** pairs, 2 mismatching **1–2** pairs and 2 mismatching **2–1** pairs, it contributes $\frac{2}{3-1} = 1$ to the $o_{1,1}$ cell, $\frac{2}{3-1} = 1$ to the $o_{1,2}$ cell and $\frac{2}{3-1} = 1$ to the $o_{2,1}$ cell. Unit 3 contains $\frac{3}{3-1} = 6$ pairs, 6 matching **3–3** pairs, $\frac{6}{3-1} = 3$ to the $o_{3,3}$ cell. Unit 4 contains $\frac{3}{3-1} = 6$ pairs, 6 matching **2–2** pairs, it contributes $\frac{6}{3-1} = 3$ to the $o_{2,2}$ cell. Unit 5 contains $\frac{3}{3-1} = 6$ pairs, 2 matching **0–0** pairs, 2 mismatching **0–1** pairs and 2 mismatching **1–0** pairs, it contributes $\frac{2}{3-1} = 1$ to the $o_{0,0}$ cell, $\frac{2}{3-1} = 1$ to the $o_{0,1}$ cell and $\frac{2}{3-1} = 1$ to the $o_{1,0}$ cell. As an example the first value in the coincidence matrix $o_{0,0}$ is the sum of all value in the five units related to $o_{0,0}$, which is rather straight forward since only unit 5 contains **0–0** pairs, hence $o_{0,0} = 1$. The coincidence matrix is as follows:

	0	1	2	3	
0	1	2	0	0	3
1	2	2	1	0	5
2	0	1	3	0	4
3	0	0	0	3	3
	3	5	4	3	15

Computing K-α is now done via Eq. 3, which means for our example:

$$\alpha = \frac{(15-1)(1+2+3+3) - [3(3-1) + 5(5-1) + 4(4-1) + 3(3-1)]}{15(15-1) - [3(3-1) + 5(5-1) + 4(4-1) + 3(3-1)]} = 0.49$$

Strict Matching, but Allow Missing Data

A second possible version build on the same example shown in Fig. 5 that allows missing data, would transfer the reliability data slightly different. Instead of 0 a * will be used indicating missing data, which won't be included in the calculation of α.

	Unit 1	Unit 2	Unit 3	Unit 4	Unit 5
Ω_A	1	1	3	2	*
Ω_B	1	1	3	2	*
Ω_C	*	2	3	2	1

Calculating the coincidence matrix would be done in the same way as before for Unit 2, Unit 3 and Unit 4, but Unit 1 and Unit 5 are different. Unit 1 contains $2(2-1) = 2$ pairs, which are 2 matching **1–1** pairs it contributes $\frac{2}{2-1} = 2$ to the $o_{1,1}$ cell. Since Unit 4 only contains a single entry, no pairable unit can be found. The coincidence matrix would therefore be:

	1	2	3	
1	3	1	0	4
2	1	3	0	4
3	0	0	3	3
	4	4	3	11

This results in a calculation of alpha with the following values:

$$\alpha = \frac{(11-1)(3+3+3)-[4(4-1)+4(4-1)+3(3-1)]}{11(11-1)-[4(4-1)+4(4-1)+3(3-1)]} = 0.75$$

Appendix 2

Further information to the historical sources:

The selected documents were already available as digitized sources. They all come from publicly accessible digital collections. These are: the digital collections of University Library Heidelberg ("Pädagogisches Skizzenbuch" [29], "Das Kunstgewerbe" [5] and "Fliegende Blätter" [2]), the Internet Archive ("Zeitschrift für Physiologie und Psychologie der Sinnesorgane" [4]), the Virtual Laboratory ("Lehre von den Tonempfindungen" [25]) and the digital collections of the Berlin State Library ("Centralblatt der Bauverwaltung" [3]).

The Pedagogical Sketchbook by Paul Klee is part of the artistic-experimental domain. It is the second volume in the Bauhaus book series. The so-called Bauhaus books are a series of books published from 1925 to 1930 by Walter Gropius and Lazlo Moholy-Nagy. Although the books appeared as a series in the same publishing house (Albert Langen Verlag), the respective layout varied widely [11]. The publication sequence was also irregular. While in 1925 alone eight publications of the series could be published, in 1926 there were only two and in 1927, 1928, 1929 and 1930 one more volume each. The publication of Klee presented not only his artwork but also presented his art theoretical knowledge. At the same time, it presented aspects of his extensive lectures on visual form at the Bauhaus and conveyed his way of thinking and working on this topic.

Both the journal "Physiology und Psychologie der Sinnesorgane" and Hermann von Helmholtz's publication "Lehre von den Tonempfindungen" are part of the domain of life sciences. The different types of publications (journal and monograph) have different but typical layout components within their domain, which is why they were both integrated into the dataset.

The journal "Das Kunstgewerbe" appeared every fourteen days from 1890 to 1895 and belongs to the domain of applied arts. The individual issues had a length of 10 pages and a manageable number of illustrations, but the pages were often designed with decorative frames and ornaments.

The illustrated magazine "Fliegende Blätter" appeared from 1844 to 1944, at first irregularly several times a month, later regularly once a week. The humorous-satirical publication was richly illustrated and held in high esteem among the German bourgeoisie. At the same time, the "Fliegende Blätter" are significant both artistically and in terms of printing, due to the high quality of its layout [50].

The "Centralblatt der Bauverwaltung" was a professional journal intended to satisfy the need for information in the construction sector. The journal was first published in April 1881 by the publishing house Ernst & Sohn, in 1931 it was merged with the "Zeitschrift für Bauwesen", in 1944 the publication was discontinued. The Ministry of Public Works acted as publisher until 1919, and from 1920 to 1931 the Prussian Ministry of Finance. The journal was to serve as a supplement to the existing trade journals and, in contrast to these, was to have a faster publication schedule. Information about construction projects and competitions, projects currently being implemented, new technologies and amended legal framework conditions were to reach the readership more quickly than before and also address international developments. At the same time, however, the journal was to be less elaborately designed than the existing trade organs and art journals. Although the Ministry of Public Works was the editor and the structure of the journal was divided into "official" and "non-official" parts, it can nevertheless not be characterized as a purely official journal of authorities [19].

Appendix 3

See Table 4.

Table 4. Benchmark results on TexBiG comparing Mask R-CNN and VSR for object detection and instance segmentation. This is the extended version of the table, including the different classes.

Task	Bounding Box		Mask	
Model	Mask R-CNN	VSR	Mask R-CNN	VSR
mAP	73.18	75.90	65.43	65.80
mAP_{50}	85.12	87.80	80.32	82.60
Advertisement	74.82	75.20	76.61	75.50
Author	52.49	55.40	47.30	47.80
Caption	44.43	52.10	45.48	49.30
Column title	86.89	89.20	85.73	82.00
Decoration	55.89	28.10	52.03	23.20
Editorial note	67.36	69.20	64.05	63.40
Equation	54.74	81.10	46.90	67.60
Footer	90.99	91.80	91.72	91.70
Footnote	83.26	84.30	83.58	82.30
Frame	91.99	91.50	0.00	0.00
Header	98.33	98.90	98.46	98.70
Heading	71.26	82.40	70.51	76.00
Image	70.45	73.10	60.99	61.80
Logo	87.78	89.80	78.33	81.40
Noise	82.57	83.30	65.59	65.60
Page number	78.29	69.30	75.33	60.70
Paragraph	86.90	90.50	86.60	89.20
Sub-heading	54.41	62.50	56.14	57.80
Table	57.58	74.40	57.88	76.30

References

1. The Virtual Laboratory. https://vlp-new.ur.de/
2. Fliegende Blätter (1845–1944). https://nbn-resolving.org/urn:nbn:de:bsz:16-diglit-35697
3. Centralblatt der Bauverwaltung (1881–1931). https://digital.zlb.de/viewer/image/14688302_1881/1/
4. Zeitschrift für Psychologie und Physiologie der Sinnesorgane (1890–1909). https://ia804503.us.archive.org/25/items/bub_gb_2dIbAAAAMAAJ/bub_gb_2dIbAAAAMAAJ.pdf
5. Das Kunstgewerbe (1890–1895). https://doi.org/10.11588/diglit.18553. http://kunstgewerDbe.uni-hd.de
6. ABBYY Development Inc.: ABBYY FineReader PDF 15. https://pdf.abbyy.com/de/finereader-pdf/
7. Artstein, R.: Inter-annotator agreement. In: Ide, N., Pustejovsky, J. (eds.) Handbook of Linguistic Annotation, pp. 297–313. Springer, Dordrecht (2017). https://doi.org/10.1007/978-94-024-0881-2_11
8. Ausiello, G., Crescenzi, P., Gambosi, G., Kann, V., Marchetti-Spaccamela, A., Protasi, M.: Complexity and Approximation: Combinatorial Optimization Problems and Their Approximability Properties. Springer, Heidelberg (2012)
9. Baumgartner, J. (ed.): Aufbrüche - Seitenpfade - Abwege: Suchbewegungen und Subkulturen im 20. Jahrhundert; Festschrift für Ulrich Linse. Königshausen & Neumann, Würzburg (2004)
10. Binmakhashen, G.M., Mahmoud, S.A.: Document layout analysis: a comprehensive survey. ACM Comput. Surv. **52**(6), 1–36 (2020). https://doi.org/10.1145/3355610. https://dl.acm.org/doi/10.1145/3355610
11. Bruening, U.: Bauhausbücher. Grafische Synthese - synthetische Grafik. Neue Bauhausbücher, pp. 281–296 (2009)
12. Carion, N., Massa, F., Synnaeve, G., Usunier, N., Kirillov, A., Zagoruyko, S.: End-to-end object detection with transformers. In: Vedaldi, A., Bischof, H., Brox, T., Frahm, J.-M. (eds.) ECCV 2020. LNCS, vol. 12346, pp. 213–229. Springer, Cham (2020). https://doi.org/10.1007/978-3-030-58452-8_13
13. Clausner, C., Antonacopoulos, A., Pletschacher, S.: ICDAR2019 competition on recognition of documents with complex layouts - RDCL2019, p. 6 (2019)
14. Clausner, C., Pletschacher, S., Antonacopoulos, A.: Aletheia - an advanced document layout and text ground-truthing system for production environments. In: 2011 International Conference on Document Analysis and Recognition, pp. 48–52 (2011). https://doi.org/10.1109/ICDAR.2011.19
15. Cohen, J.: A coefficient of agreement for nominal scales. Educ. Psychol. Meas. **20**(1), 37–46 (1960)
16. Dengel, A., Shafait, F.: Analysis of the logical layout of documents. In: Doermann, D., Tombre, K. (eds.) Handbook of Document Image Processing and Recognition, Chap. 6. Springer, London (2014). https://doi.org/10.1007/978-0-85729-859-1_6. http://link.springer.com/10.1007/978-0-85729-859-1_6
17. Devlin, J., Chang, M.W., Lee, K., Toutanova, K.: BERT: pre-training of deep bidirectional transformers for language understanding. arXiv preprint arXiv:1810.04805 (2018)
18. Flach, S., Weigel, S. (eds.): WissensKünste: das Wissen der Künste und die Kunst des Wissens = The Knowledge of the Arts and the Art of Knowledge. VDG, Weimar (2011). http://www.gbv.de/dms/weimar/toc/64247172X_toc.pdf

19. Froschauer, E.M.: "An die Leser!": Baukunst darstellen und vermitteln; Berliner Architekturzeitschriften um 1900. Wasmuth, Tübingen (2009)
20. Giedion, S.: Mechanization takes command a contribution to anonymous history. University of Minnesota (1948)
21. Gupta, A., Dollar, P., Girshick, R.: LVIS: a dataset for large vocabulary instance segmentation. In: Proceedings of the IEEE Conference on Computer Vision and Pattern Recognition (CVPR) (2019)
22. Hayes, A.F., Krippendorff, K.: Answering the call for a standard reliability measure for coding data. Commu. Methods Meas. 1(1), 77–89 (2007)
23. He, K., Gkioxari, G., Dollár, P., Girshick, R.: Mask R-CNN. In: Proceedings of the IEEE International Conference on Computer Vision (ICCV), pp. 2961–2969 (2017)
24. He, K., Zhang, X., Ren, S., Sun, J.: Deep residual learning for image recognition. In: Proceedings of the IEEE Conference on Computer Vision and Pattern Recognition (CVPR), pp. 770–778 (2016)
25. von Helmholtz, H.: Die Lehre von den Tonempfindungen als physiologische Grundlage für die Theorie der Musik. F. Vieweg, Braunschweig (1863). https://vlp-new.ur.de/records/lit3483
26. Hinton, G., Vinyals, O., Dean, J., et al.: Distilling the knowledge in a neural network. arXiv preprint arXiv:1503.02531 2(7) (2015)
27. Kann, V.: Maximum bounded 3-dimensional matching is max SNP-complete. Inf. Process. Lett. 37(1), 27–35 (1991)
28. Kay, A.: Tesseract: an open-source optical character recognition engine. Linux J. 2007(159), 2 (2007)
29. Klee, P.: Pädagogisches Skizzenbuch. Bauhausbücher; 2, Langen, München, 2. aufl. edn. (1925). https://doi.org/10.11588/diglit.26771. http://digi.ub.uni-heidelberg.de/diglit/klee1925
30. Kofax Inc.: OmniPage Ultimate. https://www.kofax.de/products/omnipage
31. Koichi, K.: Page segmentation techniques in document analysis. In: Doermann, D., Tombre, K. (eds.) Handbook of Document Image Processing and Recognition, Chap. 5. Springer, London (2014). https://doi.org/10.1007/978-0-85729-859-1_5. http://link.springer.com/10.1007/978-0-85729-859-1_5
32. Krauthausen, K.: Paul Valéry and geometry: instrument, writing model, practice. Preprint/Max-Planck-Institut für Wissenschaftsgeschichte 406, Max-Planck-Inst. für Wissenschaftsgeschichte, Berlin (2010)
33. Krippendorff, K.: Computing Krippendorff's alpha-reliability (2011). https://repository.upenn.edu/asc_papers/43
34. Lee, B.C.G., et al.: The newspaper navigator dataset: extracting headlines and visual content from 16 million historic newspaper pages in chronicling America. In: Proceedings of the 29th ACM International Conference on Information and Knowledge Management, pp. 3055–3062 (2020)
35. Li, M., et al.: DocBank: a benchmark dataset for document layout analysis. arXiv preprint arXiv:2006.01038 (2020)
36. Lin, T.Y., Dollár, P., Girshick, R., He, K., Hariharan, B., Belongie, S.: Feature pyramid networks for object detection. In: Proceedings of the IEEE Conference on Computer Vision and Pattern Recognition (CVPR), pp. 2117–2125 (2017)
37. Lin, T.-Y., et al.: Microsoft COCO: common objects in context. In: Fleet, D., Pajdla, T., Schiele, B., Tuytelaars, T. (eds.) ECCV 2014. LNCS, vol. 8693, pp. 740–755. Springer, Cham (2014). https://doi.org/10.1007/978-3-319-10602-1_48

38. Marinai, S.: Introduction to document analysis and recognition. In: Marinai, S., Fujisawa, H. (eds.) Machine Learning in Document Analysis and Recognition. SCI, vol. 90, pp. 1–20. Springer, Heidelberg (2008). https://doi.org/10.1007/978-3-540-76280-5_1

39. McCulloh, I., Burck, J., Behling, J., Burks, M., Parker, J.: Leadership of data annotation teams. In: 2018 International Workshop on Social Sensing (SocialSens), pp. 26–31 (2018). https://doi.org/10.1109/SocialSens.2018.00018

40. McLoughlin, W.G.: Revivals, Awakening and Reform. University of Chicago Press, Chicago (1978)

41. Nassar, J., Pavon-Harr, V., Bosch, M., McCulloh, I.: Assessing data quality of annotations with Krippendorff alpha for applications in computer vision. arXiv preprint arXiv:1912.10107 (2019)

42. Papadopoulos, C., Pletschacher, S., Clausner, C., Antonacopoulos, A.: The IMPACT dataset of historical document images. In: Proceedings of the 2nd International Workshop on Historical Document Imaging and Processing - HIP 2013, Washington, District of Columbia, p. 123. ACM Press (2013). https://doi.org/10.1145/2501115.2501130. http://dl.acm.org/citation.cfm?doid=2501115.2501130

43. Pattern Recognition & Image Analysis Research Lab: Aletheia document analysis system. https://www.primaresearch.org/tools/Aletheia

44. Ren, S., He, K., Girshick, R., Sun, J.: Faster R-CNN: towards real-time object detection with region proposal networks. arXiv:1506.01497 [cs], January 2016. http://arxiv.org/abs/1506.01497

45. Rezatofighi, H., Tsoi, N., Gwak, J., Sadeghian, A., Reid, I., Savarese, S.: Generalized intersection over union. In: The IEEE Conference on Computer Vision and Pattern Recognition (CVPR), June 2019

46. Ribeiro, V., Avila, S., Valle, E.: Handling inter-annotator agreement for automated skin lesion segmentation. arXiv preprint arXiv:1906.02415 (2019)

47. Richarz, J., Fink, G.A., et al.: Towards semi-supervised transcription of handwritten historical weather reports. In: 2012 10th IAPR International Workshop on Document Analysis Systems, pp. 180–184. IEEE (2012)

48. Sekachev, B., et al.: OpenCV/CVAT: v1.1.0, August 2020. https://doi.org/10.5281/zenodo.4009388

49. Shen, Z., Zhang, K., Dell, M.: A large dataset of historical Japanese documents with complex layouts. arXiv:2004.08686 [cs], April 2020. http://arxiv.org/abs/2004.08686

50. Stielau, A.: Kunst und Künstler im Blickfeld der satirischen Zeitschriften 'Fliegende Blätter' und 'Punch'. Aachen University (1976)

51. Wevers, M., Smits, T.: The visual digital turn: using neural networks to study historical images. Digital Scholarship in the Humanities, January 2019. https://doi.org/10.1093/llc/fqy085. https://academic.oup.com/dsh/advance-article/doi/10.1093/llc/fqy085/5296356

52. Wu, Y., Kirillov, A., Massa, F., Lo, W.Y., Girshick, R.: Detectron2 (2019). https://github.com/facebookresearch/detectron2

53. Xie, S., Girshick, R., Dollár, P., Tu, Z., He, K.: Aggregated residual transformations for deep neural networks. In: Proceedings of the IEEE Conference on Computer Vision and Pattern Recognition (CVPR), pp. 1492–1500 (2017)

54. Xu, Y., Li, M., Cui, L., Huang, S., Wei, F., Zhou, M.: LayoutLM: pre-training of text and layout for document image understanding. arXiv:1912.13318 [cs], June 2020. https://doi.org/10.1145/3394486.3403172. http://arxiv.org/abs/1912.13318

55. Zhang, P., et al.: VSR: a unified framework for document layout analysis combining vision, semantics and relations. In: Lladós, J., Lopresti, D., Uchida, S. (eds.) ICDAR 2021. LNCS, vol. 12821, pp. 115–130. Springer, Cham (2021). https://doi.org/10.1007/978-3-030-86549-8_8

56. Zhong, X., Tang, J., Yepes, A.J.: PubLayNet: largest dataset ever for document layout analysis. In: 2019 International Conference on Document Analysis and Recognition (ICDAR), pp. 1015–1022. IEEE (2019)

End-to-End Single Shot Detector Using Graph-Based Learnable Duplicate Removal

Shuxiao Ding[1,2(✉)] , Eike Rehder[1] , Lukas Schneider[1] , Marius Cordts[1] ,
and Jürgen Gall[2]

[1] Mercedes-Benz AG, Stuttgart, Germany
{shuxiao.ding,eike.rehder,lukas.schneider,
marius.cordts}@mercedes-benz.com
[2] University of Bonn, Bonn, Germany
gall@iai.uni-bonn.de

Abstract. Non-Maximum Suppression (NMS) is widely used to remove duplicates in object detection. In strong disagreement with the deep learning paradigm, NMS often remains as the only heuristic step. Learning NMS methods have been proposed that are either designed for Faster-RCNN or rely on separate networks. In contrast, learning NMS for SSD models is not well investigated. In this paper, we show that even a very simple rescoring network can be trained end-to-end with an underlying SSD model to solve the duplicate removal problem efficiently. For this, detection scores and boxes are refined from image features by modeling relations between detections in a Graph Neural Network (GNN). Our approach is applicable to the large number of object proposals in SSD using a pre-filtering head. It can easily be employed in arbitrary SSD-like models with weight-shared box predictor. Experiments on MS-COCO and KITTI show that our method improves accuracy compared with other duplicate removal methods at significantly lower inference time.

Keywords: End-to-end detection · learning duplicate removal · relationship modeling

1 Introduction

Object detection is a fundamental and crucial task in computer vision. In the deep learning era, most object detection algorithms can be divided into two different categories: one-stage detectors such as YOLO [17] and Single Shot Detector (SSD) [15] or two-stage detectors such as Faster-RCNN [18], Mask-RCNN [5], R-FCN [2]. In real-time applications, SSD and its variants MobileNet

---

Supplementary Information The online version contains supplementary material available at https://doi.org/10.1007/978-3-031-16788-1_23.

[8], RetinaNet [13], EfficientDet [22] have become more and more popular due to their efficiency, e.g. in robotics or automated driving. Regardless of the detection pipeline, the object detectors usually generate multiple detections for a single object. Therefore, Non-Maximum Suppression (NMS) is employed to remove these duplicates. NMS is a heuristic algorithm that solely relies on the score and overlap between detections as criterion for removal. In order to make use of the meaningful image features of the detection system, it is desirable to replace the hand-engineered NMS by a learnable component.

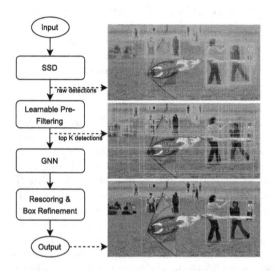

Fig. 1. We propose an end-to-end duplicate removal network for SSD. To deal with the large amount of raw detections (*top*), the network pre-filters all detections (*middle*). These are fed into a GNN to pass information between overlapping detections. Finally, the network performs a rescoring and a box refinement for each candidate, aiming to produce only one high-scoring and precise box for each instance (*bottom*). The opacity of boxes is proportional to the score. Different categories are depicted in different colors.

Following the deep learning paradigm of the end-to-end optimization, learning-based duplicate removal approaches have been proposed. Most of them use a separate network which processes raw detections with handcrafted features from an existing object detector [6,7,16]. Usually, these duplicate removal methods are not directly applicable for SSD-like architectures and, thus, can hardly be used in real time applications. The reasons for this are mainly due to two challenges: First, SSD provides significantly more raw detections (*top* image of Fig. 1) compared to its two-stage counterpart. Since all existing approaches model relations between detections, the computational complexity increases quadratically with the number of input detections. Second, image features in SSD are of lower dimensionality. Thus, they are less discriminative when embedding them into the input of a separate duplicate removal network. Since especially real time applications demand for the use of SSD architectures, these challenges have to be overcome in order to employ true end-to-end detectors.

In this paper, we propose learnable duplicate removal for SSD. To cope with the large amount of candidates, we first introduce a learned pre-filtering network that filters the highly overlapping boxes from SSD raw detections in an early stage (*middle* image of Fig. 1). We then model interactions between the top-K filtered detection candidates to eliminate those corresponding to the same object. The set of detections is regarded as an undirected graph, where an *edge* exists between two detections (*nodes*) if they overlap. In our work, node features are propagated along the edges in the graph using Graph Convolutional Network (GCN) [11] in order to obtain a single refined and rescored detection per object (*bottom* image of Fig. 1). Although existing learnable duplicate removals also model these relationships, they either rely on a deep network architecture that requires a long inference time [6,7,16] or treat the detections as a fully-connected graph [9,16]. In contrast, the architecture of GCN is simple and does not require the often uninformative fully-connected relationship. Thus it is applicable to real-time sensitive applications. To train the network, we propose to use a bipartite matching that uniquely assigns ground-truth labels to detections. It considers the localization and classification quality simultaneously instead of using a greedy matching as in existing related works.

We showcase the effectiveness of our proposed learning duplicate removal with two popular SSD models: EfficientDet [22] and RetinaNet [13]. Extensive experiments on COCO [14] and KITTI [4] show that even such a simple network architecture is still able to produce generally higher accuracy than other duplicate removal methods. While maintaining the accuracy, our approach has an extremely small complexity and does not require any post-processing other than thresholding. Consequently, it runs significantly faster: the inference of the entire model is 24.5% and 19.5% faster than NMS for EfficientDet-D0 and RetinaNet-ResNet50, respectively, while achieving better mAP.

2   Related Work

As of today, standard detection networks still employ manually engineered duplicate removal such as NMS [15,18,22]. In order to remove it, two categories of approaches exist. Either, the detector is designed to produce duplicate-free detections or they are removed by an additional network component.

NMS-Free Object Detection. Networks that can operate without an explicit NMS need to suppress duplicates within their detection pipeline. In the field of human detection in crowded situation, [20] proposed a pipeline with a CNN backbone as encoder for extracting visual features and a LSTM controller as decoder for generating detection set iteratively. Inspired by [20] and [25], DETR [1] and its successors [19,28] generate the detection set directly by implicit relationship modeling using Transformer encoder and decoder after a CNN feature extractor. CenterNet [27] identifies local maximum in the centerness score, which effectively is a NMS for box center. Our approach also learns an additional score, but it identifies non-duplicate boxes by finding global maximum due to our one-to-one target assignment. OneNet [21] uses the sum of classification and localization loss as matching cost and a one-to-one matching in target assignment. While we also consider both classification and localization in label assignment, the features in our approach is updated by explicit relationship modeling between detections.

Learning Duplicate Removal. Instead of the classical NMS, learnable duplicate removal techniques have been proposed. They can be divided into two groups. The first group employed a separate network that processes detection results from an object detector. GossipNet [7] uses handcrafted detection pair features as input and updates the representation of every detection by iterative communication between every detection pair. [16] also encodes the handcrafted features from raw detections as input and rescores detections with bidirectional RNN and self-attention. However, the network architectures of above methods are complicated and not shown to be applicable to SSD-like architectures such as RetinaNet [13] or EfficientDet [23]. A second line of these works proposed end-to-end trainable networks. For two-stage detectors, Relation Networks [9] allow learning duplicate removal using an object relation module based on scaled dot-product self-attention [25], which is easily attached to the refinement network in Faster-RCNN. For one-stage detectors, [26] proposed a positive sample selector by attaching a new head in FCOS [24] for eliminating the NMS. In this work, we show that a learning duplicate removal network can also be applied to SSD-like architectures and trained end-to-end.

3   Method

3.1   System Overview

An overview of our proposed end-to-end SSD with learned duplicate removal is shown in Fig. 2. As a central concept, we treat detections as nodes in a graph and modify their predictions through a GNN. For this, we start off with SSD as the detection architecture. To reduce the number of detection candidates, we attach a pre-filtering head to the classification branch which produces a score offset for all detections followed by a top-K sampler. The filtered detections are then fed into a Graph Convolutional Network (GCN), which updates node representations by message-passing and finally outputs a score offset and box refinement parameters. In training, the final detections are matched one-to-one with ground-truth using Hungarian Algorithm.

3.2   Local Candidate Pre-filtering

Given a standard SSD, detections are generated based on an evenly distributed grid of prior boxes with different locations, sizes, and aspect ratios for differ-ent feature map scales. Therefore, the number of detection candidates in SSD

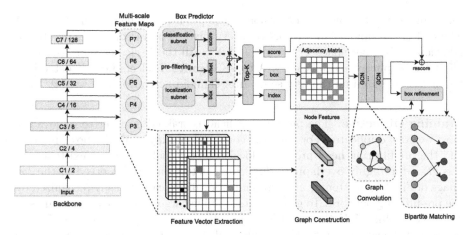

Fig. 2. An overview of our proposed network architecture. First, the base SSD model produces multi-scale feature maps using a backbone network including some feature pyramid network (FPN). Raw detections are generated by a weight-shared box predictor. The pre-filtering is done by a rescoring using an additional head and a top-K selection. The graph adjacency is constructed based on the overlap between detections, while initial node features are extracted from the feature map. The graph data is then processed by GCN layers that enable message passing between neighboring detections. The updated node representations are projected into a score offset and four box parameters. For training, the rescored and refined detection sets are matched uniquely with ground truth using a bipartite matcher.

has an obvious higher order of magnitude than Faster-RCNN that pre-filters object proposals in RPN stage using an NMS. As the learned duplicate removal relies on the relationship of overlapping detections and the computational overhead explodes when increasing the number of elements, a candidate sampling for downstream duplicate removal is necessary. A straight-forward filtering is a top-K algorithm which keeps K detections with highest scores because most detections in SSD are background. However, since high scoring detections may be highly redundant, this might discard positives with relatively low confidence. Classical NMS, on the other hand, is able to keep these by processing all detection candidates. For this reason, we aim to reduce the candidates to a reasonable amount while keeping as many potential true positives as possible.

Pre-filtering Head. Similar to previous learned NMS approaches [7], we consider the filtering as a learnable rescoring problem. To this end, we add a network which produces a score offset to indicate whether a detection candidate should be removed. Inspired by [26] for FCOS [24], we attach an additional head to the classification subnet. Parallel to the last convolutional layer that generates C binary classifications z_c^{cls} for every anchor in SSD, the new head predicts a class-agnostic confidence Δz^{pre} by a single 3×3 convolutional layer. C corresponds to the number of categories. Given a feature map $F_s \in \mathbb{R}^{H_s \times W_s \times C_F}$ with downsampling rate s, the output dimension of the pre-filtering head is $H_s \times W_s \times A$ where A is the number of anchors on every pixel. The rescoring is done by an addition in the logit space $z_c^{\mathrm{pre}} = z_c^{\mathrm{cls}} + \Delta z^{\mathrm{pre}}$. All the C classes share the same offset for simplicity and efficiency. A top-K algorithm selects best K detections for each class based on the new score after sigmoid activation $s_c^{\mathrm{pre}} = \sigma(z_c^{\mathrm{pre}})$.

Training Objective. The pre-filtering head is trained in order to remove the most obvious duplicates. For this, the convolutional layers in the box predictor and the pre-filtering head provide a local receptive field of object existence. In this case, the highly overlapping duplicated detections (as observed in the *top* image of Fig. 1) that stem from surrounding locations can be easily recognized by the pre-filtering network. To generate its training targets, we use a class-agnostic NMS with a high IoU threshold $T_1 = 0.9$. By setting a high threshold T_1, the outputs of the supervising NMS are more likely to cover all true positives while only discarding highly overlapping duplicates. Let $y_i \in \{0, 1\}$ be the result of the supervision NMS that indicates whether certain box i is kept after the class-agnostic NMS, the pre-filtering head is trained with a Binary Cross Entropy loss $\mathcal{L}_{\mathrm{pre}} = \sum_i \mathrm{BCE}(\Delta z_i^{\mathrm{pre}}, y_i)$. This training objective produces sparser detection sets which lead to a sparser adjacency matrix with less local fully-connected clusters when constructing the overlap-based graph. This is helpful to mitigate the problem caused by over-smoothing [12] in GNN.

3.3   Learning NMS Based on GCN

Graph Construction. Let $G = (V, E)$ be a graph that we construct from detection candidates, where V is the set of nodes and E is the set of edges between them. The nodes V correspond to the top K detections after pre-filtering. An adjacency matrix $\mathbf{A} \in \{0, 1\}^{K \times K}$ represents the edges between nodes. For a pair of detection boxes (b_i, b_j) from V, an edge exists (i.e. $A_{ij} = 1$) if $\mathrm{IoU}(b_i, b_j) > 0$ and otherwise $A_{ij} = 0$. Based on every filtered detection, we trace the location (x_s, y_s) in its corresponding feature map F_s at scale s and extract the feature vector $\mathbf{f}_A \in \mathbb{R}^{C_F}$ at this location as image feature. Since SSD generates multiple detections on every feature map pixel, detections that stem from the same pixel share the same image feature. For a more discriminative feature vector, we follow Relational Network [9] to use a rank feature. Concretely, all the K detections are sorted in descending order and each detection is given a rank r in $[1, K]$. This scalar is then embedded into a rank feature $\mathbf{f}_R \in \mathbb{R}^{C_F}$ using a positional encoding as demonstrated in [25]. Both feature vectors are projected into C_N-dimension and then added to build the initial node feature $\mathbf{f} = \mathbf{W}_R \mathbf{f}_R + \mathbf{W}_A \mathbf{f}_A$, where $\mathbf{W}_R$ and $\mathbf{W}_A$ are learnable weights. We found that additional handcrafted features e.g. box coordinate, score or box overlap do not lead to performance gain in our approach. Because image features are extracted from different feature map scales, an SSD architecture with weight-shared box predictor is necessary, which forces feature maps in different scales to represent an equal semantic level so that the feature vectors are comparable in the same graph.

Network Architecture. We employ the simple Graph Convolutional Network [11] for updating detection representations by propagating messages between overlapping detections. Given the adjacency matrix $\mathbf{A} \in \mathbb{R}^{K \times K}$ and an input feature matrix $\mathbf{F} \in \mathbb{R}^{K \times C_N}$, a Graph Convolutional Layer generates the output feature matrix $\mathbf{F}' \in \mathbb{R}^{K \times C'_N}$ by:

$$\mathbf{F}' = \mathbf{D}^{-1/2} \mathbf{A} \mathbf{D}^{-1/2} \mathbf{F} \mathbf{W} + \mathbf{b}, \tag{1}$$

where $\mathbf{D}$ denotes the degree matrix of $\mathbf{A}$ with $D_{ii} = \sum_j A_{ij}$. $\mathbf{W}$ and $\mathbf{b}$ are learnable weight and bias respectively. Note that we don't add the self-loop with $\hat{\mathbf{A}} = \mathbf{A} + \mathbf{I}$ because our IoU-based adjacency matrix includes it naturally. After message propagation from stacked Graph Convolutional Layers in Eq. 1, the node representations contain information on its neighborhood.

We then use a linear classifier to predict a score offset based on the updated feature representations. In a multi-class setting $(C > 1)$, the same network is operated on all classes independently and thus generates the class-specific score offset Δz_c^{gcn} for class c. Together with the class-agnostic offset from pre-filtering, the final score of a detection for category c is generated by sum in logit space followed by a sigmoid function: $s_c = \sigma(z_c^{\text{cls}} + \Delta z^{\text{pre}} + \Delta z_c^{\text{gcn}})$. The scores of duplicated boxes are strongly decreased after rescoring so that the remaining high-scoring boxes are identified as true-positives using a score threshold.

When solely applying a rescoring, a detection box with highest updated score might have an imperfect localization. Combined with our matching strategy (Sect. 3.4), a confident prediction with insufficient precise localization will be less likely to be matched. To solve this problem, a box refinement can be applied which benefits from the information of neighboring duplicated detections in message passing. Therefore, we add an additional fully-connected layer to predict four box coordinate offsets $\{\Delta x, \Delta y, \Delta w, \Delta h\}$ according to the box encoding in Faster-RCNN [18] parallel to the score offset:

$$\Delta x = (x' - x)/w, \ \Delta y = (y' - y)/h, \ \Delta w = \log(w'/w), \ \Delta h = \log(h'/h), \tag{2}$$

where $\{x, y, w, h\}$ are bounding box parameters from SSD and $\{x', y', w', h'\}$ represent the refined bounding box.

3.4 Training

Label Assignment with Bipartite Matching. The message passing network outputs a set of detections with new score and refined boxes without changing the number of detections K which is typically much larger than the number of ground truth objects N. For training, we seek an optimal assignment of a ground-truth object to the best detection determined by a combination of classification and localization accuracy. Most previous works [7,9,16] follow the simpler evaluation pipeline of Pascal VOC [3] or MS-COCO [14] for target assignment. This matching algorithm first sorts all detections in descending order and then greedily picks the detection with highest score for a ground-truth instance, when its

IoU with this ground-truth box exceeds a pre-defined threshold. However, the greedy matching selects boxes based on the classification score at an unchanged IoU level without further consideration of localization.

Following the works with set prediction [1,20], we introduce a pairwise matching cost which consists of a classification and a localization cost balanced with weights α and β:

$$L_{ij}(d_i, y_j) = -\mathbb{1}\left[\text{IoU}(\hat{b}_i, b_j) > T_2\right]\left(\alpha\hat{s}_i + \beta\text{IoU}(\hat{b}_i, b_j)\right), \tag{3}$$

given the classification score $\hat{s}_i$ and box $\hat{b}_i$ of detection d_i as well as a ground-truth annotation y_j with a bounding box b_j. The parameter T_2 is an IoU threshold that controls the positive and negative samples, similar to the one used in heuristic anchor matching in SSD. The optimal matching between the set of detections $\{d_i\}^K$ and ground truths $\{y_j\}^N$ can be represented with an assignment matrix $X \in \{0, 1\}^{K \times N}$, where $X_{ij} = 1$ indicates a matching between d_i and y_j. In a bipartite matching, each row of X is assigned at most to one column and vice versa. The optimal assignment X which minimizes the overall cost

$$\mathcal{L}_{\text{match}} = \min_X \sum_i \sum_j L_{ij} X_{ij} \tag{4}$$

can be found by the Hungarian Algorithm efficiently. With the matching cost in Eq. 3, the matcher always selects a box with both high score and precise localization, which increases the demand for the box refinement.

Overall Training Objective. We train our proposed network together with the classification loss $\mathcal{L}_{\text{cls}}$ and the localization loss $\mathcal{L}_{\text{loc}}$ in SSD. We use focal loss [13] and smooth-L1 loss as classification loss $\mathcal{L}_{\text{nms,cls}}$ and localization loss $\mathcal{L}_{\text{nms,loc}}$ in our learnable NMS network, respectively. Similar to the localization loss in SSD, the loss term $\mathcal{L}_{\text{nms,loc}}$ is only calculated for the positive (matched) samples. Note that we use the final score s_c after rescoring as the prediction in focal loss, thus the gradient from $\mathcal{L}_{\text{nms,cls}}$ also flows into the pre-filtering head and classification subnet. The overall training objective is

$$\mathcal{L} = \lambda_1(\mathcal{L}_{\text{cls}} + \mathcal{L}_{\text{loc}}) + \lambda_2\mathcal{L}_{\text{pre}} + \lambda_3\mathcal{L}_{\text{nms,cls}} + \lambda_4\mathcal{L}_{\text{nms,loc}}, \tag{5}$$

where $\lambda_1, \lambda_2, \lambda_3, \lambda_4$ are weights for each loss term.

4 Experiments

4.1 Implementation Details

We show detection results on MS-COCO [14] and KITTI 2D Object Detection [4] datasets. To avoid training instability caused by gradient domination of duplication removal components in early training, we train our model in two stages: first, the vanilla SSD model is trained alone. In the second stage, our learnable

Table 1. Results on MS-COCO *val* and *test-dev*. We compare our approach with NMS and GossipNet [7]. AP_{50} and AP_{75} are AP at 50% IoU and 75% IoU. The inference time corresponds to the entire process including pre- and post-processing and we also show the inference time of the GossipNet alone in the bracket.

Base model	Method	val			test-dev			Time [ms]
		AP	AP_{50}	AP_{75}	AP	AP_{50}	AP_{75}	
EfficientDet-D0	NMS	31.6	**50.0**	33.3	32.0	**50.5**	33.8	47.3
	GossipNet	31.6	49.7	33.7	31.5	49.9	33.7	166.1(131.1)
	Ours	**32.7**	49.9	**35.9**	**32.7**	49.8	**36.1**	**35.7**
RetinaNet-R50	NMS	34.4	52.1	36.8	34.2	**51.7**	37.2	59.7
	GossipNet	**34.7**	**52.2**	37.7	32.0	49.9	34.3	154.2(107.1)
	Ours	**34.7**	50.8	**38.7**	**34.6**	51.0	**38.5**	**48.0**

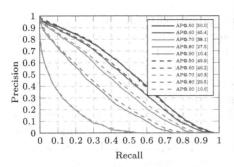

Fig. 3. Comparison of Precision-Recall Curves at different IoUs. Classical NMS is depicted in solid line, our approach in dashed line.

Fig. 4. Qualitative comparisons between our approach and classical NMS. We keep the top 100 detections for visualization. Box opacity is proportional to the score.

NMS network is attached to the base SSD network and the whole network is trained jointly according to Eq. 5 with a smaller learning rate. For a fair comparison, we also train a vanilla SSD with same total steps in a second stage and compare its performance with our approach.

To validate the generalization ability, we use two different SSD models for evaluation: EfficientDet-D0 [22] and RetinaNet-ResNet50 [13]. The numbers of initial node feature channel C_N and GCN output channel C'_N are always set to $C_N = C'_N = 4C_F$, where C_F corresponds to the channel number of feature map in the base SSD model. We stack only one GCN layer for EfficientDet and two GCN layers for RetinaNet. Furthermore, we use $K = 300$, $T_1 = 0.9$, $T_2 = 0.7$ and $\lambda_1 = \lambda_2 = \lambda_3 = \lambda_4 = 1.0$ for all baseline models.

4.2 MS-COCO Experiments

The MS-COCO is a challenging object detection dataset with 80 different categories. There are about 118k images in *train* set, 5k images in *val* set and 20k images in *test-dev* set respectively. All the models are trained on 4 NVIDIA Tesla V100-PCIE-16GB GPUs with SGD. The batch sizes are 48 for EfficientDet-D0 and 16 for RetinaNet-ResNet50. A momentum of 0.9 and cosine learning rate decay schedule are used for both stages. For EfficientDet, we train the backbone detection network for 300k steps with base learning rate 0.08 in the first stage and a further 100k steps with a base learning rate 0.015 in the second stage. For RetinaNet, the base learning rate is 0.01 for the first 200k steps and 5×10^{-4} for the next 120k steps. Unless mentioned otherwise, ablation studies are performed on the *val* set with the EfficientDet-D0 backbone.

Comparison with Baselines

Choice of Baselines. We first compare our approach with other duplicate removal methods within same backbone network architectures. For fair comparison, we train all networks with the same setup as explained above. To ensure validity of the baseline performance, we built our method based on TensorFlow Object Detection API [10] and used their EfficientDet and RetinaNet implementation trained with the same hyperparameter set as our baselines. Note that our best EfficientDet baseline falls 2.6% short on *test-dev* compared to the numbers reported in the original paper [22]. This is caused by our smaller batch size (48 vs. 128) and shorter training epochs (160 epochs vs. 300 epochs) due to hardware limitations. However, since we aim to assess only the performance improvement gained from various duplicate removal stages, this does not affect the experiments' meaningfulness.

We select the established non-maximum suppression with an IoU threshold of 0.5 as a baseline. Also, we reproduced GossipNet using the code provided by the authors. As input, the GossipNet takes the same number of SSD raw detections as in our approach ($K = 300$) because it provides not only a fair comparison but also a best performance. Other hyperparameters remain unchanged. The comparison on COCO *val* and *test-dev* sets are shown in Table 1.

Performance. For EfficientDet, our approach improves 1.1% points on *val* and 0.7 on *test-dev* against NMS. It is worth mentioning that our approach achieves a significant improvement of AP_{75}, which can be attributed to our localization refinement loss and position-aware matching cost in label assignment. We can also observe significant improvements at relatively high IoU thresholds (AP@0.70 and AP@0.80) in the Precision-Recall Curves in Fig. 3, which validates the better localization of our approach. While GossipNet achieves an improvement of AP for Faster-RCNN by 0.8% on COCO *test-dev* in our reproduction, it still can't outperform the standard NMS when applied to EfficientDet. The performance gain of our approach in RetinaNet experiments is modest everywhere comparing to EfficientDet. We argue that the RetinaNet has already achieved a better

Table 2. Ablation study of GCN layer number L and channel number of initial features C_N. The number of parameters and FLOPs include node feature generation and final dense layers. We also show the number of Params and FLOPs of the base model EfficientDet-D0.

L	C_N	AP	AP_{50}	AP_{75}	Params	FLOPs
0	256	30.2	47.4	33.2	83.72k	0.050B
1	256	**32.7**	**49.9**	**35.9**	149.51k	0.136B
2	256	32.4	49.4	35.3	215.30k	0.221B
3	256	32.3	49.4	35.4	281.09k	0.307B
1	64	32.5	49.8	35.6	29.09k	0.027B
1	128	32.4	49.6	35.6	58.37k	0.058B
1	512	32.5	49.8	35.6	430.09k	0.350B
EfficientDet-D0					3.9M	2.5B

Table 3. Ablation study of influence of pre-filtering and localization refinement. λ_1, λ_2, λ_3, λ_4 are weights of different loss terms as shown in Sect. 3.4. $\lambda_i = -$ indicates the corresponding module is disabled.

Ablation	λ_1	λ_2	λ_3	λ_4	AP	AP_{50}	AP_{75}
Full model	1.0	1.0	1.0	1.0	**32.7**	**49.9**	**35.9**
Influence of prefiltering	1.0	**0.5**	1.0	1.0	32.4	49.3	35.6
	1.0	**0.3**	1.0	1.0	32.5	49.7	35.8
	1.0	**0.1**	1.0	1.0	32.3	49.0	35.5
	1.0	**−**	1.0	1.0	31.4	48.0	34.4
Influence of loc. refinement	1.0	1.0	1.0	**0.5**	32.2	49.6	35.5
	1.0	1.0	1.0	**0.3**	31.9	49.4	35.0
	1.0	1.0	1.0	**0.1**	31.4	48.9	34.2
	1.0	1.0	1.0	**−**	30.7	48.4	33.6

localization quality than EfficientDet (3.4% AP_{75} vs. 1.2% AP_{50} improvement on *test-dev*) and thus the potential of AP improvement at a higher IoU threshold is smaller. However, our approach still performs better than the NMS baseline on both sets. It is noticed that, although GossipNet achieves the same AP as our method on *val*, the performance decreases by a large margin on *test-dev* which indicates limited generalization. A qualitative comparison with classical NMS is shown in Fig. 4. In the first example, classical NMS produces a duplicate box between second and third person from right side, while our approach is able to suppress that box in the crowded scene. In the second example, our method is able to recover low-scoring detections after rescoring.

Runtime. The last column of Table 1 shows the inference time of the entire model including pre- and post-processing on a NVIDIA RTX 2080Ti GPU. Our approach reduces 24.5% and 19.5% inference time for both models compared to using NMS, thus further accelerates the efficient SSD model and increases the ability to be embedded into real-time applications. The inference time of the pure GossipNet model without considering SSD is shown in the bracket which is significant longer (>100 ms) due to its complex architecture.

Ablation Study

Impact of the GCN Architecture. An ablation study of the number of layers in the GCN architecture for the EfficientDet-D0 base model is shown in Table 2. We observe that the network doesn't need a deep architecture, one GCN layer, $L = 1$, provides the best performance. This may be caused by the over-smoothing in GNNs if too many layers are stacked. In addition, the message from one-hop neighbors are most important in a duplicate removal problem. Without GCN

Table 4. Results on KITTI test set. The subscription E, M, H corresponds to Easy, Moderate and Hard respectively.

	Car			Pedestrian			Cyclist		
	AP_E	AP_M	AP_H	AP_E	AP_M	AP_H	AP_E	AP_M	AP_H
NMS	76.21	52.92	43.38	**52.32**	**39.46**	**35.60**	**35.72**	**23.07**	**20.54**
Ours	**78.55**	**61.93**	**53.72**	51.24	38.40	35.24	34.13	22.43	19.65

layers ($L = 0$), rescoring and refinement are made using initial node features. This leads to a significant AP drop by 2.5% which validates the importance of relation modeling in learning duplicate removal problems. For the channel count, 256 proved best. More learnable parameters don't lead to a better performance. According to the number of parameters and FLOPs, our model processes the duplicate removal and refinement with a minimal time and space overhead comparing to the EfficientDet-D0 model.

Proposed Modules. Table 3 shows an evaluation of each proposed novel module by decreasing its corresponding loss weights until it is fully disabled. The performance drop is insignificant when decreasing the pre-filtering weight λ_2, as shown in rows 2–5. This can be attributed to the gradient flow from the NMS classification loss $\mathcal{L}_{\text{nms,cls}}$ into the pre-filtering head, which jointly optimizes the pre-filtering ability. By disabling the candidate pre-filter, the mAP drops by 1.3%. We see that the AP of our approach after disabling pre-filtering (31.4%) is close to GossipNet (31.6% in Table 1), while both setting simply selects the top-K boxes with highest SSD scores as input. This shows an interpretation of the performance gap between GossipNet and our approach and indicates the importance of our pre-filtering method. In rows 6–9, we gradually decrease the weight of the NMS localization refinement loss λ_3 which also decreases performance. A reason for the performance drop is the matching cost that requires a high localization quality. It also reveals that rescoring alone cannot guarantee that high-scoring detections also have the best localization.

4.3   KITTI Experiments

For the KITTI 2D Object Detection Benchmark, we adopt experiments based on EfficientDet-D0 trained on one single GPU with a batch size of 8. The training schedule consists of a first 120k steps with a base learning rate 0.005 for training the vanilla SSD and then 40k steps with a base learning rate of 0.0005 for training the entire model. All the other settings are the same as provided in MS-COCO experiments. The results on KITTI test set are shown in Table 4. For car detection, we observe a dramatic performance improvement against classical NMS: For Moderate and Hard, our approach improves the AP by around 10% points. This can be attributed to the frequent occlusion and truncation of these objects in the traffic scenarios (e.g. closely parking cars), where our learning-based approach is able to deal with the crowded situation. For pedestrians and cyclists, however, the detection performance drops slightly when applying our approach. The reason lies in KITTI's evaluation protocols for different categories: AP_{70} is used for car but AP_{50} for pedestrian and cyclist. As shown in Fig. 3, our method outperforms NMS at AP_{70} but not at AP_{50}. Note that AP_{70} is a more accurate and difficult measure than AP_{50}.

5 Conclusion

In this paper, we proposed a novel learned duplicate removal network which can be easily embedded into SSD-like models and trained end-to-end. For duplicate removal, detection candidates are treated as nodes in a graph. Their relationship is processed by a Graph Convolutional Network (GCN) to reason about dependencies and suppression. In order to reduce the amount of candidates within this graph, a simple learnable pre-filtering head was introduced. Experimental evaluations showed that the proposed network outperforms classical NMS and other duplicate removal methods while at the same time reducing inference time significantly. Consequently, our work removes the last hand engineered component from SSD. The resulting architecture forms an entirely learned object detection pipeline within realtime constraints.

Acknowledgement. The research leading to these results is funded by the German Federal Ministry for Economic Affairs and Climate Action within the project "KI Delta Learning" (Förderkennzeichen 19A19013A). The authors would like to thank the consortium for the successful cooperation.

References

1. Carion, N., Massa, F., Synnaeve, G., Usunier, N., Kirillov, A., Zagoruyko, S.: End-to-end object detection with transformers. In: Vedaldi, A., Bischof, H., Brox, T., Frahm, J.-M. (eds.) ECCV 2020. LNCS, vol. 12346, pp. 213–229. Springer, Cham (2020). https://doi.org/10.1007/978-3-030-58452-8_13
2. Dai, J., Li, Y., He, K., Sun, J.: R-FCN: object detection via region-based fully convolutional networks. In: Advances in Neural Information Processing Systems, pp. 379–387 (2016)
3. Everingham, M., Van Gool, L., Williams, C.K., Winn, J., Zisserman, A.: The Pascal visual object classes (VOC) challenge. Int. J. Comput. Vis. **88**(2), 303–338 (2010)
4. Geiger, A., Lenz, P., Urtasun, R.: Are we ready for autonomous driving? The KITTI vision benchmark suite. In: 2012 IEEE Conference on Computer Vision and Pattern Recognition, pp. 3354–3361. IEEE (2012)
5. He, K., Gkioxari, G., Dollar, P., Girshick, R.: Mask R-CNN. In: Proceedings of the IEEE International Conference on Computer Vision (ICCV), October 2017
6. Hosang, J., Benenson, R., Schiele, B.: A convnet for non-maximum suppression. In: Rosenhahn, B., Andres, B. (eds.) GCPR 2016. LNCS, vol. 9796, pp. 192–204. Springer, Cham (2016). https://doi.org/10.1007/978-3-319-45886-1_16
7. Hosang, J., Benenson, R., Schiele, B.: Learning non-maximum suppression. In: Proceedings of the IEEE Conference on Computer Vision and Pattern Recognition, pp. 4507–4515 (2017)

8. Howard, A.G., et al.: MobileNets: efficient convolutional neural networks for mobile vision applications. arXiv preprint arXiv:1704.04861 (2017)

9. Hu, H., Gu, J., Zhang, Z., Dai, J., Wei, Y.: Relation networks for object detection. In: Proceedings of the IEEE Conference on Computer Vision and Pattern Recognition, pp. 3588–3597 (2018)

10. Huang, J.S., et al.: Speed/accuracy trade-offs for modern convolutional object detectors. In: Proceedings of the IEEE Conference on Computer Vision and Pattern Recognition, pp. 7310–7311 (2017)

11. Kipf, T.N., Welling, M.: Semi-supervised classification with graph convolutional networks. arXiv preprint arXiv:1609.02907 (2016)

12. Li, Q., Han, Z., Wu, X.M.: Deeper insights into graph convolutional networks for semi-supervised learning. In: Thirty-Second AAAI Conference on Artificial Intelligence (2018)

13. Lin, T.Y., Goyal, P., Girshick, R., He, K., Dollár, P.: Focal loss for dense object detection. In: Proceedings of the IEEE International Conference on Computer Vision, pp. 2980–2988 (2017)

14. Lin, T.-Y., et al.: Microsoft COCO: common objects in context. In: Fleet, D., Pajdla, T., Schiele, B., Tuytelaars, T. (eds.) ECCV 2014. LNCS, vol. 8693, pp. 740–755. Springer, Cham (2014). https://doi.org/10.1007/978-3-319-10602-1_48

15. Liu, W., et al.: SSD: single shot MultiBox detector. In: Leibe, B., Matas, J., Sebe, N., Welling, M. (eds.) ECCV 2016. LNCS, vol. 9905, pp. 21–37. Springer, Cham (2016). https://doi.org/10.1007/978-3-319-46448-0_2

16. Qi, L., Liu, S., Shi, J., Jia, J.: Sequential context encoding for duplicate removal. arXiv preprint arXiv:1810.08770 (2018)

17. Redmon, J., Divvala, S., Girshick, R., Farhadi, A.: You only look once: unified, real-time object detection. In: Proceedings of the IEEE Conference on Computer Vision and Pattern Recognition, pp. 779–788 (2016)

18. Ren, S., He, K., Girshick, R., Sun, J.: Faster R-CNN: towards real-time object detection with region proposal networks. arXiv preprint arXiv:1506.01497 (2015)

19. Roh, B., Shin, J., Shin, W., Kim, S.: Sparse DETR: efficient end-to-end object detection with learnable sparsity. arXiv preprint arXiv:2111.14330 (2021)

20. Stewart, R., Andriluka, M., Ng, A.Y.: End-to-end people detection in crowded scenes. In: Proceedings of the IEEE Conference on Computer Vision and Pattern Recognition, pp. 2325–2333 (2016)

21. Sun, P., Jiang, Y., Xie, E., Yuan, Z., Wang, C., Luo, P.: OneNet: towards end-to-end one-stage object detection. arXiv preprint arXiv:2012.05780 (2020)

22. Tan, M., Pang, R., Le, Q.V.: EfficientDet: scalable and efficient object detection. In: Proceedings of the IEEE/CVF Conference on Computer Vision and Pattern Recognition, pp. 10781–10790 (2020)

23. Tan, Z., Nie, X., Qian, Q., Li, N., Li, H.: Learning to rank proposals for object detection. In: Proceedings of the IEEE/CVF International Conference on Computer Vision, pp. 8273–8281 (2019)

24. Tian, Z., Shen, C., Chen, H., He, T.: FCOS: fully convolutional one-stage object detection. In: Proceedings of IEEE International Conference on Computer Vision (ICCV) (2019)

25. Vaswani, A., et al.: Attention is all you need. arXiv preprint arXiv:1706.03762 (2017)

26. Zhou, Q., Yu, C., Shen, C., Wang, Z., Li, H.: Object detection made simpler by eliminating heuristic NMS. arXiv preprint arXiv:2101.11782 (2021)

27. Zhou, X., Wang, D., Krähenbühl, P.: Objects as points. arXiv preprint arXiv:1904.07850 (2019)
28. Zhu, X., Su, W., Lu, L., Li, B., Wang, X., Dai, J.: Deformable DETR: deformable transformers for end-to-end object detection. arXiv preprint arXiv:2010.04159 (2020)

Language and Vision

Localized Vision-Language Matching for Open-vocabulary Object Detection

María A. Bravo[(⊠)], Sudhanshu Mittal, and Thomas Brox

Department of Computer Science, University of Freiburg, Freiburg im Breisgau, Germany
{bravoma,mittal,brox}@cs.uni-freiburg.de

Abstract. In this work, we propose an open-vocabulary object detection method that, based on image-caption pairs, learns to detect novel object classes along with a given set of known classes. It is a two-stage training approach that first uses a location-guided image-caption matching technique to learn class labels for both novel and known classes in a weakly-supervised manner and second specializes the model for the object detection task using known class annotations. We show that a simple language model fits better than a large contextualized language model for detecting novel objects. Moreover, we introduce a consistency-regularization technique to better exploit image-caption pair information. Our method compares favorably to existing open-vocabulary detection approaches while being data-efficient. Source code is available at https://github.com/lmb-freiburg/locov.

Keywords: Open-vocabulary Object Detection · Image-caption Matching · Weakly-supervised Learning · Multi-modal Training

1 Introduction

Recent advances in deep learning have rapidly advanced the state-of-the-art object detection algorithms. The best mean average precision score on the popular COCO [22] benchmark has improved from 40 mAP to over 60 mAP in less than 4 years. However, this success required large datasets with annotations at the bounding box level and was a achieved in a closed-world setting, where the number of classes is assumed to be fixed. The closed-world setting restricts the object detector to only discover known annotated objects and annotating all possible objects in the world is infeasible due to high labeling costs. Therefore, research of open-world detectors, which can also discover unmarked objects, has recently come into focus specially using textual information together with images for open-vocabulary detection [13,39,42].

Supplementary Information The online version contains supplementary material available at https://doi.org/10.1007/978-3-031-16788-1_24.

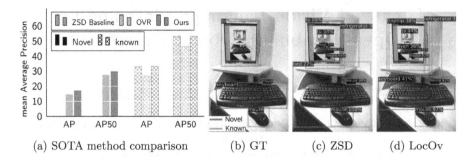

(a) SOTA method comparison   (b) GT   (c) ZSD   (d) LocOv

Fig. 1. Open-vocabulary object detection. (a) Compares our method LocOv with the baseline method (OVR) and our zero-shot baseline STT-ZSD (ZSD). LocOv improves on both novel and known classes without dropping the performance on known classes. The zero-shot method, only trained with known classes, obtains low performance (< 0.5 mAP) on novel classes. (b-d) LocOv is able to detect the novel object 'keyboard' along with known objects, shown in figure.

To learn a visual concept, humans receive the majority of the supervision in the form of narrations rather than class tags and bounding boxes. Consider the example of Figure 1 together with the annotations of mouse and tv only. Even after learning to detect these objects, finding and identifying the keyboard without any other source of information is ambitious. Instead, if we consider the image together with the caption - "A mouse, keyboard, and a monitor on a desk", it is possible to identify that the other salient object in the image is very likely a keyboard. This process involves successful localization of the objects in the scene, identification of different nouns in the narrated sentence, and matching the two together. Exploiting the extensive semantic knowledge contained in natural language is a reasonable step towards learning such open-vocabulary models without expensive annotation costs.

In this work, we aim to learn novel objects using image-caption pairs. Along with image-caption pairs, the detector is provided with box annotations for a limited set of classes. We follow the problem setting as introduced by Zareian *et al.*[39]. They refer to this problem as *Open-vocabulary Object Detection*. There are two major challenges to this problem: First, image-caption pairs themselves are too weak to learn localized object-regions. Analyzing previous works, we find that randomly sampled feature maps provide imprecise visual grounding for foreground objects, therefore they receive insufficient supervisory signals to learn object properties. Second, the granularity of the information captured by image-region features should align with the level of information captured by the text representation for an effective matching. For example, it would be ill-suited to match a text representation that captures global image information with image features that capture localized information.

In this work, we propose a method that improves the matching between image and text representations. Our model is a two-stage approach: in the first stage, *Localized Semantic Matching* (LSM), it learns semantics of objects in the image by matching image-regions to the words in the caption; and in the second stage, *Specialized Task Tuning* (STT), it learns specialized visual features for the target object detection task using known object annotations. We called our method LocOv for **Loc**alized Image-Caption Matching for **O**pen-**v**ocabulary.

For the given objects in an image, our goal is to project them to a feature space where they can be matched with their corresponding class in the form of text embeddings. We find that simple text embeddings are better candidates for matching object representations than contextualized embeddings produced by large-scale language models.

Using image-caption pairs as weak supervision for object detection requires the understanding of both modalities in a fine and a coarse way. This can be obtained by processing each modality independently in a uni-modal fashion and then matching, or using cross-modal attention to process them together. To ensure consistent training between the uni-modal and cross-modal methods, we propose a consistency-regularization between the two matching scores. To summarize, our contributions are: (1) We introduced localized-regions during the image-caption matching stage to improve visual feature learning of objects. (2) We show that simplified text embeddings match better with identified object features as compared to contextualized text embeddings. (3) We propose a consistency regularization technique to ensure effective cross-modal training.

These three contributions allow LocOv to be not only competitive against state-of-the-art models but also data-efficient by using less than 0.6 million image-caption pairs for training, ~700 times smaller than CLIP-based methods. Additionally, we define an open-vocabulary object detection setup based on the VAW [27] dataset, which offers challenging learning conditions like few-instances per object and a long-tailed distribution. Based on the above mentioned three contributions, we show that our method achieves state-of-the-art performance on both open-vocabulary object detection benchmarks, COCO and VAW.

2   Related Work

Object Detection with Limited Supervision. Semi-supervised (SSOD) [17,23,33] and weakly-supervised (WSOD) [4,8,20] object detection are two widely explored approaches to reduce the annotation cost. WSOD approaches aim to learn object localization using image-level labels only. Major challenges in WSOD approaches include differentiation between object instances [31] and precisely locating the entire objects. SSOD approaches use a small fully-annotated set and a large set of unlabeled images. Best SSOD [23,33] methods are based on pseudo-labeling, which usually suffers from foreground-background imbalance and overfitting on the labeled set of images. In this work, we address a problem which shares similar challenges with the WSOD and SSOD approaches, however they are limited to a closed-world setting with a fixed and predefined set of classes. Our method addresses a mixed semi- and weakly-supervised object detection problem where the objective is open-vocabulary object detection.

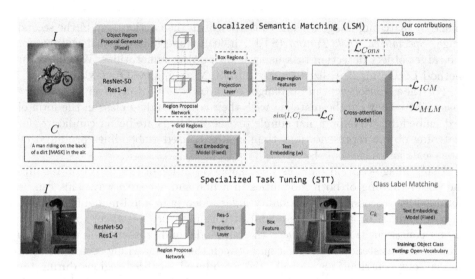

Fig. 2. Overview of LocOv . It is a two-stage model: (1) Localized Semantic Matching stage trains a Faster R-CNN-based model to match corresponding image-caption pairs using a grounding loss $\mathcal{L}_G$. We exploit the multi-modal information by using a cross-attention model and an Image-Caption matching loss $\mathcal{L}_{ICM}$, the mask language modeling loss $\mathcal{L}_{MLM}$ and a consistency-regularization loss $\mathcal{L}_{Cons}$. (2) Specialized Task Tuning stage tunes the model using the known class annotations and specializes the model for object detection. See Section 3.

Multi-modal Visual and Language Models. Over the past years, multiple works have centered their attention on the intersection of vision and language by exploiting their consistent semantic information contained in matching pairs. The success of using this pairwise information has proved to be useful for pre-training transformer-like models for various vision-language tasks [6,21,24,34,35,40,43] which process the information jointly using cross-attention. Other approaches [11,12,19,25,28,36], centered on the vision and language retrieval task use separate encoders for each modality, in a uni-modal fashion. These models give the flexibility to transfer the knowledge learned by the pairwise information to single modality tasks, which is the case of object detection. In particular Miech et al.[25] showed that combining a cross-attention model with two uni-modal encoders is beneficial for large-scale retrieval tasks. In this paper, we combine the strengths of both types of approaches to train a model using different consistency losses that exploit the information contained in image-caption pairs.

Language-Guided Object Detection. Zero-shot object detection methods learn to align proposed object-region features to the class-text embeddings. Bansal et al.[2] is among the first to propose the zero-shot object detection problem. They identified that the main challenge in ZSD is to separate the background class from the novel objects. Zhu et al.[44] trained a generative model to "hallucinate" (synthesize visual features) unseen classes and used these generated features during training to be able to distinguish novel objects from background. Rahman *et al.*[29] proposed a polarity loss to handle foreground-background imbalance and to improve visual-semantic alignment. However, such methods fail to perform well on the novel classes since the detection model has never seen these novel objects, and semantics learned by matching known object-text embeddings does not extrapolate to novel classes.

To learn the semantics of novel classes, recent methods [3,13,16,39,42] have simplified the problem by providing image-caption pairs as a weak supervision signal. Such pairs are cheap to acquire and make the problem tractable. Image-caption pairs allow the model to observe a large set of object categories along with object labels. These methods either use this model to align image-regions with captions and generate object-box pseudo labels [16,42] or as region-image feature extractor to classify the regions [13]. Many weakly-supervised [1,3,7,32, 41] approaches have been proposed to perform such object grounding. Due to the large performance gap between zero-shot/weakly-supervised and fully-supervised approaches for object detection, Zareian *et al.*[39] introduced an open-vocabulary problem formulation. It utilizes extra image-caption pairs to learn to detect both known and novel objects. Their approach matches all parts of the image with the caption, whereas we emphasize object localized regions and a consistency loss to enforce more object-centric matching.

3   Method

We propose a two-stage approach for the task of open-vocabulary object detection as shown in Figure 2. The first stage, *Localized Semantic Matching* (LSM), learns to match objects in the image to their corresponding class labels in the caption in a weakly-supervised manner. The second stage, *Specialized Task Tuning* (STT) stage, includes specialized training for the downstream task of object detection. We consider two sets of object classes: known classes O_K and novel classes O_N. Bounding box annotations, including class labels, are available for known classes whereas there are no annotations for the novel classes.

The LSM receives image-caption pairs (I, C) as input, where the caption provides the weak supervision to different image-regions. Captions contain rich information which often include words corresponding to object classes from both known and novel sets. Captions are processed using a pre-trained text-embedding model (*e.g.*BERT [10] embedding) to produce word or part-of-word features. Images are processed using an object detection network (Faster R-CNN [30]) to obtain object region features. We propose to utilize an object proposal generator OLN [18] to provide regions as pseudo-labels to train the Faster R-CNN. This helps obtaining object-rich regions which improve image region-caption matching. This way, during the LSM our model learns to match all present objects in the image in a class-agnostic way. See Section 3.1 for details. The STT stage tunes the Faster R-CNN using known object annotations primarily to distinguish foreground from background and learns corresponding precise location of the foreground objects. See Section 3.2 for details.

3.1 Localized Semantic Matching (LSM)

The LSM stage consists of three main components: (1) localized object region-text matching, (2) disentangled text features and (3) consistency-regularization.

Localized Object Region-Text Matching. Given the sets $R^I = \{ r : r$ is an image-region feature vector from the image I$\}$ and $W^C = \{ w : w$ is a word or part-of-word feature vector from the caption C$\}$, we calculate the similarity score between an image and a caption in a fine-grained manner, by comparing image-regions with words, since our final objective is to recognize objects in regions. The image is processed using a Faster R-CNN model and a projection layer that maps image-regions into the text-embedding feature space. The similarity score is calculated by taking an image composed of $|R^I|$ region features and a caption composed of $|W^C|$ part-of-word features by:

$$sim(I,C) = \frac{1}{|R^I|} \sum_{i=1}^{|R^I|} \sum_{j=1}^{|W^C|} d_{i,j}(r_i \cdot w_j) \tag{1}$$

where $d_{i,j}$ corresponds to:

$$d(r_i, w_j) = d_{i,j} = \frac{\exp(r_i \cdot w_j)}{\sum_{j'=1}^{|W^C|} \exp(r_i \cdot w_{j'})}. \tag{2}$$

Based on the similarity score (Eq. 1) , we apply a contrastive learning objective to match the corresponding pairs together by considering all other pairs in the batch as negative pairs. We define this grounding loss as:

$$\mathcal{L}_{G_r}(I) = -\log \frac{\exp(sim(I,C))}{\sum_{C' \in \text{Batch}} \exp(sim(I,C'))} \tag{3}$$

We apply this loss in a symmetrical way, where each image in the batch is compared to all captions in the batch (Eq. 3) and each caption is compared to all images in the batch $\mathcal{L}_{G_r}(C)$. The subscript r denotes the type of image-regions used for the loss calculation. We consider two types of image-regions: box-regions and grid-regions. Box-region features are obtained naturally using the region of interest pooling (RPN) from the Faster R-CNN. We make use of the pre-trained object proposal generator (OLN) to train the Faster-RCNN network. OLN is a class-agnostic object proposal generator which estimates all objects in the image with a high average recall rate. We train OLN using the known class annotations and use the predicted boxes to train our detection model, shown in Figure 2. Since captions sometimes refer to background context in the image, parallel to the box-region features, we also use grid-region features similar to the OVR [39] approach. Grid-region features are obtained by skipping the RPN in the Faster R-CNN and simply using the output of the backbone network. We apply the grounding loss to both type of image-region features. Our final grounding loss is given by:

$$\mathcal{L}_G = \mathcal{L}_{G_{box}}(C) + \mathcal{L}_{G_{box}}(I) + \mathcal{L}_{G_{grid}}(C) + \mathcal{L}_{G_{grid}}(I) \tag{4}$$

Disentangled Text Features. Many previous works [6,15,24,34] use contextualized language models to extract text representations of the sentence. Although, this might be suitable for a task that requires a global representation of a phrase or text, this is not ideal for the case for object detection, where each predicted bounding box is expected to contain a single object instance. We show that using a simple text representation, which keeps the disentangled semantics of words in a caption, gives the flexibility to correctly match object boxes in an image with words in a caption. Our method uses only the embedding module [10,26] of a pre-trained language model to encode the caption and perform matching with the proposed image-regions. For embedding model we refer to the learned dictionary of vector representations of text tokens, which correspond to words or part-of-words. For cases where the text representing an object category is divided into multiple tokens, we consider the average representation of the tokens as the global representation of the object category. We show empirically, in Section 4.4, that using such a lightweight text embedding module has better performance than using a whole large-scale language model.

Consistency-Regularization. Miech *et al.*[25] showed that processing multimodal data using cross-attention networks brings improvements in retrieval accuracy over using separate encoders for each modality and projecting over a common embedding space. However, this cross-attention becomes very expensive when the task requires large-scale retrieval. To take the benefit of cross-attention models, we consider a model similar to PixelBERT [15] to process the image-caption pairs. This cross-attention model takes the image-regions R^I together with the text embeddings W^C and matches the corresponding image-caption pairs in a batch. The image-caption matching loss ($\mathcal{L}_{ICM}$) of the cross-attention model together with the traditional Masking Language Modeling loss ($\mathcal{L}_{MLM}$) enforces the model to better project the image-region features to the language semantic space. To better utilize the cross-attention model, we propose a consistency-regularization loss ($\mathcal{L}_{Cons}$) between the final predicted distribution over the image-caption matching scores in the batch, before and after the cross-attention model. We use the Kullback-Leibler divergence loss to impose this consistency. In summary, we use three consistency terms over different image-caption pairs:

$$\mathcal{L}_{Cons} = D_{KL}(p(I_{box}, C)||q(I_{box}, C)) \\ + D_{KL}(p(I_{grid}, C)||q(I_{grid}, C)) \\ + D_{KL}(p(I_{grid}, C)||q(I_{box}, C)) \tag{5}$$

where $p(I_*, C)$ and $q(I_*, C)$ correspond to the softmax of the image-caption pairs in a batch before and after the cross-attention model respectively, and the sub-index of the image corresponds to the box- or grid-region features. Our final loss for the LSM stage corresponds to the sum of the above defined losses:

$$\mathbf{L}_{LSM} = \mathcal{L}_G + \mathcal{L}_{ICM} + \mathcal{L}_{MLM} + \mathcal{L}_{Cons} \tag{6}$$

3.2   Specialized Task Tuning (STT)

In this stage, we fine-tune the model using known class annotations to learn to localize the objects precisely. We initialize the weights from the LSM stage model, and partially freeze part of the backbone and the projection layer to preserve the learned semantics. Freezing the projection layer is important to avoid overfitting on the known classes and generalize on novel classes. To predict the class of an object, we compute the similarity score between the proposed object box-region feature vector (r_i) and all the class embedding vectors c_k and apply softmax

$$p(r_i, c_k) = \frac{\exp(r_i \cdot c_k)}{1 + \sum_{c'_k \in O_K} \exp(r_i \cdot c_{k'})}. \tag{7}$$

The scalar 1 included in the denominator corresponds to the background class, which has a representation vector of all-zeros. We evaluate the performance across three setups: (Novel) considering only the novel class set O_N, (Known) comparing with the known classes only O_K and (Generalized) considering all novel and known classes together.

4   Experiments

4.1   Training Details

Datasets. The **Common Objects in Context (COCO)** dataset [22] is a large-scale object detection benchmark widely used in the community. We use the 2017 train and val split for training and evaluation respectively. We use the known and novel object class splits proposed by Bansal *et al.* [2]. The known set consists of 48 classes while the novel set has 17 classes selected from the total of 80 classes of the original COCO dataset. We remove the images which do not contain the known class instances from the training set. For the localized semantic matching phase, we use the captions from **COCO captions** [5] dataset which has the same train/test splits as the COCO object detection task. COCO captions dataset contains 118,287 images with 5 captions each. Additionally in the supplementary material, we test LocOv using **Visual Attributes in the Wild (VAW) dataset** [27] a more challenging dataset containing fine-grained classes with a long-tailed distribution.

Evaluation Metric. We evaluate our method using mean Average Precision (AP) over IoU scores from 0.5 to 0.95 with a step size of 0.05, and using two fixed thresholds at 0.5 (AP_{50}) and 0.75 (AP_{75}). We compute these metrics separately for novel and known classes, calculating the softmax within the subsets exclusively; and in a generalized version both sets are evaluated in a combined manner, calculating the probability across all classes.

Implementation Details. We base our model on Faster R-CNN C4 [30] configuration, using ResNet50 [14] backbone pre-trained on ImageNet [9], together with a linear layer (projection layer) to obtain the object feature representations.

Table 1. Comparing mAP and AP_{50} state-of-the-art methods. LocOv outperforms all other methods for Novel objects in the generalized setup while using only 0.6M of image-caption pairs. Training dataset: [*]ImageNet1k, [§]COCO captions, [†]CLIP400M, [‡]Conceptual Captions, [⋆]Open Images, and [c]COCO

Method	Img-Cap Data Size	Constrained				Generalized					
		Novel (17)		Known (48)		Novel (17)		Known (48)		All (65)	
		AP	AP_{50}	AP	AP_{50}	AP	AP_{50}	AP	AP_{50}	AP	AP_{50}
Faster R-CNN		–	–	–	54.5	–	–	–	–	–	–
SB [2]	–	–	0.70	–	29.7	–	0.31	–	29.2	–	24.9
LAB [2]		–	0.27	–	21.1	–	0.22	–	20.8	–	18.0
DSES [2]		–	0.54	–	27.2	–	0.27	–	26.7	–	22.1
DELO [44]		–	7.6	–	14.0	–	3.41	–	13.8	–	13.0
PL [29]		–	10.0	–	36.8	–	4.12	–	35.9	–	27.9
STT-ZSD (Ours)		0.21	0.31	33.2	53.4	0.03	0.05	**33.0**	53.1	24.4	39.2
OVR[*§c] [39]		14.6	27.5	26.9	46.8	–	22.8	–	46.0	22.8	39.9
LocOv [*§c] (Ours)	0.6M	**17.2**	30.1	**33.5**	53.4	**16.6**	**28.6**	31.9	51.3	**28.1**	45.7
XP-Mask[‡§*c] [16]	5.7M	–	29.9	–	46.8	–	27.0	–	46.3	–	41.2
CLIP (cropped reg)[†] [13]	400M	–	–	–	–	–	26.3	–	28.3	–	27.8
RegionCLIP[†§c] [42]	400.6M	–	**30.8**	–	**55.2**	–	26.8	–	54.8	–	47.5
ViLD[†c] [13]	400M	–	–	–	–	–	27.6	–	**59.5**	–	**51.3**

We use Detectron2 framework [38] for our implementation. For the part-of-word feature representations, we use the embedding module of the pre-trained BERT [10] "base-uncased" model from the HuggingFace implementation [37]. To get the object proposals for the LSM stage, we train a generic object proposal network, OLN [18]. OLN is trained using only the known classes on COCO training set. We use all the proposals generated for the training images which have an objectness score higher than 0.7. For our cross-attention model, we use a transformer-based architecture with 6 hidden layers and 8 attention heads trained from scratch. We train our LSM stage with a base learning rate of 0.001, where the learning rate is divided by 10 at 45k and 60k iterations. We use a batch size of 32 and train on 8 GeForce-RTX-2080-Ti GPUs for 90k iterations. For the STT stage, we initialize the weights of the Faster R-CNN and projection layer from the LSM stage, freezing the first two blocks of ResNet50 and the projection layer. For object classes that contain more than one part-of-word representation given BERT embedding module, we consider the average of their vector representation. We use a base learning rate of 0.005 with a 10 times drop at 60k iterations and do early stopping to avoid over-fitting.

4.2 Baselines

OVR. The main baseline approach is proposed by Zareian et al.[39]. We utilize some components proposed in the work including the two-stage design, grounding loss and usage of a cross-attention model. In this work, we propose new components, which simplify and improve the model performance over OVR.

Table 2. Different image regions for the LSM stage. R^I_{grid}- grid-regions, R^I_{box}- proposed box-regions and R^I_{ann}- ground truth box-regions of (k) known or (n) novel objects use during the LSM stage

Regions			Novel (17)			Known (48)			Generalized		
R^I_{grid}	R^I_{box}	R^I_{ann}	AP	AP$_{50}$	AP$_{75}$	AP	AP$_{50}$	AP$_{75}$	AP	AP$_{50}$	AP$_{75}$
100		k+n	18.2	31.6	18.2	32.5	52.7	34.0	27.9	46.0	28.8
		k+n	16.3	28.4	15.9	32.9	53.1	34.9	27.6	45.3	28.8
100	100		**17.2**	**30.1**	**17.5**	33.5	53.4	35.5	**28.1**	**45.7**	**29.6**
200			15.5	27.1	15.4	32.2	52.1	33.9	27.1	44.5	28.2
	200		13.7	25.7	12.9	**34.2**	**53.8**	**36.5**	27.5	43.8	29.1

STT-ZSD. Our second baseline uses only the Specialized Task Tuning stage. This resembles a zero-shot object detection setting. The model is initialized with ImageNet [9] weights with a trainable projection layer.

Zero-Shot Methods. We compare to some zero-shot object detection approaches which do not include the weak supervision provided by the captions. We compare to three background-aware zero-shot detection methods, introduced by Bansal *et al.*[2], which project features of an object bounding box proposal method to word embeddings. The **SB** method includes a fixed vector for the background class in order to select which bounding boxes to exclude during the object classification, **LAB** uses multiple latent vectors to represent the different variations of the background class, and **DSES** includes more classes than the known set as word embedding to train in a more dense semantic space. **DELO** [44] method uses a generative model and unknown classes to synthesize visual features and uses them while training to increase background confidence. **PL** [29] work deals with the imbalance between positive vs. negative instance ratio by proposing a method that maximizes the margin between foreground and background boxes.

Faster R-CNN. We also compare with training the classical Faster R-CNN model only using the known classes.

Open-Vocabulary with Large Data. We compare our method with recent open-vocabulary models. RegionClip [42] uses the CLIP [28] pre-trained model to produce image-region pseudo labels and train an object detector. CLIP (cropped reg) [13] uses the CLIP pre-trained model on 400M image-caption pairs on object proposals obtained by an object detector trained on known classes. XP-Mask [16] learns a class-agnostic region proposal and segmentation model from the known classes and then uses this model as a teacher to generate pseudo masks for self-training a student model. Finally, we also compare with VILD [13] which uses CLIP soft predictions to distil semantic information and train an object detector.

(a) Ground Truth   (b) STT-ZSD   (c) OVR [39]   (d) LocOv

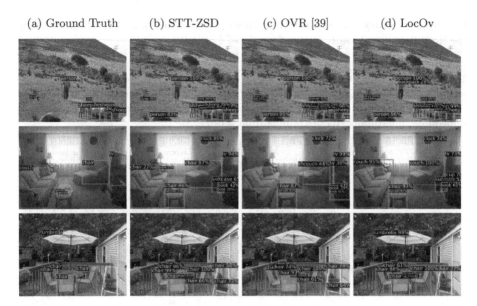

Fig. 3. Qualitative results for open-vocabulary object detection on MSCOCO dataset. Novel classes are shown in magenta while known are in green. Methods compared are described in Section 4.2. (Best viewed in color)

4.3   Results

COCO Dataset. Table 1 shows the comparison of our method with several zero-shot and open-vocabulary object detection approaches. LocOv outperforms previous zero-shot detection methods, which show weak performance on detecting novel objects. In comparison to OVR, we improve by 2.53 AP, 3.4 AP_{50} for the novel classes and 3.91 AP, 3.92 AP_{50} for the known categories. We observe open-vocabulary methods including OVR and our methods have a trade-off between known and novel class performance. Our method finds a better trade-off as compared to the previous work. It reduces the performance gap on known classes as compared to the Faster R-CNN and improves over the novel classes as compared to all previous works. Our method is competitive with recent state-of-the-art methods which use more than ∼700 times more image-captions pairs to train, which makes our method data efficient.

Figure 3 shows some qualitative results of our method compared with the STT-ZSD baseline and OVR. Known categories are drawn in green while novel are highlighted in magenta. The columns correspond to the ground truth, STT-ZSD, OVR and our method from left to right. LocOv is able to find novel objects with a high confidence, such as the dogs in the first example, the couch in the second and the umbrella in the third one. We observe that our method sometimes misclassifies objects with plausible ones, such as the case of the chair in the second example which shares a similar appearance to a couch. These examples show a clear improvement of our approach, over the other methods. In the supplementary material we include some examples of our method showing the limitations and main cause of errors of LocOv.

Table 3. Ablation study showing the contribution of our proposed consistency-regularization term ($\mathcal{L}_{Cons}$) and usage of BERT text embeddings on COCO validation set. We compared using frozen pretrained weights (fz) of the language model and embedding, fine-tuning (ft) or training from scratch

$\mathcal{L}_{Cons}$	BERT model	BERT Emb	Novel (17)			Known (48)			Generalized		
			AP	AP$_{50}$	AP$_{75}$	AP	AP$_{50}$	AP$_{75}$	AP	AP$_{50}$	AP$_{75}$
✓		fz	**17.2**	**30.1**	**17.5**	33.5	53.4	**35.5**	28.1	45.7	**29.6**
✓	fz	fz	16.7	29.7	16.7	33.4	**53.5**	**35.5**	**28.2**	45.9	29.5
✓		ft	16.9	29.5	16.9	33.4	53.0	35.4	28.1	45.7	29.4
✓		scratch	16.0	28.3	16.2	30.4	49.6	31.8	25.8	42.9	26.6
		fz	15.4	27.9	15.2	32.2	52.1	34.1	26.3	43.6	27.3

4.4 Ablation Experiments

Localized Objects Matter. Table 2 presents the impact of using box- vs grid-region features in the LSM stage. We compare our method using grid-region features R^I_{grid}, proposed box-region features R^I_{box}, and using box-region features from the known (k) or novel (n) class annotations R^I_{ann}. We find that the combination of grid- and box-regions proves to be best, showing a complementary behavior. We also considered two oracle experiments (row 1 and 2) using ground-truth box-region features from both known and novel class annotations instead of proposed box-region features. The best performance is achieved when combined with additional grid regions (row 1). The additional grid-regions help in capturing the background objects beyond the annotated classes while box-regions focus on foreground objects, which improves the image-caption matching.

Consistency Loss and Text Embedding Selection. Table 3, shows the contribution of our consistency-regularization term. We get an improvement of 1.76 AP by introducing our consistency loss. We compare the performance of using a pre-trained text embedding module vs learning it from scratch, fine-tuning it or considering the complete contextualized language model during the LSM stage in Table 3. Using the pre-trained text embedding, results in a better model.

We find out that using only the embeddings module is sufficient and better than using the complete contextualized BERT language model for the task of object detection. We argue that this is because objects are mostly represented by single word vectors, using simple disentangled text embeddings is better suited for generating object class features. In the supplementary material we include an ablation study showing that both stages of training are necessary and complementary for the success of LocOv.

Table 4. Ablation study showing the contributions LocOv. $\mathcal{L}_{Cons}$ = consistency-regularization, R_{box}^{I} = inclusion of box-regions together with grid-regions, BERT Emb. only.

$\mathcal{L}_{Cons}$	R_{box}^{I}	BERT Emb	Novel (17)			Known (48)			Generalized		
			AP	AP_{50}	AP_{75}	AP	AP_{50}	AP_{75}	AP	AP_{50}	AP_{75}
✓	✓	✓	**17.2**	**30.1**	**17.5**	**33.5**	53.4	**35.5**	28.1	45.7	**29.6**
✓	✓	✗	16.7	29.7	16.7	33.4	**53.5**	**35.5**	**28.2**	**45.9**	29.5
✓	✗	✓	15.5	27.1	15.4	32.2	52.1	33.9	27.1	44.5	28.2
✗	✓	✓	15.4	27.9	15.2	32.2	52.1	34.1	26.3	43.6	27.3
✗	✗	✗	14.3	25.6	14.4	28.1	47.8	29.3	23.7	40.9	24.5

Table 4 shows the the improvement in performance for each of our contributions. Our baseline method is our implementation of OVR [39]. Both the consistency-regularization together with the inclusion of the box-regions gives the most increment in performance for both novel and known classes. Using only the BERT Embeddings improves the novel class performance although it affects the known classes. Overall we can see that the three contributions are complementary and improve the method for open-vocabulary detection.

5   Conclusion

In this work, we proposed an image-caption matching method for open-vocabulary object detection. We introduced a localized matching technique to learn improved labels of novel classes as compared to only using grid features. We also showed that the language embedding model is preferable over a complete language model, and proposed a regularization approach to improve cross-modal learning. In conjunction, these components yield favorable results compared to previous open-vocabulary methods on COCO and VAW benchmarks, particularly considering the much lower amount of necessary data to learn from.

Acknowledgement. This work was supported by Deutscher Akademischer Austauschdienst - German Academic Exchange Service (DAAD) Research Grants - Doctoral Programmes in Germany, 2019/20; grant number: 57440921.

The Deep Learning Cluster used in this work is partially funded by the German Research Foundation (DFG) - 417962828.

References

1. Amrani, E., Ben-Ari, R., Shapira, I., Hakim, T., Bronstein, A.: Self-supervised object detection and retrieval using unlabeled videos. In: Proceedings of the IEEE/CVF Conference on Computer Vision and Pattern Recognition (CVPR) Workshops (2020)
2. Bansal, A., Sikka, K., Sharma, G., Chellappa, R., Divakaran, A.: Zero-shot object detection. In: Proceedings of the European Conference on Computer Vision (ECCV) (2018)

3. Bertasius, G., Torresani, L.: Cobe: Contextualized object embeddings from narrated instructional video. In: Advances in Neural Information Processing Systems (2020)

4. Bilen, H., Vedaldi, A.: Weakly supervised deep detection networks. In: Proceedings of the IEEE Conference on Computer Vision and Pattern Recognition (CVPR) (2016)

5. Chen, X., Fang, H., Lin, T.Y., Vedantam, R., Gupta, S., Dollár, P., Zitnick, C.L.: Microsoft coco captions: Data collection and evaluation server. arXiv preprint arXiv:1504.00325 (2015)

6. Chen, Y.C., Li, L., Yu, L., El Kholy, A., Ahmed, F., Gan, Z., Cheng, Y., Liu, J.: Uniter: Universal image-text representation learning. In: European conference on computer vision. pp. 104–120. Springer (2020)

7. Chen, Z., Ma, L., Luo, W., Wong, K.Y.K.: Weakly-supervised spatio-temporally grounding natural sentence in video. In: Proceedings of the 57th Annual Meeting of the Association for Computational Linguistics (2019)

8. Cinbis, R.G., Verbeek, J., Schmid, C.: Weakly supervised object localization with multi-fold multiple instance learning. IEEE Transactions on Pattern Analysis and Machine Intelligence (2017)

9. Deng, J., Dong, W., Socher, R., Li, L.J., Li, K., Fei-Fei, L.: Imagenet: A large-scale hierarchical image database. In: 2009 IEEE Conference on Computer Vision and Pattern Recognition (2009)

10. Devlin, J., Chang, M., Lee, K., Toutanova, K.: BERT: pre-training of deep bidirectional transformers for language understanding. arXiv preprint arXiv:1810.04805 (2018)

11. Dong, J., Li, X., Xu, C., Ji, S., He, Y., Yang, G., Wang, X.: Dual encoding for zero-example video retrieval. In: Proceedings of the IEEE/CVF Conference on Computer Vision and Pattern Recognition (2019)

12. Ging, S., Zolfaghari, M., Pirsiavash, H., Brox, T.: Coot: Cooperative hierarchical transformer for video-text representation learning. In: Advances in Neural Information Processing Systems (NeurIPS) (2020)

13. Gu, X., Lin, T.Y., Kuo, W., Cui, Y.: Open-vocabulary object detection via vision and language knowledge distillation. In: International Conference on Learning Representations (2022), https://openreview.net/forum?id=lL3lnMbR4WU

14. He, K., Zhang, X., Ren, S., Sun, J.: Deep residual learning for image recognition. In: 2016 IEEE Conference on Computer Vision and Pattern Recognition (CVPR) (2016)

15. Huang, Z., Zeng, Z., Liu, B., Fu, D., Fu, J.: Pixel-bert: Aligning image pixels with text by deep multi-modal transformers. arXiv preprint arXiv:2004.00849 (2020)

16. Huynh, D., Kuen, J., Lin, Z., Gu, J., Elhamifar, E.: Open-vocabulary instance segmentation via robust cross-modal pseudo-labeling. arXiv preprint arXiv:2111.12698 (2021)

17. Jeong, J., Lee, S., Kim, J., Kwak, N.: Consistency-based semi-supervised learning for object detection. In: Advances in Neural Information Processing Systems (2019)

18. Kim, D., Lin, T.Y., Angelova, A., Kweon, I.S., Kuo, W.: Learning open-world object proposals without learning to classify. IEEE Robotics and Automation Letters 7(2), 5453–5460 (2022)

19. Klein, B., Lev, G., Sadeh, G., Wolf, L.: Associating neural word embeddings with deep image representations using fisher vectors. In: Proceedings of the IEEE Conference on Computer Vision and Pattern Recognition (2015)

20. Kosugi, S., Yamasaki, T., Aizawa, K.: Object-aware instance labeling for weakly supervised object detection. In: Proceedings of the IEEE/CVF International Conference on Computer Vision (ICCV) (2019)
21. Li, X., Yin, X., Li, C., Zhang, P., Hu, X., Zhang, L., Wang, L., Hu, H., Dong, L., Wei, F., et al.: Oscar: Object-semantics aligned pre-training for vision-language tasks. In: European Conference on Computer Vision (2020)
22. Lin, T.Y., Maire, M., Belongie, S., Hays, J., Perona, P., Ramanan, D., Dollár, P., Zitnick, C.L.: Microsoft coco: Common objects in context. In: European conference on computer vision (2014)
23. Liu, Y.C., Ma, C.Y., He, Z., Kuo, C.W., Chen, K., Zhang, P., Wu, B., Kira, Z., Vajda, P.: Unbiased teacher for semi-supervised object detection. In: International Conference on Learning Representations (2021)
24. Lu, J., Batra, D., Parikh, D., Lee, S.: Vilbert: pretraining task-agnostic visiolinguistic representations for vision-and-language tasks. In: Proceedings of the 33rd International Conference on Neural Information Processing Systems (2019)
25. Miech, A., Alayrac, J.B., Laptev, I., Sivic, J., Zisserman, A.: Thinking fast and slow: Efficient text-to-visual retrieval with transformers. In: Proceedings of the IEEE/CVF Conference on Computer Vision and Pattern Recognition (CVPR) (2021)
26. Pennington, J., Socher, R., Manning, C.D.: Glove: Global vectors for word representation. In: Proceedings of the 2014 conference on empirical methods in natural language processing (EMNLP) (2014)
27. Pham, K., Kafle, K., Lin, Z., Ding, Z., Cohen, S., Tran, Q., Shrivastava, A.: Learning to predict visual attributes in the wild. In: Proceedings of the IEEE/CVF Conference on Computer Vision and Pattern Recognition (CVPR) (2021)
28. Radford, A., Kim, J.W., Hallacy, C., Ramesh, A., Goh, G., Agarwal, S., Sastry, G., Askell, A., Mishkin, P., Clark, J., et al.: Learning transferable visual models from natural language supervision. In: International Conference on Machine Learning. pp. 8748–8763. PMLR (2021)
29. Rahman, S., Khan, S., Barnes, N.: Improved visual-semantic alignment for zero-shot object detection. Proceedings of the AAAI Conference on Artificial Intelligence (2020)
30. Ren, S., He, K., Girshick, R., Sun, J.: Faster r-cnn: Towards real-time object detection with region proposal networks. In: Advances in Neural Information Processing Systems (2015)
31. Ren, Z., Yu, Z., Yang, X., Liu, M.Y., Lee, Y.J., Schwing, A.G., Kautz, J.: Instance-aware, context-focused, and memory-efficient weakly supervised object detection. In: Proceedings of the IEEE/CVF Conference on Computer Vision and Pattern Recognition (CVPR) (2020)
32. Sadhu, A., Chen, K., Nevatia, R.: Video object grounding using semantic roles in language description. In: Proceedings of the IEEE/CVF Conference on Computer Vision and Pattern Recognition (CVPR) (2020)
33. Sohn, K., Zhang, Z., Li, C., Zhang, H., Lee, C., Pfister, T.: A simple semi-supervised learning framework for object detection. arXiv preprint arXiv:2005.04757 (2020)
34. Su, W., Zhu, X., Cao, Y., Li, B., Lu, L., Wei, F., Dai, J.: Vl-bert: Pre-training of generic visual-linguistic representations. In: International Conference on Learning Representations (2019)
35. Tan, H., Bansal, M.: Lxmert: Learning cross-modality encoder representations from transformers. In: Proceedings of the 2019 Conference on Empirical Methods in Natural Language Processing and the 9th International Joint Conference on Natural Language Processing (EMNLP-IJCNLP) (2019)

36. Wang, L., Li, Y., Huang, J., Lazebnik, S.: Learning two-branch neural networks for image-text matching tasks. IEEE Transactions on Pattern Analysis and Machine Intelligence (2018)

37. Wolf, T., Debut, L., Sanh, V., Chaumond, J., Delangue, C., Moi, A., Cistac, P., Rault, T., Louf, R., Funtowicz, M., Davison, J., Shleifer, S., von Platen, P., Ma, C., Jernite, Y., Plu, J., Xu, C., Scao, T.L., Gugger, S., Drame, M., Lhoest, Q., Rush, A.M.: Transformers: State-of-the-art natural language processing. In: Proceedings of the 2020 Conference on Empirical Methods in Natural Language Processing: System Demonstrations (2020)

38. Wu, Y., Kirillov, A., Massa, F., Lo, W.Y., Girshick, R.: Detectron2. https://github.com/facebookresearch/detectron2 (2019)

39. Zareian, A., Rosa, K.D., Hu, D.H., Chang, S.F.: Open-vocabulary object detection using captions. In: Proceedings of the IEEE/CVF Conference on Computer Vision and Pattern Recognition (CVPR) (2021)

40. Zhang, P., Li, X., Hu, X., Yang, J., Zhang, L., Wang, L., Choi, Y., Gao, J.: Vinvl: Revisiting visual representations in vision-language models. In: Proceedings of the IEEE/CVF Conference on Computer Vision and Pattern Recognition (2021)

41. Zhang, Z., Zhao, Z., Zhao, Y., Wang, Q., Liu, H., Gao, L.: Where does it exist: Spatio-temporal video grounding for multi-form sentences. In: Proceedings of the IEEE/CVF Conference on Computer Vision and Pattern Recognition (CVPR) (2020)

42. Zhong, Y., Yang, J., Zhang, P., Li, C., Codella, N., Li, L.H., Zhou, L., Dai, X., Yuan, L., Li, Y., et al.: Regionclip: Region-based language-image pretraining. arXiv preprint arXiv:2112.09106 (2021)

43. Zhou, L., Palangi, H., Zhang, L., Hu, H., Corso, J., Gao, J.: Unified vision-language pre-training for image captioning and vqa. In: Proceedings of the AAAI Conference on Artificial Intelligence (2020)

44. Zhu, P., Wang, H., Saligrama, V.: Don't even look once: Synthesizing features for zero-shot detection. In: Proceedings of the IEEE/CVF Conference on Computer Vision and Pattern Recognition (CVPR) (2020)

Diverse Video Captioning by Adaptive Spatio-temporal Attention

Zohreh Ghaderi$^{(\boxtimes)}$, Leonard Salewski, and Hendrik P. A. Lensch

University of Tübingen, Tübingen, Germany
{zohreh.ghaderi,leonard.salewski,hendrik.lensch}@uni-tuebingen.de

Abstract. To generate proper captions for videos, the inference needs to identify relevant concepts and pay attention to the spatial relationships between them as well as to the temporal development in the clip. Our end-to-end encoder-decoder video captioning framework incorporates two transformer-based architectures, an adapted transformer for a single joint spatio-temporal video analysis as well as a self-attention-based decoder for advanced text generation. Furthermore, we introduce an adaptive frame selection scheme to reduce the number of required incoming frames while maintaining the relevant content when training both transformers. Additionally, we estimate semantic concepts relevant for video captioning by aggregating all ground truth captions of each sample. Our approach achieves state-of-the-art results on the MSVD, as well as on the large-scale MSR-VTT and the VATEX benchmark datasets considering multiple Natural Language Generation (NLG) metrics. Additional evaluations on diversity scores highlight the expressiveness and diversity in the structure of our generated captions.

Keywords: Video captioning · Transformer · Diversity scores

1 Introduction

The interplay between visual and text information has recently captivated scientists in the field of computer vision research. Generating a caption for a short video is a simple task for most people, but a tough one for a machine. In particular, video captioning can be seen as a sequence-to-sequence task [40] similar to machine translation. Video captioning frameworks aim to learn a high-level understating of the video and then convert it into text.

Since deep learning has revolutionized almost all computer vision sub-fields, it also plays a notable role in video description generation. Usually, two main Deep Neural Networks are involved, the encoder analyses visual content and the decoder generates text [17,40,46,47,53]. The employed networks often are a variety of 2D-CNN and 3D-CNNs. They extract visual features and local motion

Supplementary Information The online version contains supplementary material available at https://doi.org/10.1007/978-3-031-16788-1_25.

information between successive frames. Furthermore, a Faster RCNN object recognition (FRCNN) [37] can be used to obtain fine-grained spatial information.

Attention mechanisms are adopted to let the model build relations between local and global temporal and spatio-temporal information. This information is subsequently fed to a recurrent neural network such as an LSTM or a GRU in order to produce grammatically correct sentences [1,32,52,57]. The temporal processing is, however, somehow limited as it either involves global aggregation with no temporal resolution or is based on 3D-CNNs with a rather small temporal footprint. Transformer-based encoder-decoder architectures, on the other hand, can inherently establish relations between all components in a sequence independent of their positions [44]. After their breakthrough on language tasks, lately, transformers have been successfully applied to diverse vision applications, mainly for pure classification [3,29].

In this work, we present VASTA, an end-to-end encoder-decoder framework for the task of video captioning where transformers perform detailed visual spatio-temporal analysis of the input as well as generating the caption output.

Our encoder architecture is adopted from the Video Swin Transformer [30], which has been shown to be able to interpret non-local temporal dependencies in video-based action recognition. The task of video captioning, however, requires even more than just spatio-temporal analysis. It needs to extract all semantically relevant concepts [34,38], which will be key for the downstream text generation. We identify all relevant concepts in the captions of the training data sets and fine-tune the Swin Transformer to explicitly predict those before handing latent information to the BERT generator.

As end-to-end training of two transformers, in particular for video processing, is quite involved, we introduce an adaptive frame sampling (AFS) strategy that identifies informative keyframes for caption generation.

Our transformer-based encoder-decoder architecture harnesses the power of transformers for both the visual analysis as well as for the language generating part, rendering quite faithful descriptions to a broad range of videos. In summary, our contributions are:

a) a simple transformer-based video captioning approach, where a *single* encoder extracts all necessary spatio-temporal information. Unlike other recent works we do not employ disjoint 2D analysis (e.g. object detection) and 3D analysis (e.g. 3D convolution),
b) adaptive frame sampling for selecting more informative frames,
c) visually grounded semantic context vectors derived from all captions of each sample provide high-quality semantic guidance to the decoder,
d) state-of-the-art results on three datasets (MSVD, MSR-VTT and VATEX),
e) significantly increased diversity in the predicted captions.

2   Related Work

Existing video captioning approaches can be grouped according to the techniques used for visual analysis and text generation. See Aafaq et al. [2] for a detailed survey.

2.1   Classical Models

Classical models mainly concentrate on detecting objects, actors and events in order to fill the SVO (SVOP) structure [41]. Detection of objects and humans was accomplished by model-based shape matching including HOG, HOF and MbH, [15,48,49]. The analysis part is typically weak on interpreting dynamics and the output of these models is limited due to their explicit sentence structures [20,24–27]. Classical models have recently been outperformed by models based on deep learning.

Spatio-Temporal Analysis with CNNs. On the encoder side, a more fine-grained analysis of the spatio-temporal aspects has been enabled with the advent of 3D-convolutions and the corresponding C3D network [42]. Li et al. [53] present a 3D-CNN network for fine local motion analysis and employ soft-attention [4] for adaptive aggregation to obtain a global feature for video captioning. Methods like [1,13,39,50] combine both 2D and 3D-CNNs with attention mechanisms to obtain stronger spatial-temporal and global features. As the video captions often reflect some temporal relation between specific objects, the use of explicit object detectors [32,54,57,58] can improve the generated descriptions. Recently, the work on MGCMP [10] and CoSB [43] illustrates that extracting fine-grained spatial information followed by propagation across time frames could provide visual features as good as other methods that use external object detector features as long as their relation is adequately realized in the temporal domain. While temporally resolved features are necessary to analyse the dynamics, global aggregates can provide the proper semantic context for generating captions. In [8,34,38], semantic attributes are learned inside a CNN-RNN framework. In contrast to the work of Gan et al. [18] we condition our decoder on the semantic context vector once instead of feeding it to the decoder at every step. Still, the self-attention operation of our decoder allows it to be accessed whenever it is needed. It has been shown that selecting informative frames aids in video action recognition [19] as this reduces the overall processing cost and lets the system focus on the relevant parts only. The frame selection could be trained to optimize the input for the downstream task as in [12,19] but this would introduce further complexity to controlling the entire pipeline. In contrast to [12,19] our method is simpler and does not require to be learned.

Transformer-Based Models. Following the success of transformers [44] in text-related sequence-to-sequence tasks like translation, they have recently also been applied to vision tasks and in particular to video classification. A key ingredient of transformers is the multi-head self-attention mechanism where each head individually can attend and combine different parts of the sequence. This way, a transformer can explore both long-term and short-term dependencies in the same operation. For the task of action recognition, the ViViT transformer [3] chops the video cube into separate spatio-temporal blocks, applying multi-head self-attention. To keep the complexity at bay, factorized attention alternates between relating temporal or spatially-aligned blocks. The video Swin Transformer [30] overcomes the problem of hard partition boundaries by shifting the block boundaries by half a block in every other attention layer. Instead for action recognition, we use the Swin transformer for video captioning. On a different task, Zoha et al. [59] employ transformer in video dense captioning with long sequences and multiple events to be described. The concept of cross-attention can easily fuse the information coming in from different feature extractors. TVT [9] uses a transformer instead of a CNN-RNN network for the video captioning task. They use attentive-fusion blocks to integrate image and motion information. The sparse boundary-aware transformer method [21] explicitly performs cross-attention between the image domain and extracted motion features. In addition, a specific scoring scheme tries to tune the multi-head attention to ignore redundant information in subsequent frames. Unlike these works we do not require special fusion, as we use a single joint encoder of the input video.

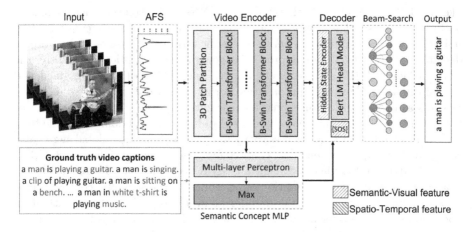

Fig. 1. VASTA (diverse Video captioning by Adaptive Spatio-Temporal Attention) The most informative 32 frames are selected by adaptive frame sampling (AFS) as input to a Swin transformer [30] for spatio-temporal video analysis. The output tokens of the encoder are used twice, once, to predict a semantic concept vector aggregating the entire sequence as start-of-sequence token for the BERT decoder, and, second, for cross-attention in the decoder. A beam search on the most likely words predicts the final caption.

3 Model Architecture

The composed architecture of our VASTA model, visualized in Fig. 1, is based on an encoder-decoder transformer [44]. First, an adaptive selection method is used to find informative frames in the whole video length. Thereafter, the model encodes the selected video frames into a contextualised but temporally resolved embedding. We modify the Swin Transformer block [30], which was originally designed for action recognition and classification tasks, to interpret the input video. The last hidden layer of this encoder is passed to the decoder. Though compressed, the output of the encoder still contains a temporal sequence. This allows the BERT [16] decoder to cross-attend to that sequence when generating the output. Besides the direct encoder-decoder connection, the encoder output is further used to predict a globally aggregated semantic context vector that is to condition the language generator.

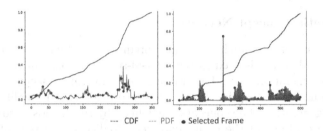

Fig. 2. Adaptive frame selection visualized for two videos from the MSR-VTT. x-axis: video length, y-axis: PDF and CDF drived from LPIPS sampling.

3.1   Adaptive Frame Selection

In videos, not all frames contribute the same information to the final caption. Some frames are rather similar to the previous ones while some contain dynamics or show new objects. In most video captioning approaches, frames are selected with fixed uniform intervals [13,42,57].

Our adaptive frame selection (AFS) performs importance sampling on the input frames based on local frame similarity. First, the similarity for each pair of two consecutive frames is computed by the LPIPS score [55]. As indicated in Fig. 2, we consider this similarity as a probability density function (PDF) f, normalizing it over all frames. Computing and inverting the cumulative density function (CDF) F with

$$F(x) = P(X \le x) = \int_{-\infty}^{x} f(t)\mathrm{d}t, \text{ for } x \in \mathbb{R} \tag{1}$$

one can sample N frames i according to f starting with a uniform distribution $j = \left\{ 0, \frac{1}{N}, \frac{2}{N}, ..., \frac{N-1}{N} \right\}$, $i = round(F^{-1}(j))$.

We select the frame i by rounding to the nearest integer. The resulting sequence forms the input to the 3D patch partition of the encoder.

3.2 Encoder

The Swin architecture is a hierarchical transformer that is able to act as general-purpose backbone in computer vision tasks [29]. The vision input is initially split into non-overlapping patches, followed by **Shifting** these **Win**dows by half the patch size in every other self-attention step to avoid artifacts from the discrete partitioning. Consequently, the swin video transformer [30] operates on shifted 3D partitions to cover both the spatial and the temporal domain. The encoder backbone is the Swin-B variant with last the hidden layer size ($BS \times 16 \times 1024$).

3.3 Semantic Concept Network

The second step of our pipeline includes predicting a semantic concept vector of the entire video that is used as the start-of-sequence token in the decoder to condition its generation on it. The training signal for this concept vector aggregates *all* ground truth captions of a video to provide a high-quality signal for the caption generation. The concepts are defined by the K most frequent words found in the captions of the entire data set. Predicting the semantic concept vector of a video is learned as a binary multi-class classification task indicating which of the frequent words are relevant to describe the video. For generating the ground truth classification vectors, we first select nouns, verbs and adverbs[1] from all captions of the training videos (see Fig. 1). Each video is labeled with the K-dimensional vector L by:

$$L_k = \begin{cases} 1, & \text{if word } k \text{ occurs in any caption} \\ 0, & \text{otherwise} \end{cases}$$

An MLP acts separately with shared weights on each of the encoder outputs. A single max-pooling layer merges them to one token. Afterwards a two-layer MLP with RELU activation predicts the K concepts. For training, the binary cross-entropy loss is minimized. In essence, the probability of each word in the concept dictionary is used as a semantic feature. Introducing the semantic concept vector provides an aggregated constant signal for each video while the decoder is trained by generating individual captions.

3.4 Decoder

Our decoder generates the language output word by word while self-attending to all already generated tokens. During training, masking ensures that BERT cannot access the future tokens while during inference it is auto-regressive.

In our architecture, we pass the semantic feature vector as start-of-sequence token to the decoder for generating the first output word. The self-attention to the first input token conditions the predicted caption on the semantic concepts which have been identified by the semantics MLP. In order to couple the hidden

---

[1] Categorizing and POS tagging using NLTK (https://www.nltk.org/).

states of the decoder to the output of the encoder, cross-modal fusion is necessary. The necessary functionality is incorporated by extending the decoder with multi-head cross-attention [44]. In 13 layers, the architecture alternates between multi-head self-attention on the language tokens, cross-attention between the language tokens and the Swin output tokens, and a feed-forward layer followed by normalization. All these steps are bridged by a residual connection. A final linear layer projects the decoder internal hidden states to the size of the BERT vocabulary, followed by a softmax to produce word probabilities for each token. The sentence is finally generated by applying beam search [36] to obtain the most likely combination of words.

4   Experiments

To show the effectiveness of our proposed architecture, we train our model on three common video captioning data sets and achieve high-ranking results.

Details on the architecture, training and optimizer [31] settings are described in the supplementary.

4.1   Datasets and Metrics

Our model is trained on MSR-VTT [51], MSVD [7] and VATEX [50]. **MSVD** [7] includes 1970 videos with an average length of 10 s. It provides up to 45 captions per video which are randomly sampled during training. **MSR-VTT** [51] contains a wide variety of open domain videos of 20 s average and 20 captions per video. **VATEX** [50] is a large-scale video description dataset. It is lexically richer, as each video has 10 unique sentences and every caption is unique in the whole corpus.

Similarity Metrics. All captions in all datasets have been annotated by humans. We utilize the MS COCO Caption Evaluation [11] protocol on both datasets and evaluate standard natural language generation metrics (NLG) as done by previous works in this field. These metrics include BLEU(4-gram)(B4) [33], METEOR(M) [5], CIDEr(C) [45] and ROUGE-L(R) [28]. Additionally, we evaluate on BERTScore [56], a more modern evaluation metric, that has shown great alignment with human judgement. Notably, it does not share the same brittleness as the n-gram based metrics [33].

Diversity Metrics. In contrast to previous work we further measure the diversity of the generated captions. Zhu et al. [60] introduced Self-BLEU (SB) to evaluate the diversity of generated sentences. It measures the BLEU value of each prediction wrt. the remaining predictions and averages the obtained BLEU values. A lower value indicates higher diversity, as on average a prediction is less similar to all other predictions. Furthermore, Dai et al. [14] proposed the concepts of Novel Captions (N), Unique Caption (U) and Vocab Usage (V) to evaluate diversity of the generated caption. Novel Caption shows the percentage of generated captions which have not been seen in the training data; Unique

Caption denotes the percentage of distinct captions among all generated captions; Vocab Usage indicates the percentage of words that are used to generate captions from the whole vocabulary.

4.2 Quantitative Results

We present quantitative results in Tables 1 and 2 and highlight that besides explanation quality also explanation diversity is important (Table 3). We ablate the components of our model in Table 4 and discuss qualitative examples in Sect. 4.4.

Comparison to Related Approaches. On the very large VATEX data set our generated captions show significant performance improvements on all scores (see Table 1). Similarly, on MSR-VTT and the even smaller MSVD we obtain high-ranking, most often top-scoring results with slightly less improvements (see Table 2). This indicates that fine tuning of the encoder and decoder transformers benefits from the additional training data.

Table 1. Natural Language Generation (NLG) and BERT scores for VATEX.

Method	Model	Year	B4 ↑	M ↑	C ↑	R ↑	BERT-S ↑
Shared Enc-Dec [50]	A	2019	28.4	21.7	45.1	47.0	-
NITS-VC [39]	A	2020	20.0	18.0	24.0	42.0	-
ORG-TRL [57]	A	2020	32.1	22.2	49.7	48.9	-
VASTA (Kinetics-backbone)	T	2022	36.25	25.32	65.07	51.88	90.76

Thus, instead of just fine-tuning the full pipeline starting with the backbone trained on Kinetics [22] for each individual data set, we trained once end-to-end on VATEX and then fine-tuned for MSVD and MSR-VTT. Through this transfer learning VASTA improves in general, particularly the CIDEr score on MSR-VTT and MSVD by a big margin. The performance on METEOR and CIDEr is relevant as both consider semantic relatedness. METEOR excepts synonyms and it exhibits a higher correlation with human judgment on captions and explanations [23]. The CIDEr score has been particularly designed for measuring the quality of descriptions for visual content. While the NLG scores are all based on n-grams the BERTScore is more semantically robust and agrees even better with human assessments. On both data sets, our model achieves the highest BERTScore.

Caption Diversity. Albeit their wide-spread use, NLG metrics only assess a few aspects of the generated captions. Maximising the scores on existing NLG metrics as presented in Table 2 can for example be achieved with focusing on the most prevalent sentence structure found in the ground truth captions. However,

Table 2. Natural Language Generation (NLG) and BERT scores for the MSR-VTT and MSVD datasets (T: Transformer, A: Attention). Darker blue indicates higher scores. For both data sets our approach improves the BERTScore and produces high-ranking NLG scores. †: BERT-score is computed on reproduced captions by the released code.

| Method | Model | Year | MSR-VTT | | | | | MSVD | | | | |
			B4	M	C	R	BERT-S	B4	M	C	R	BERT-S
Att-TVT [9]	T	2018	40.12	27.86	47.72	59.63	-	53.21	35.23	86.76	-	
GRU-EVE [1]	A	2019	38.3	28.4	48.1	60.7	-	47.9	35.0	78.1	71.5	-
OA-BTG [54]	A	2019	41.4	28.2	46.9	-	-		36.9	36.2	90.6	-
STG [32]	A	2020	40.5	28.3	47.10	60.9	-	52.2	36.9	93.0	73.9	-
STATS [13]	A	2020	40.1	27.5	43.4	60.4	-	52.6	33.5	80.2	69.5	-
SAAT [58]	A	2020	40.5	28.2	49.1	60.9	82.50	46.5	33.5	81.0	69.4	-
ORG-TRL [57]	A	2020	43.6	28.8	50.9	62.1	-	54.3	36.4	95.2	73.9	-
SAVCSS [8]	A	2020	43.8	28.9	51.4	62.4	90.00	61.8	37.8	103	76.8	91.25
DSD-3 DS-SEM [38]	A	2020	45.2	29.9	51.1	64.2	-	50.1	34.7	76	73.1	-
SBAT [21]	T	2020	42.9	28.9	51.6	61.5	-	53.1	35.3	89.5	72.3	-
SemSynAN [34]†	A	2021	46.4	30.4	51.9	64.7	82.13	64.4	41.9	111.5	79.5	82.67
MGCMP [10]	A	2021	41.7	28.9	51.4	61.0	-	55.8	36.9	98.5	74.5	-
CoSB [43]	T	2022	41.4	27.8	46.5	61.0	-	50.7	35.3	97.8	72.1	-
VASTA (Kinetics-backbone)	T	2022	43.4	30.2	55.0	62.5	90.10	56.1	39.1	106.4	74.5	92.00
VASTA (VATEX-backbone)	T	2022	44.21	30.24	56.08	62.9	90.17	59.2	40.65	119.7	76.7	92.21

we are interested in captions that are the most "human-like". Thus, we compute these diversity metrics on MSR-VTT, MSVD and VATEX and compare our model to those competitors where we have access to the generated captions for re-evaluation. As seen in Table 3, our model not only predicts highly accurate captions but also manages to predict a highly diverse set of captions. VASTA generates the most distinct captions and does not overfit to the training data, i.e. generates novel captions for some of the test videos. Our model by far exploits most of the training vocabulary. Further analysis on the diversity of sentence structures is given in the supplementary.

Analyzing the performance of SemSynAN [34] (a model which has strong similarity metrics) where the number of captions per video is limited to just five to train a predictor for the most common syntactic POS structures (see Supplementary) reveals that this comes at the cost of reduced caption diversity, sentence quality and video-caption match. Thus, we found that its diversity is much lower.

Table 3. Diversity of the generated captions.

| Method | MSR-VTT | | | | MSVD | | | | VATEX | | | |
	SB ↓	N ↑	U ↑	V ↑	SB ↓	N ↑	U ↑	V ↑	SB ↓	N ↑	U ↑	V ↑
SAVCSS [8]	95.19	44.61	33.44	1.88	84.32	**51.34**	42.08	2.07	-	-	-	-
SAAT [58]	99.99	40.46	20.06	1.33	-	-	-	-	-	-	-	-
SemSynAN [34]	96.47	42.84	18.92	1.57	83.00	47.16	37.61	2.19	-	-	-	-
VASTA (Kinetics-backbone)	92.94	**45.98**	**34.74**	2.93	81.88	30.49	42.89	3.48	86.18	97.29	85.80	7.04
VASTA (VATEX-backbone)	**92.70**	45.51	34.21	**3.00**	**76.90**	42.75	**52.16**	**3.94**	-	-	-	-

Table 4. Influence of the individual components in VASTA. Applying both, AFS and semantic vectors, yields favorable scores. UFS: uniform frame selection, AFS: Adaptive frame selection, SB: Swin BERT, SBS: Swin BERT Semantics.

	MSR-VTT								VATEX							
Method	B4↑	M↑	C↑	R↑	SB↓	N↑	U↑	V↑	B4↑	M↑	C↑	R↑	SB↓	N↑	U↑	V↑
UFS-SB	43.21	29.55	52.91	62.1	96.48	37.09	19.23	1.90	35.31	25.05	63.82	51.27	87.73	**97.62**	81.41	6.70
AFS-SB	43.07	29.72	**55.08**	62.02	93.93	38.29	27.95	2.46	35.64	**25.43**	64.98	51.53	88.57	97.51	83.33	6.50
UFS-SBS	**43.51**	29.75	53.59	62.27	94.82	42.44	26.48	2.36	35.68	25.42	**65.63**	51.58	88.40	97.35	83.38	6.43
AFS-SBS	43.43	**30.24**	55.00	**62.54**	**92.94**	45.98	34.74	2.93	**36.25**	25.32	65.04	**51.88**	**86.18**	97.29	**85.80**	**7.04**

4.3   Ablation Study

The results of Table 2 have been achieved by carefully designing our adaptive spatio-temporal encoder-decoder framework. As demonstrated by the ablation results in Table 4, introducing adaptive frame sampling (AFS) helps improve the image-description related CIDEr score while adding the semantic concept vector further improves on the more translation-related scores (BLEU-4, METEOR, ROUGE-L, CIDEr). Similarly, both AFS and the semantic concept prediction improves the diversity score. Thus, more informative and more precise encoder predictions support higher quality and more diverse language output. In the supplemental we demonstrate how the results depend on the chosen decoder model, by replacing Bert by GPTNeo Causal LM [6,35]. There, we also study different inference methods (beam search, greedy, top-k, top-p).

Uniform sampling: there is a car moving on the road

Adaptive sampling: a man is walking through the woods

Fig. 3. Adaptive Frame Selection (AFS). Uniform sampling (top) keeps frames with repetitive non-informative content (cf. frames with foliage). In contrast, adaptive sampling enhances the diversity of input frames by selecting those with activity (cf. frames with people walking). Ground truth: "Two men walking around a forest by a lake."

AFS Results. Fig. 3 exemplifies the effect of our adaptive frame selection approach. The video transformer can only take in 32 frames. Driven by the frame differences, the adaptive frame selection samples more diverse frames than simple uniform subsampling, increasing the chance of selecting informative time steps. An irregular temporal sampling pattern on the other hand leads to a non-uniform play-back speed. Still, AFS consistently improves the CIDEr result (Table 4), indicating that the gain in input information has a more positive effect than potential introducing temporal disturbance in the Swin transformer inference.

Semantic Concept Vectors. The accuracy (BCE score) of the multi-class extraction task for the semantic concept vectors is 0.88 (0.12) on the training set and 0.85 (0.15) on the test set. This indicates, that this training step generalizes well. Introducing the semantic concept vectors improves the overall performance, as one can see by the strong correlation between classification accuracy and resulting NLG scores in Table 5. Bad examples most often occur in conjunction with misclassification of the main actors or concepts in the video. In these cases, often the content of the video is not well represented by the most common 768 concepts.

Table 5. Dependency on the quality of the predicted semantic vector. Sorting all test samples of the MSR-VTT wrt. the classification accuracy of the proposed semantic vector, a strong correlation with the evaluation scores is revealed.

BCE	B4 ↑	M ↑	C ↑	R ↑
10%-best	55.67	41.25	109.4	75.44
10%-worst	31.50	21.97	22.76	49.09

Reference: a group of people are dancing and singing
Our: a group of people are dancing and singing
SymsynAN: a group of people are dancing

Reference: a dog is playing on a trampoline
Our: a dog is playing on a trampoline
SymsynAN: a dog is playing with a dog

Reference: a person is making a paper aircraft
Our: a person is making a paper airplane
SymsynAN: a person is folding paper

Fig. 4. Examples for the top-performing videos in the test set.

4.4 Qualitative Results

In Fig. 4, representative videos and the generated captions are shown. We list examples of the top 1%-percentile on the METEOR score. For positive examples, the content of the video is fully recognized leading to a description that matches one of the reference captions almost exactly. In the bad examples (see supplementary) the content is often misinterpreted or the video is so abstract that there could be many diverse explanations.

Spatio-Temporal Attention. The video in Fig. 5 on the top features a complex temporal interaction between two actors (*monkey and dog*). The generated caption correctly reflects both spatial detail (*dog's tail*) as well as multiple temporal stages (*grabbing the tail* and *running away*). Similarly, the temporal domain is also respected in the second example. Different parts of the video contribute to different sections in the generated captions (*woman talking about food* and *cooking in pot*). These examples demonstrate that high-quality detection and tracking from the Swin transformer across multiple frames goes hand-in-hand with the powerful language skills of the fine-tuned generator in our proposed framework.

Reference: A monkey pulling on a dog 's tail and running away
Generated text: a monkey grabs a dog's tail and runs away

Reference: a girl is talking about some food she is eating
Generated text: a woman is cooking in a pot and talking about it

Fig. 5. Spatio-temporal inference gathers information from different segments.

5   Limitations and Discussion

The introduced VASTA architecture performs quite well according to the commonly used evaluation metrics. Even though our model has the best diversity scores, looking at some samples of generated captions, they are often rather general and might miss some important detail about the video. This suggests, further research in the diversity aspect is important.

As indicated in Sect. 4.4, the current extraction of concepts for video captioning might need further improvement, potentially by the use of a larger training data set. Compared to the very good performance of the produced language, the visual analysis is not yet on par. The training and the evaluation are done on three data sets MSR-VTT, MSVD and VATEX, which come with their own distributions of scenes, people, objects, and actions. Any marginalization of specific social groups present in the data sets will likely also be present in our trained encoder-decoder framework. In general, our approach to automated video analysis and captioning might furthermore be trained and applied in other contexts. While we think that the application to the presented data is not problematic, ethical issues can quickly arise in surveillance or military applications.

6   Conclusion

We presented VASTA, a video captioning encoder-decoder approach which incorporates the processed visual tokens by multi-layer multi-head cross-attention. While the Swin tokens extracts separate spatio-temporal information, we introduce also a globally aggregating semantic concept vector that initializes the sentence generation in the BERT module. By proposing a content-based adaptive frame selection sampling, we can assure that the most informative frames are selected while maintaining efficient training.

This transformer-based video captioning framework introduces a new architecture that produces plausible captions that are state-of-the-art on the MSR-VTT, MSVD and VATEX benchmark data sets. Our evaluation highlights that the commonly used NLG metrics only address some of the aspects necessary to fully assess the quality of video descriptions. We demonstrate that our method produces highly diverse captions. We hope that this work will inspire further research for a better, broader assessment of the performance of caption generation algorithms.

Acknowledgements. This work has been supported by the German Research Foundation: EXC 2064/1 - Project number 390727645, the CRC 1233 - Project number 276693517, as well as by the German Federal Ministry of Education and Research (BMBF): Tübingen AI Center, FKZ: 01IS18039A. The authors thank the International Max Planck Research School for Intelligent Systems (IMPRS-IS) for supporting Zohreh Ghaderi and Leonard Salewski.

References

1. Aafaq, N., Akhtar, N., Liu, W., Gilani, S.Z., Mian, A.: Spatio-temporal dynamics and semantic attribute enriched visual encoding for video captioning. In: Proceedings of the IEEE/CVF Conference on Computer Vision and Pattern Recognition, pp. 12487–12496 (2019)
2. Aafaq, N., Mian, A., Liu, W., Gilani, S.Z., Shah, M.: Video description: a survey of methods, datasets, and evaluation metrics. ACM Comput. Surv. **52**(6) (2019). https://doi.org/10.1145/3355390
3. Arnab, A., Dehghani, M., Heigold, G., Sun, C., Lučić, M., Schmid, C.: Vivit: A video vision transformer. arXiv preprint arXiv:2103.15691 (2021)

4. Bahdanau, D., Cho, K., Bengio, Y.: Neural machine translation by jointly learning to align and translate. arXiv preprint arXiv:1409.0473 (2014)

5. Banerjee, S., Lavie, A.: METEOR: an automatic metric for MT evaluation with improved correlation with human judgments. In: Proceedings of the ACL Workshop on Intrinsic and Extrinsic Evaluation Measures for Machine Translation and/or Summarization, pp. 65–72 (2005)

6. Black, S., Gao, L., Wang, P., Leahy, C., Biderman, S.: GPT-Neo: large scale autoregressive language modeling with mesh-tensorflow. If you use this Software, Please Cite it using these Metadata **58** (2021)

7. Chen, D., Dolan, W.B.: Collecting highly parallel data for paraphrase evaluation. In: Proceedings of the 49th Annual Meeting of the Association for Computational Linguistics: Human Language Technologies, pp. 190–200 (2011)

8. Chen, H., Lin, K., Maye, A., Li, J., Hu, X.: A semantics-assisted video captioning model trained with scheduled sampling. Front. Robot. AI **7**, 475767 (2020)

9. Chen, M., Li, Y., Zhang, Z., Huang, S.: TVT: two-view transformer network for video captioning. In: Asian Conference on Machine Learning, pp. 847–862. PMLR (2018)

10. Chen, S., Jiang, Y.G.: Motion guided region message passing for video captioning. In: Proceedings of the IEEE/CVF International Conference on Computer Vision, pp. 1543–1552 (2021)

11. Chen, X., et al.: Microsoft coco captions: data collection and evaluation server. arXiv preprint arXiv:1504.00325 (2015)

12. Chen, Y., Wang, S., Zhang, W., Huang, Q.: Less is more: picking informative frames for video captioning. In: Proceedings of the European Conference on Computer Vision (ECCV), pp. 358–373 (2018)

13. Cherian, A., Wang, J., Hori, C., Marks, T.: Spatio-temporal ranked-attention networks for video captioning. In: Proceedings of the IEEE/CVF Winter Conference on Applications of Computer Vision, pp. 1617–1626 (2020)

14. Dai, B., Fidler, S., Lin, D.: A neural compositional paradigm for image captioning. NIPS **31**, 658–668 (2018)

15. Dalal, N., Triggs, B., Schmid, C.: Human detection using oriented histograms of flow and appearance. In: Leonardis, A., Bischof, H., Pinz, A. (eds.) ECCV 2006. LNCS, vol. 3952, pp. 428–441. Springer, Heidelberg (2006). https://doi.org/10.1007/11744047_33

16. Devlin, J., Chang, M.W., Lee, K., Toutanova, K.: Bert: pre-training of deep bidirectional transformers for language understanding. arXiv preprint arXiv:1810.04805 (2018)

17. Donahue, J., et al.: Long-term recurrent convolutional networks for visual recognition and description. In: Proceedings of the IEEE Conference on Computer Vision and Pattern Recognition, pp. 2625–2634 (2015)

18. Gan, Z., et al.: Semantic compositional networks for visual captioning. In: Proceedings of the IEEE Conference on Computer Vision and Pattern Recognition, pp. 5630–5639 (2017)

19. Gowda, S.N., Rohrbach, M., Sevilla-Lara, L.: Smart frame selection for action recognition. arXiv preprint arXiv:2012.10671 (2020)

20. Guadarrama, S., et al.: YouTube2Text: recognizing and describing arbitrary activities using semantic hierarchies and zero-shot recognition. In: Proceedings of the IEEE International Conference on Computer Vision, pp. 2712–2719 (2013)

21. Jin, T., Huang, S., Chen, M., Li, Y., Zhang, Z.: SBAT: video captioning with sparse boundary-aware transformer. arXiv preprint arXiv:2007.11888 (2020)

22. Kay, W., et al.: The kinetics human action video dataset. arXiv preprint arXiv:1705.06950 (2017)
23. Kayser, M., et al.: e-ViL: a dataset and benchmark for natural language explanations in vision-language tasks. In: Proceedings of the IEEE/CVF International Conference on Computer Vision, pp. 1244–1254 (2021)
24. Khan, M.U.G., Zhang, L., Gotoh, Y.: Human focused video description. In: 2011 IEEE International Conference on Computer Vision Workshops (ICCV Workshops), pp. 1480–1487. IEEE (2011)
25. Kojima, A., Tamura, T., Fukunaga, K.: Natural language description of human activities from video images based on concept hierarchy of actions. Int. J. Comput. Vis. **50**(2), 171–184 (2002). https://doi.org/10.1023/A:1020346032608
26. Krishnamoorthy, N., Malkarnenkar, G., Mooney, R., Saenko, K., Guadarrama, S.: Generating natural-language video descriptions using text-mined knowledge. In: Twenty-Seventh AAAI Conference on Artificial Intelligence (2013)
27. Lee, M.W., Hakeem, A., Haering, N., Zhu, S.C.: Save: a framework for semantic annotation of visual events. In: 2008 IEEE Computer Society Conference on Computer Vision and Pattern Recognition Workshops, pp. 1–8. IEEE (2008)
28. Lin, C.Y.: Rouge: a package for automatic evaluation of summaries. In: Text Summarization Branches Out, pp. 74–81 (2004)
29. Liu, Z., et al.: Swin Transformer: hierarchical vision transformer using shifted windows. arXiv preprint arXiv:2103.14030 (2021)
30. Liu, Z., et al.: Video Swin Transformer. arXiv preprint arXiv:2106.13230 (2021)
31. Loshchilov, I., Hutter, F.: Decoupled weight decay regularization. arXiv preprint arXiv:1711.05101 (2017)
32. Pan, B., et al.: Spatio-temporal graph for video captioning with knowledge distillation. In: Proceedings of the IEEE/CVF Conference on Computer Vision and Pattern Recognition, pp. 10870–10879 (2020)
33. Papineni, K., Roukos, S., Ward, T., Zhu, W.J.: Bleu: a method for automatic evaluation of machine translation. In: Proceedings of the 40th annual meeting of the Association for Computational Linguistics, pp. 311–318 (2002)
34. Perez-Martin, J., Bustos, B., Pérez, J.: Improving video captioning with temporal composition of a visual-syntactic embedding. In: Proceedings of the IEEE/CVF Winter Conference on Applications of Computer Vision, pp. 3039–3049 (2021)
35. Radford, A., Narasimhan, K., Salimans, T., Sutskever, I.: Improving language understanding by generative pre-training (2018)
36. Reddy, D.R., et al.: Speech Understanding Systems: a Summary Of Results of the Five-year Research Effort. Department of Computer Science, CMU, Pittsburgh, PA (1977)
37. Ren, S., He, K., Girshick, R., Sun, J.: Faster R-CNN: towards real-time object detection with region proposal networks. Adv. Neural Inf. Process. Syst. **28** (2015)
38. Shekhar, C.C., et al.: Domain-specific semantics guided approach to video captioning. In: Proceedings of the IEEE/CVF Winter Conference on Applications of Computer Vision, pp. 1587–1596 (2020)
39. Singh, A., Singh, T.D., Bandyopadhyay, S.: NITS-VC system for VATEX video captioning challenge 2020. arXiv preprint arXiv:2006.04058 (2020)
40. Sutskever, I., Vinyals, O., Le, Q.V.: Sequence to sequence learning with neural networks. In: Advances in Neural Information Processing Systems, pp. 3104–3112 (2014)
41. Thomason, J., Venugopalan, S., Guadarrama, S., Saenko, K., Mooney, R.: Integrating Language and Vision to Generate Natural Language Descriptions of Videos in

the Wild. In: Proceedings of COLING 2014, the 25th International Conference on Computational Linguistics: Technical Papers, pp. 1218–1227 (2014)

42. Tran, D., Bourdev, L., Fergus, R., Torresani, L., Paluri, M.: Learning spatiotemporal features with 3D convolutional networks. In: Proceedings of the IEEE International Conference on Computer Vision, pp. 4489–4497 (2015)

43. Vaidya, J., Subramaniam, A., Mittal, A.: Co-Segmentation aided two-stream architecture for video captioning. In: Proceedings of the IEEE/CVF Winter Conference on Applications of Computer Vision, pp. 2774–2784 (2022)

44. Vaswani, A., et al.: Attention is all you need. In: Advances in Neural Information Processing Systems, pp. 5998–6008 (2017)

45. Vedantam, R., Lawrence Zitnick, C., Parikh, D.: Cider: consensus-based image description evaluation. In: Proceedings of the IEEE Conference on Computer Vision and Pattern Recognition, pp. 4566–4575 (2015)

46. Venugopalan, S., Rohrbach, M., Donahue, J., Mooney, R., Darrell, T., Saenko, K.: Sequence to sequence-video to text. In: Proceedings of the IEEE International Conference on Computer Vision, pp. 4534–4542 (2015)

47. Venugopalan, S., Xu, H., Donahue, J., Rohrbach, M., Mooney, R., Saenko, K.: Translating videos to natural language using deep recurrent neural networks. arXiv preprint arXiv:1412.4729 (2014)

48. Wang, H., Ullah, M.M., Klaser, A., Laptev, I., Schmid, C.: Evaluation of local spatio-temporal features for action recognition. In: BMVC 2009-British Machine Vision Conference, pp. 124–1. BMVA Press (2009)

49. Wang, X., Han, T.X., Yan, S.: An HOG-LBP human detector with partial occlusion handling. In: 2009 IEEE 12th International Conference on Computer Vision, pp. 32–39. IEEE (2009)

50. Wang, X., Wu, J., Chen, J., Li, L., Wang, Y.F., Wang, W.Y.: VATEX: a large-scale, high-quality multilingual dataset for video-and-language research. In: Proceedings of the IEEE/CVF International Conference on Computer Vision, pp. 4581–4591 (2019)

51. Xu, J., Mei, T., Yao, T., Rui, Y.: MSR-VTT: a large video description dataset for bridging video and language. In: Proceedings of the IEEE Conference on Computer Vision and Pattern Recognition, pp. 5288–5296 (2016)

52. Yan, C., et al.: STAT: spatial-temporal attention mechanism for video captioning. IEEE Trans. Multimedia 22(1), 229–241 (2019)

53. Yao, L., Torabi, A., Cho, K., Ballas, N., Pal, C., Larochelle, H., Courville, A.: Describing videos by exploiting temporal structure. In: Proceedings of the IEEE International Conference on Computer Vision, pp. 4507–4515 (2015)

54. Zhang, J., Peng, Y.: Object-aware aggregation with bidirectional temporal graph for video captioning. In: Proceedings of the IEEE/CVF Conference on Computer Vision and Pattern Recognition, pp. 8327–8336 (2019)

55. Zhang, R., Isola, P., Efros, A.A., Shechtman, E., Wang, O.: The unreasonable effectiveness of deep features as a perceptual metric. In: CVPR (2018)

56. Zhang, T., Kishore, V., Wu, F., Weinberger, K.Q., Artzi, Y.: Bertscore: evaluating text generation with Bert. In: International Conference on Learning Representations (2020). https://openreview.net/forum?id=SkeHuCVFDr

57. Zhang, Z., et al.: Object relational graph with teacher-recommended learning for video captioning. In: Proceedings of the IEEE/CVF Conference on Computer Vision and Pattern Recognition, pp. 13278–13288 (2020)

58. Zheng, Q., Wang, C., Tao, D.: Syntax-aware action targeting for video captioning. In: Proceedings of the IEEE/CVF Conference on Computer Vision and Pattern Recognition, pp. 13096–13105 (2020)

59. Zhou, L., Zhou, Y., Corso, J.J., Socher, R., Xiong, C.: End-to-end dense video captioning with masked transformer. In: CVPR, pp. 8739–8748 (2018)
60. Zhu, Y., et al.: Texygen: a benchmarking platform for text generation models. In: ACM SIGIR, pp. 1097–1100 (2018)

Scene Understanding

Self-supervised Learning for Unintentional Action Prediction

Olga Zatsarynna[1(✉)], Yazan Abu Farha[2], and Juergen Gall[1]

[1] University of Bonn, Bonn, Germany
{zatsarynna,gall}@iai.uni-bonn.de
[2] Birzeit University, Birzeit, Palestine
yabufarha@birzeit.edu

Abstract. Distinguishing if an action is performed as intended or if an intended action fails is an important skill that not only humans have, but that is also important for intelligent systems that operate in human environments. Recognizing if an action is unintentional or anticipating if an action will fail, however, is not straight-forward due to lack of annotated data. While videos of unintentional or failed actions can be found in the Internet in abundance, high annotation costs are a major bottleneck for learning networks for these tasks. In this work, we thus study the problem of self-supervised representation learning for unintentional action prediction. While previous works learn the representation based on a local temporal neighborhood, we show that the global context of a video is needed to learn a good representation for the three downstream tasks: unintentional action classification, localization and anticipation. In the supplementary material, we show that the learned representation can be used for detecting anomalies in videos as well.

Keywords: Unsupervised representation learning · Contrastive learning · Unintentional action prediction · Anomaly detection

1 Introduction

Recognition of human intentions is a task that we perform easily on a daily basis. We can tell the difference between the deliberately and accidentally dropped object; between the liquid poured with intent or spilled out of carelessness. Moreover, we can easily identify the point at which a certain action turns from being intentional to an unintentional one. Our ability to do so signifies the importance of this skill in the day to day life since the intent of a particular event dictates our reaction to it. Therefore, if intelligent agents are to exist among human beings, they should possess the skill to differentiate between intentional and unintentional actions.

Supplementary Information The online version contains supplementary material available at https://doi.org/10.1007/978-3-031-16788-1_26.

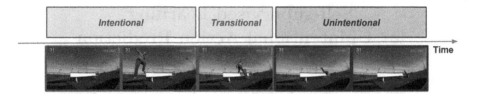

Fig. 1. Example of an unintentional action video. Unlike typical videos that are used for action recognition where the labels are fixed throughout the video, the clips labels in unintentional videos change over time. In this example, the skater intentionally jumps at the beginning of the video, but suddenly loses balance and falls down at the end. While all clips are visually similar, we can see the intent degree of the clips changing as the video progresses.

While there are large amounts of videos, which contain unintentional actions, freely available on various video platforms, they are not annotated. Since the videos contain an action that becomes unintentional over time, it would be very time-consuming to annotate the transition between an intentional and unintentional action in each video. To mitigate the effort required for annotation, Epstein et al. [9] proposed to consider unintentional action prediction from the unsupervised learning perspective. They collected a dataset of fail videos (Oops dataset [9]) from Youtube and proposed three methods for learning unintentional video features in a self-supervised way: Video Speed, Video Sorting and Video Context. Video Speed learns features by predicting the speed of videos sampled at 4 different frame rates. Video Sorting learns representations by predicting permutations of 3 clips sampled with a 0.5 s gap. Finally, Video Context relies on contrastive predictive coding to predict the feature of a clip based on its two neighboring clips. Among the proposed models, the Video Speed baseline showed the best results on the considered downstream tasks.

We notice, however, that the proposed methods do not leverage all information present in the unlabeled videos of unintentional actions. Firstly, they pay very limited attention to the distinctiveness of features along the temporal axis of the video. For instance, the Video Speed model operates on a temporal context of around one second. For the other two proposed models, the observed local temporal neighborhood is larger, but still limited - three clips of one second are sampled within 0.5 s from each other. However, since videos of unintentional actions consist of clips whose labels change throughout the video, the mere distinction of local changes in appearance is insufficient for determining how intentional the portrayed action is. For example in Fig. 1, we can see that all clips look very much alike, however, as the video progresses, the action of the skater turns from intentional to unintentional. This is barely recognizable by looking only at neighboring clips, but the global context of the video reveals that the action does not progress as expected. Secondly, we notice that information contained in the order of sampled clips has not been harnessed to the full extent since the previously proposed Video Sorting model performed only slightly better than the model initialized from scratch. Such relatively low performance, as we show in our experiments, was caused by the specifics of the chosen pre-text task formulation, and not by the lack of information in the clip order.

In this work, we address the above-mentioned limitations of [9]. First, we show that a local neighborhood is insufficient and we propose to sample the clips globally for the entire video. This is required to differentiate between local variations of an intentional action and variations between an intentional and unintentional action. Second, we revisit the poor performance of the Video Sorting approach. While a global sampling improves the learned representation of Video Sorting as well, the permutation-based approach of Video Sorting still struggles in the global setting to distinguish intentional from unintentional actions. We thus propose a pair-wise ordering loss where the features of two randomly sampled clips are concatenated and the network needs to predict which clip occurs first in the video. We demonstrate in the experiments that this loss learns a better representation than the permutation loss where the correct order of three clips needs to be predicted. Finally, we aim to learn a representation that works well for different downstream tasks, namely classification, localization and anticipation of unintentional actions. To this end, we combine a global temporal contrastive loss with a pair-wise video clip order prediction task. We show that our proposed approach outperforms all previously proposed self-supervised models for unintentional action prediction and achieves state-of-the-art results on two datasets of unintentional actions: the Oops dataset [9] and LAD2000 [32].

2   Related Work

2.1   Self-supervised Learning for Action Recognition

Self-supervised approaches for video representation learning, as noted by [7], can be generally subdivided into three types: pre-text task-based, contrastive learning-based, and combinations of the two.

Video Pretext Task Learning. The main idea behind pretext task-based learning is to utilize intrinsic properties of video data that do not require manual annotations for video representation learning. For example, video speed [4,6,39] is a commonly used cue for the pretext task formulation. These methods create several versions of the same video with different perceptual speeds by varying their sampling rate and then train the model to recognize the playback speed of the resulting clips. Benaim et al. [4] formulate this as a binary classification task (normal/sped-up), while other works [6,39] harness several different sampling rates for multi-class classification. In addition to speed, Cho et al. [6] predict the Arrow of Time (AoT) in videos, which was earlier proposed by [34]. Recognition of AoT is closely related to another commonly used pre-text task: video order classification [12,23,24,36]. Formulations of this task vary. For instance, Misra et al. [24] predict whether a sequence of frames is in the natural or shuffled order. Lee et al. [23], on the other hand, predict frame permutations. Xu et al. [36], like [23], predict permutations, but instead of frames they operate on clips. Yet another approach [12] proposes to recognize a naturally ordered sequence among the shuffled ones. Other pre-text tasks include, but are not limited to, solving spatio-temporal jigsaw puzzles [1,21], prediction of video rotations [19] and colorization of videos [31].

Video Contrastive Learning. In recent years, contrastive learning has become popular for self-supervised learning both for image and video domains. Its initial success in the image domain [5,16] has promoted the emergence of contrastive learning-based methods for video data [3,7,8,17,26,27]. These methods differ in how they sample positive and negative examples for the training procedure, as well as in the type of the used backbone network (2D or 3D CNN). For many video-based contrastive learning approaches [7,26,27], the de facto procedure of constructing examples is by considering clips from the same video as positives and clips from different videos as negatives. However, enforcing absolute temporal invariance is not beneficial for the resulting features. Therefore, Sermanet et al. [27] proposed time contrastive learning, where close frames are considered as positive examples and frames from different parts of the same video as negatives. Qian et al. [26] followed this principle and proposed an extension such that positive examples are sampled from the same video, with the gap between sampled clips drawn randomly from a monotonically decreasing distribution. Dave et al. [7] proposed to train a network with a combination of three loss terms for ensuring different levels of temporal discrimination: instance discrimination, local-local and global-local loss.

Combined Learning. Some approaches rely on the combination of pre-text task-based and contrastive-based learning. Different methods propose to combine contrastive learning with: speed prediction [33], order prediction [38], or frame rotation prediction [22]. Other methods combine several pre-text tasks simultaneously [2,18]. Our proposed approach also makes use of the multi-task learning strategy: we combine temporal contrastive learning with order prediction. However, in contrast to all previous methods that learn representations for action recognition, we learn representations for unintentional action prediction.

2.2   Self-supervised Learning for Unintentional Action Recognition

The task of self-supervised learning for unintentional action prediction has been proposed recently by Epstein et al. [9]. Previous works on unintentional action prediction or anomaly detection [11,14,28–30,35,40] do not address representation learning, but focus on predictions based on features pre-extracted from pre-trained networks. Epstein et al. [9,10] instead proposed to learn features specifically for the tasks related to unintentional action prediction. For the unsupervised learning setting, Epstein et al. [9] proposed three baselines: Video Speed, Video Sorting and Video Context. In the further work, Epstein et al. [10] have also considered fully-supervised learning, for which they combined learning on labeled examples using the standard cross-entropy loss with solving an unsupervised temporal consistency task. Two further works [37,41] addressed the fully-supervised setting for the Oops dataset. While Zhou et al. [41] proposed to model the label distribution to mine reliable annotations for training, Xu et al. [37] proposed a causal inference approach, for which they gathered additional videos with only intentional actions. In this work, we address the challenge of self-supervised representation learning for unintentional action prediction, as defined in [9].

3   Method

We propose to learn representations from videos of unintentional actions using a global temporal contrastive loss and an order prediction loss. In this section, we describe the proposed method in detail. We start by formally defining the task of representation learning for unintentional action prediction in Sect. 3.1. Then, we discuss our temporal contrastive loss in Sect. 3.2 and the order prediction loss in Sect. 3.3.

3.1   Representation Learning for Unintentionality Detection

In this work, we deal with unsupervised video representation learning for unintentional action prediction as proposed by [9]. Given a set of V unlabeled videos $(v_1, \ldots, v_V)$ of unintentional actions, partitioned into n_i short clips $\{x_i^t\}_{t=1}^{n_i}$, the goal is to learn a function $f_i^t = \phi(x_i^t)$ that maps a short clip x_i^t into a feature vector f_i^t in an unsupervised way, such that the resulting features transfer well to downstream tasks related to unintentionality detection. Epstein et al. [9] proposed three such tasks: unintentional action classification, localization and anticipation. The task of classification is to predict labels of individual video clips. The task of localization is to detect a point of transition from an intentional to an unintentional action. Finally, the task of anticipation is to predict the label of a clip located 1.5 s into the future. We describe these tasks in more detail in Sect. 4.3. For evaluating the learned features on the above mentioned tasks, a small subset of annotated data is provided with labels defined as follows. Initially, each video is annotated with a transitional time point t_i^a at which an action changes from intentional to unintentional. Based on the annotated transitional point t_i^a, clips are assigned to one of three classes: intentional, transitional and unintentional. Clip x_i^t is *intentional*, if it ends before the transitional point t_i^a; x_i^t is *transitional*, if it starts before t_i^a and ends after it. Otherwise, x_i^t is *unintentional*. An example of a video label annotation is shown in Fig. 1.

3.2   Temporal Contrastive Loss

As it is motivated in Fig. 1, we aim to learn a representation that is similar for any clip that contains the same intentional action, but that allows to differentiate if the same action is intentional or unintentional. Since we do not have any

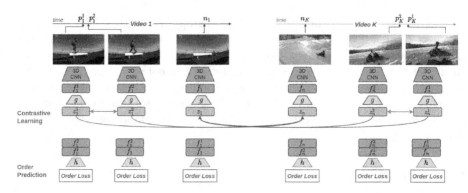

Fig. 2. We train our model with a combination of a temporal contrastive loss and an order prediction loss. For each video v_i in the batch of size K, we at first randomly sample an anchor clip p_i^1 from time step t_i. Then, we draw randomly one positive example p_i^2 from its immediate neighbors and one negative example n_i from the remaining video clips. Using a backbone 3D-CNN network and a non-linear projection head g, we extract features $\{f_i^1, f_i^2, f_i\}_{i=1}^K$ and their non-linear projections $\{z_i^1, z_i^2, z_i\}_{i=1}^K$ from the sampled clips. We use the $\{z_i^1, z_i^2, z_i\}_{i=1}^K$ to compute a temporal contrastive loss (middle row), where positive examples are drawn closer to each other *(green arrows)* and are pushed away from the negatives *(red arrows)*. Additionally, randomly-ordered pair-wise concatenations of features coming from the same videos $\{f_i^1, f_i^2, f_i\}_{i=1}^K$ are used to compute an order prediction loss with a non-linear order prediction head h (bottom row). (Color figure online)

labels, we do not know when an action in a video is intentional or unintentional. However, we can assume that sampled neighboring clips are much more likely to have the same label (intentional or unintentional) whereas clips sampled more distant are more likely to have different labels, see Fig. 2. We thus make use of the InfoNCE [13] loss function, that encourages representations of two positive views to be closer to each other in the embedding space, while pushing them away from the features of the negative examples. Formally, it is expressed as follows:

$$L_{NCE}(x, y, N) = -\log \frac{q(g(x), g(y))}{q(g(x), g(y)) + \sum_{n \in N} q(g(x), g(n))}, \quad (1)$$

where x, y are positive examples, g is a non-linear projection layer, $q(x, y) = \exp(\frac{x \cdot y}{\|x\|\|y\|}/\tau)$ measures the similarity between samples, which depends on the hyper-parameter τ, and N is the set of negative examples. For computing the temporal contrastive loss, we obtain positive and negative clips using the following sampling procedure: we sample positive examples from the immediate temporal neighborhood of a given clip while negative examples are sampled from the remaining video regions. More specifically, for a clip x_i^t from a time point t of video v_i, we consider its immediate adjacent clips $\{x_i^{t-1}, x_i^{t+1}\}$ as potential positive examples, whereas clips from the outside regions form a set of potential negative examples, i.e. $\{x_i^1, \ldots, x_i^{t-3}\} \cup \{x_i^{t+3}, \ldots, x_i^{n_i}\}$. Following [27], clips

$\{x_i^{t-2}, x_i^{t+2}\}$ form a margin zone, from which no negative examples are allowed to be sampled. Given a mini-batch of K videos $(v_1, \ldots, v_K)$, for each video v_i we randomly sample two positive and one negative examples from the set of positives and negatives accordingly. In this way, for each v_i we get a triplet of clips $\{p_i^1, p_i^2, n_i\}_{i=1}^K$, where p_i^1, p_i^2 is a positive pair and n_i is a negative example. Then, our proposed temporal contrastive loss is formulated as a symmetric InfoNCE loss in the following manner:

$$L_{temp} = \frac{1}{2K} \sum_{i=1}^{K} (L_{NCE}(p_i^1, p_i^2, N) + L_{NCE}(p_i^2, p_i^1, N)), \tag{2}$$

where $N = \{n_i\}_{i=1}^K$ is the set of all negatives, which is common for all positive pairs. Intuitively, this loss encourages that adjacent clips are close to each other in the embedding space and far apart from the remaining clips. Since we do not restrict the extent of the potential negative regions to a local neighborhood, this loss encourages discrimination between the clips on both fine-grained and more coarse levels.

3.3 Order Loss

While the temporal contrastive loss ensures that neighboring clips are close in the embedding space, it does not ensure that the relative order of the clips gets encoded in the feature vectors. However, as indicated by our experiments, order reasoning is key for improving both the classification and the localization of the unintentional moments. We therefore perform order prediction for each triplet of clips, which are sampled as described in the previous section and illustrated in Fig. 2. To this end, we do pairwise concatenation of clip features that come from the same videos. For each pair, we randomly select the order in which the representations are concatenated. This results in three concatenated feature vectors for each triplet, i.e. $m = 3K$ pairs. Using these pairs, we train a non-linear order prediction layer for recognizing whether representations of the two corresponding clips are concatenated in the correct or reversed order. Formally, for two clips $x_i^{t_1}, x_i^{t_2}$ sampled from video v_i at time steps t_1 and t_2, features $f_i^{t_1} = \phi(x_i^{t_1})$ and $f_i^{t_2} = \phi(x_i^{t_2})$ are concatenated into a single vector $f_i^{t_1 t_2} = cat(f_i^{t_1}, f_i^{t_2})$ and fed through a non-linear layer h that outputs an order prediction vector $\hat{y}_i = h(f_{l_i}^{t_1 t_2})$. The order loss is formulated as the binary cross-entropy loss between predicted labels $\hat{y}_i$ and the correct labels y_i:

$$y_i = \begin{cases} 1, & \text{if } t_1 < t_2 \\ 0, & \text{otherwise.} \end{cases} \tag{3}$$

Therefore, the final order loss has the following form:

$$L_{ord} = -\frac{1}{m} \sum_{i=1}^{m} (y_i log(\hat{y}_i) + (1 - y_i) log(1 - \hat{y}_i)). \tag{4}$$

For training the network, we sum the temporal contrastive loss (2) and the order loss (4), giving them equal weight:

$$L = L_{temp} + L_{ord}. \tag{5}$$

4 Experiments

4.1 Implementation Details

We implemented our approach using the Pytorch [25] framework. Both for the pre-training stage and downstream tasks, we follow the settings proposed by Epstein et al. [9] as close as possible for a fair comparison with the previous methods. As a backbone network, we use a randomly initialized ResNet3D-18 [15], which receives as input clips of 16 frames from videos sampled at 16 fps, so that one clip contains one second of temporal context. For the downstream tasks, the pre-trained backbone network is used as a feature extractor and a linear layer is added for the specific task. Depending on the task, the backbone network either remains fixed (linear classification and localization) or is finetuned (classification with fine-tuning and anticipation). We provide further implementation details in the supplementary material.

4.2 Datasets

We conducted our experiments on two datasets with unintentional or anomalous videos: Oops [9] and LAD2000 [32]. We present the results on the LAD2000 dataset in the supplementary material. The Oops dataset consists of fail compilation videos from YouTube that have been automatically cut. In total, it has 20723 videos, 16012 train and 4711 test videos, varying from 3 to 30 s. Most videos are unlabeled. For evaluating the learned representation on downstreams tasks, the authors provide labeled subsets of the original videos: 6065 training and 4711 test videos. Labeled videos are annotated with a time-step at which the transition from an intentional to an unintentional action happens. We further notice that a substantial number of videos in both splits contain several unrelated scenes due to failures of the automatic video cutting. Since our approach is reliant on the temporal coherency of the video data, we do not use such videos during the self-supervised pre-training stage. We therefore perform an automatic detection of videos containing such defects by training a separate model for cut recognition. We provide details about the cut detection network in the supplementary material. We emphasize that this model is trained without manual annotations. For the downstream tasks, we use all videos regardless of their quality for a fair comparison with previous methods. For the sake of completeness, we also include in the supplementary material results of our approach when pre-training is performed on all videos.

4.3   Results

In this section, we evaluate the proposed self-supervised learning approach for the different unintentional action recognition tasks. On the Oops dataset, we report the results on the three tasks proposed by [9]: classification, localization and anticipation. We adopt the protocol of [9] and compare our method with other self-supervised approaches, as well as to a network pre-trained on Kinetics [20] with action labels as supervision. Additional comparisons to fully-supervised methods are provided in the supplementary material.

Table 1. Classification accuracy on the Oops dataset.

Representation	Linear classifier		Finetune
% of Labeled videos	10%	100%	100%
Kinetics	52.0	53.6	64.0
Video speed [9]	49.9	53.4	61.6
Video context [9]	47.2	50.0	60.3
Video sorting [9]	46.5	49.8	60.2
Scratch [9]	46.2	48.2	59.4
Ours	**59.2**	**60.9**	**61.9**

Classification. The task of classification is to categorize individual one-second-long clips $\{x_i^t\}_{t=1,i=1}^{n_i,n}$ extracted from longer videos containing both intentional and unintentional actions into three categories: intentional, transitional and unintentional. The clips are uniformly sampled across the videos with increments of 0.25 s. To evaluate the proposed self-supervised approach on this task, we fit a linear classifier on top of the features extracted from the backbone pre-trained in a self-supervised way. Following [9], we evaluate the performance of our method for three classification settings. In the first setting *(Linear Classifier, 100%)*, the backbone network remains fixed and only a linear classification layer is trained on the labeled videos. The second setting *(Linear Classifier, 10%)* differs from the first one in that only 10% of the labeled videos are used during training. And finally, in the third setting *(Finetune, 100%)*, the backbone network is finetuned together with the linear layer using all labeled videos. During training, we resample the clips such that the number of clips belonging to the different classes are balanced.

We present the classification results of our approach on the Oops dataset in Table 1. All models pre-trained with self-supervision outperform the model trained from scratch for all considered classification settings, which shows the benefit of the self-supervised pre-training. For the setting, where only the linear layer is trained, our approach outperforms by a large margin all previously proposed self-supervised approaches, as well as the model pre-trained on Kinetics with full supervision. When only 10% of the labeled videos are used for training, our method improves by 9.3% and 7.2% compared to the current state-of-the-art self-supervised approach Video Speed and the representation learned fully-supervised on Kinetics. When all labeled videos are used, the improvement is 7.5% and 7.3% compared to self-supervised pre-training and pre-training on Kinetics, respectively. For the fine-tuning case, our model performs on par with the Video Speed [9] model. We notice that during the fine-tuning stage almost all self-supervised models perform similarly.

Localization. The task of localization is to detect the point of transition t_a, where the action depicted in the video turns from being intentional to unintentional. To this end, we follow the localization setting proposed by [9]. Namely, we use our previously trained linear classifier in a sliding window fashion to estimate the probability of the transitional class for the individual clips of each video. After that, the clip with the highest transitional probability score is considered as the predicted boundary and its center is considered as the predicted transition point t_a. This predicted point is deemed to be correct if it has sufficient overlap with the ground-truth transition point. For evaluation, two thresholds for such overlaps are considered: one-quarter second and one second.

Table 2. Temporal localization accuracy on the Oops dataset.

Representation	Accuracy within	
Linear	1 s	0.25 s
Kinetics	69.2	37.8
Video speed [9]	65.3	36.6
Video context [9]	52.0	25.3
Video sorting [9]	43.3	18.3
Scratch [9]	47.8	21.6
Ours	**70.5**	**41.3**

Table 2 reports evaluation results for the task of transitional point localization. For both considered thresholds our approach outperforms by a substantial margin not only all previously proposed self-supervised methods and the model trained from scratch, but also the model pre-trained in a fully-supervised way on the Kinetics dataset. Compared to the best-performing self-supervised Video Speed model [9], our approach is 5.2% and 4.7% better for one and one-quarter second thresholds, respectively. Whereas for the Kinetics pre-trained model, our method is better by 1.3% and 3.5% for the corresponding thresholds.

Anticipation. The task of anticipation is to predict labels of individual clips 1.5 s into the future. As in [9], the task of anticipation is formulated similar to that of the classification with the backbone fine-tuning. However, for this task

Table 3. Anticipation accuracy on the Oops dataset.

Representation	Accuracy	
	Reported	Reproduced
Kinetics	59.7	67.6
Video speed [9]	56.7	61.5
Ours	–	**62.4**

Table 4. Impact of the loss components on the Oops dataset.

Linear classifier		
	Localization	Classification
Loss	1 s	0.25 s	All labels
L_{temp}	65.7	37.1	52.3
L_{ord}	66.2	36.0	60.0
$L_{temp} + L_{ord}$	**70.5**	**41.3**	**60.9**

not all clips can be considered and clip labels are assigned differently. More specifically, for anticipation we can consider only those clips for which there exists a subsequent clip located 1.5 s ahead of it. Labels of those future clips are the ones that need to be predicted based on the current clips. We report the anticipation accuracy in Table 3. In our experiments, we could not reproduce the results reported in [9] for this task, which are shown in the left column (Reported). Thus, we re-evaluated the self-supervised Video Speed model [9] using the publicly available weights and the model pre-trained on Kinetics (Reproduced). Our method outperforms the previously proposed self-supervised approach Video Speed by 0.9%.

4.4 Ablation Study

In this section, we present a set of ablation experiments to study the impact of the different aspects of our approach. Firstly, we provide an analysis of the individual components of our proposed loss. Secondly, we study the impact of the temporal extent and the order loss formulation on the quality of the learned representations and thereby uncover the limitations of the previously proposed approaches. All ablation studies are performed on the Oops dataset on both the classification and localization tasks by training a linear classifier on top of the learned representations.

Effect of Loss Components. The loss function for our model consists of two components: temporal contrastive loss and order prediction loss. To analyze the impact of the individual loss terms, we train two separate models: one with temporal contrastive loss (L_{temp}), and another one with order prediction loss

(L_{ord}). The results for these models are shown in Table 4. We can observe for both downstream tasks that using both loss terms substantially outperforms the models trained with only one of the two loss terms. This supports our hypothesis that temporal cues and relative order information are complementary and both are crucial for recognizing the intentionality of human actions. We can further see that while order-based and contrastive-based models show similar performance for localization, the order-based approach achieves significantly better results on the task of classification.

Effect of Loss Formulation. For computing the temporal contrastive loss and the order prediction loss, we sample three clips per video: two positives and one negative. To analyze the impact of the temporal variety of the samples on the quality of the resulting features, we perform a set of experiments. Namely, we train the models with the corresponding loss terms but we change the temporal scope from which the negative clips are sampled. We refer to the original sampling setting as *Global*, while *Local* denotes that the sampling scope has been limited. For *Local*, potential negative examples are confined to clips that are at least 3 and at most 5 steps away from the anchor clip x_i^t, *i.e.* $\{x_i^{t-5}, \ldots, x_i^{t-3}\} \cup \{x_i^{t+3}, \ldots, x_i^{t+5}\}$. In addition to this, we also analyze how the formulation of the order prediction task affects the resulting features. More precisely, we experiment with the formulation proposed by Epstein et al. [9]. That is, instead of predicting the pairwise order of clips (*Pair Order*), we predict their random permutation (*Permutation*).

Table 5. Impact of the loss formulation on the Oops dataset.

Linear classifier				
		Localization		Classification
Loss		1 s	0.25 s	All labels
Temp. ext	Loss type			
Temporal contrastive (L_{temp})				
Global	–	65.7	37.1	52.3
Local	–	64.1	35.5	50.1
Order (L_{ord})				
Global	Pair Order	66.2	36.0	60.0
Local	Pair Order	66.6	36.9	57.4
Global	Permutation	59.7	32.1	47.2
Local	Permutation	46.5	20.1	46.6
Temporal contrastive + **Order** ($L_{temp} + L_{ord}$)				
Global	Pair Order	70.5	**41.3**	**60.9**
Local	Pair Order	**70.7**	40.8	57.2

Table 5 shows the experimental results. Firstly, we observe that limiting the temporal variety of the considered examples generally leads to a weaker performance on the downstream tasks. This confirms our hypothesis that both long-range and short-range temporal discrimination are crucial for recognizing the degree of intent in a video. Therefore loss functions should not be confined to local neighborhoods. Secondly, we can see that models trained for permutation prediction show significantly lower results than those trained with pair-wise order prediction, especially when only clips from the confined local neighborhood are considered, which is a setting similar to what is proposed by Epstein et al. [9]. This shows that our formulation of order prediction is better suited to learn representations for unintentional action prediction, since it harnesses the information available in the relative clip order more efficiently.

5   Discussion

In this work, we have presented a self-supervised approach for the task of unintentional action prediction. To address the shortcomings of the previously proposed approaches, we proposed to train a feature extraction network using a two-component loss, consisting of a temporal contrastive loss and an order prediction loss. While the temporal contrastive loss is responsible for making representations distinct, the prediction of the clip order allows to learn the relative positioning. We evaluated our approach on one video dataset with unintentional actions and we provided additional results for anomaly detection in the supplementary material. While our work shows a large improvement over the previously proposed methods, we recognize that the current evaluation setting has a number of limitations. More specifically, the Oops dataset that we used for pre-training our model consists only of videos that have been collected from fail compilation videos. These videos are biased towards very specific actions and scenes, and the temporal location of unintentional actions is biased as well. While we show in the supplementary material that learning representations on such videos can be beneficial for anomaly detection as well, it needs to be investigated in future work how well the proposed approaches perform on videos with a more general definition of unintentional actions.

Acknowledgments. The work has been funded by the Deutsche Forschungsgemeinschaft (DFG, German Research Foundation) - SFB 1502/1-2022 - Projektnummer: 450058266 and GA 1927/4-2 (FOR 2535 Anticipating Human Behavior).

References

1. Ahsan, U., Madhok, R., Essa, I.: Video jigsaw: unsupervised learning of spatiotemporal context for video action recognition. In: Proceedings of the IEEE Winter Conference on Applications of Computer Vision (WACV) (2019)
2. Bai, Y., et al.: Can temporal information help with contrastive self-supervised learning? ArXiv abs/2011.13046 (2020)

3. Behrmann, N., Fayyaz, M., Gall, J., Noroozi, M.: Long short view feature decomposition via contrastive video representation learning. In: Proceedings of the IEEE/CVF International Conference on Computer Vision (ICCV) (2021)
4. Benaim, S., et al.: Speednet: learning the speediness in videos. In: Proceedings of the IEEE/CVF Conference on Computer Vision and Pattern Recognition (CVPR) (2020)
5. Chen, T., Kornblith, S., Norouzi, M., Hinton, G.E.: A simple framework for contrastive learning of visual representations. ArXiv abs/2002.05709 (2020)
6. Cho, H., Kim, T., Chang, H.J., Hwang, W.: Self-supervised visual learning by variable playback speeds prediction of a video. IEEE Access 9, 79562–79571 (2021)
7. Dave, I.R., Gupta, R., Rizve, M.N., Shah, M.: TCLR: temporal contrastive learning for video representation. ArXiv abs/2101.07974 (2021)
8. Diba, A., et al.: Vi2clr: video and image for visual contrastive learning of representation. In: Proceedings of the IEEE/CVF International Conference on Computer Vision (ICCV) (2021)
9. Epstein, D., Chen, B., Vondrick, C.: Oops! predicting unintentional action in video. In: Proceedings of the IEEE/CVF Conference on Computer Vision and Pattern Recognition (CVPR) (2020)
10. Epstein, D., Vondrick, C.: Learning goals from failure. In: Proceedings of the IEEE/CVF Conference on Computer Vision and Pattern Recognition (CVPR) (2021)
11. Feng, J.C., Hong, F.T., Zheng, W.S.: Mist: multiple instance self-training framework for video anomaly detection. In: Proceedings of the IEEE/CVF Conference on Computer Vision and Pattern Recognition (CVPR) (2021)
12. Fernando, B., Bilen, H., Gavves, E., Gould, S.: Self-supervised video representation learning with odd-one-out networks. In: Proceedings of the IEEE/CVF Conference on Computer Vision and Pattern Recognition (CVPR) (2017)
13. Gutmann, M., Hyvärinen, A.: Noise-contrastive estimation: a new estimation principle for unnormalized statistical models. In: Proceedings of the Thirteenth International Conference on Artificial Intelligence and Statistics (2010)
14. Hanson, A., Pnvr, K., Krishnagopal, S., Davis, L.S.: Bidirectional convolutional LSTM for the detection of violence in videos. In: European Conference on Computer Vision (ECCV) Workshop (2018)
15. Hara, K., Kataoka, H., Satoh, Y.: Can spatiotemporal 3D CNNs retrace the history of 2D CNNs and imagenet? In: Proceedings of the IEEE/CVF Conference on Computer Vision and Pattern Recognition (2018)
16. He, K., Fan, H., Wu, Y., Xie, S., Girshick, R.B.: Momentum contrast for unsupervised visual representation learning. In: Proceedings of the IEEE/CVF Conference on Computer Vision and Pattern Recognition (CVPR) (2020)
17. Hoffmann, D., Behrmann, N., Gall, J., Brox, T., Noroozi, M.: Ranking info noise contrastive estimation: boosting contrastive learning via ranked positives. In: AAAI Conference on Artificial Intelligence (2022)
18. Jenni, S., Jin, H.: Time-equivariant contrastive video representation learning. In: Proceedings of the IEEE/CVF International Conference on Computer Vision (ICCV) (2021)
19. Jing, L., Yang, X., Liu, J., Tian, Y.: Self-supervised spatiotemporal feature learning via video rotation prediction. ArXiv abs/811.11387 (2018)
20. Kay, W., et al.: The kinetics human action video dataset. ArXiv abs/1705.06950 (2017)
21. Kim, D., Cho, D., Kweon, I.S.: Self-supervised video representation learning with space-time cubic puzzles. In: AAAI Conference on Artifical Inelligence (2019)

22. Knights, J., Harwood, B., Ward, D., Vanderkop, A., Mackenzie-Ross, O., Moghadam, P.: Temporally coherent embeddings for self-supervised video representation learning. In: International Conference on Pattern Recognition (ICPR) (2020)
23. Lee, H.Y., Huang, J.B., Singh, M.K., Yang, M.H.: Unsupervised representation learning by sorting sequence. In: Proceedings of the IEEE International Conference on Computer Vision (ICCV) (2017)
24. Misra, I., Zitnick, C.L., Hebert, M.: Shuffle and learn: unsupervised learning using temporal order verification. In: Proceedings of the European Conference on Computer (ECCV) (2016)
25. Paszke, A., et al.: Pytorch: an imperative style, high-performance deep learning library. Adv. Neural Inf. Process. Syst. **32**, 1–39 (2019)
26. Qian, R., Meng, T., Gong, B., Yang, M.H., Wang, H., Belongie, S.J., Cui, Y.: Spatiotemporal contrastive video representation learning. In: Proceedings of the IEEE/CVF Conference on Computer Vision and Pattern Recognition (CVPR) (2021)
27. Sermanet, P., et al.: Time-contrastive networks: self-supervised learning from video. In: Proceedings of International Conference in Robotics and Automation (ICRA) (2018)
28. Sudhakaran, S., Lanz, O.: Learning to detect violent videos using convolutional long short-term memory. In: IEEE International Conference on Advanced Video and Signal Based Surveillance (AVSS) (2017)
29. Sultani, W., Chen, C., Shah, M.: Real-world anomaly detection in surveillance videos. In: Proceedings of the IEEE/CVF Conference on Computer Vision and Pattern Recognition (CVPR) (2018)
30. Tian, Y., Pang, G., Chen, Y., Singh, R., Verjans, J.W., Carneiro, G.: Weakly-supervised video anomaly detection with robust temporal feature magnitude learning. In: Proceedings of the IEEE/CVF International Conference on Computer Vision (ICCV) (2021)
31. Vondrick, C., Shrivastava, A., Fathi, A., Guadarrama, S., Murphy, K.P.: Tracking emerges by colorizing videos. In: Proceedings of the European Conference on Computer Vision (ECCV) (2018)
32. Wan, B., Jiang, W., Fang, Y., Luo, Z., Ding, G.: Anomaly detection in video sequences: a benchmark and computational model. IET Image Process. **15**, 3454–3465 (2021)
33. Wang, J., Jiao, J., Liu, Y.-H.: Self-supervised video representation learning by pace prediction. In: Vedaldi, A., Bischof, H., Brox, T., Frahm, J.-M. (eds.) ECCV 2020. LNCS, vol. 12362, pp. 504–521. Springer, Cham (2020). https://doi.org/10.1007/978-3-030-58520-4_30
34. Wei, D., Lim, J., Zisserman, A., Freeman, W.T.: Learning and using the arrow of time. In: Proceedings of the IEEE/CVF Conference on Computer Vision and Pattern Recognition (CVPR) (2018)
35. Wu, P., et al.: Not only look, but also listen: learning multimodal violence detection under weak supervision. In: Vedaldi, A., Bischof, H., Brox, T., Frahm, J.-M. (eds.) ECCV 2020. LNCS, vol. 12375, pp. 322–339. Springer, Cham (2020). https://doi.org/10.1007/978-3-030-58577-8_20
36. Xu, D., Xiao, J., Zhao, Z., Shao, J., Xie, D., Zhuang, Y.: Self-supervised spatiotemporal learning via video clip order prediction. In: Proceedings of the IEEE/CVF Conference on Computer Vision and Pattern Recognition (CVPR) (2019)
37. Xu, J., Chen, G., Lu, J., Zhou, J.: Unintentional action localization via counterfactual examples. IEEE Trans. Image Process. **31**, 3281–3294 (2022)

38. Yao, T., Zhang, Y., Qiu, Z., Pan, Y., Mei, T.: Seco: exploring sequence supervision for unsupervised representation learning. In: AAAI Conference on Artificial Intelligence (2021)
39. Yao, Y., Liu, C., Luo, D., Zhou, Y., Ye, Q.: Video playback rate perception for self-supervised spatio-temporal representation learning. In: Proceedings of the IEEE/CVF Conference on Computer Vision and Pattern Recognition (CVPR) (2020)
40. Zhong, J.X., Li, N., Kong, W., Liu, S., Li, T.H., Li, G.: Graph convolutional label noise cleaner: train a plug-and-play action classifier for anomaly detection. In: Proceedings of the IEEE/CVF Conference on Computer Vision and Pattern Recognition (CVPR) (2019)
41. Zhou, N., Chen, G., Xu, J., Zheng, W.S., Lu, J.: Temporal label aggregation for unintentional action localization. In: IEEE International Conference on Multimedia and Expo (ICME) (2021)

Robust Object Detection Using Knowledge Graph Embeddings

Christopher Lang⊕, Alexander Braun, and Abhinav Valada(✉)⊕

Robot Learning Lab, University of Freiburg, Freiburg, Germany
{lang,valada}@cs.uni-freiburg.de

Abstract. Object recognition for the most part has been treated as a one-hot problem that assumes classes to be discrete and unrelated. In this work, we challenge the prevalence of the one-hot approach in closed-set object detection. We evaluate the error statistics of learned class embeddings from a one-hot approach with knowledge embeddings that inherit semantic structure from natural language processing or knowledge graphs, as widely applied in open world object detection. Extensive experimental results on multiple knowledge-embeddings as well as distance metrics indicate that knowledge-based class representations result in more semantically grounded misclassifications while performing on par compared to one-hot methods on the challenging COCO and Cityscapes object detection benchmarks. We generalize our findings to multiple object detection architectures by proposing a knowledge-embedded design knowledge graph embedded (KGE) for keypoint-based and transformer-based object detection architectures.

Keywords: Object detection · Knowledge graphs · Word embeddings

1 Introduction

Object detection defines the task of localizing and classifying objects in an image. Deep object detection originates from the two-stage approach [5,38,46] which first selects anchor points in the image that potentially contain objects, and second classifies and regresses the coordinates for each proposal region in isolation. This initial design was followed by end-to-end trainable networks that avoid the dependence on a heuristic suppression of multiple detections for the same object [29]. Such methods model the relationship between object proposals by formulating object detection as a keypoint detection [22,58] or a direct-set estimation problem [6,7,59]. These novel architectures along with stronger backbones [18,41] and multiscale feature learning techniques [12,26,34] have doubled the average precision on the COCO detection benchmark [28] from 21.9% by the initial Faster R-CNN architecture [38] to 54.0% achieved by Dynamic Head [7].

These astonishing benchmark performances, however, all entail the inductive bias of a set-based classification formulation, i.e., the classes are regarded as discrete and unrelated. This assumption allows using a multinomial logistic loss [38,43,58] to boost the

Supplementary Information The online version contains supplementary material available at https://doi.org/10.1007/978-3-031-16788-1_27.

B. Andres et al. (Eds.): DAGM GCPR 2022, LNCS 13485, pp. 445–461, 2022.
https://doi.org/10.1007/978-3-031-16788-1_27

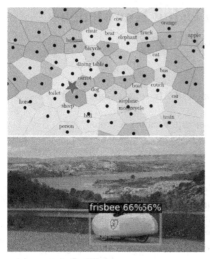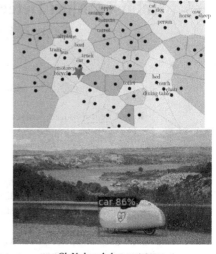

Learned class prototypes.   GloVe-based class prototypes.

Fig. 1. Voronoi diagram of 2D class prototypes (tNSE projections) and CenterNet [58] detection results for an out-of-distribution sample with an unseen object type. Segments are color-coded by their COCO stuff [4] supercategories.

classification accuracy by maximizing the inter-class distances [20]. However, it forces the model to treat each class prototype out-of-context from what it has learned about the other object types, resulting in an unstructured configuration of the classification space as can be seen in 2D tNSE projection of inter-class distances in Fig. 1 for the COCO 2017 classes. As a result, the training is prone to bias from class-imbalance [17,27], initialization, or co-occurrence statistics [40] in the training data and neglects synergies where there exist semantic similarities between classes. This closed-set formulation further requires relearning the class prototypes whenever the set of classes is extended [33,39].

Metric learning replaces learnable classification parameters with fixed class prototypes that embed object types by their semantic context in a specific domain (e.g., word embeddings generated from text corpora). The object detector thereby learns to map visual features into a semantic embedding space, encouraging to learn representations that discriminate between unrelated object types and exploits synergies between semantically related object types. The latter allows for zero-shot learning methods to recognize unseen object types only given their semantic description [3,20,36]. However, the metric learning approach has received minor attention in closed-set object detection so far, as it inherits the structural handicap that it cannot fit its class representations to maximize inter-class distances on closed-set benchmarks like COCO 2017. In this paper, we propose an extension of the metric learning approach to keypoint-based and transformer-based object detectors and built on them to challenge the necessity of the one-hot assumption in the closed-world object detection setting. Our extensive evaluations reveal that KGE can match the performance of one-hot approaches and additionally improve the quality of classifications, as misclassifications are more semantically-grounded, indicated by consistently superior mAP_{cat} scores.

In summary, our main contributions in this work are:

- a knowledge embedding formulation for two-stage, keypoint-based, and transformer-based multi-object detection architectures.
- an ablation study across distance metrics and knowledge types on COCO 2017.
- an error overlap analysis between one-hot and metric-learning based classifications.

2 Related Work

In this section, we review the related works in the research areas of object detection architectures, especially their classification losses and the usage of commonsense knowledge in computer vision.

Object Detection: Two-stage methods [5,38,43] rely on a Region Proposal Network (RPN) to first filter image regions containing objects from a set of search anchors. In a second stage, a Region of Interest (ROI) head extracts visual features from which it regresses enclosing bounding boxes as well as predicts a class label from a multi-set of classes for each object proposal in isolation.

In recent years, end-to-end trainable approaches have gained popularity. Anchorless detectors such as keypoint-based or center-based methods [22,45,58] embody an end-to-end approach that directly predicts objects as class heatmaps. Transformer-based methods [6,7,52,59] currently lead the COCO 2017 [28] object detection benchmark, pioneered by the DETR approach [6]. It builds upon ResNet as a feature extractor and a transformer encoder to compute self-attention among all pixels in the feature map.

Recently, the long-tailed object detection setting has gained interest, for instance on the LVIS V1 dataset featuring greater than 1000 object classes with highly imbalanced training samples over all classes. Here, the research interest lay in training strategies such as class-balanced sampling [14], class-frequency dependent loss formulations [25, 44,57], or data augmentation [11,54].

Knowledge-Based Embeddings: In zero-shot object detection, knowledge embeddings commonly replace learnable class prototypes in two-stage [3,13,13,36,56] and one-stage [31,50] detectors by learning a mapping from visual to semantic embedding spaces. Commonly used word embeddings are GloVe vectors [3,48] and *word2vec* embeddings [23,36,37,56], however embeddings learned from image-text pairs using the CLIP [35] recently achieved superior zero-shot performance [9,13,31,50]. The latter derive class representations from the embedding vector of a manually-tuned class prompt, while [9] propose a method for learning these prompts. The projection from visual to semantic space is done by a linear layer [3,15,23], a single [36,37,56] or two-layer MLP [13], and learned with a max-margin loss [3,10,15,36], softplus-margin focal loss [23,31], or cross-entropy loss [13,56]. Zhang *et al.* [55] suggest to rather learn the inverse mapping from semantic to visual space to alleviate the hubness problem in semantic spaces, however, our analysis of COCO 2017 class vectors suggested that the hubness phenomena does not have a noticeable impact on the COCO 2017 class embedding spaces. Another fundamental design choice in zero-shot object detection is the background representation. The majority of works rely on an explicit background representation that is either a single learned embedding vector [13,56], computed as the mean of all class vectors [15,36,37], represented by multiple word embeddings of background related concepts [3], or implicitly as a distance threshold w.r.t. each class prototype [23].

In this work, we analyze the usage of semantic relations between embeddings from the error distribution point of view and extend it to keypoint-based and transformer-based object detection architectures. We compare contrastive loss with margin-based loss functions and ablate multiple embedding sources to strengthen our analysis.

3 Technical Approach

Closed-set object detection architectures [6,19,38,58] share a classification head $\mathbb{R}^D \mapsto \mathbb{R}^C$ design incorporating a linear output layer, that projects the visual feature vector of P proposals $\mathbf{X} \in \mathbb{R}^{D \times P}$ onto a parameter matrix $\mathbf{W} \in \mathbb{R}^{D \times C}$ composed of C learnable class prototypes, from which class scores are derived as follows:

$$p(y = c|\mathbf{x}_i) = softmax(\mathbf{W}^T \mathbf{X})_i, \tag{1}$$

These class prototypes are learned with a one-hot loss formulation, incentivizing the resulting class prototypes to be pairwise orthogonal.

We replace the learnable class prototypes with fixed object type embeddings that incorporate structure from external knowledge domains in the closed-set setting. In the remainder of this section, we present the possible class prototype choices in Sect. 3.1, distance metrics in Sect. 3.2, and describe the incorporation into two-stage detectors, keypoint-based method, and transformer-based architectures in Sect. 3.3.

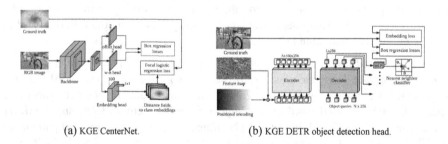

(a) KGE CenterNet.   (b) KGE DETR object detection head.

Fig. 2. Knowledge graph embedded (KGE) architecture using nearest neighbor classifiers for (a) CenterNet architecture and (b) a transformer-head. CenterNet encodes the image into a downscaled feature map from which it regresses a per-pixel class embedding vector, bounding box width and height, as well as centerpoint offset. For DETR, the decoder generates object feature vectors, which are fed into an MLP that outputs bounding box coordinates as well as an embedding vector that is used for nearest neighbor classification given semantic class prototypes.

3.1 Object-Type Embeddings

Instead of handcrafting the regression target vector or learning them from the training data, we incorporate object type embeddings from other knowledge modalities as follows:

- *GloVe* word embeddings [32] build on the descriptive nature of human language learned from a web-based text corpus.
- *ConceptNet* graph embeddings encode the conceptual knowledge between object categories entailed in the ConceptNet knowledge graphs [42].
- *COCO 2017* graph embeddings reflect the co-occurrence commonsense learned from the COCO 2017 training split. We build a heterogeneous graph from the spatial relations defined by Yatskar *et al.* [53]: {touches, above, besides, holds, on} and transform the resulting graph into node embeddings for each object prototype with an R-GCN [49].
- *CLIP* [35] are context embeddings generated by a text-encoder trained jointly with an image encoder on text-image pairs. We are using the text prompting strategy designed in [13].

3.2 Distance Metrics for Classification

We perform nearest-neighbor classification based on the distance between visual embeddings of proposal boxes and the class prototypes. We compare angular distance with the difference vector norm, as the most frequently distance measures in the metrical-learning domain. The ℓ_k norm of the difference vector between two embedding vectors is given by,

$$\ell_k(\overline{\mathbf{b}}_i, \overline{\mathbf{t}}_c) = \left(\sum_{d=1}^{D} (b_{i,d} - t_{c,d})^k \right)^{1/k}, \tag{2}$$

where $\mathbf{b}_i \in \mathbb{R}^D$ denotes the feature vector of the *i-th* proposal box and $\mathbf{t}_c \in \mathbb{R}^D$ the class prototype of the *c-th* object class. The maximum distance bound is given by the triangle inequality as $d_{k,max} \leq |\mathbf{t}_c|_k + |\mathbf{b}_i|_k$. In order to have a bound independent of D, we project all embeddings inside the unit sphere as $\overline{\mathbf{x}} = \frac{\mathbf{x}}{\max(1,|\mathbf{x}|_k)}$. Since the relative contrast in higher dimensions is largest for low values of k [2], we analyze the Manhattan distance where $k = 1$.

We further investigate nearest neighbors in terms of the cosine angle between two embedding vectors. The distance is computed using the negated cosine similarity as

$$d_{S_c}(\mathbf{b}_i, \mathbf{t}_c) = 1 - S_c(\mathbf{b}_i, \mathbf{t}_c) = 1 - \frac{\mathbf{b}_i^T \mathbf{t}_c}{|\mathbf{b}_i||\mathbf{t}_c|}. \tag{3}$$

We then interpret the negated distance as a similarity measure $sim(\mathbf{b}_i, \mathbf{t}_c) = 1 - d(\mathbf{b}_i, \mathbf{t}_c)/2$ and define the embedding losses as a contrastive loss towards the class embedding vectors is given by

$$\mathcal{L}_{embd}(\mathbf{b}_i, c_i) = -\log \left(\frac{\exp\left(sim(\mathbf{b}_i, \mathbf{t}_{c_i})/\tau\right)}{\sum_{c=1}^{C} \mathbb{1}_{[c \neq c_i]} \exp\left(sim(\mathbf{b}_i, \mathbf{t}_c)/\tau\right)} \right) \quad (4)$$

where c_i is the label of the groundtruth box to which the proposal is matched. τ denotes a fixed scaling factor of the similarity vector, commonly referred to as temperature. We follow [47] and fix $\tau = 0.07$. In the case of a feature vector $\mathbf{b}_i$ that is assigned to the background label, we set $c = 0$ and $sim(\mathbf{b}_i, \mathbf{t}_0) = 0$, as there is no class representation vector that the feature embedding should have a close distance. Please refer to the supplementary material for a comparison to a margin-based loss function.

3.3   Generalization to Existing Object Detectors

In this section, we describe the embedding extension to three types of object detectors: two-stage detectors, keypoint-based methods, and transformer-based. We intentionally chose standard object detection algorithms over state-of-the-art ones, as we wanted to compare largely distinct detection heads with a comparable amount of parameters (except for CenterNet, where the DLA-backbone consistently outperformed its ResNet-50 FPN variant). Our proposed approach however can be extended to all existing methods using a linear classification layer as their output.

Two-Stage Detectors. Such as R-CNN based methods [38] pools latent features of each object proposals regions to a fixed-size feature vector in the ROI head. These features are then processed in a box regressor and classifier to refine and classify the boxes for each proposal in isolation. The base method is trained with a standard Faster R-CNN loss, including a cross-entropy loss for bounding box classification. For the Faster R-CNN KGE method, we task the linear output layer to map from the ROI feature dimensionality to the embedding dimensionality D. We replaced the ReLU activation at the box head output layer with a hyperbolic tangent activation function (tanh) to avoid zero-capping the ROI feature vectors before the final linear layer.

Keypoint-Based Detectors. Formulate object detections as a keypoint estimation problem. CenterNet [58] uses these keypoints as the center of the bounding boxes.

For the KGE formulation, we use the filter depth of the embedding output stage according to the number of embedding dimensions, thus learning an embedding for each pixel in the output map as shown in Fig. 2a. Center point search then requires to compute a distance field of each pixel embedding to the class representation vectors.

Table 1. COCO 2017 *test-dev* and *val* results. The top section shows baseline results with learnable class prototypes and a one-hot loss, where *test-dev* results were taken from the referenced literature and *val* results were reproduced using their *detectron2* implementations. The bottom section presents results using test time augmentations for the proposed regression heads that vary in the type of class prototypes representation. For each meta architecture, we chose the best performing prediction head on the validation set. The COCO 2017 *val* columns show the average precision of predicting the correct class or category, which we could only evaluate on the validation set.

	COCO 2017 val			COCO 2017 test-dev					
	AP	AP_w	$AP_{cat,w}$	AP	AP_{50}	AP_{75}	AP_S	AP_M	AP_L
Faster R-CNN [38]	40.2	40.9	41.9	40.2	61.0	43.8	24.2	43.5	52.0
+ KGE classifier	39.3	41.6	43.5	39.4	59.7	43.4	24.1	41.3	49.8
CenterNet [58]	42.5	43.9	45.1	41.6	60.3	45.1	21.5	43.9	56.0
+ KGE classifier	**44.2**	**45.5**	**47.3**	**44.6**	63.6	**49.2**	**29.4**	**47.0**	53.5
DETR [6]	42.0	40.3	41.2	42.0	62.4	44.2	20.5	45.8	**61.1**
+ KGE classifier	43.2	42.9	43.6	43.3	**65.3**	45.8	22.9	45.9	59.8

Transformer-Based Methods. [6,59] adopt an encoder-decoder architecture to map a ResNet-encoded image to features of a set of object queries. The DETR encoder computes self-attention of pixels in the ResNet output feature map concatenated with a positional embedding. The decoder consists of cross-attention modules that extract features as values, from learned object queries and encoded visual feature keys. These are followed by self-attention modules among object queries. Each feature vector is then independently decoded into prediction box coordinates and class labels with a 3-layer perceptron with ReLU activation [6], as depicted in Fig. 2b.

We propose to replace the class label prediction with a feature embedding regression, and replace the classification cost function in the Hungarian matcher by the negative logarithm of the similarity measure, as described in Sect. 3.2. We further replace the ReLU activation function of the second-last linear layer with a tanh activation function.

4 Experimental Evaluation

We evaluate the nearest neighbor classification heads for 2D object detection on the COCO 2017 and LVIS benchmarks. We use the mean average precision (AP) metric averaged over IoU $\in [0.5 : 0.05 : 0.95]$ (COCO's standard metric) as the primary evaluation criteria. We also report the AP_w where we weight each class by the number of groundtruth instances, the average precision across scales $AP_{S,M,L}$ and the categories AP_{cat} for completeness.

The latter is a novel metric first introduced in this paper, which is based on categorizing the 80 COCO 2017 *thing* classes into a total of 19 base categories by finding common parent nodes based on Wu-Palmer similarity in the Google knowledge graph [1]. A true positive classification label is present if the correct category rather than the class was predicted by the model. Please refer to the supplementary material for an overview of object categories.

We chose the object detection task over image classification, as it additionally requires predicting whether a proposed image region contains a foreground object. Ablation studies are performed on the validation set, and an architecture-level comparison is reported on the COCO 2017 *test-dev* and LVIS *v1* datasets. For object detection algorithms, we compare Faster R-CNN [38] as representative for anchor-based methods, CenterNet [58] as keypoint-based object detector, and DETR [6] as transformer-based representative. We reserve zero-shot object detection experiments for future work, as we see the main research efforts in this domain to be in synthesizing unseen classes during training [16], or learning re-projections of the semantic embedding vectors [23,24,51]. The source of semantic embeddings currently takes up a secondary role and would require more extensive analysis.

Table 2. LIVS *val* results for various models with linear classification head and KGE classification head using ConceptNet embeddings. All methods were trained by repeat factor resampling [14] by a factor of 0.001.

Model	Loss	AP	AP_{50}	AP_{75}	AP_r	AP_c	AP_f
CenterNet2 (R-50-FPN)	FedLoss	28.2	39.2	30.0	18.8	26.4	34.4
+ KGE classifier	FedLoss	**28.7**	**40.7**	**30.8**	**19.3**	**27.0**	**34.9**
Faster R-CNN (R-50-FPN)	EQLv2	23.6	39.3	24.5	14.2	22.3	29.1
+ KGE classifier	EQLv2	22.8	38.9	24.9	13.9	21.4	28.9

Table 3. Ablation study on COCO 2017 *val* set. If not specified otherwise, ConceptNet embeddings in 100 dimensions as class prototypes, angular distance $1 - S_c$, and contrastive loss formulation (4) are used.

Model	Distance Metric		COCO 2017 val		
	$1 - S_c$	ℓ_1	AP	AP_{50}	AP_{75}
Faster R-CNN KGE	✓		40.39	**61.98**	41.58
		✓	35.99	56.88	38.87
CenterNet KGE	✓		41.37	59.23	**45.24**
		✓	16.42	22.97	18.57
DETR KGE	✓		**41.40**	61.20	43.92
		✓	40.37	60.16	42.70

(a) Results for angular distance $1 - S_c$ and Manhattan distance ℓ_1 configurations.

Model	Embeddings				COCO 2017 val		
	GV	CN	CO	CI	AP	AP_{50}	AP_{75}
Faster R-CNN KGE	✓				38.24	57.49	**41.98**
		✓			40.39	61.98	41.58
			✓		31.40	47.33	34.84
				✓	40.13	61.27	40.98
CenterNet KGE	✓				**41.37**	59.23	**45.24**
		✓			41.04	58.76	44.97
			✓		41.07	58.94	45.09
				✓	41.30	**59.27**	45.16
DETR KGE	✓				40.29	59.30	42.73
		✓			**41.40**	**61.20**	**43.92**
			✓		37.36	54.85	39.53
				✓	40.86	60.23	42.91

(b) Results using GloVe (GV), ConceptNet (CN), COCO 2017 (CO) embeddings, and CLIP (CI) (see Sect. 3.1) as class prototypes.

4.1 Datasets

COCO is currently the most widely used object detection dataset and benchmark. The data depicts complex everyday scenes containing common objects in their natural context. Objects are labeled using per-instance segmentation to aid in precise object localization [28]. We use annotations for 80 "thing" objects types in the 2017 train/val split, with a total of 886,284 labeled instances in 122,266 images. The scenes range from dining table close-ups to complex traffic scenes.

LIVS v1 builds on the COCO 2017 images but distinguishes 1203 object categories with a total of 127,0141 labeled instances in 100,170 training images. The class occurrences follow a discrete power law distribution, and therefore it is used as a benchmark for object detection under imbalanced class occurrences.

4.2 Training Protocol

We use the PyTorch framework for implementing all architectures, and we train our models on a system with an Intel Xenon@2.20GHz processor and NVIDIA TITAN RTX GPUs. All methods use a ResNet-50 backbone with weights pre-trained for image classification on the ImageNet dataset [8], and extracted multi-scale feature maps using a FPN with randomly initialized parameters. The hyperparameter settings, loss configuration, and training strategy principally follow the baseline configurations for maximum comparability, i.e., [38] for Faster R-CNN KGE, [58] for CenterNet KGE, and [6] for DETR KGE configurations. We train all networks using an Adam optimizer with weight decay [30] and gradient clipping. We use multi-scale training for all models except CenterNet-DLA [58] variants with a minimum training size of 480 pixel side length with random flipping as well as cropping for augmentation.

4.3 Quantitative Results

On the COCO 2017 test set in Table 1, we compare our results against baselines from the original methods presented in Sect. 3.3. We expected the baselines methods to outperform our proposed knowledge graph embedded (KGE) prediction heads, since the learnable class prototypes can "overfit" their classification margins on the closed-set training classes. Astonishingly, Table 1 shows that the KGE match the performance of with their baseline configurations in terms of the AP metrics. On the COCO 2017 *test-dev* benchmark, the CenterNet KGE outperforms its one-hot encoded counterparts by $+1.7\%$, while the DETR KGE variant achieves an overall AP of 43.2. The precision gain is consistently largest for AP_{75}, where the KGE methods benefit from high accuracy bounding boxes. The Faster R-CNN KGE method does not outperform its baseline performance in average precision, however, the proposed KGE methods appear to improve cross-category rankings as it is superior on AP_{cat}. We hypothesize that for Faster RCNN KGE, the proposal box classification is dominantly addressed in the box head due to the class-agnostic RPN loss, which appears to lack capacity to compensate the smaller inter-class distances. CenterNet KGE and DETR KGE seem to compensate for this within the feature extraction layers due to their class-sensitive matching of groundtruth and prediction boxes.

We attribute this competitive performance of the KGE methods to the small temperature value of $\tau = 0.07$, which was used as a hyperparameter for the contrastive loss function. As Kornblith *et al.* [20] noted, the temperature controls a trade-off between the generalizability of penultimate-layer features and the accuracy on the target dataset. We performed a grid search over temperature parameters and found that accuracy drops considerably with larger temperature values, as shown in the supplementary material. Another interesting observation is the large $AP_{cat,w}$ scores, where the KGE methods consistently outperform their baselines by more than 1.5%. These results demonstrate that misclassifications are more often within the same category, in contrast to baseline methods that appear to confuse classes across categories.

The long-tailed object detection results on the LVIS V1 *val* set are shown in Table 2. The CenterNet2 KGE variant outperformed its baseline by $+0.5\% AP$, especially for rare and common object types. This superior performance on rare classes is consistent over all configurations using KGE classification heads when compared to learnable class prototypes. We assume that semantic structure allows to leverage similarities between classes, which supports learning object types with few training samples.

4.4   Ablation Study

In this section, we compare three class prototype representations described in Sect. 3.1 to analyze which aspects of semantic context are most important for the object detection task and evaluate distance metrics used for classification.

Analysis of Object Type Representations: Table 3b shows the average precision for the object detection architectures presented in Sect. 3.3 when using various class prototype representations on the COCO 2017 *val* set. Interestingly, we observe no clear trend in which knowledge embedding is superior, the ConceptNet embedding gives the best AP over the Faster R-CNN KGE and DETR KGE configurations, however the results for using a GloVe embedding performs best for the CenterNet architecture. Embeddings extracted from the CLIP text encoder perform strong throughout all architectures. The COCO embeddings consistently perform worst of comparable KGE configurations. This is exceptional, since the COCO embeddings summarize the co-occurrence statistics without domain shift, while the ConceptNet and GloVe embeddings introduce external knowledge from textual or conceptual sources. These results indicate that the semantic contexts' role is dominated by categorical knowledge about the object classes.

Analysis of Distance Metric: In Table 3a, we further compare validation set results for Manhattan and cosine distances in the nearest neighbor classification. The results attribute consistently higher average precision values over all the architectures. The gap is largest for the CenterNet architecture, where the cosine similarity variant achieves $+24.7$ higher AP and the lowest for DETR with $+1.02 AP$. We suspect that, additionally to the sensitivity to outliers and the decreasing contrast for the L_k-norm in high dimensions [2], the convergence behavior plays a decisive role in the final model performance. Given fixed class prototypes, the *cossim* metric produces a gradient that decreases monotonous with increasing similarity to the target vector, while the ℓ_1 gradient has a constant gradient for non-zero difference vectors, which hinders iterative first-order optimization. Another interesting aspect of angular distance is the scale-invariance, which in principle could reserve the scaling dimension to account for different appearances of an object class. Further, the effect of outlier values in a single dimension only enters the distance metric at most linearly.

4.5 Misclassification Analysis

We analyze the confusion matrix of each detector on the COCO 2017 validation split. Each row in the confusion matrix $\mathbf{E} \in \mathrm{R}^{C \times C}$ corresponds to an object class, and each entry represents the counts of predicted labels for this class' groundtruth instances. For each groundtruth box, we select the predicted bounding box with the highest confidence score of all predicted boxes with an IOU ≥ 0.8, i.e., each groundtruth box is assigned to at most one prediction.

For comparing error distributions of different object detectors, we compute the Jensen-Shannon distance of corresponding rows in the confusion matrices as

$$JS(\mathbf{p}, \mathbf{q}) = \sqrt{\frac{D(\mathbf{p} \parallel \mathbf{m}) + D(\mathbf{q} \parallel \mathbf{m})}{2}}, \tag{5}$$

where $\mathbf{p}, \mathbf{q}$ are false positive distributions, $\mathbf{m}$ is the point-wise mean of two vectors as $m_i = \frac{p_i + q_i}{2}$, and D is the Kullback-Leibler divergence.

A low JS distance implies that the classification stages of the two detectors under comparison produce similar error distributions, and vice versa. Figure 3a shows the JS distances for each object detection algorithm between the baseline method and all embedding-based prediction heads. We note that the error distributions vary noticeably from the baselines methods, however all the embedding-based prediction heads appear to differ by similar magnitudes. This behavior indicates that there is a conceptual difference in the prediction characteristic of the learned (baseline) and knowledge-based class prototypes. The effect is largest for the CenterNet architecture, presumably since the embedding-based formulation affects the classification as well as localization head. To further investigate the origin of this dissimilar behavior, we quantify the inter-category confusions of different object detector architectures in Fig. 3b.

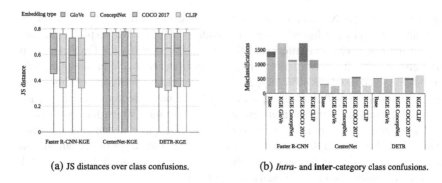

(a) JS distances over class confusions.   (b) *Intra-* and **inter**-category class confusions.

Fig. 3. Analysis of classification errors on the COCO 2017 *val* split for each detector configuration using cosine distance metric and contrastive loss. The Jensen-Shannon distances (a) are
computed w.r.t. the class confusion matrices between the baseline configurations using learnable class prototypes and the KGE method. A light color in the confusion counts (b) indicate
a common category between the matched ground truth and prediction box, full colors indicate
intercategory class confusions.

Inter-Category Confusion: Fig. 3b shows that all knowledge-embedded class prototypes, except for the *COCO 2017* class prototypes, produce lower inter-category confusions compared to their one-hot encoded configurations. This signifies that feature
embeddings derived from spatial relations between objects provide insufficient inter-
class distances when used as class prototypes. This impairment is especially noticeable
for the Faster R-CNN architecture, where class confusion of overlapping objects can
also occur during the loss computation. The ConceptNet embeddings result in the lowest counts of inter-category confusion, since its structure is derived from a conceptual
knowledge graph similar to the one used for categorization, and its inter-category confusion counts are consistently lower than the base configuration with learnable class
prototypes.

4.6 Qualitative Results

We further qualitatively evaluate methods trained on the COCO 2017 dataset and classes
with images from OpenImages [21] to demonstrate behavior on unseen objects and data
distributions. The results are shown in Fig. 4. All the methods demonstrate high object
localization accuracy, where the foreground region regression appears correlated with
the choice of the detection architecture. The KGE-based detection heads have consistently lowered confidence in the detections, however, they skew the object classification to more semantically related classes, e.g., the unknown snow mobile in Fig. 4 (a)
is assigned to related classes such as *car*, *snowboard*, or *motorcycle* by the KGE methods, rather than *airplane*, *boat*, or *truck* by the baseline methods. The KGE methods
also exhibit fewer false positives, such as the *kite* in Fig. 4 (c) for DETR, which are not
captured by the average precision metric on the object detection benchmarks.

Fig. 4. Qualitative results on images from the OpenImages [21] validation set using the configurations in Table 1. Please note that confidence scores for KGE methods describe the normalized similarity value between class prototype and visual embeddings.

5   Conclusions

In this work, we demonstrate the transfer of feature embeddings from natural language processing or knowledge graphs as class prototypes into two-stage, keypoint-based, and transformer-based object detection architectures trained using a contrastive loss. We performed extensive ablation studies that analyze the choice of class prototypes and distance metrics on the COCO 2017 and Cityscapes datasets. We showed that our resulting method can compete with their standard configurations on challenging object detection benchmarks, with error distributions that are more consistent with the object categories in the groundtruth. Especially, class prototypes derived from the ConceptNet knowledge graph [42] using a cosine distance metric demonstrate low inter-categorical confusions. Future work will investigate whether these knowledge embeddings in the classification head also benefit the class-incremental learning task in object detection.

References

1. Google Knowledge Graph. https://developers.google.com/knowledge-graph
2. Aggarwal, C.C., Hinneburg, A., Keim, D.A.: On the surprising behavior of distance metrics in high dimensional space. In: Van den Bussche, J., Vianu, V. (eds.) ICDT 2001. LNCS, vol. 1973, pp. 420–434. Springer, Heidelberg (2001). https://doi.org/10.1007/3-540-44503-X_27
3. Bansal, A., Sikka, K., Sharma, G., Chellappa, R., Divakaran, A.: Zero-shot object detection. In: Ferrari, V., Hebert, M., Sminchisescu, C., Weiss, Y. (eds.) ECCV 2018. LNCS, vol. 11205, pp. 397–414. Springer, Cham (2018). https://doi.org/10.1007/978-3-030-01246-5_24
4. Caesar, H., Uijlings, J., Ferrari, V.: Coco-stuff: thing and stuff classes in context. In: Proceedings of the IEEE Conference on Computer Vision and Pattern Recognition, pp. 1209–1218 (2018)
5. Cai, Z., Vasconcelos, N.: Cascade R-CNN: delving into high quality object detection. In: Proceedings of the IEEE Conference on Computer Vision and Pattern Recognition, pp. 6154–6162 (2018)
6. Carion, N., Massa, F., Synnaeve, G., Usunier, N., Kirillov, A., Zagoruyko, S.: End-to-end object detection with transformers. In: Vedaldi, A., Bischof, H., Brox, T., Frahm, J.-M. (eds.) ECCV 2020. LNCS, vol. 12346, pp. 213–229. Springer, Cham (2020). https://doi.org/10.1007/978-3-030-58452-8_13
7. Dai, X., et al.: Dynamic head: unifying object detection heads with attentions. In: Proceedings of the IEEE Conference on Computer Vision and Pattern Recognition, pp. 7373–7382 (2021)
8. Deng, J., Dong, W., Socher, R., Li, L.J., Li, K., Fei-Fei, L.: ImageNet: a large-scale hierarchical image database. In: Proceedings of the IEEE Conference on Computer Vision and Pattern Recognition, pp. 248–255. IEEE (2009)
9. Du, Y., Wei, F., et al.: Learning to prompt for open-vocabulary object detection with vision-language model. arXiv preprint arXiv:2203.14940 (2022)
10. Frome, A., et al.: Devise: a deep visual-semantic embedding model. In: Proceedings of the Conference on Neural Information Processing Systems, vol.26 (2013)
11. Ghiasi, G., et al.: Simple copy-paste is a strong data augmentation method for instance segmentation. In: Proceedings of the IEEE Conference on Computer Vision and Pattern Recognition, pp. 2918–2928 (2021)
12. Gosala, N., Valada, A.: Bird's-eye-view panoptic segmentation using monocular frontal view images. arXiv preprint arXiv:2108.03227 (2021)
13. Gu, X., Lin, T.Y., Kuo, W., Cui, Y.: Open-vocabulary object detection via vision and language knowledge distillation. arXiv preprint arXiv:2104.13921 (2021)
14. Gupta, A., Dollar, P., Girshick, R.: LVIS: a dataset for large vocabulary instance segmentation. In: Proceedings of the IEEE Conference on Computer Vision and Pattern Recognition, pp. 5356–5364 (2019)
15. Gupta, D., Anantharaman, A., Mamgain, N., Balasubramanian, V.N., Jawahar, C., et al.: A multi-space approach to zero-shot object detection. In: Proceedings of the IEEE/CVF Winter Conference on Applications of Computer Vision, pp. 1209–1217 (2020)
16. Hayat, N., Hayat, M., Rahman, S., Khan, S., Zamir, S.W., Khan, F.S.: Synthesizing the unseen for zero-shot object detection. In: Proceedings of the Asian Conference on Computer Vision (2020)
17. He, K., Gkioxari, G., Dollar, P., Girshick, R.: Mask R-CNN. In: International Conference on Computer Vision, pp. 2980–2988 (2017)
18. He, K., Zhang, X., Ren, S., Sun, J.: Deep residual learning for image recognition. In: Proceedings of the IEEE Conference on Computer Vision and Pattern Recognition, pp. 770–778 (2016)

19. Hurtado, J.V., Mohan, R., Burgard, W., Valada, A.: MOPT: multi-object panoptic tracking. arXiv preprint arXiv:2004.08189 (2020)
20. Kornblith, S., Lee, H., Chen, T., Norouzi, M.: Why do better loss functions lead to less transferable features?. arXiv preprint arXiv:2010.16402 (2021)
21. Kuznetsova, A., et al.: The open images dataset v4: unified image classification, object detection, and visual relationship detection at scale. Int. J. Comput. Vis. **128**(7), 1956–1981 (2020)
22. Law, H., Deng, J.: CornerNet: detecting objects as paired keypoints. In: Ferrari, V., Hebert, M., Sminchisescu, C., Weiss, Y. (eds.) Computer Vision – ECCV 2018. LNCS, vol. 11218, pp. 765–781. Springer, Cham (2018). https://doi.org/10.1007/978-3-030-01264-9_45
23. Li, Q., Zhang, Y., Sun, S., Zhao, X., Li, K., Tan, M.: Rethinking semantic-visual alignment in zero-shot object detection via a softplus margin focal loss. Neurocomputing **449**, 117–135 (2021)
24. Li, Y., Li, P., Cui, H., Wang, D.: Inference fusion with associative semantics for unseen object detection. In: Proceedings of the AAAI Conference on Artificial Intelligence, vol. 35, pp. 1993–2001 (2021)
25. Li, Y., Wang, T., Kang, B., Tang, S., Wang, C., Li, J., Feng, J.: Overcoming classifier imbalance for long-tail object detection with balanced group softmax. In: Proceedings of the IEEE Conference on Computer Vision and Pattern Recognition, pp. 10991–11000 (2020)
26. Lin, T.Y., Dollár, P., Girshick, R., He, K., Hariharan, B., Belongie, S.: Feature pyramid networks for object detection. In: Proceedings of the IEEE Conference on Computer Vision and Pattern Recognition, pp. 2117–2125 (2017)
27. Lin, T.Y., Goyal, P., Girshick, R., He, K., Dollár, P.: Focal loss for dense object detection. In: Proceedings of the IEEE Conference on Computer Vision and Pattern Recognition, pp. 2980–2988 (2017)
28. Lin, T.-Y., et al.: Microsoft COCO: common objects in context. In: Fleet, D., Pajdla, T., Schiele, B., Tuytelaars, T. (eds.) ECCV 2014. LNCS, vol. 8693, pp. 740–755. Springer, Cham (2014). https://doi.org/10.1007/978-3-319-10602-1_48
29. Liu, S., Huang, D., Wang, Y.: Adaptive NMS: refining pedestrian detection in a crowd. In: Proceedings of the IEEE Conference on Computer Vision and Pattern Recognition, pp. 6459–6468 (2019)
30. Loshchilov, I., Hutter, F.: Decoupled weight decay regularization. arXiv preprint arXiv:1711.05101 (2017)
31. Ma, Z., Luo, G., et al.: Open-vocabulary one-stage detection with hierarchical visual-language knowledge distillation. arXiv preprint arXiv:2203.10593 (2022)
32. Pennington, J., Socher, R., Manning, C.D.: GloVe: global vectors for word representation. In: Empirical Methods in Natural Language Processing, pp. 1532–1543 (2014)
33. Perez-Rua, J.M., Zhu, X., Hospedales, T.M., Xiang, T.: Incremental few-shot object detection. In: Proceedings of the IEEE Conference on Computer Vision and Pattern Recognition, pp. 13846–13855 (2020)
34. Qiao, S., Chen, L.C., Yuille, A.: Detectors: detecting objects with recursive feature pyramid and switchable atrous convolution. In: Proceedings of the IEEE Conference on Computer Vision and Pattern Recognition, pp. 10213–10224 (2021)
35. Radford, A., et al.: Learning transferable visual models from natural language supervision. arXiv preprint arXiv:2103.00020 (2021)
36. Rahman, S., Khan, S., Barnes, N.: Improved visual-semantic alignment for zero-shot object detection. In: Proceedings of the AAAI Conference on Artificial Intelligence, vol. 34, pp. 11932–11939 (2020)
37. Rahman, S., Khan, S.H., Porikli, F.: Zero-shot object detection: joint recognition and localization of novel concepts. Int. J. Comput. Vis. **128**(12), 2979–2999 (2020)

38. Ren, S., He, K., Girshick, R., Sun, J.: Faster R-CNN: towards real-time object detection with region proposal networks. In: Proceedings of the Conference on Neural Information Processing Systems, pp. 91–99 (2015)

39. Shmelkov, K., Schmid, C., Alahari, K.: Incremental learning of object detectors without catastrophic forgetting. In: International Conference on Computer Vision, pp. 3400–3409 (2017)

40. Singh, K.K., Mahajan, D., Grauman, K., Lee, Y.J., Feiszli, M., Ghadiyaram, D.: Don't judge an object by its context: learning to overcome contextual bias. In: Proceedings of the IEEE Conference on Computer Vision and Pattern Recognition, pp. 11070–11078 (2020)

41. Sirohi, K., Mohan, R., Büscher, D., Burgard, W., Valada, A.: EfficientLPS: efficient lidar panoptic segmentation. arXiv preprint arXiv:2102.08009 (2021)

42. Speer, R., Chin, J., Havasi, C.: ConceptNet 5.5: an open multilingual graph of general knowledge. In: Proceedings of the AAAI Conference on Artificial Intelligence (2017)

43. Sun, P., et al.: Sparse R-CNN: end-to-end object detection with learnable proposals. In: Proceedings of the IEEE Conference on Computer Vision and Pattern Recognition, pp. 14454–14463 (2021)

44. Tan, J., Lu, X., Zhang, G., Yin, C., Li, Q.: Equalization loss v2: a new gradient balance approach for long-tailed object detection. In: Proceedings of the IEEE Conference on Computer Vision and Pattern Recognition, pp. 1685–1694 (2021)

45. Tian, Z., Shen, C., Chen, H., He, T.: FCOS: fully convolutional one-stage object detection. In; Proceedings of the IEEE Conference on Computer Vision and Pattern Recognition, pp. 9627–9636 (2019)

46. Valverde, F.R., Hurtado, J.V., Valada, A.: There is more than meets the eye: self-supervised multi-object detection and tracking with sound by distilling multimodal knowledge. In: Proceedings of the IEEE Conference on Computer Vision and Pattern Recognition, pp. 11612–11621 (2021)

47. Wang, F., Liu, H.: Understanding the behaviour of contrastive loss. arXiv preprint arXiv:2012.09740, pp. 2495–2504 (2020)

48. Wang, X., Ye, Y., Gupta, A.: Zero-shot recognition via semantic embeddings and knowledge graphs. In: Proceedings of the IEEE Conference on Computer Vision and Pattern Recognition, pp. 6857–6866 (2018)

49. Woo, S., Kim, D., Daejeon, K., Cho, D.E., So Kweon, I.E., Kweon, I.S., Cho, D.E.: LinkNet: relational embedding for scene graph. In: Proceedings of the Conference on Neural Information Processing Systems, pp. 560–570 (2018)

50. Xie, J., Zheng, S.: ZSD-YOLO: zero-shot yolo detection using vision-language knowledge distillation. arXiv preprint arXiv:2109.12066 (2021)

51. Yan, C., Chang, X., Luo, M., Liu, H., Zhang, X., Zheng, Q.: Semantics-guided contrastive network for zero-shot object detection. IEEE Trans. Patt. Anal. Mach. Intell. pp. 1–1 (2022)

52. Yang, J., et al.: Focal self-attention for local-global interactions in vision transformers. arXiv preprint arXiv:2107.00641 (2021)

53. Yatskar, M., Ordonez, V., Farhadi, A.: Stating the obvious: extracting visual common sense knowledge. In: Conference of the North American Chapter of the Association for Computational Linguistics: Human Language Technologies, pp. 193–198 (2016)

54. cui Zhang, C., et al.: A simple and effective use of object-centric images for long-tailed object detection. arXiv preprint arXiv:2102.08884 (2021)

55. Zhang, L., Xiang, T., Gong, S.: Learning a deep embedding model for zero-shot learning. In: Proceedings of the IEEE Conference on Computer Vision and Pattern Recognition, pp. 2021–2030 (2017)

56. Zheng, Y., Huang, R., Han, C., Huang, X., Cui, L.: Background learnable cascade for zero-shot object detection. In: Proceedings of the Asian Conference on Computer Vision (2020)

57. Zhou, X., Koltun, V., Krähenbühl, P.: Probabilistic two-stage detection. arXiv preprint arXiv:2103.07461 (2021)
58. Zhou, X., Wang, D., Krähenbühl, P.: Objects as points. arXiv preprint arXiv:1904.07850 (2019)
59. Zhu, X., Su, W., Lu, L., Li, B., Wang, X., Dai, J.: Deformable DETR: deformable transformers for end-to-end object detection. arXiv preprint arXiv:2010.04159 (2020)

On Hyperbolic Embeddings in Object Detection

Christopher Lang$^{(\boxtimes)}$ ⓘ, Alexander Braun, Lars Schillingmann, and Abhinav Valada ⓘ

Robot Learning Lab, University of Freiburg, Freiburg, Germany
{lang,valada}@cs.uni-freiburg.de

Abstract. Object detection, for the most part, has been formulated in the euclidean space, where euclidean or spherical geodesic distances measure the similarity of an image region to an object class prototype. In this work, we study whether a hyperbolic geometry better matches the underlying structure of the object classification space. We incorporate a hyperbolic classifier in two-stage, keypoint-based, and transformer-based object detection architectures and evaluate them on large-scale, long-tailed, and zero-shot object detection benchmarks. In our extensive experimental evaluations, we observe categorical class hierarchies emerging in the structure of the classification space, resulting in lower classification errors and boosting the overall object detection performance.

Keywords: Object detection · Hyperbolic embeddings · Lorentz model

1 Introduction

The object detection task entails localizing and classifying objects in an image. Deep learning methods originate from the two-stage approach [5,9,32] that uses encoded visual features of an input image to first search for image regions that potentially contain objects, and then classify and refine each proposal region in isolation. Over the years, alternate approaches have challenged these initial design choices: end-to-end formulations [6,19,31,43,44] yield a real-time and fully-differentiable alternative to the two-stage approach, multi-resolution detectors [22] boost the detection accuracy for small objects, and learnable proposals [34] supersede the need for dense candidate regions. Even novel object detection paradigms have emerged, such as anchorless [43] and set-based methods [6,34] that bypass non-maximum suppression, as well as attention-based methods [6] that explicitly learn context between object proposals.

However, many design paradigms have never been questioned, first and foremost, the learnable class prototypes as well as the euclidean embedding space

---

Supplementary Information The online version contains supplementary material available at https://doi.org/10.1007/978-3-031-16788-1_28.

in the classifier head. Recently, alternative classification space formulations such as hyperbolic embeddings have outperformed their euclidean counterparts in an increasing number of domains. Gains were especially observed in tasks that underlie a hierarchical representation [24,27], including the task of image classification [14]. These successes are attributed to the exponentially growing distance ratio of hyperbolic spaces, which enables them to match the rate of growth in tree-like structures. In this paper, we analyze whether visual object detectors also benefit from a hyperbolic classification space where visual features encode information about both, object categorization and bounding-box regression.

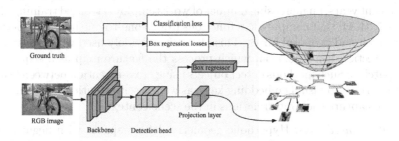

Fig. 1. General object detection architecture using classification scores embedding in the hyperboloid model. It is built on object proposal features from an arbitrary detection neck, for instance a transformer-decoder or RoI head, using operations in Euclidean space. Finally, it outputs the classification logits computed in the learned hyperbolic metric space, i.e. calculates hyperbolic distances (Eq. 5) to the learned class prototypes on the hyperboloid.

We incorporate a hyperbolic classification head into various object detectors, as can be seen in Fig. 1, including Sparse R-CNN [34], CenterNet [43], and Deformable DETR [44]. We evaluate the performance on closed-set object detection as well as long-tailed and zero-shot object detection and analyze how it copes with the task to distinguish foreground and background representations and its interaction with localization. We observe a latent class hierarchy emerging from visual features, resulting in fewer and better classification errors, while simultaneously boosting the overall object detection performance.
In summary, our main contributions in this work are:

- Formulation of a hyperbolic classification head for two-stage, keypoint-based, and transformer-based multi-object detection architectures.
- Evaluation of hyperbolic classification on closed-set, long-tailed, and zero-shot object detection.

2   Related Work

In this section, we review the relevant works in the research area of object detection architectures, with special interest in their classification heads, as well as hyperbolic embeddings in the image domain.

Object Detection: Early deep object detectors were anchor-based methods [5,32–34] that first select image regions potentially containing and object from a set of search locations and then employ a Region of Interest (RoI) head to extract visual features which are used for classification and bounding box regression. Due to its class-agnostic Region Proposal Network (RPN), such methods are nowadays widely applied in zero-shot object detection [15,30,41].

Anchor-less detectors such as keypoint-based or center-based methods [16,43] embody an end-to-end approach that directly predicts objects as class-heatmaps. Additional regression heads then estimate bounding box offset and height/width [43], instance masks [17,26] or temporal correspondences [13] in an image sequence.

In recent years, an increasing number of works employ set-based training objectives [6,7,34,44] that compute loss functions from a one-to-one matching between groundtruth and proposal boxes. This objective is widely used with transformer-based detection heads [6,7,44] which process the feature map as a sequence of image patches. Such methods detect objects using cross-attention between learned object queries and visual embedding keys, as well as self-attention between object queries to capture their interrelations in the scene context.

Hyperbolic Embeddings: Hyperbolic geometry defines spaces with negative constant Gaussian curvature. Consequently, the distance-ratio of hyperbolic spaces increases exponentially [3] - a property that is incorporated by recent works to capture parent-child relations within the data [27]. The Poincaré ball model is currently the most widely used formulation of hyperbolic space for embedding tasks [14,21,27], due to its intuitive visualization in 2D and its embedding space that is constraint based on the euclidean norm. Nickel *et al.* [27] pioneered the learning of tree-structured graph embeddings in the Poincaré ball, and surpassed Euclidean embeddings in terms of generalization ability and representation capacity. Poincaré embeddings were introduced in the image domain by Khrulkov *et al.* [14] for image classification and person re-identification tasks. They observed that mini-batches of image embeddings generated from ResNet-18 [12] feature extractors on Mini-ImageNet [8] form a hyperbolic group, as the embeddings' Caley-Graph is δ-hyperbolic. Motivated by this observation, they mapped the penultimate layer of a ResNet-18 [12] backbone onto the Poincaré ball and performed a hyperbolic multi-logistic regression, which they showed to achieve superior results compared to euclidean methods for 5-shot classification on Mini-ImageNet [8]. They further proposed a model for person re-identification tasks on proposal regions, disregarding the localization task of object detection.

For zero-shot image classification, [21] transformed image embeddings using a ResNet-101 [12] into hyperbolic vectors on the Poincaré ball model and perform classification based on distances to Poincaré embeddings of WordNet relations [27] as class prototypes. In doing so, they outperform all euclidean baselines models in terms of hierarchical precision on ImageNet. In a later work, Nickel *et al.* [28] found that the hyperboloid model, also called Lorentz model, learns embeddings for large taxonomies more efficiently and more accurately than Poincaré embeddings. Furthermore, the distance computation on the hyperboloid model is numerically stable, as it avoids the stereographic projection.

Building on embeddings in the hyperboloid model [28], we perform object detection with hyperbolic detection head for two-stage, keypoint-based, and transformer-based detectors. In addition to image classification, this requires to localize objects and distinguish between foreground and background image regions.

3   Technical Approach

SoTA closed-set object detection architectures employ linear euclidean layer design [1,32,37] that projects visual feature vectors $\mathbf{v}_i \in \mathbb{R}^D$ onto a parameter matrix $\mathbf{W} \in \mathbb{R}^{D \times C}$ composed of C class prototypes $p(y = c|\mathbf{v}_i) = softmax(\mathbf{W}^T \mathbf{v}_i)_c$.

We propose to learn class prototypes in hyperbolic space to embed latent hierarchies with lower distortion. In the remainder of this section, we introduce hyperbolic embeddings in Sect. 3.1, the modifications to the classification losses in Sect. 3.2, and describe the incorporation into two-stage detectors, keypoint-based method, and transformer-based architectures in Sect. 3.3.

3.1   Hyperbolic Embeddings

In this work, we analyze the n-dimensional hyperboloid model $\mathbb{H}^n$, also called Lorentz model, as a classification space for object detection. It is one of the several isometric models of the hyperbolic space, i.e., a Riemannian manifold with constant negative curvature $\kappa < 0$. We investigate, whether this non-zero curvature is desirable to capture latent hierarchical information due to the exponential growth of volume with distance to a point [3]. The limit case with $\kappa = 0$ would recover Euclidean geometry behavior and hence the baseline object detectors.

The n-dimensional hyperboloid model $\mathbb{H}^n$ presents points on the upper sheet of a two-sheeted n-dimensional hyperboloid. It is defined by the Riemannian manifold $\mathcal{L} = (\mathbb{H}^n, \mathbf{g}_l)$ with

$$\mathbb{H}^n = \{\mathbf{x} \in \mathbb{R}^{n+1} : \langle \mathbf{x}, \mathbf{x} \rangle_l = -1, x_0 > 0\}, \tag{1}$$

and

$$g_l(\mathbf{x}) = \mathrm{diag}(-1, 1, \ldots, 1) \in \mathbb{R}^{n+1 \times n+1}, \tag{2}$$

such that the Lorentzian scalar product $\langle \cdot, \cdot \rangle_l$ is given by

$$\langle \mathbf{x}, \mathbf{y} \rangle_l = -x_0 y_0 + \sum_{i=1}^{n} x_n y_n, \quad \mathbf{x}, \mathbf{y} \in \mathbb{R}^{n+1}. \tag{3}$$

To transform visual features $\mathbf{v} \in \mathbb{R}^{n+1}$ - extracted from euclidean modules like convolutional layers or MLP - into points on the hyperboloid, we apply the exponential map as follows:

$$\exp_0^k(\mathbf{v}) = \sinh(\|\mathbf{v}\|) \frac{\mathbf{v}}{\|\mathbf{v}\|}. \tag{4}$$

The distance between two points on the hyperboloid is then given by

$$d_{\mathbb{H}^n}(\mathbf{x}_i, \mathbf{t}_c) = \operatorname{arccosh}\left(-\langle \mathbf{x}_i, \mathbf{t}_c \rangle_l\right), \quad \mathbf{x}_i, \mathbf{t}_c \in \mathbb{H}^n. \tag{5}$$

When performing gradient optimization over the tangent space at a hyperbolic embedding $\mathbf{x} \in \mathbb{H}^n$, we employ the exponential map at $\mathbf{x}$ to the tangent vector, as shown in [38].

3.2   Focal Loss Integration

The state-of-the-art object detectors compared in this work use a focal classification loss [19] that relies on the sigmoid function for computing the binary cross entropy. Since distance metrics only span the non-negative real numbers, we compute logits by shifting the distances by a negative value as

$$s_{i,c} = \Delta - \frac{\Delta}{d_{min}} d_{i,c}, \tag{6}$$

where $s_{i,c}$ is the classification score for proposal i and class c, $d_{\mathbb{H}^n}(\mathbf{x}_i, \mathbf{t}_c)$ is the respective distance between the transformed visual feature vector and the prototype for class c. Δ is an offset that shifts the active regions of the activation function. The scaling parameter d_{min} defines the distance that accounts for a classification confidence of $p = 0.5$. It is set to the minimum inter-class distance for fixed class prototypes, or a scalar constant (here $d_{min} = 1$) for learnable class prototypes.

3.3   Generalization to Existing Object Detectors

In this section, we briefly revisit the two-stage, keypoint-based, and transformer-based object detectors that we use for the experiments with a special focus on their classification loss.

Two-stage detectors such as Sparse R-CNN [34], first extract a set of N proposal boxes that potentially contain objects from latent image features. A RoI head then processes each proposal feature vector separately to extract classification features and bounding box regression values. In the case of Sparse R-CNN [34], the RoI head takes the form of a dynamic instance interactive head, where each head is conditioned on a learned proposal feature vector. The classification scores enter the matching cost via a focal loss term. For our experiments, we replace the classification head by the hyperbolic MLR module as described in Sect. 3.1.

Keypoint-based detectors formulate object detection as a keypoint estimation problem. CenterNet [43] uses these keypoints as the center of bounding boxes. The final layer outputs a per-class heatmap as well as center point regression, bounding box width, and height, etc. We evaluate CenterNet also as a representative of one-stage detectors. It outperforms RetinaNet [19], YOLOv3 [31], and FCOS [36] on the COCO test-dev benchmark when using ResNet-50 as feature extractor or alternatives with comparable number of parameters. We modify the classification heatmap to regress towards classification embeddings for each pixel. These embeddings are then transformed into hyperbolic space, and class heatmaps are generated by computing distance fields to each hyperbolic class prototype.

Transformer-based methods were pioneered by the DETR [6] architecture that utilize a transformer encoder-decoder model that processes feature map tokens of ResNet-encoded image features. Each feature vector is then independently decoded into prediction box coordinates and class labels by a 3-layer perceptron with ReLU activation [6]. Deformable DETR [44] (DDETR) improves the computational efficiency of DETR by proposing a deformable attention module that additionally allows to aggregate multi-scale feature maps. The decoder consists of cross-attention modules that extract features as values, whereby the query elements are of N object queries and the key elements are of the output feature maps from the encoder. These are followed by self-attention modules among object queries.

4   Experimental Evaluation

Datasets. $COCO$ [20] is currently the most widely used object detection dataset and benchmark. The images cover complex everyday scenes containing common objects in their natural context. Objects are labeled using per-instance segmentation to aid in precise object localization [20]. We use annotations for 80 "thing" objects types from the 2017 train/val split, with a total of 886,284 labeled instances in 122,266 images. The scenes range from dining table close-ups to complex traffic scenes.

$LVIS$ [10] builds on the COCO 2017 images but distinguishes 1203 object categories with a total of 127,0141 labeled instances in 100,170 training images alone. The class occurrences follow a discrete power law distribution, and is used as a benchmark for long-tailed object detection.

$COCO$ $65/15$ reuses the images and annotations from COCO 2017, but holds out images with instances from 15 object types in the training set. We use the class selection as well as dataset-split from [30].

Evaluation Metrics. We evaluate our proposed hyperbolic classification head for 2D object detection on the challenging COCO 2017 *test-dev* and the long-tailed LVIS v1 benchmark. Additionally, we evaluate the visual-to-semantic mapping performance on the zero-shot detection task using the classes split proposed in [30]. Our evaluation metric is the mean average precision (mAP) which defines the area under the precision-recall curve for detections averaged over thresholds for IoU $\in [0.5 : 0.05 : 0.95]$ (COCOs standard metric). For closed-set object detection, we compare the mean over all classes, for long-tailed object detection on the LVIS v1 dataset, and we also provide the mean of frequent, common, and rare classes. For zero-shot evaluation, we report average precision as well

Table 1. COCO 2017 *val* results for methods using linear layers (top row) compared to hyperbolic (bottom row) classification heads.

Method	AP	AP_{50}	AP_{75}	AP_s	AP_m	AP_l
CenterNet (R-50-FPN) [43]	40.2	58.2	43.7	23.2	44.6	52.3
+ Hyperbolic classifier	41.1	59.3	45.2	24.2	45.0	53.8
DDETR (R-50-FPN) [44]	44.5	63.5	48.7	26.8	47.7	59.5
+ Hyperbolic classifier	45.0	64.3	48.8	27.9	47.9	59.7
Sparse R-CNN (R-50-FPN) [34]	45.0	64.1	49.0	27.8	47.5	59.7
+ Hyperbolic classifier	**46.2**	**65.9**	**50.7**	**29.2**	**49.2**	**60.7**

as recall for the 65 seen and the 15 unseen classes separately. We additionally report AP_{cat}, a modification of the average precision metric that defines a true positive detection if the IoU between the predicted and the groundtruth bounding box exceeds a threshold $\in [0.5 : 0.05 : 0.95]$ and is assigned the class label of any class with the same super-category in COCO 2017 stuff [4] label hierarchy as the groundtruth class.

Training Protocol. We use the PyTorch [29] framework for implementing all the architectures, and we train our models on a system with an Intel Xenon@2.20GHz processor and NVIDIA TITAN RTX GPUs. All the methods use the ResNet-50 backbone with weights pre-trained on the ImageNet dataset [8] for classification, and extract multi-scale feature maps using a FPN with randomly initialized parameters. The hyperparameter settings, loss configuration, and training strategy principally follow the baseline configurations for maximum comparability, i.e., [32] for Faster R-CNN KGE, [43] for CenterNet KGE, and [6] for DETR KGE configurations. Please refer to the supplementary material for a detailed overview of hyperparameter settings and schedules. We train all the networks using an Adam optimizer with weight decay [23] and gradient clipping. We use multi-scale training for all the models with a minimum training size of 480 pixel side length with random flipping and cropping for augmentation.

4.1   Benchmark Results

COCO 2017 Benchmark. To compare the behaviors of hyperbolic classification heads with their baseline configurations, we evaluate the methods on the challenging COCO 2017 dataset. All object detectors were trained on 122,000 training images and tested on 5,000 validation images following the standard protocol [34,43,44].

Baselines: We incorporate our hyperbolic classification heads into the two-stage, keypoint-based, and transformer-based object detector architectures a described in Sect. 3.3. Consequently, we compare these methods against the standard configurations using a linear classification head in the euclidean embedding space.

Table 2. COCO 2017 *val* results using single-scale testing. Each section compares the results given identical networks but a linear classification head (top row) with a Hyperbolic classification head (bottom row). The error metrics E_x were computed as proposed by Boyla *et al.* [2].

Method	mAP	mAP_{cat}	E_{cls}	E_{loc}	E_{bkg}	E_{miss}	E_{FP}	E_{FN}
CenterNet (R-50-FPN) [43]	40.2	38.8	3.1	**6.1**	3.7	5.4	21.7	12.6
+ Hyperbolic classifier	41.1	39.5	2.9	5.7	3.7	5.4	21.4	11.9
DDETR (R-50-FPN) [44]	44.5	40.7	2.3	7.5	4.2	4.4	19.6	12.2
+ Hyperbolic classifier	45.0	**47.1**	2.4	7.5	4.2	**4.0**	19.0	11.4
Sparse R-CNN (R-50-FPN) [34]	45.0	43.0	**2.1**	6.7	3.9	4.7	19.6	**11.2**
+ Hyperbolic classifier	**46.2**	45.6	2.4	6.8	**3.6**	5.0	**17.6**	11.7

Discussions: The results on the COCO 2017 *val* set in Table 1 indicate that hyperbolic classification heads consistently outperform their euclidean baseline configurations on the COCO 2017 *val* benchmark. The Sparse R-CNN configuration achieves a substantial increase in the mean average precision of +1.2%, without changes to the architecture and training strategy, only by modifying the algebra of the embedding space. The hyperbolic classification head's impact on various aspects of object detection are shown in Table 2 for the COCO 2017 *val* set. Surprisingly, the main benefits of the hyperbolic embeddings in Table 2 arise from a sharper contrast between the background and foreground detections, as the false positive error E_{FP} is consistently lower than the Euclidean baseline. The marginally increased classification error E_{cls} for DDETR and Sparse R-CNN in the hyperbolic variants is more than compensated by the lower number of false positives. Additionally, the mAP_{cat} is constantly higher for the hyperbolic methods, which we find the most striking result. This suggests that even though classification errors occur in both methods, the hyperbolic classification space appears to inherently learn a semantic structure such that classification errors are more often within the same category as for Euclidean methods. We argue that it therefore makes "better" detection errors, as the misclassifications are still within the same supercategory and therefore more related to the true class.

LVIS V1 Benchmark. The purpose of the LVIS v1 experiments is to study the behavior of hyperbolic classification heads with a large set of object types and imbalanced class occurrences. Table 3 shows the results on the LVIS v1 *val* set for baseline methods as well as their counterparts using a hyperbolic classification head.

Baselines: We compare our method against CenterNet2 using a federated loss [42], that computes a binary cross-entropy loss value over a subset of $|S| = 50$ classes. The subset S changes every iteration and is composed of all object types in the mini-batch's groundtruth and padded with randomly sampled negative classes. Additionally, we trained a Faster R-CNN model using a EQLv2 loss [35],

Table 3. LIVS *val* results for various models with linear classification head and hyperbolic classification head. All methods were trained by repeat factor resampling [10] by a factor of 0.001.

Model	Loss	AP	AP_{50}	AP_{75}	AP_r	AP_c	AP_f
CenterNet2 (R-50-FPN) [42]	FedLoss	**28.2**	39.2	**30.0**	**18.8**	**26.4**	34.4
+ Hyperbolic classifier	FedLoss	27.9	39.7	28.8	17.3	26.2	**34.9**
Faster R-CNN (R-50-FPN) [39]	EQLv2	23.6	39.3	24.5	14.2	22.3	29.1
+ Hyperbolic classifier	EQLv2	23.2	**40.1**	24.7	11.9	21.0	29.5

a mechanism to compensate class-imbalances in the dataset by equalizing the gradient ratio between positives and negatives for each class.

Discussions: We observe a consistent improvement for the detection accuracy with fine-grained object types in hyperbolic embedding space, as both hyperbolic methods outperform their euclidean counterparts on precision for frequent classes AP_f. However, the hyperbolic classifiers perform inferior on rare and common classes. This effect is largest for the Faster R-CNN model trained by an EQLv2 [35] loss, which was initially proposed for euclidean embedding spaces. We therefore suggest that methods optimized in the Euclidean space cannot be straightforwardly applied to the hyperbolic space. An improved class-balancing strategy needs to be designed for hyperbolic embeddings for long-tailed object detection, that needs to address both the class-imbalance by sampling and the impact of negatives have on the gradients.

Zero-Shot Evaluation. Next, we assess the zero-shot abilities of hyperbolic embeddings on the COCO 2017 dataset using the *65/15* classes split proposed by Rahman *et al.* [30]. Zero-shot object detection requires learning a mapping from visual to semantic feature space, such that the detector recognizes unseen object types only given their semantic representations. We investigate the behavior with semantic representations from word embeddings learned from the Wikipedia corpus by the *word2vec* method [25] in rely on the formulation for hyperbolic space by Leimeister *et al.* [18]. Recent advances in zero-shot object detection rely on synthesizing unseen classes during training [11], or learn a reprojection of the semantic embedding vectors [40]. However, we reserve these tuning strategies of the network architecture and training pipeline to future work and focus on the straight-forward mapping from vision features to semantic class prototypes and a reprojection of embedding vectors as baselines.

Baselines: We compare our method against object detectors using *word2vec* word embeddings as class prototypes and trained with a polarity loss [30] and a reconstruction loss [41]. The letter additionally learns a reprojection of semantic embedding vectors into the visual domain. We further provide results for a Sparse R-CNN method trained using *word2vec* word embeddings but using a

Table 4. Precision and recall on seen as well as unseen classes for COCO 2017 65/15 split. An IoU threshold of 0.5 is used for computing recall and average precision. *HM* refers to the harmonic mean of seen and unseen classes.

Model	Method	Embedding	Seen		Unseen		HM	
			mAP	Recall	mAP	Recall	mAP	Recall
RetinaNet	PL-vocab [30]	word2vec	34.1	36.4	12.4	37.2	18.2	36.8
Faster R-CNN	ZSI [41]	word2vec	35.8	62.6	10.5	50.0	16.2	55.6
Faster R-CNN	Hyperbolic	word2vec	36.2	52.4	13.1	40.5	19.3	45.7
Sparse R-CNN	Euclidean	word2vec	36.6	62.9	12.1	49.2	18.7	55.0
Sparse R-CNN	Hyperbolic	word2vec	**38.0**	**65.4**	**13.5**	**50.4**	**19.9**	**56.9**

classifier head in euclidean space. This method was trained with the same hyperparameters as its hyperbolic variant. We train our hyperbolic classifier using a focal loss [19].

Discussions: The zero-shot performance of the hyperbolic classification head is shown in Table 4. The hyperbolic configurations outperform their naive baselines on average precision for seen and unseen classes, even though the baseline methods rely on more sophisticated training losses. The recall of groundtruth boxes appears to be dependent on the choice of loss function, as the Faster R-CNN baseline using the reconstruction loss proposed in [41] achieves higher recall even though it yields the lowest precision on detecting unseen objects. The zero-shot performance using the hyperbolic Sparse R-CNN architecture shows superior results compared to all the baseline models and loss functions, even its euclidean counterpart trained with the exact same setting. We take this as an indication that the hyperbolic embedding space does not negatively affect the recall.

4.2   Qualitative Results

In Fig. 2, we show qualitative detection results from two classifiers trained on the COCO 2017 *train* set and classes. Detections on the left (a) were trained on object detection architectures using a learnable class prototypes in the euclidean space, while detections on the right (b) were generated by detectors using our proposed hyperbolic MLR classifier. Interestingly, the accuracies of the two detectors are comparable, even though euclidean class prototypes resulted in a false positive in Fig. 2(a). Another noticeable difference is the composition of the top-3 class scores that provide an insight in the structure of the embedding spaces. While most bounding boxes were classified correctly by both classifiers, the learned hyperbolic embeddings appear to have grouped categorically similar concepts as the detector predicts classes of *vehicle* types for the *car* object instance. For the *person* instance, there are no equivalent categorical classes, so there seems to have emerged a *living thing* neighborhood and a neighborhood of frequently co-occurring classes containing *bicycle* in the embedding space.

(a) Learned euclidean embeddings.

(b) Learned hyperbolic embeddings.

Fig. 2. Qualitative results for Sparse R-CNN model trained on full COCO 2017 classes with an (a) euclidean and (b) hyperbolic classification head.

(a) Learned euclidean embeddings.

(b) Learned hyperbolic embeddings.

Fig. 3. Qualitative results for CenterNet2 model trained on LVIS v1 classes with an (a) euclidean and (b) hyperbolic classification head. The children are wearing *ballet skirts*, a rare class in the LVIS v1 dataset with < 10 training samples.

(a) word2vec [25] euclidean embeddings.

(b) word2vec [18] hyperbolic embeddings.

Fig. 4. Qualitative results for a Faster R-CNN model trained on the seen classes of the COCO 2017 65–15 split with an (a) euclidean and (b) hyperbolic classification head on word2vec semantic embeddings. The image shows a seen *car* instance as well as an unseen *airplane* instance.

The example predictions for LVIS v1 classes are shown in Fig. 3. The hyperbolic method recognizes even partly visible objects and top-3 predictions are more semantically similar, such as *headband* and *bandanna* for the child in the center. This indicates that the embeddings capture more conceptual similarities than the euclidean classifier. However, "rare" classes are missing from the top-3 predictions, as a result the hyperbolic method fails to assign the correct class *ballet skirt* for the tutu worn by the child on the right.

Figure 4 presents the zeros-hot results for an unseen *airplane* instance. Here, the hyperbolic model also yields categorically similar predictions when given semantic word embeddings. Surprisingly, this is not as strong for the euclidean classifier (a), even though it maps the visual features to word embeddings. However, we note that the confidence by the hyperbolic method (i.e. distance in embedding space) is considerably lower (larger) for the unseen class and the *airplane* bounding box appears less accurate. This could be mitigated by using more sophisticated zero-shot pipelines such as the reconstruction loss [41] or synthetic training samples [11].

5   Conclusions

In this work, we proposed to use hyperbolic embedding spaces to learn class prototypes in object detection. We extended two-stage, keypoint-based, and transformer-based object detectors to incorporate hyperbolic classification heads. Evaluations on closed-set, long-tailed, as well as zero-shot settings showed that the hyperbolic methods outperformed their euclidean baselines on classes with sufficient training samples. The hyperbolic classification heads resulted in considerably fewer false positives, and produced "better" classification errors, misclassified labels were within the same supercategory as the true classes. We therefore conclude that hyperbolic geometry provides a promising embedding space for object detection and deserves future work to design optimized class-balancing and zero-shot training frameworks.

References

1. Besic, B., Valada, A.: Dynamic object removal and spatio-temporal RGB-D inpainting via geometry-aware adversarial learning. IEEE Trans. Intell. Veh. **7**(2), 170–185 (2022)
2. Bolya, D., Foley, S., Hays, J., Hoffman, J.: TIDE: a general toolbox for identifying object detection errors. In: Vedaldi, A., Bischof, H., Brox, T., Frahm, J.-M. (eds.) ECCV 2020. LNCS, vol. 12348, pp. 558–573. Springer, Cham (2020). https://doi.org/10.1007/978-3-030-58580-8_33
3. Bridson, M.R., Haefliger, A.: Metric Spaces of Non-positive Curvature, vol. 319. Springer, Heidelberg (2013). https://doi.org/10.1007/978-3-662-12494-9
4. Caesar, H., Uijlings, J., Ferrari, V.: Coco-stuff: thing and stuff classes in context. In: Proceedings of the IEEE Conference on Computer Vision and Pattern Recognition (2018)

5. Cai, Z., Vasconcelos, N.: Cascade R-CNN: delving into high quality object detection. In: Proceedings of the IEEE Conference on Computer Vision and Pattern Recognition, pp. 6154–6162 (2018)
6. Carion, N., Massa, F., Synnaeve, G., Usunier, N., Kirillov, A., Zagoruyko, S.: End-to-end object detection with transformers. In: Vedaldi, A., Bischof, H., Brox, T., Frahm, J.-M. (eds.) ECCV 2020. LNCS, vol. 12346, pp. 213–229. Springer, Cham (2020). https://doi.org/10.1007/978-3-030-58452-8_13
7. Dai, X., et al.: Dynamic head: unifying object detection heads with attentions. In: Proceedings of the IEEE Conference on Computer Vision and Pattern Recognition, pp. 7373–7382 (2021)
8. Deng, J., Dong, W., Socher, R., Li, L.J., Li, K., Fei-Fei, L.: Imagenet: a large-scale hierarchical image database. In: Proceedings of the IEEE Conference on Computer Vision and Pattern Recognition, pp. 248–255 (2009)
9. Gosala, N., Valada, A.: Bird's-eye-view panoptic segmentation using monocular frontal view images. arXiv preprint arXiv:2108.03227 (2021)
10. Gupta, A., Dollar, P., Girshick, R.: LVIS: a dataset for large vocabulary instance segmentation. In: Proceedings of the IEEE Conference on Computer Vision and Pattern Recognition, pp. 5356–5364 (2019)
11. Hayat, N., Hayat, M., Rahman, S., Khan, S., Zamir, S.W., Khan, F.S.: Synthesizing the unseen for zero-shot object detection. In: Proceedings of the Asian Conference on Computer Vision (2020)
12. He, K., Zhang, X., Ren, S., Sun, J.: Deep residual learning for image recognition. In: Proceedings of the IEEE Conference on Computer Vision and Pattern Recognition, pp. 770–778 (2016)
13. Hurtado, J.V., Mohan, R., Burgard, W., Valada, A.: MOPT: multi-object panoptic tracking. arXiv preprint arXiv:2004.08189 (2020)
14. Khrulkov, V., Mirvakhabova, L., Ustinova, E., Oseledets, I., Lempitsky, V.: Hyperbolic image embeddings. In: Proceedings of the IEEE Conference on Computer Vision and Pattern Recognition, pp. 6418–6428 (2020)
15. Lang, C., Braun, A., Valada, A.: Contrastive object detection using knowledge graph embeddings. arXiv preprint arXiv:2112.11366 (2021)
16. Law, H., Deng, J.: Cornernet: detecting objects as paired keypoints. In: European Conference on Computer Vision, pp. 734–750 (2018)
17. Lee, Y., Park, J.: Centermask: real-time anchor-free instance segmentation. In: Proceedings of the IEEE Conference on Computer Vision and Pattern Recognition, pp. 13906–13915 (2020)
18. Leimeister, M., Wilson, B.J.: Skip-gram word embeddings in hyperbolic space. arXiv preprint arXiv:1809.01498 (2018)
19. Lin, T.Y., Goyal, P., Girshick, R., He, K., Dollár, P.: Focal loss for dense object detection. Proceedings of the IEEE Conference on Computer Vision and Pattern Recognition, pp. 2980–2988 (2017)
20. Lin, T.-Y., et al.: Microsoft COCO: common objects in context. In: Fleet, D., Pajdla, T., Schiele, B., Tuytelaars, T. (eds.) ECCV 2014. LNCS, vol. 8693, pp. 740–755. Springer, Cham (2014). https://doi.org/10.1007/978-3-319-10602-1_48
21. Liu, S., Chen, J., Pan, L., Ngo, C.W., Chua, T.S., Jiang, Y.G.: Hyperbolic visual embedding learning for zero-shot recognition. In: Proceedings of the IEEE Conference on Computer Vision and Pattern Recognition, pp. 9273–9281 (2020)
22. Liu, W., et al.: SSD: single shot MultiBox detector. In: Leibe, B., Matas, J., Sebe, N., Welling, M. (eds.) ECCV 2016. LNCS, vol. 9905, pp. 21–37. Springer, Cham (2016). https://doi.org/10.1007/978-3-319-46448-0_2

23. Loshchilov, I., Hutter, F.: Decoupled weight decay regularization. arXiv preprint arXiv:1711.05101 (2017)
24. Meng, Y., et al.: Spherical text embedding. In: Advances in Neural Information Processing Systems, vol. 32 (2019)
25. Mikolov, T., Chen, K., Corrado, G., Dean, J.: Efficient estimation of word representations in vector space. arXiv preprint arXiv:1301.3781 (2013)
26. Mohan, R., Valada, A.: Amodal panoptic segmentation. arXiv preprint arXiv:2202.11542 (2022)
27. Nickel, M., Kiela, D.: Poincaré embeddings for learning hierarchical representations. In: Advances in Neural Information Processing Systems, vol. 30 (2017)
28. Nickel, M., Kiela, D.: Learning continuous hierarchies in the lorentz model of hyperbolic geometry. In: International Conference on Machine Learning, pp. 3779–3788 (2018)
29. Paszke, A., et al.: PyTorch: an imperative style, high-performance deep learning library. In: Proceedings of the Conference on Neural Information Processing Systems, pp. 8024–8035 (2019)
30. Rahman, S., Khan, S., Barnes, N.: Improved visual-semantic alignment for zero-shot object detection. In: Proceedings of the AAAI Conference on Artificial Intelligence, vol. 34, pp. 11932–11939 (2020)
31. Redmon, J., Farhadi, A.: Yolov3: an incremental improvement. arXiv preprint arXiv:1804.02767 (2018)
32. Ren, S., He, K., Girshick, R., Sun, J.: Faster R-CNN: towards real-time object detection with region proposal networks. In: Proceedings of the Conference on Neural Information Processing Systems, pp. 91–99 (2015)
33. Sirohi, K., Mohan, R., Büscher, D., Burgard, W., Valada, A.: Efficientlps: efficient lidar panoptic segmentation. IEEE Trans. Robot. (2021)
34. Sun, P., et al.: Sparse R-CNN: end-to-end object detection with learnable proposals. In: Proceedings of the IEEE Conference on Computer Vision and Pattern Recognition, pp. 14454–14463 (2021)
35. Tan, J., Lu, X., Zhang, G., Yin, C., Li, Q.: Equalization loss v2: a new gradient balance approach for long-tailed object detection. In: Proceedings of the IEEE Conference on Computer Vision and Pattern Recognition, pp. 1685–1694 (2021)
36. Tian, Z., Shen, C., Chen, H., He, T.: FCOS: fully convolutional one-stage object detection. In: Proceedings of the IEEE Conference on Computer Vision and Pattern Recognition, pp. 9627–9636 (2019)
37. Valverde, F.R., Hurtado, J.V., Valada, A.: There is more than meets the eye: self-supervised multi-object detection and tracking with sound by distilling multimodal knowledge. In: Proceedings of the IEEE Conference on Computer Vision and Pattern Recognition, pp. 11612–11621 (2021)
38. Wilson, B., Leimeister, M.: Gradient descent in hyperbolic space. arXiv preprint arXiv:1805.08207 (2018)
39. Wu, Y., Kirillov, A., Massa, F., Lo, W.Y., Girshick, R.: Detectron2 (2019). https://github.com/facebookresearch/detectron2
40. Yan, C., Chang, X., Luo, M., Liu, H., Zhang, X., Zheng, Q.: Semantics-guided contrastive network for zero-shot object detection. IEEE Trans. Pattern Anal. Mach. Intell. (2022)
41. Zheng, Y., Wu, J., Qin, Y., Zhang, F., Cui, L.: Zero-shot instance segmentation. In: Proceedings of the IEEE Conference on Computer Vision and Pattern Recognition, pp. 2593–2602 (2021)
42. Zhou, X., Koltun, V., Krähenbühl, P.: Probabilistic two-stage detection. arXiv preprint arXiv:2103.07461 (2021)

43. Zhou, X., Wang, D., Krähenbühl, P.: Objects as points. arXiv preprint arXiv:1904.07850 (2019)
44. Zhu, X., Su, W., Lu, L., Li, B., Wang, X., Dai, J.: Deformable DETR: Deformable Transformers for End-to-End Object Detection. arXiv preprint arXiv:2010.04159 (2020)

Photogrammetry and Remote Sensing

Probabilistic Biomass Estimation with Conditional Generative Adversarial Networks

Johannes Leonhardt[1,2]([✉]) [iD], Lukas Drees[1] [iD], Peter Jung[3] [iD],
and Ribana Roscher[1,2] [iD]

[1] Remote Sensing Group, University of Bonn, Bonn, Germany
{jleonhardt,ldrees,ribana.roscher}@uni-bonn.de
[2] AI4EO Future Lab, Technical University of Munich and German Aerospace Center,
Munich, Germany
[3] Communications and Information Theory Chair, Technical University Berlin,
Berlin, Germany
peter.jung@tu-berlin.de

Abstract. Biomass is an important variable for our understanding of
the terrestrial carbon cycle, facilitating the need for satellite-based global
and continuous monitoring. However, current machine learning methods used to map biomass can often not model the complex relationship
between biomass and satellite observations or cannot account for the estimation's uncertainty. In this work, we exploit the stochastic properties
of Conditional Generative Adversarial Networks for quantifying aleatoric
uncertainty. Furthermore, we use generator Snapshot Ensembles in the
context of epistemic uncertainty and show that unlabeled data can easily
be incorporated into the training process. The methodology is tested on
a newly presented dataset for satellite-based estimation of biomass from
multispectral and radar imagery, using lidar-derived maps as reference
data. The experiments show that the final network ensemble captures
the dataset's probabilistic characteristics, delivering accurate estimates
and well-calibrated uncertainties.

1 Introduction

An ever-growing number of satellite missions produce vast amounts of remote
sensing data, providing us with unprecedented opportunities to continuously
monitor processes on the Earth's surface. Extracting quantitative geoscientific

This work was partly funded by the Deutsche Forschungsgemeinschaft (DFG, German Research Foundation) - SFB 1502/1-2022 - Projektnummer: 450058266, by the
Deutsche Forschungsgemeinschaft (DFG, German Research Foundation) under Germany's Excellence Strategy - EXC 2070 - 390732324 and by the German Federal Ministry of Education and Research (BMBF) in the framework of the international future
AI lab "AI4EO - Artificial Intelligence for Earth Observation: Reasoning, Uncertainties,
Ethics and Beyond" (grant number: 01DD20001).

B. Andres et al. (Eds.): DAGM GCPR 2022, LNCS 13485, pp. 479–494, 2022.
https://doi.org/10.1007/978-3-031-16788-1_29

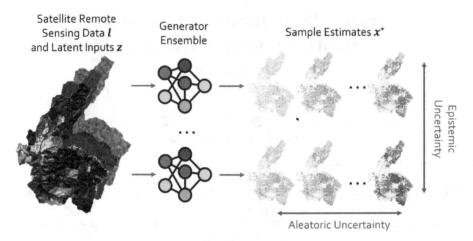

Fig. 1. Graphical summary of our methodology during inference. The observations l are fed into multiple generator neural networks along with the latent codes z. The sample estimates x^* from each generator represent individual estimates of the predictive posterior distribution and hence, aleatoric uncertainty. The variability across the generator ensemble, on the other hand is indicative of epistemic uncertainty.

information from these data requires functional models between the observations l and geographical variables of interest x. To this end, deep learning methods based on neural networks have recently established themselves due to their demonstrated capabilities to learn complex relationships. For applications like satellite-based biomass estimation, however, the inability of such methods to provide uncertainties along with their estimates represents a crucial flaw. The reason is that this problem, like many others in the field of Earth Observation, is ill-posed in the sense that there exist multiple biomass maps which are consistent with the observations. Particularly, this is due to latent variables, like tree height or tree species, which are only weakly correlated to satellite measurements but have substantial influence on biomass. This causes ambiguity, and hence, uncertainty in the estimation. While this property of our estimation task is ignored by deterministic models, probabilistic models circumvent this problem by approximating the conditional predictive posterior $P(x|l)$ instead of point estimates. By focusing on the task of accurately approximating the predictive posterior distribution, we hope to improve the informative value of the resulting biomass products for policymaking, modeling of the carbon cycle, or other downstream applications. A graphical summary of the presented methods is provided in Fig. 1.

In summary, we make the following contributions:

1. We motivate and describe the usage of *Conditional Generative Adversarial Networks* (CGANs) for non-parametric uncertainty quantification in biomass estimation. We point out that the variability across generated sample esti-

mates x^* is indicative of the dataset's intrinsic *aleatoric* uncertainty, as they follow the generator's approximation of the predictive posterior distribution.

2. We use ensembles of generator networks for capturing the *epistemic* uncertainty of CGANs, which is largely associated with instabilities of the adversarial training process. In this context, Snapshot Ensembles consisting of generators from the same network initialization turn out to be a valid, computationally inexpensive alternative to regular ensembles.

3. We show that we can use CWGANs to easily include unlabeled data in the training process. We exploit this property to fine-tune our network to the testing data.

4. We apply an implementation of our model to a novel remote sensing dataset for satellite-based biomass estimation in Northwestern USA, evaluate it regarding the quality of the estimated predictive posterior, and show that it does not negatively affect estimation accuracy.

2 Related Work

Uncertainty Quantification in Deep Learning. Since the need for reliable and accurate uncertainty measures is not limited to problems in remote sensing, the field of probabilistic deep learning has evolved rapidly in recent years. An essential distinction in this context is between aleatoric and epistemic uncertainty: Aleatoric uncertainty is caused by the nature of the data or the underlying problem and therefore cannot be explained away, even if infinitely many training samples were available. It is therefore also an intrinsic property of ill-posed problems, where the target variable cannot be recovered from the given observations in a deterministic sense [47]. On the contrary, epistemic uncertainty is caused by limitations regarding the dataset size, the neural network's architecture, or the optimization strategy. Therefore, this type of uncertainty can at least partly be reduced by, e.g. enlarging the dataset, specifying a more fitting architecture, or hyperparameter tuning [13,18].

For quantifying aleatoric uncertainty, multi-head neural networks, which output a parameterization of the predictive posterior – such as the mean and variance of a Gaussian distribution – have emerged as the favored technique [37]. The downside to such models is their limitation to the assumed parameterization and the resulting inability to represent the more varied predictive posteriors, which are present in real-world applications. A possible alternative is to have the neural network output distribution-free predictive intervals [39]. While this circumvents the problem of specifying a parameterization of the predictive posterior, such networks still only output individual statistics thereof so that the estimation of other moments is not possible.

One of the most popular techniques for the quantification of epistemic uncertainty, on the other hand, is ensembling where the estimation is aggregated from multiple independent neural networks [23]. Alternatives include explicitly Bayesian methods like Monte-Carlo Dropout, where dropout is applied during training and during inference [12], and Hamiltonian Monte Carlo, where parameter hypotheses are sampled by means of Markov Chain Monte Carlo and Hamiltonian dynamics [36].

Recently, multiple studies have also used CGANs and other conditional deep generative models for uncertainty quantification. Those models' suitability for the task is motivated by their demonstrated ability to approximate highly complex (conditional) probability distributions, such as that of natural images [14,34]. In this context, the variability in the samples generated during inference is viewed as indicative of the estimation uncertainty, as they follow the approximate predictive posterior distribution. For instance, CGANs have been applied to regression and classification tasks and were observed to produce reliable uncertainties while being more stable with respect to the backbone architecture than competing methods [27]. The technique has been especially popular in the time series domain [21], where it has been used for tasks like weather fore- and nowcasting [6,40] or pedestrian [22] and aircraft [38] trajectory prediction. In traditional regression settings, CGANs have been employed, e.g. for uncertainty quantification in medical imaging [1] and atmospheric remote sensing [28].

Biomass Estimation with Remote Sensing. As one of the World Meteorological Organization (WMO)'s *Essential Climate Variables*, large-scale and continuous estimation of biomass with satellite remote sensing is important to climate scientists and policymakers [16]. Particularly, we are interested in *Aboveground Biomass* (AGB), which by definition of the United Nations Program on Reducing Emissions from Deforestation and Forest Degradation (UN-REDD), AGB denotes all "living vegetation above the soil, including stem, stump, branches, bark, seeds, and foliage" [5]. Note that hereinafter, we will use the terms biomass and AGB interchangeably. The estimation of AGB from satellite data is less cost- and labor-intensive than obtaining ground data, but poses significant challenges due to the ill-posed nature of the problem [41].

Methodologically, classical regression techniques are still commonplace in the field of biomass estimation. These range from simple linear regression [43] to geostatistical approaches [31]. Currently, random forest regression ranks among the most popular methodologies, as they turn out to be efficient, intuitive, and not significantly more inaccurate than competing methods [29,35].

Recently, however, deep learning techniques have been used with increased frequency for biomass estimation and related tasks. For instance, neural networks were shown to better estimate biomass from Landsat data than univariate regression approaches with common vegetation indices as inputs [11]. The method was subsequently investigated in light of its spatial transferability, revealing its poor generalization capabilities [10]. Significant advances in the field were the fusion of optical imagery with Synthetic Aperture Radar (SAR) data in a deep learning-based estimation approach [2] and the use of Convolutional Neural Networks (CNNs), which can better extract information from spatial patterns in the data [8]. By taking into account textural properties of the input data, CNNs have been demonstrated to especially improve estimation of vegetation properties in cases where the pixel-wise signal saturates in the presence of tall canopies [25]. Methods from probabilistic deep learning have only recently been explored for global estimation of canopy height, which is strongly correlated to biomass, using optical and spaceborne lidar data in an ensemble of multi-head networks [24, 25]. In another recent work, CGANs are used to estimate spatially consistent biomass maps based on L-band SAR imagery [7]. Despite apparent similarities, this work significantly differs from ours, as the CGANs are only used deterministically and their stochastic possibilities are thus not fully exploited.

3   Methodology

We generally consider a supervised regression setup with a dataset of pairs of observations l and corresponding target variables x. Our approach consists of using CGANs for aleatoric uncertainty and generator Snapshot Ensembles for epistemic uncertainty. In this chapter, we will describe these two methods in detail and point out their advantages with respect to our task. Note that, for clarity, we will not explicitly distinguish between random variables and their realizations in our notation.

3.1   CGANs and Aleatoric Uncertainty

For quantifying aleatoric uncertainty, we first assume that the given samples are realizations of the conditional distribution $P(x|l)$, which is called the predictive posterior. We furthermore assume that aleatoric uncertainty is induced by the latent variable z, for which a simple prior like a standard normal distribution $P(z) = \mathbb{N}_{0,1}$ is assumed. We may view this variable as an encoding of all factors which influence x, but are inaccessible through l. In the context of biomass estimation for example, z encodes uncertainty about pertinent variables like tree height or density, which are only to some degree correlated to satellite measurements. Marginalization over these factors z results in the model

$$P(x|l) = \int P(x|l, z)dP(z). \tag{1}$$

Practically, this theoretical model is approximated by a CGAN: On the one hand, the generator $\mathcal{G}_\gamma(l, z)$, parameterized as a neural network by γ, seeks to produce sample estimates of the target variable x, which match the data-implied predictive posterior. On the other hand, a discriminator neural network $\mathcal{D}_\delta(l, x)$, parameterized by δ, evaluates the generated samples by comparing them to the real samples in the training dataset and providing a suitable metric by which the generator can be optimized.

To find optimal parameter values γ^* and δ^* for the generator and the discriminator, respectively, adversarial training is employed. In the most common variants of adversarial training, the overall objective can be formalized as a minimax game, where an objective function $L(\gamma, \delta)$ is maximized by the discriminator and minimized by the generator [14, 34]:

$$\gamma^*, \delta^* = \arg\min_\gamma \arg\max_\delta L(\gamma, \delta). \tag{2}$$

Due to major practical issues with the original GAN and CGAN implementations like vanishing gradients and mode collapse [3], recent research has mostly revolved around improving the stability of adversarial training.

In particular, the Wasserstein variant of CGAN (CWGAN) aims to solve these issues by using the objective function

$$L_{\text{CWGAN}}(\gamma, \delta) = \mathbb{E}_{(l,x)}(\mathcal{D}_\delta(l, x)) - \mathbb{E}_{(l,z)}(\mathcal{D}_\delta(l, \mathcal{G}_\gamma(l, z))) \tag{3}$$

with the additional restriction $\mathcal{D}_\delta \in \mathcal{L}_1$, where $\mathcal{L}_1$ describes the set of Lipschitz-1 continuous functions. By virtue of the Kantorowich-Rubinstein duality, the use of this particular objective leads to the minimization of the Wasserstein-1 distance between the data-implied and the generated distribution. The favorable properties of this metric regarding its gradients with respect to γ and δ have been demonstrated to mitigate the usual issues of adversarial training when compared to the Jensen-Shannon divergence used in the original GAN [4].

In implementation, the networks are alternately optimized using stochastic gradient descent and ascent, respectively. For computing the stochastic gradients of the objective with respect to γ and δ, the expectations in Eq. (3) are replaced with their empirical approximation over a minibatch. At inference, we may then theoretically generate arbitrarily many sample estimates $x^* = \mathcal{G}_{\gamma^*}(l, z)$ to approximate the predictive posterior distribution by repeatedly running generator forward passes with different z-inputs, sampled from the latent prior. CGANs therefore allow for the non-parametric and distribution-free modeling of aleatoric uncertainty, setting them apart from multi-head neural networks [37], where one is limited to the Gaussian parameterization. At the same time, they still approximate the full predictive posterior instead of single output statistics, as is the case for prediction intervals [39]. Instead, the sample estimates may be used to compute an approximation of a wide range of statistics of the predictive posterior. This also includes correlations in multi-output setups, which are entirely disregarded by the other methods. The accuracy of these approximations, however, may be limited by the number of the generated samples, which is subject to computation time and memory constraints.

Another advantageous aspect about using CGANs for probabilistic regression is the possibility to use unlabeled data at training time to train the generator network. This way, the model can be tuned not only with respect to the training data, but also the testing data without needing access to the corresponding labels. We expect that a model trained in this manner will be less likely to overfit, leading to greater generalization capabilities.

The root cause, why this procedure is feasible, lies within the CWGAN optimization objective, i.e., the minimization of the Wasserstein-1 distance between the generated and the real distribution as provided by the discriminator. We note, that the derivatives of the objective from Eq. (3) with respect to the generator's parameters are independent of any reference data x: $\nabla_\gamma L_{\text{CWGAN}} = -\mathbb{E}_{(l,z)}(\nabla_\gamma \mathcal{D}_\delta(l, \mathcal{G}_\gamma(l, z)))$ [4, Theorem 3]. This is based on the fact, that the minimization itself takes place with respect to the joint, rather than the conditional space of l and x [1]. Practically, we can therefore produce sample estimates from unlabeled data and still use the discriminator – which must still be trained on the labeled training dataset – in order to evaluate them to adjust γ accordingly. We point out that this is, in fact not just a special property of CWGAN, but is true for most variants of conditional adversarial training.

3.2   Generator Ensembles and Epistemic Uncertainty

The above described model accounts for aleatoric uncertainty in regression tasks by being able to sample from its approximation of the predictive posterior distribution, but does not model the epistemic uncertainty that arises from misspecifications of the network architecture or the optimization strategy. This is overlooked by previous works who appear to assume that CGANs capture both components of uncertainty. More specifically, the likely cause of epistemic uncertainty of our generative model is the generator's incapacity to replicate the target distribution or instabilities in the adversarial training procedure, both of which cause uncertainty in the determination of γ^*. Thus, we must not only marginalize over z, which is responsible for aleatoric uncertainty, but also over different hypotheses for γ^*. In this context, the set of optimal parameters is interpreted as a random variable, as well. For simplicity, we will simply call its distribution $P(\gamma^*)$, omitting the fact that this is actually also a conditional distribution based on the above-described factors. This extends the model in Eq. (1) to

$$P(x|l) = \iint P(x|l, z, \gamma^*)dP(z)dP(\gamma^*). \tag{4}$$

The resulting model effectively averages over possible optimal parameters, which results in so-called Bayesian Model Averages, of which ensembles represent one possible implementation [23, 46]. In our CWGAN realization of the theoretical model, each of the generators in the ensemble thus represents one individual approximation of the predictive posterior distribution. Their combination can hence be seen as a mixture model with equal weight given to each individual generator. Statistics of the predictive posterior can be approximated by again aggregating multiple sample estimates x^*, which in the combined model stem from multiple generators instead of just one.

For regular neural network ensembles, each network is initialized and trained independently from scratch. However, the training process of CGANs, and especially that of CWGANs, is time-expensive, making such a procedure impractical. We therefore turn to Snapshot Ensembles of generators, which allows for training an ensemble of networks based on a single initialization [17]. After an initial phase of T iterations of regular training with a constant learning rate λ_{max}, a cyclic learning rate schedule, particularly Cosine Annealing with Warm Restarts [30] is employed. For each cycle of T_{cyc} training iterations in this schedule, the learning rate λ_t at iteration t within the cycle is computed as

$$\lambda_t = \frac{\lambda_{max}}{2}\left(1 + \cos\left(\frac{t\pi}{T_{cyc}}\right)\right). \tag{5}$$

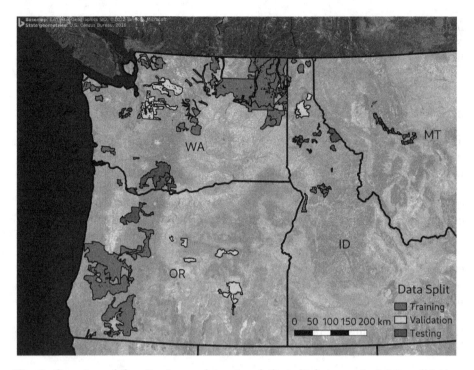

Fig. 2. Overview of the sites in our dataset and the split between training, validation and testing. For each of the sites, multispectral and SAR imagery, as well as the reference biomass map from ALS are given. The image was created using data from Bing Maps, the US Census Bureau, and the ALS reference dataset [9].

At the end of each cycle, the network is saved as one element of the ensemble and the learning rate is reset to λ_{max}. We believe that such an approach is especially suitable for the quantification of epistemic uncertainty of CGANs, because adversarial training is known to be unstable and oscillate around the optimum instead of converging to an equilibrium [33,45].

4   Application to Biomass Estimation

The next section presents the application of our methodology to the task of biomass mapping. First, we present a new dataset for satellite-based AGB estimation and afterwards apply a CWGAN implementation of our model and compare it to deterministic and multi-head neural networks in terms of the quality of the uncertainties and estimation accuracy. The code for training the models and a sample of the processed dataset are available at github.com/johannes-leonhardt/probabilistic-biomass-estimation-with-cgans-public.

4.1   Dataset

Our dataset is based on biomass maps from the US Carbon Monitoring System, which are based on airborne laserscanning (ALS) campaigns for 176 sites in Northwestern USA between 2002 and 2016, accessed through ORNL DAAC [9]. Those records are associated with multispectral imagery from the Landsat-8 satellite with its seven surface reflectance bands on the one hand and L-band SAR imagery from ALOS PALSAR-2 with HH- and HV-polarizations and the incident angle on the other. Both satellite products were subject to several pre-processing steps like athmospheric and slope corrections and were accessed through Google Earth Engine. It has been shown, that a combination of these two sensors leads to improved estimators of vegetation characteristics, because the optical signal is sensitive towards photosynthetic parts of vegetation, while SAR backscatter values correlate with physical forest properties like tree stand height. Regarding the latter, low-frequency radars are preferred, as they are to penetrate the canopy more deeply [29]. Another advantage of data from SAR and optical sensors is their global availability over long timespans. ALS records, while much more laborious to obtain than satellite data, provide far better correlation with field measurements of AGB and their use as references in this particular setup is hence justified [48].

To ensure spatial consistency between the three data sources, the multispectral and SAR images are resampled to the grid of the ALS biomass records, which have a resolution of 30 m. For temporal consistency, we choose Landsat-8 and ALOS PALSAR-2 composites for each of the sites for the year the ALS data was recorded. While there exist ready-to-use composites for ALOS PALSAR-2 [44], Landsat-8 composites were created manually by taking the 25th percentile of all images from the leaf-on season (March to September) of that respective year with a cloud cover of less than 5%. For ALS biomass records from 2013 and 2014, we allow association of the SAR composites from 2015, as the composites are only available from that point onward. All records taken before 2013, however, were discarded from the dataset. The remaining 96 sites are manually divided into geographically separated training, validation and testing datasets, as depicted in Fig. 2.

4.2   Implementation Details

As the backbone architecture for the CWGAN generator, we use a slightly modified variant of U-Net [42]. Besides the standard convolutions, we use strided convolutions in the contracting path and strided transposed convolutions in the expansive path. All hidden layers are activated with leaky ReLU, while the final output layer uses ReLU to enforce positive biomass estimates. For the Wasserstein discriminator, we use a CNN backbone with layers consisting of convolutions, strided convolutions and leaky ReLU activations. Lastly, a single, unactivated linear output layer is applied. The inputs for both networks are concatenations of the respective input tensors along the channel dimension, i.e. l and the three-dimensional z-inputs for the generator and l with either x or x^* for the discriminator.

Table 1. List of hyperparameters of the best performing models.

Method	T_{pt}	T	T_{cyc}	λ_{max}	Normalization
Deterministic	N/A	2000	N/A	5×10^{-5}	BN
Multi-head	N/A	5000	1000	5×10^{-5}	BN
CWGAN	2000	8000	1000	1×10^{-5}	None

As is usual for CWGAN training, we perform five discriminator updates for each generator update. For enforcing the Lipschitz-1 constraint in the discriminator, weight clipping to the range $[-0.01; 0.01]$ is used [4]. We additionally find that it is useful to pre-train the generator deterministically on MSE to find an initialization before the subsequent adversarial training. Afterwards, snapshot ensembles of 10 networks are then trained according to the above described procedure. For examining the advantages of using unlabeled data during training, as described above, we train another CWGAN in the same manner but sample the generator minibatches from the testing dataset, rather than the training dataset during the snapshot ensembling phase. We would like to stress again that access to the labels is not required when training the generator, and this approach is therefore implementable in practice to specifically fine-tune the generator to the dataset it shall later be applied to.

For comparison, a snapshot ensemble of multi-head neural networks is trained on an adapted variant of the MSE loss [20]. We also report results of a network that has been trained deterministically to minimize MSE as a standard regression baseline. For both the multi-head and the deterministic baselines, we use the same backbone U-Net architecture as for the CWGAN generator.

In all cases, training is performed on minibatches of 128 patches of 64×64 pixels, which are sampled from random positions in the training maps at each training iteration. Since U-Net is fully convolutional, however, the network can be applied to inputs of arbitrary size at inference. The validation dataset is used to optimize the hyperparameters individually for each method. Particularly, we conduct a search over the maximum learning rate $\lambda_{max} \in [1 \times 10^{-4}, 5 \times 10^{-5}, 1 \times 10^{-5}]$, find a suitable number of pre-training (only in the case of CWGAN), regular training and cycle iterations, T_{pt}, T and T_{cyc}, and decide whether to apply Batch Normalization (BN), Instance Normalization (IN), or neither of those in the U-Net backbone. The hyperparameters of the best performing model for each methodology are listed in Table 1.

4.3   Experimental Results

We finally evaluate the trained networks on the testing dataset. The input and reference data, as well as results of the multi-head approach and CWGAN sample estimates for one particular test site are depicted in Fig. 3.

Both methods indicate uncertainties of up to about $100t/ha$ as measured by the standard deviations in the high biomass regime of about $> 350t/ha$. For

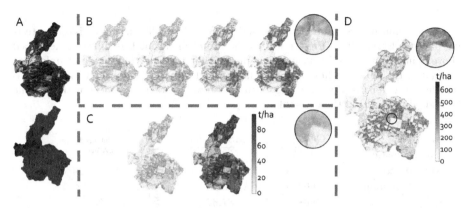

Fig. 3. Visualization of illustrative results for the test site "Big Sand Creek" in Northern Idaho. **A**: The input data, Landsat-8 in an RGB-Visualization and ALOS PALSAR-2 HH-backscatter, **B**: four sample estimates from a CWGAN, **C**: predicted Gaussian mean and standard deviation from a multi-head neural network, and **D**: the corresponding ALS-derived reference biomass map [9].

larger values, we also observe that the estimation of the predictive posterior does not significantly change for either model. We interpret this as an indication of signal saturation as there are no detectable correlations between the satellite observations and biomass. This threshold is in line with that reported in other studies on L-band SAR for biomass estimation [19, 32, 41].

For quantitative evaluation of the estimated predictive posterior distributions, we use the Quantile Calibration Error

$$\text{QCE} = \frac{1}{M} \sum_{m=1}^{M} |F(q_m) - q_m| . \tag{6}$$

This metric is derived from calibration plots [20], which describe the frequencies $F(q)$ of reference values lying within quantile q of the predicted distribution. In this context, M refers to the number of regularly spaced quantile values q_m, for which the frequency is evaluated. To determine the quantiles, the estimated cumulative distributions are evaluated at the reference values. In the case of a well-calibrated predictive posterior, the reference value should be equally likely to fall into each quantile of the predicted distribution, such that the calibration line is close to the diagonal $F(q) = q$. Intuitively, QCE describes the approximate area between this ideal diagonal and the actual calibration line. This way of quantifying calibration is preferred over other common metrics like the Expected Calibration Error [15], which only take into account a single uncertainty statistic. In contrast, QCE allows for evaluating the full approximated predictive distribution including its overall shape, making it sensitive towards possible misspecifications of the uncertainty's parametric model.

Table 2. Quantitative results for QCE and RMSE of the different methods on the testing dataset. Ensembling (Ens.) refers to the use of Snapshot Ensembles as described above. Fine-tuning (F.-T.) denotes our method for training time usage of unlabeled test data . Exemplary calibration plots used to calculate QCE are shown in the adjacent figure. For non-ensembles, the given values are averages over the metrics of the individual networks in the ensemble.

Method	QCE $[-]$	RMSE $[t/ha]$
Deterministic	N/A	86.15
Multi-Head	0.0853	85.12
+ Ensembling	0.0779	83.23
CWGAN	0.0851	87.67
+ Ensembling	0.0657	85.38
+ Fine-tuning	0.0889	89.92
+ Ens. + F.-T.	**0.0610**	86.19

Additionally, the Root Mean Squared Error

$$\text{RMSE} = \sqrt{\frac{1}{N} \sum_{n=1}^{N} \|x_n - \widehat{x}_n\|^2} \tag{7}$$

measures the accuracy across N point estimates $\widehat{x}_n$, as usual in a deterministic regression task. While the point estimate is directly provided in the multi-head setting as the distribution mean, it is computed as the average over the generator's sample estimates x^* in the case of CWGAN. Note that by using probabilistic methods we do not primarily seek to improve RMSE, but only use it to verify that the usage of a probabilistic framework does not negatively affect estimation accuracies.

Results are reported in Table 2. For CWGANs, the values are computed based on 50 sample estimates x^* from each generator. We view this number as sufficient as the metrics differ only insignificantly across multiple evaluation runs. As our main result, we observe that ensembles of CWGANs produce slightly better calibrated uncertainties than those of multi-head networks. The Snapshot Ensembling methodology is able to improve the calibration in both methods. However, while this improvement is marginal in multi-head networks, it is more significant in CWGANs and individual CWGAN generators do indeed not provide better estimates of the predictive posterior than individual multi-head networks. This insight is consistent with our expectation that Snapshot Ensembles are especially helpful in the context of CGAN-based methodologies, because fluctuations within the adversarial training process are successfully averaged out. For the multi-head approach on the other hand, snapshot ensembling cannot overcome the misspecification of the predictive posterior's parameterization.

For CWGANs, calibration is slightly improved when using our fine-tuning methodology, supporting our claim that such procedures may be helpful for training models which are tailored for application to specific data, e.g., from a particular geographical region. This approach does, however, come with the additional computational cost of retraining the network every time it is applied to a new dataset and more research may be needed to determine if the method is able to consistently improve CWGAN-based estimation.

Furthermore, it was demonstrated that both probabilistic approaches do not suffer from a significant loss in accuracy when compared to deterministic methods. In fact, our results show that snapshot ensembling consistently reduces RMSE by averaging over individual networks' epistemic uncertainties. On a final note, we observe that CWGANs deliver more consistent biomass maps than point estimators by being sensitive towards correlations in the output. This can be observed from the small scale details of the maps in Fig. 3: Whereas the point estimates of multi-head networks are rather smooth, the texture of the reference maps is at least partly replicated in the CWGAN sample estimates.

5   Conclusion and Outlook

This paper presented a new approach to uncertainty quantification in satellite-based biomass estimation. In particular, we used CGANs for non-parametric approximation of aleatoric uncertainty and Snapshot Ensembles for quantifying epistemic uncertainty. The methods were discussed theoretically, implemented and evaluated on a novel dataset consisting of optical and SAR imagery and ALS-derived references. The experiments demonstrated that our method is competitive with the commonly used parametric multi-head approach without loss in accuracy.

In light of these promising results, we envision several future research directions. From a methodological standpoint, we hope to encourage future works at the intersection of deep generative models and uncertainty quantification. Beyond biomass estimation, we consider investigations of CGANs' capabilities for uncertainty quantification in other remote sensing regression problems with similar restrictions, or even tasks from different domains like classification and segmentation to be interesting topics of future studies. Moreover, we believe that our approach to training time usage of unlabeled data is worthy of more detailed and fundamental investigation as further analyses may pave the way for general applications in the context of semi-supervised learning or domain adaptation.

Our dataset offers a starting point for the inclusion of data from more satellite missions and globally distributed biomass reference records. Such a dataset in combination with multi-sensor, probabilistic estimation methods like ours would enable the creation of reliable global and multitemporal biomass monitoring products. To improve the overall accuracy of such products, we also look forward to new spaceborne sensor technologies, such as the P-band SAR onboard the BIOMASS mission [26], which is set to launch in 2023.

References

1. Adler, J., Öktem, O.: Deep Bayesian Inversion (2018). arXiv e-Print arXiv:1811.05910
2. Amini, J., Sumantyo, J.T.S.: Employing a method on SAR and optical images for forest biomass estimation. IEEE Trans. Geosci. Remote Sens. **47**(12), 4020–4026 (2009)
3. Arjovsky, M., Bottou, L.: Towards principled methods for training generative adversarial networks. In: International Conference on Learning Representations (2016)
4. Arjovsky, M., Chintala, S., Bottou, L.: Wasserstein generative adversarial networks. In: International Conference on Machine Learning, pp. 214–223 (2017)
5. Ashton, M.S., Tyrrell, M.L., Spalding, D., Gentry, B.: Managing Forest Carbon in a Changing Climate. Springer, Dordrecht (2012). https://doi.org/10.1007/978-94-007-2232-3
6. Bihlo, A.: A generative adversarial network approach to (ensemble) weather prediction. Neural Netw. **139**, 1–16 (2021)
7. Björk, S., Anfinsen, S.N., Næsset, E., Gobakken, T., Zahabu, E.: Generation of lidar-predicted forest biomass maps from radar backscatter with conditional generative adversarial networks. In: International Geoscience and Remote Sensing Symposium, pp. 4327–4330 (2020)
8. Dong, L., et al.: Application of convolutional neural network on lei bamboo aboveground-biomass (AGB) estimation using worldview-2. Remote Sens. **12**(6), 958 (2020)
9. Fekety, P.A., Hudak, A.T.: LiDAR Derived Forest Aboveground Biomass Maps, Northwestern USA, 2002–2016. Oak Ridge National Laboratory Distributed Active Archive Center (2020)
10. Foody, G.M., Boyd, D.S., Cutler, M.E.J.: Predictive relations of tropical forest biomass from Landsat TM data and their transferability between regions. Remote Sens. Environ. **85**(4), 463–474 (2003)
11. Foody, G.M., et al.: Mapping the biomass of Bornean tropical rain forest from remotely sensed data. Glob. Ecol. Biogeogr. **10**(4), 379–387 (2001)
12. Gal, Y., Ghahramani, Z.: Dropout as a Bayesian Approximation: Representing Model Uncertainty in Deep Learning. In: International Conference on Machine Learning. pp. 1050–1059 (2016)
13. Gawlikowski, J., et al.: A survey of uncertainty in deep neural networks (2021). arXiv e-Print arXiv:2107.03342
14. Goodfellow, I., et al.: Generative adversarial nets. In: Conference on Neural Information Processing Systems, pp. 2672–2680 (2014)
15. Guo, C., Pleiss, G., Sun, Y., Weinberger, K.Q.: On calibration of modern neural networks. In: International Conference on Machine Learning, pp. 1321–1330 (Jul 2017)
16. Houghton, R.A., Hall, F., Goetz, S.J.: Importance of biomass in the global carbon cycle. J. Geophys. Res. **114**, G00E03 (2009)
17. Huang, G., Li, Y., Pleiss, G., Liu, Z., Hopcroft, J.E., Weinberger, K.Q.: Snapshot ensembles: train 1, get M for free. In: International Conference on Learning Representations (2017)
18. Hüllermeier, E., Waegeman, W.: Aleatoric and epistemic uncertainty in machine learning: an introduction to concepts and methods. Mach. Learn. **110**(3), 457–506 (2021). https://doi.org/10.1007/s10994-021-05946-3

19. Joshi, N., et al.: Understanding 'saturation' of radar signals over forests. Sci. Rep. **7**(1), 3505 (2017)
20. Kendall, A., Gal, Y.: What uncertainties do we need in Bayesian deep learning for computer vision? In: Conference on Neural Information Processing Systems, pp. 5580–5590 (2017)
21. Koochali, A., Schichtel, P., Dengel, A., Ahmed, S.: Probabilistic forecasting of sensory data with generative adversarial networks - ForGAN. IEEE Access **7**, 63868–63880 (2019)
22. Kosaraju, V., Sadeghian, A., Martín-Martín, R., Reid, I., Rezatofighi, S.H., Savarese, S.: Social-BiGAT: multimodal trajectory forecasting using bicycle-GAN and graph attention networks. In: Conference on Neural Information Processing Systems, pp. 137–146 (2019)
23. Lakshminarayanan, B., Pritzel, A., Blundell, C.: Simple and scalable predictive uncertainty estimation using deep ensembles. In: Conference on Neural Information Processing Systems, pp. 6405–6416 (2017)
24. Lang, N., Jetz, W., Schindler, K., Wegner, J.D.: A high-resolution canopy height model of the earth (2022). arXiv e-Print arXiv:2204.08322
25. Lang, N., Kalischek, N., Armston, J., Schindler, K., Dubayah, R., Wegner, J.D.: Global canopy height regression and uncertainty estimation from GEDI LIDAR waveforms with deep ensembles. Remote Sens. Environ. **268**, 112760 (2022)
26. Le Toan, T., et al.: The BIOMASS mission: mapping global forest biomass to better understand the terrestrial carbon cycle. Remote Sens. Environ. **115**(11), 2850–2860 (2011)
27. Lee, M., Seok, J.: Estimation with uncertainty via conditional generative adversarial networks. Sensors **21**(18), 6194 (2021)
28. Leinonen, J., Guillaume, A., Yuan, T.: Reconstruction of cloud vertical structure with a generative adversarial network. Geophys. Res. Lett. **46**(12), 7035–7044 (2019)
29. Li, Y., Li, M., Li, C., Liu, Z.: Forest aboveground biomass estimation using Landsat 8 and Sentinel-1A data with machine learning algorithms. Sci. Rep. **10**, 9952 (2020)
30. Loshchilov, I., Hutter, F.: SGDR: stochastic gradient descent with warm restarts. In: International Conference on Learning Representations (2016)
31. Maselli, F., Chiesi, M.: Evaluation of statistical methods to estimate forest volume in a mediterranean region. IEEE Trans. Geosci. Remote Sens. **44**(8), 2239–2250 (2006)
32. Mermoz, S., Réjou-Méchain, M., Villard, L., Le Toan, T., Rossi, V., Gourlet-Fleury, S.: Decrease of L-band SAR backscatter with biomass of dense forests. Remote Sens. Environ. **159**, 307–317 (2015)
33. Mescheder, L., Geiger, A., Nowozin, S.: Which training methods for GANs do actually converge? In: International Conference on Machine Learning, pp. 3481–3490 (2018)
34. Mirza, M., Osindero, S.: Conditional generative adversarial nets (2014). arXiv e-Print arXiv:1411.1784
35. Mutanga, O., Adam, E., Cho, M.A.: High density biomass estimation for wetland vegetation using WorldView-2 imagery and random forest regression algorithm. Int. J. Appl. Earth Obs. Geoinf. **18**, 399–406 (2012)
36. Neal, R.M.: Bayesian learning for neural networks. Ph.D. thesis, University of Toronto (1995)
37. Nix, D., Weigend, A.: Estimating the mean and variance of the target probability distribution. In: International Conference on Neural Networks, pp. 55–60 (1994)

38. Pang, Y., Liu, Y.: Conditional generative adversarial networks (CGAN) for aircraft trajectory prediction considering weather effects. In: AIAA Scitech Forum (2020)
39. Pearce, T., Brintrup, A., Zaki, M., Neely, A.: High-quality prediction intervals for deep learning: a distribution-free, ensembled approach. In: International Conference on Machine Learning, pp. 4075–4084 (2018)
40. Ravuri, S., et al.: Skilful precipitation nowcasting using deep generative models of radar. Nature **597**(7878), 672–677 (2021)
41. Rodríguez-Veiga, P., Wheeler, J., Louis, V., Tansey, K., Balzter, H.: Quantifying forest biomass carbon stocks from space. Curr. Forestry Rep. **3**(1), 1–18 (2017). https://doi.org/10.1007/s40725-017-0052-5
42. Ronneberger, O., Fischer, P., Brox, T.: U-net: convolutional networks for biomedical image segmentation. In: Navab, N., Hornegger, J., Wells, W.M., Frangi, A.F. (eds.) MICCAI 2015. LNCS, vol. 9351, pp. 234–241. Springer, Cham (2015). https://doi.org/10.1007/978-3-319-24574-4_28
43. Roy, P.S., Ravan, S.A.: Biomass estimation using satellite remote sensing data-An investigation on possible approaches for natural forest. J. Biosci. **21**(4), 535–561 (1996)
44. Shimada, M., Ohtaki, T.: Generating large-scale high-quality SAR mosaic datasets: application to PALSAR data for global monitoring. IEEE J. Sel. Top. Appl. Earth Observ. Remote Sens. **3**(4), 637–656 (2010)
45. Wang, Y., Zhang, L., van de Weijer, J.: Ensembles of generative adversarial networks. In: Conference on Neural Information Processing Systems (2016). Workshop on Adversarial Training
46. Wilson, A.G., Izmailov, P.: Bayesian deep learning and a probabilistic perspective of generalization. In: Conference on Neural Information Processing Systems, pp. 4697–4708 (2020)
47. Zhang, C., Jin, B.: Probabilistic residual learning for aleatoric uncertainty in image restoration (2019). arXiv e-Print arXiv:1908.01010v1
48. Zolkos, S.G., Goetz, S.J., Dubayah, R.: A meta-analysis of terrestrial aboveground biomass estimation using lidar remote sensing. Remote Sens. Environ. **128**, 289–298 (2013)

Time Dependent Image Generation of Plants from Incomplete Sequences with CNN-Transformer

Lukas Drees[1,2]([✉])[ID], Immanuel Weber[3][ID], Marc Rußwurm[4][ID],
and Ribana Roscher[1,2][ID]

[1] Data Science in Earth Observation, Technical University of Munich,
Munich, Germany
[2] IGG, Remote Sensing, University of Bonn, Bonn, Germany
{ldrees,ribana.roscher}@uni-bonn.de
[3] AB|EX, PLEdoc, Essen, Germany
immanuel.weber@pledoc.de
[4] ECEO Laboratory, École Polytechnique Fédérale de Lausanne (EPFL),
Lausanne, Switzerland
marc.russwurm@epfl.ch

Abstract. Data imputation of incomplete image sequences is an essential prerequisite for analyzing and monitoring all development stages of plants in precision agriculture. For this purpose, we propose a conditional Wasserstein generative adversarial network `TransGrow` that combines convolutions for spatial modeling and a transformer for temporal modeling, enabling time-dependent image generation of above-ground plant phenotypes. Thereby, we achieve the following advantages over comparable data imputation approaches: (1) The model is conditioned by an incomplete image sequence of arbitrary length, the input time points, and the requested output time point, allowing multiple growth stages to be generated in a targeted manner; (2) By considering a stochastic component and generating a distribution for each point in time, the uncertainty in plant growth is considered and can be visualized; (3) Besides interpolation, also test-extrapolation can be performed to generate future plant growth stages. Experiments based on two datasets of different complexity levels are presented: Laboratory single plant sequences with *Arabidopsis thaliana* and agricultural drone image sequences showing crop mixtures. When comparing `TransGrow` to interpolation in image space, variational, and adversarial autoencoder, it demonstrates significant improvements in image quality, measured by multi-scale structural similarity, peak signal-to-noise ratio, and Fréchet inception distance. To our knowledge, `TransGrow` is the first approach for time- and image-dependent, high-quality generation of plant images based on incomplete sequences.

Keywords: Data imputation · Transformer · Positional encoding · Image time series · Conditional GAN · Image generation · Plant growth modeling

B. Andres et al. (Eds.): DAGM GCPR 2022, LNCS 13485, pp. 495–510, 2022.
https://doi.org/10.1007/978-3-031-16788-1_30

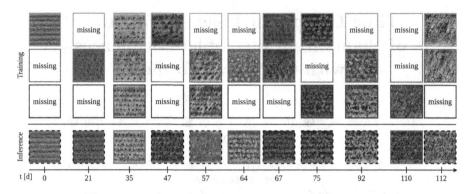

Fig. 1. TransGrow learns during training a realistic spatio-temporal model of plants, in this case of crop mixtures, from multiple irregular and incomplete sequences. Thus, at test time, it is able to substitute missing images (dashed frames) from a different number of input images (magenta frames). (Color figure online)

1 Introduction

When monitoring plants by means of image time series, corrupted, blurred, and missing images are a significant problem as plant growth is no longer holistically analyzable over the growing season [8,9,29]. This affects not only end-users, such as farmers, who plan actions in the field directly based on these images, but also researchers and model developers who may require homogeneous input data and have difficulty dealing with data gaps - especially in machine learning tasks. Sources of such gaps are manifold and, in the case of image acquisition with unmanned aerial vehicles (UAVs) in agriculture, range from an insufficient measurement setup over uncontrollable environmental influences to failures in post-processing calculation of the orthomosaic. In addition, intervals of varying size between observation times are inevitable and even desirable due to non-linear growth patterns, so that many observations fall within a range where plants are changing rapidly. There are several reasons to replace missing images instead of directly deriving target parameters and interpolating and extrapolating them, which would reduce the complexity of the task: By visualizing spatio-temporal growth evolution, classical growth models can be supported, the explainability of model outputs is substantially increased, and artificial images can be used as strong augmentations for a wide range of downstream tasks and enhance them. Hence, this work aims to generate images that can replace missing or corrupted images as artificial sensor data from irregular and incomplete sequences (Fig. 1).

Since plant growth is not exclusively deterministic but includes a large number of unobserved factors, it is also necessary to consider stochastic components in the generation. Thus, a distribution of images should be generated to indicate in each image which parts of the generated plant have high uncertainty. Traditional methods of data imputation operate directly in the image domain, like

L1 interpolation, image morphing, or optical flow, but do not allow the modeling of stochastic components. In contrast, more recently developed generative models such as variational autoencoder (VAE) or generative adversarial networks (GANs) allow interpolation in latent space that has been shown to generate more appealing images, coupled with the ability to model predictive uncertainties.

However, existing methods lack the possibility to elegantly include the time factor as a condition of the generative model, along with an incomplete image sequence. Therefore, we propose the conditional GAN TransGrow with the following contributions:

- Sharp and realistic image generation using a CNN-Transformer conditioned by an input image sequence of arbitrary length and time and by the output time, i.e., the requested growth stage of the image to be generated.
- The generation of a distribution for each point in time and from this, the visualization of predictive uncertainties on the plants in the generated image.
- The possibility to perform test-time extrapolations in addition to interpolations for data imputations in order to predict probable future expressions of the above-ground phenotypes.

2   Related Work

2.1   Interpolation Approaches for Data Imputation

In order to interpolate between two reference images, the most intuitive approaches directly operate in the image space, such as linear transformations, image warping, or optical flow. However, the resulting images are often inaccurate and not appealing since only the appearance, but no underlying features are changed for generation. This problem is addressed by mapping the essential features of the input images into a latent space and generating new images by interpolation between latent codes, for instance, enabled with autoencoders (AE) and their variants with adversarial constraints [6,26]. Still, there are three major issues: First, time is not explicitly taken into account, so assumptions about the growth process have to be made, i.e., linear interpolation, which does not hold for plant growth. Second, the additional modeling of predictive uncertainties by extending the model with a stochastic component is missing. This is essential since the observations never capture all complex growth influencing factors. Third, test-extrapolations remain impossible, which are needed, for example, to derive information from the potential future development of a plant, such as the estimation of harvest yield and date.

2.2   Conditional Generative Modeling for Data Imputation

More sophisticated methods such as various types of variational autoencoders (VAE) [21] or conditional GANs [15,19] overcome the aforementioned limitations by forming a distribution in the latent space, which allows controlled sampling. These distributions can be spanned by various combined conditions, such

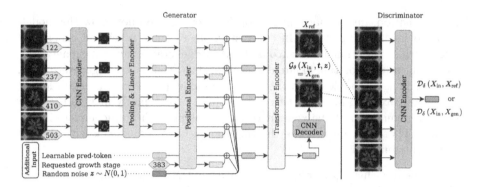

Fig. 2. TransGrow framework. In the generator an input sequence X_{in} is first spatially encoded with CNN, pooling and linear layer to dimension d_{model} and then, along with times t and stochasticity z, temporal encoded within positional encoding and a transformer stack. Out of this, an image of the requested growth stage is encoded. The CNN-based discriminator takes the input sequence with either the reference X_{ref} or the generated image X_{gen} sorted into the correct chronological position.

as stochasticity paired with images, categorical labels, or text. However, when there are sequential temporal conditions, as in this paper, most work is based on at least one of the following assumptions: Either time is modeled implicitly and is not controllable so that only a distribution for a specific point in time is generated, for example, the exclusive generation of future plant phenotypes from a fixed set of previous images [13,20,33]. Alternatively, the temporal component is inherently accounted for by equidistant or concise input intervals, such as in video frame prediction, which is nearly impossible for real-world sensor measurements in agriculture [1,28,32]. Therefore, we propose temporal positional encoding in combination with a transformer encoder [30] to control the time factor explicitly.

2.3   On Temporal Modeling with Transformer

To address the problem of non-equidistant inputs, this work uses image timestamps for positional encoding as in [14]. We call this global positional encoding since the acquisition times of the images related to a dataset reference point are used as positions. These positions deviate significantly from classical absolute positions, where the transformer is provided with indices related to their order in the sentence [30], positions of image patches related to their location in the original image [12], or with the relative timestamp of video frames [32]. Thereby, for works from the video domain, the spatial and temporal encoding is either directly combined [3,7], or initially decoupled [25]. We follow the latter idea to encode both independently and to merge them just before the transformer layer, thus creating the weighting of spatio-temporal image embeddings by self-attention (Fig. 2).

3   Methods

The TransGrow[1] model represents a conditional Wasserstein GAN with gradient penalty (CWGAN-GP) consisting of generator $\mathcal{G}_\theta$ and discriminator $\mathcal{D}_\delta$. While the different architectural components of $\mathcal{G}_\theta$ and $\mathcal{D}_\delta$ have been adopted from various state-of-the-art models, as outlined in detail in Sect. 3.2, the explicit integration of time via positional and transformer encoder allowing the generation of images of arbitrary time points is a novelty in the GAN context. The optimization as Wasserstein GAN with gradient penalty is based on Gulrajani et al. [16], but to enhance image sharpness, we regularized the generator with additional losses as explained in the following Sect. 3.1. For the remainder of the paper, one image sequence is denoted as $X = [X_1, \ldots, X_N]$ with associated time information $t = [t_1, \ldots, t_N]$, where $t_N - t_1 \leq \Delta t$.

3.1   Conditional Wasserstein GAN Objective

In the generator, a target image $X_{\text{gen}} = \mathcal{G}_\theta(X_{\text{in}}, t, z)$ is generated from an input image sequence X_{in}, times t, and noise z, whereby t is in fact split into $[t_{\text{in}}, t_{\text{gen}}]$. To divide the sample into an input image sequence $X_{\text{in}} = [X_1, \ldots, X_{N_{\text{in}}}]$ with associated times $t_{\text{in}} = [t_1, \ldots, t_{N_{\text{in}}}]$ and an image to be generated X_{ref} with its requested time t_{gen}, $N_{\text{in}} = N-1$ images and associated times are in each training step randomly sampled from X respectively t.

In the discriminator, either the reference $\mathcal{D}_\delta(X_{\text{in}}, X_{\text{ref}})$ or the generated image $\mathcal{D}_\delta(X_{\text{in}}, X_{\text{gen}})$ are presented along with the input image sequence. It outputs a score how realistic the input is, which is suitable to enforce the minimization of the Wasserstein distance within the following adversarial objective.

The adversarial objective is to optimize the parameters θ and δ by maximizing several objective functions L by $\mathcal{D}_\delta$ and minimizing them by $\mathcal{G}_\theta$.

$$\theta^*, \delta^* = \arg\min_\theta \arg\max_\delta L_{\text{GAN}}(\mathcal{G}_\theta, \mathcal{D}_\delta) \\ + \lambda_{\text{L1}} L_{\text{L1}}(\mathcal{G}_\theta) + \lambda_{\text{SSIM}} L_{\text{SSIM}}(\mathcal{G}_\theta) + \lambda_{\text{VGG}} L_{\text{VGG}}(\mathcal{G}_\theta) \tag{1}$$

Here, $L_{\text{GAN}}(\mathcal{G}_\theta, \mathcal{D}_\delta)$ represents the total CWGAN-GP objective function [16] while the other terms are further regularizations applied to the generator. Those are added with corresponding weights λ to the final objective in the form of a L_{L1} reconstruction loss, a multiscale structural similarity (SSIM) loss L_{SSIM} [31], and a perceptual content loss employing a pretrained VGG-network L_{VGG} [22]. Equation (2) represents $L_{\text{GAN}}(\mathcal{G}_\theta, \mathcal{D}_\delta)$ with the classic CWGAN objective in the first line [2], added with the gradient penalty term in the second line, one of the ways to enforce the required 1-Lipschitz continuity of $\mathcal{D}_\delta$ [16].

$$L_{\text{GAN}}(\mathcal{G}_\theta, \mathcal{D}_\delta) = \mathbb{E}_{(X_{\text{in}}, t, z)}[\mathcal{D}_\delta(X_{\text{in}}, \mathcal{G}_\theta(X_{\text{in}}, t, z))] - \mathbb{E}_{(X_{\text{in}}, X_{\text{ref}})}[\mathcal{D}_\delta(X_{\text{in}}, X_{\text{ref}})] \\ + \lambda_{\text{GP}} \mathbb{E}_{(X_{\text{in}}, \hat{X})}[(\|\nabla_{\hat{X}} \mathcal{D}_\delta(X_{\text{in}}, \hat{X})\|_2 - 1)^2] \tag{2}$$

---

[1] Source code is publicly available at https://github.com/luked12/transgrow.

For the calculation of gradient penalty, $\hat{X} = \epsilon X_{\text{ref}} + (1-\epsilon)\mathcal{G}_\theta(X_{\text{in}}, t, z)$ represents a randomly weighted average between the generated and the reference image with ϵ picked randomly between 0 and 1. The weighting of the whole term is done by coefficient λ_{GP}. It has been shown that $L_{\text{GAN}}(\mathcal{G}_\theta, \mathcal{D}_\delta)$ is able to minimize the Wasserstein-1 distance between the distribution of the real and generated samples while avoiding typical problems of the origin GAN training such as mode collapses or vanishing gradients.

3.2   Network Architecture

Generator Encoder

Spatial Encoding. For the spatial encoding of X_{in} a ResNet-18 backbone [17] is used as CNN encoder, which is pretrained on ImageNet [11]. It represents a comparatively small and thus efficient trainable model, whose embedding dimension (512) after pooling the last Conv layer also represents a reasonable latent dimension for the transformer encoder. We encode each image independently with the same shared ResNet-18 weights so that independent features result from the same latent space. In order to preserve experimentation flexibility for different latent dimensions, the pooled CNN output is linearly projected to a final latent dimension d_{model}.

Learnable Pred-Token. Inspired by [12], we add a d_{model}-dimensional learnable token, called pred-token, from which the target image is decoded. Besides, it is intended to carry firstly basic shared features of all samples of the dataset and secondly to have a container to which the positional encoded requested time t_{gen} is added and brought to the transformer encoder.

Inducing Stochasticity. To be able to generate an output distribution at fixed X_{in} and t, stochasticity in the form of random noise $z \sim \mathcal{N}(0, 1)$ is induced into the network. Therefore, the identical z of dimension d_z is scaled up to d_{model} and then added to all latent representations of the sequence together with the positional encoding. While there are various other methods to induce noise, this one has proven to be very robust in our case. Additional dropout layers are used after the positional encoding and within the transformer encoder at training time to force diversity.

Positional Encoding. In the positional encoding, the spatially encoded latent representations of the input images are provided with explicit temporal information by adding N_{in} positional encoding vectors of same dimension d_{model}. Besides, the requested growth stage in the form of a positionally encoded time point is added to the learnable pred-token. We use a global positional encoding, whereby one dataset-specific reference point is set to a reasonable time at the beginning of the growing period, such as the date of plant emergence from the soil. Thus, the global position of each image can be interpreted as the plant growth stage. This enables the transformer to capture the actual temporal information of the sample in the dataset, which is required to generate images at arbitrary points in time instead of generating fixed positions with respect to the input sequence. The positional encoding is calculated by a combination of sine-cosine signals, as in [30].

Transformer. The architecture's transformer module is a stack of multiple transformer encoder layers [30], ensuring temporal connections of the sequence elements by increasingly deeper self-attention. Each layer contains a Multi-Head Self-Attention (MSA) and a Feed-Forward Network (FFN), with layer normalization after each of them and skip-connections around each one. Any number of sequence elements can be inserted into the transformer encoder stack, which is of great importance for the flexibility of `TransGrow`. It generates an output, called memory, of the same dimension d_{model} for each incoming vector of the sequence, of which only the transformed pred-token is further used.

Generator Decoder. As a generator, we use a lightweight decoder [23], which in particular is designed to be robustly trainable with small datasets. It includes an initial ConvTranspose layer followed by BatchNorm and GLU to decode from $1^2 \to 4^2$. The subsequent upsampling modules, each quadratically enlarging the image, consist of Nearest-Upsampling, Conv, Batchnorm, and GLU layers. To counteract the weak gradient flow with deep decoders, an additional skip layer excitation between the images $8^2 \to 128^2$, $16^2 \to 256^2$, and $32^2 \to 512^2$ is used.

Discriminator. The discriminator gets the whole sequence as input, each X_{in} with either the reference X_{ref} or the generated X_{gen} target image. Before feeding through the discriminator, the target image is first sorted into the correct position of the input sequence so that the discriminator does not require positional encoding. It is built as a lightweight model from alternating convolutional layers, ReLU activation, instance normalization, and weight-sharing between all images in the sequence.

4   Experiments and Results

4.1   Data

Arabidopsis and MixedCrop. Two time series datasets are used that differ significantly in characteristics and complexity (Table 1). The larger Arabidopsis dataset [4] consists of individual plant images of the cultivar *Arabidopsis thaliana* taken in a controlled laboratory environment with a robotic arm. In contrast, the MixedCrop dataset shows multiple plants per image within real agricultural mixed cropping between faba bean and spring wheat crops captured by a UAV. Further essential differences are the intervals between the recording times and the number of different plants. While in Arabidopsis, 80 plants were observed 1676 times in a period of $836\ h \approx 35\ d$, i.e., several times per hour during the day, in MixedCrop, significantly more locations were observed, less frequently, and over a longer period (2226 locations, 11 times in 112 d). All images are processed at a pixel resolution of [256 × 256], which corresponds to a ground sampling distance (GSD) of 0.35 mm and 5.70 mm for Arabidopsis and MixedCrop, respectively. In Fig. 3 is shown how many images divided into train, validation, and test set are available at which time point. This illustrates that the sequences are neither equidistant nor that there are the same number of images per time point, i.e., the sequences are of different lengths.

Table 1. Dataset characteristics. [1]Observation period given in units of time steps of the model, i.e. [h] for Arabidopsis and [d] for MixedCrop, which is user definable. [2]Number of different time points equals the max. sequence length; for Arabidopsis greater than period, because up to 4 images were taken in one hour. [3]Number of sequences equals the number of plants in Arabidopsis and spatially separated field patches in MixedCrop.

	# imgs	period[1]	# times[2]	# seq.[3]	# train seq.	# val seq.	# test seq.	∅ imgs/seq.	img size [px]	GSD [mm]
Arabidopsis	107 078	836 h	1676	80	50	10	20	1338.5	256	0.35
MixedCrop	21 869	112 d	11	2226	1590	318	318	9.8	256	5.70

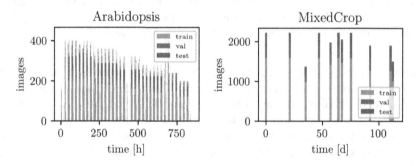

Fig. 3. Incomplete and irregular time series. Number of images over time for (left) Arabidopis and (right) MixedCrop data split into training, validation, and test set.

Preparation and Sampling. Since the time series length varies from plant to plant and is too long for efficient processing in a single sample, significantly smaller sequences of length N are randomly sampled on intervals of length Δt that lie on a random portion of the entire time series. We randomly choose the target image out of the sequence, aiming to generate interpolations, if $\min(t) < t_{gen} < \max(t)$, and extrapolations, if $t_{gen} = \min(t)$ or $t_{gen} = \max(t)$, in random alternation. This is crucial because it contributes to the positional encoding not being suppressed during the training but having an actual impact on the time of the generated image. While training on a fixed number of time points, we can still infer a variable number of images. Since transformer training benefits from high data diversity, multiple augmentations are performed on the train sets consisting of random 90°-rotations, horizontal, and vertical flippings. In addition, for Arabidopsis, comprehensive foreground (plant) and background (pot) shuffling is implemented by calculating plant masks via RGBVI [5], cutting the plant out of the image at the position of the mask, rotating it arbitrarily, and inserting it centrally on a randomly selected new image of an empty pot. Finally, all images are scaled to the value range $[0, 1]$.

4.2 Experimental Setup

Hyperparameter. For training, the input sequence length is set to $N_{in} = 3$ with the largest possible Δt for the respective data sets of 837 h and 112 d, which can be varied as needed for inference. The stochasticity and the embedding dimension are set to $d_z = 16$ and $d_{model} = 512$, as the latter is the size of the last ResNet-18 feature layer. A low dropout probability of 0.1 as suggested in [12,30] is used at all dropout positions as described in Sect. 3 to prevent overfitting. Since the transformer is intended to encode only the temporal component of the input, a low depth $L = 3$ and a number of 4 heads within the multi-head attention is experimentally selected. In the calculation of the generator loss, the additional regularizations are all equally weighted $\lambda_{L1} = \lambda_{VGG} = \lambda_{SSIM} = 1$. While in classical GANs the reconstruction loss (here: L_{L1}) is often weighted substantially higher than L_{GAN} [13,18], this did not turn out to be beneficial in this work. The weighting of gradient penalty $\lambda_{GP} = 10$ and all other WGAN-GP optimization hyperparameters are set according to [16]. Using a batch size of 32, a learning rate of 1e−4, Adam optimizer, and the settings mentioned above, it takes up to 1000 epochs for convergence, running for approximately 5 d on a single Nvidia A100 in mixed-precision mode.

Comparison Methods. As baselines, we use a variational autoencoder VAE [21] and an adversarial autoencoder AAE [24]. Previous work has shown that remarkable results can be obtained by classical interpolation between support points in latent space learned from autoencoder [26]. Furthermore, they are suitable for generating a variance in the output that follows a predefined distribution - in our case $\mathcal{N}(0, 1)$. However, unlike TransGrow, they do not allow time-dependent sampling of the latent space and, therefore, no intuitive extrapolation. For maximal comparability, VAE and AAE are provided with the same generator as TransGrow. In the encoder, only the transformer stack is omitted because VAE and AAE are not trained on sequences but on single images, and thus no explicit temporal encoding is required. Instead, the VAE-typical d_{model}-dimensional bottleneck with μ and σ is synthesized by a linear layer and decoded to the image after reparametrization from the normal distribution. In AAE, a discriminator is used with three linear layers, each followed by ReLU and final sigmoid activation. In addition to an L1-loss for VAE, the Kullback-Leibler divergence and for AAE an adversarial loss utilizing binary cross entropy are used for optimization.

Evaluation Metrics. We utilize the established metrics multi-scale structural similarity MS-SSIM [31], denoted SSIM hereafter, and a human cognition optimized signal-to-noise ratio PSNR-HVS-M [27], denoted PSNR hereafter, to compare generated and reference images of the same time point in each image domain. In addition, an improved unbiased FID score, FID_∞ [10], is used to compare the generated and real image distribution across all time points. Thereby, FID is known to correlate particularly well with human perception. While for SSIM (opt: 1), and PSNR (opt: $\sim$60 dB) the larger the better, for FID a smaller value means a higher similarity between the image distributions (opt: 0).

Table 2. Mean and std deviation of evaluation scores MS-SSIM, PSNR-HVS-M [dB], and FID for random temporal image generation divided in interpolation and extrapolation out of each two random support points on test sequences of both datasets. Best results of approaches VAE, AAE and TransGrow are indicated in bold. Additional TransGrow ablations are given with changed data parameter Δt and N_{in}.

Data	Approach	Interpolation		Extrapolation		FID
		MS-SSIM	PSNR-HVS-M	MS-SSIM	PSNR-HVS-M	
Arabidopsis	VAE	0.81 ± 0.06	47.29 ± 2.58	–	–	138.78
	AAE	**0.87 ± 0.03**	**50.57 ± 2.15**	–	–	113.23
	TransGrow	**0.87 ± 0.03**	49.88 ± 2.16	0.86 ± 0.04	49.59 ± 2.16	**58.79**
	$\Delta t = 240$ h	0.87 ± 0.03	50.03 ± 2.12	0.86 ± 0.04	49.70 ± 2.13	58.60
	$N_{in} = 10$	0.87 ± 0.03	49.95 ± 2.15	0.86 ± 0.04	49.79 ± 2.12	62.78
MixedCrop	VAE	0.63 ± 0.03	40.34 ± 1.10	–	–	344.86
	AAE	0.69 ± 0.05	44.05 ± 2.37	–	–	321.40
	TransGrow	**0.73 ± 0.02**	**45.02 ± 2.35**	0.72 ± 0.03	44.84 ± 2.57	**93.26**
	$\Delta t = 50$ d	0.74 ± 0.02	44.98 ± 2.33	0.74 ± 0.03	45.37 ± 2.47	95.90
	$N_{in} = 5$	0.74 ± 0.03	45.10 ± 2.44	0.74 ± 0.04	45.44 ± 2.82	93.99

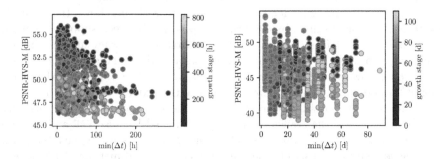

Fig. 4. PSNR-HVS-M of generated images in relation to temporal nearest support point and growth stage indicated by color of dots for Arabidopsis (left) and MixedCrop (right).

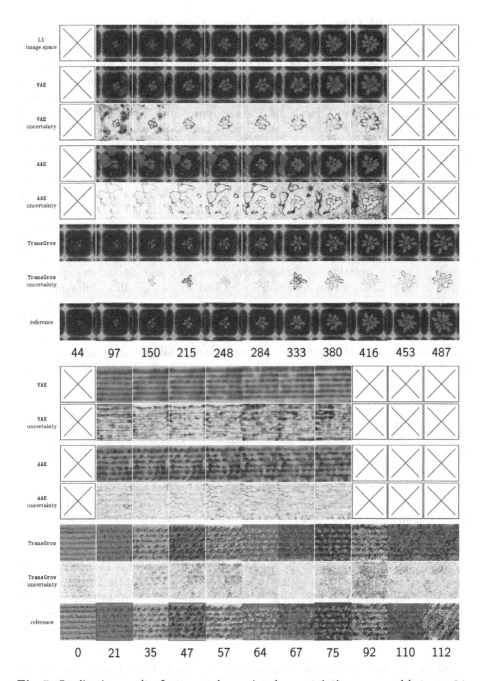

Fig. 5. Qualitative results. Images and associated uncertainties compared between L1 (image space), VAE, AAE, TransGrow, and reference for inter- and extrapolation between $N_{in} = 3$ support points (magenta frame) for (top) Arabidopsis and (bottom) Mixed-Crop. (Color figure online)

4.3   Results of Time-Dependent Image Generation

Quantitative Evaluation. To generate the quantitative results, three support points are randomly sampled from all test sequences, of which for interpolation, the temporally middle support point is generated from the edge support points (all approaches), and for extrapolation, the edge support points from the two others (only TransGrow). Hence, the scores represent an average value over all randomly sampled interpolation and extrapolation distances. When compared with VAE and AAE, Table 2 shows that TransGrow provides the best scores for SSIM (0.87 and 0.73) and FID (58.79 and 93.26) for both datasets. Only the PSNR value for Arabidopsis is slightly higher with AAE (50.57 dB) than with the other methods, but this is not necessarily reflected in good human-perceived image quality, as shown by the significantly higher FID (113.23) and also the qualitative results Fig. 5. While extrapolations cannot be performed with VAE and AAE without making specific assumptions, extrapolation is possible with TransGrow with only minimal drop in accuracy (0.01 in SSIM) and (<0.5 dB in PSNR). Further ablations to TransGrow, where N_{in} and Δt are changed compared to the training setup, demonstrate its flexibility in handling different input data dimensions, which is very practical for field applications. Although the model was trained on only two input images, the results are comparable and, in almost all cases, even slightly improve in accuracy. The FIDs are, in total, rather high because the figures are an average over all growth stages and interpolation/extrapolation distances, although there are significant differences, as discussed next.

Correlation of Accuracy with the Temporal Distance. Considering in Fig. 4 the PSNR in relation to the distance to the closest support point and the growth stage, indicated by the color of the dots, a trend is apparent: Nearby images of similar growth stages have a better PSNR, i.e., a drop in accuracy can be seen from upper left to lower right in the scatter plots. This characteristic is explained by a natural increase of the uncertainty in the plant growth with a larger distance to the last observation, which can be seen qualitatively in greater standard deviations in Fig. 5. It can be noted that smaller plants in Arabidopsis have higher scores up to 56 dB, which may be because smaller growth stages are over-represented (see Fig. 3). For MixedCrop, this trend is also evident but less clearly than expected. Possible reasons are the significantly fewer available training time points and that plant growth in this dataset from time point 57 onwards is expressed more by changing spectral information than by spatial structural changes, as in Arabidopsis.

Qualitative and Variance Evaluation. Figure 5 shows the image generation from $N_{in}=3$ images for Arabidopsis and MixedCrop. First, it is illustrated that simple L1 interpolation in the image space is inappropriate for any plant-related application since leaves do not develop at all, but contours of both early and later growth stages are blurred in one image. VAE provides decent results regarding plant size and leaf orientation for Arabidopsis, but the images are not sharp, as is the case with the MixedCrop. AAE solves this problem by making leaf edges sharper, but in return, there are substantial issues with unnaturally shaped leaves, and leaf artifacts randomly protrude into the plant. Also, for MixedCrop, the leaf surfaces themselves are not sharp. In addition, as with L1, both AE approaches fail to capture the different time-specific spectral properties of MixedCrop, e.g., generated plants at times 57 and 64 have the same color. Finally, TransGrow provides both sharp and realistic results in terms of leaf structure and orientation. Extrapolation also works, although there are limitations if one moves too far away from the support point, e.g., $t = 112$ in MixedCrop. In addition, reliable uncertainty maps at each time point can be generated by producing a distribution of generations (here: 10 samples) at varying z but otherwise constant input conditions. While many classical conditional GANs tend to suppress noise and thus degrade to a deterministic one-to-one mapping model, the possibility to generate a distribution relies in particular on the optimization as a Wasserstein GAN. In contrast to VAE and AAE, where the variance is more scattered in the image, it produces images with pronounced standard deviations at the leaf edges, i.e., at the locations where naturally the greatest variance exists.

5 Conclusion and Outlook

In this work, we have shown that our conditional Wasserstein generative adversarial network TransGrow with a combined generator of convolutional neural networks and transformers enables high-quality and realistic image generation for incomplete and irregular sequences. For two datasets showing single plants of *Arabidopsis thaliana* and crop mixtures of faba bean and spring wheat, it was demonstrated that the time-dependent sampling in the latent space ensures a substantial reduction of Fréchet inception distance compared to variational and adversarial autoencoder approaches utilizing linear latent space interpolation. In addition to interpolation, TransGrow is also capable of test-extrapolation with only a minimal decrease in multiscale structural similarity and peak signal-to-noise ratio. This allows farmers to forecast a future probable above-ground phenotype from a flexible number of images and any time points in the growing season. Furthermore, the pixel-wise uncertainty for each time can be indicated, showing reliable pronounced variance at the leaf edges, where the variance of plant growth is naturally highest.

Future work will take a detailed view on the transformer attention maps to better understand the mechanisms of temporal generation. Challenges of transferability of one model to another location or growth period, especially due to different environmental conditions affecting crop growth and varying lighting affecting the homogeneity in the image sequence appearances, will be addressed. We also plan to scale up from the close-range to satellite imagery time series to analyze the vegetation development field- rather than crop-wise.

Acknowledgment. This work was funded by the Deutsche Forschungsgemeinschaft (DFG, German Research Foundation) under Germany's Excellence Strategy - EXC 2070 - 390732324 and partly funded by the German Federal Ministry of Education and Research (BMBF) in the framework of the international future AI lab "AI4EO – Artificial Intelligence for Earth Observation: Reasoning, Uncertainties, Ethics and Beyond" (Grant number: 01DD20001).

References

1. Aigner, S., Körner, M.: Futuregan: Anticipating the future frames of video sequences using spatio-temporal 3d convolutions in progressively growing GANs. In: Proceedings of the ISPRS International Archives of the Photogrammetry, Remote Sensing and Spatial Information Sciences, vol. XLII-2/W16, pp. 3–11 (2019). https://doi.org/10.5194/isprs-archives-XLII-2-W16-3-2019

2. Arjovsky, M., Chintala, S., Bottou, L.: Wasserstein GAN. arXiv preprint arXiv:1701.07875 (2017)

3. Arnab, A., Dehghani, M., Heigold, G., Sun, C., Lučić, M., Schmid, C.: Vivit: A video vision transformer. arXiv preprint arXiv:2103.15691 (2021)

4. Bell, J., Dee, H.M.: Aberystwyth leaf evaluation dataset (2016). https://doi.org/10.5281/zenodo.168158

5. Bendig, J., et al.: Combining UAV-based plant height from crop surface models, visible, and near infrared vegetation indices for biomass monitoring in barley. Int. J. Appl. Earth Obs. Geoinf. **39**, 79–87 (2015). https://doi.org/10.1016/j.jag.2015.02.012

6. Bengio, Y., Courville, A., Vincent, P.: Representation learning: A review and new perspectives. IEEE Trans. Pattern Anal. Mach. Intell. **35**(8), 1798–1828 (2013). https://doi.org/10.1109/TPAMI.2013.50

7. Bertasius, G., Wang, H., Torresani, L.: Is space-time attention all you need for video understanding? arXiv preprint arXiv:2102.05095 (2021)

8. Burkart, A., Hecht, V.L., Kraska, T., Rascher, U.: Phenological analysis of unmanned aerial vehicle based time series of barley imagery with high temporal resolution. Precision Agric. **19**(1), 134–146 (2017). https://doi.org/10.1007/s11119-017-9504-y

9. Chang, S., Lee, U., Hong, M.J., Jo, Y.D., Kim, J.B.: Time-series growth prediction model based on U-net and machine learning in Arabidopsis. Front. Plant Sci. **12** (2021). https://doi.org/10.3389/fpls.2021.721512

10. Chong, M.J., Forsyth, D.: Effectively unbiased fid and inception score and where to find them. In: Proceedings of the IEEE/CVF Conference on Computer Vision and Pattern Recognition (CVPR), June 2020. https://doi.org/10.1109/CVPR42600.2020.00611

11. Deng, J., Dong, W., Socher, R., Li, L.J., Li, K., Fei-Fei, L.: ImageNet: A large-scale hierarchical image database. In: Proceedings of the IEEE Conference on Computer Vision and Pattern Recognition (CVPR), pp. 248–255. IEEE (2009). https://doi.org/10.1109/CVPR.2009.5206848

12. Dosovitskiy, A., et al.: An image is worth 16x16 words: transformers for image recognition at scale. arXiv preprint arXiv:2010.11929 (2020)

13. Drees, L., Junker-Frohn, L.V., Kierdorf, J., Roscher, R.: Temporal prediction and evaluation of brassica growth in the field using conditional generative adversarial networks. Comput. Electron. Agric. **190**, 106415 (2021). https://doi.org/10.1016/j.compag.2021.106415

14. Garnot, V.S.F., Landrieu, L., Giordano, S., Chehata, N.: Satellite image time series classification with pixel-set encoders and temporal self-attention. In: Proceedings of the IEEE/CVF Conference on Computer Vision and Pattern Recognition (CVPR), pp. 12325–12334 (2020). https://doi.org/10.1109/CVPR42600.2020.01234
15. Goodfellow, I., et al.: Generative adversarial nets. In: Proceedings of the Advances in Neural Information Processing Systems (NeurIPS), pp. 2672–2680 (2014)
16. Gulrajani, I., Ahmed, F., Arjovsky, M., Dumoulin, V., Courville, A.: Improved training of Wasserstein GANs. In: Proceedings of the International Conference on Neural Information Processing Systems. NIPS 2017, pp. 5769–5779. Curran Associates Inc., Red Hook (2017)
17. He, K., Zhang, X., Ren, S., Sun, J.: Deep residual learning for image recognition. In: Proceedings of the IEEE Conference on Computer Vision and Pattern Recognition, pp. 770–778 (2016)
18. Isola, P., Zhu, J.Y., Zhou, T., Efros, A.A.: Image-to-image translation with conditional adversarial networks. In: Proceedings of the IEEE Conference on Computer Vision and Pattern Recognition (CVPR), pp. 1125–1134 (2017). https://doi.org/10.1109/CVPR.2017.632
19. Karras, T., Laine, S., Aila, T.: A style-based generator architecture for generative adversarial networks. In: Proc. of the IEEE/CVF Conference on Computer Vision and Pattern Recognition (CVPR). pp. 4401–4410 (2019). https://doi.org/10.1109/CVPR.2019.00453
20. Kierdorf, J., Weber, I., Kicherer, A., Zabawa, L., Drees, L., Roscher, R.: Behind the leaves-estimation of occluded grapevine berries with conditional generative adversarial networks. arXiv preprint arXiv:2105.10325 (2021)
21. Kingma, D.P., Welling, M.: Auto-encoding variational Bayes. arXiv preprint arXiv:1312.6114 (2013)
22. Ledig, C., et al.: Photo-realistic single image super-resolution using a generative adversarial network. In: Proceedings of the IEEE Conference on Computer Vision and Pattern Recognition (CVPR), pp. 4681–4690 (2017). https://doi.org/10.1109/CVPR.2017.19
23. Liu, B., Zhu, Y., Song, K., Elgammal, A.: Towards faster and stabilized GAN training for high-fidelity few-shot image synthesis. In: Proceedings of International Conference on Learning Representations (ICLR) (2020)
24. Makhzani, A., Shlens, J., Jaitly, N., Goodfellow, I., Frey, B.: Adversarial autoencoders. arXiv preprint arXiv:1511.05644 (2015)
25. Neimark, D., Bar, O., Zohar, M., Asselmann, D.: Video transformer network. arXiv preprint arXiv:2102.00719 (2021)
26. Oring, A., Yakhini, Z., Hel-Or, Y.: Autoencoder image interpolation by shaping the latent space. arXiv preprint arXiv:2008.01487 (2020)
27. Ponomarenko, N., Silvestri, F., Egiazarian, K., Carli, M., Astola, J., Lukin, V.: On between-coefficient contrast masking of DCT basis functions. In: Proceedings of the Third International Workshop on Video Processing and Quality Metrics, vol. 4. Scottsdale USA (2007)
28. Shi, Z., Xu, X., Liu, X., Chen, J., Yang, M.H.: Video frame interpolation transformer. arXiv preprint arXiv:2111.13817 (2021)
29. Tsaftaris, S.A., Minervini, M., Scharr, H.: Machine learning for plant phenotyping needs image processing. Trends Plant Sci. 21(12), 989–991 (2016). https://doi.org/10.1016/j.tplants.2016.10.002
30. Vaswani, A., et al.: Attention is all you need. arXiv preprint arXiv:1706.03762 (2017)

31. Wang, Z., Simoncelli, E.P., Bovik, A.C.: Multiscale structural similarity for image quality assessment. In: Proceedings of the Asilomar Conference on Signals, Systems and Computers, vol. 2, pp. 1398–1402. IEEE (2003). https://doi.org/10.1109/ACSSC.2003.1292216

32. Yan, W., Zhang, Y., Abbeel, P., Srinivas, A.: VideoGPT: Video generation using VQ-VAE and transformers. arXiv preprint (2021). https://doi.org/10.48550/arXiv.2104.10157

33. Yasrab, R., Zhang, J., Smyth, P., Pound, M.P.: Predicting plant growth from time-series data using deep learning. Remote Sens. **13**(3), 331 (2021). https://doi.org/10.3390/rs13030331

Pattern Recognition in the Life and Natural Sciences

I-MuPPET: Interactive Multi-Pigeon Pose Estimation and Tracking

Urs Waldmann[1,2(✉)] , Hemal Naik[1,2,3,4] , Nagy Máté[1,2,3,5,6] ,
Fumihiro Kano[2,3] , Iain D. Couzin[1,2,3] , Oliver Deussen[1,2] ,
and Bastian Goldlücke[1,2]

[1] University of Konstanz, Konstanz, Germany
[2] Centre for the Advanced Study of Collective Behaviour, University of Konstanz,
Konstanz, Germany
urs.waldmann@uni-konstanz.de
[3] Max Planck Institute of Animal Behavior, Konstanz, Germany
[4] Technische Universität München, Munich, Germany
[5] Hungarian Academy of Sciences, Budapest, Hungary
[6] Eötvös Loránd University, Budapest, Hungary

Abstract. Most tracking data encompasses humans, the availability of annotated tracking data for animals is limited, especially for multiple objects. To overcome this obstacle, we present I-MuPPET, a system to estimate and track 2D keypoints of multiple pigeons at interactive speed. We train a Keypoint R-CNN on single pigeons in a fully supervised manner and infer keypoints and bounding boxes of multiple pigeons with that neural network. We use a state of the art tracker to track the individual pigeons in video sequences. I-MuPPET is tested quantitatively on single pigeon motion capture data, and we achieve comparable accuracy to state of the art 2D animal pose estimation methods in terms of Root Mean Square Error (RMSE). Additionally, we test I-MuPPET to estimate and track poses of multiple pigeons in video sequences with up to four pigeons and obtain stable and accurate results with up to 17 fps. To establish a baseline for future research, we perform a detailed quantitative tracking evaluation, which yields encouraging results.

Keywords: Pose estimation · Multi-object tracking · Animals · Applications

We acknowledge funding by the Deutsche Forschungsgemeinschaft (DFG, German Research Foundation) under Germany's Excellence Strategy - EXC 2117 - 422037984, the Office of Naval Research (Research Grant to I.D.C, #N00014-64019–1-2556) and the European Union's Horizon 2020 research and innovation programme under the Marie Skłodowska-Curie grant agreement (to I.D.C; #860949). Ethics: Animal experiments were approved by the Regierungspräsidium Freiburg under the permit number Az. 35–9185.81/G-19/107. Full author affiliations are in our supplemental material.

Supplementary Information The online version contains supplementary material available at https://doi.org/10.1007/978-3-031-16788-1_31.

B. Andres et al. (Eds.): DAGM GCPR 2022, LNCS 13485, pp. 513–528, 2022.
https://doi.org/10.1007/978-3-031-16788-1_31

Fig. 1. *Interactive multi-pigeon pose estimation and tracking (I-MuPPET). Left*: Estimated complex pose (beak tip, nose, left and right eye, left and right shoulder and tail) of a pigeon with its ID from tracking. Left body side of pigeon in red, right one in blue and beak in orange. *Right*: Facility with cameras and Vicon motion capture system where our pigeon datasets were recorded. © CASCB Uni Konstanz.

1   Introduction

Accurate quantification of behavior is critical to understand the underlying principles of social interaction and the neural and cognitive underpinnings of animal behaviour [1,5,7,31,38]. While researchers conventionally analyzed animal behaviour manually using a predefined catalogue of behaviours called ethograms, the recent advances in computer vision, as well as the increasing demands for a large data set involving the analysis on the fine-scaled and rapidly-changing behaviours of animals, encourage automated tracking methods [2,12,18,38]. The CVPR workshop in 2021 on "Computer Vision for Animal Behavior Tracking and Modeling" [43] emphasized the increasing interest in computer vision tools in the field of animal behaviour. While existing automatic methods range from object detection [16], behavior analysis [10,42], segmentation [11], 3D shape and pose fitting [3,9] to pose estimation [19,33] and tracking [45,49], reliable tracking of multiple moving animals in real-time and estimating their pose remains a challenging task.

One of the limiting factors in the field of animal pose estimation is the small amount of annotated training data compared to its human counterpart (for example 3.6 million in [25]). DeepLabCut [38], LEAP [46] and DeepPoseKit [20] overcome this lack of training data by introducing a method to manually label few data that is then used to train a neural network. With that network the authors predict body parts of additional unlabeled material creating more and more annotated training data for animals. Creatures Great and SMAL [9] instead creates synthetic silhouettes for training and extracts silhouettes [52,53] from real data for inference. We are aware of only three data sets for birds [3,50,54]. Clearly, methods need to be developed that exploit few training data in an efficient way.

In this paper, we present I-MuPPET, an interactive multi-pigeon pose estimation and tracking system. We can acquire training data for a single pigeon in a semi-automated way and demonstrate that training on an annotated dataset containing only a single pigeon is sufficient for our framework to predict seven keypoints of a complex pose for multiple pigeons and track the individuals at interactive speed ($\geqslant 1$ fps). We track up to four pigeons (at the moment the upper limit in our dataset) with $12 - 17$ fps, and report detailed results for speed and accuracy. Our framework is comparable with state of the art 2D animal pose estimation methods in terms of Root Mean Square Error (RMSE) .

2 Related Work

2.1 Animal Pose Estimation

2D Single Animal Pose Estimation. With the huge success of DeepLabCut [38] and LEAP [46], animal pose estimation has been developing into its own research branch parallel to human pose estimation. DeepLabCut and LEAP both introduce a method for labelling animal body parts and training a deep neural network for predicting 2D body part positions. DeepPoseKit [20] improved the inference speed by a factor of approximately two, while maintaining the accuracy of DeepLabCut. In 3D Bird Reconstruction [3], they predict 2D keypoints to estimate the pose and shape of cowbirds from a single view. Since manual annotations are time-consuming, labor-intensive, and prone to errors, we use a framework that uses semi-automatically labeled data.

2D Multi-Animal Pose Estimation. DeepLabCut is extended in [34] to predict 2D body parts of multiple animals. This extension uses training data with annotations of multiple animals. The authors will release four datasets with annotations containing mice, pups, marmosets and fish. Similarly SLEAP [47] provides several architectures to estimate 2D body parts of multiple animals. These two approaches [34,47] work well but are trained on multi-animal annotated data. Since this kind of data is limited in its availability, we overcome this limitation by training a framework on annotated single animal data and still predict complex poses of multi-animal video sequences at interactive speed.

3D Animal Pose Estimation. In [15] Dunn *et al.* use a 3D CNN similar to [26] to infer 3D poses of single rodents from multi-view. This approach comes at the cost of longer run times. In [4,21,28,30,40] the authors use a 2D pose estimator (e.g. [38,41]) to predict 2D keypoints that they then triangulate to 3D. We notice that all these 3D frameworks exploit 2D keypoints, and can thus also use our method as a base.

2.2 Animal Tracking

Romero-Ferrero *et al.* in [49] and Heras *et al.* in [24] use the software idtracker.ai [17] to track up to 100 zebrafish at once. The software needs to know the number of individuals beforehand since it performs an individual identification in each frame. Idtracker.ai does not predict keypoints of the individuals, whereas TRex [51] estimates 2D head and rear of bilateral animals while tracking up to 256 individuals in real-time using background subtraction.

2D Animal Pose Estimation and Tracking. DeepLabCut [38] is further extended in [34] to track multiple mice, pups, marmosets and fish. The authors split the workflow in local and global animal tracking. For local animal tracking they build on SORT [8], a simple online tracking approach. For animals that are closely interacting or in case of occlusions they introduce a global tracking method by optimizing the local tracklets with a global minimization problem using multiple cost functions on the basis of the animals' shape or motion for example. In contrast to this work, we focus on online tracking thus using only SORT [8]. In principal our method can also be post-processed to optimize the local tracklets obtained from SORT [8].

SLEAP [47] uses a tracker based on Kalman filter or flow shift inspired by [55] for candidate generation to track multiple individuals. As mentioned beforehand they also do 2D multi-animal pose estimation.

3   Technical Framework

We will explain the data acquisition of our pigeon data, introduce briefly the two datasets with which we train I-MuPPET in order to compare our framework to [38] and [3] (cf. Sects. 4.2 and 4.3), describe the technical framework behind I-MuPPET and discuss several ablation studies.

3.1   Datasets

Data Acquisition. Our pigeon data is recorded with a Vicon motion capture system. The system consists of six Vue 2, four Vantage 5 and 26 Vero 2.2 sensors covering a volume of approximately $15 \times 7 \times 4$ meters, see Fig. 1 and the supplemental material. Two Vue cameras were used to record the RGB video sequences of single pigeons, while the 30 infrared sensors captured the positions of the pigeons within an area of approximately 5×5 meters.

Single Pigeon Data. In total we have 27730 annotated RGB frames (13532 frames from one camera view, 14198 from the other) with a resolution of $1920 \times 1080 \times 3$ pixels available on which only one single pigeon is present (cf. Figure 2, first row). The annotated frames contain the 2D positions of seven distinct body landmarks (beak tip, nose, left and right eye, left and right shoulder and tail, cf. Figure 1) plus the coordinates of a bounding box containing the object. These annotations are obtained in a semi-automatic manner (cf. [39]). For more details regarding our data see our supplemental material.

Multi-Pigeon Data. In addition, we have RGB video sequences of multiple pigeons available (cf. Figure 2, second row). At the moment we do not have ground truth annotations for individual keypoints of the multi-pigeon video sequences. We do have bounding boxes for the multi-pigeon sequences that we use as ground truth for a quantitative tracking evaluation (cf. Sect. 4.4). To

Fig. 2. *Pigeon Data.* Sample frames of our data set. First row shows images from our annotated single pigeon data set. Second row from our multi-pigeon data. Best viewed in color version online.

obtain these bounding boxes we perform a simple background subtraction and validate the bounding boxes with the 3D Vicon positions of the pigeons projected into the camera images.

Data set (upon request) along with accompanying source code to reproduce the results of this paper are publicly available at https://urs-waldmann.github.io/i-muppet/.

Odor Trail Tracking Data. This data from [38] contains single mice following an odor and contains 1080 manually annotated samples. The samples are random, distinct frames from multiple sessions observing seven different mice [38] and the resolution of the images is 640×480 or 800×800 since the data were recorded with two different monochromatic cameras.

Cowbird Data. This data from [3] contains single cowbirds. Their original images have a maximum resolution of 1920×1200 containing multiple birds. For 2D pose estimation they use 1000 cropped samples of single individuals from a subset of 18 moments across six of the 10 days [3] with a resolution of 256×256.

For more details on these two datasets we refer to [3,38]. We use them to train I-MuPPET in order to compare the accuracy in pose estimation to that of [38] and [3].

3.2 Pose Estimation and Tracking

The core components of our framework are a Keypoint R-CNN [22] and the SORT tracker [8], see Fig. 3.

The Keypoint R-CNN is a PyTorch [44] implementation of a Mask R-CNN [22], which is modified to output seven keypoints (beak tip, nose, left and right eye, left and right shoulder and tail) for each detected instance, in addition to a score, label (background vs. object) and bounding box. Like DeepLabCut [38], our network has a ResNet-50-FPN [23,36] backbone that was pretrained on ImageNet [14], similar to [22]. For details, we refer to [22]. The input to the network are RGB images (cf. Figure 3) normalized to mean and standard deviation of 0.5. The network is trained in a fully supervised manner using

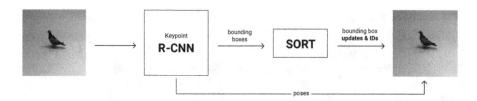

Fig. 3. *I-MuPPET.* For inference the input image (here one pigeon cropped for better view) is passed to the Keypoint R-CNN [22] that predicts bounding boxes and poses of all instances. The bounding boxes are passed to SORT [8] that returns bounding box updates with their associated ID.

stochastic gradient descent with learning rate decay, momentum and weight decay. For training, the network expects ground truth labels, bounding boxes and keypoints in addition to the normalized RGB images.

We also implement data augmentation for training in order to avoid overfitting and to mimic other conditions than those present in the single pigeon data. This expands the training set, which turns out to also lead to better results in multi-pigeon pose estimation when trained on data with only single pigeons present. Specifically, our input data has a specific probability to be flipped, scaled within a specified range, and changed in brightness or sharpness.

The SORT tracker [8] accepts the bounding boxes from all pigeon instances in every frame that exceed a given score threshold and outputs updated bounding boxes with their associated ID using a combination of Kalman Filter [29] and Hungarian algorithm [32]. We chose this method since we are primarily interested in online tracking and high inference speed, and SORT [8] can run up to 260 fps. We use standard parameters and refer to [8] for details.

3.3   Network Training and Ablation Studies

Data Augmentation for Pigeons. For data augmentation we find that changing brightness, flipping or scaling do not enhance performance, but changing sharpness with a probability of 0.2 results in the best performance (for numbers cf. supplemental material). This is intuitive since we train and test on the single pigeon data (cf. Figure 2, first row) where the training data already contains a wide range of different pigeon positions and lightning conditions, and thus covers most of the scaling and brightness. Also the training data already include most body orientations (with respect to the camera), thus flipping does not improve test accuracy. Since the depth of field of the cameras is limited the pigeons are sometimes slightly out of focus and therefore blurring the input image with a small probability of 0.2 improves the accuracy of the test set.

In case of multi-pigeon video sequences, however, we find that the best data augmentation parameters are not the same as for the single pigeon data set. We keep the parameters from the single pigeon analysis but find that randomly jittering brightness by a factor chosen uniformly from [0.4, 1.6] and a flipping probability of 0.5 is best. This is intuitive because the single pigeon data (cf.

Figure 2, first row) does not cover the range of brightness found in the multi-pigeon data (cf. Figure 2, second row) plus the flipping makes the pose estimation in new situations more robust. A small scaling range of ±5% is sufficient since the single pigeon data covers already a large range of pigeon sizes. Also, if the scaling range is too large, we find multiple (mis-)detections if pigeons are nearby. This is also the case in situations where the pigeons occlude or are close to each other even if we do not apply scaling.

Data Augmentation for Cowbirds. The cowbird data set is recorded in outdoor aviaries [3]. Thus different day light and season conditions are present. To consider these different conditions inherent in the data, we use different data augmentation parameters. We find that randomly changing brightness by a factor chosen uniformly from $[0.7, 1.3]$, and a sharpness probability of 0.1, works best (for numbers cf. supplemental material).

Training Hyperparameters. To find out the best network configuration for I-MuPPET we perform several experiments (see supplemental material). From this analysis we find that using a learning rate of 0.005 and reducing it by $\gamma = 0.5$ every given step size to reach a final learning rate of 0.0003 at the end of training works best.

4   Evaluation

We quantitatively evaluate I-MuPPET on our annotated single pigeon data (RMSE in Sect. 4.2, PCK in Sect. 4.3). In addition we evaluate our framework on the odor trail tracking data set from [38] and the cowbird data set from [3]. In this way we can compare the performance of I-MuPPET to the 2D pose estimators used in [3,38]. We also evaluate the I-MuPPET tracking performance in terms of accuracy, precision and speed on a workstation with an nVidia Titan RTX, 64 GB DDR4 RAM, an Intel Xeon E5-2620 at 2.10 GHz and a 2 TB Samsung SSD 850.

4.1   Metrics

Pose Estimation. Two widely used metrics, also in human pose estimation, are the Root Mean Square Error (RMSE), in human pose estimation better known as Mean Per Joint Position Error (MPJPE, cf. e.g. [26]), and the Percentage of Correct Keypoints (PCK, cf. e.g. [56]). DeepLabCut [38] uses the former, 3D Bird Reconstruction [3] the latter. Note that PCK properly takes into account scale, and thus this accuracy measure is more meaningful than RMSE. Both metrics assume that all keypoints in all frames can be predicted.

Tracking. There are three sets of tracking performance measures that are widely used in the literature [13]: the CLEAR-MOT metrics introduced in [6], the metrics introduced in [35] to measure track quality, and the trajectory-based metrics proposed in [48]. Additionally, we report the new Higher Order Tracking

Accuracy (HOTA). It was introduced in [37] because the other metrics overemphasize the importance of either detection or association. HOTA measures how well the trajectories of matching detections align, and averages this over all matching detections, while also penalising detections that do not match [37].

For further details we refer to [13,37]. We use [27] for evaluation.

4.2   Comparison with DeepLabCut

DeepLabCut [38] is state of the art for 2D animal pose estimation. In the article the authors evaluate and report numbers in terms of RMSE on their odor trail tracking data where they estimate the pose (snout, left and right ear and tail base) of single mice. That is why we also report RMSE only in this section. The networks are trained a total of 650K iterations with batch size 1 for three splits of 0.8/0.2 (training/test) and evaluated every 50K iterations. The authors also report the average of the three splits. For more details see [38].

Table 1. *Comparison with DeepLabCut (DLC).* RMSE on the odor trail tracking test set from [38]. Values for DLC from [38]. We report precision within ±0.2 because we have to read values from Fig. 2c in [38].

Model, iterations	RMSE [px]
I-MuPPET, 200K iterations	4.2
DLC, 200K iterations	3.6 ± 0.2
DLC, 350K/600K iterations	$\mathbf{3.2 \pm 0.2}$

In order to compare I-MuPPET to DeepLabCut, we train their odor trail tracking data set with our framework. In addition we randomly sample 1000 frames from our full single pigeon data set. This sub data set represents our four sessions in the same way as our full single pigeon data set. We train our framework on the DeepLabCut and our sub-sampled single pigeon data with the configuration that we report in Sect. 3.3. We train for 250 epochs with a batch size of 20 instead of 1 to exploit our hardware and fine-tune twice for another 250 epochs with training configurations that lower the learning rate further to compare our results to those of DeepLabCut after 200K, 400K and 600K iterations.

Table 1 compares results for DeepLabCut from [38] with our framework. We obtained the results for DeepLabCut from Fig. 2c in [38]. These results were achieved with a network based on ResNet-50. We report their values for 200K iterations and their absolute lowest RMSE on test set averaged over the three 0.8/0.2 splits. For our framework we report numbers with the same precision as we are able to read for DeepLabCut. We report numbers for 200K iterations only because our network does not improve the accuracy of pose estimation in the test set when trained for more iterations: 4.2 px@200K (cf. Table 1) on the odor trail tracking test set from DeepLabCut averaged over the three splits, 3.2 px@200K on our sub-sampled single pigeon test set averaged over the three splits.

I-MuPPET is comparable with DeepLabCut in terms of RMSE meaning that we also achieve a RMSE of about 4 px on the odor trail tracking test set. In addition, we achieve a RMSE of about 3 px for our sub-sampled single pigeon data set, both after 200K training iterations. Overall, this comparison shows that I-MuPPET achieves performance on par with state-of-the-art.

4.3   Comparison with 3D Bird Reconstruction

3D Bird Reconstruction [3] is state of the art for 3D bird shape recovery, and they also report on accuracy on 2D bird pose estimation. The authors evaluate and report numbers in terms of PCK (cf. Sect. 4.1) on their cowbird data, where they estimate the pose (bill tip, right and left eyes, neck, nape, right and left wrists, right and left wing tips, right and left feet and the tail tip) of single cowbirds. Their network is trained for 60 epochs (private e-mail communication with the authors) with a train/test split of 0.75/0.25. For more details see [3].

Table 2. *Comparison with 3D Bird Reconstruction (3DBR).* PCK on the cowbird test set from [3]. Values for 3DBR from [3].

Model, epochs	@0.05	@0.1
I-MuPPET, 45 epochs	0.39	0.56
I-MuPPET, 60 epochs	0.36	0.54
3DBR, 60 epochs	**0.46**	**0.64**

In order to compare I-MuPPET to 3D Bird Reconstruction, we train their single cowbird data with our framework. In addition we take the same single pigeon sub data set containing 1000 frames (cf. Sect. 4.2) to report PCK on our pigeon data. We remind the reader that PCK properly takes into account scale, and thus this accuracy measure is more meaningful than RMSE (cf. Sect. 4.1) reported in Sect. 4.2. We train our framework (cf. Sect. 3.2) on the cowbird and our sub-sampled pigeon data with the configuration that we report in Sect. 3.3. We train for 60 epochs with a batch size of 20 to compare our results to those of 3D Bird Reconstruction. Our framework achieves best performance on the cowbird data after 45 epochs, which is why we report PCK for these as well.

Sect. 2 compares results for 3D Bird Reconstruction from [3] with our framework. While I-MuPPET achieves lower accuracy by 7% (PCK@0.05) and 8% (PCK@0.1) on the cowbird data set than 3D Bird reconstruction, I-MuPPET converges faster (45 epochs vs. 60 epochs). In addition, we achieve a PCK of 0.94@0.05 and 0.97@0.1 for our sub-sampled single pigeon data set after 60 training epochs.

Table 3. *Combined Quantitative Tracking Evaluation.* We test 24 video sequences quantitatively with the metrics specified in Sect. 4.1. Here we report the combined results for different detection confidence scores of the Keypoint R-CNN (cf. Sect. 3.2). The space is unfortunately not sufficient to explain all abbreviations and metrics in detail, please refer to our supplemental material.

conf. score	HOTA↑	MOTA↑	MOTP↑	Rcll↑	Prcn↑	MT↑	ML↓	FP↓	IDS↓	Frag↓	IDF1↑
0	0.53	0.48	**0.61**	**0.83**	0.70	**0.64**	**0.01**	0.99	24	292	0.75
0.5	**0.57**	0.65	**0.61**	**0.83**	0.83	**0.64**	**0.01**	0.49	**8**	278	0.82
0.75	**0.57**	0.67	**0.61**	**0.83**	0.84	**0.64**	**0.01**	0.44	11	280	**0.83**
0.9	0.56	**0.68**	**0.61**	0.82	**0.85**	**0.64**	**0.01**	**0.39**	14	**277**	**0.83**

Fig. 4. *Qualitative Results of I-MuPPET.* Cropped sample frames of our pipeline. Left body side of pigeon in red, right one in blue and beak in orange. First and second, third and fourth row are from video sequences with one, two, three and four pigeons present respectively. Sometimes not all pigeons are present in cropped frame for a better view.

4.4 I-MuPPET Tracking Performance

The availability of annotated data from animals is limited, especially for multiple individuals. To overcome this obstacle, we train our Keypoint R-CNN (cf. Sect. 3.2) on our single pigeon data (cf. Sect. 3.1) and infer 2D keypoints on multi-pigeon video sequences. In addition we track the individuals with SORT (cf. Sect. 3.2). We do so for up to four pigeons present in the videos. The video sequence with one pigeon present is not from our labeled single pigeon data set.

Figure 4 shows results of the 2D pose estimation and tracking task for multiple pigeons. The 2D keypoint locations show a very good accuracy even though I-MuPPET was trained on single pigeon data only. The individuals are tracked correctly. See also our supplementary video sequences.

Quantitative Tracking Evaluation. We test I-MuPPET quantitatively on 24 video sequences recorded with 50 fps. They contain between one and four pigeons and 7872 frames and 70 objects in total. For evaluation we use the metrics specified in Sect. 4.1. In Table 3 we report the combined results of the 24 video sequences for different detection confidence scores. We see that tracking does not improve much when setting the detection score from 0.5 to 0.75. We get the best tracking results for a confidence score of 0.9. Detailed results for this detection confidence score of 0.9 are shown in Table 4. We achieve an overall good result with I-MuPPET on the video sequences (HOTA: 0.56, MOTA: 0.68, MOTP: 0.61, Recall: 0.82, Precision: 0.85 and IDF1: 0.83).

By far the worst sequence with respect to tracking accuracy is 4_pigeons_8. In this sequence the four pigeons walk towards the edge of the facility that in the camera view appears darker than it does otherwise. In cases of high fragments (frag), e.g. sequences 2_pigeons_3 and 4_pigeons_9, the video sequences show the same darker regions. Please note that this can be solved by simply setting the SORT [8] parameter to keep alive a track without associated detections to a value higher than 1. We leave it at 1 since we are interested in online tracking and not in re-identification. Thus early deletion of lost targets improves efficiency.

Table 4. *Detailed Quantitative Tracking Evaluation.* We test 24 video sequences quantitatively with the metrics specified in Sect. 4.1. The threshold for the confidence score of the Keypoint R-CNN (cf. Sect. 3.2) is set to 0.9.

Video seq.	HOTA↑	MOTA↑	MOTP↑	Rcll↑	Prcn↑	MT↑	ML↓	FPF↓	IDS↓	Frag↓	IDF1↑
1_pigeon_1	0.64	1	0.65	1	1	1	0	0	0	0	1
1_pigeon_2	0.58	0.89	0.62	0.94	0.94	1	0	0.06	0	2	0.94
1_pigeon_3	0.57	0.96	0.59	0.98	0.98	1	0	0.02	0	7	0.98
2_pigeons_1	0.53	0.57	0.56	0.78	0.78	0.50	0	0.43	0	1	0.78
2_pigeons_2	0.56	0.99	0.57	0.99	0.99	1	0	0.01	0	2	0.99
2_pigeons_3	0.57	0.76	0.58	0.88	0.88	0.50	0	0.24	0	30	0.88
2_pigeons_4	0.60	0.94	0.60	0.97	0.97	1	0	0.06	0	2	0.97
2_pigeons_5	0.65	0.99	0.66	0.99	1	1	0	0	1	1	0.99
2_pigeons_6	0.69	1	0.69	1	1	1	0	0	0	0	1
3_pigeons_1	0.57	0.50	0.60	0.75	0.75	0.67	0	0.74	0	27	0.75
3_pigeons_2	0.57	0.81	0.59	0.90	0.91	0.67	0	0.28	0	11	0.91
3_pigeons_3	0.59	0.91	0.60	0.96	0.96	1	0	0.13	0	7	0.96
3_pigeons_4	0.64	0.73	0.66	0.87	0.87	0.67	0	0.40	0	17	0.87
3_pigeons_5	0.62	0.82	0.64	0.91	0.91	0.67	0	0.27	0	7	0.91
4_pigeons_1	0.47	0.49	0.56	0.73	0.75	0.50	0	0.95	2	23	0.72
4_pigeons_2	0.46	0.32	0.55	0.60	0.68	0.25	0	1.14	2	19	0.64
4_pigeons_3	0.48	0.75	0.57	0.84	0.90	0.75	0	0.36	3	16	0.82
4_pigeons_4	0.59	0.62	0.65	0.80	0.82	0.75	0	0.73	1	6	0.80
4_pigeons_5	0.63	1	0.64	1	1	1	0	0	0	0	1
4_pigeons_6	0.54	0.77	0.60	0.85	0.91	0.50	0	0.33	0	5	0.88
4_pigeons_7	0.55	0.53	0.63	0.76	0.76	0.50	0	0.93	1	12	0.76
4_pigeons_8	0.29	−0.09	0.55	0.26	0.42	0	0	1.38	1	25	0.29
4_pigeons_9	0.50	0.47	0.59	0.73	0.74	0.25	0	1	1	52	0.71
4_pigeons_10	0.46	0.44	0.58	0.69	0.74	0.75	0.25	0.97	2	5	0.63
Combined	0.56	0.68	0.61	0.82	0.85	0.64	0.01	0.39	14	277	0.83

Inference Speed. We also benchmark the inference speed of I-MuPPET (cf. Sect. 3.2) with the four videos from our supplemental material. The benchmark includes the complete pipeline except for loading the model. It includes also I/O times reading the images from our AVI video sequences (encoded with libx264). We loop three times over the full video sequence, repeat this procedure three times and calculate the average. We obtain an interactive speed of about $12 - 13$ fps (cf. Table 5) for our full pipeline. Interestingly, speed is almost independent from the number of pigeons present in the video.

Table 5. *I-MuPPET Inference Speed.* Benchmark for our complete pipeline. We process our pipeline frame by frame which also includes I/O times reading the images from our AVI video sequences. Values for different number of pigeons differ by 1 fps at most.

	1 pigeon	2 pigeons	3 pigeons	4 pigeons
Frame rate [fps]	13.1	13.0	12.5	12.1

We also benchmark the scenario where we preload the video sequence in memory and are thus independent of disk I/O, with otherwise the same procedure, see Table 6 for results. We report values for batch sizes up to 32, after which we do not observe any speed-up. The speed of our pipeline increases for a batch size of 1 by about 1 fps (comparing Table 5 with Table 6) if we preload the video to memory. The maximum speed is at batch size 16 and 32 with an interactive speed of about $16 - 17$ fps depending on the number of pigeons present in the video sequence.

There are two frameworks which also perform 2D keypoint prediction of complex poses and tracking: maDLC [34] and SLEAP [47]. maDLC [34] does not report numbers on inference speed. SLEAP [47] instead reports numbers and also compares to a SLEAP version of a DLC ResNet model for multi-instance pose estimation. Their benchmark procedure and hardware is comparable to

Table 6. *I-MuPPET Inference Speed.* Benchmark for our in-memory pipeline. We benchmark our pipeline with our AVI video sequences preloaded in memory and report values for different batch sizes.

Batch size	frame rate [fps]			
	1 pigeon	2 pigeons	3 pigeons	4 pigeons
1	14.5	14.1	13.8	13.5
2	15.2	14.4	14.6	14.4
4	15.6	15.3	14.9	14.8
8	16.1	15.5	15.5	15.0
16	17.1	16.8	**16.3**	**16.1**
32	**17.4**	**16.9**	16.2	15.9

Fig. 5. *Limitations.* Cropped frames of failure cases. See Fig. 1 for an explanation of colors and labels.

ours. For details we refer to [47]. A rough comparison yields that I-MuPPET is comparable in inference speed with the DLC ResNet version of SLEAP. SLEAP [47] instead is about an order of magnitude faster than our framework (numbers read off from [47], Figs. 2b, 3e and Extended Data Fig. 6c; considering the fact that the pigeon image resolution is higher than the one of the flies and mice (open field) and thus we process more data through the whole pipeline). While I-MuPPET solves the substantially harder task of a 'generalist' approach of training a single model that works on all datasets, SLEAP uses a 'specialist' paradigm where small, lightweight models have just enough representational capacity to generalize to the low variability typically found in scientific data [47]. The approach of I-MuPPET comes with an additional cost of compute resource requirements. Albeit with I-MuPPET we want to offer a framework that works with both low and high variability data at the same time, depending on the application, one can easily change the pose estimator of I-MuPPET to achieve frame rates comparable to SLEAP.

4.5 Limitations and Future Work

From Fig. 5 we see that in some frames of the multi-pigeon video sequences, pose estimation is not accurate. In addition the bounding box detector fails in cases where pigeons are too close together, or occlude each other, since we trained it only on single pigeon data. This also affects the pose estimation in this case. Both of these situations can probably be improved by exploiting labeled multi-instance data. Since availability is limited one approach is to synthetically exploit the single instance data. There currently are no instances of occlusions in our multi-pigeon video sequences, we intend to create more varied datasets to assess performance in more complex scenarios.

5 Conclusion

In this work we present I-MuPPET, an interactive multi-pigeon pose estimation and tracking system. While training a neural network only on single pigeon training data, we demonstrate that we can still predict keypoints of a complex pose (seven distinct keypoints) for multiple pigeons and track the individuals at interactive speed of 12.1 − 17.4 fps. I-MuPPET has also a comparable accuracy with DeepLabCut [38] in terms of RMSE with respect to the estimation of

2D animal keypoints. Furthermore we perform a quantitative tracking evaluation on 24 video sequences and obtain good results (HOTA: 0.56, MOTA: 0.68, MOTP: 0.61, Recall: 0.82, Precision: 0.85 and IDF1: 0.83). We hope that this work inspires researchers to improve upon our baseline and pose estimation and tracking of multiple animals in general. As discussed above, we have strived to give a fair comparison, but due to the limitations in the reported data and the different domains of the methods, this comparison can not be fully rigorous. However, it gives, in our opinion, sufficient information to indicate the competitive performance of the proposed framework. Nevertheless, our future work will additionally focus on more datasets for a more comprehensive quantitative performance comparison of animal pose estimation and tracking across different species, which we believe is necessary to make further systematic progress.

References

1. Altmann, J.: Observational study of behavior: sampling methods. Behaviour **49**(3–4), 227–266 (1974)
2. Anderson, D., Perona, P.: Toward a science of computational ethology. Neuron **84**(1), 18–31 (2014)
3. Badger, M., et al.: 3d bird reconstruction: a dataset, model, and shape recovery from a single view. In: ECCV, pp. 1–17 (2020)
4. Bala, P.C., Eisenreich, B.R., Yoo, S.B.M., Hayden, B.Y., Park, H.S., Zimmermann, J.: Automated markerless pose estimation in freely moving macaques with open-MonkeyStudio. Nat. Commun. **11**, 4560 (2020)
5. Berman, G.J.: Measuring behavior across scales. BMC Biol. **16**(23), 1–11 (2018)
6. Bernardin, K., Stiefelhagen, R.: Evaluating multiple object tracking performance: the clear mot metrics. EURASIP J. Image Video Process. **2008**, 1–10 (2008)
7. Bernshtein, N.: The Co-ordination and Regulation of Movements. Pergamon Press (1967)
8. Bewley, A., Ge, Z., Ott, L., Ramos, F., Upcroft, B.: Simple online and realtime tracking. In: ICIP, pp. 3464–3468 (2016)
9. Biggs, B., Roddick, T., Fitzgibbon, A., Cipolla, R.: Creatures great and SMAL: recovering the shape and motion of animals from video. In: Jawahar, C.V., Li, H., Mori, G., Schindler, K. (eds.) ACCV 2018. LNCS, vol. 11365, pp. 3–19. Springer, Cham (2019). https://doi.org/10.1007/978-3-030-20873-8_1
10. Bolaños, L.A., et al.: A three-dimensional virtual mouse generates synthetic training data for behavioral analysis. Nat. Methods **18**, 378–381 (2021)
11. Chen, X., Zhai, H., Liu, D., Li, W., Ding, C., Xie, Q., Han, H.: SiamBOMB: a real-time AI-based system for home-cage animal tracking, segmentation and behavioral analysis. In: IJCAI, pp. 5300–5302 (2020)
12. Dell, A.I., et al.: Automated image-based tracking and its application in ecology. Trends Ecol. Evol. **29**(7), 417–428 (2014)
13. Dendorfer, P., et al.: MOTChallenge: a benchmark for single-camera multiple target tracking. Int. J. Comput. Vis. **129**(4), 845–881 (2020). https://doi.org/10.1007/s11263-020-01393-0
14. Deng, J., Dong, W., Socher, R., Li, L.J., Li, K., Fei-Fei, L.: ImageNet: a large-scale hierarchical image database. In: CVPR, pp. 248–255 (2009)
15. Dunn, T.W., et al.: Geometric deep learning enables 3D kinematic profiling across species and environments. Nat. Methods **18**(5), 564–573 (2021)

16. Duporge, I., Isupova, O., Reece, S., Macdonald, D.W., Wang, T.: Using very-high-resolution satellite imagery and deep learning to detect and count African elephants in heterogeneous landscapes. Remote Sens. Ecol. Conserv. **7**(3), 369–381 (2021)

17. Ferrero, F.R., Bergomi, M.G., Heras, F.J., Hinz, R., de Polavieja, G.G.: The champalimaud foundation: idtracker.ai (2017). https://idtrackerai.readthedocs.io/en/latest

18. Gomez-Marin, A., Paton, J.J., Kampff, A.R., Costa, R.M., Mainen, Z.F.: Big behavioral data: psychology, ethology and the foundations of neuroscience. Nat. Neurosci. **17**, 1455–1462 (2014)

19. Gosztolai, A., et al.: Liftpose3D, a deep learning-based approach for transforming two-dimensional to three-dimensional poses in laboratory animals. Nat. Methods **18**, 975–981 (2021)

20. Graving, J.M., et al.: Deepposekit, a software toolkit for fast and robust animal pose estimation using deep learning. eLife **8**, e47994 (2019)

21. Günel, S., Rhodin, H., Morales, D., Campagnolo, J., Ramdya, P., Fua, P.: Deepfly3D, a deep learning-based approach for 3D limb and appendage tracking in tethered, adult Drosophila. eLife **8**, e48571 (2019)

22. He, K., Gkioxari, G., Dollar, P., Girshick, R.: Mask R-CNN. In: ICCV (2017)

23. He, K., Zhang, X., Ren, S., Sun, J.: Deep residual learning for image recognition. In: CVPR (2016)

24. Heras, F.J.H., Romero-Ferrero, F., Hinz, R.C., de Polavieja, G.G.: Deep attention networks reveal the rules of collective motion in zebrafish. PLOS Comput. Biol. **15**(9), 1–23 (2019)

25. Ionescu, C., Papava, D., Olaru, V., Sminchisescu, C.: Human3.6M: large scale datasets and predictive methods for 3D human sensing in natural environments. IEEE Trans. Pattern Anal. Mach. Intell. **36**(7), 1325–1339 (2014)

26. Iskakov, K., Burkov, E., Lempitsky, V., Malkov, Y.: Learnable triangulation of human pose. In: ICCV (2019)

27. Jonathon Luiten, A.H.: Trackeval. https://github.com/JonathonLuiten/TrackEval (2020)

28. Joska, D., et al.: AcinoSet: a 3D pose estimation dataset and baseline models for cheetahs in the wild. In: 2021 IEEE International Conference on Robotics and Automation (ICRA), pp. 13901–13908 (2021). https://doi.org/10.1109/ICRA48506.2021.9561338

29. Kalman, R.E.: A new approach to linear filtering and prediction problems. J. Basic Eng. **82**(1), 35–45 (1960)

30. Karashchuk, P., et al.: Anipose: a toolkit for robust markerless 3D pose estimation. Cell Rep. **36**(13), 109730 (2021)

31. Kays, R., Crofoot, M.C., Jetz, W., Wikelski, M.: Terrestrial animal tracking as an eye on life and planet. Science **348**(6240), aaa2478 (2015)

32. Kuhn, H.W.: The Hungarian method for the assignment problem. Naval Res. Logist. Q. **2**(1–2), 83–97 (1955)

33. Labuguen, R., et al.: MacaquePose: a novel "in the wild" macaque monkey pose dataset for markerless motion capture. Front. Behav. Neurosci. **14**, 268 (2021)

34. Lauer, J., et al.: Multi-animal pose estimation, identification and tracking with DeepLabCut. Nat. Methods **19**, 496–504 (2022)

35. Li, Y., Huang, C., Nevatia, R.: Learning to associate: HybridBoosted multi-target tracker for crowded scene. In: CVPR, pp. 2953–2960 (2009)

36. Lin, T.Y., Dollar, P., Girshick, R., He, K., Hariharan, B., Belongie, S.: Feature pyramid networks for object detection. In: CVPR (2017)

37. Dendorfer, P., et al.: HOTA: a higher order metric for evaluating multi-object tracking. Int. J. Comput. Vis. **129**(2), 548–578 (2021). https://doi.org/10.1007/s11263-020-01375-2

38. Mathis, A., et al.: DeepLabCut: markerless pose estimation of user-defined body parts with deep learning. Nat. Neurosci. **21**, 1281–1289 (2018)

39. Naik, H.: XR For all: Closed-loop Visual Stimulation Techniques for Human and Non-Human Animals. Dissertation, Technische Universität München, München (2021)

40. Nath, T., Mathis, A., Chen, A.C., Patel, A., Bethge, M., Mathis, M.W.: Using DeepLabCut for 3D markerless pose estimation across species and behaviors. Nat. Protoc. **14**, 2152–2176 (2019)

41. Newell, A., Yang, K., Deng, J.: Stacked hourglass networks for human pose estimation. In: ECCV, pp. 483–499 (2016)

42. Nourizonoz, A., et al.: EthoLoop: automated closed-loop neuroethology in naturalistic environments. Nat. Methods **17**, 1052–1059 (2020)

43. Park, H.S., Rhodin, H., Kanazawa, A., Neverova, N., Nobuhara, S., Black, M.: Cv4Animals: computer vision for animal behavior tracking and modeling (2021). https://www.cv4animals.com/

44. Paszke, A., et al.: PyTorch: an imperative style, high-performance deep learning library. In: NeurIPS (2019)

45. Pedersen, M., Haurum, J.B., Bengtson, S.H., Moeslund, T.B.: 3D-ZeF: a 3D zebrafish tracking benchmark dataset. In: CVPR (2020)

46. Pereira, T.D., et al.: Fast animal pose estimation using deep neural networks. Nat. Methods **16**, 117–125 (2019)

47. Pereira, T.D., et al.: SLEAP: a deep learning system for multi-animal pose tracking. Nat. Methods **19**, 486–495 (2022)

48. Ristani, E., Solera, F., Zou, R., Cucchiara, R., Tomasi, C.: Performance measures and a data set for multi-target, multi-camera tracking. In: ECCV, pp. 17–35 (2016)

49. Romero-Ferrero, F., Bergomi, M.G., Hinz, R.C., Heras, F.J.H., de Polavieja, G.G.: idtracker.ai: tracking all individuals in small or large collectives of unmarked animals. Nat. Methods **16**, 179–182 (2019)

50. Van Horn, G., et al.: Building a bird recognition app and large scale dataset with citizen scientists: the fine print in fine-grained dataset collection. In: CVPR (2015)

51. Walter, T., Couzin, I.D.: Trex, a fast multi-animal tracking system with markerless identification, and 2D estimation of posture and visual fields. eLife **10**, e64000 (2021)

52. Wang, J., Yuille, A.L.: Semantic part segmentation using compositional model combining shape and appearance. In: CVPR (2015)

53. Wang, P., Shen, X., Lin, Z., Cohen, S., Price, B., Yuille, A.L.: Joint object and part segmentation using deep learned potentials. In: ICCV (2015)

54. Welinder, P., et al.: Caltech-UCSD Birds 200. Tech. Rep. CNS-TR-2010-001, California Institute of Technology (2010)

55. Xiao, B., Wu, H., Wei, Y.: Simple baselines for human pose estimation and tracking. In: ECCV (2018)

56. Yang, Y., Ramanan, D.: Articulated human detection with flexible mixtures of parts. IEEE Trans. Pattern Anal. Mech. Intell. **35**(12), 2878–2890 (2013)

Interpretable Prediction of Pulmonary Hypertension in Newborns Using Echocardiograms

Hanna Ragnarsdottir[1], Laura Manduchi[1], Holger Michel[2], Fabian Laumer[1], Sven Wellmann[2], Ece Ozkan[1(✉)], and Julia E. Vogt[1]

[1] Department of Computer Science, ETH Zürich, Zürich, Switzerland
ece.oezkanelsen@inf.ethz.ch
[2] Department of Neonatology, University Children's Hospital Regensburg (KUNO), Regensburg, Germany

Abstract. Pulmonary hypertension (PH) in newborns and infants is a complex condition associated with several pulmonary, cardiac, and systemic diseases contributing to morbidity and mortality. Therefore, accurate and early detection of PH is crucial for successful management. Using echocardiography, the primary diagnostic tool in pediatrics, human assessment is both time-consuming and expertise-demanding, raising the need for an automated approach. In this work, we present an interpretable multi-view video-based deep learning approach to predict PH for a cohort of 194 newborns using echocardiograms. We use spatio-temporal convolutional architectures for the prediction of PH from each view, and aggregate the predictions of the different views using majority voting. To the best of our knowledge, this is the first work for an automated assessment of PH in newborns using echocardiograms. Our results show a mean F1-score of 0.84 for severity prediction and 0.92 for binary detection using 10-fold cross-validation. We complement our predictions with saliency maps and show that the learned model focuses on clinically relevant cardiac structures, motivating its usage in clinical practice.

Keywords: Echocardiography · Pediatrics · Computer Assisted Diagnosis (CAD) · Interpretable machine learning

1 Introduction

Pulmonary hypertension (PH) is a complex condition that can affect newborns and children as well as adults and is formally defined as an increased mean pulmonary artery pressure (PAP) at rest [13]. The level of PAP in newborns is

H. Ragnarsdottir and L. Manduchi—Shared first authorship
E. Ozkan and J. E. Vogt—Shared last authorship

Supplementary Information The online version contains supplementary material available at https://doi.org/10.1007/978-3-031-16788-1_32.

frequently high and it is expected to decrease after birth to reach a level comparable to healthy adult values [4]. When the normal cardiopulmonary transition fails to occur, the newborns are affected by persistent pulmonary hypertension of the newborn (PPHN), which is associated with bronchopulmonary dysplasia in older premature infants and various chronic pulmonary, cardiac, and systemic diseases for newborns at term contributing to morbidity and mortality [9,13,28].

The gold standard for PH diagnosis is right heart catheterisation (RHC). However, due to its invasive nature of this costly procedure and the resulting high risk of related complications, especially in the pediatrics age group [24], RHC is not a screening procedure. Echocardiography, on the other hand, is recommended as a non-invasive screening tool for PH using its two modes: 2D echocardiography videos (ECHOs) and Doppler echocardiograms [20,23]. It is one of the most common and growing diagnostic tools due to its low-cost, portable, and non-invasive technology, which makes it an ideal choice for pediatrics [20].

Screening of PH typically involves estimating PAP with Doppler echocardiography; however, the measurements may frequently be inaccurate, thus, it is not the ultimate predictive tool to assess and manage PH [11]. Since elevated PAP can result in abnormalities in the shape and structure of the heart, subjective evaluation on ECHOs is often performed as well, i.e. to detect the abnormalities in the shape of the septal wall and changes in the right-ventricular area [12].

The aforementioned procedures for PH estimation are time-consuming and expertise-demanding, which may delay care to a more advanced stage of illness, potentially decreasing the chance of survival [2]. Thus, there is a clear need for an automatic and streamlined method to assist clinicians in the assessment of PH in newborns. With little effort being directed towards automatic approaches for PH diagnostics, this need is not being met. The few existing methods for PH prediction are only proposed for the adult population and do not assess the PH severity nor propose methods to explain the predictions [21,31].

Our Contributions. In this work, we propose a robust and interpretable deep learning approach – _i_ntepretable _p_rediction of _p_ulmonary _h_ypertension in _n_ewborns (IP-PHN) to predict and classify the severity of PH by utilising spatio-temporal patterns of the ECHOs from multiple views. To the best of our knowledge, this is the first work on multi-view video-based automated assessment of PH in newborns. To increase its clinical usability, we complement our predictions with saliency maps that highlight how the learned model focuses on clinically relevant cardiac structures. We show that these learned localization maps align with how clinicians subjectively assess PH.

To ensure the reproducibility of our work, the code was made publicly available under https://github.com/hanna15/echo_classification.

2   Related Work

Although several machine learning methods have been proposed to automatically estimate PH in adults using different input modalities, such as chest X-rays

[18,33], ECGs [19,22], heart sounds recorded by sensors [15], CTs [30], and MRIs [3,8], not much effort has been directed towards the automatic assessment of PH using echocardiography.

The two exceptions are the work of Leha et al. [21] and Zhang et al. [31], where the authors show the potential of using deep learning for predicting PH using ECHOs. The former approach relies on manually extracted ECHO parameters and applies various machine learning algorithms to predict PH. The main drawback is that the ECHO parameters must still be measured and estimated by highly trained specialists; thus, this approach does not help reduce the workload of experts. The latter approach [31], shows the potential of using deep learning for predicting PH using ECHOs, requiring no manual feature extraction. This method, however, has several limitations. First of all, it works on static frames of the ECHO videos and does not exploit the spatio-temporal patterns in the sequence. Second, it only uses a single view of the heart (apical 4-chamber view), although the literature has shown that considering multiple views improves accuracy for the manual assessment of PH [25]. Furthermore, these previous works on automatic PH detection focus on binary classification, limiting clinical usability. The determination of the severity of PH from ECHOs is crucial for correct treatment, but is a challenge for cardiologists [7,11]. Moreover, the morbidity rate is significantly increased for increased severity of PH, and thus the severity of PH determines the urgency of a treatment [6,12].

In recent years, interpretability and explainability of machine learning (ML) models have attracted much attention, and various methods aimed to help explain the reasons for a model's prediction have been proposed. This is especially true for the application of ML to healthcare, where achieving high predictive accuracy is often as important as understanding the prediction. However, the applicability of deep learning methods, such as [31], is still limited in the medical domain due to their black-box nature that makes their internal mechanisms and their results opaque.

3   Materials and Methods

3.1   Dataset

The dataset in this work consists of 2D transthoracic echocardiography videos (ECHOs) in 5 different standard views. Retrospectively, 194 newborns were examined and 536 ECHOs were performed in a single centre by a pediatric cardiologist from the Hospital Barmherzige Brüder Regensburg between the years 2019–2020. All ECHOs were performed with the GE Logic S8 ultrasound machine using the transducer S4-10 at 6 MHz.

A single ECHO contains a sequence of ultrasound images of the patient's heart at a specific view. The five views include a parasternal long-axis view (PLAX), apical four-chamber view (A4C), and three parasternal short-axis views; at the level of papillary muscles (PSAX-P), at the level of semilunar valves (PSAX-S), and on the apical short-axis view (PSAX-A). The ECHOs operate on 25 frames-per-second, and the average video length is 5 s, whereby each ECHO consists of around ten heartbeats.

Table 1. Characteristics of the dataset. It includes 194 newborns and 536 2D transthoracic echocardiography videos (ECHOs) from 5 different standard views.

Feature	Value
PH (#None (%)/#Mild(%)/#Severe(%))	126(65%)/32(16%)/36(19%)
Age (days) (Mean ± SD)	56 ± 160
Maturity in birth (days) (Mean ± SD)	230 ± 46
Patient's weight (kg) (Mean ± SD)	2.9 ± 1.5
Spatial size of original 2D images (pixels)	1440 × 866
Video length (frames)	122 ± 2
Video FPS	25 fps
Manufacturer (Ultrasound Machine/Transducer)	GE Logic S8/S4-10 at 6 MHz

The ground truth for each ECHO was manually annotated by a senior pediatric cardiologist based on the visual evaluation. The ground truth labels differentiate between none (65%), mild (16%), and moderate to severe (19%) PH. Grading was done using PSAX-P view, annotating no PH if there is no septal flattening; mild PH, if there is a decent septal flattening (curvature into the right ventricle); and moderate to severe PH if septum is bowing into the left ventricle. Furthermore, for each ECHO, its corresponding view is also annotated. A detailed overview of the data is provided in Table 1. The study was approved by the local ethics committee. In addition, all data is pseudonymized.

3.2   Preprocessing and Data Augmentation

As the first step in pre-processing the available data, we crop and mask the ECHOs to eliminate information (such as additional text or signals) outside the scanning sector and resize them to 224 x 224 pixels using bilinear interpolation. We then apply histogram equalization to distribute the pixel intensities to the full range of gray-scale values and normalize them.

During training, two types of image transformations are applied: intensity transformations so that the learned model is invariant to intensity variations, and spatial transformations to increase resilience against different zoom settings of the US machine, actual size of the heart, and/or placements of the transducer. In particular, we apply the following random transformations to each sequence: sharpness and brightness adjustment, gamma correction, addition of salt and pepper or Gaussian noise, variation of the background with different amounts of speckle noise, rotation up to 15°, translation up to 0.1x, scaling down to 0.8x, zooming up to 1.2x.

3.3   Proposed Method

We introduce an end-to-end deep learning approach, IP-PHN, to automatically assess PH severity without needing tedious manual measurements of the ventricles used in the standard clinical workflow. The dataset is inherently imbalanced

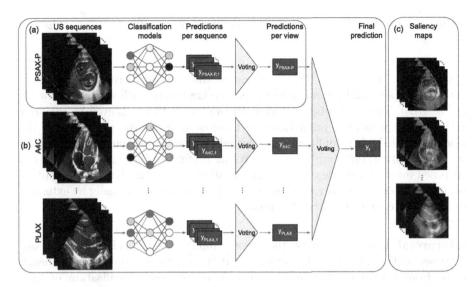

Fig. 1. Overview of our proposed method, IP-PHN, to automatically assess PH severity of a patient using (a) single view and (b) multi-view approach with majority voting utilising spatio-temporal patterns of ECHOs. Spatio-temporal saliency maps (c) are provided from each view to increase clinical usability.

as mild and severe cases are rare compared to the healthy cases, increasing the complexity of the problem.

We assume that for each patient, we have access to multiple ECHOs showing the heart from different views, which should contribute to the patient-level prediction. Even though a single view is commonly used for subjective assessment of PH in newborns, recent works have shown that using multiple views is beneficial for the assessment [9,25]. The proposed framework is depicted in Fig. 1.

Single-View. We first process each view separately. In particular, we employ a 3D-CNN architecture with residual connections and spatio-temporal convolutions across frames [14] using a ResNet-18 as the model backbone [5] (see Fig. 1(a)). In contrast to previous work [31], our approach integrates spatial as well as temporal information into the learning process. This mitigates the frame-level variations that can occur due to external changes, such as the position or the contact of the transducer, or in the cardiac function itself. To overcome the scarcity of the annotated data, common in the medical domain, from each ECHO, we extract n shorter video sequences by randomly choosing a frame as their starting frame followed by $k - 1$ consecutive frames, with total k frames, covering on average one heartbeat. We then aggregate sequence-level predictions $\{y_{\text{view},i}\}_{i=1,...,n}$ through majority voting, i.e. by selecting the most frequently predicted label, to a view-level prediction y_{view}. The view-level confidence is then defined as $C = |y^*_{\text{view}}|/n$, where $|y^*_{\text{view}}|$ is the count of the most frequently predicted label from the list of predictions for the n sequences of a given ECHO per view.

Multi-view. To increase the robustness of the method further, we employ a multi-view approach by combining the models trained on each available view (as in Fig. 1(b)). The final subject-level prediction, y_f, is then achieved by majority voting of the view-level predictions. In the case of a tie, the prediction of the model(s) with higher confidence is selected. We tried different approaches for view aggregation, but simple majority voting performed the best. Note that our proposed method uses view annotations to differentiate the distinct modalities. Following recent work on view classification [31], IP-PHN can easily be extended to incorporate ECHOs without annotation.

Interpretability. To increase the accountability and clinical usability of our proposed method, we complement our predictions with spatio-temporal saliency maps from each view (as in Fig. 1(c)). The automatic localisation of relevant pixels in the video sequence for the model's prediction provides an interpretable explanation that mimics the clinical workflow. Among different methods [26, 27, 32], we chose to use Grad-CAM (Gradient-weighted Class Activation Mapping), which exploits the gradients of any target concept flowing into a given convolutional layer to produce a coarse localization map highlighting the important regions in the image for predicting the label [26]. Recent works [1, 16] have shown how pixel-space gradient visualizations, such as Guided Backpropagation and Guided Grad-CAM, could be rather insensitive to model and data, making them similar to simple edge detectors. Grad-CAM is one of few saliency methods that pass the insensitivity check, making it our saliency method of choice [1].

However, Grad-CAM was originally proposed for 2D-CNNs. We, therefore, extend Grad-CAM to 3D-CNNs processing spatio-temporal video inputs. This allows us to identify the spatio-temporal regions on the video sequence that the network finds most informative for its prediction, which are the regions in both spatial and time domains. We do this by assigning each neuron a relevance score for the class prediction at the output layer, and backpropagate this information to the last convolutional layer to produce a coarse spatio-temporal localization map highlighting spatio-temporal areas of the ECHO video sequence.

4 Experiments and Results

4.1 Implementation Details

Our method was developed using the Python programming language with the PyTorch deep learning library. Experiments were run on a cluster containing different NVIDIA GeForce graphic cards: GTX 1080, GTX 1080 Ti, RTX 2080 Ti with 2048 MB RAM per processor core.

For each view, we extracted $n = 10$ video sequences and each sequence was composed of $k = 12$ consecutive frames, covering on average one heartbeat in every sequence. To deal with class imbalance, we employed a weighted random sampler, which samples elements from the dataset using their inverse class weight as their sample weight, ensuring that for every epoch, the model sees approximately equal number of samples from each class. Additionally, during training, we continuously augmented each sample with a probability of 90%. Each model was trained for around 150 epochs per view minimizing the (categorical) cross-entropy loss with the Adam [17] optimiser. Both the learning rate and weight decay were set to 0.001, while the batch size was set to 8 video sequences.

4.2   Experimental Setup

For all experiments, a stratified 10-fold cross-validation was performed, such that the data was randomly split ten times into 20% validation set and 80% training set. Note that, the splitting into training and validation sets was done on a patient basis. As classification metrics, we evaluated the area under the receiver operation characteristic (AUROC, one-vs-one), balanced accuracy, frequency-weighted F1-score, weighted precision, and weighted recall, as commonly used metrics. The multi-view AUROC was computed from the output probabilities of the most confident model selected by the majority voting. Results were averaged over the folds, and the mean and standard deviation are reported on patient level.

4.3   Results and Discussions

We hereby provide an empirical assessment of IP-PHN for PH severity prediction on the dataset described in Sect. 3.1. We report in Table 2(a) the quantitative performance from each of the three major views (A4C, PLAX, PSAX-P) (see Fig. 1(a)) and two minor views (PSAX-S, PSAX-A), as well as from the multi-view approach (see Fig. 1(b)) obtained through majority voting using different combinations of views. In particular, we combined (i) the 3 major views (MV-3) and (ii) all views for a total of 5 different views (MV-All).

   Among the single-view methods, the parasternal short-axis view at the level of papillary muscles (PSAX-P) shows the best performance in PH severity prediction and achieves an F1-score of 0.81 and Balanced Accuracy of 0.73, followed by the parasternal long-axis view (PLAX). We observed that both PSAX-P and PLAX are fairly confident in their prediction, with an average confidence of correct predictions of 0.92 and 0.90, respectively, while it decreases to 0.83 and 0.84 for wrong predictions. Although the apical four-chamber view (A4C) is one of the most commonly used views for cardiovascular disease diagnosis, our evaluation shows that it is not as discriminative as PSAX-P and PLAX, yielding an F1-score of 0.72 and Balanced Accuracy of 0.65, which are clearly lower than the other two views. This is also in line with the neonatal echocardiography teaching manual [9], where it is stated that subjective assessment of PH from the A4C view in a 2D ECHO is usually only possible for moderate to severe PH cases, and quantitative evaluation is difficult.

   The PH severity prediction problem is challenging, not only due to the hard task at hand but also because of the data imbalance. In this case, the robustness

Table 2. Results from both spatio-temporal (a,b) and spatial (c,d) approaches for PH severity prediction (a,c) and binary PH detection (b,d). *MV-3* refers to majority voting of A4C, PLAX, and, PSAX-P views. *MV-All* refers to majority voting of all five views. The best results for each task have been highlighted in **bold**. In both cases, these are spatio-temporal approaches.

	View	AUROC	F1-Score	Precision	Recall	Balanced accuracy
(a) Spatio-temporal Severity Prediction	A4C	0.77 ± 0.03	0.72 ± 0.05	0.75 ± 0.05	0.72 ± 0.05	0.65 ± 0.06
	PLAX	0.85 ± 0.04	0.78 ± 0.05	0.82 ± 0.06	0.79 ± 0.06	0.72 ± 0.05
	PSAX-P	0.85 ± 0.04	0.81 ± 0.05	0.83 ± 0.06	0.82 ± 0.04	0.73 ± 0.06
	PSAX-S	0.73 ± 0.07	0.68 ± 0.08	0.69 ± 0.09	0.69 ± 0.08	0.62 ± 0.07
	PSAX-A	0.77 ± 0.07	0.74 ± 0.06	0.77 ± 0.04	0.74 ± 0.06	0.67 ± 0.06
	MV-3	0.84 ± 0.08	0.83 ± 0.05	0.86 ± 0.04	0.83 ± 0.05	0.76 ± 0.07
	MV-All	**0.86 ± 0.09**	**0.84 ± 0.06**	**0.86 ± 0.05**	**0.85 ± 0.05**	**0.78 ± 0.07**
(b) Spatio-temporal Binary PH Detection	A4C	0.83 ± 0.05	0.81 ± 0.04	0.84 ± 0.03	0.81 ± 0.04	0.81 ± 0.04
	PLAX	0.90 ± 0.07	0.86 ± 0.09	0.88 ± 0.07	0.86 ± 0.09	0.86 ± 0.08
	PSAX-P	**0.95 ± 0.04**	**0.92 ± 0.03**	**0.93 ± 0.03**	**0.92 ± 0.03**	**0.94 ± 0.03**
	PSAX-S	0.79 ± 0.04	0.81 ± 0.03	0.82 ± 0.04	0.81 ± 0.03	0.80 ± 0.04
	PSAX-A	0.88 ± 0.05	0.87 ± 0.03	0.88 ± 0.03	0.87 ± 0.03	0.87 ± 0.04
	MV-3	0.90 ± 0.03	0.87 ± 0.04	0.88 ± 0.03	0.87 ± 0.04	0.87 ± 0.04
	MV-All	0.90 ± 0.03	0.89 ± 0.02	0.90 ± 0.02	0.89 ± 0.02	0.89 ± 0.02
(c) Spatial Severity Prediction	A4C	0.79 ± 0.04	0.75 ± 0.05	0.77 ± 0.04	0.75 ± 0.06	0.67 ± 0.06
	PLAX	0.84 ± 0.04	0.76 ± 0.04	0.78 ± 0.05	0.77 ± 0.04	0.70 ± 0.05
	PSAX-P	0.83 ± 0.03	0.81 ± 0.02	0.82 ± 0.03	0.81 ± 0.03	0.74 ± 0.03
	PSAX-S	0.74 ± 0.07	0.68 ± 0.06	0.70 ± 0.07	0.70 ± 0.08	0.62 ± 0.06
	PSAX-A	0.80 ± 0.03	0.75 ± 0.04	0.76 ± 0.04	0.76 ± 0.05	0.66 ± 0.04
	MV-3	0.84 ± 0.03	0.81 ± 0.03	0.83 ± 0.04	0.82 ± 0.03	0.74 ± 0.06
	MV-All	0.84 ± 0.03	0.82 ± 0.03	0.83 ± 0.04	0.83 ± 0.03	0.73 ± 0.04
(d) Spatial Binary PH Detection	A4C*	0.87 ± 0.04	0.83 ± 0.04	0.85 ± 0.03	0.83 ± 0.04	0.83 ± 0.03
	PLAX	0.92 ± 0.05	0.88 ± 0.04	0.89 ± 0.04	0.88 ± 0.04	0.88 ± 0.04
	PSAX-P	0.93 ± 0.04	0.91 ± 0.03	0.92 ± 0.03	0.91 ± 0.03	0.92 ± 0.03
	PSAX-S	0.83 ± 0.03	0.81 ± 0.03	0.83 ± 0.02	0.81 ± 0.03	0.81 ± 0.03
	PSAX-A	0.86 ± 0.04	0.85 ± 0.03	0.85 ± 0.03	0.85 ± 0.03	0.84 ± 0.03
	MV-3	0.91 ± 0.02	0.88 ± 0.02	0.88 ± 0.02	0.88 ± 0.02	0.88 ± 0.02
	MV-All	0.92 ± 0.02	0.90 ± 0.02	0.91 ± 0.01	0.90 ± 0.02	0.90 ± 0.01

and accuracy can be increased by utilising more views. By combining results from the PSAX-P, PLAX, and A4C views using majority voting, the F1-score improves from 0.81 to 0.83, while the Balanced Accuracy from 0.73 to 0.76 with a relative increase ratio of 2.5% and 4.1%, respectively. When the other two short-axis views are furthermore included, we get an F1-score of 0.84 and a Balanced Accuracy of 0.78. The majority voting is not only helpful to enhance the performance, but it is also useful in case a single view has an unsatisfactory quality for a given subject, a common scenario in many real-world applications.

Moreover, we performed an additional ablation, where we simplified the problem setting to a binary classification. We then discriminated between no PH (65% of the data) and PH, combining mild, moderate, and severe cases, in line with previous work [31]. Even though the assessment of the severity of PH is crucial for a correct treatment, as the morbidity rate significantly increases for higher degrees of PH [6,12], the clinicians might also be interested in simply discriminating between healthy and unhealthy patients as an initial screening procedure. In such a case, the data imbalance would be less significant. We report the binary PH detection results in Table 2(b). PSAX-P view is still the most discriminative one, which yields improved accuracy compared to the severity prediction, with an F1-score of 0.92 and Balanced Accuracy of 0.94. Given the substantial prediction accuracy of the PSAX-P view alone for binary PH detection, including more views to the aggregated model does not result in increased performances. This is due to the larger number of weaker models and high performance of the PSAX-P single view. The voting strategy is then driven by weaker models rather than the single best performing PSAX-P view.

As an alternative approach to combining various views with majority voting, we also explored an end-to-end approach joining the views in the embedding space. This improved results compared the best single view with Balanced Accuracy from 0.73 to 0.75, but did not improve compared to the majority voting, which has Balanced Accuracy of 0.78. Furthermore, we also tried using confidence weighted majority voting. Although the confidence is higher on average for correct predictions, in some cases the models are confidently wrong, which is why we decided not to use voting weighted by confidence.

The existing method [31] for binary PH detection in adults does not exploit the spatio-temporal patterns. Thus, as a comparison, we also evaluated the spatial-only approach, which proved to be inferior in both, severity prediction and binary detection tasks. The results are reported in Table 2(c)-(d). We achieve similar results as the state-of-the-art method using A4C view as in [31], with an AUROC of 0.87 compared to 0.85, when evaluating a similar task in adults.

We evaluated different spatio-temporal architectures, such as R(2+1)D [29] and SlowFast [10]. In Table 3 we provide an empirical evaluation for binary PH detection using PSAX-P view. The 18-layer ResNet3D (same results as in Table 2(b)) shows superior performance compared to the other two architectures, with SlowFast being slightly better than R(2+1)D. Although the 50-layer Slow-Fast network has shown superior performances on various video classification tasks [10], it seems to lead to over-fitting in our dataset. Furthermore, factoring the 3D convolutional filters into separate spatial and temporal components, as in R(2+1)D, does not improve accuracy in our case.

Interpretability. To increase the clinical usability, our method contains a post-hoc analysis of the single-view spatio-temporal convolutions. For each ECHO view, we highlight the pixels that are the most relevant for the assessment of PH severity. In Fig. 2 we show the original ECHO frames with different levels of PH (left column) combined with saliency maps using Grad-CAM (right column) corresponding to the significant views, in (a) PSAX-P and in (b) PLAX.

Table 3. Results from different both spatio-temporal architectures for binary PH detection using PSAX-P view. The best results for each task have been highlighted in **bold**.

Architecture	AUROC	F1-Score	Precision	Recall	Balanced accuracy
R(2+1)D - 18 layers	0.90 ± 0.06	0.90 ± 0.03	0.91 ± 0.03	0.90 ± 0.03	0.90 ± 0.05
SlowFast - 50 layers	0.93 ± 0.04	0.90 ± 0.04	0.91 ± 0.04	0.90 ± 0.04	0.90 ± 0.05
ResNet3D - 18 layers	**0.95 ±0.04**	**0.92 ±0.03**	**0.93 ±0.03**	**0.92 ±0.03**	**0.94 ±0.03**

According to the neonatal echocardiography teaching manual [9], for PSAX-P view, PH results in change in intraventricular septum (IVS) morphology and left ventricle (LV) shape, which stems from the change in right ventricle (RV) pressure. In mild to moderate PH the IVS becomes flat during systole and in moderate to severe PH the septum bows into the LV, such that the LV becomes D-shaped, or crescentic. We show in Fig. 2(a) that our PSAX-P severity prediction model evaluates the change in shape of LV, which is the result of enlarged RV. Thus, our model focuses on the same clinically relevant features as are recommended for diagnosis.

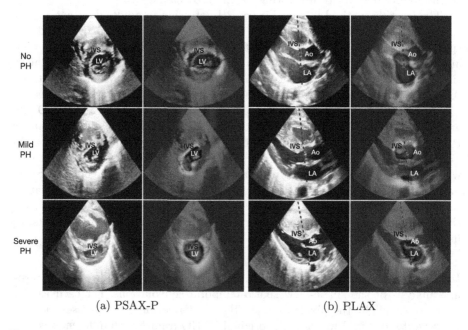

(a) PSAX-P   (b) PLAX

Fig. 2. ECHO frames of subjects with no, mild and severe PH (left), as well as the IP-PHN saliency maps (right), for (a) the PSAX-P view, and (b) the PLAX view. The yellow line shows how the M-mode for the LA:Ao measurement is extracted. The highlighted pixels feature crucial cardiac structures. (Color figure online)

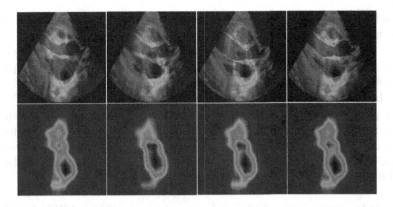

Fig. 3. Spatio-temporal Grad-CAM saliency maps (bottom) imposed on the original frames (top) for frames corresponding to systole, mid, diastole, mid in a PLAX ECHO.

Subjective evaluation of the IVS morphology is also possible from the PLAX view [9]. Furthermore, quantitative assessments are frequently performed on this view, including measurements of the aortic valve (AV) annulus diameter, and left atrial-to-aortic root diameter ratio (LA:Ao) by extracting the M-mode as demonstrated with the yellow line in Fig. 2(b). When exploring the saliency map of the PLAX severity model, we see in Fig. 2(b) that the model focuses on the area around the LA, AV and Ao, and IVS. This suggests that the model is able to consider both the relevant quantitative features and the subjective ones.

Note that, for simplicity, we show the visualisation results of a single frame per patient in Fig. 2. In a clinical setting, the visualizations can be viewed as a video containing spatio-temporal explanation. In Fig. 3, we show more examples of how the focus changes along the frames of a sequence.

We would like to stress that, although we only plotted a few random individuals, we analyzed saliency maps of the entire population to draw meaningful conclusions. Provided code can be used to test such findings.

5   Conclusion

In this work we developed an automated and streamlined approach, IP-PHN, to assist clinicians in the assessment of PH in newborns. We achieved optimal performance for the severity prediction of PH when using a multi-view approach with spatio-temporal convolutional architectures using majority voting of several views. The severity estimation of PH from ECHOs is critically important as it determines the urgency of a treatment [6,12], but it remains a challenge for cardiologists [7,11]. Thus, IP-PHN may have a considerable clinical impact in increasing the accuracy and steadiness of ECHO examinations by reducing the number of late or missed diagnoses of PH. Furthermore, it may assist less trained specialists and thereby reduce the workload of highly trained experts. Finally, by highlighting the input features that are crucial for the PH assessment, the proposed approach provides interpretable explanations for the clinicians, which in turn makes the system accountable.

Note that, this was a retrospective study and we focused on the shape change and motion of the ventricles and septum by using 2D ECHOs in standard planes. The extension to detect abnormalities in cardiac functions could be easily performed by integrating other modalities, such as ECGs.

Our proposed method is not only limited to newborns and can be applied ECHOs from the adult population as well, where re-training would be needed. Furthermore, due to the multi-view setup, one can adapt the pipeline to other kinds of disease predictions in the medical context, where the clinicians benefit from different views of the heart in their clinical routine.

Acknowledgements. LM and FL have been supported by PHRT - SHFN/SWISSHE-ART Failure Network, project number 2018-122. EO has been supported by the Hasler Foundation grant #21050.

References

1. Adebayo, J., Gilmer, J., Muelly, M., Goodfellow, I., Hardt, M., Kim, B.: Sanity checks for saliency maps. In: Proceedings of the 32nd International Conference on Neural Information Processing Systems, NIPS 2018, pp. 9525–9536. Curran Associates Inc., Red Hook (2018)
2. Barst, R.J., McGoon, M.D., Elliott, C.G., Foreman, A.J., Miller, D.P., Ivy, D.D.: Survival in childhood pulmonary arterial hypertension. Circulation **125**(1), 113–122 (2012)
3. Bello, G.A., et al.: Deep-learning cardiac motion analysis for human survival prediction. Nat. Mach. Intell. **1**(2), 95–104 (2019)
4. de Boode, W.P., et al.: Application of neonatologist performed echocardiography in the assessment and management of persistent pulmonary hypertension of the newborn. Pediatric Res. **84**(S1), 68–77 (2018)
5. Carreira, J., Zisserman, A.: Quo vadis, action recognition? a new model and the kinetics dataset, pp. 4724–4733 (2017)
6. Corris, P., Degano, B.: Severe pulmonary arterial hypertension: treatment options and the bridge to transplantation. Eur. Resp. Rev. **23**(134), 488–497 (2014)
7. Dasgupta, S., Richardson, J.C., Aly, A.M., Jain, S.K.: Role of functional echocardiographic parameters in the diagnosis of bronchopulmonary dysplasia-associated pulmonary hypertension. J. Perinatol. **42**(1), 19–30 (2021)
8. Dawes, T.J.W., et al.: Machine learning of three-dimensional right ventricular motion enables outcome prediction in pulmonary hypertension: a cardiac MR imaging study. Radiology **283**(2), 381–390 (2017)
9. EL-Khuffash, A.: Neonatal echocardiography teaching manual (2014)
10. Feichtenhofer, C., Fan, H., Malik, J., He, K.: SlowFast networks for video recognition. In: 2019 IEEE/CVF International Conference on Computer Vision (ICCV) (2019)
11. Fisher, M.R., et al.: Accuracy of doppler echocardiography in the hemodynamic assessment of pulmonary hypertension. Am. J. Resp. Crit. Care Med. **179**(7), 615–621 (2009)

12. Galiè, N., et al.: 2015 ESC/ERS guidelines for the diagnosis and treatment of pulmonary hypertension. Eur. Resp. J. **46**(4), 903–975 (2015)
13. Hansmann, G.: Pulmonary hypertension in infants, children, and young adults. J. Am. Coll. Cardiol. **69**(20), 2551–2569 (2017)
14. Hara, K., Kataoka, H., Satoh, Y.: Learning spatio-temporal features with 3D residual networks for action recognition, pp. 3154–3160 (2017)
15. Kaddoura, T., et al.: Acoustic diagnosis of pulmonary hypertension: automated speech- recognition-inspired classification algorithm outperforms physicians. Sci. Rep. **6**(1) (2016)
16. Kindermans, P.-J., et al.: The (Un)reliability of saliency methods, pp. 267–280. Springer International Publishing, Cham (2019)
17. Kingma, D.P., Ba, J.: Adam: a method for stochastic optimization. arXiv preprint arXiv:1412.6980 (2014)
18. Kusunose, K., Hirata, Y., Tsuji, T., Kotoku, J., Sata, M.: Deep learning to predict elevated pulmonary artery pressure in patients with suspected pulmonary hypertension using standard chest X-ray. Sci. Rep. **10**(1) (2020)
19. Kwon, J.M., et al.: Artificial intelligence for early prediction of pulmonary hypertension using electrocardiography. J. Heart Lung Transplant. **39**(8), 805–814 (2020)
20. Lang, R., et al.: Recommendations for cardiac chamber quantification by echocardiography in adults: an update from the American Society of echocardiography and the European Association of cardiovascular imaging. Eur. Heart J. Cardiovasc. Imaging **16**(3), 233–70 (2015)
21. Leha, A., et al.: A machine learning approach for the prediction of pulmonary hypertension. PLOS ONE **14**(10), e0224453 (2019)
22. Mori, H., Inai, K., Sugiyama, H., Muragaki, Y.: Diagnosing atrial septal defect from electrocardiogram with deep learning. Pediatric Cardiol. **42**(6), 1379–1387 (2021)
23. Ni, J.R., et al.: Diagnostic accuracy of transthoracic echocardiography for pulmonary hypertension: a systematic review and meta-analysis. BMJ Open **9**(12), e033084 (2019)
24. Rosenkranz, S., Preston, I.R.: Right heart catheterisation: best practice and pitfalls in pulmonary hypertension. Eur. Resp. Rev. **24**(138), 642–652 (2015)
25. Schneider, M., et al.: Multi-view approach for the diagnosis of pulmonary hypertension using transthoracic echocardiography. Int. J. Cardiovasc. Imaging **34**(5), 695–700 (2018)
26. Selvaraju, R.R., Cogswell, M., Das, A., Vedantam, R., Parikh, D., Batra, D.: Grad-CAM: visual explanations from deep networks via gradient-based localization. In: 2017 IEEE International Conference on Computer Vision, pp. 618–626 (2017)
27. Springenberg, J.T., Dosovitskiy, A., Brox, T., Riedmiller, M.A.: Striving for simplicity: the all convolutional net. CoRR abs/1412.6806 (2015)
28. Steinhorn, R.H.: Neonatal pulmonary hypertension. Pediatric Crit. Care Med. **11**, S79–S84 (2010)
29. Tran, D., Wang, H., Torresani, L., Ray, J., LeCun, Y., Paluri, M.: A closer look at spatiotemporal convolutions for action recognition. In: 2018 IEEE/CVF Conference on Computer Vision and Pattern Recognition (2018)
30. Vainio, T., Mäkelä, T., Savolainen, S., Kangasniemi, M.: Performance of a 3D convolutional neural network in the detection of hypoperfusion at CT pulmonary angiography in patients with chronic pulmonary embolism: a feasibility study. Eur. Radiol. Expe. **5**(1) (2021)
31. Zhang, J., et al.: Fully automated echocardiogram interpretation in clinical practice. Circulation **138**(16), 1623–1635 (2018)

32. Zhou, B., Khosla, A., Lapedriza, À., Oliva, A., Torralba, A.: Learning deep features for discriminative localization. 2016 IEEE Conference on Computer Vision and Pattern Recognition (CVPR), pp. 2921–2929 (2016)
33. Zou, X.L., et al.: A promising approach for screening pulmonary hypertension based on frontal chest radiographs using deep learning: a retrospective study. PLOS ONE **15**(7), e0236378 (2020)

Systems and Applications

A Framework for Benchmarking Real-Time Embedded Object Detection

Michael Schlosser, Daniel König, and Michael Teutsch[✉]

HENSOLDT Optronics GmbH, Oberkochen, Germany
{michael.schlosser,daniel.koenig,michael.teutsch}@hensoldt.net

Abstract. Object detection is one of the key tasks in many applications of computer vision. Deep Neural Networks (DNNs) are undoubtedly a well-suited approach for object detection. However, such DNNs need highly adapted hardware together with hardware-specific optimization to guarantee high efficiency during inference. This is especially the case when aiming for efficient object detection in video streaming applications on limited hardware such as edge devices. Comparing vendor-specific hardware and related optimization software pipelines in a fair experimental setup is a challenge. In this paper, we propose a framework that uses a host computer with a host software application together with a light-weight interface based on the Message Queuing Telemetry Transport (MQTT) protocol. Various different target devices with target apps can be connected via MQTT with this host computer. With well-defined and standardized MQTT messages, object detection results can be reported to the host computer, where the results are evaluated without harming or influencing the processing on the device. With this quite generic framework, we can measure the object detection performance, the runtime, and the energy efficiency at the same time. The effectiveness of this framework is demonstrated in multiple experiments that offer deep insights into the optimization of DNNs.

Keywords: Generic evaluation · Optimization · Efficient deployment

1 Introduction

Algorithm benchmarking is a crucial step during the development of computer vision systems and applications. In applications that have to meet requirements for minimum latency (i.e. real-time requirements) on limited hardware (i.e. edge devices), not only the algorithm effectiveness is important but also the efficiency. Facilitating recent state-of-the-art techniques such as deep learning and Deep Neural Networks (DNNs) as a very powerful tool in computer vision nowadays, authors try to find the sweet spot between processing speed and algorithm accuracy [13,19]. Relevant fields of application for finding such a trade-off range from robotics [15] and autonomous driving [10] to smartphones [34]. Accompanying this progress, several vendors of specific inference hardware provide specialized

© The Author(s), under exclusive license to Springer Nature Switzerland AG 2022
B. Andres et al. (Eds.): DAGM GCPR 2022, LNCS 13485, pp. 545–559, 2022.
https://doi.org/10.1007/978-3-031-16788-1_33

software based optimization pipelines that enable scientists and developers to strongly reduce the latency of certain algorithms, while preserving the effective performance at the same time [14,21,31]. Since these optimization software frameworks and pipelines are highly specific, however, benchmarking certain rather generic computer vision algorithms for certain applications with related hardware limitations such as miniaturized edge devices can be challenging.

In this paper, we propose a generic framework for benchmarking low-latency computer vision algorithms for their application on vendor-specific inference hardware. We use object detection as our considered computer vision task. Utilizing the popular You Only Look Once (YOLO) object detector [25] in its version YOLOv4 [3] as reference detection algorithm and MS Common Objects in Context (COCO) [17] as reference dataset, we aim to measure detection performance and algorithm runtime simultaneously. This is achieved by separating data distribution and evaluation from data processing. A host app running on a desktop computer distributes the video data via the light-weight Message Queuing Telemetry Transport (MQTT) protocol. This data is processed by a target app on the target board. The results are then sent back via MQTT to the host app for evaluation and benchmarking. In this way, we can efficiently compare different vendor-specific hardware and optimization software pipelines, which usually contain software tools for quantization and pruning of DNNs [5]. Furthermore, we can integrate new hardware and/or software updates easily into our framework to measure their performance and runtime gains, respectively.

Our proposed framework is not the first of its kind, of course. Several approaches exist for evaluating the performance of object detection, but most related literature either does not measure all important metrics relevant for the use on embedded systems [28,30], which are primarily the accuracy, the runtime and the power consumption, or the proposed frameworks are less generic compared to ours as they only refer to a single hardware [28,30] or vendor [27]. Other authors compare embedded hardware for certain computer vision tasks but they do not use or mention a unified evaluation framework at all [18,29,36]. Another relevant aspect is that our MQTT based publish-subscribe approach is more flexible than server-client based architectures [27]: in this way, we can evaluate a computer vision algorithm on multiple target platforms simultaneously. Server-client architectures instead usually have higher communication overhead since requests have to be sent to the host from each individual target device. Furthermore, MQTT is very light-weight, simpler, and with higher throughput compared to other protocols or interfaces such as Hypertext Transfer Protocol (HTTP) or Advanced Message Queuing Protocol (AMQP) [8,11,20,35]. The application behind the framework is to provide a generic test bed for benchmarking optimized computer vision algorithms on highly efficient edge devices. In this way, we can effectively find the trade-off between processing speed and algorithm accuracy.

Our contributions are:

1. We propose a generic evaluation framework for different embedded devices using a lightweight concept that can be deployed with little effort and that

provides remote access from the host app without the need to send requests from the target side.

2. To the best of our knowledge this is the first framework of its kind that uses the highly efficient publish-subscribe protocol MQTT instead of less flexible or efficient communication protocols and/or interfaces such as HTTP or Representational State Transfer (REST). In this way, we can evaluate an algorithm on multiple target devices simultaneously and efficiently.

3. We demonstrate the usefulness of our framework by evaluating two different embedded devices from two vendors utilizing their specific optimization pipelines for the task of generic object detection.

The remainder of this paper is organized as follows: related work is presented in Sect. 2. Our proposed framework together with the related methodology is presented in Sect. 3. Experimental results are described in Sect. 4 followed by a discussion in Sect. 4.4. We conclude in Sect. 5.

2 Related Work

Several approaches exist for evaluating the performance of object detection, but most proposed works either do not measure all important metrics for use on embedded systems, which are primarily the accuracy, the runtime and the power consumption, or are not generic enough, because they only refer to a single hardware or manufacturer.

Stäcker et al. [28] evaluate object detection on embedded systems using RetinaNet [16]. The detection model is optimized using Nvidia TensorRT and deployed on an Nvidia Jetson AGX Xavier. Accuracy and runtime, but not power consumption, are measured during the experimental evaluation. The Robot Operating System (ROS) is used to communicate with the target and to receive the detection results. Only an Nvidia Jetson AGX Xavier is used as hardware platform and the comparison to other platforms is not considered here. Rungsuptaweekoon et al. [27] utilize the object detector YOLOv2 on different embedded devices such as the Jetson TX1 and TX2. In addition to Frames Per Second (FPS) and mean Average Precision (mAP), the power consumption is also measured. A benchmark environment based on a server-client model is provided, where the target board acts as a client and requests the image data from a host PC. A system based on a client-server architecture is proposed, which requires the direct access of the target board to communicate with the server and the authors only consider Nvidia hardware.

Besides the evaluation of GPU-based hardware accelerators, there are also works dealing with the evaluation of object detection on Field Programmable Gate Arrays (FPGAs). Wang et al. [30] evaluate a YOLOv3 object detector, which is optimized using the recommended optimization framework Vitis AI on a Xilinx Zynq UltraScale+ MPSoC ZCU104 evaluation board. The performance results of the Xilinx MPSoC are compared to the performance of a Nvidia GeForce GTX 1080 GPU on a desktop computer. The power consumption and the FPS are measured, but no accuracy, which means that it is not verified whether the model still has an acceptable accuracy after optimization. Furthermore, there is no uniform evaluation framework for the different system environments that are compared, so implementation mismatches between the platforms are possible. In [36], Yu et al. propose a comparison of several object detectors such as YOLO, Faster RCNN and SSD, on multiple platforms, including Nvidia TK1, Xilinx Zynq 7045 and Xilinx KU115. They measure power consumption, throughput, and accuracy. However, they provide an incomplete comparison as not all models are evaluated on all boards. Furthermore, they also do not use an uniform evaluation framework for different implementations. Blott et al. [2] propose a theoretical and experimental evaluation of different DNNs for several computer vision tasks on a variety of different acceleration platforms, such as FPGAs, GPUs and TPUs. The authors point out that measurement methods are often unclear and complicated by the large variety of deployment parameters. For this purpose, a large experimental study is conducted on how different DNN topologies behave with different deployment settings (e.g., batch size or power modes) and optimization methods (e.g., pruning and quantization), in terms of throughput, inference time, hardware utilization, power consumption, and accuracy. Accordingly, a detailed study on the comparison of DNNs, especially in the use case of image classification, is presented here. Lin et al. [18] provide a benchmark for different SSD models deployed on an Intel Arria 10 FPGA for traffic sign detection. In addition to an analysis of the training framework, they evaluate the models deployed on the FPGA in terms of inference time, accuracy, and power efficiency, varying critical parameters such as floating point precision and batch size. They found that the inference time on the GPU is faster in most cases and that the FPGA is better in terms of power efficiency. As with most of the publications just presented, the focus here is an experimental evaluation of the results for the given models, optimization methods and hardware platforms rather than the methodology of a generic evaluation framework. Verucchi et al. [29] propose a detailed comparison between object detectors, such as YOLOv3, CenterNet, and SSD deployed on an Nvidia Jetson AGX Xavier, a Xilinx Zynq UltraScale+ MPSoC ZCU102, and an industrial PC. High attention is paid to the fairness of the comparison between the detectors deployed on different hardware platforms. All important metrics mentioned before are considered, which include accuracy, runtime, and power consumption. However, no uniform evaluation framework is implemented and the accuracy is directly measured on the target device.

3   Proposed Evaluation Framework

Our proposed framework enables the evaluation of object detection algorithms for such a stream on arbitrary target hardware and shifts the responsibility of providing input data and calculating evaluation measures to a separate host PC. The framework itself, however, is generic and thus not limited to the task of object detection. We choose an MQTT-based approach, because it is a lightweight protocol and often used in embedded devices [20]. Since MQTT uses a publish-subscribe mechanism, it is even possible to evaluate object detection on multiple target devices simultaneously. The MQTT broker manages message distribution and decouples the communication of host and target. Hence, requests do not have to be sent directly to the host from each individual target device as is the case with a commonly used server-client architecture. As Fig. 1 depicts, with the proposed evaluation framework image data is sent from a host computer to the target via MQTT. The target is the platform that performs the inference, the associated pre-processing, which consists of resizing and normalizing the input image data, and post-processing, which consists of the conversion of the model output to bounding box coordinates and confidence values, and Non-Maximum Suppression (NMS). The results are sent back to the host PC for evaluation.

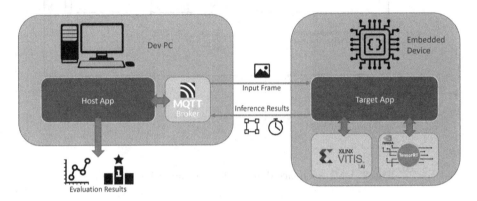

Fig. 1. Architecture of the proposed evaluation framework consisting of the development PC with the host application and the embedded device with the target application. MQTT serves as communication protocol between the devices.

The use of such a framework allows to evaluate a DNN directly on a platform that is used for deployment in operational systems. Thus, we are able to verify the conversion from common deep learning frameworks such as PyTorch or TensorFlow into the proprietary optimization frameworks of the hardware vendors such as Xilinx or Nvidia. In this work, without limitation of generality, we focus on Xilinx Vitis AI and Nvidia TensorRT. Furthermore, we can provide accuracy measures of a final deep learning application deployed on the embedded device. Various proprietary profiler tools are provided by Xilinx and Nvidia that support measuring of runtime and throughput. However, to evaluate complete accuracy measurements locally, the entire test dataset would have to be installed on the target. This can be impractical especially for large datasets such as the COCO test dataset that is used in this work and consists of over 20,000 images. We avoid this with the proposed evaluation framework. The responsibility of storing and providing the input data can thus be transferred to an external device (i.e. the host PC) together with the calculation of evaluation measures.

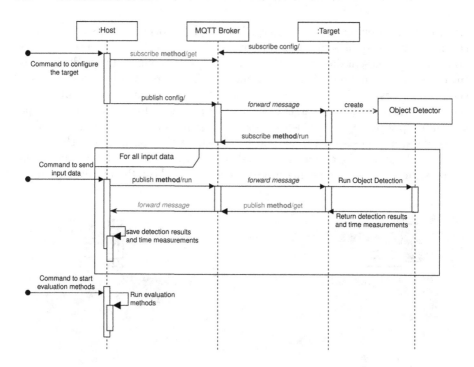

Fig. 2. UML sequence diagram for an evaluation session.

Figure 2 depicts the flow of an evaluation session as a Unified Modeling Language (UML) sequence diagram. In the first preparatory step, the host sends the desired configuration of the experiment setup to the MQTT broker. The target subscribes to this configuration topic, whereupon messages are distributed that contain, for example, the algorithm to be used and the topics to be subscribed to, on which the input data is sent. This procedure simplifies the setup of the target, because the target component only has to be started, which can also be automated in the boot process, and all further steps can be done remotely from the desktop PC. The host app sends the input data to the MQTT broker in a next step. For this purpose, the input image is read in as an OpenCV [4] image matrix and serialized for transfer to the target device using Msgpack [12]. These input messages are then successively forwarded to the target component, processed there and the results are sent back. These results include the measured times of pre- and post-processing and inference, as well as the determined bounding boxes. For demonstration purposes, the processed image with the bounding boxes plotted can be sent back to the host via MQTT. The host can then display the processed images at runtime if required. After all desired input data has been processed, the results can be further processed using the selected evaluation modules. For example, the received detection results can now be compared with the annotations of the test dataset that was just processed in order to measure the accuracy.

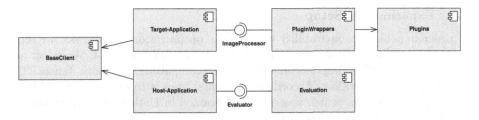

Fig. 3. UML component diagram for the evaluation framework.

Due to the decoupling and the modularized structure of the framework, as Fig. 3 depicts, it is possible to integrate further object detection algorithms or evaluators without much effort. Hence, no additional dependencies arise for the communication of the two components via MQTT and the actual object detection application. Functionality relevant to both target and host such as data transfer in particular, is implemented in the BaseClient component. By implementing the evaluator interface, a plugin can be developed for the host component that has access to the result message. This allows further processing of all existing measurements. Similarly, the object detector interface can be implemented on the target board, which receives and processes an OpenCV image matrix and provides access to various information such as the predicted bounding box coordinates and time measurements. The target part of the evaluation framework only depends on an MQTT library, such as Eclipse Paho MQTT [7] and Msgpack, which is used for the standardization and de/serialization of the message. All other dependencies are dependent on the respective plugin. For example, the Vitis AI Runtime must be installed as a dependency for controlling an application for the Xilinx Deep Learning Processor Unit (DPU), which is a programmable engine for accelerating deep learning tasks on an FPGA [33]. Since host and target are completely decoupled from each other, modifications to the host component are not necessary when including a new target device.

4 Experiments

In this work, we choose a YOLOv4 object detector [3] as baseline model. For the Xilinx Zynq UltraScale+ MPSoC ZCU104 [32] it is optimized using Xilinx Vitis AI [31] and for the Nvidia Jetson AGX Xavier [22] we utilize Nvidia TensorRT [21]. By varying different parameters within the vendor-specific optimization frameworks, we can analyze the effects on the then deployed DNN. This for example includes steps such as quantization, which is the approximation of a neural network in floating point precision by means of a new neural network with a smaller bit width [9], and pruning, in which the size of the neural network is reduced by the systematical removal of elements [1]. In addition, a cross-platform comparison between the models on different target devices is performed.

4.1 Experimental Setup

In order to achieve comparability between the optimization frameworks, we set up the conversion and optimization process as visualized in Fig. 4. We select a model trained with a deep learning framework compatible with both TensorRT and Vitis AI: TensorFlow. Accordingly, the first step is to convert a YOLOv4 model to TensorFlow, which was originally trained in Darknet [24], to create a baseline for the optimization pipeline.

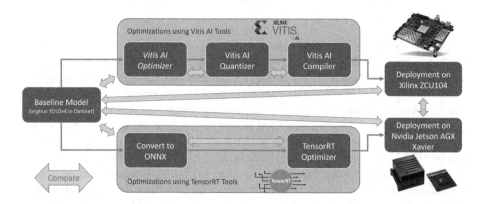

Fig. 4. Optimization pipelines for Xilinx Vitis AI and Nvidia TensorRT.

Vitis AI provides three separate optimization tools. The Vitis AI Optimizer, which applies the pruning, the Vitis AI Quantizer, which quantizes the model into INT8-precision and the Vitis AI Compiler, which compiles the model for the underlying DPU design. Pruning with the Vitis AI Optimizer is not considered in the optimization pipeline directly, since the related software tool is not free of charge. Its effects are nevertheless analyzed in a separate experiment. If the validation results are satisfactory and only a slight or even no loss of accuracy can be noted, the quantized model must be compiled using the Vitis AI compiler.

For optimization with TensorRT, we convert the TensorFlow model into ONNX format as a first step. For this purpose, the command line tool onnx-tf [23] is used. Subsequently, the ONNX model is optimized for utilization on inference hardware using TensorRT. According to the official documentation of the tool, onnx-tf not only provides a portable intermediate format that increases the interoperability of the model, but it also performs optimization steps during the conversion that are intended to reduce the inference time. Pruning is already performed in this step: unused ONNX operators (e.g., neurons of the DNN) are removed and similar operators are merged. The TensorRT Optimizer processes the converted ONNX model. Therefore, the optimizer must be executed directly on the target hardware, since various hardware-specific optimizations are performed.

As evaluation measures, we choose the inference time, FPS, the energy consumption in watts, the energy efficiency in FPS/watt, and the mAP 0.5:0.95 for the accuracy. For the measurement of the inference time, the object detector plugins were provided with time measurements, which are sent to the host along with the result message. The measurement of power consumption in watts is realized by reading a multimeter, which is connected in series with the hardware platform to be evaluated. To measure the power in watts, the constant set voltage is multiplied by the current. A distinction is made between absolute and relative power consumption during the execution of object detection. To determine the relative power, the idle power, which is the power consumption of the target device without running an application, is subtracted from the absolute power used to actually execute the application. This increases the comparability between the inference hardware since the absolute power of the two platforms differs greatly as shown in Table 1. Energy efficiency indicates the FPS in relation to the power consumption. This enables us to analyze how efficiently the resources of the inference hardware are used in terms of power consumption. Due to the diversity of the compared hardware in terms of computing power and power consumption, measuring the energy efficiency allows for a cross-platform comparison, which puts the energy consumption of the platform in relation to the runtime performance. Accuracy is measured by averaging the mAP for Intersection-over-Union (IoU) thresholds from .5 to .95 in steps of .05. mAP is a standard metric for evaluating object detectors and used for the COCO benchmark [17].

4.2   Implementation Details

The baseline model is available in resolutions of 416×416, 512×512, and 608×608 pixels. It was found that the 512×512 resolution provides the best compromise between accuracy and runtime. Therefore, this model is used as the baseline model for the majority of the experiments. Nevertheless, in a separate experiment (see Fig. 6a, b and c), the other two variants are also evaluated and included in the final comparison. All executions of the object detection algorithm are performed with similar pre- and post-processing, which are based on reference implementations of the respective framework. For example, for Vitis AI, the pre- and post-processing is implemented following the example of the Vitis AI Library, which is a highly optimized variant. For TensorRT and ONNX, pre- and post-processing is implemented via Python numpy. For a fair comparison, we verify that all implementations are similar across all frameworks. For each evaluation session, object detection with the COCO validation dataset consisting of 5,000 frames of image data is run six times in total and the evaluation results are averaged to ensure more stable results in terms of runtime. For the measurement of the accuracy, the confidence threshold is uniformly set to 0.25. For the execution of the NMS in post-processing, a threshold of 0.45 was set. The choice of threshold values was taken from existing implementations of a YOLOv4 object detection application [6,31]. Accuracy measurements on the test dataset, consisting of about 20,000 frames of image data, are performed only once. The annotations of the test dataset are not freely available, since they are used for participation in the COCO challenge, and the related website allows to upload results to the COCO server just up to five times a day. In the context of this work, accuracy measurements have been performed with the test dataset for each optimization level in this way. For optimizations that have no influence on the accuracy, only the validation dataset, consisting of 5,000 frames of image data, is entered several times for the evaluation, since the annotations of the validation dataset are freely available and the accuracy can thus be determined using the proposed evaluation framework. The confidence threshold was reduced to .05 for the measurements on the test dataset, since this setting is used to evaluate the original darknet YOLOv4. It is a common practice to set the confidence threshold for evaluating the accuracy that low to achieve a higher mAP [26].

4.3   Experimental Results

For the evaluation of the TensorRT optimizer, the model was quantized to all possible precisions such as Integer representations using 8 Bits (INT8) and floating point representations using 32 Bits (FP32) and 16 Bits (FP16), respectively.

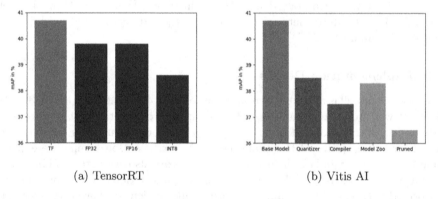

(a) TensorRT   (b) Vitis AI

Fig. 5. Accuracy comparison of optimized DNN models after all optimization steps. A higher bar indicates higher mAP and thus better DNN performance. TF is the reference DNN run in TensorFlow at FP32 precision.

Figure 5a shows the accuracy loss when quantizing to all available precisions. It could be observed that optimization with TensorRT in FP32 format results in accuracy losses. However, when quantizing the model converted to FP16 format, the same effects on the accuracy could be observed. But the inference time could be almost halved compared to the FP32 variant as we show in Table 1. In addition, a lower energy consumption is evident. The INT8 quantization causes a loss of accuracy compared to the FP32 and FP16 models, but the average inference time was reduced. The Jetson AGX Xavier offers the possibility to configure the maximum clock rate, and therefore the maximum power consumption of the device, through so-called Jetson Power Modes. Mode 1, 2, and 5 budget the maximum power of the Jetson to 10, 15, and 30 W, respectively. Mode 0 or mode MAXN is selected by default and sets the maximum possible power of the Jetson. The INT8 model optimized with TensorRT is used for the experiment as it shows the highest energy efficiency and by adjusting the power mode, this can be further optimized. As shown in Table 2, the power modes have a direct impact on the overall runtime of the object detection application. Please note that there is a time difference for the same experiment reported in Table 2 with 70.23 ms and in Table 1 with 69.75 ms since we run the same experiment multiple times. In addition, a lower energy consumption is evident. The INT8 quantization causes a loss of accuracy compared to the FP32 and FP16 models, but the average inference time was reduced. The Jetson AGX Xavier offers the possibility to configure the maximum clock rate, and therefore the maximum power consumption of the device, through so-called Jetson Power Modes. Mode 1, 2, and 5 budget the maximum power of the Jetson to 10, 15, and 30 W, respectively. Mode 0 or mode MAXN is selected by default and sets the maximum possible power of the Jetson. The INT8 model optimized with TensorRT is used for the experiment as it shows the highest energy efficiency and by adjusting the power mode, this can be further optimized. As shown in Table 2, the power modes have a direct impact on the overall runtime of the object detection application. Please note that there is a time difference for the same experiment reported in Table 2 with 70.23 ms and in Table 1 with 69.75 ms since we run the same experiment multiple times.

Table 1. Comparison of the optimized models across all used frameworks using all available quantization modes.

Framework	Device	Precision	Inference time	Absolute power	Relative power	Efficiency	mAP
TensorFlow	CPU	FP32	767.16 ms	N/A	N/A	N/A	40.7
TensorRT	Jetson	FP32	69.75 ms	28 W	18.5 W	0.45 $\frac{FPS}{W}$	39.8
	Jetson	FP16	35.32 ms	20 W	10.5 W	1.17 $\frac{FPS}{W}$	39.8
	Jetson	INT8	22.0 ms	16.5 W	7.0 W	2.05 $\frac{FPS}{W}$	38.6
Vitis AI	ZCU104	INT8	54.42 ms	23 W	7.0 W	1.31 $\frac{FPS}{W}$	37.5
Vitis AI Zoo	ZCU104	INT8	67.84 ms	22.5 W	6.5 W	1.40 $\frac{FPS}{W}$	38.3
Zoo Pruned	ZCU104	INT8	48.42 ms	21.6 W	5.6 W	1.97 $\frac{FPS}{W}$	36.5

Table 2. Runtime on Nvidia Jetson in different power modes.

	MAXN	30 W	15 W	10 W
Pre-process	8.78 ms	10.91 ms	16.43 ms	17.11 ms
Inference	22.0 ms	26.22 ms	33.75 ms	61.76 ms
Post-process	39.45 ms	48.62 ms	68.12 ms	71.71 ms
Total	70.23 ms	85.75 ms	118.3 ms	150.58 ms

For the optimization with Vitis AI, the Vitis AI Quantizer was applied first. The quantized model is also executed on the desktop PC and evaluated with respect to accuracy and inference time. Figure 5b shows the accuracy loss after all optimization steps for Vitis AI. It was found that the Vitis AI Quantizer reduces the mAP by 2.2 %. This result can be verified by checking against reference instructions for optimizing a YOLOv4 model as similar results are obtained. Compared to the baseline model, a significantly higher runtime of the quantized model was observed on the desktop PC. However, it is noticeable that only one processor core is used when executing the model on the Desktop PC. When executing the baseline model, all available cores are used. Thus, the inference of the Vitis AI quantized model is not optimally parallelized. After compiling the model, using the Vitis AI compiler, it is subsequently installed on the ZCU104 and executed by the evaluation framework. It can be seen that the mAP is lower in comparison with the base model, but also inference time is reduced to 54.4 ms (see Table 1. For the optimization via Vitis AI Optimizer, already optimized models from the Vitis AI Model Zoo [31] are used and their results are evaluated. We utilize a YOLOv4 model trained on COCO, which is provided pruned and unpruned with an input resolution of 416 × 416. In the information provided about each model in Model Zoo, it is described that the number of operations in the model was reduced by 36% using the Vitis AI Optimizer. The two models are also integrated and evaluated in this experiment. When comparing the similarly optimized models in different input resolutions, it can be seen that the optimizations of the model in different resolutions result in similar improvements in terms of inference time and energy efficiency. Thus, after applying the optimizations, similar results are obtained as shown in Fig. 6a and Fig. 6b. No improvements in terms of power consumption could be identified, as shown in Fig. 6c. It can be concluded that the input resolution has no direct influence on the effectiveness of the applied optimization tools. If a low inference time at an acceptable cost of accuracy is required, a smaller input resolution is preferable.

4.4   Discussion

The results just described show that significant improvements in runtime and energy efficiency can be achieved by optimizing with TensorRT and Vitis AI. However, a small loss of accuracy can be expected for most optimization operations. Since FP16 quantization with TensorRT does not result in any loss of accuracy, it outperforms all other optimized models when the highest possible accuracy is required. The FP16 model already has a lower runtime than all optimizations in Vitis AI as shown in Fig. 6a. For the INT8 quantization operations, similar accuracy losses could be observed in TensorRT and Vitis AI. Nevertheless, after the compilation process with the Vitis AI compiler, the accuracy is further reduced. Accordingly, all TensorRT models outperform the Vitis AI models in terms of accuracy. The TensorRT optimized INT8 model with an input resolution of 416 × 416 outperforms all other models in terms of inference time at the expense of an acceptable loss of accuracy. Significant improvements in

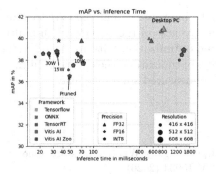

(a) Accuracy vs. Inference Time

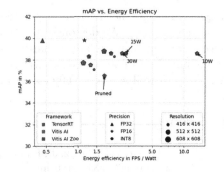

(b) Accuracy vs. Energy Efficiency

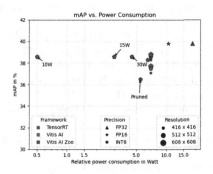

(c) Accuracy vs. Power Consumption

Fig. 6. Comparison of all optimized models with respect to the chosen evaluation measures accuracy, inference time, power consumption and energy efficiency.

energy efficiency and inference time can be observed with the Vitis AI Optimizer. On the other hand, the largest accuracy loss of all optimizations is noted here. The measurements of the pruned model in terms of energy efficiency are the only ones that provide similarly good results as the TensorRT-INT8 model. Figure 6a, b and c also show the measurements at different power budgets in the Jetson. Power budgeting can increase energy efficiency at the expense of inference time. Hence, a power budget of 15 W is preferable for the requirement of high energy efficiency instead of 10W Mode, since the inference time is only 11.75 ms higher in comparison to MAXN Mode.

5   Conclusion

We described a generic evaluation framework for computer vision algorithms deployed on an embedded device. As an exemplary task we chose object detection. The framework is *flexible* as different vendor-specific optimization pipelines are supported, *scalable* as multiple edge devices can be connected to the host computer and evaluated in parallel, and *light-weight* as basically only some

MQTT messages need to be supported (i.e. interpreted and replied) to integrate new devices. We demonstrate the effectiveness of the framework in multiple experiments using reference hardware and optimization software from Nvidia and Xilinx. Performance deterioration during optimization, the effective runtime reduction as well as energy efficiency can be measured simultaneously.

References

1. Blalock, D., Gonzalez Ortiz, J., Frankle, J., Guttag, J.: What is the state of neural network pruning? arXiv preprint arXiv:2004.10934 (2020)
2. Blott, M., et al.: Evaluation of optimized CNNs on heterogeneous accelerators using a novel benchmarking approach. IEEE Trans. Comput. **70**(10), 1654–1669 (2021)
3. Bochkovskiy, A., Wang, C., Liao, H.: YOLOv4: optimal speed and accuracy of object detection. arXiv preprint arXiv:2004.10934 (2020)
4. Bradski, G.: The OpenCV library. Dobb's J. Softw. Tools (2000)
5. Cai, Z., He, X., Sun, J., Vasconcelos, N.: Deep learning with low precision by half-wave gaussian quantization. In: IEEE CVPR (2017)
6. david8862: keras-yolov3-model-set. https://github.com/david8862/keras-YOLOv3-model-set/tree/v1.3.0
7. Eclipse: Eclipse paho mqtt c++ client library. https://github.com/eclipse/paho.mqtt.cpp
8. Gemirter, C., Senturca, C., Baydere, S.: A comparative evaluation of AMQP, MQTT and HTTP protocols using real-time public smart city data. In: 6th International Conference on Computer Science and Engineering (UBMK) (2021)
9. Gholami, A., Kim, S., Dong, Z., Yao, Z., Mahoney, M., Keutzer, K.: A survey of quantization methods for efficient neural network inference. arXiv preprint arXiv:2103.13630 (2021)
10. Gog, I., Kalra, S., Schafhalter, P., Wright, M., Gonzalez, J., Stoica, I.: Pylot: a modular platform for exploring latency-accuracy tradeoffs in autonomous vehicles. In: Proceedings of the IEEE International Conference on Robotics and Automation (ICRA) (2021)
11. Gündogan, C., Kietzmann, P., Lenders, M., Petersen, H., Schmidt, T., Wählisch, M.: NDN, CoAP, and MQTT: a comparative measurement study in the IoT. In: Proceedings of the 5th ACM Conference on Information-Centric Networking (ICN) (2018)
12. Hamerski, J.C., Domingues, A.R., Moraes, F.G., Amory, A.: Evaluating serialization for a publish-subscribe based middleware for mpsocs. In: 2018 25th IEEE International Conference on Electronics, Circuits and Systems (ICECS) (2018). https://doi.org/10.1109/ICECS.2018.8618003
13. Huang, J., et al.: Speed/accuracy trade-offs for modern convolutional object detectors. In: IEEE CVPR (2017)
14. Intel: OpenVINO Repository. https://github.com/openvinotoolkit/openvino
15. Jung, S., Hwang, S., Shin, H., Shim, D.: Perception, guidance, and navigation for indoor autonomous drone racing using deep learning. IEEE Rob. Autom. Lett. **3**(3), 2539–2544 (2018)
16. Lin, T., Goyal, P., Girshick, R., He, K., Dollar, P.: Focal loss for dense object detection. In: IEEE ICCV (2017)

17. Lin, T.-Y., et al.: Microsoft COCO: common objects in context. In: Fleet, D., Pajdla, T., Schiele, B., Tuytelaars, T. (eds.) ECCV 2014. LNCS, vol. 8693, pp. 740–755. Springer, Cham (2014). https://doi.org/10.1007/978-3-319-10602-1_48
18. Lin, Z., Yih, M., Ota, J., Owens, J., Muyan-Özcelik, P.: Benchmarking deep learning frameworks and investigating FPGA deployment for traffic sign classification and detection. IEEE Trans. Intell. Veh. **4**(3), 385–395 (2019)
19. Liu, D., Kong, H., Luo, X., Liu, W., Subramaniam, R.: Bringing AI to edge: from deep learning's perspective. Neurocomputing **485**, 297–320 (2022)
20. Mishra, B., Kertesz, A.: The use of MQTT in M2M and IoT systems: a survey. IEEE Access **8**, 201071–201086 (2021)
21. NVIDIA: TensorRT Repository. https://github.com/NVIDIA/TensorRT/
22. Nvidia: Jetson agx xavier developer kit - user guide (2019). https://developer.download.nvidia.com/embedded/L4T/r32-3-1_Release_v1.0/jetson_agx_xavier_developer_kit_user_guide.pdf
23. ONNX: Tensorflow backend for onnx. https://github.com/onnx/onnx-tensorflow/
24. Redmon, J.: Darknet: Open source neural networks in c (2013–2016). http://pjreddie.com/darknet/
25. Redmon, J., Divvala, S., Girshick, R., Farhadi, A.: You only look once: unified, real-time object detection. In: IEEE CVPR (2016)
26. Redmon, J., Farhadi, A.: Yolov3: an incremental improvement. CoRR abs/1804.02767 (2018). http://arxiv.org/abs/1804.02767
27. Rungsuptaweekoon, K., Visoottiviseth, V., Takano, R.: Evaluating the power efficiency of deep learning inference on embedded gpu systems. In: International Conference on Information Technology (INCIT) (2017)
28. Stäcker, L., et al.: Deployment of deep neural networks for object detection on edge ai devices with runtime optimization. In: IEEE International Conference on Computer Vision Workshops (ICCVW) (2021)
29. Verucchi, M., et al.: A Systematic assessment of embedded neural networks for object detection. In: 2020 25th IEEE International Conference on Emerging Technologies and Factory Automation (ETFA), vol. 1, pp. 937–944 (2020). https://doi.org/10.1109/ETFA46521.2020.9212130
30. Wang, J., Gu, S.: FPGA implementation of object detection accelerator based on Vitis-AI. In: 2021 11th International Conference on Information Science and Technology (ICIST), pp. 571–577 (2021)
31. Xilinx: Vitis AI Repository. https://github.com/Xilinx/Vitis-AI/
32. Xilinx: Zcu104 board user guide (2018). https://www.xilinx.com/support/documentation/boards_and_kits/zcu104/ug1267-zcu104-eval-bd.pdf
33. Xilinx: Dpuczdx8g for zynq ultrascale+ mpsocs (2021). https://www.xilinx.com/content/dam/xilinx/support/documentation/ip_documentation/dpu/v3_3/pg338-dpu.pdf
34. Xiong, Y., et al.: MobileDets: searching for object detection architectures for mobile accelerators. In: IEEE CVPR (2021)
35. Yokotani, T., Sasaki, Y.: Comparison with HTTP and MQTT on required network resources for IoT. In: International Conference on Control, Electronics, Renewable Energy and Communications (ICCEREC) (2016)
36. Yu, J., et al.: Real-time object detection towards high power efficiency. In: Design, Automation & Test in Europe Conference & Exhibition (DATE) (2018)

ArtFID: Quantitative Evaluation
of Neural Style Transfer

Matthias Wright[1][✉] and Björn Ommer[1,2]

[1] Ludwig Maximilian University of Munich, Munich, Germany
m.wright@campus.lmu.de
[2] IWR, Ruprecht Karl University of Heidelberg, Heidelberg, Germany
https://github.com/matthias-wright/art-fid

Abstract. The field of neural style transfer has experienced a surge of research exploring different avenues ranging from optimization-based approaches and feed-forward models to meta-learning methods. The developed techniques have not just progressed the field of style transfer, but also led to breakthroughs in other areas of computer vision, such as all of visual synthesis. However, whereas quantitative evaluation and benchmarking have become pillars of computer vision research, the reproducible, quantitative assessment of style transfer models is still lacking. Even in comparison to other fields of visual synthesis, where widely used metrics exist, the quantitative evaluation of style transfer is still lagging behind. To support the automatic comparison of different style transfer approaches and to study their respective strengths and weaknesses, the field would greatly benefit from a quantitative measurement of stylization performance. Therefore, we propose a method to complement the currently mostly qualitative evaluation schemes. We provide extensive evaluations and a large-scale user study to show that the proposed metric strongly coincides with human judgment.

Keywords: Neural style transfer · Image synthesis · Quantitative evaluation

1 Introduction

Style transfer and texture transfer have been researched at least since the early 2000s [20,25]. In 2016, Gatys et al. proposed a novel method for style transfer based on the features of a pretrained convolutional neural network. The recent years have seen a surge of research exploring different avenues including, but not limited to, optimization-based approaches [23,36,40,41], feed-forward models [33,72], universal feed-forward models [7,30,32,44,46,50,57,65], ultra-resolution techniques [11,75], meta-learning approaches [64,85], and video style transfer [6,10,29,60].

Supplementary Information The online version contains supplementary material available at https://doi.org/10.1007/978-3-031-16788-1_34.

The developed techniques have not just progressed the field of style transfer, but also led to breakthroughs in other areas of computer vision, such as visual synthesis. For example, the perceptual loss [23,33] has been applied to tasks ranging from photographic image synthesis [9] to motion transfer [4], the generator architecture employed by Johnson et al. [33] has been used to synthesize photo-realistic images from semantic label maps [76] or for unpaired image-to-image translation [88], and the AdaIN layer [30] was a key ingredient for the StyleGAN generator [35] that produced state-of-the-art results in unconditional generative image modeling.

In contrast to other areas of computer vision research such as classification or even natural image synthesis, where quantitative evaluation and benchmarking are already common practice, quantitative assessment of style transfer models is still lacking.

Currently, the most common method for evaluating these models is a qualitative comparison for a few, commonly used, style and content images. This is generally useful for an initial impression, however, the performance of style transfer models greatly varies across different style and content images. For example, Fig. 1 shows stylized images from AdaIN [30] and WCT [46] for two different style/content pairs. One can argue that AdaIN [30] outperforms WCT [46] for the first pair and vice versa for the second pair.

Some papers provide a quantitative comparison using measurements for speed, memory, or control [11–13,28,30,46,49,51,54,64,72,79,82,85]. These measurements are very helpful to highlight a model's performance with respect to a specific property such as speed, but are generally not intended to measure stylization performance. A few works [28,37,52,82] also employ classical perceptual metrics such as PSNR or SSIM [77], however, these metrics are generally not consistent with human perception [86].

Sanakoyeu et al. [62] proposed the *Deception rate* to measure the quality of stylized images. It is the fraction of stylized images that an artist classification network has assigned to the artist, whose artwork has been used for stylization. The deception rate can be useful in some cases but also suffers from certain drawbacks and is not widely used as a result. First, it only works for style images belonging to an artist for which the artist classifier network has been trained and thus cannot be used for arbitrary styles. And second, it completely disregards content preservation.

In the absence of a suitable quantitative measurement of stylization performance, many authors have turned to human evaluation studies [5,7,8,15,16, 28,37,40,41,43,50,54,57,62,75,80–83], where users are asked to compare stylized images of different models and specify their preference. These studies give better insights into a model's stylization performance in comparison to other methods, especially when conducted with many users and for many different style and content images. Nonetheless, there are cases where a user study is not feasible. Large-scale crowdsourcing can be expensive and may not be an option for researchers with limited funding. Furthermore, there are cases where a quantitative measurement is simply more suitable. As an example, consider the closely-related field of image synthesis, where quantitative measurements for image quality are used, not just for evaluation, but also as a core part of the approach. Recent examples include work by Mokady et al. [56], where Fréchet Inception Distance (FID) [26] and Learned Perceptual Image Patch Similarity (LPIPS) [86] measurements are employed for self-filtering a collection of images, work by Karras et al. [34] that use the FID to detect GAN [24] overfitting, or a large-scale GAN study by Lucic et al. [53] that utilize the FID to compare the sensitivity of different GAN models to hyper-parameters. A quantitative measurement of stylization performance would facilitate similar studies to further analyze and improve style transfer methods. In this work, we propose a method that fills this role and call it *ArtFID*. Our goal is not to replace the current evaluation techniques, but rather to complement them.

Stylization performance is mostly determined by two factors: *content preservation* and *style matching*. Content preservation refers to the extent to which the semantic content from the content images is preserved in the stylized images. Style matching refers to the extent to which the style of the generated images resembles the style of the target style images. Measuring content preservation is straightforward using the well-established perceptual loss [23,33], CLIP loss [59], or LPIPS metric [86]. However, measuring style matching is more challenging because it confronts us with the question "what is style?", a question that has been debated relentlessly by art historians [1,42,55,63,73]. However, a commonly used definition is that style is the "distinctive manner which permits the grouping of works into related categories" [21]. This definition gives rise to a representation learning approach, where artworks are classified into categories by a neural network to obtain representations that reflect their stylistic similarity. To this end, we collect a large-scale dataset of artworks, labeled by artist and stylistic period. We make use of both labels by employing an architecture with two classification heads. Having obtained the image representations in the form of neural network features, we return to the issue of measuring style matching. As shown by Li et al. [45], the task of style transfer corresponds to aligning feature distributions of neural networks. To measure style matching, we can thus measure how well the feature distribution of style images matches the feature distribution of stylized images. Following the work by Heusel et al. [26], we measure the distance between these two feature distributions with respect to the first two moments using the Fréchet distance [18,22].

Our contributions are as follows:

- We propose a method for quantitatively evaluating style transfer models with respect to stylization performance that strongly coincides with human judgment.
- We introduce a large-scale dataset, containing 250k images of labeled artworks.
- We provide extensive evaluations and a large-scale human evaluation study to support our claims.

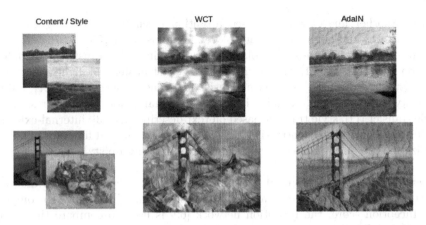

Fig. 1. AdaIN [30] (arguably) performs better on the top style/content pair, while WCT [46] (arguably) performs better on the bottom style/content pair.

2 Related Work

Style Transfer. Research in the fields of style transfer and texture transfer goes back to the early 2000s. Efros and Freeman [20] proposed texture synthesis and transfer using image quilting and Hertzmann et al. [25] proposed *image analogies* based on a simple multi-scale autoregression. Other work in this area includes a method for synthesizing directional textures [74].

In 2016, Gatys et al. [23] proposed an iterative optimization algorithm for style transfer that leverages the representations learned by convolutional neural networks. In the following, Johnson et al. [33] and Ulyanov et al. [72] used feed-forward networks to approximate the optimization problem formulated by Gatys et al. [23] for a specific style image.

In order to use multiple styles with a single network, Dumoulin et al. [19] proposed conditional instance normalization. Huang and Belongie [30] proposed the first method for arbitrary style transfer, using adaptive instance normalization. Li et al. [46] introduced another arbitrary style transfer model, based on whitening and colouring transformations.

Li et al. [45] provided insights into the mechanics of style transfer by proving that matching the Gram matrices of feature maps is equivalent to minimizing the Maximum Mean Discrepancy with the second order polynomial kernel.

Li et al. [47] proposed a closed-form solution for photorealistic stylization that is based on the aforementioned whitening and colouring transformations. Sheng et al. [65] introduced a method that semantically aligns content features to trade off generalization and efficiency and Li et al. [44] proposed a linear transformation for image and video style transfer.

Shen et al. [64] and Zhang et al. [85] employed meta-learning approaches to handle the trade-off between speed, flexibility, and quality, and Svoboda et al. [68] used graph neural networks to recombine style and content in latent space. Another line of research used attention mechanisms to integrate local style patterns and align content and style manifolds [16,32,50,54,57].

Recent work includes exemplar-based portrait style transfer [83], online motion style transfer [71], transformer-based style transfer [15], lightweight photorealistic style transfer [13], style transfer for scene reconstruction [27], industrial style transfer [82], thumbnail instance normalization for ultra-resolution style transfer [11], style transfer based on text descriptions [43], internal-external style transfer with two contrastive losses [7], reversible neural flows for unbiased stylization [2], and a unified architecture for domain-aware style transfer [28].

Inception Score. Salimans et al. [61] proposed the *Inception score*, an evaluation metric for generated images that correlates with human judgment. To compute the Inception score, the Inception network [69] is used to compare the conditional label distribution to the marginal distribution of the generated images. A downside of the Inception score is that the statistics of the generated images are not compared to the statistics of real images [26].

Fréchet Inception Distance. Heusel et al. [26] proposed the *Fréchet Inception Distance (FID)* that improves the Inception score by computing the Fréchet distance [18,22] between the Gaussian distribution of Inception features of generated images and the Gaussian distribution of Inception features of real images.

3   Approach

3.1   ArtFID

As stated before, the stylization quality is determined by content preservation and style matching. In contrast to previous work, we measure both factors and combine them to form a quantitative metric.

Let X_c denote the set of content images, X_s the set of style images, and X_g the set of stylized images, generated from a particular style transfer model. To measure content preservation for a particular stylized image, we compute a distance $d(X_c^{(i)}, X_g^{(i)})$ between the content image $X_c^{(i)}$ and the corresponding stylized image $X_g^{(i)}$. Possible choices for $d(\cdot)$ are the VGG perceptual loss [23,33], the CLIP loss [59], or the LPIPS metric [86]. We select LPIPS and show in Sect. 4.5 that it slightly outperforms the alternatives.

Measuring the content preservation for a style transfer model then simply corresponds to evaluating $d(X_c^{(i)}, X_g^{(i)})$ for a large batch of stylized images and taking the mean.

As stated above, to measure style matching for a model, we first learn suitable image representations by training a classifier on a large-scale artwork dataset (Sect. 3.3). For the classifier, we use the Inception network [69]. The architecture is modified by using two classification heads instead of one. In doing so, we are able to harness the information from both the artist labels as well as the labels for the stylistic period that are present in the dataset. For more information about the classifier training, see Sect. 3.4. The image representations are the Inception features from the last layer before the classifier heads. These features are computed for both the style images X_s and the stylized images X_g. To measure style matching between the style images X_s and the stylized images X_g, we measure the distance between these two feature distributions. This is motivated by work from Li et al. [45] that shows that the task of style transfer corresponds to aligning feature distributions of deep neural networks. Similar to Heusel et al. [26], we measure the distance between these two feature distributions with respect to the first two moments using the Fréchet distance [18,22]

$$\text{FID}(X_s, X_g) = ||\mu_s - \mu_g||_2^2 + \text{Tr}(\Sigma_s + \Sigma_g - 2(\Sigma_s\Sigma_g)^{\frac{1}{2}}), \qquad (1)$$

where (μ_s, Σ_s) and (μ_g, Σ_g) are the mean and covariance of the Inception features of the style images X_s and the stylized images X_g, respectively.

Having obtained a measure for content preservation and a measure for style matching, we combine these measures to form the ArtFID, formulated as follows

$$\text{ArtFID}(X_g, X_c, X_s) = \left(1 + \frac{1}{N}\sum_{i=1}^{N} d(X_c^{(i)}, X_g^{(i)})\right) \cdot \left(1 + \text{FID}(X_s, X_g)\right) \quad (2)$$

Ones are added to both factors to avoid a degenerate minimum when $X_c = X_g$ or $X_s = X_g$. The measures are combined to ensure that only models that perform well on both content preservation and style matching achieve a low ArtFID score. Multiplication lends itself well to this purpose. We also tested the addition operation but the effect on the overall ranking was negligible.

3.2   Unbiased ArtFID Computation

Chong and Forsyth [14] showed that the FID computed with a finite number of samples N, denoted FID_N, is biased. This bias in FID_N vanishes when $N \to \infty$. The authors [14] propose a method for computing $\overline{\text{FID}}_\infty$, an unbiased estimate of FID_∞, using N samples. The FID is computed K times, each time with a different number of samples $M_1, \ldots, M_K$. The $M_1, \ldots, M_K$ are evenly spaced numbers over the interval $[5000, N]$. A linear regression model is then fitted to the points $(1/M_1, \text{FID}_{M_1}), \ldots, (1/M_K, \text{FID}_{M_K})$. To obtain $\overline{\text{FID}}_\infty$, the linear regression model is evaluated at 0. For an in-depth analysis, we refer to the work of Chong and Forsyth [14].

We use $\overline{\text{FID}}_\infty$ for computing the ArtFID and denote it as ArtFID_∞. Table 2 shows that it performs slightly better than the biased ArtFID.

3.3   Data

The dataset used for training the Inception network consists of 250K images, labeled by artist and stylistic period. The images were collected from public datasets (e.g. WikiArt [70]), as well as museum databases and art collections (e.g. Art UK[1]). See Sec. A of the supplementary for more details about the dataset.

---

[1] https://artuk.org/.

3.4 Training

We broadly follow the methodology described by Szegedy et al. [69] for training the Inception network. The classifier head is replaced by two separate heads, one for each label (artist and stylistic period). We use the Adam optimizer [38] with a learning rate of 0.0001 and $\beta = (0.9, 0.999)$. The batch size is set to 64 and the weight of the auxiliary classifier is set to 0.3. See Sect. B of the supplementary for more information about the training and evaluation.

4 Experiments

4.1 ArtFID Evaluation

We evaluate the ArtFID with 13 different style transfer methods from the literature [7,11,16,23,30,32,44,46,50,54,57,65,68], some of which are well-established, some are recently published, and some are in between. For each method, we generate stylized images using the same pairs of content and style images. Content images are sampled from the Places365 dataset [87] and the COCO dataset [48]. Style images are sampled from the WikiArt dataset [70] and the BAM dataset [78]. Images are sampled from multiple datasets to increase the variability of style and content images. Following the recommendations by Heusel et al. [26], we compute the ArtFID with samples of 50k images. Both style and content images are resized to 512 × 512, a commonly used image size for style transfer methods. As proposed by Parmar et al. [58], we resize style and content images with bicubic interpolation and antialiasing and save the stylized images using the PNG format.

For each style transfer method, the ArtFID is computed with 5 different samples containing 50k images each. The results are reported in Table 1.

4.2 Large-Scale Human Evaluation

In order to test the validity of the ArtFID, we conduct a large-scale human evaluation study on Amazon Mechanical Turk (AMT). We use the same 13 style transfer methods as before. Similar to [36,40], we chose a pairwise comparison, where the outputs of two methods are compared head-to-head. This choice is in line with recent work from the field of psychology that provides evidence that human perceptual decision-making is significantly impaired when presented with multiple alternatives, rather than just two alternatives [84]. We compare each possible pairing of style transfer methods. For each pairing, we perform 80 comparisons. Each comparison is voted on by 5 workers and the winner is decided by majority vote. In total there were 31200 tasks and workers were rewarded $0.03 for each task. Figure 2 shows the interface that was shown to the AMT workers for a particular task.

Fig. 2. The interface shown to the ATM workers for the user study.

4.3 Correlation with Human Judgment

We evaluate the results of the AMT user study with the widely-used Bradley-Terry model [3]. Given m entities that are repeatedly compared with each another in pairs, the Bradley-Terry model yields an overall score γ_i for each entity i that induces a global ranking of the entities. The model works under the assumption that if we partition the set of entities into two non-empty subsets, some entity in the first subset is compared to some entity in the second subset at least once [31]. This requirement is easily satisfied by comparing each entity with all the other entities, as described in Sect. 4.2. We can then estimate the scores $\gamma_1, \ldots, \gamma_m$ using the log-likelihood of the Bradley-Terry model

$$l(\gamma_1, \ldots, \gamma_m) = \sum_{i=1}^{m} \sum_{j=1}^{m} [w_{ij} \log(\gamma_i) - w_{ij} \log(\gamma_i + \gamma_j)], \qquad (3)$$

where w_{ij} denotes the number of times that entity i was preferred over entity j, and we assume that $w_{ii} = 0$ and $\sum_i \gamma_i = 1$ [31]. There exists a simple iterative algorithm that yields a unique maximum of Eq. 3. See Sec. C of the supplementary for an outline of the algorithm and [31] for a study of its convergence properties.

To measure how well the ArtFID coincides with human judgment, we compute the correlation between the ranking of style transfer methods obtained from the human evaluation study and the ranking of the same methods induced by the ArtFID. A commonly-used measure for this is *Spearman's rank correlation coefficient (Spearman's ρ)* [66, 67], a non-parametric measure of correlation between rankings. Spearman's ρ is calculated by replacing the actual observations with the corresponding ranks in the formula for the correlation coefficient [39]. Spearman's ρ is often used as a hypothesis test to determine if there is a relation between two random variables [17]. For the two-sided test, the null hypothesis is that both random variables are mutually independent and the alternative hypothesis is that there is either a positive or a negative correlation. For the one-sided test, the null hypothesis is that both random variables are mutually independent and the alternative hypothesis is that there is a positive correlation. We report both the Spearman's ρ as well as the p-values of the hypothesis tests in Table 2.

To validate our results, we rely not only on our AMT user study but also consider user studies from other style transfer works. We observe that the ranking induced by the ArtFID coincides with the majority of user studies reported in the literature [7,15,16,44,50,54,57]. For example, Chen et al. [7] report that users preferred IEContraAST [7] over SANet [57], Gatys et al. [23], LST [44], AdaAttN [50], WCT [46], and Avatar-Net [65]. Luo et al. [54] report that users preferred PAMA [54] over AdaAttN [50], MANet [16], SANet [57], MAST [32], and AdaIN [30]. Park and Lee [57] report that users preferred SANet [57] over Gatys et al. [23], Avatar-Net [65], AdaIN [30], and WCT [46], Liu et al. [50] report that users preferred AdaAttN [50] over LST [44], SANet [57], MAST [32], AdaAttN [50], and Avatar-Net [65]. Deng et al. [16] report that users preferred MANet [16] over SANet [57] and AdaIN [30].

4.4   Consistency with Increasing Perturbations

Heusel et al. [26] showed that the FID is consistent with respect to increasing levels of perturbations that are applied to the images. We verify that the ArtFID$_\infty$ inherits this property. Figure 3 shows the ArtFID$_\infty$ evaluated using the same image transformations as Heusel et al. [26]. The results for the ArtFID are comparable.

4.5   Ablations

We perform the following ablation experiments. All results are reported in Table 3.

Using ImageNet Features for ArtFID Computation. Instead of using the modified Inception network trained on the art dataset (Sect. 3.3), we use the ImageNet features from the original Inception network to measure style matching. This shows the effectiveness of learning image representations that reflect stylistic similarity for the style matching task.

Training the Inception Network Only with Artist Labels. We only use the artist labels when training the Inception network on the art dataset. This experiment highlights the importance of harnessing the information from both labels.

Training the Inception Network Only with Style Labels. We only use the style labels when training the Inception network on the art dataset. Again, this shows the importance of using the information from both labels.

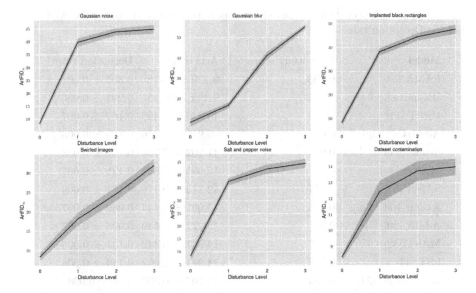

Fig. 3. The ArtFID$_\infty$ is consistent with respect to increasing perturbations applied to the stylized images. The stylized images for this experiment were generated using the algorithm proposed by Gatys et al. [23]. The line represents the mean and the shaded area the standard deviation over 4 trials.

Using CLIP for Measuring Content Preservation. Instead of using the LPIPS metric [86] to measure content preservation, we use CLIP [59]. We observe that the LPIPS metric performs slightly better.

Using VGG for Measuring Content Preservation. Instead of using the LPIPS metric [86] to measure content preservation, we use the VGG perceptual loss [23,33]. Again, the LPIPS metric performs slightly better.

5   Limitations

Obtaining accurate ArtFID measurements is computationally expensive. It requires evaluating the Inception network and the LPIPS metric for several thousands of images.

Table 1. For each style transfer model, we report the user study score, the ArtFID$_\infty$ and the Deception rate.

Model	User study score γ ↑	ArtFID$_\infty$ ↓	Deception rate ↑
PAMA [54]	0.103	9.129 ± 0.478	0.307 ± 0.001
IEContraAST [7]	0.105	9.495 ± 0.495	0.291 ± 0.006
URST [11]	0.092	10.846 ± 0.426	0.167 ± 0.007
AdaAttN [50]	0.093	10.911 ± 0.356	0.108 ± 0.008
Svoboda et al. [68]	0.073	11.202 ± 0.766	0.127 ± 0.008
MANet [16]	0.08	12.095 ± 0.878	0.128 ± 0.007
SANet [57]	0.077	12.373 ± 0.179	0.171 ± 0.003
Avatar-Net [65]	0.075	13.065 ± 0.844	0.089 ± 0.007
AdaIN [30]	0.065	13.222 ± 0.549	0.096 ± 0.007
MAST [32]	0.067	14.937 ± 0.442	0.131 ± 0.005
LST [44]	0.066	14.941 ± 1.062	0.146 ± 0.008
Gatys et al. [23]	0.054	15.707 ± 0.307	0.16 ± 0.008
WCT [46]	0.05	25.495 ± 0.665	0.06 ± 0.006

Table 2. The correlation between the rankings induced by the different evaluation methods (ArtFID, ArtFID$_\infty$, and Deception rate) and the ranking induced by the AMT user study. The ranking from the ArtFID$_\infty$ strongly correlates with the ranking from the user study.

Metric	Spearman's ρ ↑	Two-sided p-value ↓	One-sided p-value ↓
ArtFID$_\infty$	**0.939**	**1.87e−06**	**9.39e−07**
ArtFID	0.934	2.99e−06	1.49e−06
Deception rate	0.549	0.051	0.025

Table 3. Ablation experiments. (A) ArtFID as described in Sect. 3, (B) the Inception network is trained on ImageNet instead of the art dataset, (C) the modified Inception network is trained using only the artist labels, (D) the modified Inception network is trained using only the style labels, (D) content preservation is measured using CLIP, and (D) content preservation is measured using the VGG perceptual loss.

Configuration	Spearman's ρ ↑		Two-sided p-value ↓		One-sided p-value ↓	
	ArtFID	ArtFID$_\infty$	ArtFID	ArtFID$_\infty$	ArtFID	ArtFID$_\infty$
A Full	**0.934**	**0.939**	**2.99e−06**	**1.87e−06**	**1.49e−06**	**9.39e−07**
B ImageNet features	0.302	0.329	0.316	0.271	0.158	0.136
C Only artist labels	0.868	0.868	0.0001	0.0001	5.95e−05	5.95e−05
D Only style labels	0.851	0.851	0.0002	0.0002	0.0001	0.0001
E CLIP for content	0.917	0.917	9.91e−06	9.91e−06	4.95e−06	4.95e−06
F VGG for content	0.928	0.923	4.61e−06	6.85e−06	2.30e−06	3.42e−06

6   Conclusion

In this work, we propose a method for quantitatively evaluating style transfer models. The goal of this work is to complement the currently used evaluation schemes by promoting the automatic comparison of different style transfer approaches and to study their respective strengths and weaknesses through in-depth analyses. A given model is evaluated by measuring content preservation and style matching across many different style and content images. Content preservation is quantified using the well-established LPIPS metric. To measure style matching, we first learn suitable image representations using a large-scale art dataset. We then measure the distance between the feature distributions of the stylized images and style images with respect to the first two moments. We evaluate our method by conducting a user study on Amazon Mechanical Turk and show that it strongly coincides with human judgment.

Acknowledgements. This work has been funded by the Deutsche Forschungsgemeinschaft (DFG, German Research Foundation) within project 421703927.

References

1. Ackerman, J.S.: A theory of style. J. Aesthet. Art Critic. **20**(3), 227–237 (1962)
2. An, J., Huang, S., Song, Y., Dou, D., Liu, W., Luo, J.: ArtFlow: unbiased image style transfer via reversible neural flows. In: Conference on Computer Vision and Pattern Recognition (CVPR) (2021)
3. Bradley, R.A., Terry, M.E.: Rank analysis of incomplete block designs: I. The method of paired comparisons. Biometrika **39**(3/4), 324–345 (1952)
4. Chan, C., Ginosar, S., Zhou, T., Efros, A.A.: Everybody dance now. In: International Conference on Computer Vision (ICCV) (2019)
5. Chandran, P., Zoss, G., Gotardo, P., Gross, M., Bradley, D.: Adaptive convolutions for structure-aware style transfer. In: Conference on Computer Vision and Pattern Recognition (CVPR) (2021)
6. Chen, D., Liao, J., Yuan, L., Yu, N., Hua, G.: Coherent online video style transfer. In: International Conference on Computer Vision (ICCV) (2017)
7. Chen, H., et al.: Artistic style transfer with internal-external learning and contrastive learning. In: Conference on Neural Information Processing Systems (NeurIPS) (2021)
8. Chen, H., et al.: Diverse image style transfer via invertible cross-space mapping. In: International Conference on Computer Vision (ICCV) (2021)
9. Chen, Q., Koltun, V.: Photographic image synthesis with cascaded refinement networks. In: International Conference on Computer Vision (ICCV) (2017)
10. Chen, X., Zhang, Y., Wang, Y., Shu, H., Xu, C., Xu, C.: Optical flow distillation: towards efficient and stable video style transfer. In: Vedaldi, A., Bischof, H., Brox, T., Frahm, J.-M. (eds.) ECCV 2020. LNCS, vol. 12351, pp. 614–630. Springer, Cham (2020). https://doi.org/10.1007/978-3-030-58539-6_37
11. Chen, Z., Wang, W., Xie, E., Lu, T., Luo, P.: Towards ultra-resolution neural style transfer via thumbnail instance normalization. In: AAAI Conference on Artificial Intelligence (AAAI) (2022)

12. Chiu, T.-Y., Gurari, D.: Iterative feature transformation for fast and versatile universal style transfer. In: Vedaldi, A., Bischof, H., Brox, T., Frahm, J.-M. (eds.) ECCV 2020. LNCS, vol. 12364, pp. 169–184. Springer, Cham (2020). https://doi.org/10.1007/978-3-030-58529-7_11

13. Chiu, T.Y., Gurari, D.: PCA-based knowledge distillation towards lightweight and content-style balanced photorealistic style transfer models. In: Conference on Computer Vision and Pattern Recognition (CVPR) (2022)

14. Chong, M.J., Forsyth, D.: Effectively unbiased fid and inception score and where to find them. In: Conference on Computer Vision and Pattern Recognition (CVPR) (2020)

15. Deng, Y., et al.: StyTr^2: image style transfer with transformers. In: Conference on Computer Vision and Pattern Recognition (CVPR) (2022)

16. Deng, Y., Tang, F., Dong, W., Sun, W., Huang, F., Xu, C.: Arbitrary style transfer via multi-adaptation network. In: ACM International Conference on Multimedia (2020)

17. Dodge, Y.: The Concise Encyclopedia of Statistics. Springer, New York (2008). https://doi.org/10.1007/978-0-387-32833-1

18. Dowson, D., Landau, B.: The Fréchet distance between multivariate normal distributions. J. Multivar. Anal. **12**(3), 450–455 (1982)

19. Dumoulin, V., Shlens, J., Kudlur, M.: A learned representation for artistic style. In: International Conference on Learning Representations (ICLR) (2017)

20. Efros, A.A., Freeman, W.T.: Image quilting for texture synthesis and transfer. In: Proceedings of the 28th Annual Conference on Computer Graphics and Interactive Techniques, SIGGRAPH 2001, pp. 341–346. Association for Computing Machinery, New York, NY, USA (2001)

21. Fernie, E.: Art History and Its Methods. Phaidon Press, New York (1995)

22. Fréchet, M.: Sur la distance de deux lois de probabilité. C. R. Acad. Sci. Paris **244**, 689–692 (1957)

23. Gatys, L.A., Ecker, A.S., Bethge, M.: Image style transfer using convolutional neural networks. In: Conference on Computer Vision and Pattern Recognition (CVPR) (2016)

24. Goodfellow, I., et al.: Generative adversarial nets. In: Conference on Neural Information Processing Systems (NeurIPS) (2014)

25. Hertzmann, A., Jacobs, C.E., Oliver, N., Curless, B., Salesin, D.H.: Image analogies. In: Proceedings of the 28th Annual Conference on Computer Graphics and Interactive Techniques, SIGGRAPH 2001, pp. 327–340. Association for Computing Machinery, New York, NY, USA (2001)

26. Heusel, M., Ramsauer, H., Unterthiner, T., Nessler, B., Klambauer, G., Hochreiter, S.: GANs trained by a two time-scale update rule converge to a Nash equilibrium. In: Conference on Neural Information Processing Systems (NeurIPS) (2017)

27. Höllein, L., Johnson, J., Nießner, M.: StyleMesh: style transfer for indoor 3D scene reconstructions. In: Conference on Computer Vision and Pattern Recognition (CVPR) (2022)

28. Hong, K., Jeon, S., Yang, H., Fu, J., Byun, H.: Domain-aware universal style transfer. In: International Conference on Computer Vision (ICCV) (2021)

29. Huang, H., et al.: Real-time neural style transfer for videos. In: Conference on Computer Vision and Pattern Recognition (CVPR) (2017)

30. Huang, X., Belongie, S.J.: Arbitrary style transfer in real-time with adaptive instance normalization. In: International Conference on Computer Vision (ICCV) (2017)

31. Hunter, D.R.: MM algorithms for generalized Bradley-Terry models. Ann. Stat. **32**(1), 384–406 (2004)
32. Huo, J., et al.: Manifold alignment for semantically aligned style transfer. In: International Conference on Computer Vision (ICCV) (2021)
33. Johnson, J., Alahi, A., Fei-Fei, L.: Perceptual losses for real-time style transfer and super-resolution. In: Leibe, B., Matas, J., Sebe, N., Welling, M. (eds.) ECCV 2016. LNCS, vol. 9906, pp. 694–711. Springer, Cham (2016). https://doi.org/10.1007/978-3-319-46475-6_43
34. Karras, T., Aittala, M., Hellsten, J., Laine, S., Lehtinen, J., Aila, T.: Training generative adversarial networks with limited data. In: Conference on Neural Information Processing Systems (NeurIPS) (2020)
35. Karras, T., Laine, S., Aila, T.: A style-based generator architecture for generative adversarial networks. In: Conference on Computer Vision and Pattern Recognition (CVPR) (2019)
36. Kim, S.S.Y., Kolkin, N., Salavon, J., Shakhnarovich, G.: Deformable style transfer. In: Vedaldi, A., Bischof, H., Brox, T., Frahm, J.-M. (eds.) ECCV 2020. LNCS, vol. 12371, pp. 246–261. Springer, Cham (2020). https://doi.org/10.1007/978-3-030-58574-7_15
37. Kim, S., Kim, S., Kim, S.: Deep translation prior: test-time training for photorealistic style transfer. In: AAAI Conference on Artificial Intelligence (AAAI) (2022)
38. Kingma, D.P., Ba, J.: Adam: a method for stochastic optimization. In: International Conference on Learning Representations (ICLR) (2015)
39. Kokoska, S., Zwillinger, D.: CRC Standard Probability and Statistics Tables and Formulae. Chapman & Hall, New York (2000)
40. Kolkin, N., Salavon, J., Shakhnarovich, G.: Style transfer by relaxed optimal transport and self-similarity. In: Conference on Computer Vision and Pattern Recognition (CVPR) (2019)
41. Kotovenko, D., Wright, M., Heimbrecht, A., Ommer, B.: Rethinking style transfer: from pixels to parameterized brushstrokes. In: Conference on Computer Vision and Pattern Recognition (CVPR) (2021)
42. Kubler, G.: Towards a reductive theory of visual style. In: Meyer, L.B., Lang, B. (eds.) The Concept of Style, pp. 119–127. University of Pennsylvania Press (1979)
43. Kwon, G., Ye, J.C.: CLIPstyler: image style transfer with a single text condition. In: Conference on Computer Vision and Pattern Recognition (CVPR) (2022)
44. Li, X., Liu, S., Kautz, J., Yang, M.H.: Learning linear transformations for fast image and video style transfer. In: Conference on Computer Vision and Pattern Recognition (CVPR) (2019)
45. Li, Y., Wang, N., Liu, J., Hou, X.: Demystifying neural style transfer. In: Twenty-Sixth International Joint Conference on Artificial Intelligence (IJCAI) (2017)
46. Li, Y., Fang, C., Yang, J., Wang, Z., Lu, X., Yang, M.H.: Universal style transfer via feature transforms. In: Conference on Neural Information Processing Systems (NeurIPS) (2017)
47. Li, Y., Liu, M.-Y., Li, X., Yang, M.-H., Kautz, J.: A closed-form solution to photorealistic image stylization. In: Ferrari, V., Hebert, M., Sminchisescu, C., Weiss, Y. (eds.) ECCV 2018. LNCS, vol. 11207, pp. 468–483. Springer, Cham (2018). https://doi.org/10.1007/978-3-030-01219-9_28
48. Lin, T.-Y., et al.: Microsoft COCO: common objects in context. In: Fleet, D., Pajdla, T., Schiele, B., Tuytelaars, T. (eds.) ECCV 2014. LNCS, vol. 8693, pp. 740–755. Springer, Cham (2014). https://doi.org/10.1007/978-3-319-10602-1_48
49. Liu, S., et al.: Paint transformer: feed forward neural painting with stroke prediction. In: Conference on Computer Vision and Pattern Recognition (CVPR) (2021)

50. Liu, S., et al.: AdaAttN: revisit attention mechanism in arbitrary neural style transfer. In: International Conference on Computer Vision (ICCV) (2021)
51. Liu, X.C., Yang, Y.L., Hall, P.: Learning to warp for style transfer. In: Conference on Computer Vision and Pattern Recognition (CVPR) (2021)
52. Liu, X., Wu, W., Wu, H., Wen, Z.: Deep style transfer for line drawings. In: AAAI Conference on Artificial Intelligence (AAAI) (2021)
53. Lucic, M., Kurach, K., Michalski, M., Gelly, S., Bousquet, O.: Are GANs created equal? A large-scale study. In: Conference on Neural Information Processing Systems (NeurIPS) (2018)
54. Luo, X., Han, Z., Yang, L., Zhang, L.: Consistent style transfer. arXiv preprint arXiv:2201.02233v1 (2022)
55. Meyer, L.B., Lang, B.: The Concept of Style. University of Pennsylvania Press, Philadelphia (1979)
56. Mokady, R., et al.: Self-distilled StyleGAN: towards generation from internet photos. arXiv preprint arXiv:2202.12211 (2022)
57. Park, D.Y., Lee, K.H.: Arbitrary style transfer with style-attentional networks. In: Conference on Computer Vision and Pattern Recognition (CVPR) (2019)
58. Parmar, G., Zhang, R., Zhu, J.Y.: On aliased resizing and surprising subtleties in GAN evaluation. In: Conference on Computer Vision and Pattern Recognition (CVPR) (2022)
59. Radford, A., et al.: Learning transferable visual models from natural language supervision. In: International Conference on Machine Learning (ICML) (2021)
60. Ruder, M., Dosovitskiy, A., Brox, T.: Artistic style transfer for videos and spherical images. Int. J. Comput. Vision 126, 1199–1219 (2018)
61. Salimans, T., Goodfellow, I., Zaremba, W., Cheung, V., Radford, A., Chen, X.: Improved techniques for training GANs. In: Conference on Neural Information Processing Systems (NeurIPS) (2016)
62. Sanakoyeu, A., Kotovenko, D., Lang, S., Ommer, B.: A style-aware content loss for real-time HD style transfer. In: Ferrari, V., Hebert, M., Sminchisescu, C., Weiss, Y. (eds.) ECCV 2018. LNCS, vol. 11212, pp. 715–731. Springer, Cham (2018). https://doi.org/10.1007/978-3-030-01237-3_43
63. Schapiro, M.: Style. University of Chicago Press, Chicago (1953)
64. Shen, F., Yan, S., Zeng, G.: Neural style transfer via meta networks. In: Conference on Computer Vision and Pattern Recognition (CVPR) (2018)
65. Sheng, L., Lin, Z., Shao, J., Wang, X.: Avatar-Net: multi-scale zero-shot style transfer by feature decoration. In: Conference on Computer Vision and Pattern Recognition (CVPR) (2018)
66. Spearman, C.: The proof and measurement of association between two things. Am. J. Psychol. 15(1), 72–101 (1904)
67. Spearman, C.: Demonstration of formulae for true measurement of correlation. Am. J. Psychol. 18(2), 161–169 (1907)
68. Svoboda, J., Anoosheh, A., Osendorfer, C., Masci, J.: Two-stage peer-regularized feature recombination for arbitrary image style transfer. In: Conference on Computer Vision and Pattern Recognition (CVPR) (2020)
69. Szegedy, C., Vanhoucke, V., Ioffe, S., Shlens, J., Wojna, Z.: Rethinking the inception architecture for computer vision. In: Conference on Computer Vision and Pattern Recognition (CVPR) (2016)
70. Tan, W.R., Chan, C.S., Aguirre, H.E., Tanaka, K.: Ceci n'est pas une pipe: a deep convolutional network for fine-art paintings classification. In: International Conference on Image Processing (ICIP) (2016)

71. Tao, T., Zhan, X., Chen, Z., van de Panne, M.: Style-ERD: responsive and coherent online motion style transfer. In: Conference on Computer Vision and Pattern Recognition (CVPR) (2022)
72. Ulyanov, D., Lebedev, V., Vedaldi, A., Lempitsky, V.S.: Texture networks: feedforward synthesis of textures and stylized images. In: International Conference on Machine Learning (ICML) (2016)
73. Wallach, A.: Meyer Schapiro's essay on style: falling into the void. J. Aesthet. Art Critic. **55**(1), 11–15 (1997)
74. Wang, B., Wang, W., Yang, H., Sun, J.: Efficient example-based painting and synthesis of 2D directional texture. Trans. Vis. Comput. Graph. **10**(3), 266–277 (2004)
75. Wang, H., Li, Y., Wang, Y., Hu, H., Yang, M.H.: Collaborative distillation for ultra-resolution universal style transfer. In: Conference on Computer Vision and Pattern Recognition (CVPR) (2020)
76. Wang, T.C., Liu, M.Y., Zhu, J.Y., Tao, A., Kautz, J., Catanzaro, B.: High-resolution image synthesis and semantic manipulation with conditional GANs. In: Conference on Computer Vision and Pattern Recognition (CVPR) (2018)
77. Wang, Z., Bovik, A.C., Sheikh, H.R., Simoncelli, E.P.: Image quality assessment: from error visibility to structural similarity. In: Transactions on Image Processing, vol. 13, no. 4 (2004)
78. Wilber, M.J., Fang, C., Jin, H., Hertzmann, A., Collomosse, J., Belongie, S.: BAM! The behance artistic media dataset for recognition beyond photography. In: International Conference on Computer Vision (ICCV) (2017)
79. Wu, X., Hu, Z., Sheng, L., Xu, D.: StyleFormer: real-time arbitrary style transfer via parametric style composition. In: International Conference on Computer Vision (ICCV) (2021)
80. Wu, Z., Song, C., Zhou, Y., Gong, M., Huang, H.: EFANet: exchangeable feature alignment network for arbitrary style transfer. In: AAAI Conference on Artificial Intelligence (AAAI) (2020)
81. Xu, W., Long, C., Wang, R., Wang, G.: DRB-GAN: a dynamic ResBlock generative adversarial network for artistic style transfer. In: International Conference on Computer Vision (ICCV) (2021)
82. Yang, J., Guo, F., Chen, S., Li, J., Yang, J.: Industrial style transfer with large-scale geometric warping and content preservation. In: Conference on Computer Vision and Pattern Recognition (CVPR) (2022)
83. Yang, S., Jiang, L., Liu, Z., Loy, C.C.: Pastiche master: exemplar-based high-resolution portrait style transfer. In: Conference on Computer Vision and Pattern Recognition (CVPR) (2022)
84. Yeon, J., Rahnev, D.: The suboptimality of perceptual decision making with multiple alternatives. Nat. Commun. **11**(3857), 1–12 (2020)
85. Zhang, C., Zhu, Y., Zhu, S.C.: MetaStyle: three-way trade-off among speed, flexibility, and quality in neural style transfer. In: AAAI Conference on Artificial Intelligence (AAAI) (2019)
86. Zhang, R., Isola, P., Efros, A.A., Shechtman, E., Wang, O.: The unreasonable effectiveness of deep features as a perceptual metric. In: Conference on Computer Vision and Pattern Recognition (CVPR) (2018)

87. Zhou, B., Lapedriza, A., Khosla, A., Oliva, A., Torralba, A.: Places: a 10 million image database for scene recognition. IEEE Trans. Pattern Anal. Mach. Intell. **40**, 1452–1464 (2017)
88. Zhu, J.Y., Park, T., Isola, P., Efros, A.A.: Unpaired image-to-image translation using cycle-consistent adversarial networks. In: International Conference on Computer Vision (ICCV) (2017)

GazeTransformer: Gaze Forecasting for Virtual Reality Using Transformer Networks

Tim Rolff[1,2]([✉]) [ID], H. Matthias Harms[1], Frank Steinicke[2] [ID],
and Simone Frintrop[1] [ID]

[1] Computer Vision Group, Universität Hamburg, Hamburg, Germany
{Tim.Rolff,Simone.Frintrop}@uni-hamburg.de, harmmatthias.harms@gmail.com
[2] Human Computer Interaction Group, Universität Hamburg, Hamburg, Germany

Abstract. In this paper, we propose *GazeTransformer*, a transformer architecture for forecasting egocentric gaze points in virtual environments (VEs) presented on immersive head-mounted displays (HMDs). In contrast to previous architectures, we do not rely on information that depends on the application state, but rather focus on data modalities provided by the eye-tracker or sent to the HMD. GazeTransformer allows to forecast multiple types of eye-movements, including saccades and fixations, by creating two unfiltered datasets, using the raw gaze from the eye-tracker for forecasting. Moreover, we analyze six different image encoding backends in their quality to forecast gaze positions. To evaluate the performance of our model, we compared all architectures on the generated datasets. The results show that our architecture with all chosen backends outperforms the current state-of-the-art approaches in forecasting egocentric gaze points in VEs.

Keywords: Virtual reality · Transformers · Gaze forecasting

1 Introduction

With the recent increase in interest in virtual reality (VR), in particular, driven by hype around the metaverse [9,23,53], as training tool for medical experts and manufacturing jobs [22,49], or as a platform for social interactions and meetings [58,61], gaze and eye movements of users has shown to be an integral part for several VR technologies and applications [15,21,39,42,52,57]. For example, it is still challenging to provide highly realistic and immersive dynamic virtual environments (VE) on mobile VR platforms [35,68] due to limited GPU performance and battery capacity [68]. Utilizing gaze data from an eye-tracker can be a potential solution for this problem, as the eye has only a small area, the

Supplementary Information The online version contains supplementary material available at https://doi.org/10.1007/978-3-031-16788-1_35.

fovea, in which humans perceive a sharp image [26]. With foveated rendering [18,51,57] a high-resolution image is only rendered in the foveal region, whereas the rest of the image is rendered with lower resolution and quality, resulting in reduced requirements on GPU and battery performance. Besides foveated rendering, there are several other proposed methods that try to solve reoccurring challenges of VR using information provided through gaze data, such as, redirected walking by performing changes to the VE during saccades or eye blinks [42,67], gaze-contingent rendering [39,52], gaze behavior analysis [64], or content compression [64]. Many of these solutions rely on knowledge about the human gaze to alter the VE without user detecting such manipulations. For instance, the duration of saccadic movements range from 30 to 80 ms [26] where the visual input is usually suppressed for >100 ms [11], such that the user will not notice slight changes to the VE. However, it may take up to 50 ms to detect saccades [66], the possibility to predict them would greatly improve applicability of suppression techniques. Hence, knowledge about the user's eye gaze has enormous advantages, as it can be utilized for the aforementioned algorithms.

A commonly utilized method to capture the gaze for the previously listed methods is by utilizing a video-based eye-tracker built in into the head-mounted displays (HMD). These eye-trackers, however, can only report historic gaze data, as the output of them often has a latency of several milliseconds due to the required preprocessing [1,66]. This latency is often due to the eye-tracker itself or due to applied algorithms when estimating the gaze. While there are recent attempts to reduce latency through the proposal of hardware-based solutions [2,43], the latency of eye-trackers in widespread commercially available HMD's often hinders the direct usage of gaze data for VR applications, especially for fast eye-movements such as saccades or blinks. Therefore, directly utilizing the gaze data in downstream tasks might miss such eye movements or requiring unnatural actions, such as intentional blinking [42] or long saccades [1,67].

As a software-based solution, Hu et al. [27,29] proposed a neural network for forecasting the gaze of individual users. They define gaze prediction as a multimodal time series prediction problem, utilizing past gaze, head velocities, object positions, and saliency, to predict gaze positions. While [29] focuses more on the prediction of current gaze positions under the assumption that no information on past gaze data is available, they additionally perform ablation studies, showing that their method can forecast gaze positions when given information about the user past gaze. In [27], they extend this work by predicting future fixation points using a pre-filtered dataset, but do not evaluate on other common eye-movements, such as saccades or smooth pursuits.

We build upon this idea by proposing a different architecture for gaze prediction. In our case, we do not only focus on gaze fixations, but rather include further important types of eye-movements: saccades, fixations and smooth pursuits [26]. For the prediction, we propose the utilization of transformer networks that have shown recent success in multiple tasks, such as natural language processing [4,12,13,70] or image classification [7,14,38]. As Hu et al. [27,29] only analyzed saliency as an additional data modality, we will evaluate six different image modalities through pretrained networks, including saliency, RGB and grayscale images, or the output of ResNet.

To summarize, our work addresses the following contributions:

- We propose *GazeTransformer*, a state-of-the-art transformer architecture for egocentric gaze forecasting in VR handling different eye-movements, like fixations or saccades from raw gaze data.
- We analyze six different image processing techniques and backends, such as saliency, grayscale and RGB images, DINO [7] or ResNet [24] on their ability to predict the task at hand. We optimize *GazeTransformer* for each backend independently to find a set of good hyperparameters.

The paper is structured such that we will first explain related work in the upcoming section. Afterwards, Sect. 3 will describe our method in detail, containing explanations on input representation and architecture. Next, we will go over our results along with the utilized datasets and metric in Sect. 4. At last, we will discuss those results in Sect. 5 along with limitations and future work.

2   Related Work

In this section, we will provide an overview about previous work on visual attention and visual saliency, as well as gaze prediction and gaze forecasting.

2.1   Visual Attention and Visual Saliency

Human gaze is generally considered to be controlled by mechanisms of visual attention, which drive the human visual system to focus on regions of general interest [56]. This attention can computationally be modelled through saliency methods, which are generally divided into two categories of *bottom-up* and *top-down* attention.

Bottom-up refers to the visual attention based on low-level image features, such as color, shape or contrast [10]. In fact, earlier computation saliency models compute several feature maps from low-level features and fuse them together for the final saliency prediction [19,32]. Some of these models are based on work by Treisman and Gelade [69], who theorized that visual features are registered in parallel early in the vision process, whereas objects are formed in later stages from the collected features. More recent approaches rely on modeling fixations through the help of deep-learning [3] by capturing the datasets either through the use of eye-trackers [5,72] or by recording mouse input [34]. A recent trend for these deep-learning-based saliency predictors is the utilization of transfer learning [33,46] that employing pretrained backend networks, mostly trained for image classification, such as ResNet [24], NASNet [74] or VGG [63].

Top-down is, in contrast to *bottom-up*, driven through high-level features, such as task-specific information [10]. Here, multiple works have shown that gaze is heavily influenced by task or context information that drives the attention. This also includes prior knowledge or instructions, with a study by Yarbus [73] showing considerably different eye-movements depending on the information about the same scene supplied beforehand.

2.2   Gaze Prediction and Gaze Forecasting

Gaze prediction describes the process of predicting the next gaze positions, based on a set of data points. These data points can either be task information [27], mouse input [41], hand positions [44], or close up images of the eye [50]. This problem closely relates to visual saliency. However, although gaze and saliency prediction are similar problems, they both differ in that gaze prediction describes the process of predicting the gaze point of individuals given a set of input features, whereas saliency maps tries to model the general distribution of fixation points. Gaze prediction has been researched for sometime on a variety of different applications, such as in the use of action recognition [44], in 360° videos [54,71], or in video games [41]. However, the research on gaze prediction in VR is fairly recent, with prior work focusing on multiple aspects, like dataset collection, architecture proposal, and data analysis [29,30].

Gaze forecasting can be interpreted as an extension of gaze prediction. While gaze forecasting still outputs a gaze point like gaze prediction, the gaze points should be predicted several milliseconds into the future. This forecasting allows mitigating often found challenges with eye-trackers in commercial HMD's that often only support low frequency update rates [66]. This lead to other research studies relying on low latency gaze data in VR to mitigate those challenges by intentional blinking [42] or relying on long saccade durations [1,67]. Another recently proposed approach to mitigate latency was proposed by Rolff et al. [59]. They estimate when future gaze shifts will occur by performing time-to-event analysis on each captured sample, rather than predicting the gaze points directly. However, this approach does not report gaze points that can potentially be used in other downstream tasks.

3   GazeTransformer

In this section, we will give an overview of our *GazeTransformer*. We start with an overview of the input representation (Sect. 3.1) and present afterwards the proposed architecture for the gaze forecasting transformer (Sect. 3.2).

3.1   Input Representation

As gaze datasets often provide different data modalities, such as gaze positions, head orientations, IMU data, videos, depth, EEG, or task data [17,20,25,27,29, 36,40,45], our model should be able to handle those different data modalities. Therefore, it is required to represent the input, such that the model can interpret it. Fortunately, most of the listed data modalities can either be represented as images or as a temporal sequence, containing an individual feature vector for each time step. Since the aforementioned datasets provide different representations, we choose to represent each sample point as a concatenation of different data modalities, with each modality having a fixed length. As most modalities like gaze or IMU data are already captured as a sequence, we can directly utilize those

(a) Saliency map, generated through the   (b) Attention scores generated through
saliency backend described in Sec. 3.1.   the DINO backend described in Sec. 3.1.

Fig. 1. Visualization of the different backends described in Sect. 3.1 overlaid on
the original image. These are used as input for the transformer model explained in
Sect. 3.2. Note that we only use the center cropped part for saliency and attention score
prediction.

for our model. Here, we focus on four different modalities: the horizontal and
vertical gaze, the head velocity, and depending on the dataset, the current task
and the last rendered frames. For image data, we employ an additional feature
extraction network that processes a sequence of frames to extract 1-dimensional
vectors first. We explicitly choose these data modalities as they are provided
from or, in case of frames, to the HMD without requiring information about the
internal application state, like object positions [29], The only exception is task
information, but recent work [28] has shown that it is possible to infer the task
information from the eye-in-head, gaze-in-world and head data without requiring
the application state. In general, we provide the network with the last 400 ms of
input samples to forecast the sample 150 ms ahead. As a result, we can describe
our input I as follows:

$$I = \begin{pmatrix} d_{t-39} \\ d_{t-38} \\ \vdots \\ d_t, \end{pmatrix}, \text{ with } d_{t-i} = \left(\text{gaze}_{t-i}, \text{head}_{t-i}, \text{task}_{t-i}, \text{frame}_{t-i}\right), \quad (1)$$

where $i \in [0, \dots, 39]$, and t denotes the index of the last captured sample. To
extract 1-dimensional feature representations from the input frames, we will analyze the following image-to-sequence backends:

Grayscale: As a baseline image method, we flatten a grayscale image of the input into a 1-dimensional vector. This restricts the input to images of the same size, as otherwise spatial information between image pixels are lost. Furthermore, if the chosen image size is too large, we hypothesize that the network might not pick up information on the other modalities. Thus, we transform the input frames to 32×32 grayscale images, resulting in 1024 features for each sample. Here, we concatenate the full 1-dimensional flattened vector onto each step in the sequence, as formulated in Eq. 1, differing from previous approaches, like [8], as they use the individual pixel values of the image as the input sequence.

Patch: To preserve the color information of the image, we transform the image into a singular 64×64 patch, similar to Dosovitskiy et al. [14]. In [14], they generate input vectors for their transformer architecture by dividing the original image into multiple patches. Afterwards, each patch is flattened and processed as part of multiple patches. However, due to the chosen representation of the input, as formulated in Eq. 1, this is not feasible. Instead, we resize the input image down to a singular 64×64 pixel image patch, conserving the color information, resulting in a 12288-dimensional feature representation of the input.

Saliency: Since saliency is used by multiple gaze prediction and forecasting methods [27,29–31,71], we also analyze the use of saliency as input modality. To generate the saliency map of each frame, we employ the approach proposed by Jia and Bruce [33], acquiring the information on the fixation distribution of the input image. Other work by Einhäuser and Nuthmann [16] has shown that the usage of saliency data is beneficial as they correlate with fixation durations. This correlation might potentially be valuable in case of an upcoming saccade, as it might contain information on the duration about the currently performed fixation. However, as we only provide saliency, the latter network layers might have no awareness of the original content of the image, therefore, losing information on color, intensity, or shape. As shown in Fig. 1a, we follow the approach of Hu et al. [27,29] and generate the saliency maps from the center-cropped region of each frame and resizing the output to 24×24 pixels.

ResNet: A different approach for the generation of sequence data from images was explored by Carion et al. [6]. They evaluated multiple ResNet [24] architectures by prepending the ResNet module in front of a transformer for feature extraction. In our work, we extend their idea by utilizing a ResNet50 architecture that was pretrained on ImageNet [60]. First, we extract the image features for each input image and pass the extracted features into the transformer architecture. However, to avoid output that fully resembles the class distribution of in the input image, we discard the final classification layer, resulting in a feature vector of 2048.

DINO: As the last evaluated backend, we utilize a vision transformer that is trained through DINO [7], a recently proposed self-supervised training approach. They interpret self-supervised learning as a form of self-distillation. They train a student and a teacher model, where the teacher model is provided with the full image and the student model with a randomly augmented and cropped region of

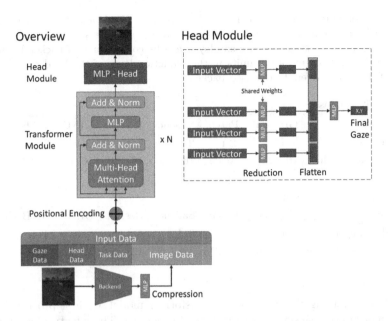

Fig. 2. Overview of our *GazeTransformer* architecture. A backend network extracts a 1D feature vector from the input frames and concatenates it with other data. Positional encoding is concatenated, and the data is fed into multiple (N) transformer encoder layers. A head module, consisting of multiple feedforward layers, reduces the dimensionality of the features and performs the final prediction of gaze points (see Sect. 3 for details).

the same image. To perform gradient back propagation, they compute the loss as the negative log likelihood between the student and the centered output of the teacher model and propagate the error back through the student network. Then the exponential moving average of the students gradients is used to update the weights of the teacher network. They have shown that the attention weights of the transformer architecture closely correlates with semantic segmentation. Hence, we use the inner attention state, depicted in Fig. 1b, of a pretrained model as the input to our transformer, resulting in feature vectors of size 376.

3.2   Transformer Model

We base our architecture on the popular transformer architecture proposed by Vaswani et al. [70]. For clarity, we divide our proposed architecture into three modules, see Fig. 2 for an overview. The first module is the input encoder module that constructs the input representation for later modules (cf. Sect. 3.1). Next, the transformer encoder module utilizes the transformer architecture of [70] by stacking multiple transformer layers. At last, the head module is used for dimensionality reduction and the final gaze forecasting.

Table 1. Configurations used to report final results. *Heads* and *layers* refer to the number of heads and layers in the transformer layers. *Compress* refers to the number of units in the linear layer that are employed for the compression of backend features. *Reduce* refers to the number of units in the reduction layer of the head module. The name of the model refers to the used backend.

DGaze [29] dataset

Backend	Grayscale	Patch	Saliency	ResNet	DINO	No Backend
Heads – Layers	4–1	4–1	2–1	4–1	6–1	6–4
Compress – Reduce	16–128	16–64	16–128	16–128	16–128	/– 64

FixationNet [27] dataset

Backend	Grayscale	Patch	Saliency	ResNet	DINO	No Backend
Heads – Layers	8–1	1–1	6–1	4–1	6–1	4–4
Compress – Reduce	256–256	32–256	32–256	128–256	32–128	/– 256

Before providing the data to the transformer model, we first process frames through one of the backend networks listed in Sect. 3.1. These features are further compressed using a feedforward layer followed by a ReLU [55] and a dropout layer [65]. These result in 1-dimensional feature representations of the processed images that we concatenate with the other data samples. Here, we provide the network with the last 400 ms of previous gaze positions, head velocities and task-related object information, following the previous approach of [27]. This leads to an input of 40 1-dimensional feature vectors. After the construction of the input data from the different modalities, we perform positional encoding, allowing the transformer model to distinguish between different time-steps of the input.

As we expect the different input data modalities to have different sampling rates, the implementation of our positional encoding is based on [37]. They propose a trainable model-agnostic representation of time that also depends on the input and which is concatenated with a scalar interpretation of time. The entire encoded sequence is fed into the encoder model consisting of multiple stacked transformer layers. In addition, we follow previous work [4,14] which has shown that a decoder model is not required. Note that the number of utilized layers and transformer heads depend on the backend, see Table 1 for more details.

Lastly, the head module consists of a multi-layer perceptron network that predicts the final visual angle from the screen center. As the transformer architecture does not reduce the sequence length, it outputs the same number of 1-dimensional feature vectors that are input into the architecture. Thus, we reduce the dimensionality through a feedforward layer in the head module with the number of units listed in Table 1. Afterwards, we reduce the number of features to two, resulting in an output of 40 × 2. To apply a non-linearity, we additionally add a ReLU and a dropout layer after the output of both linear layers. Afterwards, we flatten the outputted matrix into a 1-dimensional vector that we then utilize to forecast the final horizontal and vertical gaze position.

For training the network, we follow the approach of Hu et al. [27], using the angular error as the loss function, which is defined as the mean angular difference between the line of sight of the ground truth and the forecasted gaze position. For the hyperparameters and optimizer, we choose to employ the AdamW [48] with a learning rate of 0.001, a batch size of 256, dropout of 0.1, and the weight decay set to 0.01. While training, we monitor the loss on the validation set and use early stopping after three epochs, if the loss has not decreased. To find a set of good of hyperparameters for layers, transformer heads, compression, and reduction units for each backend separately, we evaluate our proposed architecture on multiple configurations that can be found in the ablation studies, found in the supplementary. We did not perform additional hyperparameter optimization for other parameters, such as batch size or weight decay. Then we utilize the best performing configuration as our parameters, which are reported in Table 1. For further details on these results and the evaluated parameters, see the supplementary material.

4   Evaluation

4.1   Metric

For the error metrics, we follow Hu et al. [27], by using the angular error as our primary metric that describes the angular distance between the ground truth line of sight and the predicted line of sight, with a smaller value indicating better performance.

4.2   Datasets

We evaluate our model on two different egocentric datasets fully captured in VR, namely the *DGaze* [29] and *FixationNet* [27] dataset. For capturing the first-mentioned *DGaze* dataset, each participant was asked to freely explore 2 out of 5 randomly assigned VEs containing different dynamic visual distractors in the form of animals. For the recording, each participant was instructed to record at least 3 min of data without any further instructions on a task or explanation of the environment. In total, the dataset contains 86 samples from 43 participants with an average sequence length of over 20,000 data points per session. The *FixationNet* dataset captures the same data modalities as the *DGaze* dataset, but additionally provides information on the current task of each participant.

Fig. 3. Sequence of frames showing a prediction of *GazeTransformer* (red dot) on the FixationNet dataset [27] along with the ground truth (green dot) and the last captured gaze position (blue dot). The frames are cropped to the relevant region. As participants were tasked to search for targets, the left animal disappears due to its correct classification. (Color figure online)

Here, all participants were instructed to solve a specific search task, pointing the VR controller onto the target. In total, the *FixationNet* dataset contains 162 samples from 27 participants containing on average 12,000 head and gaze points per trial.

However, as the evaluated task of Hu et al. [27] is the prediction of fixation points, the authors provide a pre-processed dataset with filtered gaze positions that correspond to the fixation points of the participants. Therefore, we generate a custom dataset from the raw data of both datasets that do not compute fixation points and therefore account for other eye-movements. We also follow the same methodology for the *DGaze* dataset. Both datasets contain videos, gaze, head velocities captured through the IMU of the HMD, and object positions of the nearest objects. In these generated datasets, we made sure not to utilize any internal information only known to the running application, such as object positions, but rather focused on the information already provided from or to the HMD, with the only exception being the task information. As both datasets do not contain gaze events, we follow the methodology of [59] to generate fixation and saccade events, using the I-VT algorithm [62].

4.3   Results

Table 2 shows the result of our proposed *GazeTransformer* architecture with all backends introduced in Sect. 3.1. As described in Sect. 4.2, we evaluate our approach against the state-of-the-art *DGaze* and *FixationNet*. As the baseline, we choose the last known gaze position that is lagging the target by 150 ms. For the evaluation, we choose a cross validation approach by validating across users and scenes. For computational reasons, we only evaluate across the data of 3

Table 2. Results for the FixationNet [27] and DGaze datasets [29] using the raw gaze as input. We name the models of *GazeTransformer* according to their image-to-sequence backend. The error metric is computed through the angular error (*Mean*: mean angular error; *Std.*: mean standard deviation over different folds). Best results in **underlined blue bold**.

Model	DGaze dataset				FixationNet dataset			
	Cross-user		Cross-scene		Cross-user		Cross-scene	
	Mean	Std.	Mean	Std.	Mean	Std.	Mean	Std.
Baseline								
Current gaze	5.12°	8.00°	5.85°	9.77°	3.67°	7.17°	3.66°	7.14°
State-of-the-art								
DGaze [29]	10.28°	6.87°	10.24°	7.65°	8.66°	6.89°	8.76°	6.92°
FixationNet [27]	10.31°	6.91°	10.41°	7.70°	8.49°	6.71°	8.56°	6.76°
Gaze transformer								
Grayscale	4.91°	6.80°	5.27°	7.76°	3.58°	6.08°	3.63°	6.06°
Patch	4.75°	**6.74°**	5.10°	7.77°	3.49°	6.09°	3.46°	6.05°
Saliency	4.85°	6.77°	5.20°	**7.75°**	3.49°	**6.07°**	3.51°	**6.04°**
ResNet	4.84°	6.76°	5.16°	7.77°	3.49°	6.10°	3.58°	6.05°
DINO	4.81°	6.76°	5.15°	7.76°	3.55°	6.06°	3.62°	**6.04°**
No Backend	**4.71°**	6.75°	**5.05°**	7.77°	**3.47°**	6.10°	**3.44°**	6.06°

participants as the test sets and used the rest either as our training or validation data and compute the final results as the mean over all folds.

Overall, Table 2 shows that all selected backends outperform the baseline, as well as the methods introduced by Hu et al. [27,29]. When utilizing the image data provided by a backend network, we found that the *Patch* backend shows the best performance. Surprisingly, we discovered that utilizing image data does not improve the predictive performance, as the model that does not use frame data performs the best on all datasets. The reported mean standard deviation across all methods is similar, regardless of the employed backend. Surprisingly, the standard deviation of the best performing *GazeTransformer* is also not the most optimal among all our *GazeTransformers*. As mentioned in Sect. 3, we performed multiple ablation studies to find a good set of parameters for our architecture, dependent on the used backend. For more information on these results, see the supplementary material. Table 3 also shows the separate errors for fixations and saccades between the current state-of-the-art and our *No Backend* model. Here, we compute the error metrics on saccades and fixations separately using the estimate gaze event label. Due to space restrictions we only compare the performance on fixations and saccades on the *No Backend* model and include the other models in the supplementary.

Table 3. Individual results for saccades and fixations measured on the FixationNet [27] and DGaze datasets [29] using the raw gaze as input. The error metric is computed through the angular error seperatly across all saccades and fixations (*Mean*: mean angular error; *Std.*: mean standard deviation over different folds). Best results in **underlined blue bold**.

	Model	DGaze dataset				FixationNet dataset			
		Cross-user		Cross-scene		Cross-user		Cross-scene	
		Mean	Std.	Mean	Std.	Mean	Std.	Mean	Std.
Saccades	*State-of-the-art*								
	DGaze [29]	12.81°	10.94°	14.81°	**11.07°**	12.91°	9.92°	13.04°	**9.93°**
	FixationNet [27]	14.45°	**9.56°**	15.06°	11.17°	12.86°	**9.86°**	12.96°	9.96°
	Gaze transformer								
	No Backend	**10.80°**	10.22°	**11.74°**	12.26°	9.96°	10.57°	**9.93°**	10.57°
Fixations	*State-of-the-art*								
	DGaze [29]	9.17°	5.45°	9.00°	5.35°	7.85°	5.80°	7.94°	5.84°
	FixationNet [27]	9.18°	5.43°	9.20°	5.46°	7.67°	5.56°	7.72°	5.58°
	Gaze transformer								
	No Backend	**3.02°**	**4.01°**	**2.96°**	**3.80°**	**2.23°**	3.64°	**2.20°**	**3.57°**

Additionally, we performed a qualitative evaluation on the output of *Gaze-Transformer* and FixationNet. Here, we discovered that the performance of FixationNet is due to its design choice to only predict fixations and often shifts towards salient regions. It is unable to handle strong gaze shifts, even though the network was retrained on our dataset. In contrast, although not instantaneous with the target, our model can perform these shifts by reacting faster than the baseline, with an example shown in Fig. 3.

When running in inference, we achieve real-time performance running at approximately 329 predictions per second when using the *No Backend* model on the GPU. To measure the timings, we use a system equipped with an AMD Ryzen Threadripper 3960X with 128 GB RAM and an NVIDIA RTX 3090 and performed the execution on the GPU. The other timings, including CPU performance metrics, can be found in the supplementary. When estimating the run-time, we included the full backend and predict image features twice per second.

5   Conclusion and Discussion

In this paper, we proposed *GazeTransformer* a state-of-the-art transformer architecture for forecasting gaze points in VR using the raw gaze data and IMU data provided by the HMD's with built-in eye-trackers. For the prediction of future gaze points, we only utilize data provided from or send to the HMD, without dependencies on the internal state of the application through object locations except for task data, which itself has shown to be predictable without the application state [28]. We forecast the gaze positions 150 ms into the future, allowing us to compare our method against existing literature [27,29]. To evaluate our proposed architecture, we analyzed its ability on two state-of-the-art VR datasets. Furthermore, we analyzed multiple image backends, such as grayscale or RGB images, saliency, attention weights of DINO, and ResNet. Overall, we discovered that our approach, regardless of the backend, significantly outperformed all previous state-of-the-art methods when using the raw gaze as input to the network.

Surprisingly, we found that the best performing approach did not utilize image data. This contrasts with previous literature [27,29], which found that utilizing the saliency directly does improve the final performance of the network, or with other work heavily relying on RGB data of captured frames [44]. There are several potential reasons for this finding. First, some utilized backends, like ResNet, might not provide meaningful information to the transformer layers and head module. This is since ResNet was pretrained for image classification, and therefore high-level features will most likely contain information on the estimated class. Another reason might be that only two frames are used over the entire input sequence. As the input of *GazeTransformer* is split by time instead of splitting by features, like [29] or [27], this causes the duplication of frames that might potentially result in over weighting the image features, as the size of the other modalities is significantly smaller than the image feature space. Moreover, due to memory requirements and analysis on the different backends, we did not train the backend networks in combination with the transformer architecture. This might have further impacted the performance of the image-dependent architectures. At last, this may also be due to the rather small dataset size, as transformers rely on huge datasets when trained from scratch to capture meaningful correlations between features [47]. Given this, we also expect that the need to use different hyperparameters for each data set to achieve optimal performance will be eliminated if the data set is large enough. However, we also suspect that conducting a final calibration phase for each user before using a pre-trained model is a worthwhile research direction, as it could lead to a more optimal model.

Investigating these observations maybe valuable directions for future work, as we expect the image data to have a positive impact on the final performance of the architecture, even though we could not confirm this in our paper. Here, training these backend networks may be a good initial step on verifying if performance can further be improved when image modalities are used. This, however, might be bound by the memory of the GPU. Therefore, another direction might be to analyze other virtual and real-world datasets that are similar to the data in the datasets commonly used for pre-training, such as ImageNet, to make better use of the pre-trained networks. With those, it would also be possible to explore additional image modalities, for example depth data or EEG input. Besides, extending the architecture to directly work with image data that is split by time as well as by feature would remove the need for duplicated input frames. Moreover, adding multi-horizontal forecasting, to predict multiple future short-term and long-term gaze points would be helpful, as we expect the network to perform better on shorter forecast durations. Besides the surprising results on image modalities, we found that *GazeTransformer* significantly outperforms the state-of-the-art regardless of the backend utilized.

References

1. Albert, R., Patney, A., Luebke, D., Kim, J.: Latency requirements for foveated rendering in virtual reality. ACM Trans. Appl. Percept. (TAP) **14**(4), 1–13 (2017)
2. Angelopoulos, A.N., Martel, J.N., Kohli, A.P., Conradt, J., Wetzstein, G.: Event-based near-eye gaze tracking beyond 10,000 hz. IEEE Trans. Vis. Comput. Graph. (TVCG) **27**(5), 2577–2586 (2021)
3. Borji, A.: Saliency prediction in the deep learning era: successes and limitations. IEEE Trans. Pattern Anal. Mach. Intell. (TPAMI) **43**(2), 679–700 (2019)
4. Brown, T., et al.: Language models are few-shot learners. Adv. Neural Inf. Process. Syst. (NeurIPS) **33**, 1877–1901 (2020)
5. Bylinskii, Z., et al.: Mit saliency benchmark (2015)
6. Carion, N., Massa, F., Synnaeve, G., Usunier, N., Kirillov, A., Zagoruyko, S.: End-to-end object detection with transformers. In: Vedaldi, A., Bischof, H., Brox, T., Frahm, J.-M. (eds.) ECCV 2020. LNCS, vol. 12346, pp. 213–229. Springer, Cham (2020). https://doi.org/10.1007/978-3-030-58452-8_13
7. Caron, M., Touvron, H., Misra, I., Jégou, H., Mairal, J., Bojanowski, P., Joulin, A.: Emerging properties in self-supervised vision transformers. In: Proceedings of the IEEE/CVF International Conference on Computer Vision (ICCV), pp. 9650–9660 (2021)
8. Chen, M., et al.: Generative pretraining from pixels. In: Proceedings of the 37th International Conference on Machine Learning, vol. 119, pp. 1691–1703. PMLR (2020)
9. Cheng, R., Wu, N., Chen, S., Han, B.: Reality check of metaverse: a first look at commercial social virtual reality platforms. In: IEEE Conference on Virtual Reality and 3D User Interfaces Abstracts and Workshops (VRW), pp. 141–148. IEEE (2022)
10. Connor, C.E., Egeth, H.E., Yantis, S.: Visual attention: bottom-up versus top-down. Curr. Biol. **14**(19), R850–R852 (2004)
11. Crevecoeur, F., Kording, K.P.: Saccadic suppression as a perceptual consequence of efficient sensorimotor estimation. eLife **6**, e25073 (2017)
12. Dai, Z., Yang, Z., Yang, Y., Carbonell, J., Le, Q.V., Salakhutdinov, R.: Transformer-xl: Attentive language models beyond a fixed-length context. arXiv preprint arXiv:1901.02860 (2019)
13. Devlin, J., Chang, M.W., Lee, K., Toutanova, K.: Bert: pre-training of deep bidirectional transformers for language understanding. arXiv preprint arXiv:1810.04805 (2018)
14. Dosovitskiy, A., et al.: An image is worth 16×16 words: transformers for image recognition at scale. In: 9th International Conference on Learning Representations (ICLR). OpenReview (2021)
15. Duchowski, A.T.: Gaze-based interaction: a 30 year retrospective. Comput. Graph. **73**, 59–69 (2018)
16. Einhäuser, W., Nuthmann, A.: Salient in space, salient in time: fixation probability predicts fixation duration during natural scene viewing. J. Vision **16**(11), 13–13 (2016)
17. Emery, K.J., Zannoli, M., Warren, J., Xiao, L., Talathi, S.S.: OpenNEEDS: a dataset of gaze, head, hand, and scene signals during exploration in open-ended vr environments. In: ACM Symposium on Eye Tracking Research and Applications (ETRA). ACM, New York (2021)

18. Franke, L., Fink, L., Martschinke, J., Selgrad, K., Stamminger, M.: Time-warped foveated rendering for virtual reality headsets. In: Computer Graphics Forum, vol. 40, pp. 110–123. Wiley Online Library (2021)
19. Frintrop, S.: VOCUS: A Visual Attention System for Object Detection and Goal-Directed search, vol. 3899. Springer, Heidelberg (2006). https://doi.org/10.1007/11682110
20. Fuhl, W., Kasneci, G., Kasneci, E.: TEyeD: over 20 million real-world eye images with pupil, eyelid, and iris 2D and 3D segmentations, 2D and 3D landmarks, 3D eyeball, gaze vector, and eye movement types. In: IEEE International Symposium on Mixed and Augmented Reality (ISMAR), pp. 367–375. IEEE (2021)
21. Guenter, B., Finch, M., Drucker, S., Tan, D., Snyder, J.: Foveated 3D graphics. ACM Trans. Graph. (TOG) 31(6), 1–10 (2012)
22. Gurusamy, K.S., Aggarwal, R., Palanivelu, L., Davidson, B.R.: Virtual reality training for surgical trainees in laparoscopic surgery. Cochrane Database Syst. Revi. (CDSR) (1) (2009)
23. Han, D.I.D., Bergs, Y., Moorhouse, N.: Virtual reality consumer experience escapes: preparing for the metaverse. In: Virtual Reality, pp. 1–16 (2022)
24. He, K., Zhang, X., Ren, S., Sun, J.: Deep residual learning for image recognition. In: Proceedings of the IEEE Conference on Computer Vision and Pattern Recognition (CVPR), pp. 770–778 (2016)
25. Hollenstein, N., Rotsztejn, J., Troendle, M., Pedroni, A., Zhang, C., Langer, N.: ZuCo, a simultaneous EEG and eye-tracking resource for natural sentence reading. Sci. Data 5(1), 1–13 (2018)
26. Holmqvist, K., Nyström, M., Andersson, R., Dewhurst, R., Jarodzka, H., Van de Weijer, J.: Eye Tracking: A Comprehensive Guide to Methods and Measures. OUP Oxford, Oxford (2011)
27. Hu, Z., Bulling, A., Li, S., Wang, G.: FixationNet: forecasting eye fixations in task-oriented virtual environments. IEEE Trans. Vis. Comput. Graph. (TVCG) 27(5), 2681–2690 (2021)
28. Hu, Z., Bulling, A., Li, S., Wang, G.: EHTask: recognizing user tasks from eye and head movements in immersive virtual reality. IEEE Trans. Vis. Comput. Graph. (TVCG) (2022)
29. Hu, Z., Li, S., Zhang, C., Yi, K., Wang, G., Manocha, D.: DGaze: CNN-based gaze prediction in dynamic scenes. IEEE Trans. Vis. Comput. Graph. (TVCG) 26(5), 1902–1911 (2020)
30. Hu, Z., Zhang, C., Li, S., Wang, G., Manocha, D.: SGaze: a data-driven eye-head coordination model for realtime gaze prediction. IEEE Trans. Vis. Comput. Graph. (TVCG) 25(5), 2002–2010 (2019)
31. Huang, Y., Cai, M., Li, Z., Lu, F., Sato, Y.: Mutual context network for jointly estimating egocentric gaze and action. IEEE Trans. Image Process. (TIP) 29, 7795–7806 (2020)
32. Itti, L., Koch, C.: A saliency-based search mechanism for overt and covert shifts of visual attention. Vision Res. 40(10–12), 1489–1506 (2000)
33. Jia, S., Bruce, N.D.B.: EML-NET: an expandable multi-layer network for saliency prediction. Image Vision Comput. 95, 103887 (2020)
34. Jiang, M., Huang, S., Duan, J., Zhao, Q.: SALICON: saliency in context. In: Proceedings of the IEEE Conference on Computer Vision and Pattern Recognition (CVPR), pp. 1072–1080 (2015)
35. Kanter, D.: Graphics processing requirements for enabling immersive vr. In: AMD White Paper, pp. 1–12 (2015)

36. Kastrati, A., Plomecka, M.B., Pascual, D., Wolf, L., Gillioz, V., Wattenhofer, R., Langer, N.: EEGEyeNet: a simultaneous electroencephalography and eye-tracking dataset and benchmark for eye movement prediction. In: Proceedings of the Neural Information Processing Systems (NIPS) Track on Datasets and Benchmarks (2021)
37. Kazemi, S.M., et al.: Time2vec: learning a vector representation of time. arXiv preprint arXiv:1907.05321 (2019)
38. Khan, S., Naseer, M., Hayat, M., Zamir, S.W., Khan, F.S., Shah, M.: Transformers in vision: a survey. ACM Comput. Surv. (2021)
39. Konrad, R., Angelopoulos, A., Wetzstein, G.: Gaze-contingent ocular parallax rendering for virtual reality. ACM Trans. Graph. (TOG) **39**(2), 1–12 (2020)
40. Kothari, R., Yang, Z., Kanan, C., Bailey, R., Pelz, J.B., Diaz, G.J.: Gaze-in-wild: a dataset for studying eye and head coordination in everyday activities. Sci. Rep. **10**(1), 1–18 (2020)
41. Koulieris, G.A., Drettakis, G., Cunningham, D., Mania, K.: Gaze prediction using machine learning for dynamic stereo manipulation in games. In: IEEE Virtual Reality, pp. 113–120. IEEE (2016)
42. Langbehn, E., Steinicke, F., Lappe, M., Welch, G.F., Bruder, G.: In the blink of an eye: leveraging blink-induced suppression for imperceptible position and orientation redirection in virtual reality. ACM Trans. Graph. (TOG) **37**(4), 1–11 (2018)
43. Li, R., et al.: Optical gaze tracking with spatially-sparse single-pixel detectors. In: IEEE International Symposium on Mixed and Augmented Reality (ISMAR), pp. 117–126. IEEE (2020)
44. Li, Y., Fathi, A., Rehg, J.M.: Learning to predict gaze in egocentric video. In: Proceedings of the IEEE International Conference on Computer Vision (ICCV), pp. 3216–3223 (2013)
45. Li, Y., Liu, M., Rehg, J.M.: In the eye of beholder: joint learning of gaze and actions in first person video. In: Proceedings of the European Conference on Computer Vision (ECCV), pp. 619–635 (2018)
46. Linardos, A., Kümmerer, M., Press, O., Bethge, M.: DeepGaze IIE: Calibrated prediction in and out-of-domain for state-of-the-art saliency modeling. In: Proceedings of the IEEE/CVF International Conference on Computer Vision (ICCV), pp. 12919–12928 (2021)
47. Liu, Y., Sangineto, E., Bi, W., Sebe, N., Lepri, B., Nadai, M.: Efficient training of visual transformers with small datasets. Adv. Neural Inf. Process. Syst. (NeurIPS) **34** (2021)
48. Loshchilov, I., Hutter, F.: Decoupled weight decay regularization. arXiv preprint arXiv:1711.05101 (2017)
49. Matsas, E., Vosniakos, G.C.: Design of a virtual reality training system for human-robot collaboration in manufacturing tasks. Int. J. Interact. Design Manuf. (IJIDeM) **11**(2), 139–153 (2017)
50. Mazzeo, P.L., D'Amico, D., Spagnolo, P., Distante, C.: Deep learning based eye gaze estimation and prediction. In: 2021 6th International Conference on Smart and Sustainable Technologies (SpliTech), pp. 1–6. IEEE (2021)
51. Meng, X., Du, R., Zwicker, M., Varshney, A.: Kernel foveated rendering. Proc. ACM Comput. Graph. Interact. Tech. (PACMCGIT) **1**(1), 1–20 (2018)
52. Murphy, H.A., Duchowski, A.T.: Gaze-contingent level of detail rendering. In: Eurographics 2001 - Short Presentations. Eurographics Association (2001)
53. Mystakidis, S.: Metaverse. Encyclopedia **2**(1), 486–497 (2022)
54. Naas, S.A., Jiang, X., Sigg, S., Ji, Y.: Functional gaze prediction in egocentric video. In: Proceedings of the 18th International Conference on Advances in Mobile Computing & Multimedia (MoMM), pp. 40–47. ACM, New York (2020)

55. Nair, V., Hinton, G.E.: Rectified linear units improve restricted boltzmann machines. In: Proceedings of the 27th International Conference on International Conference on Machine Learning (ICML). ACM, New York (2010)

56. Pashler, H.E.: The Psychology of Attention. MIT Press, Cambridge (1999)

57. Patney, A., et al.: Towards foveated rendering for gaze-tracked virtual reality. ACM Trans. Graph. (TOG) 35(6), 1–12 (2016)

58. Perry, T.S.: Virtual reality goes social. IEEE Spectr. 53(1), 56–57 (2015)

59. Rolff, T., Steinicke, F., Frintrop, S.: When do saccades begin? prediction of saccades as a time-to-event problem. In: ACM Symposium on Eye Tracking Research and Applications, ETRA 2022. ACM, New York (2022)

60. Russakovsky, O., et al.: ImageNet large scale visual recognition challenge. Int. J. Comput. Vision (IJCV) 115(3), 211–252 (2015)

61. Rzeszewski, M., Evans, L.: Virtual place during quarantine-a curious case of vrchat. Rozwój Regionalny i Polityka Regionalna 51, 57–75 (2020)

62. Salvucci, D.D., Goldberg, J.H.: Identifying fixations and saccades in eye-tracking protocols. In: Proceedings of the 2000 Symposium on Eye Tracking Research & Applications, ETRA 2000, pp. 71–78. Association for Computing Machinery, New York (2000). https://doi.org/10.1145/355017.355028

63. Simonyan, K., Zisserman, A.: Very deep convolutional networks for large-scale image recognition. In: 3rd International Conference on Learning Representations (ICLR) (2015)

64. Sitzmann, V., et al.: Saliency in VR: how do people explore virtual environments? IEEE Trans. Vis. Comput. Graph. (TVCG) 24(4), 1633–1642 (2018)

65. Srivastava, N., Hinton, G., Krizhevsky, A., Sutskever, I., Salakhutdinov, R.: Dropout: a simple way to prevent neural networks from overfitting. J. Mach. Learn. Res. 15(1), 1929–1958 (2014)

66. Stein, N., et al.: A comparison of eye tracking latencies among several commercial head-mounted displays. i-Perception 12(1), 1–16 (2021)

67. Sun, Q., et al.: Towards virtual reality infinite walking: dynamic saccadic redirection. ACM Trans. Graph. (TOG) 37(4), 1–13 (2018)

68. Sun, Y., Chen, Z., Tao, M., Liu, H.: Communications, caching, and computing for mobile virtual reality: modeling and tradeoff. IEEE Trans. Commun. 67(11), 7573–7586 (2019)

69. Treisman, A.M., Gelade, G.: A feature-integration theory of attention. Cogn. Psychol. 12(1), 97–136 (1980)

70. Vaswani, A., et al.: Attention is all you need. In: Advances in Neural Information Processing Systems (NIPS), vol. 30. Curran Associates, Inc. (2017)

71. Xu, Y., et al.: Gaze prediction in dynamic 360 immersive videos. In: proceedings of the IEEE Conference on Computer Vision and Pattern Recognition (CVPR), pp. 5333–5342 (2018)

72. Yang, C., Zhang, L., Lu, H., Ruan, X., Yang, M.H.: Saliency detection via graph-based manifold ranking. In: 2013 IEEE Conference on Computer Vision and Pattern Recognition (CVPR), pp. 3166–3173. IEEE (2013)

73. Yarbus, A.L.: Eye Movements and Vision. Springer, Heidelberg (2013). https://doi.org/10.1007/978-1-4899-5379-7

74. Zoph, B., Vasudevan, V., Shlens, J., Le, Q.V.: Learning transferable architectures for scalable image recognition. In: Proceedings of the IEEE Conference on Computer Vision and Pattern Recognition (CVPR), pp. 8697–8710 (2018)

Improving Traffic Sign Recognition by Active Search

Sami Jaghouar[1], Hannes Gustafsson[2], Bernhard Mehlig[3], Erik Werner[4(✉)], and Niklas Gustafsson[4]

[1] University of Technology of Compiègne, Compiègne, France
[2] Chalmers University of Technology, Gothenburg, Sweden
[3] University of Gothenburg, Gothenburg, Sweden
[4] Zenseact, Gothenburg, Sweden
werner.erik@gmail.com

Abstract. We describe an iterative active-learning algorithm to recognise rare traffic signs. A standard ResNet is trained on a training set containing only a single sample of the rare class. We demonstrate that by sorting the samples of a large, unlabeled set by the estimated probability of belonging to the rare class, we can efficiently identify samples from the rare class. This works despite the fact that this estimated probability is usually quite low. A reliable active-learning loop is obtained by labeling these candidate samples, including them in the training set, and iterating the procedure. Further, we show that we get similar results starting from a single synthetic sample. Our results are important as they indicate a straightforward way of improving traffic-sign recognition for automated driving systems. In addition, they show that we can make use of the information hidden in low confidence outputs, which is usually ignored.

Keywords: Rare traffic signs · Active learning · Active search

1 Introduction

Deep neural networks are the standard choice for perception systems in self-driving cars [33]. However, they can perform poorly on *rare* classes, for which there are few samples in the training set. This is problematic for traffic-sign recognition, since some signs occur much less often than others. As an example, Fig. 1 shows samples from the 25 rarest classes in the Mapillary traffic-sign data set [9]. One way to improve the performance is to find more samples of these rare signs in the raw data, label them, and add them to the training set. However, finding the rare traffic signs in the raw, unlabeled dataset is a challenge in itself, a task that has been likened to finding a needle in a haystack [7,32].

In this paper, we describe an active-learning algorithm for finding rare traffic signs in a large unlabeled data set. The algorithm is based on a standard ResNet [12], trained on a heavily imbalanced training set, which contains one sample of

B. Andres et al. (Eds.): DAGM GCPR 2022, LNCS 13485, pp. 594–606, 2022.
https://doi.org/10.1007/978-3-031-16788-1_36

Fig. 1. Samples of the 25 rarest traffic signs in the Mapillary data set (see text).

each rare class from Fig. 1. The algorithm finds more samples of each rare sign in the unlabeled data set, by simply selecting the samples with the highest estimated probability of belonging to the rare class.

This works quite well, despite the fact that this estimated probability is often low. We show that the low probabilities estimated by the network nevertheless contain important information – sorting the unlabeled set by this probability reveals that a large fraction of the highest scoring samples belongs to the rare class (Fig. 2). By labeling these samples, and adding them to the training set, we can rapidly improve the performance of our model on the rare classes. This algorithm works well even when the single sample from each rare class is a synthetic image.

The motivation for this research was to improve the recognition of rare traffic signs for automated driving. Apart from the practical significance of these results, an interesting finding of our study is that it is possible to make use of the information present in very low estimated probabilities. We explain this phenomenon by analysing a two-dimensional toy model.

2   Related Work

Active learning describes a collection of iterative methods to expand the training set for neural networks. Since manual labeling is expensive, the goal of active learning is to use the output of the network to find the most useful samples to add to the training set [26].

A common approach is the pool-based active learning loop [4]. The network is trained on a labeled training set, and used to select samples from an unlabeled dataset, or *pool*, commonly via uncertainty sampling using e.g. entropy [26]. The samples are labeled and added to the training set. This loop can be repeated a number of times.

The process of searching the unlabeled dataset for rare samples, in order to add them to the training set to improve performance on those classes, is called *active search* [7,15,16]. While active learning has been used to tackle the traffic sign recognition problem [22], to the best of our knowledge there is no published research on active search for rare traffic sign recognition.

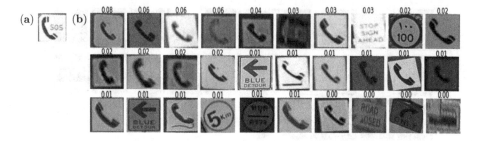

Fig. 2. An illustration of an essential step in the algorithm to find rare traffic signs, for the sign shown in panel (**a**). Panel (**b**) shows the 30 signs in the unlabeled data set with the highest probability of belonging to the same class as this sign, as estimated by the neural network. This probability is indicated above each sample.

Few-shot learning algorithms can learn to recognize an image from only few examples [31]. The algorithm can grasp the essential features of a sample and generalise them, enabling the algorithm to correctly classify e.g. traffic signs it has only seen a few times before, perhaps even only once. These algorithms tend to follow the meta-learning paradigm [10,25], meaning they *learn to learn* by training on small classification problems called episodes. The algorithms commonly rely on a feature extractor that represents the essential traffic-sign features in a high-dimensional feature space. Distance based techniques [27,28,30] or smart optimisers [2] are then used to interpret clusters in feature space in order to correctly classify rare traffic signs.

Class imbalance is a well-known problem in machine learning. A classification model may achieve excellent overall performance, e.g. accuracy, yet fail on classes which are underrepresented in the training set. A common explanation for this is that the few rare samples will make a small contribution to the total training loss [17]. One could use oversampling [3] to artificially increase this contribution. Instead, we show that one can find meaningful information in the low softmax outputs for the rare classes.

3 Methods

3.1 Datasets

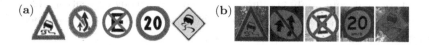

Fig. 3. (**a**) Synthetic samples of rare traffic signs from wikipedia [1]. (**b**) Corresponding signs from the Mapillary data set.

Algorithm 1. Python-style pseudocode for our active learning algorithm

```
# training_set: initial training set
# unlabeled_set: initial unlabeled set
# validation_set: initial validation set
# rare_classes: list of rare class indices
# model: neural network
# N: #frames to label per class in each iteration
# T: #iteration steps

F1 = []

model.fit(training_set)
F1.append(f1_metrics(model, validation_set))

for t in range(T): # active-learning loop
    for i in rare_classes:
        scores = [model(x)[i] for x in unlabeled_set]
        indices = scores.argsort()[:N]
        selected_frames = unlabeled_set[indices]
        labeled_frames = label(selected_frames)
        training_set.extend(labeled_frames)
        unlabeled_set.remove(selected_frames)

    model.fit(training_set)
    F1.append(f1_metrics(model, validation_set))
```

The Mapillary dataset [9] was used in all of our experiments. It consists of images of scenes with traffic signs in them. The bounding box for each sign was used to extract all image patches with a traffic sign. All patches smaller than 30×30 pixels were discarded, resulting in a labeled dataset of 59150 traffic signs, belonging to 313 different classes. Lastly, all patches were reshaped to 128×128 pixels.

The data was split into three sets. A training and validation set, and a third set to use as an unlabeled dataset. The training set contained 18306 samples, and the validation set contained 2560 samples. The remaining 38284 traffic signs were used as a pool of unlabeled traffic signs.

The 25 rarest traffic-sign classes shown in Fig. 1 were used to test the algorithm. For each rare class a single, randomly selected, sample was added to the training set, while two to three randomly selected ones were added to the validation set. The remaining ones, between four and fifty samples per class, were added to the unlabeled set.

Experiments were also performed using synthetic data. In these experiments, a single synthetic sample [Fig. 3(a)] corresponding to one of the five rare classes shown in Fig. 3(b) was added to the training set instead of a randomly selected sample from the dataset. We limited the number of samples in the unlabeled dataset to fifty for each rare class.

3.2   Neural-Network Model

In all experiments, the torchvision [20] implementation of ResNet18 [12] was used. The network was pretrained on ImageNet [8], except for the last classifi-

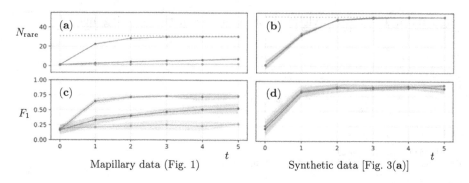

Fig. 4. Performance of Algorithm 1. (**a**) Number N_{rare} of rare samples in the training set, averaged over the rare classes in Fig. 1, as a function of the iteration number t of the active loop. Shown are results of Algorithm 1 (green); entropy method (Sect. 3.5), blue; random selection (Sect. 3.5), orange. The dotted gray line shows the average number of rare samples in the unlabeled data set. (**c**) Same, but for the F_1 score of the rare classes. In panels (**b**) and (**d**), we show the corresponding results, but using synthetic samples for the five rare classes in Fig. 3 (black). For comparison, we also show the result when using Mapillary samples in Fig. 3 (red), instead of synthetic ones. In each panel, we report the results with 95% confidence intervals obtained from five runs. (Color figure online)

cation layer which was randomly initialized. Random cropping was applied as data augmentation. The network was trained using the ADAM optimizer [18] with a learning rate of 10^{-3} and a batch size of 256 for 20 epochs.

3.3 Active-Learning Algorithm

One iteration of the active-learning algorithm consists of three steps. First, the network is trained on the training set. Second, the network is used to predict the class of each unlabeled sample. Lastly, for each rare class, the samples are sorted in descending order using the estimated probability of belonging to the rare class as shown in Fig. 2, and the N first samples are assigned their previously hidden labels and moved to the training dataset. The algorithm is summarised in Algorithm 1, and our implementation is available on github. Two experiments were conducted, one using the rare classes from Fig. 1 and one on synthetic data using the rare classes shown in Fig. 3. In these experiments N was set to 50, resulting in $50 \times K$ samples being moved from the unlabeled dataset to the training dataset in each iteration, where K is the number of rare classes. This means $50 \times 25 = 1250$ samples were moved in the experiment using the Mapillary data, while $50 \times 5 = 250$ samples were moved in the experiments on synthetic data.

3.4   Evaluation of Performance

The F_1 score on the rare classes was used to evaluate the performance of the algorithm described in Sect. 3.3. In addition, the number of training samples per class averaged over all of the rare classes was computed. This is denoted by N_{rare}. At the first iteration we have $N_{rare} = 1$, since there is one sample for each rare class in the training set. When rare samples are found and added to the training set, N_{rare} increases.

3.5   Benchmarks

The results of Algorithm 1 are compared against random selection and a commonly used active-learning method - selecting the samples with the highest entropy [26]. In Appendix A, we also show the result of applying two few-shot learning techniques [27,28] to our problem.

4   Results

Figure 4 illustrates how the algorithm iteratively finds more and more samples of the rare class. The figure shows N_{rare}, the number of training samples per class averaged over the rare classes from Fig. 1, as well as the F_1 score. Both quantities are plotted versus the iteration number t of the active loop (see Sect. 3.5). Also shown are the results of selecting the samples with highest entropy and random selection (Sect. 3.5). The new algorithm significantly outperforms the other two methods.

The value of N_{rare} tells us how many new rare samples were added in each iteration of the active loop. Figure 4(a) shows that in the first iteration, our method finds on average 22 new training samples per rare class in the unlabeled dataset. The two other two algorithms, by contrast, find fewer than five of them, and after five iterations, N_{rare} remains below ten for both of these algorithms.

Now consider the F_1 score [Fig. 4(c)]. For Algorithm 1, the F_1 score on the rare classes increases from 0.17 for the initial training set, to 0.72 after the third active learning iteration. For the entropy and the random-selection methods, the F_1 score for the rare classes increases more slowly [Fig. 4(c)].

In the first two iterations, Algorithm 1 finds more and more rare samples to add to the training set. Naturally, this helps increase the recognition performance, as measured by the F_1 score on the rare classes. However, the F_1 score starts to plateau after the first two iterations. The reason is that Algorithm 1 manages to find almost all of the rare samples in the unlabeled dataset in the first two iterations. Therefore, in the later iterations it is impossible to add more than a small number of new rare samples, and as a result there is only a small improvement for the last three iterations. The confidence intervals in Fig. 4(a,c) are quite small. This indicates that the method is quite robust.

Figure 4(b,d) compares the performance for two different initializations: using a rare sample from the Mapillary data set in the training set (red), and using a synthetic sample (black) [Fig. 3(**b**)]. The figure shows that it does not matter much whether the algorithm first sees an actual Mapillary sample or a synthetic one, it works as efficiently. The final F_1 score is higher in Fig. 4(**d**) than in Fig. 4(**c**). This indicates that the 5 classes for which there are synthetic samples [Fig. 3(**a**)] are on average easier to recognize than the 25 classes used in the non-synthetic experiment (Fig. 1). Moreover, these 5 classes have more samples in the unlabeled dataset than the 25 rarest classes, and thus at the end of the fifth iteration there are more training samples for these classes [Fig. 4(**b**)].

In Appendix B, we analyse the performance of our active-search algorithm when the standard supervised training is replaced by two few-shot learning methods. Contrary to what one might expect, there is no performance gain when incorporating these techniques. This is in line with recent work indicating that standard neural networks may do just as well at few-shot learning, and that what really matters is the quality of the feature extraction [5,6,19,24,29,34].

5   Discussion

Figure 2 shows something unintuitive. The classification network does a very good job at finding samples from the rare class – e.g. 16 out of the top 20 belong to this class. However, the probability assigned to this class is always very low, below 0.1 for all samples. In this Section we explain why there is relevant information in the small softmax outputs, and how it can be used.

We can analyse the classification of a given input x in two steps. First, the ResNet model maps the input x to a 512-dimensional feature vector z. Then, the final layer of ResNet maps the feature vector to a probability estimate by passing it through a softmax function [21]

$$P_i = \frac{\exp(\boldsymbol{w}_i \cdot \boldsymbol{z} + b_i)}{\sum_j \exp(\boldsymbol{w}_j \cdot \boldsymbol{z} + b_j)} . \tag{1}$$

Here P_i is the estimated probability that input x belongs to class i, $\boldsymbol{w}_i$ is the weight vector of the output unit corresponding to the rare class, b_i is its bias.

Consider the output for a rare class. If the network is trained with a normal cross-entropy loss, as in our case, the rare class can only make a limited contribution to the loss function. As a result, the rare class has a quite limited influence on the feature vector z. Further, the network quickly learns to output a small probability for the rare class, for all samples with a different label. E.g. by assigning a large negative value to b_i. However, to avoid a very high loss on the few samples with the rare label, the network learns to minimise this loss by updating $\boldsymbol{w}_i$ to point along the direction in feature space that gives the highest probability for class i. In other words, even if the probability $P(y_i)$ is small for all samples in the training set, it will still be largest for those samples that have the label i. If the features of the unseen samples of the rare class are also in the direction of $\boldsymbol{w}_i$, the new active-learning algorithm has a large chance of finding these samples in the unlabeled data set. To illustrate this point, we consider a toy model for classification [Fig. 5(**a**)], with one rare class and two common ones in two-dimensional input space. The samples of each class are generated by Gaussian distributions $\mathcal{N}(\mu, \sigma^2)$, where $\mu = (-1, \pm 1)$ for the common classes, $\mu = (0, 0)$ for the rare class, and $\sigma = 0.5$. This two-dimensional space is a highly idealised model of the feature space of a deep neural network.

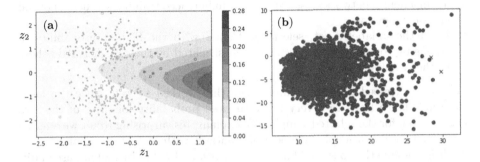

Fig. 5. (a) A toy model of a feature space with one rare class (red points), and two common ones (yellow and green points). We trained a one-layer perceptron with cross-entropy loss, and show a contour plot of the estimated probability that a point belongs to the rare class. The network is trained on all inputs represented by filled symbols. The other points (empty symbols) represent the unlabeled dataset. (b) A two-dimensional projection of the 512-dimensional feature space of the ResNet model trained on traffic signs. To obtain a projection that brings out the difference between the rare class and the others, we performed uncentered PCA for the 6 *training* samples of the rare class, and used this projection to map out the feature space of the *validation* set. The two blue crosses are the samples of the same rare class, and the green circles are all the other samples in the validation set. Note that despite the large class imbalance, the two samples corresponding to the rare class are among the four rightmost points. (Color figure online)

On this toy dataset we train a linear classifier with a cross-entropy loss. The color map of Fig. 5(a) shows the estimated probability for the rare class, Eq. 1, for each point in input space. We want to highlight three aspects of this output: First, the estimated probability is small (≤ 0.2) for all input samples. Second, it is largest for inputs in the right-hand part of the plane, corresponding to the direction of the rare cluster. Third, despite the large class imbalance, if we were to sort all unlabeled samples according to this probability, a large fraction of the highest scoring ones would belong to the rare class. In Fig. 5(b) and Appendix A we show that the feature space of our ResNet model is similar to this toy model. In particular, we show that the feature space is expressive enough that all samples of a rare class are in a consistent direction in feature space.

6   Conclusions

In this work, we considered the problem of how to learn to classify rare traffic signs. Our main result is that we obtain very good results using a simple active learning scheme, which can be summarised as[1]

1. Train a neural network classifier on your imbalanced training set, using normal cross-entropy loss.
2. From the unlabeled set, select the frames with the highest probability of belonging to one of the rare classes, as estimated by the classifier. Add these to the training set.

We were surprised that this simple algorithm worked so well, since the large class imbalance leads to a very low estimated probability for most of the rare classes, even for the selected samples. To explain this surprising result we analyse a simple two-dimensional toy model of a dataset with high class imbalance.

It is possible that one could improve our results further by making use of different techniques that have been employed to improve the performance of neural network classifiers under strong class imbalance. In Appendix B we describe results obtained incorporating two commonly used few-shot learning algorithms into our method. We found that the added complexity does not lead to improved results. However, there are many more few-shot learning methods we did not try [13], as well as other techniques such as loss reweighting that may be worth investigating in the future.

Finally, in this paper we focused on the problem of traffic sign classification. We believe that a similar method could work well for other classification problems as well, yet it is worth keeping in mind that traffic signs are special. In contrast with naturally occurring objects such as different animal and plant species, traffic signs are designed to be easily distinguishable by a neural network (the human visual cortex). This could be the reason why even rare classes can be rather well separated from the other classes, even when training on just one or a few samples from the rare class.

Acknowledgments. The results presented in this manuscript were obtained by S. Jaghouar and H. Gustafsson in their joint MSc project [11,14]. This work would not have been possible without the help of Mahshid Majd and her expertise on traffic-sign recognition. The research of BM was supported by Vetenskapsrådet (grant number 2021-4452) and by the Knut-and-Alice Wallenberg Foundation (grant number 2019.0079).

Appendices

A   Feature-Space Dissection

We discussed in Sect. 5 how it can be possible for a standard neural network, trained with unweighted cross-entropy loss, to identify samples from the rare

---

[1] For a detailed description of the algorithm used, we refer to Sect. 3.3 and Algorithm 1.

class with such high precision, despite a low estimated probability. However, this requires first that the feature space is expressive enough that the training samples of the rare class share a consistent direction in feature space, second that unseen samples from this class are also preferentially found in this direction. Figure 5(b) shows that this is indeed the case for our trained ResNet model. In this figure, we show a two-dimensional linear projection of the feature space, which has been designed to bring out the dimension along which the training samples belonging to the rare class differ the most from the other samples. This is the x-axis of Fig. 5(b). In this figure, we see the projection of the *validation* set. The two samples from the rare class that are present in this set are both very far to the right. This is consistent with Ref. [23], where they show that different samples from a rare class tend to lie in a consistent direction in feature space, even when this class is not present in the training set. Following the discussion above, this also indicates that we can expect good results by using the output probability of this class to search for samples. This is exactly what we found in Sect. 4.

B   Comparison with Few-Shot Learning

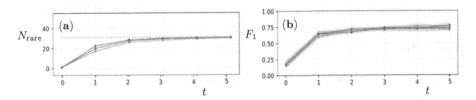

Fig. 6. Performance of Algorithm refalgo:activepsloop with few-shot learning. (a) Number N_{rare} of training samples per class, averaged over the rare classes in Fig. 1, as a function of the number of iterations t in the active loop. The dotted gray line in panel (a) shows the number of rare samples in the unlabeled data set. Training methods used: Standard cross-entropy training (green), ProtoNet (blue), RelationNet (orange). Each experiment was conducted five times, and the corresponding 95% confidence intervals are shown as shaded areas. (b) Same, but for F_1 score. (Color figure online)

The efficiency of our algorithm is explained by the fact that it recognizes rare traffic signs after seeing only a single rare sample amongst a large number of common traffic signs. The algorithm works so well because it uses features learned from the common traffic signs to identify rare ones. This is quite similar to the problem of few-shot learning. We therefore tested whether we could improve the performance of our active-search algorithm by using few-shot learning methods when training the network used for searching. We tested two few-shot learning methods, ProtoNet [27] and RelationNet [28]. For each active learning iteration, we trained a network using the respective method, and used it for selecting what frames to move to the training set. RelationNet and ProtoNet were trained in a one-shot scenario with training episodes containing 50 classes and 8 queries. ProtoNet and RelationNet take a query sample and one or more support samples as input. ProtoNet predicts the distance between the query and the support samples, and RelationNet the similarity between the two. Therefore, to perform the search, the training samples of a given rare class are used as support samples, while each sample in the unlabeled set is used as a query to compute a distance/similarity between the two. For ProtoNet, the samples with the smallest distance are moved to the training set. For RelationNet, the samples with highest similarity are moved. To evaluate the performance of these methods, a normal ResNet model was trained on the new training set, and used to calculate the F_1 score. To get a fair comparison, we used the same ResNet backbone pretrained on ImageNet for both few-shot models. Our implementations are available in a github repository.

In Fig. 6, we compare the performance of Algorithm 1 with and without the use of few-shot methods. In Fig. 6(**a**), we show that the few-shot methods do a little bit worse than the standard training method, when it comes to how many samples from the rare classes that they manage to identify. In Fig. 6(**b**), we show the performance (F_1 score) of a classification model trained on the resulting training sets. Here, we see no clear difference between the models, when it comes to how well they can classify rare classes. In sum, there is no benefit from incorporating these techniques into our active-search algorithm.

References

1. https://en.wikipedia.org/wiki/Comparison_of_European_road_signs . Accessed 21 Sept 2021
2. Andrychowicz, M., et al.: Learning to learn by gradient descent by gradient descent. In: Proceedings of the 30th International Conference on Neural Information Processing Systems. NIPS 16, pp. 3988–3996. Curran Associates Inc., Red Hook (2016)
3. Buda, M., Maki, A., Mazurowski, M.A.: A systematic study of the class imbalance problem in convolutional neural networks. Neural Netw. **106**, 249–259 (2018). https://doi.org/10.1016/j.neunet.2018.07.011
4. Budd, S., Robinson, E.C., Kainz, B.: A survey on active learning and human-in-the-loop deep learning for medical image analysis. Med. Image Anal. **71**, 102062 (2021). https://doi.org/10.1016/j.media.2021.102062, arXiv:1910.02923
5. Chen, W.Y., Liu, Y.C., Kira, Z., Wang, Y.C.F., Huang, J.B.: A closer look at few-shot classification. In: International Conference on Learning Representations (2019)
6. Chowdhury, A., Jiang, M., Chaudhuri, S., Jermaine, C.: Few-shot image classification: just use a library of pre-trained feature extractors and a simple classifier. In: 2021 IEEE/CVF International Conference on Computer Vision (ICCV), pp. 9425–9434 (2021). https://doi.org/10.1109/ICCV48922.2021.00931
7. Coleman, C., et al.: Similarity search for efficient active learning and search of rare concepts. In: Proceedings of the AAAI Conference on Artificial Intelligence, vol. 36, pp. 6402–6410 (2022)

8. Deng, J., Dong, W., Socher, R., Li, L.J., Li, K., Fei-Fei, L.: ImageNet: a large-scale hierarchical image database. In: 2009 IEEE Conference on Computer Vision and Pattern Recognition, pp. 248–255 (2009). https://doi.org/10.1109/CVPR.2009.5206848

9. Ertler, C., Mislej, J., Ollmann, T., Porzi, L., Neuhold, G., Kuang, Y.: The Mapillary traffic sign dataset for detection and classification on a global scale. In: Vedaldi, A., Bischof, H., Brox, T., Frahm, J.M. (eds.) Computer Vision – ECCV 2020. LNCS, vol. pp. 68–84. Springer, Cham (2020). https://doi.org/10.1007/978-3-030-58592-1_5, arXiv:1909.04422

10. Finn, C., Abbeel, P., Levine, S.: Model-agnostic meta-learning for fast adaptation of deep networks. In: Precup, D., Teh, Y.W. (eds.) Proceedings of the 34th International Conference on Machine Learning. Proceedings of Machine Learning Research, vol. 70, pp. 1126–1135. PMLR (2017). arXiv:1703.03400

11. Gustafsson, H.: Searching for rare traffic signs. Master's thesis, Chalmers University of Technology (2021)

12. He, K., Zhang, X., Ren, S., Sun, J.: Deep residual learning for image recognition. In: 2016 IEEE Conference on Computer Vision and Pattern Recognition (CVPR), pp. 770–778 (2016). https://doi.org/10.1109/CVPR.2016.90, arXiv:1512.03385

13. Hu, Y., Gripon, V., Pateux, S.: Leveraging the feature distribution in transfer-based few-shot learning. In: Farkaš, I., Masulli, P., Otte, S., Wermter, S. (eds.) Artificial Neural Networks and Machine Learning - ICANN 2021. LNCS, vol. , pp. 487–499. Springer, Cham (2021). https://doi.org/10.1007/978-3-030-86340-1_39, arXiv:2006.03806

14. Jaghour, S.: Finding a needle in a haystack, using deep learning to enrich a dataset with important edge cases. Master's thesis, University of Technology of Compiègne (UTC) (2021)

15. Jiang, S., Garnett, R., Moseley, B.: Cost effective active search. In: Wallach, H., Larochelle, H., Beygelzimer, A., d'Alché-Buc, F., Fox, E., Garnett, R. (eds.) Advances in Neural Information Processing Systems, vol. 32. Curran Associates, Inc. (2019)

16. Jiang, S., Malkomes, G., Converse, G., Shofner, A., Moseley, B., Garnett, R.: Efficient nonmyopic active search. In: Precup, D., Teh, Y.W. (eds.) Proceedings of the 34th International Conference on Machine Learning. Proceedings of Machine Learning Research, vol. 70, pp. 1714–1723. PMLR (2017)

17. Johnson, J.M., Khoshgoftaar, T.M.: Survey on deep learning with class imbalance. J. Big Data 6(1), 1–54 (2019). https://doi.org/10.1186/s40537-019-0192-5

18. Kingma, D., Ba, J.: Adam: a method for stochastic optimization. In: International Conference on Learning Representations (2014). arXiv:1412.6980

19. Kolesnikov, A., et al.: Big transfer (BiT): general visual representation learning. In: Vedaldi, A., Bischof, H., Brox, T., Frahm, J.-M. (eds.) ECCV 2020. LNCS, vol. 12350, pp. 491–507. Springer, Cham (2020). https://doi.org/10.1007/978-3-030-58558-7_29

20. Marcel, S., Rodriguez, Y.: Torchvision the machine-vision package of torch. In: Proceedings of the 18th ACM International Conference on Multimedia. MM 2010, pp. 1485–1488. Association for Computing Machinery, New York (2010). https://doi.org/10.1145/1873951.1874254

21. Mehlig, B.: Machine Learning with Neural Networks: An Introduction for Scientists and Engineers. Cambridge University Press, Cambridge (2021). https://doi.org/10.1017/9781108860604

22. Nienhuser, D., Zöllner, J.M.: Batch-mode active learning for traffic sign recognition. In: 2013 IEEE Intelligent Vehicles Symposium (IV), pp. 541–546 (2013). https://doi.org/10.1109/IVS.2013.6629523
23. Qi, H., Brown, M., Lowe, D.G.: Low-shot learning with imprinted weights. In: Proceedings of the IEEE Conference on Computer Vision and Pattern Recognition, pp. 5822–5830 (2018)
24. Raghu, A., Raghu, M., Bengio, S., Vinyals, O.: Rapid learning or feature reuse? Towards understanding the effectiveness of MAML. In: International Conference on Learning Representations (2020). https://openreview.net/forum?id=rkgMkCEtPB
25. Ren, M., et al.: Meta-learning for semi-supervised few-shot classification. In: Proceedings of 6th International Conference on Learning Representations ICLR (2018)
26. Ren, P., et al.: A survey of deep active learning. ACM Comput. Surv. **54**(9) (2021). https://doi.org/10.1145/3472291, arXiv:2009.00236
27. Snell, J., Swersky, K., Zemel, R.: Prototypical networks for few-shot learning. In: Guyon, I., et al. (eds.) Advances in Neural Information Processing Systems, vol. 30. Curran Associates, Inc. (2017). arXiv:1703.05175
28. Sung, F., Yang, Y., Zhang, L., Xiang, T., Torr, P.H., Hospedales, T.M.: Learning to compare: relation network for few-shot learning. In: 2018 IEEE/CVF Conference on Computer Vision and Pattern Recognition, pp. 1199–1208 (2018). https://doi.org/10.1109/CVPR.2018.00131, arXiv:1711.06025
29. Tian, Y., Wang, Y., Krishnan, D., Tenenbaum, J.B., Isola, P.: Rethinking few-shot image classification: a good embedding is all you need? In: Vedaldi, A., Bischof, H., Brox, T., Frahm, J.-M. (eds.) ECCV 2020. LNCS, vol. 12359, pp. 266–282. Springer, Cham (2020). https://doi.org/10.1007/978-3-030-58568-6_16
30. Vinyals, O., Blundell, C., Lillicrap, T., Kavukcuoglu, K., Wierstra, D.: Matching networks for one shot learning. In: Lee, D., Sugiyama, M., Luxburg, U., Guyon, I., Garnett, R. (eds.) Advances in Neural Information Processing Systems, vol. 29. Curran Associates, Inc. (2016), arXiv:1606.04080
31. Wang, Y., Yao, Q., Kwok, J.T., Ni, L.M.: Generalizing from a few examples: a survey on few-shot learning. ACM Comput. Surv. **53**(3) (2020). https://doi.org/10.1145/3386252, arXiv:1904.05046
32. Yue, Z., Zhang, H., Sun, Q., Hua, X.S.: Interventional few-shot learning. In: Proceedings of the 34th International Conference on Neural Information Processing Systems. NIPS 2020. Curran Associates Inc., Red Hook (2020). arXiv:2009.13000
33. Yurtsever, E., Lambert, J., Carballo, A., Takeda, K.: A survey of autonomous driving: common practices and emerging technologies. IEEE Access **8**, 58443–58469 (2020). https://doi.org/10.1109/ACCESS.2020.2983149, arXiv:1906.05113
34. Zhai, X., Kolesnikov, A., Houlsby, N., Beyer, L.: Scaling vision transformers. In: Proceedings of the IEEE/CVF Conference on Computer Vision and Pattern Recognition, pp. 12104–12113 (2022)

Author Index

Printed in the United States
by Baker & Taylor Publisher Services